American Military
Cemeteries

SECOND EDITION

American Military Cemeteries

Second Edition

Dean W. Holt

McFarland & Company, Inc., Publishers

Jefferson, North Carolina

The present work is a reprint of the illustrated case bound edition of American Military Cemeteries, *2nd ed. first published in 2010 by McFarland.*

LIBRARY OF CONGRESS CATALOGUING-IN-PUBLICATION DATA

Holt, Dean W., 1927–
American military cemeteries / Dean W. Holt.— 2nd ed.
p.   cm.
Includes index.

ISBN 978-1-4766-8176-4
paperback : acid free paper ∞

1. National cemeteries— United States— History.
2. Cemeteries— United States— History.   3. National cemeteries, American — History.   4. United States— History, Local.
5. United States— Genealogy.   I. Title.
UB393.H65   2020   363.7'5 — dc22   2009044640

British Library cataloguing data are available

Front cover © 2020 Shutterstock

Printed in the United States of America

McFarland & Company, Inc., Publishers
Box 611, Jefferson, North Carolina 28640
www.mcfarlandpub.com

To the men and women
who have devoted themselves
to caring for these hallowed grounds
in which rest those who sacrificed so much
to keep America free, united and independent.

Acknowledgments

The help of many cemetery superintendents, directors, and employees who helped me gather information about "their" cemeteries is gratefully acknowledged. Space does not permit me to thank each by name. To all of them, I extend my sincere thanks and appreciation. Over the years we wrote, rewrote and edited the material on individual cemeteries that we handed out to the visiting public. Now at last, the entire story of national cemeteries and memorials is in one place. This second edition brings the story up-to-date.

I again thank all those who helped with the first edition.

Fred Boyles, superintendent of Andersonville National Cemetery, provided information on the National Park Service National Cemeteries.

My thanks also to Steve Muro, National Cemetery Administration. I feel quite pleased that we left the system in such capable hands when we retired.

And of course, Wil Ebel, who kept telling me to get to work on this edition. Thanks, Wil.

Contents

Preface

Four million of the United States' honored dead are buried in the hallowed grounds of national military cemeteries. These grounds are, by law, national shrines to the men and women who fought our nation's wars. Veterans of every war and conflict in which the United States has been engaged are interred in its national cemeteries. Abraham Lincoln and the American people recognized at the beginning of the Civil War that the casualties of battle must be properly memorialized, so the National Cemetery System was established in 1862. It has been said that the location of the early cemeteries was an accident of geography — on battlefields and at central points where the remains of those who fell in remote battles and skirmishes could be brought for proper burial.

The National Cemetery Administration is completing the largest expansion since the Civil War. On January 7, 2009, with the simultaneous interment of seven veterans at the new Jacksonville National Cemetery, the NCA opened its one hundred-thirty-first national cemetery. In the years since the publication of *American Military Cemeteries*, interments have risen from about 55,000 per year, to 103,275 in fiscal year 2008. The cemeteries now cover more than 18,000 acres, nearly double what it was in 1989. With this expansion, I began to receive inquiries from National Cemetery personnel and veteran groups urging me to bring "the green book," as the cemetery personnel call it, up to date. In the first edition, I stated that I had walked over 10,000 acres of national cemeteries. Since then, and after much urging, I have visited and walked over a number of established cemeteries as well as an additional 3,000 plus acres. I can't even count the number of telephone conversations and e-mail messages to and from cemetery personnel. In this endeavor, I've met a lot of old friends, and made a lot of new friends.

One thing that always intrigued me, both when I worked in the cemetery system and later after I retired and visited new and old cemeteries, was the attitude of the personnel. There was always a sense of service to honor the veterans and their families. Never was there anything less than a total devotion to caring for the final resting place of our nation's heroes.

Note on cemetery records: The National Cemetery System has always been meticulous about the accuracy of burial records. Unfortunately, the same cannot be said for the records of former superintendents and directors. In a number of cemeteries, records covering many years could not be found, and in some cases, names were spelled differently or initials changed. One man's name was changed from Placide Rodriguez in one cemetery to Rodrigues Placide in another cemetery. The names are listed as shown as the individual cemetery records.

All illustrations courtesy National Cemetery System.

Bivouac of the Dead

Theodore O'Hara (1820–1867) wrote this poem in 1847 in memory of the Kentuckians who fell at the Battle of Buena Vista. At one time almost every national cemetery had several bronze plaques containing two lines of verse from this poem placed at strategic points. Two-line verses used on plaques in national cemeteries are indicated by an asterisk before the first line.

The muffed drum's sad roll has beat
  The soldier's last tattoo;
*No more on Life's parade shall meet
  That brave and fallen few.
*On Fame's eternal camping-ground
  Their silent tents to spread,
*And Glory guards, with solemn round,
  The bivouac of the dead.

*No rumor of the foe's advance
  Now swells upon the wind;
*No troubled thought at midnight haunts
  Of loved ones left behind;
*No vision of the morrow's strife
  The warrior's dream alarms;
*No braying horn nor screaming fife
  At dawn shall call to arms.

Their shriveled swords are red with rust,
  Their plumed heads are bowed;
Their haughty banner, trailed in dust,
  Is now their martial shroud.
And plenteous funeral tears have washed
  The red stains from each brow,
And the proud forms, by battle gashed,
  Are free from anguish now.

*The neighing troop, the flashing blade,
  The bugle's stirring blast,
*The charge, the dreadful cannonade,
  The din and shout, are past;
Nor war's wild note nor glory's peal
  Shall thrill with fierce delight
Those breasts that nevermore may feel
  The rapture of the flight.

Like the fierce northern hurricane
  That sweeps his great plateau,
Flushed with the triumph yet to gain,
  Came down the serried foe.

Who heard the thunder of the fray
  Break o'er the field beneath,
Knew well the watchword of that day
  Was "Victory or death."

Long had the doubtful conflict raged
  O'er all that stricken plain,
For never fiercer flight had waged
  The vengeful blood of Spain;
And still the storm of battle blew,
  Still swelled the gory tide;
Not long, our stout old chieftain knew,
  Such odds his strength could bide.

Twas in that hour his stern command
  Called to a martyr's grave
The flower of his beloved land,
  The nation's flag to save.
By rivers of their fathers' gore
  His first-born laurels grew,
And well he deemed the sons would pour
  Their lives for glory too.

Full many a norther's breath has swept
  O'er Angostura's plain–
And long the pitying sky has wept
  Above its mouldered slain.
The raven's scream, or eagle's flight,
  Or shepherd's pensive lay,
Alone awakes each sullen height
  That frowned o'er that dread fray.

Sons of the Dark and Bloody Ground
  Ye must not slumber there,
Where stranger steps and tongues resound
  Along the heedless air.
*Your own proud land's heroic soil
  Shall be your fitter grave;
*She claims from war his richest spoil–
  The ashes of her brave.

Thus 'neath their parent turf they rest,
  Far from the gory field,
Borne to a Spartan mother's breast
  On many a bloody shield;
The sunshine of their native sky
  Smiles sadly on them here,
And kindred eyes and hearts watch by
  The heroes sepulchre.

*Rest on, embalmed and sainted dead!
  Dear as the blood ye gave;
*No impious footstep shall here tread
  The herbage of your grave;

Nor shall your glory be forgot
  While fame her records keeps,
Or Honor points the hallowed spot
  Where Valor proudly sleeps.

Yon marble minstrel's voiceless stone
  In deathless song shall tell,
When many a vanished ago hath flown,
  The story how ye fell;
Nor wreck, nor change, nor winter's blight,
  Nor Time's remorseless doom.
Shall dim one ray of glory's light
  That gilds your deathless tomb.

Introduction: The National Cemetery System/Administration

History and Operations

Since very early times, those who died in the defense of their state or nation have been deemed worthy of special commemoration for their service on the field of battle. The outbreak of the Civil War forced two issues on the people of the United States—the survival of the Union, and care of the casualties, both wounded and dead. The Southern surrender at Appomattox settled the first issue, but the nation grappled with the second issue for many years thereafter.

Prior to the Civil War the American people gave little if any thought to a standing military force. The Army served more as a police force than an army; it provided protection on the frontier for settlers and prospectors as they pushed west and southwest into Indian territories, helped settle land disputes, and helped police lawless mining camps. Numerous small Army garrisons were established along the most heavily traveled trails and in areas where trouble was likely to occur. Some of these posts were manned by only a company of troops. When a soldier was killed or died of some illness, he was buried in a corner of the post designated by the commander for that purpose. The Army had no problem giving a proper burial to these soldiers.

In 1861 when President Lincoln issued his call to the loyal states to provide volunteers to fight the rebellion, the response was not merely a collection of individual volunteers— indeed, whole companies and regiments were formed within the towns and states. All of the unit members were from the same area, usually knew each other, elected their own officers and usually selected their unit designation. They were close-knit organizations and morale was important. The onset of hostilities introduced an urgency into the situation of caring for casualties that had not existed before. The large number of casualties, from both battlefields and hospitals, brought the issue to the public's attention and created a clamor among members of Congress for some national policy. President Lincoln recognized that maintaining a high national morale was necessary to the war effort and that providing a decent burial for those who gave their lives in defense of the Union would help boost morale.

The initial legislation that led to the establishment of the National Cemetery System was enacted by the 37th Congress. On July 17, 1862, President Abraham Lincoln signed an Omnibus Act covering legislation on a variety of subjects. Section 18 of the act provided "That the President of the United States shall have power, whenever in his opinion it is expedient, to purchase cemetery grounds and cause them to be securely enclosed, to be used as a national cemetery for the soldiers who shall die in the service of the country." This Act was the necessary final step in assuring a proper burial for military dead—an effort the War Department had begun over a year earlier, when responsibility for burial of officer and soldier dead was delegated to commanding officers of military corps and departments. They were also responsible for providing names for a registered headboard to be placed at each soldier's grave.

The act itself was a means of legitimating the actions of military commanders in the field who had, prior to July 1862, simply buried the dead where they fell and declared the land a military burying ground without compensating the owner. Often condemnation proceedings on these burial grounds were not completed and the property legally acquired by the government until many years after the end of the war. For example, a clear title to Alexandria, Virginia, one of the first national cemeteries, was not acquired until 1875.

Fourteen national cemeteries were established in 1862 after passage of the legislation. The huge encampment around Washington, D.C., dictated the establishment of a cemetery at Alexandria, and when that space began to fill up, Soldiers' Home was designated a national cemetery. Fort Leavenworth and Fort Scott, Kansas, had their post cemeteries incorporated into the system because of their importance as military operation centers. Seven cemeteries were established at troop concentration and training camps: Annapolis, Maryland; Camp Butler, Illinois; Danville, Kentucky; Keokuk, Iowa; Loudon Park, Maryland; New Albany, Indiana; and Philadelphia, Pennsylvania. A cemetery at Cypress Hills, New York, was opened for interment of Confederate prisoners of war and their guards who perished in a train wreck. Two battlefield cemeteries, Antietam, Maryland, and Mill Springs, Kentucky, were the first in which the dead were buried almost where they fell. The original national cemeteries were established both to bury the dead from general hospitals near large troop training camps and to bury the battlefield dead.

When the Civil War ended, Quartermaster General Meigs ordered a massive search of every battlefield, isolated churchyard, farm, plantation, railroad siding, or any other place combat operations had occurred and where Union dead might lie in temporary graves. This effort covered five years and brought nearly 300,000 remains to national cemeteries, with 58 percent identified. In many instances, combat areas became national cemetery sites as the hastily buried dead were reburied as part of a formally designed cemetery. Several cemeteries which had been established near Army general hospitals to care for those who died of wounds or disease were designated as national cemeteries. Post cemeteries at frontier garrisons were enlarged and designated as national cemeteries to receive the dead from Civil War skirmishes in their areas. Three national cemeteries established during the period 1862–1870 — Andersonville, Georgia; Florence, South Carolina; and Salisbury, North Carolina — were located adjacent to Confederate military prisons. By 1870, it was believed that all of the Union dead, whether killed in action or having died of wounds or illness in hospitals during the war, had been interred in private or national cemeteries. The number of national cemeteries had grown from 14 in 1862 to 73 in 1870.

In March 1873, Congress extended the right of burial in a national cemetery to all honorably discharged Union veterans of the Civil War. Cemeteries were established beyond the battlefield and hospital sites to accommodate the newly eligible. In 1884, San Francisco National Cemetery became the first national cemetery on the Pacific Coast.

The Spanish-American War in 1898 and the Philippine Insurrection in 1900–1901 marked a new era in the history of American burial policy. It was probably the first time in history that a country at war with a foreign power had disinterred its soldiers who died on foreign soil and brought them home to family and friends. The Quartermaster Burial Corps, made up of civilian morticians, performed disinterments and identified and prepared remains for shipment to the United States for final interment in either a private or national cemetery. The Graves Registration Service, Army Quartermaster Corps, performed outstanding service at the end of both world wars. After disinterment and identification of a decedent, the next of kin was given the option of having the remains returned home for burial or having the deceased interred in a permanent American military cemetery overseas (see American Battle Monuments Commission). The United States is the only nation to give such an option to the fallen warrior's next of kin.

Over the years, Congress has passed legislation that gradually extended burial privileges to a larger portion of the population. A War Department survey in 1929 reported that in the 84 national cemeteries the annual interment rate was 2,779, and even with the nearly five million World War I veterans, grave space would be available until 1993. Unfortunately, over half of the available gravesites were located in remote cemeteries. The survey also found that over half of the annual interments took place in nine national cemeteries located in metropolitan areas. Of the seven cemeteries established during the 1930s, three were intended to supplement existing cemeteries, two were constructed at the request of the Navy and the Army to meet current burial needs of the armed forces, and one — Fort Snelling, Minnesota — was built to accommodate the veteran population of a large metropolitan area. Fort Snelling marked the first time that veterans service organizations banded together to raise a public outcry and apply pressure on members of Congress to secure a national cemetery for a specific location. This technique has been used successfully many times since then, and in a few instances it has resulted in excessive expenditures of taxpayer dollars.

World War II introduced "group burials," a new term to the cemetery vocabulary and a new type of burial to the national cemeteries. Prior to this time there had been multiple interments in a single grave, such as the trench burials during the Civil War and the mass graves for Indian massacre victims. In those cases, the remains could not be identified, either individually or as a group. Group burials are the result of a common disaster, such as an airplane or helicopter crash, when it is known with certainty the names of the decedents but their individual remains cannot be identified because of the circumstances of their death. The special group marker on their gravesite lists the names and ranks of each of the deceased.

World War II added some 15 million veterans eligible for burial in a national cemetery, and Congress debated numerous proposals for expanding the National Cemetery System. The proposals ranged from one cemetery in every state, territory and possession, to one every 250-mile population radius. Private cemetery owners and associations jumped into the fray with cries of "socialism" and invasion of private enterprise rights. The Department of the Army, after proposing the development of 79 new national cemeteries at a cost of $120 million, retreated into a policy it had earlier adopted and then abandoned. The Army believed, based on studies it had performed, that the majority of interments in national cemeteries were of veterans whose military service had long since been completed, and spouses and dependents of those veterans. Therefore, it was a civilian issue, and Congress should make the decision as to where and when new national cemeteries would be established. The Army, in effect, adopted a nonexpansion policy for national cemeteries. Congress did take the initiative, and after being pressured by local political groups and veterans service organizations, mandated five new cemeteries during the 1950s. An administration policy was announced in February 1962 that there would be no more national cemeteries established, and no more lands acquired for expansion of existing cemeteries except Arlington National Cemetery. This announcement resulted from a mutual agreement by the Army, the White House and Congress.

Historically, for 111 years the development and operation of the National Cemetery System was a command responsibility of the War Department (later the Department of the Army), Office of the Quartermaster General. In 1933, by presidential executive order, 11 national cemeteries located on Civil War battlefields were transferred to the jurisdiction and care of the National Park Service, Department of the Interior. In August 1962, the Office of the Chief of Support Services, Department of the Army, assumed responsibility for the operation and maintenance of the 85 national cemeteries still assigned to the Department of Defense. Subsequently, the U.S. Army Memorial Affairs Agency was designated the successor organization to the Chief of Support Services.

In every session of Congress after the nonexpansion policy was announced, bills were introduced calling for a new national cemetery in some location. The Army, speaking for the administration, opposed them, and none of the bills was enacted. After being rebuffed several times, the veterans supporters in Congress took a different approach. They succeeded in getting the legislative oversight responsibility transferred from the House Committee on Interior and Insular Affairs to the Committee on Veterans Affairs. Then they set about introducing bills to transfer the National Cemetery System from the Department of the Army to the Veterans Administration where, in the judgment of millions of veterans, it more properly belonged. Such a bill was passed in the 92nd Congress but vetoed by the president. Another attempt was made in the 93rd Congress, and it passed. On June 18, 1973, the president signed Public Law 93–43, The National Cemeteries Act of 1973. It has been said that the most important interment that year was the burial of the nonexpansion policy.

Under the provisions of the Act of 1973, 82 of the 84 national cemeteries, 21 soldiers' lots, 7 Confederate cemeteries, 3 monument sites, and 1 special installation under the jurisdiction of the U.S. Army Memorial Affairs Agency were transferred to the Veterans Administration (VA). The Army retained Arlington National Cemetery and the Soldiers' Home National Cemetery. The transfer was effective September 1, 1973. In addition, the 21 cemeteries operated by the Veterans Administration in conjunction with its medical centers were incorporated into the Veterans Administration National Cemetery System.

There was no equitable distribution of grave space throughout the nation. More than half of the Army cemeteries, 42, had already been closed for interment. Some states had several cemeteries and some states had none. The state of Virginia had 14 national cemeteries including five in Richmond.

The National Cemeteries Act of 1973 contained a provision that directed the Administrator of Veterans Affairs to conduct a study and submit recommendations to Congress not later than January 3, 1974, on the criteria to govern the development and operation of a national cemetery system. The study recommended an expansion of the system by providing a regional cemetery in each of the 10 standard federal regions, (SFR) which encompass the entire United States, including Puerto Rico, and a 50 percent grant-in-aid for veterans cemeteries developed by the states. Since Arlington was not included in the National Cemetery System, and the eligibility criteria were more restrictive than for other cemeteries, the study recommended that another national cemetery should be established in or near the District of Columbia. The concept was that since the nation could not afford to build new cemeteries in such numbers as to meet the needs of all veterans in every state, there would in lieu thereof be established regional cemeteries to serve the particular regions. Although the plan was never formally approved by Congress, it was adopted by the VA and implemented by the National Cemetery System as the "regional concept" for cemetery expansion and development.

In the late 1980s and early 1990s the National Cemetery System was renamed the

National Cemetery Administration. With this change began the largest expansion since the Civil War. Along with the expansion in the number of cemeteries came numerous changes in organization and management . Some of these are:

1. The National Cemetery System has relied on on-the-job training for cemetery employees. On August 24, 2004, The VA National Cemetery Training Center was opened in St, Louis, Missouri, near the Jefferson Barracks National Cemetery. The Center provides formal training and practical experience for cemetery directors, assistant directors, equipment operators, groundskeepers, cemetery representatives, and other employees. The program covers management subjects and other topics to assure a well-prepared staff to carry out the mission and functions of the NSA.
2. The three Area Offices for management of field operations have been changed to five Memorial Service Areas. This more evenly divides the responsibilities for management of field operations.
3. The more active cemeteries now have stone masons on their staffs to expedite the preparation and installation of headstones.

Another provision of the National Cemetery Act of 1973 directed the Administrator of Veterans Affairs to appoint an Advisory Committee on Cemeteries and Memorials. Its purpose is to advise and consult with the administrator on administration of national cemeteries, selection of cemetery sites, erection of appropriate memorials, and the adequacy of federal burial benefits. The first chairman of the committee was Admiral John McCain, U.S. Navy, Retired.

As the National Cemetery System set about implementing the regional concept, two policy decisions were made which had a significant impact on the future. First, four existing national cemeteries with substantial undeveloped land for gravesites were designated regional cemeteries, and second, land for the seven additional cemeteries would have to be acquired at no cost to the government. The Advisory Committee on Cemeteries and Memorials played a significant role in identifying suitable federally owned land that could be excessed and transferred, at no cost, to the National Cemetery System for the seven new cemeteries. They also provided valuable advice on the master planning and development, and selecting names for the new sites. Since its establishment, the advisory committee has been consulted on major policy changes prior to their implementation.

The four designated regional cemeteries are as follows: Houston National Cemetery, Houston, TX (Region VI); Jefferson Barracks National Cemetery, St. Louis, MO (Region VII); Fort Logan National Cemetery, Denver, CO (Region VIII); and Willamette National Cemetery, Portland, OR (Region X).

Since 1974, seven large regional cemeteries have been constructed: Massachusetts National Cemetery, Bourne, MA (Region I); Calverton National Cemetery, Calverton, Long Island, NY (Region II); Indiantown Gap National Cemetery, Annville, PA (Region III); Fort Mitchell National Cemetery, Phoenix City, AL (Region IV); Fort Custer National Cemetery, Augusta, MI (Region V); Riverside National Cemetery, Riverside, CA (Region IX); and Quantico National Cemetery, Triangle, VA (Washington, DC region).

The opening of Fort Mitchell National Cemetery in 1987 completed implementation of the regional concept. During this same period, a number of previously closed cemeteries were reopened through acquisition and development of adjacent land donated by civic and service organizations.

Two additional national cemeteries were established by political directive rather than the usual careful planning. Senator Robert Byrd spearheaded a legislative move to mandate a cemetery in West Virginia and succeeded in having the necessary funds appropriated. West Virginia National Cemetery is located at Pruntytown, West Virginia. The Florida National Cemetery was established by executive order shortly after President Jimmy Carter returned from a campaign trip seeking to capture the large veteran vote in Florida during his reelection campaign in 1980. The Florida National Cemetery is located at Bushnell, Florida.

It became apparent even before the last of the seven cemeteries were opened that the regional concept was not the final answer to meeting veterans' burial needs. It is a well-accepted fact that Americans will not bury a loved one more than 50–75 miles from home, except in the most unusual circumstances, and are unlikely to cross state lines to reach the cemetery. With over 27 million veterans and their eligible spouses and dependents, the National Cemetery System once more began planning for the future despite the objection of the White House Office of Management and Budget (OMB), which insisted that the regional concept was the end of national cemetery expansion. Internal studies indicated that there were ten areas of the United States with large veteran populations not served by an existing national cemetery. The OMB would not permit the initial study to be sent to Congress. As often happens, the unofficial report was leaked to congressional staff members, and then to Congress members themselves. At one point there must have been about 100 copies floating around Capitol Hill. The predictable result was that the House of Representatives Veterans Affairs Committee directed the National Cemetery System to study future burial needs of the nation's veterans and submit recommendations for meeting these needs. A modified report was submitted to Congress and hearings were held, but the committee took no action.

The report on locating national cemeteries where the need existed spurred individual congressmen who represented the ten areas to begin introducing bills requiring the VA to prepare environmental impact statements (EIS) on those areas. Several of the bills were passed and funds appropriated to pay for the EIS. Administrator of Veterans Affairs Thomas Turnage reversed the policy prohibiting the VA from buying land, and Secretary of Veterans Affairs Edward Derwinski subsequently affirmed this decision. As of this writing, land has been purchased to expand the Fort Smith, Santa Fe, Willamette and Fayetteville national cemeteries. Construction is now under way on a new national cemetery in Los Banos, California — a site rejected by the VA when studying sites for locating a cemetery for Standard Federal Region IX. A friend of former Congressman Tony Coelho and Senator Alan Cranston donated the land and the two members of Congress urged the VA to accept it. The San Joaquin Valley National Cemetery was scheduled to be opened on Veterans Day 1991 to serve the veterans of northern California.

Environmental impact statements are under way in Albany, New York; Chicago; Dallas/Fort Worth; Cleveland; and Seattle. The EIS process is projected to be started in the near future in Oklahoma City and Pittsburgh. It is anticipated that when an EIS is approved and a site selected, funds for development and construction will be included in VA budget requests submitted to Congress. Despite the nonexpansion policy so rigidly adhered to by the OMB, eight of the ten areas cited in the report to Congress will someday, barring total economic disaster, have national cemeteries. The long-range goal of the National Cemetery System, as stated by Secretary of Veterans Affairs Edward Derwinski, is that by the year 2000, there will be an open national cemetery within 75 miles of 75 percent of the veteran population.

Funeral customs have changed with the passage of time. Four cemeteries have beautiful chapels where funeral services were conducted at one time. Golden Gate, Los Angeles, and Houston National Cemetery chapels were built prior to 1973. Only Jefferson Barracks has a chapel constructed since that date. Most funeral services are held in a church or funeral home chapel. Services in a national cemetery are considered "committal services" and all cemeteries provide small shelters for this purpose. Except for those few instances when a family requests a graveside service, all services are conducted at these "committal shelters" located centrally in the cemetery away from the gravesites. After the service, cemetery employees remove the remains to the actual gravesite.

The increasing acceptance of cremation as a form of burial has dictated changes in cemetery development plans. As the trend toward cremation grew, the National Cemetery System developed "Garden Niches," small plots (usually three feet by three feet) in areas of the cemetery where casketed remains could not be interred. These plots were suitable for the in-ground burial of urns containing cremated remains. Several older national cemeteries had columbariums but space was limited. It is interesting to note that at some locations where cemeteries now have both in-ground and columbarium niches, the families prefer the in-ground niches. They say that they feel closer to their departed loved one. All national cemeteries constructed since 1973 have both facilities available. In fiscal year 1989, cremated remains accounted for 20 percent of the total interments in national cemeteries. That year, interment of casketed remains increased 2.5 percent over the previous year, while interment of cremated remains increased by 9.5 percent. The development of smaller columbarium units will permit their placement in almost all cemeteries where the need exists. The National Cemetery System has 20 such units scheduled for construction within the next 5 years, and 21 units planned for construction beyond that date.

As part of the 1976 Bicentennial program, the National Cemetery System implemented four new initiatives to further honor our nation's veterans:

- Lighting was installed around the flagpoles in all national cemeteries so that the United States flag can be flown 24 hours a day.
- Special headstones were provided for all Medal of Honor recipients. The headstone contains a golden reproduction of the Medal incised into the stone, and is provided to all recipients regardless of where they are interred. The original headstones at the graves of recipients interred in national cemeteries were replaced with the special headstone.
- A Bicentennial tree, of a species common to the area, was planted in each national cemetery. A small bronze plaque on a stone pillar base was placed at the planting site, dedicating the tree to all Medal of Honor recipients.
- The Avenue of Flags program, established earlier at Fort Smith National Cemetery, was expanded to all national cemeteries. Under this program the next of kin may donate the veteran's casket flag to the cemetery. These flags are flown on ten-foot flagstaffs placed at intervals along cemetery roadways and walkways on Memorial Day, Veterans Day and other special occasions.

The Presidential Memorial Certificate program, started in 1980 under the Department of Veterans Benefits, was reassigned to the National Cemetery System in 1987. A special certificate signed by the president is sent to the next-of-kin of a deceased veteran when the notification of death is received by the VA. The certificate is inscribed, "The United States of America honors the memory of (veteran's name). This certificate is awarded by a grateful nation in recognition of devoted and selfless consecration to the service of our country in the Armed Forces of the United States." Over 300,000 certificates are furnished to next-of-kin each year.

In February 1978, the administrator of veterans affairs reorganized the VA with the concept that all organizational elements having a direct "hands-on" responsibility for veterans benefits should be a department within the VA. The National Cemetery System was elevated to become the Department of Memorial Affairs within the VA. In 1988 the legislation that created the cabinet-level Department of Veterans Affairs changed the name back to the National Cemetery System — a name it has proudly carried for 126 years.

In 1987 the Department of Memorial Affairs adopted the "DMA Credo." It is a profound statement of mission and purpose, not only for the present but for the future. Cemetery system employees placed copies on bulletin boards, and a framed copy was prominently displayed in every office. The credo instantly became the standard for the conduct of all cemetery activities. It reads as follows:

> We are the Department of Memorial Affairs.
> We pledge to conduct the memorial affairs of eligible veterans and dependents with dignity and compassion.
> We treat each National Cemetery as a national shrine created in tribute to the sacrifices made by over 39 million Americans who served in the U.S. Armed Forces.
> We believe that National Cemeteries are as much for the living as for the deceased, a place to rejoice as much as to grieve, and to that end we solemnly vow to preserve and perfect these sacred grounds in perpetuity.
> We dedicate ourselves, individually and collectively, to improved quality of service and increased productivity in meeting the needs of veterans and their families.
> We encourage community participation in enhancement and beautification projects and to that end we strive constantly to improve public awareness and understanding of our mission.
> We take great pride in our past accomplishments and freely promise to continue to fulfill our responsibilities to America's veterans as a matter of professional pride and personal honor.

Very briefly stated, eligibility for burial in a national cemetery is available to any veteran who was discharged from active service under conditions other than dishonorable. A veteran's eligibility for burial is inviolable no matter what turns his life takes after his military service. A case in point is the veteran who held the Washington Monument captive for several hours threatening to blow it up. He was killed by police officers and later interred in Arlington National Cemetery. He had been awarded the Purple Heart Medal for wounds received in combat. Discharges other than honorable must be adjudicated by the Secretary of Veterans Affairs to determine eligibility. Also eligible are spouses of active-duty members or veterans, minor children and unmarried adult children who become physically or mentally disabled before attaining the age of 21. Members of reserve components, commissioned officers of the National Oceanic and Atmospheric Administration and public health service officers may also be eligible. Complete information on eligibility and availability of grave space may be obtained at the nearest national cemetery, VA regional office, or VA medical center.

The growth and evolution of the National Cemetery System since its transfer from the Department of the Army to the Veterans Administration from military to civilian management is a tribute to the outstanding leadership of the appointed directors of the National Cemetery System. Each of them has had a particular agenda and methods of getting the job done, and each has made a positive impact on the system. One thing they have all shared is the compelling desire to improve service to the veterans of the United States. Neither should any criticism be made of the military management of the system for the previous 111 years. The administrators did an outstanding job.

- Rufus H. Wilson, February 1974 to January 1975
- John W. Mahan, January 1975 to April 1977

- Carl T. Noll, May 1977 to January 1981
- Paul T. Bannai, December 1981 to December 1986
- Wilfred L. Ebel, July 1987 to April 1989
- Jo Ann K. Webb, October 1989 to 1991
- Allen B. Clark, 1991 to 1993
- Jerry W. Bowen, 1993 to 1998
- Robert M. (Mike) Walker, 2000 to 2001
- Robin L. Higgins, 2001 to 2002
- J. W. Nicholson. 2003 to 2005
- William F. Tuerk, 2005 to 2009
- Steve L. Muro, 2009–

As of September 30, 2008, the total area of the open and under construction national cemeteries under the jurisdiction of the National Cemetery Administration. Department of Veterans Affairs, exceeded 18,000 acres. From 1862 to September 30, 2008, 3,511,068 interments had been made in these cemeteries. Earlier it was noted that 2,779 burials were made in 1929. In fiscal year 2008, there were a total of 103,275 interments, and this number is expected to increase to over 125,000 by the year 2010. The National Cemetery Administration is in the midst of the largest expansion since the Civil War. When the six cemeteries under construction are opened for interments, the VA will be operating 131 cemeteries in 39 states and Puerto Rico.

This is but a brief synopsis of the history and background of the National Cemetery System/Administration. Each cemetery has its own rich history. Each has a story to tell on why it came to be, why it is located at a particular site, and the notable individuals and characters interred therein. The national cemeteries of the United States offer perpetual testimony of the concern of a grateful nation that the lives and services of members of the armed forces, who served their nation well, will be appropriately commemorated. Here in cemeteries diverse in size and location, the flag of the United States is proudly flown 24 hours each day. It bows its colors briefly to acknowledge the presence of a newly fallen warrior. Here well-kept grounds and ordered rows of headstones and monuments mark each site as one of dedication and serenity.

Cemetery Support Organizations

Visitors to national cemeteries are impressed by many different things. For some, it is a rifle squad firing a volley over the grave of a fallen comrade; for others it may be the beautiful music played by the electronic carillon. Most people accept these things as part of the national cemetery program. But they are not. They are there because of the support of volunteers who make up the various organizations that support the cemeteries. Listing each support organization at every cemetery would require too much space. It is more appropriate to describe the various organizations and the type of support they provide.

National Veterans Service Organizations

Many of these organizations are chartered by Congress to provide service to veterans. Their national headquarters offices provide testimony and support cemetery officials appearing before legislative and oversight committee hearings. They conduct outreach programs to acquaint veterans with current burial benefits; serve, as appointed, on the Advisory Committee on Cemeteries and Memorials; and consult with and advise cemetery officials.

On the local level, posts and auxiliaries plan and conduct ceremonies on Memorial Day, Veterans Day and other special occasions, and furnish continuing support to the local cemetery. In several cities such as Bath, New York; Fayetteville and Fort Smith, Arkansas; Florence, South Carolina; Culpeper, Virginia; and Camp Nelson, Kentucky, they have banded together to raise funds to purchase land and donate it to the cemetery to add additional gravesites. Some volunteers work in the cemetery office greeting visitors and providing information. At every cemetery dedication, volunteers work tirelessly to assure that the program is conducted with dignity and reverence befitting the occasion. Local veterans organizations have donated electronic bell carillons at Fort Snelling and Fort Sam Houston national cemeteries.

At a number of cemeteries, local veterans organizations have united to form memorial rifle squads. These squads provide honor guards, fire the last volley and sound taps for any veteran. Probably the most active is at Fort Snelling National Cemetery. It has served at more than 10,000 funerals.

There are at least six cemeteries, and possibly more, that exist as the direct result of concerted efforts by members of the American Legion. They saw the need, solicited public support and lobbied their congressional delegation until action was taken to establish a national cemetery. Their members have also donated electronic bell carillons at the Black Hills, Fort Logan, and Puerto Rico National Cemeteries. The National Service Foundation of the American Veterans of World War II, Korea and Vietnam (AMVETS) have donated electronic bell carillons to 24 national cemeteries. At 22 of these cemeteries they have also donated bell towers so that the music can be heard throughout the cemetery. Where rifle squads are not available, the carillon sounds a rifle volley and plays taps when the next of kin requests it. In addition, suitable music is played at various times during the day.

Veterans service organizations led the successful effort to have the National Cemetery System transferred to the Veterans Administration. They were also in the forefront in securing legislative action and White House approval to elevate the Veterans Administration to the cabinet level as the Department of Veterans Affairs.

Garden Clubs

The flower beds that adorn the entrances and grounds of many national cemeteries are the work of garden clubs in the area. These clubs select the plants after consultation with the cemetery director, prepare the beds and care for them throughout the growing season. Some cemeteries have rose gardens cared for by a local garden club. At Willamette National Cemetery, statewide clubs are involved. The Federated Garden Clubs of Oregon donated an electronic bell carillon to the cemetery, and, for the past several years, have planted undeveloped areas with wildflowers.

Boy Scouts of America and Girl Scouts of America

Each year just prior to Memorial Day, thousands of Boy and Girl Scouts flock to national cemeteries to place a small flag (about 24 inches high) at the head of each grave. The flags are carefully placed one foot in front of the headstone. Many troops use this as a community service project, and at a number of locations, each participant is given a cloth badge to wear on the uniform.

Gold Star Mothers and Gold Star Wives

These ladies serve as volunteers assisting visitors and taking part in ceremonies at cemeteries. At Jefferson Barracks National Cemetery, they spearheaded a campaign to raise funds for the construction of the Memorial Chapel. After several design changes, the Veterans Administration funded and built the chapel. The Jefferson Barracks Chapel Association contributed the dossal curtain, kneeling bench covers, a 60 by 8 foot stained glass skylight, 20 Venetian nave windows, and a 30 by 10 foot laminated glass panel, and has plans to present a large statue for the grounds outside the chapel.

The Arlington Ladies

This group was founded by Gladys Vandenburg, wife of General Hoyt Vandenburg, chief of staff of the Air Force, in 1948. Initially, the group represented the Air Force chief of staff at the funeral of each Air Force decedent buried at Arlington National Cemetery. They now represent the chief of staff of each branch of the Armed Forces. At the conclusion of the graveside service, the group presents the next of kin with a personal note of sympathy on behalf of the chief of staff of the deceased's branch of service.

The United States Armed Forces

Military installations across the country provide honor guards and rifle squads, personnel for traffic control, bands and marching units.

The list should also include the community groups who support their local cemetery. Most communities furnish police protection and emergency medicine during all large ceremonies. The bench on which visitors rest and the water fountain from which they drink were furnished by some support group. If these groups did not exist, much of what you see in a national cemetery, other than interments and grounds maintenance, would not be there.

PART I

Department of Veterans Affairs (VA) National Cemeteries and Related Sites

National Cemeteries

Abraham Lincoln National Cemetery
27034 South Diagonal Road
Elwood, Illinois 60421

The Abraham Lincoln National Cemetery is located in Elwood, Illinois, about 50 miles south of Chicago. The cemetery includes 982 acres located in the northwestern area of the former Joliet Army Ammunition plant, and when fully developed, will provide 400,000 burial spaces.

Dedicated on October 3, 1999, as the 117th National Cemetery, the 150 acre initial development will provide 25,000 gravesites, 2,000 lawn crypts, 3,000 columbaria sites, and 2,300 garden niches for cremated remains. As of September 30, 2008, there were 18,479 interments.

The Cemetery contains 21 memorials, mostly commemorating veterans of the twentieth century wars. An 18-foot granite obelisk crowned by a bronze eagle with outstretched wings was donated by the Pearl Harbor Survivors Association, and dedicated on May 12, 2001. It honors the Americans who died in the surprise attack on Pearl Harbor. The Blue Star Memorial Marker was donated by the District VIII Garden Club of Illinois and dedicated on September 15, 2000.

One Medal of Honor recipient is interred in the cemetery:

> **Theodore Hyatt**, Section 1, Grave 1613. First Sergeant, Company D, 127th Illinois Infantry, 2nd Division, 15th Army Corps. Place and date: Battle of Vicksburg, May 22, 1863.
> Citation: Gallantry in the charge of the "volunteer storming party."

Directors:
Billy Murphy, 1998–2001
Roseann Santore, April 2007–Present

Alabama National Cemetery
3133 Highway 119
Montevallo, Alabama 35115

The new 479 acre Alabama National Cemetery is approximately 15 miles south of Birmingham, just north of the town of Montevallo and west of Interstate 65. The initial development of 45 acres will provide 7,395 full-casket gravesites, 999 in-ground cremation sites, and about 2,700 columbarium niches.

The cemetery was dedicated on July 13, 2008, and officially opened on June 25, 2009. The new cemetery will serve about 200,000 veterans and dependents when it is fully developed.

Quincey Whitehead was appointed in December 2007 to be the first director of the cemetery. She was previously the Director of the Barrancas National Cemetery.

Alexandria National Cemetery
209 Shamrock Avenue
Pineville, Louisiana 71360

Alexandria National Cemetery is actually located in Pineville, Louisiana. It was established in 1867 on a site about one mile east of the Pineville landing on the Red River, immediately opposite Alexandria. The village of Pineville has grown over the years to a town of more than 12,000 residents. The cemetery is only one block off the main street, near the center of town.

In 1968, Congressman Speedy O. Long introduced a bill to change the name of the cemetery to Pineville National Cemetery. This change was resisted by the Army. Colonel C.A. Shaunsey said that the name Alexandria was chosen deliberately, even though the cemetery was known to be located in Pineville, due to the importance of Alexandria to travelers. The present name had acquired meaning for over a century. Another reason might be that the surveyed center of the state of Louisiana is located in the cemetery. The spot is identified by a square marble marker.

The 8.23-acre site was appropriated in 1867 from Francious Poussin. In1874, a suit was filed by heirs of Poussin. Judge W.B. Woods ordered an appraisal of the appropriated land and subsequently ordered the United States to pay the heirs $1,200 for title to the property. The growth of the town of Pineville has prohibited any further expansion of the cemetery.

The official reason for selecting this site is not recorded; nor is the name of the officer who selected it. It appears, however, that since it was established as a concentration point for deceased Union Civil War soldiers, its location on the Red River was the decisive factor. Bodies were removed from Mount Pleasant, Cheneyville, Cotile Landing, Fort De Russy, Yellow Bayou, Bayou Delplase, Grand Ecore, Natchitoches, Shreveport, and other places in Louisiana; and from Jefferson and Tyler, Texas.

The report of the inspector of national cemeteries dated February 24, 1871, lists interments in the cemetery as follows:

Commissioned officers, known	19
Commissioned officers, unknown	6
White Union soldiers, known	412
White Union soldiers, unknown	616
Colored Union soldiers, known	62
Colored Union soldiers, unknown	141
Sailors, known	14
Citizens, known and unknown	12
Soldiers, not classified	96
Total	1,378

In later years, 25 remains from Fort Jessup, Louisiana, 16 remains from Fort Ringgold, Texas, and 1,537 remains from Fort Brown, Texas, were brought to the cemetery. The remains from Fort Brown were disinterred from the Brownsville National Cemetery, which was abandoned in 1911. It is interesting to note that the inspector's report in 1872 listed a total of 1,532 known and 1,195 unknown interments in the Brownsville National Cemetery. There is no record of the disposition of the other 1,190 remains. The remains at Brownsville had been moved there from Indianola, Galveston, Lavaca, Victoria, Ringgold Barracks, Laredo, Brazos, Santiago, and other places in Texas. The Brownsville cemetery was located about 200 yards southeast of Fort Brown, on a little island, formed by a lagoon, about 100 yards from the bed of the Rio Grande. Each of these three reinterments was in a common grave, each one marked by a large gray granite marker inscribed "Unknown."

Three known remains from the Brownsville National Cemetery are interred here. Major Jacob Brown, for whom the fort was named, is interred in Section B, Grave 1. He died of wounds received during a skirmish with Mexican soldiers in 1846. In Graves 7 and 8 are two civilian Civil War casualties, Captain William Montgomery and Lieutenant Jackson of the Texas Rangers. The kidnapping and subsequent hanging of Captain Montgomery by Confederate Texans threatened to close the border trade between Texas and Mexico. Captain Montgomery's remains were reinterred in the Brownsville National Cemetery from another location in Texas. His story, and why he was hanged, is buried with him.

In February 1946, five German prisoners of war were reinterred in the national cemetery from Camp Fannin, Texas.

Congressman Gillis Long is interred in Section B beside his favorite tree, a crepe myrtle.

As of September 30, 1990, there was a total of 19,256 interments in the cemetery. Alexandria National Cemetery has space for cremated remains and may be able to inter casketed remains in the same gravesite with a previously interred family member.

Former superintendents/directors are:

G. Fitzgerald, Unknown–1874
Frank Burrows, Unknown–October 1886
C. Taylor, October 1886–January 1891
Ernest Mittenhouse, January 1891–April 1894
R.C. Taylor, April 1894–December 1898
J.S. Brian, December 1898–December 1906
John A. Reeves, December 1906–August 1908
Eric E. George, April 1909–April 1911
W.H. Thrift, April 1911–May 1914
E.T. Eagle, May 1914–September 1914
William M. Hammonds, October 1914–July 1924
L.L. Davis, July 1924–December 1925
Rodriques Placide, December 1925–May 1926
George W. May, May 1926–August 1939
Rodriques Placide, September 1939–October 1941
Thomas E. Swain, October 1941–December 1943

Allen H. Keel, December 1943–June 1945
John W. Cox, June 1945–January 1947
Charles S. Stroup, January 1947–October 1955
Rudolph F. Staude, October 1955–April 1964
Thomas N. McLain, April 1964–December 1967
Andrew F. Szilvasi, January 1968–March 1972
Bill Haynie, Jr., April 1972–May 1974
Robert Bevering, September 1974–December 1975
Velva L. Melton, May 1976–January 1978
Dennis E. Kuehl, January 1978–June 1979
Stuart S. Sowers, September 1979–September 1980
Ronald Pemberton, June 1981–November 1982
Rodney L. Dunn, September 1983–July 1985
Mark P. Maynard, August 1985–October 1987
Kimberly M. Wright, 1988–1991
Joe Nenally, 1991–1996

In 1996, Alexandria became a satellite cemetery assigned to Natchez National Cemetery.

Alexandria (Va.) National Cemetery
Wilkes Street
Alexandria, Virginia 22314

Alexandria National Cemetery is located in the suburbs of Alexandria at the end of Wilkes Street surrounded by several other privately owned cemeteries. The original cemetery consisted of approximately four acres known as Spring Garden Farm. The land was sold in lots at auction in 1794. Two acres of this tract belonged to the city of Alexandria and were conveyed to the United States on June 1, 1862. The remainder of the land was sold to the United States by John H. Baggett in two parcels, one on November 8, 1865, and the second on November 24, 1870. Another 1.5 acres were added later to bring the cemetery to its present size of 5½ acres.

Alexandria was the site of one of the principal camps for the Northern troops sent to defend Washington, D.C., at the outbreak of the Civil War. These troops were physically unprepared, hastily trained, and composed mainly of "three months volunteers" whose terms were about to expire. When they tried to turn the Southern advance on the south bank of Bull Run, they were decisively defeated and beat a hasty retreat to Washington. At that time, Washington was surrounded by a cordon of field works, which included Alexandria. At one point later in the war, General Lee and his staff rode the outskirts of Alexandria and viewed the Capitol dome.

As the tide of battle turned, especially after Gettysburg, the battle zone was moved south and west and away from Washington. The fortress area nonetheless continued to serve as a major supply and replacement center throughout the remainder of the war.

Alexandria National Cemetery is one of the original 14 national cemeteries established in 1862. (Antietam, near Sharpsburg, Maryland, now under the jurisdiction of the National Park Service, and Soldiers' Home National Cemetery, administered by the Department of the Army, are the two not under the jurisdiction of the National Cemetery System.) The first burials made in the cemetery were soldiers who died incident to training or from sick-

Alexandria (Va.) National Cemetery, ca. 1903.

ness or disease in the many hospitals around Alexandria. The small cemetery was nearly filled to capacity by 1864. This was one of the considerations leading to the establishment of Arlington National Cemetery. The report of the inspector of national cemeteries, dated October 13, 1871, states that cemetery records listed the following interments:

White Union soldiers	3,277
Colored Union soldiers	249
Rebel soldiers, prisoners	29
Total	3,555

As of September 30, 2008, there was a total of 4,247 interments. Since the 1871 report, interments have averaged about five each year.

The lodge was designed and built by the U.S. Army Quartermaster Department about 1870. It was built of red sandstone and is still in use today, leased to a national veterans service organization. The lodge is on the National Register of Historic Places.

In 1879, the remains of 34 Confederate soldiers, originally interred in the cemetery, were disinterred and moved to the Christ Church Cemetery in Alexandria.

Near the flagpole and rostrum are four markers and a special monument erected by the United States Government on July 7, 1922. It commemorates four Quartermaster Corps employees who drowned in the Potomac River while in pursuit of President Lincoln's assassin, John Wilkes Booth, on April 24, 1865: Samuel N. Gosnell, Sec A, Grave 3174; Christian Farley, Sec A, Grave 3175; George W. Huntington, Sec A, Grave 3176; and Peter Carroll, Sec A, Grave 3177.

Former superintendents/directors of the cemetery are:

Frederick Kaufman, August 1867–January 1872
Charles R. Thomas, July 1939–February 1947
Eugene B. Taylor, March 1947–March 1948
William J. Costine, May 1948–November 1949
Carl W. Schaller, November 1949–February 1955
Albion H. McLellan, Jr., August 1955–February 1958
Samuel H. Davis, Jr., February 1958–September 1960

Oscar P. Findley, October 1960–December 1961
Thomas L. Hoefelmeyer, April 1964–August 1970
Romaldo F. Lucero, August 1970–August 1973
James D. Simms, August 1973–March 1975
William E. Rodgers, Jr., July 1976–December 1977
Robert L. Brake, January 1978–November 1979
Dennis P. Gura, December 1979–August 1980

The cemetery is closed for interments except for those in reserved gravesites or second interments in existing gravesites under the single gravesite per family policy. The cemetery is assigned to the director, Quantico National Cemetery for administration, management, and maintenance.

Alton National Cemetery
600 Pearl Street
Alton, Illinois 62003

The cemetery is located in the Alton City Cemetery, in Madison County.

The report of the inspector of national cemeteries dated June 28, 1870, includes a comment, "In the City Cemetery, near Alton, there is a soldiers' lot owned by the Government, in which are buried one hundred and sixty-three white Union soldiers, twelve being unknown, the rest known." The government did not own the 0.48-acre property until it was donated on July 1, 1940, by the Alton Cemetery Association, as one of the conditions prior to its designation as a national cemetery.

During the Civil War, the remains of Union soldiers who died at the post hospital and on steam boats passing up the Mississippi River were interred in a plot in the City Cemetery. The government paid the cemetery $30 a year to care for the plot. After the Civil War ended, when national cemeteries were being established, remains were removed from many plots in civilian cemeteries. The War Department planned to move the 163 soldiers at Alton to the Springfield National Cemetery, but the community protested and exerted sufficient influence to prevent the removal of these remains.

The initial offer by the Alton Cemetery Association was made in 1938. The offering was for land for "a national cemetery site," along with a proviso that the government would build a rostrum, or permanent speaker's stand, for use on Memorial Day and other national holidays. After the title was cleared and the offer accepted, the Works Progress Administration constructed the permanent rostrum. The first interments in the Alton National Cemetery occurred in 1941. In 1941–42, the remains of 49 Union soldiers interred in a separate section of the City Cemetery were moved to Sections A and G of the national cemetery.

The cemetery is maintained under private contract supervised by the director of the Jefferson Barracks National Cemetery. As of September 30, 2006, there were 526 interments. The cemetery is closed for interments except for those in reserved gravesites or second interments in existing graves.

Annapolis National Cemetery
West Street
Annapolis, Maryland 21401

The cemetery is located in Anne Arundel County, within the city of Annapolis. Annapolis was one of the 14 national cemeteries established in 1862, and one of the 7 established at Union troop concentration points. Land was leased from Nichalas Brewer in August 1862, December 1865, and August 1865, for a period of 99 years, but purchased from his heirs in 1871.

Disease, accidents and violence took its toll in the large recruitment and training camps. Epidemics of smallpox and ague (chills and malaria-like fever) occurred regularly in Annapolis, but the most consistent causes of death in the hospitals were typhoid and chronic diarrhea.

During the War of 1812, the practice of "paroling" prisoners of war was well established since neither side wanted the expense of holding and maintaining the other's troops for any period of time. In July 1862, an agreement between Union and Confederate forces continued this practice. City Point, Virginia, was selected as the site for the official exchange. The agreement specified Annapolis as the site where paroled Union prisoners would be held until they could be exchanged one-for-one for Confederate prisoners. Because of the conflict between the paroled prisoners and local town people, the Army established Camp Parole about two miles outside the town. This did very little to quell the turmoil and disruption in the town.

Records indicate that of all the units stationed at Annapolis, the 2nd Maryland Cavalry Regiment and the 67th Pennsylvania Infantry Regiment suffered the most casualties. The 2nd Maryland served only 6 months on guard duty in Annapolis and Anne Arundel Counties, yet during that time 12 men died. The regiment was composed of only 5 companies instead of the usual 12. The 67th Pennsylvania served as military policemen in Annapolis for 10 months before they were transferred to Harpers Ferry and then to Winchester. At Winchester the entire command was taken prisoner and held at Belle Isle prison camp at Richmond. They were paroled in July 1863 and returned to Annapolis. Later they were officially exchanged and returned to the fighting. During its two stays in Annapolis, 24 men of the 67th died.

Original interments were those men who died while encamped nearby, and later decedents from the hospitals at Camp Parole, near Annapolis, who were mostly returned prisoners of war. The report of the inspector of national cemeteries dated July 13, 1871, indicated a total of 2,505 interments 2,371 known and 134 unknown. The inspection report dated August 1, 1874, notes that the cemetery register showed 11 Confederates died at Annapolis, but only 10 graves could be located. A Russian sailor who died at Annapolis in 1864 while serving on a Russian man-of-war is interred in the cemetery.

National Archives records indicate that one Medal of Honor recipient, Coxswain Thomas Jones (U.S. Navy; died December 11, 1892) is buried here, but his gravesite cannot be located.

As of September 30, 2008, there was a total of 2,996 interments. The cemetery was closed for interments during fiscal year 1961, except for those in reserved gravesites and second interments in existing graves under the single gravesite per family policy. The cemetery is under the supervision of the Director, Baltimore National Cemetery.

Former superintendents/directors of the cemetery are:

W. Wakenshaw, 1874–Unknown
Robert R. Dye, April 1910–August 1911
Andrew K. Hill, March 1938–May 1938
Claude J. Huff, July 1940–September 1941
Roy B. Donahoe, October 1941–November 1946
James E. Bryars, November 1946–August 1948
James E. Wolstenholme, October 1948–March 1956
Ernest L. Fusse, March 1956–August 1957

Charles H. Culver, August 1957–June 1959
Charles E. Kilgore, July 1959–November 1959
Donald E. Eason, November 1959–January 1961
Andrew K. Hill, January 1961–April 1962
John T. Dowd, April 1962–November 1970
Eugene C. Goodman, November 1970–August 1975
G. Michael Heiman, May 1976–October 1976

Bakersfield National Cemetery
30338 East Bear Mountain Boulevard
Arvin, California 93203

The 500 acre Bakersfield National Cemetery is located about 25 miles east of SR 99 near Arvin along SR 223 in Kern County. The ground breaking ceremony for the cemetery was held on December 7, 2008, at 2:00 P.M.

The 50 acre Phase I development, when completed, will provide 4,800 gravesites, 4,000 pre-placed crypts, 4,000 in-ground cremation sites, and 3,000 columbarium niches. The National Cemetery Administration anticipates that interments will begin in he spring of 2009.

In February 2008, Wesley Jones was appointed the first director of the Bakersfield National Cemetery.

Balls Bluff National Cemetery
Leesburg, Virginia 22075

The cemetery is located about two miles from Leesburg in Loudon County, Virginia. A direction sign is on U.S. Highway 15, about two miles north of the intersection with Route 7. From the sign, one proceeds 1.3 miles down a narrow roadway to the cemetery.

The government owns 4.63 acres of land here, but only about a half acre is occupied by the cemetery. It is probably the least known and least visited of all the national cemeteries. The government acquired the land by donation in 1865 and received a quit-claim deed from the heirs of the owners in 1904. Because of its location and size, no superintendent has ever been assigned to this cemetery. The facility is maintained by private contract supervised by the director of Culpeper National Cemetery.

Within the enclosed area are the remains of 54 soldiers, interred in 25 graves, who fell during the Battle of Balls Bluff on October 21, 1861. Only one of these is known. James Allen, Company H, 15th Massachusetts Infantry, is interred in Grave 13. Outside the wall, but on government property, rests the lone Confederate buried here. On his headstone, commissioned by the Commonwealth of Virginia, is the inscription, "Clinton Hatcher, 1840–1861, Co. F, 8th Va. Regt., CSA Fell Bravely Defending His Native State." About 65 feet away, in a small clearing on private property, a government marker has been erected to the memory of Colonel Edward D. Baker, the Union commander in the battle. His remains are interred in San Francisco. Colonel Baker was a close personal friend of President Abraham Lincoln, who introduced him at the inauguration ceremonies and had him ride in his carriage as his chosen companion.

The Battle of Balls Bluff occurred when rather vague orders from General George B. McClellan to conduct a small reconnaissance were interpreted by officers in the field to conduct a full-scale assault into enemy territory. The operation was so poorly conceived and executed that it resulted in a staggering rout of the federal forces with nearly 1,000 dead, wounded or captured, including Colonel Baker. Coming only two months after the defeat at Bull Run, the battle prompted Congress to set up a joint committee to investigate the possibility of treason at Balls Bluff. As a result, Brigadier General Charles P. Stone, who had received General McClellan's orders and then issued the reconnaissance orders so grievously misunderstood, was arrested and jailed for 189 days before being released. No formal charges were ever filed against him. General Stone's reputation never fully recovered, although he later performed courageously in the war as commander of a combat brigade when General Grant moved east to take over the top command.

Another prominent Union officer in the Battle of Balls Bluff was Colonel Charles Devens, commanding the 15th Massachusetts Regiment. Colonel Devens, a lawyer from Boston, compiled a distinguished war record and later became U.S. attorney general under President Rutherford B. Hayes.

Among the wounded abandoned on the Virginia shore when the Union forces

Grave of Clinton Hatcher, Balls Bluff National Cemetery, 1951.

retreated into Maryland was a young first lieutenant in the 20th Massachusetts, Oliver Wendell Holmes. Although wounded several times during the Civil War, he survived and later became an outstanding justice of the United States Supreme Court.

Also in the 20th Massachusetts was Major Paul Revere, a descendent of the Revolutionary War patriot and silversmith. Major Revere was captured and sent off to the infamous Libby Prison in Richmond. He and other prisoners taken at Balls Bluff were later released in exchange for the crew of a Confederate privateer captured by the U.S. Navy.

Since the 1950s the War Department, and later the Veterans Administration, has been interested in moving the bodies in this cemetery to Culpeper National Cemetery, and disposing of the cemetery property. Public sentiment to maintain the cemetery as a landmark of the Battle of Balls Bluff, as well as congressional disfavor, has blocked any action. A bill to disestablish the national cemetery and remove the remains to another national cemetery was passed by the Senate on March 31, 1958, but no action was taken by the House of Representatives.

Baltimore National Cemetery
Frederick Avenue
Baltimore, Maryland 21228

The cemetery is located in the southwest section of the city of Baltimore, about ¾ mile from Loudon Park National Cemetery.

When it became apparent that Loudon Park National Cemetery was filling up rapidly and there was no other veterans cemetery close by, the Baltimore department of the American Legion enlisted the aid of Senator Millard E. Tydings to spearhead the fight to get a new national cemetery in Baltimore.

Before the War of 1812, there was a well constructed house on Frederick Avenue called "Cloud Capped." The coming of the British fleet to attack Baltimore in 1814 was watched from the top of the house, and a messenger dispatched to the town to announce its arrival, before the bombardment of Fort McHenry and the battle of North Point. The cemetery occupies 72.227 acres of rolling, tree-studded land once known as Cloud Capped. More than seven acres in the cemetery are too steep for interment purposes.

The property was purchased on September 18, 1936, from Blanchard and Susan K.B. Randall. During the American Revolution the property was held by the Baltimore Iron Ore Mining Company. It passed through several owners before becoming the summer home of the Randalls in 1890. The bulk of materials in the director's lodge was salvaged from the old mansion. The lodge is a duplication of the left wing of the old mansion.

One recipient of the Medal of Honor is buried in Baltimore National Cemetery:

Loddie Stupka, Grave 1, Distinguished Service section. Fireman, First Class, U.S. Navy.
Citation: Serving onboard the *USS Leyden*; for heroism at the time of the wreck of that vessel, 21 January 1903. [His special Medal of Honor headstone spells his name Laddie, but the citation spells it as above. He died on February 20, 1946.]

The cemetery was closed for interments on October 16, 1970, except for those burials in reserved gravesites or second interments in existing graves under the single gravesite per family policy. As of September 30, 2008, there were 44,883 interments, and there were still over 2,600 reservations.

Rostrum, Baltimore National Cemetery.

Former superintendents/directors of the cemetery are:

G.B. Alexander, March 1937–March 1938
Andrew K. Hill, May 1938–June 1938
John Bierman, July 1938–April 1942
Harold Montague, April 1942–April 1945
Claude J. Huff, April 1945–May 1945
George M. Hoswell (Actg), May 1945–
 September 1945
Thomas O. Moore, September 1945–November
 1946
Roy B. Donnahoe, November 1946–June 1959
Adolph P. Bernhardt, June 1959–November
 1968

Rudolph F. Staude, November 1968–June 1973
John H. Richardson, July 1973–July 1974
Harold A. Johnson, September 1974–February
 1976
Charles R. Weeks, February 1976–November
 1977
Harlon R. Sheets, January 1978–May 1979
Thomas E. Costanzo, May 1979–August 1980
Clifford E. Filteau, August 1980–July 1981
Leroy Newhouse, Jr., July 1981–June 1987
Lawrence Mitchell, August 1987–September 1988
Arthur E. Bath, October 1988–

Barrancas National Cemetery
Naval Air Station
Pensacola, Florida 32508

    Barrancas National Cemetery is located within the boundaries of the United States Naval Air Station. It is situated in Escambia County, eight miles southwest of downtown Pensacola and about two miles south of Warrington, Florida.

    The Pensacola Naval Air Station is the site of the United States Naval Air Training Command. The station covers almost 12,000 acres of land. It was established in 1914 on the site of the old United States Navy Yard at Pensacola. A small cemetery had been maintained in conjunction with the Marine Hospital which was located near Fort Barrancas. In 1838, the cemetery was expanded and established as a Naval cemetery. During the Civil War years, many casualties were interred in this cemetery in grave sites initially set aside for personnel on duty at the Navy yard.

Following the election of Abraham Lincoln in 1860, Florida became the third state to secede from the Union, on January 10, 1861. It had been a state for only 16 years, and it would be 7 more years before it was readmitted to the Union. Pensacola Bay provided the best harbor along the Gulf of Mexico. Its entrance was guarded by three United States Army forts; Fort McRae and.

Fort Barrancas on the land side, and Fort Pickens at the western tip of Santa Rosa Island. On the day of Florida's secession from the Union, Lieutenant Adam J. Slemmer, commanding Company G, 1st United States Artillery, spiked the guns at Fort Barrancas, blew up the ammunition at Fort McRae, and occupied Fort Pickens. Fort Pickens remained under control of the Union forces throughout the Civil War. Reinforcements for Lieutenant Slemmer's small garrison of 81 men arrived after the attack on Fort Sumter in April 1861 and brought the strength of the fort to 500 men. On April 18, 1861, Colonel Harvey Brown established the headquarters of the newly created Department of Florida at Fort Pickens.

On the mainland of Pensacola Bay the United States Navy Yard was surrendered intact to Confederate forces on April 12, 1861. Effective use by the Confederacy of the most important Navy yard south of Norfolk was considerably nullified by Union control of Fort Pickens. In May 1862, Confederate forces abandoned the Navy yard, Fort Barrancas, and Fort McRae.

A number of actions took place in and around Pensacola Bay before the Confederates evacuated the area. On September 2, 1861, Colonel Brown senta boat crew of 11 men from Fort Pickens to destroy the dry dock at the Navy yard, thus forestalling a Confederate plan to sink the dock and block the channel opposite Fort McRae. In a night expedition on September 14, 1861, Union sailors burned the Confederate cruiser *Judah* at the Navy yard after a hand-to-hand fight with her crew. Confederate General Braxton Bragg hit back with a raid on Santa Rosa Island on October 8–9, 1861. On November 22–23, 1861, the United States war vessels *Niagara* and *Richmond* joined Fort Pickens in attacking the Confederate steamer *Time* as she entered Pensacola harbor. The accompanying bombardment from Fort Pickens almost destroyed Fort McRae. The continuing presence of a strong federal force at Fort Pickens no doubt was a significant factor influencing the Confederate decision to abandon the Pensacola Bay area.

Many of those lost in these engagements were interred in Barrancas National Cemetery. As the war continued, the remains of other casualties were brought to the national cemetery for final burial.

By agreement between the Secretary of the Navy and the Secretary of War, on January 30, 1868, the cemetery was transferred to the War Department and became a national cemetery.

General Lorenzo Thomas, inspector of national cemeteries, reported in1869 that some 1,310 burials had been made in the cemetery. In addition to burials of troops stationed at forts Barrancas and Pickens, remains had also been reinterred in the cemetery from Pensacola, Bayou Chico, Gunboat Point, Santa Rosa Island, Appalachicola in Franklin County, and Mariannain Jackson County. This total included the remains of 673 unknown Union soldiers. However, the inspector's report of February 16, 1871, shows the following:

	Known	*Unknown*
White Union soldiers	379	271
Colored Union soldiers	154	98
Citizens	21	47
Rebel soldiers	60	12
Officers and sailors of the U.S. Navy	<u>112</u>	<u>225</u>
Total	726	653

General Thomas, in 1869, also reported that some 290 remains of the Civil War dead were yet to be removed to Barrancas. These remains were subsequently disinterred from Santa Rosa Island, San Juan Island, and St. Andrew's Bay in Washington County and brought to Barrancas for reinterment.

Grave 1496, Section 18, marks the grave of Ga-Ah, second wife of the Apache Chief Geronimo. Geronimo was born in southern Arizona. His Indian name was Goyathloy, meaning one who yawns. The Mexicans gave him the name Geronimo, which is Spanish for Jerome. He was not a chief by birth but rose to the ranks of leadership by his courage, determination and skill in successive raids on Mexican troops who had killed his mother, first wife, and children in 1858. He was considered perhaps the most cunning Indian fighter in American history. He led devastating raids in Arizona and New Mexico before the U.S. government intervened and caused him to surrender to General George F. Crook in May 1883. The elusive Geronimo escaped and conducted further raids in both the United States and Mexico before his capture by General Nelson A. Miles in 1886.

Following the capture of Geronimo, the Chiricahuas were removed as prisoners of war to Florida, and then resettled in Fort Pickens where Ga-Ah died of pneumonia on September 29, 1887.

In 1887, the Apache exiles were transferred to Mount Vernon Barracks, Alabama, and some 100 of their children were sent to the Carlisle Indian School in Pennsylvania. Cli-

Director's lodge, Barrancas National Cemetery, 1959.

matic conditions in Alabama caused many deaths among the Indians, including Chappo, Geronimo's son, and Larry (Lanny) Fun, Geronimo's cousin. Both of them are interred in Mobile National Cemetery. In 1894 the entire group was relocated to Fort Sill, Oklahoma, as wards of the U.S. government. Many of these Indians, including Geronimo, another of his wives, a son and a daughter are interred in the Apache Cemetery at Fort Sill. While at Fort Sill, Geronimo enlisted in the U.S. Army and served as an Indian scout with Troop L of the 7th Cavalry. He died of pneumonia at Fort Sill on February 17, 1909, at the age of 80.

Adm. John Walter Reeves, Jr., recipient of several citations during World War II, was interred in Section 26, Grave 814, on July 18, 1967. For his outstanding tactical leadership of his troops against the enemy Japanese forces, he was awarded the Distinguished Service Medal and two Gold Stars in lieu of the second and third Distinguished Service Medals, and the Legion of Merit with Combat "V" and a Gold Star in lieu of the second Legion of Merit with Combat "V." Following his distinguished World War II service, Adm. Reeves reported to the Naval Air Station at Pensacola where he served as chief of Naval basic training.

There are three known Medal of Honor recipients interred in the Barrancas National Cemetery. A dagger before the name indicates that the recipient was killed in action.

Clyde Everett Lassen, Sec. 38, Grave 113. Lieutenant, U.S. Navy, Helicopter Support Squadron 7, embarked in U.S.S. Preble (DLG-15). Place and date: Republic of Vietnam, 19 June 1968.
Citation: For conspicuous gallantry and intrepidity at the risk of his life above and beyond the call of duty as pilot and aircraft commander of a search and rescue helicopter attached to Helicopter Support Squadron 7, during operations against enemy forces in North Vietnam.

Stephen W. Pless, Sec 21, Grave 929A. Major (then Capt.), U.S. Marine Corps, VMD-6, Mag-36, 1st Marine Aircraft Wing. Place and date: Near Quang Nai, Republic of Vietnam, 19 August 1967.
Citation: For conspicuous gallantry and intrepidity at the risk of his life above and beyond the call of duty while serving as a helicopter gunship pilot attached to Marine Observation Squadron 6 in action against the enemy forces. During an escort mission Maj. Pless monitored an emergency call that four American soldiers stranded on a nearby beach were being overwhelmed by a large Viet Cong force. Maj. Pless flew to the scene and found 30 to 50 enemy soldiers in the open. Some of the enemy were bayonetting and beating the downed Americans. Major Pless displayed exceptional airmanship as he launched a devastating attack against the enemy force, killing and wounding many of the enemy and driving the remainder back into a treeline. His rocket and machinegun attacks were made at such low levels that the aircraft flew through debris created by explosions from its rockets. Seeing one of the wounded soldiers gesture for assistance, he maneuvered his helicopter into a position between the wounded men and the enemy, providing a shield which permitted his crew to retrieve the wounded. During the rescue the enemy directed intense fire at the helicopter and rushed the aircraft again and again, closing to within a few feet before being beaten back. When the wounded men were aboard, Maj. Pless maneuvered the helicopter out to sea. Before it became safely airborne, the overloaded aircraft settled four times into the water. Displaying superb airmanship, he finally got the helicopter aloft. Major Pless' extraordinary heroism coupled with his outstanding flying skill prevented the annihilation of the tiny force. His courageous actions reflect great credit upon himself and uphold the highest traditions of the Marine Corps and the U.S. Naval Service.

Clifford Chester Sims, Sec 29, Grave 546. Staff Sergeant, U.S. Army, Company D, 2d Battalion (Airborne), 501st Infantry, 101st Airborne Division. Place and date: Near Hue, Republic of Vietnam, 21 February 1968.
Citation: For conspicuous gallantry and intrepidity in action at the risk of his life above and beyond the call of duty. Staff Sergeant Sims distinguished himself while serving as a squad leader with Company D. Company D was assaulting a heavily fortified enemy position concealed within a dense wooded area when it encountered strong enemy defensive fire. Once within the wood line, S/Sgt. Sims led his squad in a furious attack against the enemy which had pinned down the 1st Platoon and threatened to overrun it. His skillful leadership provided the platoon with freedom of movement and enabled it to regain the initiative. Staff Sergeant Sims was then ordered to move

his squad to a position where he could provide covering fire for the company command group and to link up with the3rd Platoon, which was under heavy enemy pressure. After moving no more than 30 meters S/Sgt. Sims noticed that a brick structure in which ammunition was stocked was on fire. Realizing the danger, S/Sgt. Sims took immediate action to move his squad from this position. Though in the process of leaving the area two members of his squad were injured by the subsequent explosion of the ammunition, S/Sgt. Sims' prompt actions undoubtedly prevented more serious casualties from occurring. While continuing through the dense woods amidst heavy enemy fire, S/Sgt. Sims and his squad were approaching a bunker when they head the unmistakable noise of a concealed booby trap being triggered immediately to their front. Staff Sergeant Sims warned his comrades of the danger and unhesitatingly hurled himself upon the devise as it exploded, taking the full impact of the blast. In so protecting his fellow soldiers, he willingly sacrificed his life. Staff Sergeant Sims' extraordinary heroism at the cost of his life is in keeping with the highest traditions of the military service and reflects great credit upon himself and the U.S. Army.

Other recent war casualties:

Seven of the fourteen crewmembers of the C-130 Hercules Gun-Ship shot down during the Persian Gulf War are buried alongside each other in Section 38. Two aircrew members who served in direct support of Somalia when their C-130 "Jockey 14" Hercules crashed during taleoff from the coast of Kenya. They are interred next to each other in Section 38. Two local airmen killed by terrorists at the Saudi Arabia Housing Compound in Dhahran, June 25, 1996, are interred in Section 40, Graves 81 and 82. The remains of three repatriated aviators from Vietnam are interred in Sections 38 and 41. Ten British aviators killed during training at a naval air station during World War II, are interred in Section 23.

A large monument in Section 22 of the cemetery brings to mind the toll taken by a yellow fever epidemic. This disease, happily now almost unknown, was a prevalent threat in the Southern states throughout the 19th century. This monument was erected in 1884 by the Marine Guard of the Navy Yard in memory of eight comrades who died in an epidemic during late August and early September 1883. The names of the fever victims, whose ages ranged from 20 to 29 years, are inscribed on the four faces of the monument.

In 1944, 1950, 1986, and 1990, additional acreage was set apart from the land of the Naval Air Station to expand the cemetery. Today the Barrancas National Cemetery encompasses 94.9 acres. An old civilian cemetery (Warrington) with approximately two acres is incorporated within this cemetery. As of September 30, 2008, 36,165 interments had been made in the cemetery.

Former superintendents/directors of the Barrancas National Cemetery are:

L.B. Gould, Unknown–May 1898
Albert Gale, Unknown–October 1919
John H. Black, dates unknown
Thomas P. Boston, January 1943–June 1946
Harold A. Johnson, July 1946–June 1955
Curtis W. Spence, June 1955–March 1956
Pearl O. Crawford, March 1956–September 1956
Norman W. Kelly, September 1956–August 1961
John W. Clemons, August 1961–February 1964

Steve L. Bukovitz, March 1964–June 1974
Mack Cochenour, Jr., July 1974–August 1975
Raymond B. Schuppert, September 1975–May 1988
Sandra M. Beckley, May, 1988–March 2003
Jeffrey Teas, July 2003–June 2005
Quincy Whitehead, September 2005–December 2007

Bath National Cemetery
Bath, New York 14810

The Bath National Cemetery is located in Steuben County, New York, adjacent to the Department of Veterans Affairs Medical Center. The grounds consist of 24.9 acres of hilly terrain with a commanding view of the countryside.

The cemetery was originally a part of the New York State Soldiers and Sailors Home, established in 1877. The cemetery was dedicated on December 25, 1879. In 1930, the Soldiers and Sailors Home became the Veterans Administration Medical Center (VAMC) and the cemetery became a part of the VAMC. When the National Cemetery System was transferred from the Department of the Army to the Veterans Administration in 1973, the VAMC cemetery at Bath was transferred to the National Cemetery System and designated a national cemetery. The Veterans Administration became the Department of Veterans Affairs in 1988.

The first interment in the cemetery was Private William O. Terrell, on February 12, 1879. He is interred in Section G, Grave 13. The initial interments in the cemetery were conducted according to military custom with a home company acting as escort. The chaplain conducted services first at the chapel and then at the gravesite, where a parting salute and the sounding of taps accompanied the final resting of yet another veteran. This custom is still continued by the dedicated veterans at the domiciliary located at the VAMC.

In 1892 a granite monument 40 feet high was erected by Samuel Dietzand dedicated to the "Memory of the soldiers and sailors of the War for Preservation of the Union who died in the Soldiers and Sailors Home."

Until July 1, 1974, the cemetery was maintained by the Engineering Service of the VAMC. The first superintendent was Ray C. Van Tassel, Sr.

Local veteran and civic organizations raised funds to purchase six acres of land adjacent to the cemetery, and donated it to the Veterans Administration in April 1984. This donation extended the availability of gravesites for many years. Total interments as of September 30, 2008, were 13,842.

What has been described as "the first and oldest United States MIAs"(missing in action) were brought to Bath National Cemetery and interred on June 30, 1988. The story started on October 26, 1987, on land owned by a school teacher in Lake Erie, Canada. That day archeologists found a skeleton on the site where he planned to build a house. At that point, scientists and military historians took over the task of uncovering, classifying and studying the bones. A total of 28 remains were uncovered. The soldiers had been buried in their

Fort Erie Repatriates, Bath National Cemetery.

uniforms, without coffins, and their uniform buttons became the method by which unit identification was made. When the bones were first found, they were believed to be those of Indians. Later, when buttons were found, they were thought to be British. Identification of the buttons proved that they were Americans. A total of 438 buttons was found.

The 28 soldiers were buried in the traditional Christian method, bodies lying east-west with hands crossed. This indicated that they were buried during a lull in the fighting by their comrades and not by their enemies. Most of the men were in their mid-teens to early twenties, and the remains showed that they had been driven hard, carrying heavy weights, marching long distances, and living on meager rations. This was typical of the way their commanding officer, General Winfield Scott, used his men. Few of them were taller than 5 feet 6 inches, and some bore evidence of earlier infections or wounds.

The buttons told their story. These men had fought the Niagara Campaign with clashes at Chippawa and Lundy's Lane before the Fort Erie battle. They died at Snake Hill, a battery overlooking Fort Erie. According to military historians, they probably died on the night of August 15, 1814. The British had besieged the fort for two weeks and, thinking they had weakened the Americans, launched a night attack. At dawn the British had gone, their attack a failure. It is believed that the Americans buried their dead on the spot. The siege continued until November 5, when the Americans abandoned Fort Erie and moved back across the river, leaving these 28 behind them for 174 years. Before leaving, the Americans destroyed most of the fort's earthworks, which may have caused the graves to remain hidden for so long.

The Department of the Army, working with Canadian officials, held a repatriation ceremony at Fort Erie, Canada, on June 30, 1988. The author was privileged to participate in the ceremony. On behalf of the government of Canada, the minister of veterans affairs released the remains to the United States ambassador to Canada. Ambassador Thomas Niles turned the remains over to Major General Jones for transport to the Bath National Cemetery. The Third United States Infantry, the "Old Guard," Fife and Drum Corps, served as escort at Fort Erie. The remains were moved by hearse to Bath, escorted by the New York State police. At Bath, they were interred with full military honors performed by the tomb guards who guard the Tomb of the Unknown Soldier at Arlington National Cemetery. Each of the remains is marked by an "Unknown" headstone. In addition, a bronze plaque on a granite base reads as follows:

> To the memory of those American fighting men who lost their lives in the Niagara Campaigns of the War of 1812. These hallowed grounds hold the remains of soldiers who died at Fort Erie, Ontario during the period August to October 1814. Under the leadership of Major General Jacob Brown they gallantly withstood and ultimately broke a British siege of their fortifications. Their earthly remains lay long forgotten until rediscovered in 1987 and reburied at this site 30 June 1988.

There are five Medal of Honor recipients interred in Bath National Cemetery:

George Grueb, Sec A, Grave 2–3. Private, Company F, 158th New York Infantry. Place and date: Chapins Farm, Va., 29 September 1864.
Citation: Gallantry in advancing to the ditch of the enemy's works.

John Kiggins, Sec H, Grave 32–9. Sergeant, Company D, 149th New York Infantry. Place and date: Lookout Mountain, Tenn., 24 November 1863.
Citation: Waved the colors to save the lives of the men who were being fired upon by their own batteries, and thereby drew upon himself a concentrated fire from the enemy.

George Ladd, Sec C, Grave 6–6. Private, Company H, New York Cavalry. Place and date: Waynesboro, Va., 2 March 1865.
Citation: Captured a standard bearer, his flag, horse and equipment.

James Roberts. Seaman, U.S. Navy. G.O. No.: 45, 31 December 1864.

Citation: Roberts served on board the *USS Agawan*, as one of a volunteer crew of a powder boat which was exploded near Fort Fisher, 23 December 1864. The powder boat, towed in by the *Wilderness* to prevent detection by the enemy, castoff and slowly steamed to within 300 yards of the beach. After fuses and fires had been lit and a second anchor with short scope let go to assure the boat's tailing inshore, the crew again boarded the *Wilderness* and proceeded a distance of 12 miles from shore. Less than two hours later the explosion took place, and the following day fires were observed still burning at the fort.

Charles E. Morse, Sec J, Grave 4–20. Sergeant, Company I, New York Infantry. Place and date: Wilderness, Va., 5 May 1864.

Citation: Voluntarily rushed back into the enemy's lines, took the colors from the color sergeant, who was mortally wounded, and although himself wounded, carried them through the fight.

Former superintendents/directors of the cemetery are:

Ray C. Van Tassell, Sr., July 1974–Unknown   Mark E. Maynard, 1987–1990
Robert C. Bennett, February 1984–August 1987   William L. Livingston, 1990–

Baton Rouge National Cemetery

220 North 19th Street
Baton Rouge, Louisiana 70806

The cemetery is located in East Baton Rouge Parish within the corporate limits of the city of Baton Rouge. It is about one mile from the Mississippi River, between Florida and Convention streets on 19th Street.

During the Civil War, soldiers were buried in this place, which was then just a forest. They were also buried in the adjacent city-owned Magnolia Cemetery. The interment of deceased Union soldiers in this tract was started in January 1867, and the U.S. government purchased the 7.5-acre property from Mr. Pierre Barronne and Madame Simonia Bareno in 1868. The cemetery has not been expanded since that time. It was designated a National Cemetery in 1867.

Situated 130 miles north of New Orleans, Baton Rouge is an important port on the Mississippi River, the principal shipping waterway of the inland area of the United States. Chattanooga, Tennessee, and Vicksburg, Mississippi, were keys to the Union strategy during the Civil War Chattanooga because it was the doorway between Richmond and the Southwest, Vicksburg because it not only commanded the Mississippi River, but was also the rail connection with Texas, where the Confederacy obtained much of its food and munitions for its armies fighting in the east. It was imperative that Union forces control the Mississippi River if the war was to be won. New Orleans fell to the combined land and naval attacks of General Benjamin F. Butler and Flag Officer, later Admiral, David G. Farragut, on April 29, 1862. General N.P. Banks occupied Baton Rouge in December 1863. Vicksburg fell on July 4, 1863. Control of the Mississippi was assured and a vital artery of the Confederate supply line was severed.

After the national cemetery was established, remains were brought here from the battlefields near Baton Rouge. Bodies were also removed from Plaquemine, Louisiana, and interred here, as were 116 from Camden, Arkansas. At the end of the Civil War, it was reported that the government paid a bonus to anyone who discovered the grave of a Union soldier. The recovered remains were buried in the cemetery.

The report of the inspector of national cemeteries dated February 28, 1871, listed interments at that time as follows:

Baton Rouge National Cemetery.

	Known	*Unknown*
Commissioned officers	24	4
White Union soldiers	2,231	485
Colored Union soldiers	173	3
Sailors	3	0
Citizens	2	0
Total	2,433	492

There are three Confederate soldiers buried in the cemetery.

In 1870 the city of Jerusalem presented a "Cedar of Lebanon" tree to the cemetery. Later, when workers wanted to cut down the tree to make way for the rostrum, permission was denied. At last report, the old cedar tree still stands south of the old rostrum.

The cemetery was originally enclosed by a "substantial wooden fence." In 1878 the government let a contract to Michael and Bernard Jodd to build a brick wall around the cemetery in place of the picket fence. It is thought that the Jodds were from Boston, Massachusetts. They brought with them a crew of bricklayers and hired local men to carry brick and mortar. At this time yellow fever was widespread in the South, and, before the wall was completed, both of the Jodds had contacted the fever and died in September 1878. They are interred in Section 44 of the cemetery. The wall was completed later by local workmen.

In 1882, 20 bodies were removed from the old Baton Rouge Barracks Post Cemetery and interred in the cemetery. They were adults and children, presumably, family members of officers stationed there. Their graves are marked by inscribed flat granite grave covers. The old barracks grounds are now part of the new state capitol grounds.

In 1886, the remains of General Philemon Thomas were disinterred from the old post cemetery and reinterred in the national cemetery. General Thomas was born in Virginia on February 9, 1763, and died in Baton Rouge on November 18, 1847. He fought in both the Revolutionary War and the War of 1812. He commanded the forces that captured the Spanish fort at Baton Rouge in 1810. General Thomas had served as a member of the legislatures of Kentucky and Louisiana, and twice was elected to the United States Congress.

In 1908 the state of Massachusetts authorized the erection of a monument in memory of the officers of the 31st and 41st Infantry and the men from Massachusetts who lost their lives in the Department of the Gulf during the Civil War. The monument was dedicated November 16, 1909.

The cemetery was closed during fiscal year 1960, except for interments in reserved gravesites and second interments in existing graves under the single gravesite per family policy. As of September 30, 2008, there was a total of 5,476 interments in the cemetery.

In the early years, the tour of duty for most superintendents was from two to three years. The reason some of them disliked this station was the damp climate, which they considered unhealthy. Two of them, a Mr. King and John Carroll, are buried in the cemetery. Former superintendents/directors are:

Fred Schmidt, 1882–1885
John Carroll, 1888–1889
Mr. King, 1920–1924
Captain Church, 1924–1927
Mr. Moody, 1927–1930
L.S. Porter, 1932–1934
John Sasser, 1934–1937
Victor A. Bolsius, 1937–1940
Floyd Wilcox, 1940–1941

C. Roy Handley, June 1941–November 1947
Jacob H. Wade, November 1947–February 1960
Paul B. Porter, February 1960–March 1977
Clifford E. Filteau, December 1977–September 1980
Eugene L. Chambers, November 1980–January 1984
Steve L. Muro, January 1984–January 1985

Since January 1985, the cemetery has been under the jurisdiction of the director of Port Hudson National Cemetery.

Bay Pines National Cemetery
Veterans Administration Center
Bay Pines, Florida 33504

The cemetery is located on the grounds of the Veterans Administration Center (VAC) in Pinellas County, about 15 miles south of St. Petersburg, Florida. The VAC includes a hospital and domiciliary.

On March 15, 1933, the cemetery was dedicated and officially opened as a burial ground for those who died in the Bay Pines VAC hospital and domiciliary. When the 21.248-acre site was opened it was laid out in 42 symmetrical sections. The first interment was made on April 25, 1933, and by January 1964, all available gravesites had been used. A survey in 1984 reported that over 4,000 gravesites could be gained by removing the hedges that divided the center of the cemetery and reducing the space between the aisles separating the sections. The survey also found that 12.25 acres were not suitable for gravesites because of the high water table, although some of the land was suitable for the in-ground burial of cremated remains.

The cemetery was transferred to the National Cemetery System on May 28, 1984, and reopened for interments on July 2, 1984. This change in status to an open national cemetery permitted the interment of all eligible veterans, spouses and dependents. By Septem-

Monument at Bay Pines National Cemetery.

ber 1987 the only remaining gravesites were those for cremated remains and gravesites set aside for surviving spouses of those already interred. As of September 30, 2008, there were 27,369 interments.

A large monument constructed of pink Etowah marble in 1937, dedicated to "the memory of those who served their country," stands guard at the entrance to the cemetery grounds. A polished granite bench, dedicated to the memory of World War I veterans, sits just outside the cemetery entrance, facing the new POW/MIA monument. The maple tree planted in Section 53 in 1976 commemorates the bicentennial of our country's Declaration of Independence.

Former directors of the cemetery are:

Betty L. Whitaker, June 1984–July 1988
Gilberto Lopez, August 1988–1990
Jeffrey Teas, 1990–

Beaufort National Cemetery
1601 Boundary Street
Beaufort, South Carolina 29902

Beaufort National Cemetery is located within the city limits of Beaufort, South Carolina. All land traffic enters Beaufort on U.S. Highway 21, and Boundary Street is part of

Beaufort National Cemetery, 1954.

this highway in the downtown portion of the city. The cemetery is surrounded by a six-foot-high red brick wall and is laid out in the shape of a half wheel. The large iron gates are set at the hub with the oyster shell roads forming the spokes. The cemetery files contain a copy of an unsigned letter from President Abraham Lincoln, dated February 10, 1863, personally authorizing the establishment of this national cemetery.

The city of Beaufort is located on Port Royal Island, one of the 64 islands that make up Beaufort County. Jean Ribaut discovered and named Port Royal Island in 1562, and the city of Beaufort was founded in 1711.

South Carolinians strongly supported states' right to free trade. They opposed federal tariffs because their economy depended heavily on trade with the European nations, and high tariffs discouraged this trade. In 1828 Congress passed a law raising the tariff. Vice President John C. Calhoun, a South Carolinian, wrote the "Exposition and Protest." His paper declared that a state was not bound by any federal law which that state considered unconstitutional. Congress compromised with a reduced tariff bill in 1833. As the controversy boiled during the 1850s over whether slavery should be allowed in parts of the West, South Carolina threatened to secede from the Union, but got little support from other Southern states.

As the 1860 election approached, South Carolinians feared that if elected, Abraham Lincoln would use federal power to abolish slavery. Following the election South Carolina on December 20, 1860, became the first state to secede from the Union. Lincoln was inaugurated on March 4, 1861. By late spring of that year, ten other states had joined South Carolina in the secession movement and formed the Confederate States of America. After Confederate troops fired on Fort Sumter on April 12, 1861, fighting along the South Carolina coast continued throughout the war.

Beaufort was a center of culture and affluence prior to the Civil War. Great fortunes were made in the cultivation of rice and indigo, and later, in long staple sea island cotton. The South Carolina historian McCrady wrote that the plantation owners in this area, who had summer homes in Beaufort, made that city "the wealthiest, most aristocratic and cultivated town of its size in America." It was also a hotbed of secessionist sentiment. The original Ordinance of Secession, by which South Carolina led the withdrawal of Southern states from the Union, was drawn up in Beaufort in 1860. As a result, Beaufort was made an early object for repression and reprisal by the United States government.

Port Royal Sound, about 60 nautical miles southwest of Charleston, provided one of the best harbors along the south Atlantic coast. Its entrance was guarded by two Confederate forts; Fort Beauregard to the north and Fort Walker to the south. In late October 1861 the federal fleet steamed out of the Chesapeake Bay heading south with 50 ships and troop transports under the command of Flag Officer Samuel F. DuPont. The troop transports carried 1,500 Union soldiers under the command of General William T. Sherman. After nine days, the flotilla reached Port Royal Sound. On November 5, a Union reconnaissance revealed batteries at Bay Point (Fort Beauregard) and Hilton Head Island (Fort Walker), as well as a number of Confederate gun boats. On November 6, a skirmish between opposing naval vessels took place. The next day, Fort Walker opened fire on the fleet with its 13 guns. The ensuing Union amphibious assault succeeded in capturing the area.

Beaufort became headquarters for the U.S. Army, Department of the South, and the chief base for the South Atlantic Blockading Squadron. From here both coastal and inland operations were conducted. Federal troops were not withdrawn from South Carolina until 1877.

The report of the inspector of national cemeteries from May 17, 1870, lists interments in the cemetery as follows:

	Known	*Unknown*
Commissioned officers	84	0
White Union soldiers	3,621	3,353
Colored Union soldiers	795	950
Sailors	91	109
Employees and citizens	78	0
Total	4,669	4,412

In the years before and during the Civil War, there was a strong sense of regionalism. Most of the Civil War veterans were interred in sections according to their state of origin. Section D was designated for "colored" enlisted burials.

Original interments in the cemetery were those who died in the Union hospital during the occupation and bodies removed from several places in East Florida, from the vicinity of Savannah, Georgia, and from Charleston, Morris Island, Hilton Head, and other places in South Carolina. About 2,800 remains were removed from Millen, Georgia, a prison cemetery at Lawton, Georgia, and reinterred in the national cemetery. There are also 117 Confederate soldiers interred here.

One German World War II prisoner of war is interred here. He was a crew member of the German submarine *U-Rathke*, which was sunk on May 9, 1942, off Cape Lookout, North Carolina, by the Coast Guard cutter *Icarus*. He died en route to Charleston.

In May 1987, souvenir hunters on Folly's Island, near Charleston, using metal detectors to locate relics, discovered the remains of 19 Union soldiers. The remains were discovered on what was believed to be the winter encampment of the 55th Regiment and the First North Carolina Infantry. Both units were made up of black troops who fought side by side with the 54th Regiment. The 54th and 55th Infantry regiments were from Massachusetts. The South Carolina Institute of Archaeology and Anthropology directed the excavation and unit identification of the remains. When found, the enlisted soldiers were wearing standard U.S. Army uniforms and buried in individual graves, some in wooden coffins. Others were wrapped in rubber blankets in what appeared to be a formal cemetery.

The 1989 Memorial Day program at Beaufort National Cemetery featured the reinterment of the 19 black Union soldiers missing in action since 1863. The Honor Guard for the service were members of the cast who were filming the movie *Glory* nearby. Massachusetts Gov. Michael Dukakis led a group of dignitaries and served as principal speaker at the ceremony. He quoted General Sherman: "If it had not been for so much talk in Massachusetts and so much hot blood in Carolina, this war would not have come upon us." He unveiled a bronze plaque for the 19 Massachusetts soldiers that reads as follows:

> The governor of the Commonwealth of Massachusetts, Michael Dukakis, and descendents of the African-American Civil War volunteers of the 54th and 55th Infantry Regiments of Massachusetts, accompanied by citizens of the Commonwealth, came on this day to Beaufort, South Carolina, National Cemetery, to honor members of the black 55th Massachusetts Regiment of Volunteer Infantry, whose remains were found on Folly Island, S.C., in 1987 and reinterred this day with full military honors befitting American soldiers.
>
> Duty well performed, glory and reward won.

At the end of the center road in the cemetery, a large granite monument honoring those who died for the Union cause bears the legend, "Immortality to Hundreds of the Defenders of American Liberty Against the Great Rebellion."

A marble tablet in Section 64 is mounted on a brick base and inscribed with the names of 174 unknown Union dead who are presumed to be buried in the cemetery, but whose graves are not identified other than by unknown markers. In the lower right-hand corner is the inscription "Hundreds of Others Names Unknown." The monument was erected by Mrs. L.T. Potter of Charleston, South Carolina, shortly after the Civil War.

In Section 6, Grave 368, Ord. Sgt. James Smith is interred. His headstone lists "U.S. Navy," and Section 6 is an all–Civil War Navy section. His record of interment, however, indicates that he was a member of the U.S. Marine Corps stationed aboard the *USS New Hampshire.*

The commanding general of the Union occupation forces purchased the 28.92-acre tract, once known as Jolly's Grove, at a tax sale on March 11, 1863, for $75. As of September 30, 2008, there were 19,759 interments in the cemetery.

Brigadier General George William McCaffrey, U.S. Army, Ret., was buried on April 6, 1990. General McCaffrey's military career included combat service in World War II, Korea and Vietnam. He also served as chief of the U.S. Military Advisory Group in Ethiopia.

There is one known Medal of Honor recipient interred in Beaufort National Cemetery. Ralph H. Johnson was reinterred on March 20, 1990, from a rural cemetery near Charleston, S.C. The dagger indicates that he was killed in action.

†**Ralph H. Johnson**, Sec 3, Grave 21. Private First Class, U.S. Marine Corps, Company A, 1st Reconnaissance Battalion, 1st Marine Division (Rein), FMF. Place and date: Near the Quan Duc Valley, Republic of Vietnam, 5 March 1968.

Citation: For conspicuous gallantry and intrepidity at the risk of his life above and beyond the call of duty while serving as a reconnaissance scout with Company A, in action against the North Vietnamese Army and Viet Cong forces. In the early morning hours during Operation ROCK, Pfc. Johnson was a member of a 15-man reconnaissance patrol manning an observation post on Hill 146 overlooking the Quan Duc Valley deep in enemy-controlled territory. They were attacked by a platoon-size hostile force employing automatic weapons, satchel charges and hand grenades. Suddenly, a hand grenade landed in the three-man fighting hole occupied by Pfc. Johnson and two fellow Marines. Realizing the inherent danger to his two comrades, he shouted a warning and unhesitatingly hurled himself upon the explosive device. When the grenade exploded, Pfc. Johnson absorbed the tremendous impact of the blast and was killed instantly. His prompt and heroic act saved the life of one Marine at the cost of his life and undoubtedly prevented the enemy from penetrating his sector of the patrol's perimeter. Pfc. Johnson's courage, inspiring valor and selfless devotion to duty were in keeping with the highest traditions of the Marine Corps and the U.S. Naval service. He gallantly gave his life for his country.

OTHERS: Joseph Simmons, Master Sergeant, 25th Infantry, Buffalo Soldiers, World War I and World War II. (Section 2, Grave 2) Fought on three fronts in France, and was awarded the Legion of Honor Medal by the Republic of France. (The French equivalent of the U.S. Medal of Honor). He died on 24 September 1999, 21 days before his 100th birthday.

Former superintendents/directors of Beaufort National Cemetery are:

John G. Voss, Dates unknown
Neils Christensen, Dates unknown
W.A. Donaldson, Dates unknown
George Ford, Unknown–1906
Frank Barrows, Dates unknown
George Hess, Dates unknown
R. Dickson, Dates unknown
J.B. Erion, Dates unknown
Richard B. Hill, Dates unknown
Fillmore M. Brist, Dates unknown
O. Wright, Dates unknown
R.C. McCzacken, Dates unknown
R. Rodriquiz, Dates unknown
William M. Darby, August 1942–February 1947

Curtis W. Spence, March 1949–June 1955
John T. Spelman, June 1955–August 1957
Bernie Bowse, 2006–Present
Francis M. Brooke, August 1957–November 1962
Harold A. Johnson, November 1962–October 1965
William A. Rossbach, October 1965–August 1968
Allen G. Farabee, August 1968–October 1977
Willie B. Smith, November 1977–April 1980
Robert E.L. St. Clair, April 1980–February 1984
Gilberto Lopez, March 1984–July 1988
Virgil M. Wertenberger, 1988–1992
Ramona L. Vaughn, 1992–1993

Herbert D. Stanley, February 1947–December
  1947
Robert A. Spence, January 1948–March 1949

Dennis O'Gorman, 1993–1994
Rafael Rodriguez, 1994–1995
Walter Gray, 1995–2006

Beverly National Cemetery
R.D. #1, Bridgeboro Road
Beverly, New Jersey 08010

The cemetery is situated in Burlington County, in Edgewater Park near the intersection of Mt. Holly and Bridgeboro Roads.

The original tract consisted of one acre which was purchased from Mr. Christian Weymann when the cemetery was established in 1864. The plot was located in the northwest corner of the village cemetery and surrounded by a picket fence painted black. Additional lands were acquired in 1936, 1937, 1948 and 1951. As of September 30, 2008, the cemetery comprised 64.55 acres and included 42,080 interments. Beverly National Cemetery serves the large veteran population in the metropolitan area of Philadelphia.

The cemetery was established for the burial of veterans who died in the Federal Army Hospital located nearby and in one of the convalescent hospitals established in the old brick buildings of the Wall Rope Factory. Although this was a convalescent hospital, many operations and amputations were performed here. The original 147 Union soldiers buried here, 137 known and 10 unknown, came from that hospital. Until 1946, Beverly National Cemetery handled only a few interments each month, but as Philadelphia National Cemetery became filled, interments increased steadily and the government expanded its size and facilities.

Little is known about Warner Haskell, the first veteran to be interred in the cemetery. He died in August 1864, at the height of the Civil War. He was originally interred in Section 1, Grave 1, located by the north gate of the cemetery, but the section and grave were moved to allow for the widening of the entrance road.

Seven unknown Revolutionary War soldiers who were initially interred in the rear of the fire station, 5th and Arch streets, Camden, New Jersey, were reinterred in the national cemetery in July 1955. Their remains are located in Section F, Grave 1879-H.

The State of New Jersey Monument, erected in 1872, was dismantled in 1951 and donated to the American Legion of Beverly. It was removed from the cemetery by the donee on May 13, 1953.

Directly north of the administration building is the lodge. This building was constructed in 1879 and is still used as the home of the cemetery director.

Seven group burials from World War II contain 22 remains. One group burial from Vietnam contains three remains. In Section J, Graves 2912, 2913, and 2914, are the remains of two soldiers and two civilians killed in a Nike missile explosion on May 28, 1958.

Beverly National Cemetery is closed for future interments other than those in previously reserved gravesites or second interments in existing graves under the single gravesite per family policy. The last available gravesite was used on February 4, 1966, for the wife of a veteran.

There are four Medal of Honor recipients interred in the cemetery. Daggers before three names indicate that the deceased were killed in action.

†**Edward Claude Benford**, Section 8, Grave 804. Hospital Corpsman Third Class, U.S. Navy, attached to a company of the 1st Marine Division. Place and date: Korea, 5 September 1952.

Citation: For gallantry and intrepidity at the risk of his life above and beyond the call of duty while serving in operations against enemy aggressor forces. When his company was subjected to heavy artillery and mortar barrages, followed by a determined assault during the hours of darkness by an enemy force estimated at battalion strength, HC3c Benford resolutely moved from position to position in the face of intense hostile fire, treating the wounded and lending words of encouragement. Leaving the protection of his sheltered position to treat the wounded when the platoon area in which he was working was attacked from bot the front and rear, he moved forward to an exposed ridge where he observed two Marines in a large crater. As he approached the two men to determine their condition, an enemy soldier charged the position. Picking up a grenade in each hand, HC3c Benford leaped out of the crater and hurled himself against the onrushing hostile soldiers, pushing the grenades against their chests and killing both the attackers. Mortally wounded while carrying out this heroic act, HC3c Benford, by his great personal valor and resolute spirit of self-sacrifice in the face of almost certain death, was directly responsible for saving the lives of his two comrades. His exceptional courage reflects the highest credit upon himself and enhances the finest traditions of the U.S. Naval Service. He gallantly gave his life for others.

†**Nelson Vogel Brittin**, Section DS, Grave 2. Sergeant First Class, U.S. Army, Company I, 19th Infantry Regiment. Place and date: Vicinity of Yonggong-ni, Korea, 7 March 1951.

Citation: Sergeant Brittin, member of Company I, distinguished himself by conspicuous gallantry and intrepidity above and beyond the call of duty in action. Volunteering to lead his squad up a hill, with meager cover against murderous fire from the enemy, he ordered his squad to give him support and, in the face of withering fire and bursting shells, he tossed a grenade at the nearest enemy position. On returning to his squad, he was knocked down and wounded by an enemy grenade. Refusing medical attention, he replenished his supply of grenades and returned, hurling grenades into hostile positions and shooting the enemy as they fled. When his weapon jammed, he leaped without hesitation into a foxhole and killed the occupants with his bayonet and the butt of his rifle. He continued to wipe out foxholes and, noting that his squad had been pinned down, he rushed to the rear of a machine gun position, threw a grenade into the nest, and ran around to its front, where he killed all three occupants with his rifle. Less than 100 yards up the hill, his squad again came under vicious fire from another camouflaged, sandbagged, machine gun nest well flanked by supporting riflemen. Sergeant Brittin again charged this new position in an aggressive endeavor to silence this remaining obstacle and ran directly into a burst of automatic fire which killed him instantly. In his sustained and driving action, he had killed 20 enemy soldiers and destroyed 4 automatic weapons. The conspicuous courage, consummate valor, and noble self-sacrifice displayed by Sfc. Brittin enabled his inspired company to attain its objective and reflect the highest glory on himself and the heroic traditions of the military service.

†**John W. Dutko**, Section DS, Grave 1. Private First Class, U.S. Army, 3d Infantry Division. Place and date: Near Ponte Rotto, Italy, 23 May 1944.

Citation: For conspicuous gallantry and intrepidity at the risk of life above and beyond the call of duty, on 23 May 1944, near Ponte Rotto, Italy. Pfc. Dutkoleft the cover of an abandoned enemy trench at the height of an artillery concentration in a single handed attack upon three machine guns and an 88-mm. Mobile gun. Despite the intense fire of these four weapons which were aimed directly at him, Pfc. Dutko ran 100 yards through the impact area, paused momentarily in a shell crater, and then continued his one-man assault. Although machine gun bullets kicked up the dirt at his heels, and 88-mm. shells exploded within 30yards of him, Pfc. Dutko nevertheless made his way to a point within 30 yards of the first enemy machine gun and killed both gunners with a hand grenade. Although the second machine gun wounded him, knocking him to the ground, Pfc. Dutko regained his feet and advanced on the 88-mm. gun, firing his Browning automatic rifle from the hip. When he came within ten yards of this weapon he killed its five-man crew with one long burst of fire. Wheeling on the machine gun which had wounded him, Pfc. Dutko killed the gunner and his assistant. The third German machine gun fired on Pfc. Dutko from a position 20 yards distant, wounding him a second time as he proceeded toward the enemy weapon in a half run. He killed both members of its crew with a single burst from his Browning automatic rifle, continued toward the gun and died, his body falling across the dead German crew.

Beverly National Cemetery

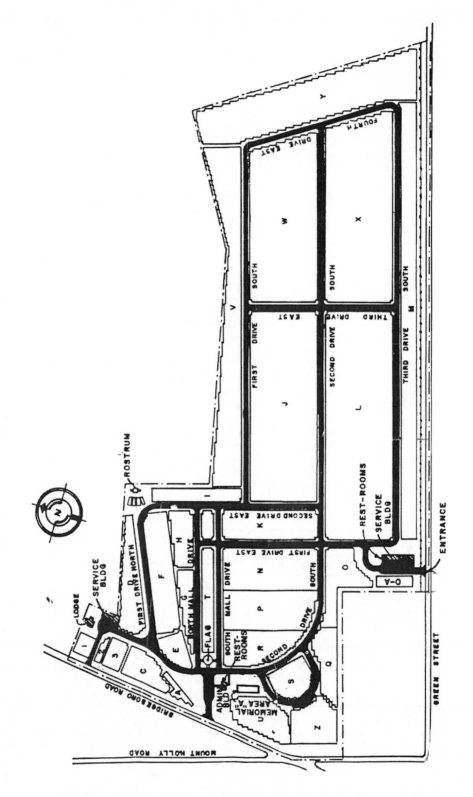

Bernard A. Strausbaugh, Section G, Grave 102. First Sergeant, Company A 3rd Maryland Infantry, Place and date: At Petersburg, Virginia, 17 June 1864.

Citation: Recaptured the colors of 2d Pennsylvania Provisional Artillery.

Former superintendents/directors of the cemetery are:

Jos. Gearing, August 1869–August 1871

Wesley Markwood, April 1875–December 1884

Jas. Murphy, July 1885–September 1885

Harry Emmert, Unknown–October 1917

Mrs. Marie Emmert, October 1917–November 1917 (Actg)

John T. Ross, November 1917–November 1917

Robert Archibald, November 1917–January 1918

John Harrigan, January 1918–March 1919

Louis Whitson, March 1919–September 1919

Elmer E. Johnson, September 1919–March 1928 (Actg)

John W. Willson, March 1920–November 1921

Unknown, December 1921–June 1922

Michael Casey, July 1922–July 1922

Milton Aronson, October 1922–July 1927

Geo. H. Christie, July 1927–November 1927 (Actg)

James Brierly, February 1931–1941

Floyd Wilcox, September 1942–1942

Walter Hanns, 1942–January 1943

Unknown, July 1943–February 1947

Joseph J. Walsh, February 1947–January 1948

Frank A. Lockwood, January 1948–February 1948

Andrew K. Hill, February 1952–June 1953

Frank A. Lockwood, June 1953–June 1956

Robert H. Schmidt, July 1956–May 1961

John T. Spelman, May 1961–December 1964

Samuel H. Davis, Jr., December 1964–October 1969

William J. Costine, October 1969–December 1977

Robert L. Whitfield, December 1977–July 1982

David Rivera-Guzman, September 1982–February 1985

Robert L. Brake, March 1985–February 1986

Eddie Walker, 1986–1990

Delores Blake, 1990–Present

Biloxi National Cemetery

P.O. Box 4968

Biloxi, Mississippi 39535

The cemetery is located in Harrison County, about five miles west of the center of Biloxi, on the grounds of the Department of Veterans Affairs Medical Center (VAMC) and adjacent to the Keesler Field Air Force Base.

The first burial in what was originally established in 1934 as a VAM Cemetery was made on March 24 of that year. Edgar A. Ross, who had served from May to September 1898 as a private in the 1st Regiment, Tennessee Infantry, was the first interment. The cemetery was established to provide a burying ground for those who died in the medical center. These patients came primarily from Florida, Alabama, Mississippi and Louisiana.

With the passage of the National Cemeteries Act of 1973, Public Law 93-43, the National Cemetery System was transferred from the Department of the Army to the Veterans Administration. Biloxi was one of 21 cemeteries operated by VA Medical Centers added to the system in 1973. This transfer opened all cemeteries to any eligible veteran and dependents.

The original cemetery covered 25 acres; its size has been increased by a 17-acre addition from the VAMC reservation in 1982, and an additional 12 acres in 1996. The cemetery is currently 54 acres. The first interment after the facility was designated Biloxi National Cemetery was Chief Master Sergeant Robert E. Callender, USAF. As of September 30, 2008, there were 17,360 interments.

The sole Medal of Honor recipient interred here is a Spanish-American War veteran, 2nd Lt. Ira C. Welborn (U.S. Army; died July 3, 1956). His grave is 12-4-12.

From its establishment in 1934 until October 2, 1983, the cemetery was operated and

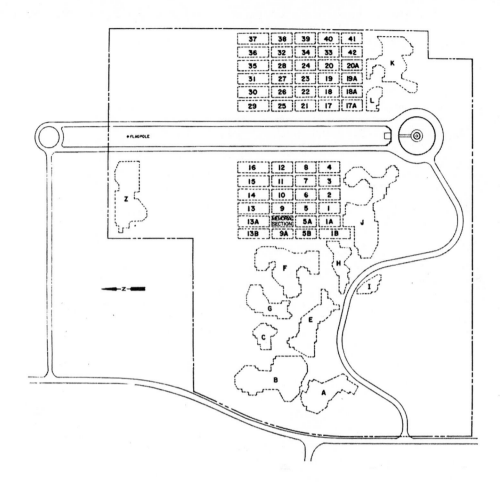

Biloxi National Cemetery.

maintained by the engineering service personnel of the medical center. Directors of the cemetery since that date are:

Jimmy T. Jackson, September 1983–September 1988
Jorge L. Lopez, September 1988–November 1990
Jeff S. Barnes, 1991–1997

Black Hills National Cemetery
P.O. Box 640
Sturgis, South Dakota 57785

The cemetery is located 3 miles east of Sturgis and 25 miles west of Rapid City, South Dakota. It lies in the shadows of the Black Hills where legend has it that the hoof beats of Custer's 7th Cavalry may be faintly heard to this day.

The Sioux Indians called this area, which was once part of the Sioux reservation, the Black Hills because the slopes of the hills were covered with pine trees which made them appear black when viewed from the plains. In the summer of 1874, Lieutenant Colonel

George Custer led the 7th Cavalry into the Black Hills, thereby breaking the Treaty of Fort Laramie. Ostensibly, his mission was to test the soil for its gold content. His favorable report brought on a horde of miners which the government was powerless to stop. Some Indian leaders like Sitting Bull and Crazy Horse refused to sell their land in 1875, and the government ordered all Indians to move to reservations by January 31, 1876, or face military action. This was the first step toward the Little Big Horn River, where Colonel Custer and his 250-man 7th Cavalry were wiped out on June 25, 1876.

As the miners discovered other minerals and mining towns sprang up, the pine forests were cut down and farmers began raising crops. The Homestake mine, the largest gold producer in the Western Hemisphere, is located in the town of Lead, about 10 miles from Sturgis. Also close by is the town of Deadwood, which quickly became the center of mining operations and was known as the most lawless town on the frontier. It was in Deadwood that Calamity Jane and Wild Bill Hickok became legends.

In 1947 Congressman Francis Case endorsed the concept of a National Cemetery in this part of the country. With the support of various South Dakota veterans organizations, and the South Dakota Veterans Department, the site just outside Sturgis, on the Fort Meade, South Dakota Military Reservation was selected. The 105.9-acre tract was transferred to the Department of the Army in April 1948 and designated the Fort Meade National Cemetery. It was dedicated under this name on October 3, 1948.

The name was changed in 1949 to avoid confusion with the existing active military installation in the State of Maryland, and with the Fort Meade, South Dakota, Veterans Administration Hospital. The cemetery was designated the Black Hills National Cemetery in recognition of its location within an area of great historical significance. The first interments, made on September 27, 1948, were four World War II remains representing the Army, Navy and the Air Force. On September 30, three more interments were made, bringing the total of interments to seven at the time of dedication. As of September 30, 2008, there were 21,238 interments. The cemetery is projected to have available gravesites beyond the year 2030.

A simple white marble headstone in Section A, Grave 239, marks the burial place of Sgt. Charles Windolph, the only Medal of Honor recipient interred in the cemetery. Born December 9, 1851, in New York State, Sgt. Windolph was a member of Troop H, 7th Regiment, U.S. Cavalry. He was awarded the Medal of Honor while serving during the Battle of Little Big Horn about five miles from where Lt. Col. Custer and his troops were massacred on June 25, 1876, while serving with Captain Frederick Benteen and Major Marcus A. Reno, Sgt. Windolph displayed courageous action and disregard for his personal safety while holding a position that secured water for the command. After retirement at Fort Meade, he worked as a blacksmith with the Homestake Mining Company. During his life of 99 years, he saw the Civil War, the Indian Wars, the Spanish-American War, and World Wars I and II, and became part of the history of his country. Sgt. Windolph died on March 11, 1950.

Grave 10, Section D, marks the burial place of Brigadier General Richard E. Ellsworth, Class of 1935, U.S. Military Academy. He served in World War II and was awarded the Legion of Merit, two Distinguished Flying Crosses, and three Air Medals. While serving as commanding general o the Rapid City, South Dakota, Air Force Base, he was killed in an air accident over Newfoundland on March 18, 1953. The Air Force base was renamed Ellsworth Air Force Base in his honor.

The South Dakota Medal of Honor was dedicated and presented to Black Hills National Cemetery on Memorial Day, May 30, 1985, by Governor William J. Janklow, on behalf of

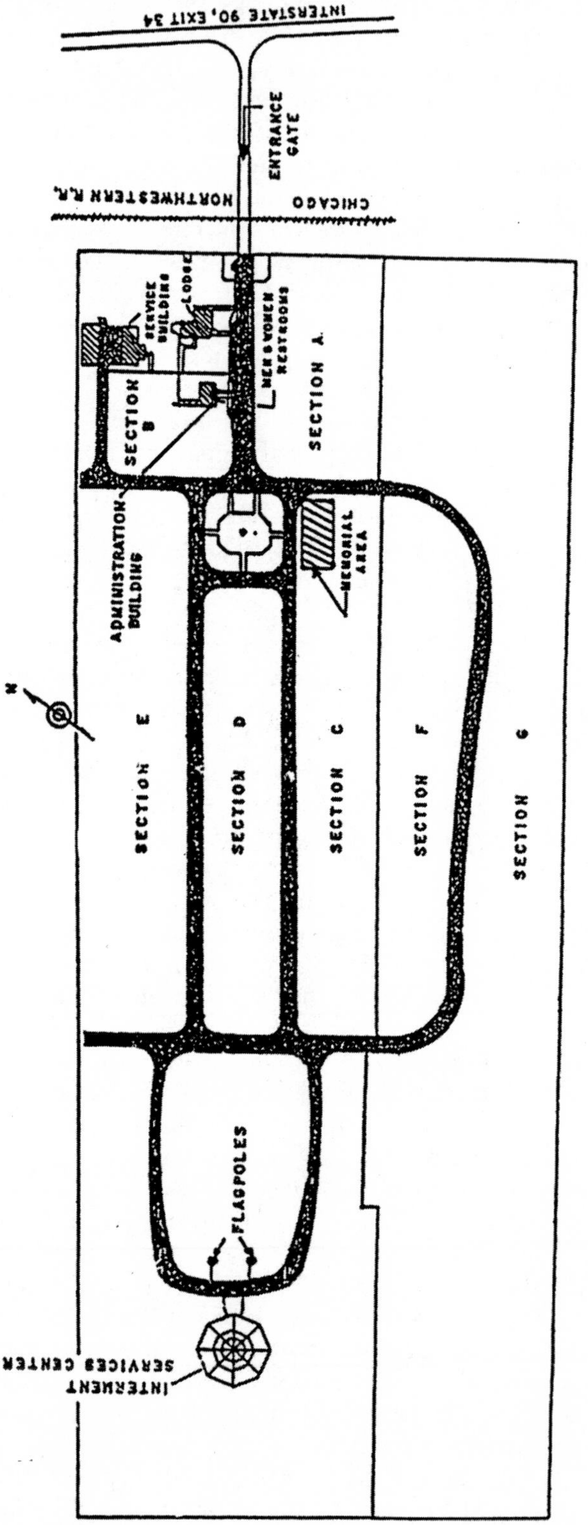

BLACK HILLS NATIONAL CEMETERY
STURGIS, SOUTH DAKOTA

INTERSTATE 90, EXIT 34

ENTRANCE GATE

NORTHWESTERN R.R.

CHICAGO

SERVICE BUILDING

LODGE

MEN & WOMEN RESTROOMS

SECTION B

SECTION A

ADMINISTRATION BUILDING

MEMORIAL AREA

N

SECTION E

SECTION D

SECTION C

SECTION F

SECTION G

FLAGPOLES

INTERMENT SERVICES CENTER

the people of South Dakota. There were three South Dakota Medal of Honor Commemoratives struck: the one located at the national cemetery, the one remaining on display in the Rotunda of the capitol building in Pierre, and the one on display in Arlington National Cemetery. The inscription of the medal reads, "They came from the Hills, the Valleys, the Plains of South Dakota. Remember These Men & Women Who Served So Well. To Their Sacrifice This Medal Is Dedicated."

Former superintendents/directors of the cemetery are:

Ernest C. Schanze, September 1948–November 1961
Grover R. Neal, November 1961–May 1968
John H. Richardson, June 1968–July 1973
Andrew F. Szilvasi, July 1973–June 1976
John C. Metzler, Jr., June 1976–April 1977
Andrew F. Szilvasi, August 1977–July 1988

Daniel L. Nelson, August 1988–1995
Douglas Miner, 1995–1998
Robert Poe, 1998–2004
Douglas Voorhees, 2004–2005
Daniel Cassidy, 2005–2007
Sara Elton, 2007–Present

Calverton National Cemetery
Route 25
210 Princeton Boulevard
Calverton, New York 11933

Calverton National Cemetery is located on the eastern end of Long Island near Calverton, New York. It is situated in Suffolk County within the town of Riverhead. Arrowheads and crude stone-cutting tools can still be found in the area, remnants of the culture of its first inhabitants, the Algonquin Indians.

Ever since Cypress Hills National Cemetery was established in Brooklyn in 1862, there has been a national cemetery in New York. A second cemetery was opened at Pinelawn in 1937. The Calverton National Cemetery became the third national cemetery on Long Island when the site was dedicated on September 10, 1978.

The need for a third cemetery to serve the 2,956,000 veterans and their dependents in the New York City metropolitan area was realized in 1974 when NCS officials estimated that the Long Island National Cemetery would reach its burial capacity in 1978. Plans were set in motion to establish a new regional national cemetery within the greater New York area. This cemetery would serve veterans in the Standard Federal Region II, which includes New York and New Jersey. The U.S. Naval Weapons Industrial Reserve Plant at Calverton had excess land that was among the sites considered. On December 7, 1977, a 902-acre tract was transferred to the Veterans Administration for use as a national cemetery. Today, the cemetery covers 1,045 acres.

This area saw fighting in the Battle of Long Island on August 26, 1776, the day British forces landed at Fort Hamilton. General Howe, commander of the British troops, quickly realized that of the four roads leading to Brooklyn, three were guarded by American troops, but the fourth, the Jamaica Pass, was neglected. He then silently marched his men toward the Jamaica Road until he reached Howard's Half-Way House. The innkeeper and his son, being English sympathizers, willingly acted as their guides to Flatbush. There they came upon the rear echelon of American General Sullivan's men and forced them to retreat. This situation almost dashed America's hopes for independence. Only George Washington's escape across the East River to New York enabled the Americans to fight again.

It was in this area of Long Island that the American patriot and spy for General Wash-

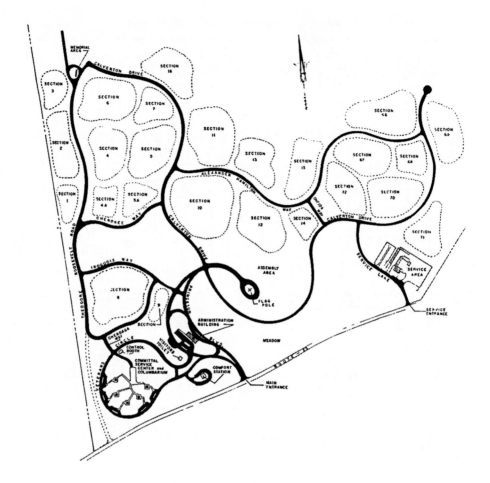

Calverton National Cemetery.

ington, Captain Nathan Hale, was captured on September 21, 1776. Without benefit of a trial, he was summarily sentenced to death and hanged in New York City the following morning. The British, trying to avoid making him a martyr, secretly disposed of his body, which has never been found. His last words became a slogan for his surviving fellow American patriots: "I regret that I have but one life to give to my country." In June 1988, the Veterans Administration erected a memorial monument in the cemetery in his honor.

The planners of Calverton National Cemetery knew that it would be very active. For that reason, they designed and built a feature called a committal wheel which permits multiple burial services to be held simultaneously. Around Veterans Circle to the left of the main entrance are five shelters for services. From the committal shelter, after the service, the remains are moved into the nave of the wheel and then transported to the gravesite. No funeral flowers are taken to the gravesite. The walls of the committal shelters were reconstructed in 1983 to become columbaria for the inurnment of cremated remains.

Calverton is the largest, and third most active national cemetery in the National Cemetery System. The cemetery averages 28 interments per day, and On December 31, 1990, the staff made 64 burials in one day. As of September 30, 2008, there were 207,719 total interments, including over 600 inurnments in the columbaria. Grave space will be available beyond the year 2030. Each fall, about 1,000 graves are dug and prepared for winter interments when the ground is frozen several feet deep.

There is one Medal of Honor recipient interred in the cemetery.

†**Michael P. Murphy**, Lieutenant, U.S. Navy, Place and date: In the vicinity of Asadabad, Konar Province, Afghanistan, on 28 June 2005.

Citation: For conspicuous gallantry and intrepidity at the risk of his life above and beyond the call of duty as the leader of a special reconnaissance element with Special Warfare Task Unit Afghanistan on 27 NS 28 June 2005. While leading a mission to locate a ligh-level anti-coalition militia leader, Lieutenant Murphy demonstrated extraordinary heroism in the face of great danger in the vicinity of Asadabad, Konar Province, Afghanistan. On 28 June 2005, operating in an extremely rugged enemy-controlled area, Lieutenant Murphy's team was discovered by anti-coalition militia sympathizers who revealed their position Taliban fighters. As a result, between 30 and 40 enemy fighters besieged his four-member team. Demonstrating exceptional resolve, Lieutenant Murphy valiantly lead his men in engaging the large enemy force. The ensuing fierce firefight resulted in numerous casualties, as well the wounding of all four members of the team. Ignoring his own wounds and demonstrating exceptional composure, Lieutenant Murphy continued to lead and encourage his men. When the primary communicator fell mortally wounded, Lieutenant Murphy repeatedly attempted to call for assistance for his beleaguered teammates . Realizing the impossibility of communicating in the extreme terrain, and in the face of almost certain death, he fought his way into open terrain to gain a better position to transmit a call. This deliberate, heroic act deprived him of cover, exposing him to direct enemy fire. Finally achieving contact with his Headquarters, Lieutenant Murphy maintained his exposed position while he provided his location and requested immediate support for his team. In his final act of bravery, he continued to engage the enemy until he was mortally wounded, gallantly giving his life for his country and for the cause of freedom. By his selfless leadership, courageous actions, and extraordinary devotion to duty, Lieutenant Murphy reflected great credit upon himself and upheld the highest traditions of the United States Naval Service.

Former directors of the national cemetery are:

Theodore J. Nick, January 1978–April 1980
John C. Metzler, Jr., July 1980–June 1985
Fred I. Haselbarth, Jr., September 1985–
February 1986
Robert A. Wilk, May 1986–June 1990

Floyd J. Parker, June 1990–August 1994
Patrick Hallinan, August 1994–June 2003
Rick Boyd, June 2005–September 2005
Michael G. Picerno, December 2005–Present

Camp Butler National Cemetery
RFD No. 1
Springfield, Missouri

Camp Butler National Cemetery is located in Sangamon County near Riverton, Illinois, six miles northeast of Springfield on U.S. Highway 36. The area the cemetery occupies is a portion of what was the second largest military training camp in Illinois during the Civil War.

With the fall of Fort Sumter, S.C., on April 13, 1861, war between the United States and the Confederacy of seceding states became a fact. President Lincoln issued a proclamation calling for troops to defend the Union. Resultant demands for troops made upon the states of the North found many of them totally unprepared to assume the responsibility so suddenly thrust upon them. For Governor Richard Yates of Illinois the urgency of the situation became clearly evident when on April 15, 1861, he received a message from

Camp Butler National Cemetery.

Lincoln's secretary of war, Simon Cameron, requesting six regiments of militia for immediate service.

This request and succeeding demands for more troops necessitated the establishment of facilities for receipt and training of war recruits. General William Tecumseh Sherman was sent to Springfield by the War Department to select a site for such a camp. Governor Yates directed William Butler, state treasurer of Illinois and a longtime resident of Springfield, and Mr. O.M. Hatch, a former Illinois secretary of state, to assist General Sherman in his search for a suitable training camp site. The three men drove by carriage to the vicinity of Riverton, some six miles northeast of Springfield, where a site was located which appeared to meet the qualifications for a troop concentration and training camp. The land chosen had high ground for camping purposes and lower, more level ground for drill and training, as well as space for a cemetery.

The Sangamon River was in close proximity for water and the Wabash Railroad was conveniently located nearby. Also, it was believed that the distance of the site from the city of Springfield would be a favorable factor in the maintenance of discipline at the camp. General Sherman was greatly pleased with the location and surroundings. He immediately selected this site and named it Camp Butler in honor of the Illinois state treasurer. The original camp consisted of 6.2 acres, most of which lay directly west of the cemetery tract. The old parade ground is now a level field easily identified from the road leading to the cemetery.

The first troops arrived at Camp Butler on August 5, 1861, and by the end of the month there were more than 5,000 men in camp with hundreds more arriving daily. The camp functioned as an important center for training and dispatching Union troops until the last Illinois troops were mustered out of service in 1866.

As the war progressed, the facilities of Camp Butler were used for the confinement of Confederate prisoners of war. Those captured at Fort Henry and Fort Donelson were among the first to arrive. Some 2,000 Confederates who were captured when General Buckner surrendered Fort Donelson to General Grant on February 16, 1862, arrived at Camp Butler on February 23. More than 1,000 prisoners of war captured by General Pope at Island No. 10 (a fortified island in the Mississippi River, just below New Madrid, Missouri) arrived at Camp Butler on April 14, 1862. As the prisoners began to arrive, officers and men at Camp Butler were put to work constructing a stockade and a hospital. The prisoner of war population continued high throughout the war even though many of these prisoners were subsequently exchanged for Union soldiers held in the prison camps of the Confederacy.

The Confederate prisoners came from all of the eleven southern states except Florida. The early arrivals were from Tennessee, Alabama, and Arkansas. Later they came from as far away as Texas and the Carolinas. The barracks were inadequate and poorly constructed. Sanitation facilities were primitive, and the daily ration of food often consisted of hard biscuits and a cup of thin coffee. Almost immediately, death became an everyday affair. The heat of summer, the severe cold of northern winter, as well as poor discipline among the prisoners which prevented proper care and policing of quarters were among the factors which encouraged the spread of contagious diseases such as smallpox, typhus, and pneumonia. About 700 died in a smallpox epidemic during the summer of 1862. Another 123 died the month before a group of survivors were paroled in exchange for Union prisoners.

Camp Butler National Cemetery, located within the area of the wartime training center and prison camp, was established in 1862. At that time there were 714 interments, 549 known and 165 unknown. The first death at Camp Butler occurred on August 21, 1861. A Private Willard of the Mason City Company of Infantry died of "lung fever." A Private Johnson was drowned on September 17, 1861. A total of 848 Confederate soldiers is interred in the cemetery.

The six acres initially appropriated by the United States for cemetery use were purchased in 1865. Subsequent land purchases have increased the cemetery to its present size of 53 acres.

The cemetery is projected to close for initial interments in the year 2013.

Along with those members of the Union and Confederate forces of the Civil War who are interred here are those who fought in other wars. Veterans of the Spanish-American War, World Wars I and II, and the Korean and Vietnamese wars are among the 11,703 interred at Camp Butler National Cemetery as of September 30, 1989. For many who met death on the far-flung battlefields of World War II, Camp Butler became their final resting place with the return of their remains from overseas for reinterment here. The first Springfield deceased veteran to be returned was William Evans, Jr., Fireman1/C, USN. He was interred on October 31, 1947, in Section 3, Grave 408-B. Included among these decedents of World War II are 9 group burials for 30 remains. Circumstances of their death precluded identification for individual burial. A total of 499 war dead was returned from overseas and reinterred at Camp Butler.

John Hugh Catherwood is the only Medal of Honor recipient interred at Camp Butler. He was originally interred in the Oak Ridge Cemetery, Springfield, Illinois, in 1930. At the request of his family, his remains were moved to Camp Butler and reinterred on July 17, 1987. The citation for his Medal of Honor reads as follows:

Ordinary Seaman, U.S. Navy. Citation: While attached to the *USS Pampang*, Catherwood was one of a shore party moving in to capture Mundang, on the island of Basilan, Philippine Islands, on the morning of 24 September 1911. Advancing with the scout party to reconnoiter a group of nipa huts close to the trail, Catherwood unhesitatingly entered the open area before the huts, where his party was suddenly taken under point-blank fire and charged by approximately 20 enemy Moros coming out from inside the native huts and from other concealed positions. Struck down almost instantly by the outlaws' deadly fire, Catherwood, although unable to rise, rallied to the defense of his leader and fought desperately to beat off the hostile attack.

OTHERS: Colonel Otis B. Duncan, a native of Springfield, Ill. Was the highest ranking African American during World War I. He is interred in Section 3, Grave 835.

One of the five private monuments in the old section of the cemetery is that of George W. Ford. He was appointed superintendent of Camp Butler National Cemetery in 1906 and served for 24 years until he retired at age 82 in 1930. He had previously served as superintendent at Chattanooga, Beaufort, Fort Scott, and Port Hudson national cemeteries. A veteran of the Indian wars, he served as a major in the Spanish-American War.

There are 30 German, 1 Korean, 4 Italian POW's interred in the cemetery. Two of the remains were reinterred from Camp Grant, Illinois, in June 1946, 3 from Camp McCoy, Wisconsin, in June 1947, 11 from Fort Robinson, Nebraska, in July 1947, and 19 from Camp Atterbury, Indiana, in June 1970. As of September 30, 2008, a total of 21,697 interments had been made in the cemetery.

Former superintendents/directors of the cemetery are:

George W. Ford, 1906–August 1930
Samuel Sharp, August 1930–Unknown
Bernard J. Slade, Unknown–May 1937
Joseph Schwar, May 1937–November 1945
Andrew K. Hill, November 1945–April 1947
Louis B. Hellmeyer, April 1947–June 1949
Fred Rover, July 1949–June 1951
Andrew K. Hill, June 1951–February 1952
Louis B. Hellmeyer, February 1952–January 1962
Harold F. Hammer, January 1962–June 1971
John W. Cox, June 1971–October 1977

Mack Cochenour, Jr., November 1977–November 1979
Leroy C. Newhouse, November 1979–July 1981
Gary W. Smith, August 1981–January 1985
Elmer D. Nygaard, February 1985–August 1987
Jack D. Shaw, Unknown–1990
Kurt Rotar, June 1990–July 1995
Leon B. Murphy, August 1995–February 1999
Dane B. Freeman, March 1999–September 2004
William E. Rhoades, March 2005–October 2006
Claude F. Rivers, October 2006–March 2008

Camp Nelson National Cemetery
6980 Danville Road
Nicholasville, Kentucky 40356

On the crest of a small knoll surrounded by numerous native trees is the serene and beautiful Camp Nelson National Cemetery. It is located about seven miles southeast of Nicholasville, Jessamine County, Kentucky, and about ⅜ of a mile off U.S. Highway 27. A description from the *Lexington Herald* dated April 5, 1898, provides this picture:

> From the turnpike, which passes through the Camp, may be seen on a hill a quarter of a mile away, the United States' flag flying. Here is located the National Cemetery. A beautiful graveled driveway shaded by double row of poplar trees leads to it from the pike. The cemetery is a level grass, shaded plot. In it are buried the men who died at Camp Nelson and those men killed in a number of battles fought in Kentucky.

In 1866 the United States appropriated about 8½ acres in Jessamine County for cemeterial purposes. Of the original tract, about 7¼ acres constituted the cemetery proper, and the remainder formed a driveway extending from the Lexington and Danville turnpike to the main entrance to the cemetery grounds. An additional acre, adjoining the southeast

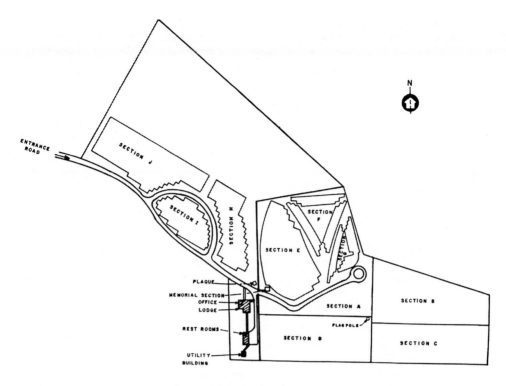

Camp Nelson National Cemetery.

corner, was purchased in 1874. In 1975, the Committee to Reopen and Expand Camp Nelson National Cemetery donated 10 acres to the Veterans Administration. On May 26, 1985, the Jessamine County Industrial Board announced their intention to donate an additional 10+ acres of land to the cemetery. The donation extended the boundary of the cemetery to U.S. Highway 27. Today, the cemetery encompasses 30 acres and includes 13,236 interments. It is projected to close for initial interments not before the year 2030.

The cemetery had its beginnings in the middle stages of the Civil War. The country was divided over slavery and other issues. After the conflict erupted at Fort Sumter on April 13, 1861, 23 northern states answered President Lincoln's call to arms. Eleven southern states responded to the call of Jefferson Davis under the flag of the Confederacy. Kentucky lay between the Union and Confederate forces and became a state divided, in spite of its efforts to avoid war. It was in the border states, such as Kentucky, that great heartache was felt when the issues of the war separated families into different loyalties. Brother fought against brother and fathers fought against sons. The Union armies gathered about 90,000 Kentucky men and the Confederacy about 40,000, to bear arms.

The Union army established camps at various locations in Kentucky as recruiting and training areas. It was for this purpose that Camp Nelson was located on the Jessamine County side of the Kentucky River in early 1863. Although no battles were fought in the immediate area of the camp, many men trained there later fought in the many battles of the Civil War. The area was selected for its proximity to the river and the bluffs of the river which provided for defense south of the camp. The camp extended about two miles from the river toward Nicholasville and was fortified with cannon emplacements around its perimeter.

On a high bluff overlooking the river, on the Jessamine County side, an earthen breast works was developed as a protective fort. It was complemented by many cannons that could pour shells on the river from either direction either on the Garrard County side of the river, or on the turnpike and open fields leading to the camp. The emplacement came to be known as Fort Bramlette, after a Union general of the time. It is now on the National Register of Historic Places. Smaller emplacements were built on the Garrard County side of the river, which allowed additional firepower and an early warning, should the Confederacy muster an attack from that direction.

In those days life in a military training camp was harsh and creature comforts were few. Despite the efforts of camp commanders and sympathetic organizations, many men fell victim to disease and common illnesses, especially smallpox. Although a large hospital was eventually located on the grounds that served not only the immediate camp but battlefield injured who were brought there, other means to separate the smallpox cases from the rest of the area had to be taken. Separated from the main camp, but within the protected area, a hospital and a graveyard were located on what was then known as the Moss property. In the burial records the location is described as "Small graveyard ¼ of a mile west of the Lexington-Danville Turnpike at Camp Nelson, Jessamine County, Kentucky. In a ravine 100 yards on the North bank of the river on land belonging to John Moss."

The site was designated in the records as graveyard =1. There were 379 men buried there between June 2, 1863, and July 6, 1865. It is evident that not all of them died of smallpox. While no cause of death is usually listed in the burial records, on one burial a side note indicated that death resulted from a "falling tree." It is believed that this graveyard was originally established with the camp, and that graveyard #2, also listed in the burial records, was a later addition but is the present location of the national cemetery. From the old records it can be determined that there were 1,183 men buried in graveyard #2 who died between July 28, 1863, and February 4, 1866. It is probable that many of them died of wounds received in battle. Some were reinterments from battlefield sites. One hundred forty-three men were listed in the old records as having been disinterred from surrounding towns and family plots on farms.

The earliest death listed in the old burial records is James Sexton, Company G, 1st Kentucky Cavalry, who died on October 14, 1861. He was disinterred from a farm near Stanford, Kentucky, on the Knoblick Turnpike, in an old family burying ground belonging to the family of G. Lackey. The grave of the soldier was listed as having been "under an appletree" on this farm. Hewas reinterred in the national cemetery sometime between 1868 and 1870 in Section A, Grave 131. Of the 1,605 burials recorded in the early log book, 88 were listed as unknown. It is most likely that these were disinterments from other locations and their names were lost or weathered away from the crude wooden headboards erected at the time of original burial.

Within five years after the Civil War ended, the Army had complete the program to locate and concentrate the Union dead in national cemeteries. During June and July 1868, a total of 2,023 remains were removed from five areas in Kentucky and reinterred at Camp Nelson National Cemetery: 104 from Frankfort, 241 from Richmond, 266 from London, 437 from Covington, and 975 from Perryville (see Perryville National Cemetery). The remains of Confederate prisoners of war originally buried in the national cemetery were all removed, either to the Confederate lot in the cemetery at Nicholasville, or elsewhere possibly to their homes. With the exception of the two graves removed from Covington and supposed to be Confederate soldiers, there are no Confederates interred in the cemetery. In the cemetery at Nicholasville the Confederate dead are buried in a separate section. The Confederate Associations marked these graves with granite markers. The old register includes 37 names, but 7 have not been located.

The stone wall around the original cemetery was built in 1867–68 and encloses 9.75 acres. The remainder of the cemetery is enclosed with chain link fencing. The lodge was constructed in 1875 and now serves as the cemetery office and the director's residence. It is the second such structure erected in the cemetery after the initial building was razed. The utility building in the cemetery was originally a stable for the horses used in the maintenance of the cemetery.

The only Medal of Honor recipient interred in the cemetery is:

William M. Harris, Sec. U, Grave 3, Private, Company D, 7th U.S. Calvary. Place and date: At Little Big Horn River, Montana, 25 June 1876.
    Citation: Voluntarily brought water to the wounded under fire from the enemy.

Former superintendents/directors of the cemetery are:

Fred Rover, June 1939–November 1946
Benjamin Pruitt, November 1946–April 1955
Francis M. Brooke, May 1955–August 1957
Russell K. Hamilton, August 1957–November 1961
Oscar P. Findley, December 1961–July 1968
William G. Kaiser, August 1968–July 1973
Ronald F. Houska, July 1973–December 1974

Dorrance A. Long, January 1975–April 1979
Dellas L. Atchinson, June 1979–January 1980
Robert L. Scoggins, February 1980–January 1988
Eileen G. Harrison, 1988–1993
Kimberly M. Wright, February 1993-March 1994
Jeffrey L. Teas, May 1994-September 1998
Patrick H. Lovett, November 1998–March 2003
Patrick H. Lovett, July 2005–Present

Cave Hill National Cemetery

701 Baxter Avenue
Louisville, Kentucky 40204

The national cemetery is located in the northwest corner of the Cave Hill Cemetery, in Jefferson County, Louisville, Kentucky.

The original reservation of 0.65 acre was acquired by donation in 1861 from the Cave Hill Cemetery Company, the land having been dedicated by them as a burial place for soldiers who died in the service of the United States. An additional donation in 1897 and purchases in 1863, 1864, and 1867 brought the national cemetery to its present size of 4.108 acres. All land donations and purchases are subject to the rules and regulations of the Cave Hill Cemetery Co.

The first interment occurred in the cemetery on November 4, 1861, and the National Cemetery was established in 1863. Original interments were soldiers who died at camps and hospitals around Louisville. In the spring of 1867, 732 additional interments were made of the dead gathered up at various points on the Louisville and Nashville Railroad as far south as Rowlett Station, and from points on the Kentucky side of the Ohio River as far southwest as Henderson. Most of these remains were interred in Section D, with a few in Section C.

Interred in graves 1–12 in Section C are 12 men of the 32nd Indiana Infantry Regiment, commanded by Brigadier General August Willich, who were killed during a battle at Rowlett Station on December 17, 1861. They were originally buried within the enclosure are Fort Willich, near Munfordsville, and the graves were marked by a stone tablet bearing the following inscription neatly sculpted in German: "Here rest the first heroes of the 32nd Indiana German Regiment, who laid down their lives for the preservation of the free Constitution of the republic of the United States of North America. They were killed December 17, 1861, in a fight with the rebels at Rowlett Station, Kentucky, in which one regiment of Texas rangers, two regiments of infantry, and a battery of six cannon (over 3,000 strong) were defeated by 500 German soldiers."

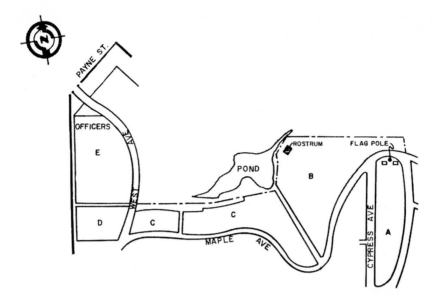

Cave Hill National Cemetery. Within Cave Hill Private Cemetery Louisville Kentucky, September 1969.

The state of Kentucky recognized the sacrifice of these men by purchasing the ground on which they were buried. With the consent of the governor of Indiana, they were removed to Cave Hill National Cemetery and reinterred in the order of their original burial. The stone tablet was also transferred, and mounted on a solid stone pedestal contributed by the loyal Germans of Louisville.

There are 37 Confederate soldiers buried in the cemetery.

As of September 30, 2008, there were a total of 5,977 interments. The cemetery is maintained by contract with the Cave Hill Cemetery Company which is one of the provisions of the donation and sale of land to the government. Operation of the cemetery is supervised by the director of Zachary Taylor National Cemetery, Louisville, Kentucky.

An 1867 land purchase of 0.22 acres was a site for a "keeper's lodge," but as far as can be determined, no lodge was ever constructed. The land was conveyed to the Highland Co. in June 1940. Cemetery records list only one former superintendent, James R. Martin, who served from March 1924 until October 1929.

Chattanooga National Cemetery
1200 Bailey Avenue
Chattanooga, Tennessee 37404

The Chattanooga National Cemetery is located in the city of Chattanooga, Hamilton County, Tennessee, about one mile south of the old Union Railway Station. Major General George H. Thomas, "The Rock of Chickamauga," may be called the founder of this national cemetery. It was his General Order No. 296, dated December 25, 1863, which established a military cemetery "in commemoration of the Battles of Chattanooga, November 23–27, 1863." General Thomas selected the site during the assault of his troops which carried Missionary Ridge and brought to victorious conclusion a campaign of far-reaching importance to the Union cause. The exigencies of war necessitated the appropriation of the area in

Monument to the Andrews Raiders, Chattanooga National Cemetery.

which General Thomas established his military cemetery in 1863. However, in 1870, the land the cemetery occupied was purchased by the United States from Joseph Ruohs, Robert M. Hooke, and J.R. Slayton for $25,579.

Following the defeats at Gettysburg and Vicksburg in July 1863, victory at Chickamauga on September 19–20, 1863, had given new hope to the Confederacy. These hopes were dimmed as the hard-fought and costly Chattanooga campaign was resolved in favor of the Union. Under the command of Major General Ulysses S. Grant, commanding the newly organized Military Division of the Mississippi; Major General George H. Thomas, commanding the Army of the Cumberland; Major General Joseph Hooker, commanding a detachment of the Army of the Potomac; and General William T. Sherman, commanding the Army of the Tennessee, the Union forces secured for the Union the important railway center of Chattanooga, a vital point of departure for the start of Sherman's Atlanta Campaign in May 1864.

The site chosen by General Thomas for the military cemetery included some 75 acres consisting of a round hill rising with a uniform slope to a height of 100 feet. It is directly in front of Missionary Ridge on one side and Lookout Mountain on the other. General Grant established his headquarters on the summit of the hill during the early phase of the four-day battle for Lookout Mountain.

Chaplain Thomas B. Van Horne, U.S. Army, was placed in charge of development of the cemetery. In his report of May 14, 1866, to Brigadier General W.D. Whipple, chief of staff of the military division of the Tennessee, the chaplain indicated that probably one-third of the cemetery area could not be used for burial purposes because of the outcropping of large rock ledges. The plan for laying out the grounds for cemetery purposes was suggested by the undulating terrain of the area. "Where nature suggested avenues," Chaplain Van Horne reported, "they have been made, and their curves define the sections. It has given marked individuality to each, and has allowed a well sustained unity of expression to the whole, as nature has nowhere been opposed."

Much was accomplished during the period that Chaplain Van Horne was in charge of the cemetery. Flowering shrubs, evergreens and other trees were planted to replace a portion of the dense forest of live oak trees which had been cut down when the area became a part of the battleground of the Chattanooga campaign. Interment sections were developed with each section having a central plot for a monument around which were arranged plots for officers with the graves of enlisted personnel arranged in concentric circles about them.

This military cemetery, established as a last resting place for the many casualties of the Chattanooga campaign, was designated a national cemetery in 1867. There is no record to indicate that the cemetery has ever been officially named. Frederick Buntley, a discharged sergeant of Company D, Thirteenth Regiment of Infantry, was appointed the first superintendent as of January 10, 1868.

The chaplain's report of 1866 noted the existence of a large rock cave along the northwest boundary which could be used as a receiving vault, and from which stone for the cemetery boundary wall had been quarried. In later years exploration of this cave by one of the cemetery superintendents indicated that it penetrated nearly a mile beneath the surface of the cemetery. The cave entrance is now sealed. The original stone wall marking the boundary of the original 75 acres of the cemetery has been removed with the acquisition and development of additional cemetery land.

By 1870, more than 12,800 interments had been made in the cemetery, 8,685 known and 4,189 unknown. The dead included those who fell on the battlefields of Chickamauga, Missionary Ridge and Lookout Mountain, as well as reinterments from Athens and Charleston in Tennessee; Bridgeport, Alabama; and other locations along the line of Sherman's march to Atlanta. Chaplain Van Horne's report of 1866 furnishes information concerning the very large number of unknowns interred as a result of the Battle of Chickamauga. He stated that some 800 Union dead were left on the field to be buried there by Union burial parties when possession of the battleground was recovered from the Confederates. Identification of the remains of these Union soldiers was made chiefly from the blue uniform blouse or trousers, or from residual blue mould left by their decay. When these and other remains were disinterred from the Chickamauga battleground for reinterment in the Chattanooga military cemetery, 1,798 burials were made as unknowns and 154 burials were made as those of identified remains.

The report of the inspector of national cemeteries dated December 1, 1870, notes that "During the past year two bodies have been exhumed and delivered to friends, and two removed from the place of original burial and interred in the cemetery; and during the same time eleven soldiers of the garrison (nearby) have been buried here." It also reports that 14 employees were buried in the cemetery. There is no indication as to whether they were employees of the cemetery or of the Army garrison.

In 1884 the War Department directed that the Military Post of Chattanooga, known as Fyffe Barracks, be made a part of the national cemetery.

A large granite private monument, located in Section H, is a familiar landmark in the Chattanooga National Cemetery. This monument, topped by a bronze replica of a tall-stacked, wood-burning Civil War locomotive known as the General, was erected by the state of Ohio in 1890. It commemorates an 1862 Civil War raid repleted with thrills and misadventures in the best traditions of a "cops and robbers" chase. The Disney movie *The Great Locomotive Chase* was based on this most daring and famous escapade of the Civil War. The group was officially called Mitchell's Raiders, but the popular name, especially after the movie was released, became Andrews' Raiders.

The possible consequence to the Union cause, had this April 1862 foray of James J. Andrews and his fellow conspirators been successful, is now just one of those interesting "ifs" of history. Yet, it does appear that if Andrews and his men had been successful in their attempt to cut the important railroad line between Atlanta, Georgia and Chattanooga, the Civil War might possibly have been brought to a swifter conclusion, and Georgia (Atlanta in particular) might have been spared the ravages and destruction that occurred during Sherman's March to the Sea.

During the period April 7–12, 1862, James J. Andrews, a civilian federal spy, and his company of volunteer soldiers from Ohio disguised themselves as civilians and penetrated nearly 200 miles south into Confederate territory (100 miles south of Chattanooga). Their objective was to initiate a daringly conceived plan to destroy rail and telegraph communication lines between Atlanta and Chattanooga. Briefly, the plan of the raiders entailed the boarding of a northbound train at Marietta, Georgia; seizure of the locomotive, the General, at Big Shanty (now Kennesaw), Georgia; a breakfast stop; and a wild northward run to Chattanooga leaving destroyed railroad tracks, burned trestles, and clipped telegraph wires in their wake.

The conductor of the train, William A. Fuller, his breakfast rudely interrupted by the sight of the engine and part of his train heading northward, set off in hot pursuit on foot, then by hand car and finally with another engine and some Confederate soldiers picked up along the way. The pursued and the pursuer finally met when the General ran out of fuel some 87 miles later near Ringgold, Georgia, and the raiders continued their flight on foot, but within a week Confederate troops captured all of them, including Andrews. Two others who had overslept and missed the chase were also captured. Trials were held, and Andrews and seven of the Ohio soldiers were hanged on June 7, 1862, and buried in Atlanta. Later, the seven soldiers' remains were moved to Chattanooga. In 1887, after months of intensive search by the quarter master general's office in Atlanta, Andrews' remains were located beneath a street in one of the suburbs of Atlanta and shipped to Chattanooga for interment with his co-conspirators.

Soon after their capture, eight of the raiders escaped. Six remained in jail and were finally paroled at City Point, Virginia, on March 17, 1863. The eight executed spies are interred around the monument that so appropriately honors the courageous action of the raiders. They are James J. Andrews, civilian, Grave 12992; Sgt. Samuel Slavens, Grave 11176; Pvt. Samuel Robertson, Grave 11177; Pvt. George D. Wilson, Grave 11178; Sgt. Major Marion A. Ross, Grave 11179; Cook William H. Campbell, Grave 11180; Pvt. Perry G. Shadrack, Grave 11181; and Sgt. James M. Scott, Grave 11182.

Though the daring raid of Andrews and his fellow conspirators failed, those who participated in it were regarded as heroes in the North. Shortly after their parole, the six members of the band who had been imprisoned by the Confederates were ordered to Washington to report to the judge advocate general, Major General Ethan Allen Hitchcock. There, on March 25, 1863, Secretary of War Edwin M. Stanton personally awarded the Medal of Honor to Pvt. William Bensinger, Pvt. Robert Buffum, Sgt. Elihu H. Morgan, Pvt. Jacob Parrott, Sgt. William Pittinger, and Cpl. William A. Reddick. The little ceremony for the six surviving members of Andrews' raid marked the first presentation of the Army Medal of Honor. Private Jacob Parrott, the youngest member of the raiders, became the first to be awarded the nation's highest military decoration. His Medal of Honor is permanently on display in the crypt area beneath the Great Rotunda of the capitol.

Posthumous awards of the Medal of Honor were made to four of the eight members of the raiders who are interred in Chattanooga National Cemetery: Pvt. Samuel Robertson, Co. G, 33d Ohio Infantry; Sgt. Major Marion A. Ross, 2d Ohio Vol. Infantry; Sgt. John M. Scott, Co. F, 21st Ohio Vol. Inf.; and Sgt. Samuel Slavens, Co. E, 33d Ohio Vol. Inf.

In addition, nine other members of the Andrews raid received the Medal of Honor: Pvt. Wilson Brown, Co. F, 21st Ohio Infantry; Cpl. Daniel Dorsey, Co. H, 33d Ohio Infantry; Cpl. Martin J. Hawkins, Co. A, 33d Ohio Inf.; Pvt. William Knight, Co. E, 21st Ohio Infantry; Pvt. John R. Porter, Co. G, 21st Ohio Infantry; Pvt. James Smith, Co. I, 2d Ohio Infantry; Pvt. John A. Wilson, Co. C, 21st Ohio Infantry; Pvt. John Wollam, Co. C, 33d Ohio Infantry; and Pvt. Mark Wood, Co. O, 21st Ohio Infantry.

Official records indicate that corporals Martin J. Hawkins and Daniel Allen Dorsey are the only members of the Andrews raiders to be interred in a national cemetery other than Chattanooga. Corporal Hawkins died on February 7, 1886, and was interred in Quincy National Cemetery, Quincy, Illinois. Corporal Dorsey died on May 10, 1918, and is interred in Leavenworth National Cemetery.

Throughout Chattanooga National Cemetery, amid the silent rows of uniform white headstones, are scattered monuments that were erected in memory of past deeds and lost lives. A granite obelisk was erected by the Fourth Army Corps "In Memory of Their Fallen Comrades." The date of their deaths remains a mystery, but it quite probably was some time after the Civil War ended, as various volunteer regiments from many states are inscribed on the four sides of the monument's base.

In 1935, a monument was erected by the German government in honor of 78 German soldiers whose military careers and lives ended in an American prisoner of war camp during World War I. Of the 78 German POWs interred in the Section, 22 are unknown remains disinterred from the Hot Springs, North Carolina, cemetery and reinterred at Chattanooga. The 22 were interred in three gravesites in the post section on February 4, 1933.

Pursuant to provisions included in the peace treaty between the United States and Germany signed on August 25, 1921, and ratified on October 21, 1921, the German government initiated a request to learn the location and status of graves of German soldiers, sailors and nationals who died while interned in the United States during World War I and were buried in the United States. The War Department, acting primarily through the adjutant general's office and the office of the quartermaster general, cooperated in securing this information.

This survey disclosed that the largest number of deceased German prisoners of war (56) were interred in the Chattanooga National Cemetery. Consideration was, at one time, given to the removal of all other German prisoners of war located in the United States to the Chattanooga National Cemetery. But the Department of State was notified on October 25, 1932, and the War Department on December 21, 1932, by the German Embassy that.

> It will not be necessary to remove all the graves of German prisoners of war, located in the United States, to Chattanooga, since the majority of these graves are well taken care of. Only the 23 graves in the Odd Fellows Cemetery, Hot Springs, [North Carolina] are in a very bad condition. We would, therefore, be grateful if they could be removed to the National Cemetery, Chattanooga.

At the time of disinterment only 22 remains were located. The German government assumed the cost of disinterment and transportation to the national cemetery. Many of the German World War I prisoners of war were interned at a camp set up in Hot Springs, North

Carolina, where an old mountain resort hotel was taken over for the officer prisoners and barracks were erected on the hotel grounds for enlisted personnel. Most of those who died while interned here were the victims of a severe typhoid fever epidemic in 1918. Many of the victims were taken to the Army General Hospital in Asheville, North Carolina.

The German government, after receiving permission from the War Department to erect a monument to commemorate the prisoners of war, submitted a photograph and sketch of the proposed monument, and a list of 92 decedents whose names were to be inscribed on the monument. It was this sketch and listing which the quartermaster general approved on March 21, 1935. Both the listing and the monument inscription contain 92 names, but 14 of the individuals are not interred in the cemetery. They are Emil Behrendt, Otto Berner, Joh. Halenkamp, August Katzinsky, George Lenz, Johann Lintermann, Christian Mueller, Guenther Muenchen, William C. Ohle, F. Pohlin, Johannes Schoenawa, Karl Schoener, H. Staupe, and P. Wagner. The German inscription on the face of the monument reads, "During the war years died here far from home, and Germany will ever remember you."

In addition to the World War I prisoners of war, 108 World War II prisoners of war are interred here, including 105 Germans, 1 Frenchman, 1 Italian, and 1 Pole. Cemetery records indicate that this cemetery is the only National Cemetery in which both World War I and World War II POWs are interred. Ninety-four of the Germans were reinterred from Crossville, Tennessee, two were interred directly in the national cemetery, and the remainder of the POWs were reinterred from Camp Butler, North Carolina, in 1947.

Under the Government Reorganization Act of 1933, the cemetery was transferred to the Department of the Interior, National Park Service. In 1944, it was returned to the jurisdiction of the War Department.

As of September 30, 2008, the cemetery encompasses 120.8 acres and includes 46,601 interments. The projected closing date for initial interments is 2019.

There are seven Medal of Honor recipients, including the four members of Mitchell's Raiders, interred in the cemetery. A dagger before the first name denotes that the recipient was killed in action.

†**Ray E. Duke,** Sec Z, Grave 272. Sergeant First Class, U.S. Army, Company C, 21st Infantry Division. Place and date: Near Mugok, Korea, 26 April 1951.
Citation: Sergeant Duke, a member of Company C, distinguished himself by conspicuous gallantry and outstanding courage above and beyond the call of duty in action against the enemy. Upon learning that several of his men were isolated and heavily engaged in an area yielded by his platoon when ordered to withdraw, he led a small force in a daring assault which recovered the position and the beleaguered men. Another enemy attack in strength resulted innumerous casualties but Sfc. Duke, although wounded by mortar fragments, calmly moved along his platoon line to coordinate fields of fire and to urge his men to hold firm in the bitter encounter. Wounded a second time, he received first aid and returned to his position. When the enemy attacked again shortly after dawn, despite his wounds, Sfc. Duke repeatedly braved withering fire to ensure maximum defense of each position. Threatened with annihilation and mounting casualties, the platoon was again ordered to withdraw when Sfc. Duke was wounded a third time in both legs and was unable to walk. Realizing that he was impeding the progress of two comrades who were carrying him from the hill, he urged them to leave him and seek safety. He was last seen pouring devastating fire into the ranks of the onrushing assailants. The consummate courage, superb leadership, and heroic actions of Sfc. Duke, displayed during intensive action against overwhelming odds, reflect the highest credit upon himself, the infantry, and the U.S. Army.

Samuel Robertson, Sec H, Grave 11177. Private, Company G, 33d Ohio Infantry. Place and date: Georgia, April 1862.

Citation: One of the 19 of 22 men* (including 2 civilians) who by direction of Gen. Mitchell (or Buell) penetrated nearly 200 miles south into enemy territory and captured a railroad train at Big Shanty, Ga., in an attempt to destroy the bridges and track between Chattanooga and Atlanta.

Marion A. Ross, Sec H, Grave 11179. Sergeant Major, 2d Ohio Infantry. Place and date: Georgia, 1862.

Citation: Nineteen of 22 men (including 2 civilians) who, by direction of Gen. Mitchell (or Buell), penetrated nearly 200 miles south into enemy's territory and captured a railroad train at Big Shanty, Ga., in an attempt to destroy the bridges and track between Chattanooga and Atlanta.

James M. Scott, Sec H, Grave 11182. Sergeant, Company F, 21st Ohio Infantry. Place and date: Georgia, April 1862.

Citation: One of the 19 of 22 men (including 2 civilians) who, directed by Gen. Mitchell (or Buell), penetrated nearly 200 miles south into enemy territory and captured a railroad train at Big Shanty, Ga., and attempted to destroy the bridges and track between Chattanooga and Atlanta.

Samuel Slavens, Sec H, Grave 11176. Private, Company E, 33d Ohio Infantry. Place and Date: Georgia, April 1862.

Citation: One of the 19 of 22 men (including 2 civilians) who, by direction of Gen. Mitchell (or Buell), penetrated nearly 200 miles south into enemy territory and captured a railroad train at Big Shanty, Ga., in an attempt to destroy the bridges and track between Chattanooga and Atlanta.

William F. Zion, Sec U, Grave 40. Private, U.S. Marine Corps. G.O. No.: 55, 19 July 1901.

Citation: In the presence of the enemy during the battle of Peking, China, 21 July to 17 August 1900. Throughout this period, Zion distinguished himself by meritorious conduct.

†**Desmond T. Doss**, Sec. P. Grave. Private First Class, U.S. Army Medica; Department, 307 the Infantry, 77th Division. Place and Date: Near Urasol Mua, Okinawa, Ryukyu Islands, 29 April–21 May 1945.

Citation: He was a Company Aid man when the 1st Battalion assaulted a jagged escarpment 400 feet high. Through his outstanding bravery and unflinching determination in the face of desperately dangerous conditions, Pfc Doss saved the lives of many soldiers. His name became a symbol throughout the 77th Infantry Division for outstanding gallantry far above the call of duty.

Former superintendents/directors of Chattanooga National Cemetery are:

Frederick Buntley, January 1868–Unknown
Robert R. Dye, January 1914–July 1919
Walter L. Henderson, July 1931–March 1956
Curtis W. Spence, April 1956–January 1962
Walter N. Mick, January 1962–February 1965
William J. Boyer, May 1965–June 1967
Charles J. Horten, July 1967–June 1970
Oscar P. Findley, August 1970–December 1975
Andrew F. Szilvasi, June 1976–August 1977

Raymond L. Cordell, August 1977–January 1980
Robert E. Bevering, February 1980–May 1988
Jimmy S. Adamson, 1988–1990
James Wallace III, 1990–1999
Candice Underwood, August 1999–February 2005
Sandra Beckley, March 2005–June 2005 (Acting)
Paul H. Martin, June 2005–Present

City Point National Cemetery
500 North 10th Avenue
Hopewell, Virginia 23860

The cemetery is situated in Prince George County, on the south bank of the Appomattox River at City Point, Virginia. (Hopewell, which includes City Point, is an independent city.)

*This is the exact wording of the citation. The meaning of this phrase is not clear, though 19 is taken to refer to the number of soldiers in the group. The man unaccounted for may be one who slept through the raid.

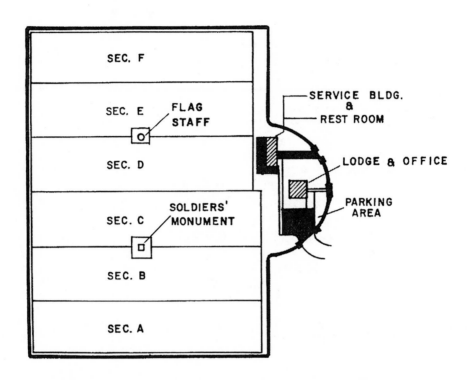

Map of the City Point National Cemetery, Hopewell, Va., October 1969.

The existence of military burial grounds at City Point and the subsequent establishment of City Point National Cemetery in 1866 reflects another aspect in the struggle for the capital city of the Confederacy. Here at City Point on the James River the Union Army established a large supply depot for receipt of troops and vast quantities of all manner of war materiel in preparation for another attempt to capture Richmond. General Grant's objective was to capture Petersburg, a vital communications center, and then to advance upon Richmond from south of the James River. From June 1864 to April 1865, heavy siege action by Union forces and desperate and stubborn defense tactics by Lee's Army of Northern Virginia characterized the campaign which brought Grant's forces to Petersburg and ultimately into the streets of Richmond.

The result of this all-out thrust for Richmond was a large number of casualties. A large general hospital at City Point cared for some of the sick and wounded. The death rate from wounds and disease was high, and many of the combatants of the 1864–65 siege of Petersburg and Richmond were interred in burial grounds near this and other hospitals of the Army of the Potomac and the Army of the James. Following cessation of hostilities, this burial ground became a part of the City Point National Cemetery.

The land for the cemetery, about seven acres, was appropriated in 1866 and purchased in 1868 from Edward Comer of Prince George County. Remains not originally buried in the cemetery were recovered from another burial ground at City Point, from Point of Rocks in Chesterfield County, and a few from Harrison's Landing in Charles City County.

City Point differs from the other five cemeteries of the Richmond area in that the number of identified remains exceeds the number of unknown remains. Initial interments included 3,753 known remains and 1,454 unknowns. As of September 30, 2008, total interments were 6,028. There are 118 Confederate soldiers interred in the cemetery.

In 1955 the remains of 17 unknown soldiers of the Civil War were discovered during an excavation of some vacant lots in Hopewell, Virginia. Apparently the site was an abandoned cemetery. Buttons from both Union and Confederate uniforms were found in some of the graves. The 17 remains were reinterred in the national cemetery.

The remains of two Union soldiers killed in the Battle of Petersburg 1864–65 were recovered from shallow graves in the path of Interstate Highway 95, and reinterred in the cemetery on August 12, 1959.

Inside the boundaries of City Point National Cemetery is a white marble monument approximately 20 feet high erected in 1865 to the memory of the dead of the Army of the James, by direction of Major General B.F. Butler, commander of the Army of the James from April 1864 to January 1865.

The cemetery was closed for interments on July 26, 1971, except for those in reserved gravesites and second interments in existing graves under the single gravesite per family policy. The director of Richmond National Cemetery, is responsible for the operation, maintenance, and administration of the cemetery.

Former superintendents/directors of the cemetery are:

John Delacray, June 1868–Unknown	John T. Spelman, April 1948–1955
Walter A. Donaldson, 1880–Unknown	Harold A. Johnson, June 1955–November 1962
T.D. Godman, 1886–Unknown	William A. Miller, November 1962–September
John Amrein, 1909–Unknown	1964
Johan T. Vandre, 1912–Unknown	Jack A. Morris, September 1964–August 1970
Roy B. Shupp, October 1941–1947	Henry L. Hoefelmeyer, August 1970–June 1972

Cold Harbor National Cemetery
Route 156 North
Mechanicsville, Virginia 23111

The cemetery is located in Hanover County, on Virginia Highway 156 about nine miles east of Richmond, Virginia. It fronts on White House Road and may be approached on the Nine Mile Road from Richmond.

This little cemetery is truly a battlefield cemetery. A portion of the fighting of two Union campaigns to reach Richmond occurred in this area. General George R. McClellan's Peninsula Campaign to reach Richmond virtually collapsed as a result of the fighting of the Seven Days' Battles of June 26–July 2, 1862. The fighting at Gaines' Mill (Cold Harbor) on June 26–27 has been described as the most costly and vicious of the Seven Days' battles with heavy losses inflicted on both Union and Confederate forces. Then in early June 1864, a mighty army under General Ulysses S. Grant met General Robert E. Lee's forces, fewer in number but strongly entrenched, at Cold Harbor, a strategic crossroad guarding the approaches to Richmond. Fighting from June 1 through June 3 assured the security of Richmond for another 10 months, but only at the cost of tremendous casualties for both the Union and Confederate armies. Writing of the operations at Cold Harbor during those

Marker for unknown Union soldiers, Cold Harbor National Cemetery.

hot days of early June, General Lee's biographer, Douglas Southall Freeman, states that Lee "had won his last great battle in the field."

Some historians believe that Cold Harbor was the only battle that General Grant ever regretted having fought.

The U.S. government appropriated the ground upon which the cemetery is located and established the cemetery in January 1866. The original site of 1⅙ acres was purchased in 1870 from Miss Indian H. Slaughter. An additional strip of land extending around 3 sides of the cemetery was purchased in 1871 from Miles Garthright and Gustavus Lange, bringing the cemetery to its present size of 1.4 acres.

With the establishment of Cold Harbor National Cemetery in 1866, an extensive search over a 22-mile area located the initial burial places of many who were killed in action and buried on the battlefield. Lack of identification on the remains and the time lapse from the hasty battlefield burial made it impossible to identify by name and rank many of the remains interred in the national cemetery. As of July 25, 1871, a total of 1,851 interments had been made. Of these, 576 were identified and 1,275 were unknown. A total of 2,114 interments had been made in the cemetery as of September 30, 2008, including 1,313 unknowns.

On the north side of the cemetery are two long trenches, one containing the remains of 568, and the other 321 Union soldiers, all unknown by name. A large white marble sarcophagus erected by the U.S. government in 1877 bears the following inscription in tribute to these unknowns: "Near this stone rest the remains of 889 Union soldiers gathered from the Battlefields of Mechanicsville, Savage Station, Gaines Mills and the vicinity of Cold Harbor."

A tall granite monument bearing the figure of a soldier at parade rest was erected at the cemetery in 1909 by the Commonwealth of Pennsylvania "To all Pennsylvania Regiments which participated in the operations from May 31st to June 12th 1864 incident to and during the Battle of Cold Harbor, Virginia June 1–3, 1864."

Another large commemorative monument erected in 1909 under the auspices of the New York State Monuments Commission bears a large bronze plaque listing the names of 219 members of the Eighth New York Heavy Artillery who were killed or died of wounds received in the Battle of Cold Harbor, June 2–12, 1864. The 8th Heavy Artillery was organized at Lockport and recruited principally in the counties of Niagara, Orleans and Genesee. It was originally the 129th New York Infantry, and was part of General Hancock's Second Corps. At Cold Harbor it was commanded by Colonel Peter A. Porter. He was killed there and succeeded by Lieutenant Colonel W.W. Bates.

There is one Medal of Honor recipient interred here:

> **Augustus Barry**, Section A, Grave 309. Sergeant Major, 16th U.S. Infantry. Place and date: Unknown, 1863–65.
> Citation: Gallantry in various actions during the rebellion.

Former superintendents/directors of the cemetery are:

Augustus Barry, Unknown	Grover R. Neal, May 1960–November 1961
Harry Painting, March 1940–April 1945	Gerald C. Nelson, November 1961–August 1967
John Brewer, June 1945–May 1948	Henry A. Hartwig, August 1967–January 1968
Marvin F. Ellerman, June 1948–December 1958	George C. Miller, January 1968–August 1970

The Cold Harbor National Cemetery was closed to interments on February 27, 1970, except for burial in reserved gravesites and second interments in existing graves under the single gravesite per family policy. The director of Richmond National Cemetery is responsible for the administration and management of this cemetery.

Corinth National Cemetery
1551 Horton Street
Corinth, Mississippi 38834

The cemetery is located in Alcorn County within the city limits of Corinth, Mississippi, about 89 miles east of Memphis, Tennessee. It is situated about ¾ mile southeast of the Alcorn County Court House.

The Confederate stronghold of Corinth was of strategic importance in General U.S. Grant's western campaign. It served to guard one approach to Memphis, Vicksburg, and the Mississippi. It also was an important railroad center. Following the Battle of Shiloh, Tennessee, on April 6–7, 1862, in which Confederate General Albert Sidney Johnson was killed, the Confederate forces retreated to Corinth. In late April, the Union supreme commander, General Henry W. Halleck, took command of Grant's army and started moving south toward Corinth. The Confederate commander, General Pierre Gustave Toutant Beauregard, recognizing the importance of Corinth, engaged in many skirmishes and battles as Halleck moved cautiously southward. Finally, Halleck had the city surrounded and forced Beauregard to evacuate his forces from the city. On September 19, 1862, generals Sterling Price and Earl Van Dorn attacked and captured Iuka, south of Corinth, hoping to move

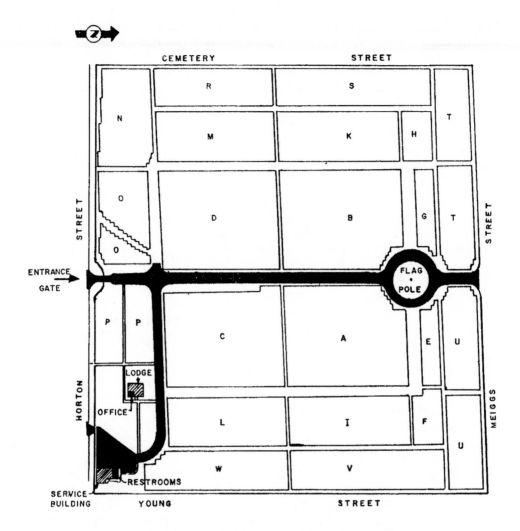

Corinth National Cemetery, Corinth, MS.

back to Corinth. They were decisively defeated in a battle in October, and never again seriously threatened Union control of the area.

The Confederate commander, General P.G.T. Beauregard, was a native of New Orleans and a West Point graduate of 1838. He was a veteran of the Mexican War, commanded the bombardment of Fort Sumter, share the Confederate command at Shiloh, and later fought in the Battle of Petersburg. He had served as Superintendent of West Point for five days in early 1861, but was removed after he said that he would join the South if war started. He did resign his commission and joined the Confederate army where he rose to the rank of full general.

Corinth National Cemetery was established in 1866 to consolidate the casualties of the battles of Corinth, Iuka, Holly Springs and other battles and skirmishes in the area. The cemetery grounds occupy a 20-acre portion of the battlefield. The land was owned by C.F. Vance, F. Menhite, and James H. Walker until appropriated and later purchased by the United States.

Original interments were remains gathered from some 15 to 20 battlefields or skirmish sites. In addition to Corinth, Iuka, and Holly Springs, remains were brought from

Grenada, Guntown and Farmington, Mississippi; from Parkers Crossroads, Middlebury, and Brittans Lane, Tennessee; from Florence, Tuscumbia, Decatur and Cullman, Alabama; and from various scattered camps and hospitals in Tennessee and Mississippi. When the reinterment program was virtually complete in late 1870, there were 5,688 interments in the cemetery 1,793 known and 3,895 unknown. These dead represented 273 regiments from 15 states, including the 63rd Regiment of Ohio Volunteers, 4th Regiment of Illinois Volunteers, and Michigan Volunteers. As far as possible, interments were made by states. There are three Confederate soldiers interred in the cemetery, two known and one unknown.

Originally, the cemetery was enclosed with a wooden picket fence, which was replaced by a brick wall in 1872. The first lodge was a wooden cottage which was replaced in 1872 and again in 1934. The first superintendent, Joseph Berrigan, a discharged private of Company B, 43rd Regiment of Infantry, was appointed on November 26, 1867.

As of September 30, 2008, there were 7,295 interments in the cemetery. It is projected to have available grave space beyond the year 2030. Corinth National Cemetery is a beautiful area with large oak and magnolia trees throughout the grounds. Perhaps one reason for the low interment rate in the cemetery might be as expressed by several local residents: "This is a Yankee cemetery and we don't want to have anything to do with it."

Former superintendents/directors of the cemetery are:

Joseph Berrigan, November 1867–Unknown
Claude B. Ryburn, April 1934–January 1947
Walter Hanns, January 1947–October 1955
Charles J. Horton, October 1955–August 1957
Ernest L. Fusse, August 1957–November 1967

Allen H. Long, December 1967–October 1969
John Clemmons, November 1969–July 1981
Lonnie Nelms, August 1981–December 1988
Jeffrey S. Barnes, January 1989–

Crown Hill National Cemetery
3402 Boulevard Place
Indianapolis, Indiana 46208

This cemetery consists of the 1.37-acre Section No. 10 of the Crown Hill Incorporated Cemetery, situated on Michigan Road. It was established as a national cemetery in 1866.

During the Civil War those soldiers who died while stationed in the various camps near the city of Indianapolis, and those who died in the general hospitals, were temporarily buried in the old city graveyard known as the Greenlawn Cemetery. With the expansion of the city, it became apparent that the old cemetery would be abandoned within a few years. Indiana Governor Oliver P. Morton suggested to the secretary of war in 1866 that the remains should be removed to the Crown Hill Cemetery, whose management had offered to donate land for the reinterments on condition that the U.S. government would expend a certain sum for improvements. Since no funds were available for improvements, it was considered preferable that the United States purchase the ground and the cemetery company expend the purchase price in improvements.

Brigadier General James A. Ekin, deputy quartermaster general, came to Indianapolis for the ceremony attending the reinterment of the first remains. Matthew Quigley, Company A, 13th Regiment, was the first of 709 remains removed from the Greenlawn Cemetery and reinterred here between October 1866 and March 1867. As of September 30, 2008, there were only 795 total interments.

For the first few years there was a superintendent here. Sergeant A.S. Diol, serving in 1867, was probably the first. In 1868, Sergeant John Trindle was appointed, but because he was incapacitated by the loss of one leg and was also quite illiterate, he was dismissed. The cemetery was placed under the care of the superintendent of the Crown Hill Cemetery, who still manages it today.

Lot 285, Section 32, in Crown Hill Cemetery is a Confederate cemetery lot owned by the United States.

Both Crown Hill National Cemetery and the Confederate cemetery lot are maintained by Crown Hill Cemetery at no cost to the United States, except for headstone maintenance.

Culpeper National Cemetery
305 U.S. Avenue
Culpeper, Virginia 22701

Culpeper National Cemetery is a small cemetery, originally occupying about 6½ acres, located about one-half mile from the courthouse in the town of Culpeper, Culpeper County, Virginia. The cemetery was established in 1866 and designated a national cemetery in 1867. The right and title to the property was acquired from E.B. Hill of Culpeper on May 10, 1867, for the sum of $1,400.

The area around Culpeper was the scene of many battles and engagements during the Civil War years as armies advanced and retreated between Washington, D.C., and Richmond, Virginia.

The tempo of military activity was greatly stepped up during the late summer of 1862. Following its reverses in the Peninsular Campaign for Richmond in June and July, General McClellan's Army of the Potomac was back at Harrison's Landing, still within striking distance of Richmond. It did not appear however, that the Army of the Potomac would be used further for such a purpose. Accordingly, General Lee now felt that the best defensive action would be an offensive movement northward. The Battle of Cedar Mountain, south of Culpeper, on August 9, 1862, was an early manifestation of this strategy. The encounter was a disaster for the Union forces commanded by General Nathaniel Banks against a superior number of Confederates under the command of General Stonewall Jackson. The remains of more than 300 Union soldiers, casualties of this battle, are interred at Culpeper National Cemetery. Many of these are among the 912 unknowns now interred in the cemetery.

During the late summer of 1862 the Confederate push northward moved beyond Cedar Mountain and Culpeper toward Manassas and the second Battle of Bull Run, in late August. Eventually, they moved into Maryland and the fierce fighting and heavy casualties of the Antietam (Sharpsburg) Campaign. Following this, General Lee withdrew southward into Virginia. The summer of 1863 found Lee and his Army of Northern Virginia once more advancing northward. The advance was finally checked after three momentous days of fighting at a little Pennsylvania town Gettysburg. Among the incidents of the pre–Gettysburg campaign was a fierce cavalry engagement in and about the area of Brandy Station, Virginia, on June 9, 1863. It has been described as the largest and first true cavalry engagement of the Civil War. Casualties on both sides were heavy. Records compiled after the war, as Culpeper National Cemetery was being established, indicate burial in the cemetery of at least two Union Cavalry officers who lost their lives at Brandy Station. Lieutenant Colonel Virgil Broderick, 1st New Jersey Cavalry, died on June 9, 1863. He was buried near Brandy Station at a site described in Army records as George L. Stewart's farm. His remains were subsequently disinterred and moved to Grave 451 in the national cemetery. The second, 1st Lieutenant Isaac M. Ward, 6th United States Cavalry, was killed on the same day and also interred on Mr. Stewart's farm. His remains are now interred in Grave 438.

Culpeper National Cemetery.

The Army of the Potomac camped at Brandy Station during the winter of 1863–64. The remains of soldiers who died in the military hospital set up there were subsequently interred in Culpeper.

For the most part, the dead from these encounters were interred in hastily prepared graves where they fell. In many instances there was little or no marking of the burial place of a soldier killed in battle. With the ending of hostilities came the search of combat areas, hospital areas, church yards, plantations, and other locations for remains of the war dead so that they might receive a final proper burial in one of the national cemeteries established for that purpose. Identification in 1866 and 1867 of the dead given battlefield burial during the war years was not an easy matter. The report of the inspector of national cemeteries dated August 8, 1871, indicated that a total of 1,349 interments had been made in the cemetery. Of that number, 448 were identified by name and rank and 901 were interred as unknowns. Remains were brought to Culpeper from Cedar Mountain, Trevilians Station, Gordonsville, Brandy Station, and several other places in that vicinity.

Within the Culpeper National Cemetery are five large monuments commemorating those who died at Cedar Mountain. They were erected by the states of Maine, Massachusetts, New York, Ohio, and Pennsylvania. The inscriptions read as follows:

Maine monument: "To the memory of twenty-two officers and soldiers of the Tenth Maine Volunteer Infantry killed at Cedar Mountain, Virginia, August 9, 1862." The sponsor and date are not known.

Massachusetts monument: "The Second Mass. Infantry raised this stone in memory of their dead who fell in the battle of Cedar Mountain, Virginia, August 9, 1862. Erected by the Second Massachusetts Infantry, 1893."

New York monument: "28th Regiment New York State Volunteer Infantry, 1st Brig., 1st Div. 12th Corps Army of the Potomac. Erected by the State of New York Regimental Association, 1902." The 28th was organized in Albany and recruited in the counties of Orleans, Niagara, Ontario, Genesee, and Sullivan. It was commanded at Cedar Mountain by Colonel Dudley Donnelly and was part of General Banks' 12th Corps.

Ohio monument: "Erected by the Seventh Ohio Regimental Association in honor of the Officers and Soldiers of that Regiment who fought in the battle of Cedar Mountain, Virginia, August 9, 1862, many of whom are buried in unknown graves in this cemetery. Killed 37, Wounded 153. Total loss of 190 out of 307 present. Erected by the Seventh Ohio Regimental Association." The date is not known.

Pennsylvania Monument: "Pennsylvania remembers with solemn pride her heroic sons who here repose in known and unknown graves. May their sacrifices be an inspiration to the people and promote civic virtue, love of liberty, peace, prosperity and happiness in all the States. 'DULCE ET DECORUM EST PROPATRIA MORI.' Erected by the State of Pennsylvania, 1910."

The Burton-Hammond Post 2524, Veterans of Foreign Wars, donated a memorial plaque which reads as follows: "Civil War soldiers were originally buried where they bravely fought and died during battles at Cedar Mountain, Trevilians Station, Gordonsville, Brandy Station and surrounding area. Following the Civil War the remains of 912 soldiers whose names are unknown were reinterred here in Sections C and D."

It is definitely known that at least one Confederate soldier is buried in the cemetery. Burial records and headstones indicate that there could be quite a few more.

Culpeper National Cemetery closed to new interments on November 17, 1972, when there were no more available interment sites except for reserved gravesites and second interments in existing graves. The Veterans of Foreign Wars, Burton-Hammond Post 2524, appointed a National Cemetery Committee to investigate the possibility of acquiring additional property. The committee was instrumental in arranging the donation of 10.51 acres of land from Joe H. Gardner, president of Bingham & Taylor Corp., as a memorial to all corporation employees who served in the armed forces. The property was accepted by the Veterans Administration on October 21, 1975, and the cemetery reopened on January 16, 1978. The first interment in the new area was Edward H. Maxwell, cemetery director, who died suddenly in December 1977.

The cemetery now encompasses 29.5 acres and includes a total of 10,595 interments. Former superintendents/directors of Culpeper National Cemetery are:

Herbert Rhodes, August 1940–July 1944
John J. Carr, January 1945–September 1947
Ralph L. Fischetti, November 1947–September 1948
William J. Boyer, September 1948–March 1959
Edward E. Douglas, Jr., March 1959–October 1960
Harold D. Stabler, October 1960–February 1961
James H. Carson, February 1961–October 1965
Unknown, October 1965–August 1971

David L. Bartlett, August 1971–October 1972
Edward H. Maxwell, November 1975–December 1977
Dellas L. Atchinson, February 1978–June 1979
Dennis L. Kuehl, June 1979–February 1980
Eugene L. Chambers, March 1980–November 1980
Kevin J. Taylor, November 1980–September 1985
Delores T. Blake, 1985–1990
David R. Wells, 1990–

Cypress Hills National Cemetery
Jamaica Avenue
Brooklyn, New York

By the summer of 1862 it was increasingly evident to the governments of both the Union and the Confederacy that the war, begun with such confidence on both sides in 1861, would be a long and difficult struggle. Casualty lists of the dead, the wounded, and the sick reflected all too poignantly the intensity of the great struggle. Metropolitan areas such as New York City, though distant from the sites of armed conflict, saw the establishment of military hospitals to care for the wounded and sick from the battlefields of the war.

Burial space for the dead from these hospitals became a necessity. It was under these conditions that Cypress Hills National Cemetery had its beginnings as a Zone of the Interior Military Cemetery. It was located within the boundaries of the Cypress Hills Cemetery, a large private cemetery in Brooklyn, New York, which had been established in 1849. The site set aside for the burial of Civil War dead occupied 2.75 acres and became known a the Union Grounds. The Union Grounds were deeded to the United States by the Cypress Hills Cemetery Corporation on March 29, 1870, for a consideration of $9,600.

Private Alfred Mitchell, a young soldier of the 1st New York Engineers who died on April 13, 1862, was the first Civil War casualty to be interred in this designated cemetery area. The report of the inspector general dated 2 September 1870 indicated that 3,170 Union soldiers and 461 Confederate prisoners of war were then interred in the cemetery. Burials were of the dead from various military hospitals in and about New York City. Reinterments were made of remains previously interred at Hart's and David's islands in Long Island Sound, and from the soldiers' burial ground near Providence, Rhode Island. The first superintendent of Cypress Hills National Cemetery was John Bryson, a former private with the Thirtieth New York Volunteers.

Prior to 1873, eligibility for burial in national cemeteries was restricted to the soldiers of the United States who fell in battle during the Civil War, or who died in hospitals of wounds received in battle. In 1873 legislation was approved which gave burial rights to surviving honorably discharged soldiers, sailors and Marines who served during the war in either the regular or volunteer forces.

Cypress Hills National Cemetery, by its location in a large metropolitan area, felt a

Cypress Hills National Cemetery, 1933.

great impact from the liberalized burial regulations. It became evident that additional land would be necessary to supplement the 2.75 acres utilized since 1862 and acquired by purchase in 1870. An additional tract of land of slightly more than 15 acres was purchased in 1884. This property, on Jamaica Avenue, is approximately one mile from the Union Grounds. In 1941 a small plot in the old Cypress Hills Cemetery, known as the Mount of Victory Plot, was donated to the United States by the State of New York. The Cypress Hills National Cemetery today consists of three tracts of land: the Union Grounds, the larger area on Jamaica Avenue, and the Mount of Victory Plot. The three tracts total 18.197 acres and, as of September 30, 2008, a total of 21,112 interments.

In 1887 a residence/office structure was erected on the Jamaica Avenue property, replacing a smaller structure in the old portion of the cemetery. The last assigned cemetery director vacated the lodge in November 1978 and the building has been vacant since then. The Department of Veterans Affairs is negotiating with the Cypress Hills Development Corporation, which wants to use the lodge as a museum and a community center building. The corporation plans to spend approximately $125,000 to restore the severely vandalized structure to meet historic restoration requirements.

Though Cypress Hills National Cemetery was established to provide a burial place for Civil War soldiers who died in military hospitals, its present boundaries include the graves of individuals who fought in all wars in which our country has been engaged. One of the graves in the Mount of Victory Plot is that of Private Hiram Cronk. He is thought to be the last survivor o the War of 1812. He died in 1905 at the age of 105 years.

A total of 488 Confederate soldiers is interred here. In addition to those who died at nearby Hart's and David's islands, others are interred here who died while prisoners of war at Fort Columbus, Willet's Point, Fort Lafayette, and Fort Wood, New York, and at Portsmouth Grove, Rhode Island.

A distinguishing landmark in the Mount of Victory Plot is a pyramid of fieldstone topped by a large stone eagle with wings outspread. The stone pyramid was constructed by laborers at the cemetery about 1934. The eagle, which was the property of the cemetery, was erected on top of the pyramid by the Londino Construction Company during the same year.

In 1885, remains from Fort Hamilton were removed to Cypress Hills. Subsequently, remains from Governor's Island and Fort Wadsworth (1886), Fort Wood (about 1889), and Mount Hope Cemetery at Otisville (1921), were reinterred in the cemetery. Veindovi, a Fiji Island Chief, died in the Brooklyn Naval Hospital on June 11, 1842, and was interred in the hospital cemetery. When the hospital cemetery closed in 1926, Veindovi's remains and the remains of other decedents interred there were reinterred in the National Cemetery.

A large granite monument at Grave 36, Plot 4, Post Section, bears the names of 14 officers and men of the British Navy who perished off the coast of Sandy Hook, New Jersey, on December 31, 1783. Inasmuch as a treaty of peace between Great Britain and the United States was signed on September 3, 1783, ending the Revolutionary War, perhaps the ship bearing these men might have been homeward bound when disaster overtook it on the final day of 1783. They were originally interred in the Fort Hancock Post Cemetery, New Jersey. A century and a quarter later their remains were unearthed and were reinterred in Cypress Hills National Cemetery on March 5, 1909.

Other special monuments include the Garfield Memorial Site, the location of which was marked by an oak tree planted November 3, 1881, by the James A. Garfield Oak Society of Brooklyn, New York, in memory of President Garfield. In 1944 the original oak, which had been destroyed by a hurricane, was replaced with a red oak.

A large cross near the cemetery's rostrum was erected by the Franco-American Society in 1920 to commemorate 25 French sailors who died in the Brooklyn Naval Hospital during influenza epidemics from 1914 through 1918.

Sergeant Major Daniel Joseph Daly, interred in Grave 70, Section 5, is considered by many the greatest hero to bear the name "Marine." During his career he received two Medals of Honor, the Army Distinguished Service Cross, the Navy Cross, the French Medaille Militaire, and the French Croix de Guerre with Palm. The Medal of Honor citations do not do justice to his deeds. Daly joined the Marine Corps in 1899, at age 27, in hope of seeing action in the Spanish-American War, but he did not get into action until he arrived in China as a private during the Boxer Rebellion. He was awarded his first Medal of Honor for his valiant one-man stand in which he single handedly defended the extension of the American Legation Wall in Peking against the onslaught of hundreds of Boxers. Fourteen years later as a Gunnery Sergeant in the Haitian Campaign, he received his second Medal of Honor for rescuing a machine gun from a Haitian Caco at great personal risk and enabling his patrol to fight off a mass attack by fanatical warriors. During June 1918, with the Marine Expeditionary Force at Belleau Woods, he spurred his men into a bayonet charge with the battle cry, "Come on, you sons-a-bitches. Do you want to live forever?" This cry has been handed down through the years as one of the finest expressions of Marine *esprit de corps* ever uttered. Sergeant Major Daly died of a heart attack in 1937 at the age of 65.

There are 24 recipients of the Medal of Honor interred at Cypress Hills National Cemetery. Their names and citations follow. A dagger indicates that the recipient was killed in action.

John Mapes Adams (a.k.a. George Lawrence Day), Sec 2, Grave 8262. Sergeant, U.S. Marine Corps. G.O. No.: 55, 19 July 1901.
Citation: In the presence of the enemy during the battle near Tientsin, China, 13 July 1900, Adams distinguished himself by meritorious conduct.

†**Wilbur E. Colyer,** Sec 2, Grave 8588. Sergeant, U.S. Army, Company A, 1st Engineers, 1st Division. Place and date: Near Verdun, France, 9 October 1918.
Citation: Volunteering with two other soldiers to locate machine gun nests, Sgt. Colyer advanced on the hostile positions to a point where he was half surrounded by the nests, which were in ambush. He killed the gunner of one gun with a captured German grenade and then turned this gun on the other nests, silencing all of them before he returned to his platoon. He was later killed in action.

John Cooper (a.k.a. John Mather), Sec 2, Grave 5022. Coxswain, U.S. Navy. G.O. No.: 45, 31 December 1864.
First Award Citation: On board the *USS Brooklyn* during action against rebel forts and gunboats and with the ram *Tennessee*, in Mobile Bay, 5 August 1864. Despite severe damage to his ship and the loss of several men on board as enemy fire raked her decks from stem to stern, Cooper fought his gun with skill and courage throughout the furious battle which resulted in the surrender of the prize rebel ram *Tennessee* and in damaging and destruction of batteries at Fort Morgan.
Second Award Citation: Served as quartermaster on Acting Rear Admiral Thatcher's staff. During the terrific fire at Mobile, on 26 April 1865, at the risk of being blown to pieces by exploding shells, Cooper advanced through the burning locality, rescued a wounded man from certain death, and bore him back to a place of safety. G.O. No.: 62, 29 June 1865.

Daniel Joseph Daly, Sec 5, Grave 70. Private, U.S. Marine Corps. G.O. 55, 19 July 1901. Other Navy Awards: Second Medal of Honor, Navy Cross.
Citation: In the presence of the enemy during the battle of Peking, China, 14 August 1900, Daly distinguished himself by meritorious conduct.
Second Award: Gunnery Sergeant, U.S. Marine Corps. Citation: Serving with the 15th Company of Marines on 22 October 1915, Sgt. Daly was one of the company to leave Fort Liberte, Haiti, for a 6-day reconnaissance. After dark on the evening of 24 October, while crossing the river in a deep ravine, the detachment was suddenly fired upon from 3 sides by about 400 Cacos concealed in bushes about 100 yards from the fort. The Marine detachment fought its way forward to a good position, which it maintained during the night, although subjected to continuous fire from the Cacos. At daybreak the Marines, in three squads, advanced in three different directions, surprising and scattering the Cacos in all directions. G/Sgt. Daly fought with exceptional gallantry against heavy odds throughout this action.

James Dougherty, Sec 6, Grave 12374. Private, U.S. Marine Corps. G.O. No.: 169, 8 February 1872.
Citation: Onboard the *USS Carondelet* in various actions of that vessel. Wounded several times, Dougherty invariably returned to duty, presenting an example of constancy and devotion to the flag.

Christopher Freemayer, Sec 2, Grave 5259. Private, Company D, 5th U.S. Infantry. Place and date: Cedar Creek, etc., Mont., 21 October 1876 to 8 January 1877.
Citation: Gallantry in action.

Joseph John Franklin, Private, U.S. Marine Corps. G.O. No.: 521, 7 July 1899.
Citation: Onboard the *USS Nashville* during the operation of cutting the cable leading from Cienfuegos, Cuba, 11 May 1898. Facing the heavy fire of the enemy, Franklin set an example of extraordinary bravery and coolness throughout this action.

Frederick W. Gerber, Sec 2, Grave 6101. Sergeant Major, U.S. Engineers. Date: 1839–71.
Citation: Distinguished gallantry in many actions and in recognition of long, faithful, and meritorious services covering a period of 32 years.

Patrick Golden. Sergeant, Company B, 8th U.S. Cavalry. Place and date: Arizona, August to October 1868.
Citation: Bravery in scouts and actions against Indians.

Edward P. Grimes, Sec 2, Grave 7210. Sergeant, Company F, 5th U.S. Cavalry. Place and date: Milk River, Colo., 29 September to 5 October 1879.

Citation: The command being almost out of ammunition and surrounded on three sides by the enemy, he voluntarily brought up a supply under heavy fire at almost point blank range.

Bernhard Jetter, Sec 5, Grave 1. Sergeant, Company K, 7th U.S. Cavalry. Place and date: At Sioux campaign, December 1890.
Citation: Distinguished bravery.

Johannes J. Johannessen, Sec 2, Grave 7425. Chief Watertender, U.S. Navy. G.O. No.: 182, 20 March 1905.
Citation: Serving onboard the *USS Iowa,* for extraordinary heroism at the time of the blowing out of the manhole plate of boiler D onboard that vessel, 25 January 1905.

Edward (Edwin) S. Martin, Grave 5966. Quartermaster, U.S. Navy; died December 23, 1901.

Mons Monssen, Sec OS, Grave 190. Chief Gunner's Mate, U.S. Navy. G.O. No.: 160, 26 May 1904.
Citation: While serving aboard the *USS Missouri,* for extraordinary heroism in entering a burning magazine through the scuttle and endeavoring to extinguish the fire by throwing water with his hands until a hose was passed to him, 13 April 1904.

John Nihill, Private, Company F, 5th U.S. Cavalry. Place and date: Whetstone Mountains, Ariz., 13 July 1872.
Citation: Fought and defeated four hostile Apaches located between him and his comrades.

Anton Olsen, Sec 2, Grave 9158. Ordinary Seaman, U.S. Navy. G.O. No.: 529, 2 November 1899.
Citation: Onboard the *USS Marblehead* during the operation of cutting the cable leading from Cienfuegos, Cuba, 11 May 1898. Facing the heavy fire of the enemy, Olsen displayed extraordinary bravery and coolness throughout this period.

Henry Rodenburg, Sec 2, Grave 5825. Private, Company A, 5th U.S. Infantry. Place and date: Cedar Creek, etc., Mont., 21 October 1876 to 8 January 1877.
Citation: Gallantry in action.

Valentine Rossbach, Sec 2, Grave 5427. Sergeant, 34th New York Battery. Place and date: Spotsylvania, Va., 12 May 1864.
Citation: Encouraged his cannoneers to hold a very dangerous position, and when all depended on several good shots it was from his piece that the most effective was delivered, causing the enemy's fire to cease and thereby relieving the critical position of the Federal troops.

John Schilling (Schiller), Grave 5–3. Private, U.S. Army; died June 3, 1926.

Eugene P. Smith, Sec 2, Grave 7742. Chief Watertender, U.S. Navy. G.O. No.: 189, 8 February 1916.
Citation: Attached to *USS Decatur;* for several times entering compartments onboard of *Decatur* immediately following an explosion onboard that vessel, 9 September 1915, and locating and rescuing injured shipmates.

Wilhelm Smith, Sec 2, Grave 9492. Gunner's Mate First Class, U.S. Navy. G.O. No.: 202, 6 April 1916.
Citation: Onboard the *USS New York;* for entering a compartment filled with gases and rescuing a shipmate on 24 January 1916.

Peter Stewart, Sec 2, Grave 7303. Gunnery Sergeant, U.S. Marine Corps. G.O. No.: 55, 19 July 1901.
Citation: In action with the relief expedition of the Allied forces in China during the battles of 13, 20, 21, 22 June 1900. Throughout this period and in the presence of the enemy, Stewart distinguished himself by meritorious conduct.

James Webb, Sec 2, Grave 7410. Private, Company F, 5th New York Infantry. Place and date: Bull Run, Va., 30 August 1862.
Citation: Under heavy fire voluntarily carried information to a battery commander that enabled him to save his guns from capture. Was severely wounded, but refused to go to the hospital and participated in the remainder of the campaign.

Henry Wilkens, Sec 2, Grave 5325. First Sergeant, Company L, 2nd U.S. Cavalry. Place and date: At Little Muddy Creek, Mont., 7 May 1877; at Camas Meadows, Idaho, 20 August 1877.
Citation: Bravery in actions with Indians.

Louis Williams, Sec 6, Grave 12616. Captain of the Hold, U.S. Navy. G.O. No.: 326, 18 October 1884.

First Award Citation: For jumping overboard from the *USS Lackawanna*, 16 March 1883, at Honolulu, T.H., and rescuing from drowning Thomas Moran, landsman.

Second Award Citation: Serving onboard the *USS Lackawanna*, Williams rescued from drowning William Cruse, who had fallen overboard at Calleo, Peru, 13 June 1884.

In fiscal year 1954, the cemetery was closed for interments except those in reserved gravesites, or second interments in existing graves under the single gravesite per family policy. In 1978, the cemetery was assigned for administration and management to the director of Long Island National Cemetery.

Former superintendents/directors of Cypress Hills National Cemetery are:

John Bryson, Unknown

Carlos B. Trotter, October 1939–April 1940

Leon P. Leonard, May 1940–June 1948

Ralph R. Dea, June 1948–September 1948

Ralph Fischetti, October 1948–June 1953

Oberlin H. Carter, June 1953–February 1955

Raymond J. Costanzo, February 1955–August 1955

Carl W. Schaller, August 1955–March 1957

Winston J. Stratton, March 1957–March 1962

Edward B. McFarland, March 1962–February 1964

James F. Wolstenholme, February 1964–May 1967

Harry W. Blake, May 1967–August 1968

Roland E. Lex, August 1968–May 1969

Eddie Walker, May 1969–November 1974

Earl R. White, February 1975–November 1978

Dallas–Fort Worth National Cemetery

2000 Mountain Creek Parkway

Dallas, Texas 75211

The Dallas–Fort Worth National Cemetery was dedicated and opened for interments on May 12, 2000. The 638.5 acre cemetery overlooks picturesque Mountain Creek Lake. It is located in the southwest corner of Dallas, Texas, midway between Interstate 20 and Interstate 30, just off Spur 408.

The first phase of construction consisted of 110 acres to include 12,000 gravesites, 2,000 lawn crypts, and 2,200 columbarium or garden niches for cremated remains. When fully developed, the cemetery will provide burial space for approximately 280,000 eligible veterans and their dependents. As of September 30, 2008, there have been 22,397 interments in the cemetery.

The cemetery features a memorial walkway lined with a variety of memorials honoring America's veterans. Most of these commemorate events and troops of the twentieth century wars.

Cloyde Pinson, Sr., founder of the Texas National Cemetery Foundation, is interred in Section 76, Grave 1702B.

Danville (Ill.) National Cemetery

1900 East Main Street

Danville, Illinois 61832

The cemetery is located in Vermilion County, Danville, Illinois, at the eastern side of the Department of Veterans Affairs Medical Center (VAMC). Entrance to the cemetery is through the VAMC grounds.

While no battles of the Civil War were fought near Danville, the state did contribute a great number of men who fought in the war. After the war they came home, many sick, wounded, or disabled. In 1897 Congress authorized the establishment of the National Home for Disabled Volunteer Soldiers in Danville. In 1898, a small plot of land northwest of the present cemetery was set aside for burial of those who died in the Soldiers' Home. It was referred to as the Home Cemetery, and 99 interments were made in the burying ground. In 1901, the present cemetery was plotted and the 99 remains were moved to the new cemetery. National Cemetery System records indicate that the Danville National Cemetery was established in 1898.

In 1909, the remains of the first governor of the Danville National Home for Volunteer Soldiers, Colonel Isaac Clements, were interred in the cemetery center circle. On September 22, 1922, the remains of Colonel Clements were disinterred and moved to Spring Hill Cemetery. A large monument honoring the dead of the nation's wars was erected over his gravesite.

In 1930, the Soldiers' Home was transferred to the Veterans Administration (VA), and the cemetery became a part of the VA Cemetery System. An internal study of the VA Cemetery System in 1948 recommended that the cemetery be offered for transfer to the Department of the Army. No action was taken, however, and in 1973 when the National Cemetery System was transferred from the Department of the Army to the Veterans Administration, the cemetery, along with 19 others operated by the VA, was merged into the National Cemetery System.

Nancy Timm, a nurse at the Soldiers' Home, was interred in the cemetery on October 12, 1930. During World War I Timm served in government hospitals in England, caring for British wounded brought home from France. She was born in Birmingham, England, and after World War I she moved to the United States.

The memorial section was dedicated on Memorial Day, May 26, 1980, with the unveiling of the first headstone in memory of S 2/c Donald Jay Blake, U.S. Navy.

In April 1984, a Medal of Honor headstone was erected for Army Lieutenant Morton A. Read. The standard headstone marking his grave was replaced after research disclosed that he had been awarded the Medal of Honor. Lt. Read was interred in the cemetery on July 11, 1921.

> **Morton A. Read,** Section 10, Grave 3033. Lieutenant, Company D, 8th New York Cavalry. Place and date: At Appomattox Station, Va., 8 April 1865.
> Citation: Capture of flag of 1st Texas Infantry (C.S.A.).

On April 15, 1985, the remains of Sgt. Robert C. Sherman, USMC, were interred in Section 6, Grave 1324A. Sgt. Sherman's remains were returned to the United States from Vietnam. He was reported to have been captured in South Vietnam on June 24, 1967. It was the wish of family members to have November 28, 1968, listed as his date of death.

As of September 30, 2008, a total of 10,526 interments had been made in the cemetery. It is projected that the 63 acre site will remain open for interments beyond the year 2030.

The cemetery was operated and maintained by the Soldiers' Home from 1898 until 1930. From 1930 until 1973, operations and maintenance were performed by the Engineering Service of the VA Medical Center. Since the cemetery was transferred to the National Cemetery System in 1973, the following have served as superintendents/directors:

Eddie Walker, November 1974–August 1977   Freddie Watson, December 1978–January 1979
Ralph Church, October 1977–November 1978   Richard J. Pless, February 1979–

Danville (Ky.) National Cemetery

377 North First Street
Danville, Kentucky 40442

The cemetery is situated in Boyle County, in the Bellevue Cemetery at Danville, Kentucky. The government appropriated 18 cemetery lots from the town of Danville consisting of a plot of ground lying within the limits of the Danville City Cemetery. Payment for the land was made on June 12, 1868. The soldiers lot was established as a national cemetery in 1862.

The lots constituting the United States property cover an area of 13,800 square feet (approximately 0.31 acre), and are laid off in the form of a rectangle. A square post of dressed limestone with the letters "U.S." on the upper face marks each corner. The plot is divided into six sections, five of which are for the burial of soldiers and one for the interment of civilians.

Original interments were Union soldiers who died in the hospital at Danville. Other remains from South Danville, Hustonville, and Middleburg were reinterred in the cemetery.

A Confederate lot in the city cemetery with 66 interments adjoins the national cemetery. This Confederate lot and Danville National Cemetery are under the jurisdiction of the director of Camp Nelson National Cemetery for operation, maintenance, and administration. As of September 30, 2008, there were 394 interments. The cemetery is closed for interments except for one reserved gravesite.

No superintendents have ever been assigned to this site.

Danville (Va.) National Cemetery

721 Lee Street
Danville, Virginia 24541

The cemetery is situated in Pittsylvania County, Virginia. Danville is approximately 144 miles southwest of Richmond, Virginia, only a few miles from the North Carolina border.

During the Civil War, Danville served as a railroad center through which passed great quantities of recruits, supplies and war materiel for the Army of Northern Virginia. As a railroad center it was also a logical place for a Confederate prisoner of war camp.

Danville National Cemetery was established on December 15, 1866, on 2.63 acres of land about a mile from the R & D railroad station. The land was conveyed to the United States on July 19, 1873, by George C. Ayres, president of the Danville town council. On the same date the federal government acquired an additional ⅘ acre from Thos. D. Stokes, executor of N.D. Greene, deceased. The *Roll of Honor* (1868) refers to the property as part of "the Widow Greene's estate."

With the exception of the remains of four soldiers of the Sixth Army Corps, all of the original interments in the cemetery were Union prisoners of war who died in the Confederate prison. The seven tobacco warehouses that made up the prison were located about ½ to ¾ mile north of the cemetery.

The *Roll of Honor* (1868) lists the principal causes of death as pneumonia, chronic diarrhea, and a disease indicated as "scorbutus," which is similar to scurvy. Deaths of these decedents were principally during the latter part of 1864 and the early months of 1865.

Danville (Va.) National Cemetery, 1970.

Those who died at Danville as prisoners of war and were interred in the national cemetery were for the most part privates, corporals and sergeants. Many state regiments were represented: Connecticut, Maine, Massachusetts, Pennsylvania, Ohio, Wisconsin, Michigan, New Jersey, Tennessee, Kentucky, Indiana, New York, New Hampshire, Vermont, and various regiments of the U.S. Colored Troops.

The report of the inspector of national cemeteries dated August 18, 1871, lists interments as follows:

	Known	Unknown
Commissioned officers	4	0
White Union soldiers	1,098	131
White Union soldiers, regulars	19	0
White Union sailors	4	0
Colored soldiers	37	12
Citizens, etc.	8	0
Total	1,170	143

As of September 30, 2008, the cemetery covered 3.5 acres and contained 2,290 interments. It is maintained by private contract under the supervision of the director of Salisbury National Cemetery. There are 4 group burials containing 16 remains. The cemetery was closed for interments on October 23, 1970, except for those in reserved gravesites and second interments in existing graves under the single gravesite per family policy.

The first superintendent of the cemetery, appointed August 6, 1867, was Francis

O'Donohoe, a discharged sergeant of the Fifth New York Volunteers. Former superintendents/directors of the cemetery are:

Francis O'Donohoe, August 1867–Unknown

Morris Keim, 1874–Unknown

Harry H. Williamson, March 1939–December 1958

Howard J. Ferguson, January 1959–October 1960

Harold F. Hammer, October 1960–January 1962

Henry L. Hoefelmeyer, February 1962–April 1964

Milton T. Kelly, Jr., April 1964–October 1967

Theodore J. Nick, Jr., October 1967–December 1968

Ronald G. Andrews, December 1968–June 1976

Fred I. Haselbarth, June 1976–December 1977

Leroy C. Newhouse, January 1978–November 1979

Arthur E. Bath, November 1979–April 1981

Dayton National Cemetery
4100 West Third Street
Dayton, Ohio 45428

The cemetery is located on the northern side of the Department of Veterans Affairs Medical Center in Montgomery County, Dayton, Ohio. Dayton is one of the 21 Veterans Administration Medical Center cemeteries transferred to the National Cemetery System in 1973.

In 1862 the U.S. Sanitary Commission proposed the creation of a national home for soldiers who had served their country during times of war. On March 3, 1865, Congress passed an act establishing a National Asylum for Disabled Volunteer Soldiers and Seamen. It was one of the last acts signed by President Abraham Lincoln. The law provided for a corporation of 100 men, named in the act, to build and administer such an asylum. After 5 unsuccessful attempts to establish a quorum, the law was amended on March 21, 1866, establishing a board of managers consisting of 12 men. Nine were to be elected and the other three the president, the chief justice of the Supreme Court, and the secretary of war were to serve *ex officio*. The first asylum authorized by the board of managers was the Eastern Branch at Togus, Maine, on September 6, 1866; the second at Milwaukee, Wisconsin, on December 7, 1866; and the third the Home at Dayton on April 11, 1867.

Camp Chase in Columbus, Ohio, where the Tripler Military Hospital (a gift to Ohio from the federal government) and the Camp Chase Confederate Stockade were located, was given back to the government. The buildings there, approximately 3.5 million feet of lumber and $6,169.62 in cash, became available to the managers of the Central Branch. The buildings were dismantled and transported along with the occupants of the hospital, 450 war veterans, to the National Home at Dayton in September 1867. The cemetery was established as the permanent burial site for residents of the Central Branch when the home opened.

The first interment, on September 11, 1867, was Civil War veteran Cornelius Solly. The last veterans of three wars are buried here: Theodore Witts, the last Civil War veteran, on February 13, 1974; Josiah Pence, the last Mexican War veteran, on October 9, 1914; and Peter Miller, the last Ohio veteran of the War of 1812, on December 27, 1889.

On the highest ground within the cemetery stands the Soldier's Monument. It was first proposed by the Monumental and Historical Association, formed by the veterans of the home, to perpetuate the memory of those buried in the cemetery. The association proposed the memorial and, with the aid of the soldiers of the home, raised all the funds for the project except $2,000 donated by the federal government to complete the project in

Committal shelter, Dayton National Cemetery.

1877. The cornerstone was laid on July 4, 1873, and covers a time capsule containing a Bible, a copy of the Constitution of the United States, photographs, coins, a muster roll of officers and men of the Home, copies of major newspapers from 10 cities and other historic memorabilia. The pillar, one of the colonnades from the U.S. Bank of Philadelphia, was a gift to the state of Ohio from the federal government. Atop the 48-foot pillar stands a 10-foot statue of a Civil War soldier at parade rest, surrounded at the base by four statues, carved in Italy, representing the Infantry, the Cavalry, the Artillery and the Navy. President Rutherford B. Hayes delivered the dedication address and unveiled the monument on September 12, 1877, with about 25,000 visitors attending the ceremonies. Unfortunately, on December 8, 1990, two youthful vandals toppled and desecrated the four statues. The estimated cost of repairs is about $300,000, and replacements would cost over $500,000. Local veterans organizations are forming a fund-raising organization to rebuild the monument.

The National Home was transferred to the newly formed Veterans Administration in 1930.

A large boulder monument in the cemetery was erected as a "Memorial to thirty-three Soldiers of the War of 1812 Buried in this Cemetery.... Erected by the Ohio United States Daughters of 1812 on the Anniversary of Perrys Victory September 10, 1936."

Although he is not buried here, Chaplain William Earnshaw exerted considerable influence on this and other national cemeteries. Chaplain Earnshaw marched with the first occupants of the National Home from Camp Chase, arriving on September 9, 1867. He served as chaplain of the home until his death on July 17, 1885. He is responsible for locating and establishing the cemetery grounds. He entered the Army at the outbreak of the Civil War and was commissioned as a chaplain. He served in the Army of the Potomac until, after the Battle of Gettysburg, he was assigned to the Army of the Cumberland under General George H. Thomas. During his service under General Thomas, he was appointed superintendent at Stones River and Nashville cemeteries where he gathered and interred the remains of 22,000 soldiers. He was subsequently appointed, with two other officers, to select sites and purchase land for the national cemeteries at Fort Donelson, Shiloh, Corinth, and Memphis.

A number of individuals who achieved special recognition for their heroic deeds, special assignments or the nature of their civilian lives are interred here. Among them are the following:

Marsina Rudolph Patrick, Civilian Section, Row 3, Grave 1. General, U.S. Army, served during the Florida Indian War, Mexican War and Civil War. Fourth governor of the National Home, Central Branch, from September 23, 1880, to July 27, 1888.

Jerome Beers Thomas, Civilian Section, Row 2, Grave 2. Colonel, U.S. Army, served during the Civil War. Fifth governor of the home, from November 17, 1888, to March 5, 1905.

Louis Margolis, Section 15, Row 17, Grave 15. Private, U.S. Army, served during both World Wars. Margolis was a boxer who fought under the name Kayo Mars.

Edmund Burke Magner, Section 10, Row 12, Grave 48. Lieutenant, U.S. Navy R.F. Served during World War I. Magner played baseball as an infielder with the New York Yankees in 1911.

A rock grave marker in the Civilian Section designates the burial place of Mrs. Emma L. Miller. She was superintendent of the Dayton Clothing Depot, which supplied clothes for all the national homes, until her death on January 18, 1914. Mrs. Miller became the first woman to receive a commission in the United States Army. The Miller Cottage for women members at the VA Center is her enduring monument.

There are six Medal of Honor recipients buried in Dayton National Cemetery:

Henry W. Downs, Sec Q, Row 7, Grave 24. 2nd Lieutenant, then Sergeant, Company I, 8th Vermont Infantry. Place and date: Winchester, Virginia, on 19 September 1864.
Citation: He and one comrade twice crossed open fields with raking enemy fire and returned with ammunition.

Oscar Wadsworth Field, Sec Q, Row A, Grave 9. Corporal, USMC. Place and date: Onboard the *USS Nashville* during the operation of cutting the cable leading from Cienfuegos, Cuba, on May 11, 1898.
Citation: Facing heavy enemy gun fire he set an example of extraordinary courage and behavior.

John H. James, Sec 1, Row 19, Grave 58. Seaman, then Captain of the Top, U.S. Navy. Place and date: Onboard the *USS Richmond* at Mobile Bay, Alabama, on 5 August 1864.
Citation: During a furious two hour battle and despite heavy damage to his ship and the loss of several men, he continued to fire his gun causing heavy damage to Fort Morgan and the subsequent surrender of the [Confederate ship] *Tennessee.*

John C. Matthews, Sec 3, Row 7, Grave 50. Corporal, Company A, 61st Pennsylvania Infantry. Place and date: Petersburg, Virginia, on 2 April 1865.
Citation: He voluntarily took the colors from the injured bearer and despite being severely injured himself, held the colors until the enemy surrendered.

Charles A. Taggart, Sec R, Row 9, Grave 14. Private, Company B, 37th Massachusetts Infantry. Place and date: At Sayler's Creek, Virginia, on 6 April 1865.
Citation: For capturing the enemy's flag.

George Geiger, Sec N, Row 20, Grave 47. Private, Troop H, 7th U.S. Cavalry. Place and date: At the Battle of Little Big Horn on 25 June 1876.

Citation: With three comrades he held his position and secured water for the command.

Dayton National Cemetery covers 98.2 acres. As of September 30, 2008, there were 44,175 interments.

Former superintendents/directors of the cemetery are:

Henry Hartwig, July 1974–June 1976
Ronald F. Houska, August 1976–January 1978
Eddie Walker, February 1978–November 1979
Lyle Norby, November 1979–July 1988
Richard L.R. Boyd, August 1988–1991

Karen Duhart, April 1993–September 2000
Sean Baumgartner, October 2002–March 2003
Patrick H. Lovett, March 2003–July 2005
Karl McDonald, August 2005–September 2007
Bernard A. Blizzard, January 2008–Present

Eagle Point National Cemetery
2763 Riley Road
Eagle Point, Oregon 97524

The cemetery is located 14 miles northeast of Medford and a mile east of Eagle Point, in Jackson County. It was started in 1952 as an adjunct to the Veterans Administration Domiciliary at White City, Oregon, about four miles away. The land was originally acquired from the Department of the Navy. It probably was part of Camp White, established in the early 1940s as a training camp. Over 30,000 troops trained here. The 4-million-gallon water tank used to supply those troops was sold to the City of Eagle Point in 1990 for $1 and, according to press reports, the city fathers are still trying to find some use for it. It is located across Riley Road from the cemetery.

Private Albert Paull, a U.S. Army veteran, was the first to be interred on March 7, 1952. The cemetery was one of the 21 cemeteries transferred to the National Cemetery System in 1973 by the Veterans Administration. Upon its transfer in 1973 it was named the White City National Cemetery. On March 19, 1985, the name was changed to the Eagle Point National Cemetery since it is situated in the city of Eagle Point. As of September 30, 2008, the cemetery encompassed 43.4 acres and contained 14,153 interments. It is projected to remain open for interments beyond the year 2030.

Major General Roy V. Rickard, U.S. Army, was interred in 1975 in Section 24, Grave 108. He served in World Wars I and II.

Lieutenant George R. Tweed, U.S. Navy, was interred in Section 14, Grave 170, on January 20, 1989, next to his son who was also a veteran. A former Navy radioman, the father was the sole survivor of a group which was captured and killed by the Japanese after their occupation of Wake Island during World War II. Tweed hid out on the island for two years and seven months, evading capture and supplying valuable information to the Allied forces. During this time he was the object of a massive manhunt by the Japanese. His ordeal inspired several books and the movie *No Man Is an Island*.

In 1985, when the Oregon state flag was stolen from the cemetery, the director began writing to the state governments to obtain flags. Emblem Club #420, an Elks affiliate, took on the project and at the Memorial Day services on May 29, 1990, all 50 state flags were flown at the cemetery.

From its establishment in 1952 until 1978 the cemetery was operated by the Veterans Administration Domiciliary at White City, Oregon. In 1978, the National Cemetery System took over the operation and management of the cemetery. Former directors of the cemetery are:

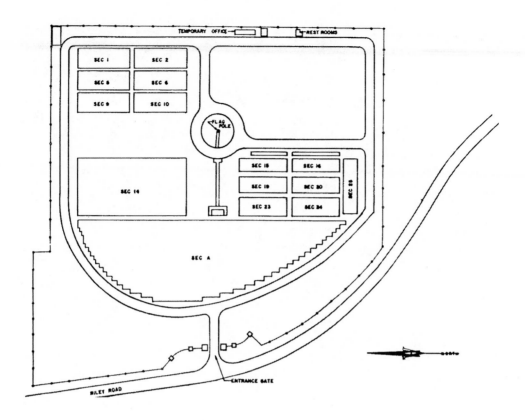

Eagle Point National Cemetery.

Stephen Jorgensen, April 1978–December 1979
Bernard G. Rice, December 1979–August 1984
Oliver Creswick, Nov, 1984–December 1986

Carla S. Williams, March 1987–July 1988
Marvin J. Krause, 1988–1990
Gilbert Gallo, 1990–

Fayetteville National Cemetery
700 Government Avenue
Fayetteville, Arkansas 72701

The Fayetteville National Cemetery is located on the south side of Fayetteville in Washington County, Arkansas, about one mile southwest of the old courthouse.

In 1867 about five acres were purchased from David Walker and Stephen K. Stone for use as a burying ground. In 1875, an additional 1.11 acres was purchased from them. About 5⅓ acres are enclosed within the brick wall constructed in 1873.

The cemetery, established in 1867, is nearly square in shape. The flagpole is located on the summit of a small hill from which the cemetery flows downward in all directions. The original layout of the cemetery, according to old blueprints, consisted of the outer circle and a six-pointed star with diamonds between the points of the star, and the flagpole in the center forming a hub of a complete wheel. There were 18 sections with an estimated capacity of 1,800 graves. During World War II, the layout was revised and five sections were added. This increased the estimated number of gravesites to 3,665.

Circular burial sections in Fayetteville National Cemetery.

The first burials were remains disinterred from the Civil War battles of Pea Ridge, Prairie Grove, Elk Horn Tavern, Cane Hill, and other places in the vicinity of Fayetteville. Interments are made with the head facing the flagpole. Layout of interments and setting of headstones are in a circular pat tern with inscriptions on the headstones facing the flagpole. When the five sections were added, the placement of headstones was changed so that the inscription now faces the interred remains. The report of the inspector of national cemeteries dated May 29, 1871, shows that there were 1,210 interments in the cemetery, "the greater portion being unknown white soldiers." As of September 30, 2008, a total of 7,785 interments had been made. Thirty-nine states and the Republic of Ireland are represented on the headstone inscriptions.

Two interesting notations in the original interment records are "Killed in the act of arresting horse thieves" and "Citizen prisoner brought from Missouri and murdered by Reb soldiers."

The Regional National Cemetery Improvement Corporation, a group of citizens, veterans, and officials of the city of Fayetteville, Washington County, and the state of Arkansas formed to raise funds to purchase land for the expansion of the cemetery, advised the Department of Veterans Affairs that they had acquired three parcels of land adjacent to the cemetery that they wished to convey to the department. After all historic and environmental clearances were received, the secretary of veterans affairs accepted the property on January 26, 1990. Additional donations will be made as the property is acquired by the corporation. These donations will provide grave space for some decades.

There is one Medal of Honor recipient interred here:

Clarence B. Craft, Sec.17, Grave 120, Private First Class, U.S. Army, Company G, 382nd Infantry, 96th Infantry Division. Place and date: Hen Hill, Okinawa, Ryukyu Islands, 31 May 1945.

Citation: He was a rifleman when his platoon spearheaded an attack on Hen Hill, the tactical position on which the entire Naha-Shuri-Yanaburu line of Japanese defense Okinawa, Ryukyu Islands was hinged. His contribution to the campaign on Okinawa was of much more far-reaching for Hen Hill was the key to the entire defense line, which rapidly crumbled after his utterly fearless and heroic attack.

Former superintendents/directors of Fayetteville National Cemetery are:

Josiah Nutting, April 1869–February 1871
Henry Smith, 1871–June 1871
Mical J. McPartridge, 1871–1873
Henry Warel, 1873–1875
Patrick Hart, 1875–1879
J.M. Bryant, March 1879–June 1883
William O'Brien, 1883–1889
Richard B. Hill, 1890–1893
D.M. Bryant, 1893–1900
Harrison C. Magoon, 1902–1903
Winslow H. Barger, 1905–1908
John Amrein, 1908–1909
L.H. Bow, 1909–1912
F.M. Davis, January 1912–1914
J.H. Thompson, February 1914–November 1918
E.W. Grisson, 1918–November 1921
H.D. Stanley, November 1921–November 1925
Vivian Bell, November 1925–1927
Drue C. Wilks, June 1928–October 1929

Jack H. Howard, January 1930–September 1956
Lester C. Harvey, October 1956–January 1975
John C. Metzler, Jr., February 1975–June 1976
Ralph E. Church, June 1976–September 1977
Dellas L. Atchinson, December 1977–February 1978
Arthur L. Conklin, April 1978–May 1979
Billy D. Murphy, November 1979–December 1979
Raymond J. Reynolds, January 1980–1990
L. Karen Browne, 1990–1991
Edward Marshall, 1991–1992
Larry Bibbs, Jr., 1992–1994
James Fitzgerald, 1995–1997
Darrell Lindsey, 1997–2002
Arleen Vincenty, 2002–2004
Dan Cassidy, 2004–2005
Tommy Monk, 2005–Present

Finn's Point National Cemetery
RFD #3, Fort Mott Road
Salem, New Jersey 08079

The cemetery is situated in Salem County about six miles northwest of Salem, New Jersey, at the northerly end of the former Fort Mott Military Reservation, and is surrounded by the Killcohook National Wildlife Refuge, administered by the Department of the Interior.

Finn's Point National Cemetery is but a small part of an area which was at one time considered an important coastal defense location. The Finn's Point Military Reservation was fortified in 1896 with the construction of emplacements for heavy coastal defense guns. The name was changed to Fort Mott on December 16, 1897, to honor Major General Gershom Mott, Commander of the New Jersey Volunteers during the Civil War.

Finn's Point National Cemetery is a small 4.6 acre site, located far from any battlefield of the Civil War, but its existence reflects one important aspect of that war. This hallowed ground is the resting place for the remains of 2,436 Confederate prisoners of war. These men were among those interred at Fort Delaware on Pea Patch Island in the Delaware River about 1½ miles from Finn's Point. Many of these prisoners were captured during the Battle of Gettysburg on July 1–3, 1863. The death toll among the prisoners at Fort Delaware was high, especially in the latter part of 1863 and during 1864. Crowded conditions on the

Finn's Point National Cemetery.

small island, combined with a high water table, rendered the area unsuitable for burial of the dead and necessitated transfer of the deceased to a more suitable location.

The area selected for burial of the Confederate dead took its name from a Swedish colony established about 1660 and said to have included among its settlers some of Sweden's Finnish subjects. A tract of about 104 acres in this vicinity was purchased by the United States to establish the Finn's Point Battery for the protection of the Port of Philadelphia.

The remains of the prisoners of war were transported across the river for burial in this ground set aside on the military reservation. There were times, however, when inclement weather or ice in the river made such trips to the mainland hazardous, necessitating initial burial on Pea Patch Island and reinterment at Finn's Point after the war.

On May 12, 1875, Virginia Governor James L. Kemper wrote to the secretary of war concerning the neglected conditions of the graves in which Southern soldiers were buried during the war on land near Fort Delaware. In response to this letter, Adjutant General E.D. Townsend, advised Governor Kemper that the burial ground at Finn's Point would be announced in general orders as a national cemetery, and the quartermaster general would be directed to have the remains of the soldiers both Union and Confederate buried on Pea Patch Island transferred to the Finn's Point cemetery. Finn's Point was established as a national cemetery on October 3, 1875.

Frederick Schmidt, a discharged Union soldier who had lost an arm in the war, was appointed the first superintendent of Finn's Point National Cemetery. When Schmidt entered on duty he requested permission to rent a lodge in Salem, N.J., at a cost of $8.50 per month. His salary was $60 per month. He also requested authority to hire a horse and cart for $2.50 a day, and a laborer to go with it for $1 to $1.50 per day to help with the planting of needed trees and grass. He listed the 1876 prices for some of the trees which he wished to plant. A Norway maple cost 75 cents, silver maples 50 cents, and Norway pines 3 to 6 feet in height could be purchased for 50 cents each.

Superintendent Schmidt's successor, when he left on March 1, 1882, to become superintendent at the Baton Rouge National Cemetery, was Charles F. Eichwurzel. Eichwurzel was assistant superintendent at the Chattanooga National Cemetery and a former fighter in the Indian campaigns in Nebraska and Wyoming from 1876 to 1879.

As of September 30, 2008, a total of 3,033 interments had been made in the cemetery. The absence of long rows of white marble headstones, characteristic of many military cemeteries with similar numbers of interments, reflects the conditions under which most of the interments were made. Burials of deceased Confederate prisoners of war account for 2,436 interments, and 135 other burials are Union soldiers who died at Pea Patch Island while serving as guards at the prison camp. Their remains, like those of many of the prisoners, were removed from the island. Initially, the graves of the Union soldiers were marked with wooden headboards, many of which had deteriorated by the time the burial grounds were made a national cemetery. The Confederate prisoners were interred in long trenches, with the location marked with evergreen trees.

In 1879 the U.S. government erected a marble monument to the memory of the Union soldiers, showing the names of 105 individuals and indicating that the identification of 30 other remains could not be determined. The erection of a Grecian columnar cupola over this monument by the government in 1936 gave the Union Memorial its present appearance.

The monument to the Confederate dead was erected by the U.S. government in 1910, pursuant to 1906 legislation authorizing the marking of Confederate graves for those who died in prison camps and hospitals, and who were buried near their place of confinement.

The names of 2,436 Confederate prisoners of war are inscribed on bronze plates affixed to the base of the monument. This obelisk was built of reinforced concrete with Pennsylvania white granite facing and stands about 85 feet high.

In the northeast corner of the post section of the cemetery, 13 white marble headstones mark the burial place of German prisoners of war of World War II who died while confined at Fort Dix, New Jersey.

Former superintendents/directors of the cemetery are:

Frederick Schmidt, October 1875–March 1882
Charles F. Eichwurzel, March 1882–June 1884
John Laun, June 1884–February 1892
Theodore Joseph, February 1892–February 1894
C.P. Rodgers, February 1895–March 1895
David Whitney, March 1895–October 1903
John Tomlin, October 1903–April 1912
James W. Bodley, April 1912–October 1912
William Hammond, October 1912–October 1914
Henry Donaldson, October 1914–November 1917
Ed. A. Carlin, November 1917–January 1919
John Harrigan, 1919–August 1925
James Breierly, August 1925–June 1930
Charles W. Cripps, June 1930–December 1942
Walter Hanns, January 1943–July 1943

William C. MacMurray, November 1943–July 1954
Daniel R. Ulmer, August 1954–November 1961
William A. Byers, November 1961–January 1964
Brice E. Bowen, January 1964–July 1964
Raymond Cordell, July 1964–April 1965
Allen C. Farabee, Sr., May 1965–August 1965
Andrew Szilvasi, August 1965–October 1965
Edward H. Maxwell, October 1965–November 1965
Stephen J. Satow, December 1965–June 1966
Ray C. Van Tassell, August 1966–March 1967
William Kaiser, March 1967–June 1967
Theodore J. Nick, Jr., June 1967–October 1967
Dorrance A. Long, October 1967–February 1969
Harlon R. Sheets, February 1969–October 1974

Since October 1974, the cemetery has been under the supervision of Johnny V. Carr, cemetery caretaker.

Florence National Cemetery

803 E. National Cemetery Road
Florence, South Carolina 29501

Florence National Cemetery is located in Florence County in the city of Florence, South Carolina. The land, about 5¾ acres, was appropriated, and later purchased from the estate of James H. Jarrott. It was outside the town limits and about 1½ miles southeast of the post office. In those days the town of Florence consisted of about 700 inhabitants. Its importance, and in fact its existence, is attributed to the fact that it was a railroad center of the South. Rail lines crossed here running both north to south and east to west.

During the Civil War one of the largest Confederate prisoner of war camps was located about ¾ mile south of the present cemetery site. Here between 7,000 and 12,000 federal troops were held, and in October 1864, the number exceeded 12,000. Due to lack of food, shelter, and medical supplies, about 3,000 prisoners died in the winter of 1864 and the early part of 1865.

In 1864 a prisoner of war exchange agreement collapsed and large numbers of prisoners were held by both sides. The camps located in Andersonville and Macon, Georgia, Charleston, South Carolina, and Salisbury, North Carolina, were severely overcrowded. General Sam Jones, at Charleston, issued orders to a Major Warley to build a large stockade in Florence. A yellow fever epidemic had broken out in the city and was threatening the prisoners, and General Jones wanted them moved out of danger. Major Warley had been captured by Union troops, and after a few months in prison he was paroled in exchange for a Union prisoner. He had returned to his home in Darlington, South Carolina, when General Jones ordered him back to active duty in charge of building the stockade with all possible speed.

The stockade was constructed by digging a trench on all sides of the 15–16 acres, embedding logs on end in the trench, and filling up the trench from the outside. This made a wall about 12 feet high on the inside, with an embankment on the outside reaching to about 3 feet from the top of the wall. The embankment provided a walkway for the guards to keep their eyes on everything that went on inside the stockade. The ditch from which this earth was taken was sufficiently deep to prevent the prisoners from digging escape tunnels. Five acres of the stockade were too swampy for the prisoners to use. No tents or shelter of any kind were furnished to the prisoners. The early arrivals from Charleston cut down trees which had been left standing inside the compound. They used the wood for firewood and to build huts for shelter. The 5th Georgia Regiment, which had guarded the camp at Charleston, was transferred to Florence for the same purpose. In addition, there were several battalions of conscripts or reserves stationed there for guard duty. These battalions were made up mostly of old men and young boys.

On two occasions, the U.S. Sanitary Commission sent supplies to the prison camp. The first shipment contained clothing, food, blankets, and items considered comforts for the sick. The second shipment included a large quantity of new fine quality sheets. Since there were no beds to put them on, the principal surgeon decided to trade them to the local farmers for

Marker for Florena Budwin in Florence National Cemetery.

sweet potatoes. When this notice was posted, it is reported that ladies young and old flocked in from all the surrounding communities to make the exchange. Scurvy was prevalent throughout the camp and the sweet potatoes were considered important in treating it.

Prisoners began to arrive so fast from Andersonville and Charleston that it was impossible to keep accurate records. There were 500 soldiers buried in Florence whose names were known but whose graves cannot be identified. It was reported that the people of Florence knew a record of prisoner deaths was kept, but despite considerable searching, it was never found.

When a contingent of prisoners arrived from Andersonville they found that many of the earlier arrivals had already taken an oath of allegiance to the Confederacy and joined the Southern army. They were told that many more had indicated their intention to do the same. Outside the prison stockade was a camp occupied by those prisoners who had transferred allegiance. Their fellow prisoners did not find it too difficult to understand their decision since they were ragged, half-starved, and facing death in the stockade.

Disease and deprivation took a large toll among the prisoners. It was said at the time that "diarrhea and scurvy carried off from twenty to fifty a day." On October 12, 1864, there were 800 sick in the hospital. A wealthy plantation owner, Dr. James H. Jarrott, allowed the dead to be buried in trenches on a portion of his property near the camp. Dr. Jarrott owned many slaves and worked them on his plantation, but he was believed to be a Union sympathizer.

The first interment is believed to have been made on September 17, 1864. Original interments were made in two separate burial grounds, one containing 416 remains and the other approximately 2,322 remains. Interments in the larger burial ground were made in 16 trenches. In 1865, the larger burial ground was designated a national cemetery, and the remains from the smaller burial ground were reinterred therein. Remains were disinterred from Darlington, Cheraw, the Marion Districts, and the Magnolia Cemetery in Charleston and reinterred here. The wooden headboards marking the trenches were replaced by 2,167 marble "unknown" headstones six inches square and set approximately six inches apart. In 1955, all but 5 of these markers were replaced with 32 upright marble headstones, set at each end of the trenches. One of the five known interments in the trenches is Florena Budwin. She was buried in the prison cemetery on January 25, 1865. Her head stone is set in Section D, Grave 2480. Heroism takes many forms and certainly Florena Budwin was a heroine, though who she really was and exactly what she did may never be fully known. One thing is certain, she was given a hero's burial in the Florence National Cemetery. The simple headstone engraved with her name, date of death, and number 2480 holds a mystery which will probably never be solved.

Florena Budwin was the bride of a Captain Budwin from Pennsylvania. No other records of him can be found. After Captain Budwin joined the Union Army, his bride disguised herself as a man and donned a uniform hoping to find her husband. There are no records giving her date of birth, date or place of her enlistment in the Union Army. She was captured near Charleston, South Carolina, in 1864 and sent to Florence in the autumn of that year. She arrived in Florence with several thousand Union prisoners as the stockade was being built. Rations were meager and medical supplies scarce. Florena Budwin fell ill. During a routine medical examination the camp physician found that one of his patients was a woman. Mrs. Budwin was moved to separate quarters and given food and clothing by the sympathetic women of Florence. When she recovered she told a most remarkable story of how she had donned a Federal uniform to serve at the side of her husband, and how he had been killed and she captured. After Florena grew strong she stayed at the prison as a nurse. Her devotion to her husband was bestowed on the hundreds of soldiers who were suffering from the lack of food and medicine. A few months later she fell sick a second time and did not recover. Florena Budwin, as she is listed on the Army rolls, was buried with full military honors, the first female service member to be buried in a national cemetery. There are no records in the National Archives to verify this story, except the burial register entry. In the *Roll of Honor*, Volume XIX, page 222, the data reads: "Baduine, Florence, date of death, January 23, 1865."

In the report of the inspector of national cemeteries dated May 14, 1870, Brevet Colonel Oscar A. Mack reports that "The Union prisoners of war confined at Florence were treated with decency and humanity, in striking contrast to the shameful barbarities practiced at Andersonville and Salisbury, and consequently the ratio of deaths is very small compared with the mortality at those places."

Florence National Cemetery was expanded in 1942, and again in 1984, to a total of 10.4 acres. It has been expanded to 24.9 acres and occupies land on both sides of National Cemetery Road. As of September 30, 2008, there was a total of 9,772 interments in the cemetery.

One Medal of Honor recipient is interred here:

James Elliott Williams, Sec. F, Grave 177. Boatswain's Mate, First Class (PO/c), U.S. Navy, River Section 531, My Tho, Republic of Vietnam. Place and date: Mekong River, Republic of Vietnam, 31 October 1966.
Citation: For conspicuous gallantry and intrepidity in action at the risk of his life above and beyond the call of duty.

Former superintendents/directors of the Florence National Cemetery are:

Francis D. Smith, Dates unknown
Robert Wood, Dates Unknown
P.R.R.M. Sattes, 1868–February 1873
Frederick Osborne, March 1873–April 1873
Samuel McKeown, April 1873–October 1882
William J. Elgie, November 1882–March 1890
W.M. Jones, April 1890–October 1895
M.P. Foley, November 1895–August 1897
Unknown may have been Foley, August 1897– April 1899
John Delacroy, April 1899–December 1905
Erie E. Georgia, Acting, January 1906–June 1906
John A. Reeves, Acting, June 1906–November 1906
John B. Russell, November 1906–March 1909
W.H.H. Garritt, March 1909–September 1913
William Davis, September 1913–April 1917
H.W. Pond, May 1917–June 1919
Geo. W. Thornburg, Acting, June 1919–1925
Unknown, 1925–July 1940
Henry R. Cole, July 1940–February 1946

Jarold L. Keogh, February 1946–July 1946
John M. Baker, July 1946–June 1947
Robert Ashley Spence, June 1947–March 1949
Slifford E. Larkins, March 1949–August 1955
Lester A. Smith, August 1955–August 1956
Lionel M. Rippy, October 1956–November 1957
Ronald L. McCulloch, January 1958–Unknown
Gary W. Smith, May 1979–May 1980
Patricia K. Novak, November 1980–February 1982
Elmer D. Nygaard, April 1982–May 1983
Delores Blake, May 1983–March 1984
Sandra M. Beckley, April 1984–May 1988
Kenneth LaFever, 1988–2001
Gregory Whitney, September 2001–July 2002
Wayne Ellis, September 2002–December 2003
Wayne Kenny, January 2004–February 2005
Elfrieda Robinson, March 2005–March 2007
Mishelle Kochel, March 2007–December 2007
Lynnette Parker, January 2008–Present

Florida National Cemetery
P.O. Box 337
Bushnell, Florida 33513

The cemetery is located in Sumter County, about 55 miles north of Tampa, Florida, at exit 62 on Interstate 75. The site is in part of the Withlacoochee State Forest adjacent to the Sumter County Correctional Institute.

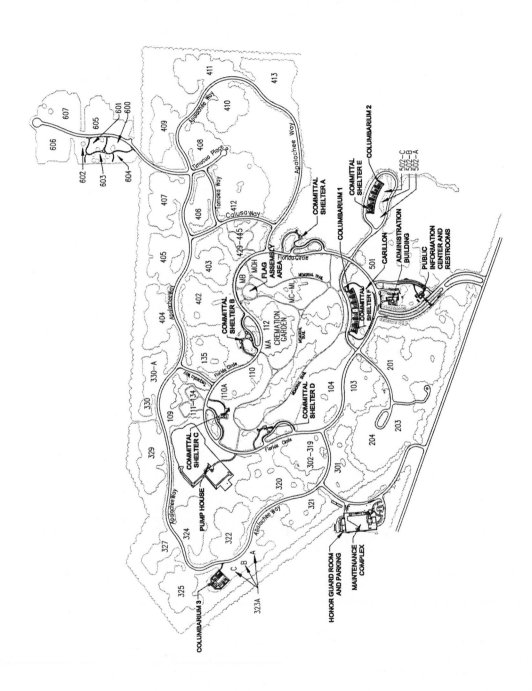

Florida National Cemetery.

Because Florida is one of the states that make up Standard Federal Region IV, which is centered in Atlanta, Georgia, it appeared unlikely that a site in Florida would be selected for a new national cemetery. In 1980, when President Jimmy Carter was campaigning for re-election and the polls indicated that he would be defeated, he made a short visit to the state in October, hoping to pick up support in the November election. Upon his return to Washington he issued an executive order establishing a national cemetery in Florida, in addition to the regional cemetery. This gesture did not get him enough votes to carry the state in the election. Hindsight indicates that it was a good decision since in fiscal year 2008, Florida is the second most active National Cemetery in the United States, with 97,303 interments as of September 30, 2008. There is a project under way to develop 113 acres of newly acquired land, to include 28,000 pre-placed crypts for casket interments. Although it has been operation for less than 20 years, this is the fourth major expansion project.

Because of the dramatic increase in the veteran population and the fact that the only open national cemetery was on the Panhandle, veterans organizations had been trying for over 20 years to get a new cemetery established in central Florida. In early 1979, the state of Florida agreed to donate land, and in May, it set aside up to 1,300 acres in the Withlacoochee State Forest. In 1983, the Veterans Administration (VA) selected a specific 400-acre site in the state forest and the state transferred it to the VA. The cemetery now occupies 512.9 acres. The Florida National Cemetery was dedicated on May 29, 1988, with Governor Robert Martinez, Senator Lawton Chiles, Representative Buddy McKay and Veterans Administration head Thomas Turnage present. The author was also privileged to participate in this ceremony.

The site selected in Sumter County is rich in Indian lore, since the Seminoles once occupied this territory. The Wild Cow Prairie Cemetery, which was consecrated by the Seminoles, is located and preserved within the national cemetery. The second Seminole war started near here with the massacre of Major Francis L. Dade and his troops in December 1835. Major Dade was marching from Tampa to reinforce General Wiley Thompson at Fort King in Ocala (see St. Augustine National Cemetery). Most of the Seminole Indian nation was wiped out in this war which lasted until 1842, and it was not until 1934 that the remaining Seminoles finally signed a peace treaty with the United States.

The use of in-ground crypts was introduced at this cemetery. These were double-depth crypts of poured concrete, cast at the site and set in rows in one section. Early problems with pre-placed grave liners have been overcome and their use is extensive in all new cemeteries.

There are two Medal of Honor recipients interred in the cemetery:

Franklin D. Miller, Sec. ML, Grave 1, Sergeant Major, U.S. Army 5th Special Forces Group, 1st Special Forces. Place and Date: Kontum Province, Republic of Vietnam, January 5, 1970.
Citation: "For conspicuous gallantry and intrepidity in action at the risk of his life above and beyond the call of duty."

James R. Hendrix, Sec. MOH, Grave 1. Master Sergeant, U.S. Army, Company C, 53rd Armored Infantry Battalion, 4th Armored Division. Place and Date: Near Assenois, Belgium, December 26, 1944.
Citation: On the night of 26 December 1944, near Assenois, Belgium, he was the leading element in the final thrust to break through the besieged garrison at Bastoigne.

Other notables:

Major David Moniac, Sec. MD, Grave 1. (2nd Seminole War) 6th U.S. Infantry Alabama Mounted Creek Volunteers, First Native American Graduate, USMA Class of 1822. Killed in action at Wahoo Swamp 1836 (December 25, 1802–November 21, 1836).

First Lieutenant Thomas Buchanan, Sec. MD, Grave 39. (Civil War) (October 7, 1825–June 13, 1863).

Private Albert J. Emery, Sec. 103, Grave 383. (Spanish American War) 7th U.S. Cavalry, 14th Division (September 15, 1877–August 30, 1957).

Former directors of the cemetery are:

Ralph E. Church, 1987–1990
Fred Haselbarth, 1990–1995

Ron Pemberton, 1995–2001
Billy D. Murphy, 2001–2009

Fort Bayard National Cemetery
Bayard, New Mexico 88036

Fort Bayard is located in dry southwestern New Mexico. It is adjacent to the Apache National Forest, just east of Silver City, New Mexico, in the foothills of the Pinos Altos Mountains.

A Lieutenant Kerr, 125th Infantry (Negro), selected the site in 1863, because of its springs and because it commanded a view of the Apache war trails surrounding the numerous mining camps. In 1866, General Bell, commander of the Department of Missouri at Santa Fe, ordered that a military post be established to protect the important gold camp of Pinos Altos. The garrison was named Fort Bayard in honor of General G.D. Bayard, who had died from wounds received during the Battle of Fredericksburg, Virginia. General Bayard had previously served in New Mexico and Arizona and had been wounded on several occasions by Indian arrows. Many campaigns were launched against the Apaches from this fort during the 1870s and 1880s ending only with the surrender of their chief, Geronimo, to General Nelson A. Miles in September 1886.

Second Lieutenant John J. Pershing was assigned to Fort Bayard with the 6th Cavalry in 1866, upon his graduation from West Point.

Sergeant David H. Boyd, Company M, 3rd U.S. Cavalry, was the first known interment on October 10, 1866. A noted civilian interred here is Walter Foote Sellers, author of the poem "The Kneeling Nun." He was the stepson of Brigadier General Walter I. Duggan.

In 1899, the Army deactivated Fort Bayard, and a government tuberculosis hospital and research center was established. During World War I, an Army hospital was located here, and frequently had a patient load of over 1,700. The U.S. Public Health Service operated the hospital from 1920 to 1922, when it was transferred to the Veterans Bureau, which became a part of the new Veterans Administration in 1930. The Veterans Administration turned the facility over to the state of New Mexico in 1965. The old buildings, formerly called "ships," have been removed and replaced with a modern general medical and surgical hospital.

The cemetery was established in 1922 when the Veterans Bureau assumed responsibility for the hospital and grounds. The cemetery was transferred to the National Cemetery System in 1973, when the system was transferred from the Department of the Army to the Veterans Administration. As of September 30, 2008, it covers 18.8 acres and includes 4,091 interments. The terrain is hilly with sandy topsoil with underlying soft rock in many places. The remaining gravesites in the cemetery must be blasted open, which is a very expensive procedure. As a result of a joint effort between the National Cemetery System and the state of New Mexico, in mid–1990 the state donated about 3.95 acres of land with soils which will allow for routine excavation.

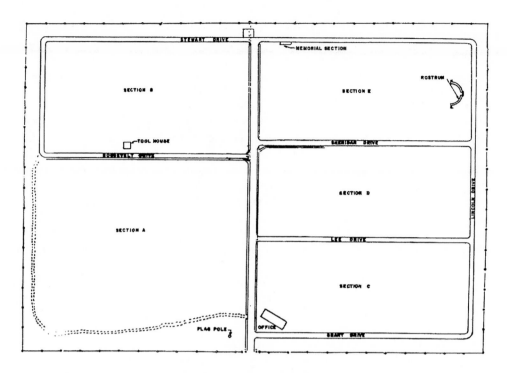

Fort Bayard National Cemetery.

Two known Medal of Honor recipients are interred in the cemetery

Alonzo Bowman, Sec. A, Grave I-31. Sergeant, U.S. Army. Company D, 6th U.S. Calvary. Place and date: At Cibicu Creek, Arizona, 30 August 1881.
Citation: Conspicuous and extraordinary bravery in attacking mutinous scouts. Died October 4, 1885.

John Schnitzer, Sec A-O, Grave 43. Wagoner, Troop G, 4th U.S. Cavalry. Place and date: Horseshoe Canyon, N. Mex., 23 April 1862.
Citation: Assisted, under heavy fire, to rescue a wounded comrade.

The cemetery was operated by the Veterans Bureau from 1922 to 1930; from 1930 to 1965 by personnel of the Fort Bayard VA Hospital; from 1965 to 1973 by personnel of the VA Hospital, Albuquerque, New Mexico; and, by private contract until 1988 when personnel from Fort Bliss National Cemetery were assigned. The cemetery is under the jurisdiction of the director of Fort Bliss National Cemetery, who is responsible for administration and management.

Fort Bliss National Cemetery
P.O. Box 6342
Fort Bliss, Texas 79906

Situated in El Paso County within the Fort Bliss Military Reservation, the cemetery is located on the north side of the Fort Bliss Army Base on Fred Wilson Highway.
Stations at Franklin, later known as El Paso, were occupied by U.S. troops from 1849

to 1853. The first Army post was established on the left bank of the Rio Grande River, 1½ miles above El Paso during this period. In January 1854 the post was named Fort Bliss after Lieutenant Colonel William S. Bliss, Assistant Adjutant General, U.S. Army, who died on August 5, 1853. The troops were withdrawn at the beginning of the Civil War, but the post was reoccupied on March 1, 1868, under the name of Camp Concordia. On July 1, 1872, 100 acres were leased about ½ mile farther north for the accommodation of a small garrison. This post was abandoned on December 31, 1876, and a new post established about five miles northeast of the city. The old cemetery was granted to the city in 1894. No definite records are available as to when a cemetery was established at the new post, but records of interment indicate that the first interment was made in 1883, and 16 burials were made prior to 1890.

In February 1903, Fort Bliss was recommended as a permanent post for four companies of infantry and two troops of cavalry. In 1911, all public lands making up Dona Ana (Artillery and Small Arms) Target Range, Dona Ana County, New Mexico, about 28 miles northwest of the fort, were set aside for military purposes. This range totals over 46,000 acres.

In 1914, the status of Fort Bliss was changed from an infantry post to a cavalry post. At that time the area set aside as a post cemetery, 2.2 acres with a capacity of 800 graves, was enclosed with a stone wall.

All troops at Fort Bliss joined with other troops near Columbus, New Mexico, and

Rostrum, Fort Bliss National Cemetery.

crossed the international border on March 16, 1916, in pursuit of the bandits who had raided the town of Columbus. After the punitive expedition returned in February 1919, approximately 40,000 regular and National Guard soldiers were encamped in and around Fort Bliss. During World War I, Fort Bliss was used as a training center for cavalry detachments and a gathering point for recruits. After the Armistice, it was used as a demobilization camp.

The post cemetery was enlarged by 2.24 acres in 1935, increasing its capacity to 2,400 graves. The stone wall was extended around this new area.

Congress authorized the establishment of a national cemetery at Fort Bliss in June 1936, but did not appropriate funds for construction until fiscal year 1938. This special act of Congress established a new policy in the War Department regarding national cemeteries. The War Department would do the necessary research regarding any proposed cemetery to be established but leave the final decision to Congress. From July 1936 until March 1939, the commanding general of Fort Bliss and the Office of the Quartermaster General could not agree on a site for the cemetery. On or about March 1, 1939, a plan approved by the quartermaster general was received at Fort Bliss, and the debate ended. The polo field, a railroad spur and power lines crossing the area were relocated, and construction proceeded. The cemetery was dedicated on March 17, 1939. The first interment in the new cemetery, on March 7, 1940, was Sergeant First Class James F. Featherstone.

In the fall of 1944 Chinese authorities officially selected the post section as the place of interment for Chinese Air Force cadets who died while in training in the United States. Beginning in 1942, 12 cadets had been buried in the post section. There are now 55 cadets interred here.

During the existence of the prisoner of war camp at Fort Bliss, four German prisoners were interred in the post section. In February 1946, a German civilian scientist on duty with research activities at Fort Bliss was buried here. During April 1946, the bodies of two German prisoners, one Italian prisoner and three Japanese civilian internees were disinterred at Lordsburg, New Mexico, and brought here. That same month, five deceased German prisoners were brought from Roswell, New Mexico. In June 1946, 10 German, 3 Austrian and 18 Italian POWs were brought here from Florence, Arizona.

In January 1947, the military establishment at Marfa, Texas, was abandoned and the remains of 4 enlisted men and 11 dependents were removed to this cemetery.

On November 22, 1955, the remains of Lieutenant Colonel William Wallace Smith Bliss were interred in the cemetery. Lieutenant Colonel Bliss had served in operations against the Cherokee Indians, taught at West Point, served in the Florida Indian War, was assistant adjutant general of the 16th Military Department, was chief of staff to General Zachary Taylor in the war with Mexico, and served as adjutant general of the Western Division at New Orleans. He married Zachary Taylor's daughter Elizabeth in 1848, and served as private secretary to President Taylor. He died at age 38 of yellow fever in Pascagula, Mississippi, on August 5, 1853. In January 1854, his remains were removed from Pascagula and interred in a crypt in the Girard Street Cemetery in New Orleans. In the fall of 1955, the city of New Orleans notified the Army that all monuments in the Girard Street Cemetery must be removed as the land had been condemned for the construction of a new federal building and highway.

The original monument, a 20-foot marble shaft which bears Bliss' name and the battles in which he distinguished himself during the Mexican War, was moved to the military reservation at Fort Bliss, and the "mummy-type" cast iron casket in which he was buried was placed in the museum at Fort Bliss. It was reported that when a small metal covering was removed from the casket, the head and face of LTC Bliss were clearly visible through the glass-covered aperture commonly constructed in caskets used by wealthy families in the early 19th century.

As of September 30, 2008, the cemetery encompassed 82.1 acres and included 46,020 interments.

There are two Medal of Honor recipients interred in the cemetery:

†**Ambrosio Guillen**, Sec E, Grave 9171. Staff Sergeant, U.S. Marine Corps, Company F, 2nd Battali7th Marines, 1st Marine Division (Rein).
Citation: Gallantry in action near Songuch-on, Korea, on July 25, 1953. Sergeant Guillen led his platoon in defense of a forward outpost against an estimated enemy force of two battalions, and although severely wounded, refused medical aid until the enemy was defeated and thrown into disorderly retreat. He succumbed to his wounds a few hours later.

Benito Martinez, Sec B, Grave B-366A. Corporal, U.S. Army; Company A, 27th Infantry Regiment, 27th Infantry Division. Place and Date : Near Satae-ri, Korea, September 6, 1952. (Reinterred from a private cemetery in Fort Hancock, Texas.)

Memorial headstones honor Medal of Honor recipients Cpl. Frank Bratling (U.S. Army; died July 13, 1873) and 1st Lt. George W. Hooker (U.S. Army; died January 22, 1873).

Former superintendents/directors of the cemetery are:

Elmer E.E. Swanton, March 1939–June 1940
Dewey S. Brown, June 1940–April 1944
Anthony J. Nettke, April 1944–September 1945
Carl J. Sonstelie, September 1945–March 1956
William R. Rossback, March 1956–August 1964
Charles H. Culver, August 1964–October 1977
Joe D. Willard, November 1977–July 1980
Fred I. Haselbarth, August 1980–November 1983
Dennis E. Kuehl, November 1983–September 1985

Patricia K. Novak, October 1985–1990
Oakland A. DeMoss, 1990
Gil Gallo, 1990–1992
Eileen Harrison, 1992–1996
Gerald Vitela, 1996–January 2002
Robert Flitcraft, Jr., May 2002–April 2006
Gene Linxwiler, September 2006–October 2007
Cindy Van Bibber, January 2008–Present

Fort Custer National Cemetery
15501 Dickman Road
Augusta, Michigan 49012

The cemetery is located eight miles west of downtown Battle Creek on M-96 Dickman Road, and about eight miles from the National Cemetery exit on Interstate 94 in Kalamazoo County, south of the Kalamazoo River.

The original Camp Custer was established in 1917 as part of the military mobilization effort for World War I, on a 130-acre leased parcel of land made up of small farms. The land was purchased two years later. Construction started in July 1917, and 5 months later 2,000 buildings were ready to accept some 36,000 men for training. The 85th Infantry Division was organized and trained here under the guidance of Major General Joseph Dickman. The first "Doughboys" came from the cities and towns of Michigan and Wisconsin. During World War I, some 90,000 troops passed through Camp Custer. Following the Armistice of 1918, the camp became a demobilization base for over 100,000 men. Some of the troops passed through here twice, going to war and returning home.

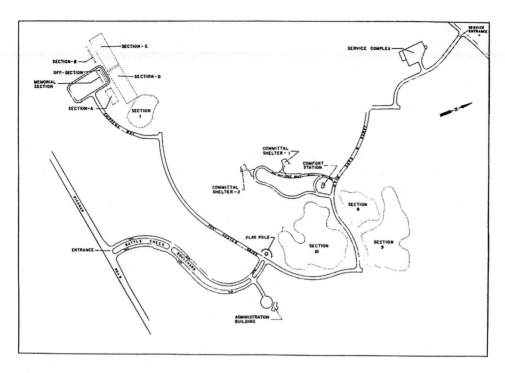

Fort Custer National Cemetery.

On May 10, 1923, an executive order transferred 675 acres to the Veterans Bureau, predecessor organization to the Veterans Administration, for the construction of the Battle Creek Veterans Hospital, which was completed in 1924. At one time, about 200 acres of the site were farmed by the staff and patients from the hospital. It was considered good therapy and helped the hospital to be reasonably self-sufficient. During this early period, many pine trees were planted which today present an attractive cathedral-like feature area in the northeast corner of the cemetery.

In August 1940, General George C. Marshall, Army chief of staff, transmitted orders from the secretary of the Army making the area a permanent military installation, and officially changed the name to Fort Custer. An additional 6,166 acres were acquired, a new camp constructed, and over 700 of the old buildings were replaced. The first division-size unit to train at the "new" fort was the famed 5th Infantry Division, better known as the Red Diamond Division. They completed training in 1941 and were shipped to Iceland before going into battle in Europe where the Germans referred to them as the "Red Devils." Later, Fort Custer became headquarters of the provost Marshal general's 350th Military Police Escort Guard and a processing center for prisoners of war. The Fort Custer Post Cemetery was established with the first interment on September 18, 1943.

During World War II, the fort was expanded to over 14,000 acres. In addition to its use as a training base, over 5,000 German prisoners of war captured in Tunisia, Italy, France, Belgium and Germany were interned at Fort Custer. Finding able farm labor during the war had become a problem as the labor force had been drawn into the military or was at work in factories producing war materials. Workers were needed to harvest Michigan's crops, and the prisoners, whatever their background soldier, auto mechanic, carpenter, or opera singer were recruited to the farms. They were good workers and were well treated.

In fact, many of them gained from 20 to 40 pounds while held. The last prisoners repatriated to their homeland departed from Fort Custer in 1946. They left behind 26 of their comrades buried in the old post cemetery. Sixteen of the German soldiers were killed in a truck-train accident near Blissfield, Michigan, in 1945, as they were returning from a work detail in the sugar beet fields.

On Memorial Day 1953, the first *Volkstrauertag*, which means day of National mourning and is the equivalent of Memorial Day, was held at the cemetery. Elmer Beck, a former German prisoner at Fort Custer and now an American citizen, was a guest at the ceremony. The principal speaker that day was Lieutenant Governor Swainson, who said that when he woke up in an American Field Hospital and realized he had lost his legs after stepping on a German land mine, he would never have imagined that he would one day be lieutenant governor of Michigan and, as such, would be addressing a memorial service that honored the very people responsible for the loss of his legs.

As early as the 1960s, area political figures and all veterans organizations were active in obtaining a national cemetery at Fort Custer. The National Cemeteries Act of 1973, signed by President Nixon, transferred the National Cemetery System from the Department of the Army to the Veterans Administration (VA) and directed the VA to develop a plan by which all veterans who so desired could be interred in a national cemetery. After much study, the system adopted what came to be called the regional concept designate or construct one large national cemetery in each of the 10 Standard Federal Regions which had been established by the General Services Administration. A policy was also established that new cemeteries would be created only on land already owned by the federal government.

The Fort Custer site, located midway between Chicago and Detroit, was the VA's choice of a location for the Region V national cemetery (Region V includes Michigan, Wisconsin, Ohio, Illinois, Indiana and Minnesota). In February 1981 the Department of the Army transferred 770 acres to the VA, including the 8.25 acres of the old post cemetery. There were approximately 2,600 gravesites available in the post cemetery which made it possible for veterans to be buried there while the new cemetery was being developed. On Memorial Day 1982, more than 33 years after the first resolution had been introduced in Congress, impressive ceremonies marked the official opening of the cemetery. The first interment took place on June 1, 1982, and the cemetery was formally dedicated on September 23, 1984. In the summer of 1983, Dennis J. Johnson was named the first director of the Fort Custer National Cemetery, and served until the summer of 1988.

On Veterans Day, November 11, 1986, a unique and moving ceremony took place when an unknown black soldier of the Civil War, whose remains had been disinterred from an isolated grave in Grand Rapids, Michigan, was reinterred here. He was accorded full military honors, carried out by men dressed in Civil War uniforms.

As of September 30, 2008, there were 23,863 interments. The cemetery is projected to remain open for interments beyond the year 2030. Because of soil conditions, the cemetery is under the Adjacent Gravesite Set-Aside Program. This means that double-depth interments cannot be made, and when one interment is made, the adjacent gravesite is set aside for the surviving spouse.

Former directors of the cemetery are:

Helen Szumylo (Acting), April 1982–August 1983
Dennis J. Johnson, August 1983–July 1988
Eugene L. Chambers, August 1988–April 1993

Robert Poe, April 1993–October 1998
John Bacon, January 1999–June 2006
William Rhoades, October 2006–February 2008

Fort Gibson National Cemetery
Route 2 Box 47
Fort Gibson, Oklahoma 74434

Fort Gibson National Cemetery is situated in Muskogee County, 1½ miles northeast of Fort Gibson, Oklahoma. It is located on land that was once part of the military reservation and is within the limits of the Cherokee Nation. Old records indicate that the area was probably called Ketona prior to 1824.

In mid–April 1824, Colonel Matthew Arbuckle was ordered to descend the Arkansas River, locate a suitable site, and establish a military post at some strategic point for keeping the peace between the Osage and Cherokee Indians. About three miles from the mouth of the Neosho River, Colonel Arbuckle found a wide ledge of shelving rock on the east bank which formed a natural wharf. It was here that he established Cantonment Gibson, Indian Territory, named after Colonel George Gibson, then commissary general of subsistence. The post was one of the several established along the "permanent Indian frontier" which ran from Minnesota to Louisiana. In the years preceding 1824, the government had exiled eastern tribes westward beyond the line of white settlement and assigned them land that had been part of the Osage nation. For the Cherokees, Creeks and Seminoles, Fort Gibson was the end of the Trail of Tears. The purpose of the new garrisons was to keep peace among the Indian tribes and to provide protection for the immigrants and traders.

Cantonment Gibson, the oldest town in Oklahoma, was established April 24, 1824, approximately 60 miles northwest of Fort Smith (established in 1817) and 2½ miles from the Arkansas River. Prior to 1824, Fort Smith had been the westernmost U.S. military post. In May 1824, the western boundary line of the Arkansas Territory was changed and it was deemed expedient by the War Department to move the military garrison at Fort Smith far-

Fort Gibson National Cemetery, just before Memorial Day.

ther west. The new post was garrisoned by five companies (B, C, G, H, and K) of the 7th U.S. Infantry stationed at Fort Smith, and commanded by Colonel Arbuckle. In 1832, all cantonments were ordered to change their names to forts. Colonel Arbuckle remained at Fort Gibson for 17 years.

On February 14, 1833, a treaty was made with the Indians regarding use of the land near the fort. Later the Cherokees made a determined effort to have the garrison removed, claiming that the fort had served its purpose as a protecting agent. They further claimed that the site of Fort Gibson would serve the community better if it were changed into a town. This location was important because of the natural rock, and the river was a most important highway. The Cherokees eventually prevailed, and on June 8, 1957, Fort Gibson was abandoned by the 7th Infantry. Old Army records indicate that the troops were withdrawn in the interest of the health of the soldiers.

The Cherokees created a town called Kec-tee-wah which proved short lived because of the strategic importance of the location for military forces. Early in 1863, the post was reestablished by Brigadier General James G. Blunt, commander of the District of the Frontier and the 1st Division, Army of the Frontier. The name of the post was officially changed to Fort Blunt. Later in 1863 the name was again changed back to Fort Gibson. From 1863 until 1890, the fort was garrisoned by different small detachments of troops. In 1868 and 1869, the 10th Cavalry (Colored) Regiment Headquarters was here. The 10th was moved from Fort Gibson to Camp Wichita, which later was renamed Fort Sill. The reservation was relinquished by the War Department in 1891 and turned over to the Department of the Interior.

The history of Fort Gibson is very impressive even though the fort was active for only a total of about 60 years. Among the many officers stationed at Fort Gibson were Colonel Leavenworth (veteran of the War of 1812), Captain Benjamin Eulalie de Bonneville (the Pathfinder), Lieutenant Jefferson Davis, General Zachary Taylor, Brigadier General J.G. Blunt, and Captain Nathan Boone, son of Daniel Boone. An interesting anecdote still told around the area is that Lieutenant Jefferson Davis, later president of the Confederacy, eloped from Fort Gibson with the daughter of Zachary Taylor, later president of the United States. In fact, Jefferson Davis and Sarah Knox Taylor were married in a home off Brownsboro Road in Louisville, Kentucky.

There are at least 16 forts and camps across the United States that were named after individuals who served at Fort Gibson. These include Fort Leavenworth, Fort Bliss, Fort Bragg, Fort Hood, Fort Arbuckle, Fort Davis, Fort Rucker, Fort Sam Houston, Fort Belknap, Fort Brown, Fort Mason, Fort Custer, Camp Cooper, Camp McIntosh, and Fort Riley. Since Fort Gibson was for many years the westernmost outpost, many distinguished visitors came to the fort. These included Washington Irving, Henry Longfellow, General Robert E. Lee, John Payne, Henry M. Stanley (the noted African explorer), and Sequoyah, inventor of the Cherokee alphabet.

Due to the great tolls exacted by fever, three successive post cemeteries were established at Fort Gibson. Original interments in the national cemetery were mostly remains of soldiers removed from old and abandoned post cemeteries. Other interments were Union dead who died on the battlefields of the southwest. Of the Union soldiers, 156 are known and 2,208 are unknown. Most of the unknowns were moved to Fort Gibson from Fort Towson, Fort Arbuckle, Fort Washita, Fort Tallequah, and other nearby towns. In 1868 a plot of seven acres east of Fort Gibson was converted into a national cemetery. The soldiers stationed at the fort had previously used the ground for cemeterial purposes, and a few civilians were buried there prior to 1850. The oldest recorded interment is that of Lieutenant

John W. Murray, 7th U.S. Infantry, who died on February 14, 1831. There are three other officers who died in 1831 buried around the circle with Murray. Among them is Colonel John Nicks, 7th U.S. Infantry, and the first postmaster at Fort Gibson. Colonel Nicks was a native of North Carolina.

Within the confines of the Fort Gibson National Cemetery is interred at least one veteran of every war in which the United States has fought. And there are others, perhaps not quite so famous or well known, but each of them has a story to tell. Graves of the known and unknown are intermingled with soldiers, Indians, scouts, civilians, wives, and children. Their stories of hardship, danger, laughter, and tears are buried with them, but their legacy lives on. Some of the stories have been passed on to succeeding generations so they will not be forgotten.

Brigadier General Noah P. Wood, U.S. Marine Corps and Major General Samuel C. Russell, U.S. Army, are interred here. So is Captain Billy Bowlegs, an intrepid Seminole scout in an Indian regiment. Acee Blue Eagle, Creek Indian artist, and John Reese, Medal of Honor recipient, share these grounds with comrade-in-arms Marvin Bradley, cemetery caretaker, who devoted over 20 years of his life to caring for the cemetery's gravesites, and Francis M. Brooke, cemetery director, who served veterans for nearly 35 years.

Montfort Stokes, a Revolutionary War hero and former governor and U.S. Senator from North Carolina, died in 1842 and is interred in the cemetery. Captain John P. Decatur, brother of Commodore Stephen Decatur, naval hero of the War of 1812, was the sutler at Fort Gibson and is interred in Section OC, Grave 2101. Mary Eliza Mix, reputedly a spy for the U.S. government is interred in Section OC, Grave 2110. Since she died before the Mexican War, the only war in which she could have been a spy was the War of 1812 or some of the Indian skirmishes. Her secrets are buried with her.

In 1845, Lieutenant Daniel Henry Rucker, who was stationed at Fort Gibson, was married to Flora Fields, a member of a distinguished Cherokee family. Four years later while he was on duty in Arizona and New Mexico, his wife died in Little Rock, Arkansas. Lt. Rucker subsequently remarried, and a daughter of the second marriage later became the wife of General Phil Sheridan. Some years later, Lt. Rucker had the remains of his first wife removed and reinterred in the Fort Gibson National Cemetery in Section OC, Grave 2108. Lt. Rucker had a distinguished military career, achieving the rank of major general, and served for several years as the quartermaster general of the Army.

Major Joel Elliott is buried in Section OC, Grave 2233. He was a member of General George Armstrong Custer's Seventh Cavalry. Major Elliott commanded the Seventh Cavalry during the year Custer was suspended from his command and rank after being court-martialed on seven charges growing out of desertion of his command at Fort Wallace to hurry to his wife at Fort Riley after receiving reports of cholera there. General Custer led a troop of 800 men against a Cheyenne village at the Washita River. Major Elliott took a detachment of 19 men in pursuit of a group of Indians escaping from the village. Over a considerable period of time, shots were heard in the distance. The fact was fully reported to General Custer several times, but he made no effort to send troops to rescue Elliott's detachment. He later explained that, among other reasons, there was a shortage of ammunition. Yet, Custer's men were engaged in shooting 875 captured Indian ponies at the time. Major Elliott and the 19 men with him were all killed. Custer's official report of the Seventh Cavalry's losses that day listed 2 officers and 19 men killed, 3 officers and 11 men wounded.

On February 2, 1990, Nelson Fonseca was interred in the cemetery with full military honors. He was a survivor of the Bataan Death March during World War II. He served his country under the most extreme conditions as a prisoner of war in a Japanese prison camp, and later in Korea.

Talahina Rogers Houston, the second wife of General Sam Houston, is interred in Section OC, Grave 2467. She was born in 1799 and died in 1833. There is some controversy over the correct spelling of her name, and many articles have been written on this subject. "Talahina" is a Choctaw word, and Mrs. Houston was Cherokee. Many people believe the correct spelling of her name is Tiana. Her headstone still bears the spelling of "Talahina."

After Sam Houston was divorced from Eliza Allen Houston, about 1829, he met and married Talahina Rogers. He bought a large farm on the Neosho River about two miles northeast of Fort Gibson, and there they lived for a while. Houston grew restless and soon was off again to the southwest where he became president of the Republic of Texas. Talahina died of pneumonia in 1833. One story says that she died of a broken heart when General Houston left her with her people to go down to Texas and Mexico to seek new frontiers. Another version states that he sent runners back to Talahina asking her to join him, saying, "I have built a kingdom for you." Talahina always answered him by saying that he had returned to his people and she would stay with hers. The truth lies buried with her. She was originally interred at Wilsons Rock, near Muldrow, Oklahoma, and subsequently was removed to Fort Gibson.

One of the most interesting and far-fetched stories surrounding someone interred in a national cemetery concerns Vivia Thomas, who is interred in Section OC, Grave 2119. One of the many versions of her legend is that she was a high-spirited daughter of wealthy Boston parents, and attended Boston society's finest affairs. At a ball following the Civil War, she met and fell in love with a handsome young lieutenant. After several months of courtship, they announced their engagement. Shortly before the wedding date the lieutenant, more intrigued by Vivia's wealth and place in society than by her beauty, suddenly left. His note stated that he desired to go west in search of adventure, that marriage and Boston society were not for him.

Broken-hearted and bitter over the embarrassment caused her and her family, Vivia left home in search of her lover. Learning from the military that the lieutenant was stationed at Fort Gibson, Indian Territory, her long journey began. The trip was extremely hard, especially for a girl who had known only luxury, but her vengeful heart pushed her on to her destination. She cut her hair, dressed in men's clothing, and joined the Army. She avoided recognition by the young lieutenant, although she frequently observed him. She discovered that he had an Indian girlfriend that he visited each evening. One cold evening in December, Vivia trailed, ambushed, and killed him. An intensive investigation was conducted to no avail and the matter was dropped. However, Vivia became remorseful. Disturbed over the killing, she began visiting the grave at night. She contracted pneumonia from the continued exposure, and one night she collapsed near his grave. She died shortly thereafter on January 7, 1870. Her comrades were so impressed with her courage in coming alone to the frontier and carrying out a successful disguise as a male that, rather than condemning her, they awarded her a place of honor for burial in the Officers' Circle.

As of September 30, 2008, the cemetery contains a total of 48.3 acres and includes 19,102 interments.

There are two known Medal of Honor recipients interred in the cemetery. The dagger denotes that he was killed in action.

†**John N. Reese, Jr.,** Sec 2, Grave 1259-E. Private First Class, U.S. Army, Company B, 148th Infantry, 37th Infantry Division. Place and date: Paco Railroad Station, Manila, Philippine Islands, 9 February 1945.

Citation: He was engaged in the attack on the Paco Railroad Station, which was strongly defended by 300 determined enemy soldiers with machine guns and rifles, supported by several pillboxes, three 20-mm. guns, one 37-mm. gun, and heavy mortars. While making a frontal assault across an open field, his platoon was halted 100 yards from the station by intense fire. On his own initiative he left the platoon, accompanied by a comrade, and continued forward to a house 60 yards from the objective. Although under constant enemy observation, the 2 men remained in this position for an hour, firing at targets of opportunity, killing more than 35 Japanese and wounding many more. Moving closer to the station and discovering a group of Japanese replacements attempting to reach the pillboxes, they opened heavy fire, killed more than 40 and stopped all subsequent attempts to man the emplacements. Enemy fire became more intense as they advanced to within 20 yards of the station. From that point Pfc. Reese provided effective covering fire and courageously drew enemy fire to himself while his companion killed seven Japanese and destroyed a 20-mm. gun and heavy machine gun with hand grenades. With their ammunition running low, the two men started to return to the American lines, alternately providing cover for each other as they withdrew. During this movement, Pfc. Reese was killed by enemy fire as he reloaded his rifle. The intrepid team, in 2½ hours of fierce fighting, killed more than 82 Japanese, completely disorganized their defense and paved the way for subsequent complete defeat of the enemy at this strong point.

Jack C. Montgomery, Sec. 20, grave 963. First Lieutenant, U.S. Army, 45th Infantry Division. Place and Date: Near Padiglione, Italy, 22 February 1945.

Citation: For conspicuous gallantry and intrepidity at the risk of life above and beyond the call of duty.... The selflessness and courage exhibited by First Lieutenant Montgomery in alone attacking 3 strong enemy positions inspired his men to a degree beyond estimation.

A memorial headstone honors another recipient, Cpl. John Haddoo (U.S. Army; died September 30, 1877), and is interred in the Custer Battlefield National Cemetery.

Former superintendents/directors are:

Patrick Hart, September 1885–April 1887
William N. Jones, April 1887–March 1890
C.M. Doty, November 1890–December 1890
J.A. Dickson, December 1890–May 1894
D.F. Stephens, May 1894–April 1898
Harrison C. Magoon, April 1898–July 1902
William W. Morris, July 1902–February 1903
Austin J. Chapman, February 1903–July 1914
Theodore F. Robinson, July 1914–September 1930
William E. Brindley, September 1930–January 1931
Charles H. Hunter, January 1931–January 1932
Harry H. Williamson, February 1932–November 1937

Marion M. Coffee, November 1937–June 1939
Anthony J. Nettke, July 1939–March 1944
David W. Senters, March 1944–March 1952
Theodore Nick, June 1952–June 1953
Clifton Cockrell, June 1953–February 1964
John W. Clemmons, February 1964–July 1967
Francis M. Brooke, July 1967–June 1981
Patricia K. Novak, March 1982–December 1985
Jimmy S. Adamson, February 1986–May 1988
Carla Stipe Williams, 1988–1992
Candice Underwood, July 1992–August 1999
Kenny Rader, October 1999–October 2001
Timothy L. Spain, April 2002–Present

Fort Harrison National Cemetery
8620 Varina Road
Richmond, Virginia 23231

Fort Harrison National Cemetery, situated on Varina Road in Henrico County, is approximately eight miles southeast of Richmond. It is a small cemetery of only 1.6 acres whose location was dictated by the exigencies of the Civil War. Here honored sepulture is accorded the members of the Army of the Potomac who perished on the fields of battle or died in hospitals as the relentless push toward Richmond continued during late 1864 and the early months of 1865.

From June 1864 until 1865 siege operations before Petersburg commanded the atten-

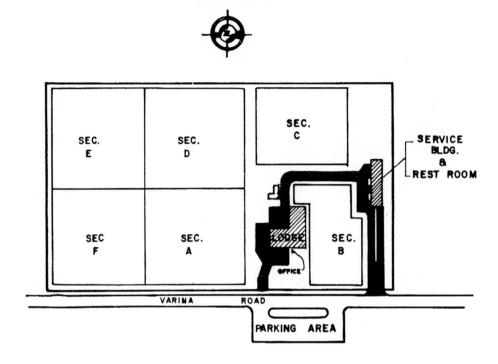

Map of the Fort Harrison National Cemetery, Fort Harrison, Va., October 1969.

tion of General U.S. Grant and the Army of the Potomac. However, several unsuccessful attempts were made to reach Richmond from north of the James River. Forts Harrison and Gilmer, two strongly fortified positions in the outer defense of the city, were the objectives of a surprise attack by Union forces during the early morning hours of September 29, 1864. Fort Harrison was captured by eight o'clock that morning, but the attempt to capture Fort Gilmer, about one mile to the north, was repulsed with heavy losses. Confederate attempts on September 30 to retake Fort Harrison were unsuccessful, and the fort remained under Union control until the evacuation of Richmond in April 1865. During this period, it was renamed Fort Burnham in honor of Union General Hiram Burnham, who was killed at Chapin's Farm during the Federal attack on Fort Harrison.

With the cessation of hostilities a site near Fort Harrison was appropriated by the United States for use as a cemetery. Purchases of the various portions of the 1.73-acre site were made in 1869, 1872 and 1873, from Alpheus Childrey and wife, and from Mattie E. Cox and husband. Remains interred in the national cemetery after its establishment in 1866 were recovered from the battlefields of forts Harrison and Gilmer, and from some 40 locations within a five-mile area surrounding the cemetery. Here again, the number of unknown decedents exceeded the known. The 814 interments as of July 26, 1871, included 239 known and 575 unknowns. As of September 30, 2008, a total of 1,582 interments had been made in the cemetery.

There are four Confederate prisoners of war interred among the unknown from the Civil War.

There is one Medal of Honor recipient interred in the cemetery. As stated in the citation, he was killed in action.

†**George A. Buchanon,** Sec A, Grave 224. Private, Company G, 148th New York Infantry. Place and date: At Chapin's Farm, Va., 29 September 1864.

Citation: Took position in advance of the skirmish line and drove the enemy's cannoneers from their guns; was mortally wounded.

The cemetery was closed for interments on March 7, 1967, except those in reserved gravesites, or second interments in existing graves under the single gravesite per family policy. Fort Harrison National Cemetery is assigned for administration and management to the director of Richmond National Cemetery.

Former superintendents/directors of the cemetery are:

Shelby A. Robbins, April 1932–1933

William H. Green, May 1933–July 1933 (Actg)

Charles M. Smith, August 1933–September 1934

John M. Polley, September 1934–December 1934 (Actg)

Carl O. Gruel, December 1934–April 1936

Nathan E. Numbers, April 1936–September 1936

James R. Martin, September 1936–June 1964

Brice E. Bowen, July 1964–June 1966

Allan M. Long, June 1966–December 1967

Forrest W. Gore, December 1967–February 1969

Robert L. Whitfield, February 1969–September 1971

Fort Jackson National Cemetery

4170 Percival Road

Columbia, South Carolina 29229

The 585-acre national cemetery is Richland County, South Carolina, on property formerly part of Fort Jackson. Currently under construction, the first phase development of 50 acres will provide 5,000 full casket gravesites, including 4,200 pre-placed crypts, 1,100 in-ground cremation sites, and 2,000 columbarium niches.

The cemetery was dedicated on October 26, 2008

Gene B. Linxwiler was appointed the first director of the cemetery.

Fort Leavenworth National Cemetery

Fort Leavenworth, Kansas

Fort Leavenworth National Cemetery, just north of Leavenworth, Kansas, is situated almost in the center of the historic Fort Leavenworth Military Reservation. Because of its associations with the legendary figures who helped open up and develop the Old West, Fort Leavenworth is an important part of U.S. history. It is the oldest continuously active military post west of the Missouri River.

When Mexico obtained independence from Spain in 1821, trading routes were opened to supply goods and merchandise to the Mexican people. Conflict with the Indians was inevitable since the routes crossed their lands. The traders were soon appealing to the United States government for protection and help. The government responded by establishing a series of military posts west of the Missouri River.

In 1827 the War Department directed Colonel, later Brigadier General, Henry Leavenworth, one of the Army's most distinguished officers, to ascend the Missouri River until he reached a point on its left bank near the mouth of the Little Platte River. Within a range of 20 miles above or below its confluence, he was to select a position which in his judgment was best calculated for the site of a permanent cantonment. After exploring the east-

General Leavenworth Monument at Fort Leavenworth National Cemetery.

ern bank of the Missouri, Colonel Leavenworth determined that the Kansas side offered a more advantageous location and, crossing the river, picked the site for Cantonment Leavenworth, which became Fort Leavenworth in 1832.

In 1827 Colonel Leavenworth received orders which approved the selection of the site for the post. Construction had already begun with a tent camp and small huts of logs and bark. A stone wall, which still stands today, was built for protection against Indian attacks.

In the history of Kansas as well as in the history of the Army, Fort Leavenworth has played a prominent role. A branch of the famous Oregon Trail led through here from the steep hills of Missouri. The corrals and supply yards for a branch of the Santa Fe Trail were located on flat land near the river. From there traders and wagon trains began their long journey into Mexico territory. On June 29, 1829, Major Bennett Riley, leading a battalion of the 6th Infantry, for the first time provided the protection service for a wagon train leaving the fort.

In 1828 the first post office in Kansas was established here with Mr. Philip Rand as postmaster. Prior to that time the nearest post office was in Liberty, Missouri, a 26-mile trip on horseback, or a long boat ride down river.

Beginning as early as 1834, the First Dragoons, organized in 1833 as the first cavalry regiment in the Army, was ordered to Fort Leavenworth and acquitted themselves well in quelling Indian uprisings. When the Mexican War broke out, Fort Leavenworth became the outfitting post for troops moving to the Southwest, and later outfitted the gold seekers heading for California. The Army of the West, under the command of newly promoted Brigadier General Stephen W. Kearney, was headquartered here. General Kearney left Fort Leavenworth on June 26, 1846, to carry out President Polk's plan to conquer the northern provinces of Mexico and California. On August 19 he accepted the formal surrender of New Mexico in the plaza at Santa Fe (see Santa Fe National Cemetery).

Wars and skirmishes with the Indians and later between the Free Traders and the pro-slavery settlers justly earned the territory the title Bloody Kansas. In the 1850s when the territory was opened for settlement, states' rights and slavery were hot issues often fought over. On 13 June 1854 a company was organized at Weston, Missouri, for the establishment of a new town near the fort. Leavenworth is the oldest incorporated city in the state of Kansas. From 7 October to 24 November 1854, the first territorial governor, Andrew J. Reeder, maintained his executive headquarters in a building located on the present site of Pope Hall. He lived at 14 Sumner Place, which is still used for officers' family housing.

William F. Cody, who later gained fame as plainsman Buffalo Bill, helped outfit wagon trains as a boy working in the yards here. James Butler "Wild Bill" Hickok and Kit Carson were other familiar figures on the streets of Leavenworth in the middle 1880s. In 1858 a new lawyer named William Tecumseh Sherman put out his shingle. In 1859 the telegraph was extended to the post from Saint Louis, Missouri.

With the outbreak of the Civil War, Fort Leavenworth achieved additional importance because of its strategic location on the border of two states with opposing sympathies. In 1861 Camp Lincoln was established on the post and thousands of volunteers were equipped and trained for the Union Army, establishing a precedent for the role the fort was to play in America's later wars.

In 1874 the United States Disciplinary Barracks was established at Fort Leavenworth, adding to the national importance of the post. In 1881, General William T. Sherman was instrumental in the establishment of the School of Application for Infantry and Cavalry. The school began with correct reading, writing, grammar and arithmetic as its primary subjects. The name has been changed to the U.S. Army Command and General Staff College, and its mission is to provide instruction that will give student officers a comprehensive grasp of the working of the combined arms of the Army, together with supporting services. Today, the Command and General Staff College is known worldwide and its name is synonymous with higher military education.

Fort Leavenworth National Cemetery is the direct product of the development of the fort and its changing requirements. The ravages of malaria and other diseases among the original personnel at the garrison necessitated the establishment of a burying ground as early as 1827. Actually, there were two burying grounds in which interments were made until 1858. One, used for burial of soldiers, was located near the present site of the commanding general's quarters, and the other, reserved for officers, was located near the present site of the Command and General Staff College Library. Between 1852 and 1860, the use of these burying grounds was discontinued and the remains transferred to the present national cemetery location. The cemetery was designated a national cemetery in 1862.

After Civil War hostilities ceased, the remains of Union soldiers were concentrated in the national cemetery from Saint Joseph, Kansas City and Independence, Missouri, from the old arsenal grounds at Fort Leavenworth and from cemeteries located at frontier posts and stations in Kansas, New Mexico, Arizona, Colorado, and southern Wyoming. The November 7, 1870, report of the inspector of national cemeteries shows that there were 354 known white Union soldiers; 731 unknown white Union soldiers; and 178 known citizens, women, and children interred in the cemetery. There are seven Confederate prisoners of war buried here.

The oldest known grave in the cemetery is that of Clarinda Dale, who died on 21 September 1844. She was originally interred in the Fort Leaven worth Arsenal Cemetery and later moved to the national cemetery. She is listed as a civilian. The oldest known military grave in the cemetery is that of Captain James Allen of the 1st U.S. Dragoons, who died on 23 August 1846. He also was originally interred in the arsenal cemetery and later moved to the national cemetery. A most interesting and significant chapter in the history of this cemetery occurred in 1886, when the remains of those interred at Fort Craig, New Mexico, were moved to the Fort Leavenworth National Cemetery. This consolidating movement was made practical by completion of the Atchison, Topeka and Santa Fe Railroad between Kansas City and the Rio Grande in 1882.

Following the close of the Indian Wars, the Army had many small military posts that it no longer needed. During the period 1885 to 1907 the federal government moved nearly 2,000 remains from 24 post cemeteries to Fort Leavenworth National Cemetery. They came from forts Dodge, Downer, Harker, Hays, Larned, and Wallace in Kansas; from forts Defiance, Goodwin, and Thomas in Arizona; forts Bascom, Craig, Cummings, Seldon, and Union in New Mexico; forts Garland and Lyons in Colorado; forts Randall and Sully in South Dakota; Fort Niobraro in Nebraska; Fort Gibson in Indian Territory; Fort Washakie in Wyoming; and the cemetery at Little Big Horn River in Wyoming.

The remains of Brigadier General Henry Leavenworth, the fort's founder, were disinterred from Woodland Cemetery, Delhi, New York, his boyhood home, and reinterred in the national cemetery on Memorial Day 1902. General Leavenworth died in 1834 at Cross Timbers, Indian Territory, without knowing that he had been promoted from colonel to brigadier general. An impressive monument topped by an eagle in repose, perched on a granite cairn, now marks his gravesite.

One hero buried here is Colonel Edward Hatch. During his 23-year military career he was considered one of the best cavalry officers in the Army. His monument at Fort Leavenworth National Cemetery indicates that he participated in over 50 battles and skirmishes in southern Missouri, Tennessee, Mississippi and northern Alabama. He was wounded only once. He was shot in the chest in an encounter at Moscow, Tennessee, but remained on the battlefield in an ambulance until the rebel force was finally routed. The wound hospitalized him for three months. After the Civil War he was commissioned a Regular Army colonel in the 9th U.S. Cavalry, and for a time he commanded the Department of Arizona and New Mexico. Still in the active Army at age 57, Colonel Hatch was thrown from his carriage and severely injured. He died on April 11, 1889, at Fort Robinson, Nebraska.

Interred in the national cemetery are the remains of Hiram Rich, who was sutler in 1841, and four members of his family. Private John Urquhart, one of the soldiers who fought in the first Civil War battle at Fort Sumter, is buried here. Also interred here is an Indian guide, Shango Hango, of the convoys to Laramie during the 1850s.

In 1854, a young 2nd lieutenant, John L. Grattan, arrived at Fort Laramie, Wyoming, with the conviction that Indians were cowards and that he could easily clear the Plains of them. It was this attitude that caused him to volunteer, against the better judgment of his commanding officer, to locate and bring to justice an Indian who had killed an immigrant's cow. He and 28 men arrived at the Indian village and angrily demanded that the chiefs turn the man over to him for punishment. It will never be known whether what happened next was the fault of a nervous "shavetail" or an angry, indignant warrior, but shots were exchanged and soon Grattan and all his men lay dead. News of the massacre spread quickly across the nation, and demands were made for retribution. Troops under the command of Colonel William L. Harney, known for his hatred of Indians, were ordered to seek out the responsible Indians. In pursuit of the guilty parties, Harney encountered a group of Sioux warriors, women and children. He had scarcely commanded them to give up the Indians he was after when he ordered a charge into the group. Over 86 Indians were killed in the attack; unfortunately, there was no evidence that the wanted Indians were among those killed.

Lieutenant Grattan and his men, brave but foolhardy, were initially interred at the post cemetery in Fort Laramie, Wyoming, and then reinterred at Fort McPherson, Nebraska, where a monument was erected in memory of the Grattan Massacre. Subsequently, Lieutenant Grattan's remains were again removed, and his final resting place is Grave 290 in the officers' section at Fort Leavenworth National Cemetery.

Near the front of the cemetery is a marker honoring ten U.S. Army soldiers and an "unknown citizen guide." Their remains had been removed from Fort Wallace during the 1880s. They were a party led by Lieutenant Lyman S. Kidder who were on a mission to locate Lt. Col. George Custer and warn him to "beware of hostiles" in the area. They were killed at Beaver Creek, Kansas, on July 1, 1867, in what historians now refer to as the Kidder Massacre. In 1987, a Wichita newspaper photographer proved that the "unknown citizen guide" was in fact an Indian scout named Red Bead. On July 1, 1987, a ceremony was held to dedicate a plaque giving appropriate recognition to the Indian scout. Chief Glittering Rainbow, great-grandson of Geronimo, accepted the burial flag on behalf of the Mid-America Indian Center in Wichita.

In a long row near the wall of the prison cemetery at Fort Leavenworth, 14 German prisoners of war are buried. They were executed by hanging during July and August 1945 for murdering a fellow prisoner in three widely separated POW camps. In these camps the inmates discovered, tried, and executed three men of their number who had become American informers. The first execution took place within a POW camp for former Afrika Korpsmen in Oklahoma. Five German prisoners were convicted for this. Two prisoners were convicted of strangling an informer at a camp in Aiken, South Carolina. The last murder took place in a camp for U-boat crewmen in Papago Park, Arizona. Seven men were found guilty of the crime. On July 10, 1945, Walter Beyer, age 32; Berthold Seidel, age 30; Hans Schomer, age 27; Hans Demme, 23; and Willi Scholz, 22, were hanged. On July 14 the trap was sprung on Rudolf Straub, 39, and Erich Gauss, 32. The last executions on August 14 were: Otto Stengel, 26; Heinrich Ludwig, 25; Helmut Fischer, 22; Guenther Kuelsen, 22; Fritz Franke, 21; Bernard Reyak, 21; and Rolf Wizuy, 20. The official witnesses at the execution were impressed by the discipline and stolid acceptance of their fate that the prisoners exhibited. All of them had proclaimed their innocence. They argued that they had acted under orders, and otherwise would have been punished in Germany.

Possibly the most famous battle between the United States Cavalry and the Indians was Little Big Horn, which took place on June 25, 1876. Four officers of the 7th U.S. Cavalry Regiment, who perished with General George Custer in that tragic clash, are interred in Section A of the cemetery. Two of these four casualties were related to General Custer. Captain James Calhoun, interred in Grave 1489, was his brother-in-law, and Captain Thomas W. Custer, in Grave 1488, was his brother. Long before Thomas Custer died in the Valley of Little Big Horn he had won recognition for his valor. During the Civil War he was twice awarded the Medal of Honor.

There are ten Medal of Honor recipients interred in the cemetery:

Harry Bell, Sec Off., Grave 167. Captain, 36th Infantry, U.S. Volunteers. Place and date: Near Porac, Philippine Islands, 17 October 1899.
Citation: Led a successful charge against a superior force, capturing and dispersing the enemy and relieving other members of his regiment from a perilous position.

Thomas W. Custer, Sec A, Grave 1488. Second Lieutenant, Company B, 6th Michigan Cavalry. Place and date (first award): At Namozine Church, Va., 10 May 1863.
First award citation: Capture of flag on 10 May 1863. Place and date (second award): At Sailor Creek, Va., April 1865.
Second award citation: Second Lieutenant Custer leaped his horse over the enemy's works and captured two stands of colors, having his horse shot from under him and receiving a severe wound.

William F. Hall, Sec. I, Grave 286. Lieutenant Junior Grade, U.S. Naval Reserve. Place and date: Coral Sea, 7 and 8 May 1945.
Citation: For extreme courage and conspicuous heroism in combat above and beyond the call of duty as a pilot of a scouting plane in action against enemy Japanese forces in the Coral Sea.

John Kyle, Section H, Grave 3341. Corporal, Company M, 5th U.S. Cavalry. Place and date: Near Republican River, Kansas, 8 July 1869.
Citation: This soldier and 2 others were attacked by 8 Indians, but beat them off and badly wounded 2 of them.

Fitz Lee, Sec G, Grave 3183. Private, Troop M, 10th U.S. Cavalry. Place and date: At Tayabacoa, Cuba, 30 June 1898.
Citation: Voluntarily went ashore in the face of the enemy and aided in the rescue of his wounded comrades; this after several attempts had been frustrated.

George Miller, Memorial Section, Number 29. Private, Company H, 5th U.S. Infantry. Place and date: At Cedar Creek, etc., Montana, 21 October 1876 to 8 January 1877.
Citation: Gallantry in action.

Edward Pengally, Sec G, Grave 3032. Private, Company B, 8th U.S. Cavalry. Place and date: At Chiricahua Mountains, Ariz., 20 October 1869.
Citation: Gallantry in action.

Joseph Robinson, Sec D, Grave 12690. First Sergeant, Company D, 3d U.S. Cavalry. Place and date: At Rosebud River, Mont., 17 June 1876.
Citation: Discharged his duties while in charge of the skirmish line under fire with judgment and great coolness and brought up the lead horses at a critical moment.

Albert Sale. Private, U.S. Army; died November 29, 1874; originally interred at Fort Union, N.M.

Jacob Widmer, Sec G, Grave 3529. First Sergeant, Company D, 5th U.S. Cavalry. Place and date: At Milk River, Colo., 29 September 1879.
Citation: Volunteered to accompany a small detachment on a very dangerous mission.

As of September 30, 2008, the cemetery contained 36.1 acres and 23,058 interments, including 73 remains interred in 15 group burials. The cemetery was closed for interments during fiscal year 1981 except those in reserved gravesites and second interments in existing graves under the single gravesite per family policy.

Former superintendents/directors of the cemetery are:

Edward E. Collins, Unknown–June 1928

Wayne Smeltz, May 1934–November 1947

Ret. Adolph P. Bernhardt, November 1947–August 1955

Charles S. Stroup, October 1955–March 1962 Ret.

Francis M. Brooke, November 1962–July 1967

Metro Kowalchick, August 1967–January 1969

James D. Simms, January 1969–July 1973

Gerald C. Nelson, July 1973–September 1974

Donald L. Polston, January 1975–December 1978

Raymond Van Tassel, December 1978–February 1981

Velva Melton, February 1981–1997

Jeff S. Barnes, 1997–2005

William A. Owensby, Jr., 2005–Present

Fort Logan National Cemetery
3698 South Sheridan Boulevard
Denver, Colorado 80235

Situated in Denver County, near the southwest boundary of the city of Denver, Colorado.

The city of Denver was incorporated in 1861, following the consolidation of Denver and a neighboring town of Auraria in 1860. Denver was founded during the Pikes Peak gold rush of 1858 when gold was discovered at Cherry Creek. The city was named for James William Denver, governor of the Territory of Kansas in 1858. Part of the territory is now the state of Colorado. After the outbreak of the Mexican War Denver raised a company for the 12th U.S. Volunteer Infantry and was commissioned captain. His company joined General Scott's army at the Battle of Pueblo. When the Civil War erupted, Denver was commissioned a brigadier general by President Lincoln and placed in command of troops in Kansas. He resigned his commission in 1863, and moved to Washington, D.C., where he died in 1892.

Fort Logan was originally established as a military post in 1887. It was named for Major General John Alexander Logan, a brilliant military leader and eloquent politician. He served in the U.S. House of Representatives before the Civil War and in the Senate after the war. Logan was wounded in the battle at Fort Donelson and served gallantly in action at Vicksburg. While serving in the Senate he was one of the managers of the impeachment proceeding against President Andrew Johnson. In 1868, Logan became the second commander-in-chief of the Grand Army of the Republic. His famous Order #11, dated May 5, 1868, inaugurated the observance of Memorial Day. General Logan died on December 27, 1886, and was buried in Rock Creek Cemetery in Washington, D.C. In 1888, his remains were removed to Soldiers' Home National Cemetery.

During 1946 and 1947, land at nine military reservations was declared surplus. Headquarters, Fifth Army, requested the War Department staff to set aside nine acres at Fort Logan, pending legislation authorizing the use of such military land for national cemetery purposes. Legislation was submitted by the War Department in 1948, but was not passed by Congress. During the first session of the 81st Congress a bill was introduced by senators Eugene D. Millikin and Edwin C. Johnson of Colorado to provide for a national cemetery at Fort Logan. Congress passed the bill on March 10, 1950, but limited the size to no more than 160 acres and did not prescribe a name for the cemetery.

After considering the names Pikes Peak National Cemetery, Rocky Mountain National Cemetery and Mt. Evans National Cemetery, the War Department chose the name Denver National Cemetery. The old post cemetery was immediately designated National Cemetery North, transferred to Office of the Quartermaster General, and used for burials until the new cemetery was built. Through the efforts of local citizens, the name was changed in 1952

Old burials at Fort Logan National Cemetery.

to Fort Logan National Cemetery and Fort Logan National Cemetery, North. Subsequently, with the expansion of the cemetery, the "North" was dropped and the entire site became Fort Logan National Cemetery.

The first recorded burial in the old post cemetery was Mable Peterkin, daughter of Private Peterkin, Company E, 18th Infantry, who died on June 28, 1889. The first interment in the newly established national cemetery occurred on November 1, 1950. Master Sergeant Harry C. Miller, 45th Bombing Squadron, 40th Bomber Group, U.S. Army Air Corps, died October 25, 1944. His remains were returned to the U.S. for final burial after World War II ended.

The cemetery has been expanded from the original 160 acres authorized by Congress to 214 acres. At the time of its establishment as a national cemetery, there were 378 graves in the post cemetery. As of September 30, 2008, there were 95,905 interments, and it is estimated that the cemetery will remain open beyond the year 2030. Thanks to the foresight of the Army engineers in the late 1800s, the cemetery is the majority stockholder in a series of lakes and ditches that control water rights in the Fort Logan area.

One World War II German prisoner of war is buried in the national cemetery.

A sun dial, presented by the Veterans of World War I of the U.S.A. Inc., was erected on March 15, 1961.

A fund-raising campaign using the title "Bells of Hope," sponsored by patriotic and veterans organizations and chaired by Mrs. Mary M. McDonald, raised funds through public contributions and purchased a Schulmerich electronic carillon for the cemetery. It was dedicated on November 17, 1967.

Medal of Honor recipients interred in Fort Logan National Cemetery are:

†**William Edward Adams**, Sec P, Grave 3831. Major, U.S. Army, A/227th Assault Helicopter Company, 52nd Aviation Battalion, 1st Aviation Brigade. Place and date: Kontum Province, Republic of Vietnam, 25 May 1971.

Citation: Major Adams volunteered to fly a lightly armed helicopter in an attempt to rescue three seriously wounded soldiers from a small fire base under heavy enemy attack. Despite ever-increasing enemy fire, he landed the helicopter and took the wounded on board. As the aircraft departed the fire base, it was struck by anti-aircraft fire and began descending. Major Adams regained control of the aircraft and attempted a controlled landing. Despite his valiant efforts the helicopter exploded, overturned and plummeted to the ground amid the hail of enemy fire.

†**Maximo Yabes**, Sec R, Grave 369. First Sergeant, U.S. Army, Company A, 4th Battalion, 9th Infantry, 25th Infantry Division. Place and date: Near Phu Hoa Dong, Republic of Vietnam, 26 February 1967.

Citation: First Sgt. Yabes distinguished himself with Company A, which was providing security for a land clearing operation. The company was suddenly attacked on three sides by a battalion-sized enemy assault. First Sergeant Yabes used his body as a shield to protect others in the command bunker against enemy grenades thrown into the bunker. Although painfully wounded, he remained there while the others relocated. When the command group had reached a new position, he moved through withering fire to another bunker 50 meters away. There he secured a grenade launcher from a fallen comrade and fired point blank into the attacking Viet Cong, stopping further penetration of the perimeter. Noting two wounded men in the fire swept area, he moved them to a safer position. As the battle continued, he noticed a machine gun which threatened the whole position. He dashed across the exposed area, assaulted the machine gun, killed the crew, destroyed the weapon, and fell mortally wounded.

John Davis, Section MB, Grave 280, Private, Company F, 17th Indiana Mounted Infantry. Place and date: Culloden, GA., April 1865.

Citation: Capture of flag of Worrill Grays (CSA).

Former superintendents/directors of the cemetery are:

James Davis, October 1950–August 1960
William F. Spivey, August 1960–February 1964
Edward B. McFarland, February 1964–
  September 1970
Howard J. Ferguson, October 1970–May 1980
Joe D. Willard, July 1980–April 1982
Robert L. Whitfield, August 1982–October 1984
Ronald F. Houska, July 1984–November 1987
Daniel L. Nelson, December 1987–August 1988

Robert L. Brake, September 1988–1990
Jimmy S. Adamson, 1990–1991
Robert McCollum, 1992–1995
Arthur Smith, 1996–1998
Leon Murphy, 1999–2001
Gerald Vitela, 2002–2004
Tricia Blocker, 2004–2006
Joseph Turnbach, 2006–Present

Fort Lyon National Cemetery
Veterans Administration Hospital
Fort Lyon, Colorado 81038

Situated in Bent County, Fort Lyon, Colorado, Fort Lyon National Cemetery is entered by traveling seven miles east from Las Animas, Colorado, on U.S. Highway 50, then turning onto Highway 183 (the state's shortest highway, stretching only one mile) to the VA Hospital's stone gate entrance on Gate Road. The cemetery is located at the end of Northeast Road.

Fort Lyon was first called Fort Wise in honor of Henry A. Wise, governor of Virginia. With the outbreak of the Civil War in April, 1861, and the secession of Virginia, the Army high command decided that the name of a governor of that state was hardly appropriate for a Union fort. The name was accordingly changed by General Orders No. 11, Department of Kansas, to Fort Lyon, after Brevet Brigadier General Nathaniel Lyon. He was killed at

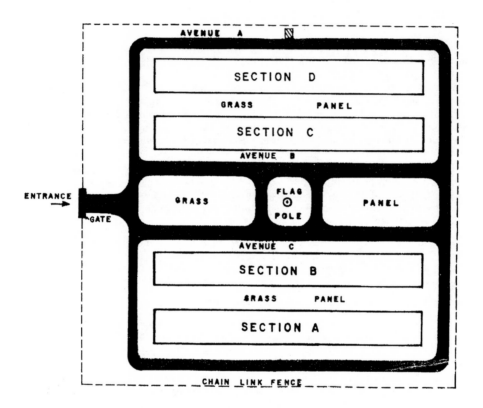

Map of the Ft. Lyon National Cemetery, Ft. Lyon, Colorado.

the Battle of Wilson Creek, Missouri, on August 10, 1861, the first Union general to die in battle in the Civil War.

The fort was originally established in 1867 as a military post with Captain W.H. Penrose commanding. The floods in 1867 made moving the troops imperative. On June 9, 1867, the troops and their equipment and personal belongings were moved to the present location of the fort, just below the mouth of the Purgatoire River. Even before the move was completed, Captain Penrose had men at work erecting new buildings. The parade ground was located where it is now, and the officers' quarters, constructed of adobe on the north side of the parade ground, are still being used as housing for key hospital personnel. The two stone buildings constructed for commissary stores and quartermaster supplies still stand just south of the present-day A Street.

In the middle of May 1868, Christopher (Kit) Carson, the noted Army scout, former trapper, a brevet brigadier general, and, at one time, commanding officer at Fort Garland, was brought to the quarters of Dr. Henry R. Tilton for treatment of an illness that had been aggravated by a trip to Washington, D.C., the preceding winter in behalf of peaceable relations with the Ute Indians. Carson died of a ruptured aneurism of a large blood vessel near his heart on May 23, 1868.

The building in which Carson died eventually fell into disrepair. During Navy days, it was rebuilt enough to serve as a blacksmith shop. Under later administrations, it was fully restored and used as a meeting hall and, later, as a museum. In 1959, funds were obtained to convert the building into a small chapel. As the Kit Carson Memorial Chapel, it is now an American shrine. Dr. Tilton, major and surgeon, U.S. Army, who treated Kit Carson, was awarded the Medal of Honor in 1895 for gallantry in action at Bear Paw Mountain, Montana, on September 30, 1877.

William F. "Buffalo Bill" Cody served as a scout out of Fort Lyon with Major Carr's 5th Cavalry.

The U.S. Army abandoned Fort Lyon in 1897 along with Fort Laramie, Wyoming, and Fort Hays, Kansas. The troops were transferred to other stations, and the bodies of soldiers buried at the post were disinterred and moved to Fort McPherson National Cemetery, south of Maxwell, Nebraska. In 1906, the U.S. Navy, looking for a mild, dry climate, established the U.S. naval hospital at Fort Lyon as a tuberculosis sanitarium for treating sailors and Marines afflicted with the illness.

It remained a naval hospital until 1922, when, for five months, it became a U.S. Public Health Service Hospital. On June 22, 1922, the Veterans Bureau assumed operation of the hospital to treat veterans for tuberculosis and general medical illnesses. In 1930, President Hoover, by executive order, established the Veterans Administration (VA) to replace the Veterans Bureau. Three years later Fort Lyon was designated by the VA as a neuropsychiatric hospital.

Burials in the original cemetery were started in 1907 as the Naval hospital burying ground, and continued under the Veterans Bureau operation. Cemetery records indicate that the first veteran interred here was Youayoshi Hoshi, a Japanese American from Pennsylvania who served as a Navy warrant officer steward during the Spanish-American War. He was interred on October 21, 1907. There is a small fenced civilian cemetery in the southeast section between the national cemetery and the protective dike (John Martin Dam water backup protection). This small cemetery contains 26 graves.

Of the four graves marked with stone markers, only two are legible. The other graves are marked with old wooden markers. Several naval hospital employees, Veterans Bureau employees, and wives and infant children of some of these employees are interred here. Burials in the civilian cemetery were discontinued in 1930, but the area is still maintained in good condition as many present-day employees of the VA Hospital have family members or relatives interred there.

During World War I, German prisoners of war who had contracted tuberculosis were entitled to treatment in American hospitals under the Geneva Convention. A number of these prisoners were sent to the U.S. naval hospital at Fort Lyon, and they were allowed considerable freedom on their word of honor. Rear Admiral G.H. Barber, commanding officer at the time, apparently approved of fraternization between the Americans and the Germans. A custom established during that time of decorating the graves of the two members of the German Imperial Navy, Carl H. Jastrau and H. Dereggenbucke, interred in the national cemetery with the German flags on Memorial Day when the graves of the American dead are decorated still continues.

There are no known Medal of Honor recipients interred in the cemetery.

The two spruce trees at the main entrance to the cemetery were donated by the Colorado American War Mothers, and dedicated on May 17, 1973.

The cemetery was transferred to the National Cemetery System in September 1973. Cemetery records indicate that Fort Lyon, as a national cemetery, was established in 1867. The chief of engineering services at the VA hospital serves as superintendent of Fort Lyon National Cemetery. The cemetery encompasses 51.896 acres, of which only 14.7 acres have been developed for interments. As of September 30, 2008, there had been a total of 2,192 interments. Projected closing date for initial interments is beyond the year 2030.

Fort McPherson National Cemetery

12004 S. Spur 56A
Maxwell, Nebraska 69151

Located in Lincoln County, Nebraska, about four miles south of Maxwell, the cemetery is situated on State Spur No. 56A two miles south of Interstate 80.

The cemetery was established on the Fort McPherson Military Reservation by General Order No. 103, War Department, dated October 13, 1873. The order set aside a tract of land containing about 107 acres within the limits of the reservation. By Executive Order 3364, December 1, 1920, all of the National cemetery except 20 acres constituting the present cemetery was transferred to the Department of the Interior for disposition as provided by law. Eighty-seven acres were sold in 1925. An easement was granted to Lincoln County for a road through the cemetery in 1920.

The Platte River Valley was the avenue by which early pioneers traveled from the Mississippi River to the Pacific coast. The valley had an easy grade, the river and its tributaries furnished water, the broad prairies were heavy with grass, and the buffalo provided meat. The Indians were not troublesome to the early travelers. The Pawnees, living from the forks of the Platte River (near the present North Platte airport) eastward, were more concerned with begging and occasionally stealing a horse. The Sioux, living from the forks westward, had but lately moved into that territory and were fascinated by the wagon trains and eager for the trade goods which they brought. However, when travelers on the Oregon Trail increased from a few hundred to many thousand within a single year, and the rifles of the immigrants began the swift extermination of the buffalo, the Sioux and their allies watched with growing apprehension. Fort McPherson was built, as were others, along the route to the west. Scarcely a wagon train went through without some trouble with the Indians. More and more, troops were called upon for assistance to the settlers and immigrants.

Major General George M. O'Brian, 7th U.S. Cavalry, arrived on September 27, 1863, and selected the site for the military post. This camp was primarily to provide military protection for the construction of a railroad against actions of unfriendly Indians. Many burials in Fort McPherson were of these frontier soldiers stationed at the post during this period. The old post burying ground embraced about an acre on the sloping side of a hill one-eighth mile southeast of the post. A new cemetery site about one-fourth mile southwest of the post, on top of a bald bluff, was selected, and some 50 remains were moved from the original site to the new location.

When Major H.H. Heath, commanding Company G, 7th Iowa Volunteer Cavalry, arrived in 1863, the garrison was known as Fort McKean, in honor of Major General Thomas J. McKean, commanding officer for the military district of which that post was a part. In early 1866, the post name was changed to the Post at Cottonwood Springs. On February 20, 1866, the name was changed again to Fort McPherson, in honor of Major General James B. McPherson. General McPherson, commander of the Army of the Tennessee, was killed

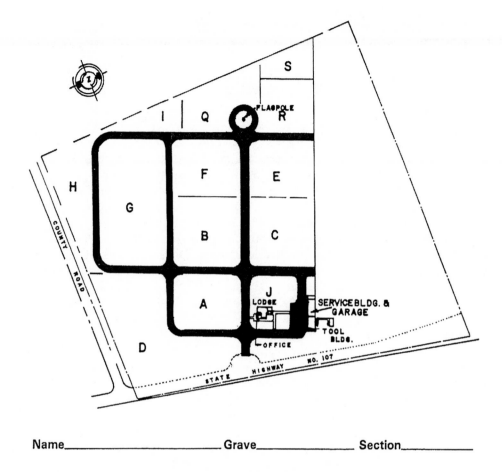

Name_____ Grave_____ Section_____

Fort McPherson National Cemetery.

on July 22, 1864, during the Battle of Atlanta. Fort McPherson was an active military post from its establishment in 1863 to 1880.

When the Union Pacific Railroad was completed and wagon train travel began to decrease, the need for protection of settlers and travelers declined. As a result, many military posts were abandoned, leaving isolated post cemeteries exposed to deterioration and neglect. With the establishment of Fort McPherson National Cemetery in 1873, space and facilities were available for the removal and reinterment of the remains from many of these abandoned cemeteries. In disinterring these bodies it was not uncommon to find the remains strung with wire or rope, bearing silent witness as to the manner in which death was administered by the Indians. Burial records from many of these stations testify that life on the frontier had hardships and dangers similar to those of the camps and battlefields of war. Diseases, such as smallpox, typhoid, fever and pneumonia, attacks by the Indians, drowning, lightning, murder, and suicide all claimed their victims at these lonely outposts.

Initial interments in the national cemetery were disinterments from the post cemetery at Fort McPherson and abandoned post cemeteries at Fort Kearney, Nebraska, and Fort Sedgwick, Colorado. Later, remains were exhumed and reinterred at Fort McPherson from forts Sidney, Hartsuff, and Robinson, Nebraska; forts Bridger, Laramie, Sanders, Steele,

Halleck, Fetterman, and Independence Rock, Wyoming; Fort Hall, South Dakota; forts Crawford and Lewis, Colorado; and Fort Hall, Idaho. In addition, the remains of eight unknown soldiers supposed to belong to either the 7th or 11th Ohio troops were reinterred on May 26, 1896, from La Bonte Station, Wyoming.

The cemetery lodge, built in 1876, was remodeled in 2000 and is now the cemetery's administrative offices. The wall around most of the cemetery is built of bricks made from local clay by the reservation Indians while Fort McPherson was an active frontier post.

There are many noteworthy individuals interred here. Section B Grave 541 contains the remains of Patrick J. O'Rourke. He was born in Cork, Ireland, and married Mary Hodgson in England. With his wife he immigrated to the United States and settled in Lancaster County, Pennsylvania. In 1861 he enlisted in the U.S. Army. He was captain, Company E, 1st Regiment, Pennsylvania Reserves, and was cited for gallantry in action during the Battle of Fredericksburg. Captain O'Rourke was superintendent of Fort McPherson National Cemetery from August 15, 1877, until his death on January 20, 1885.

Section C Grave 800 belongs to Benjamin F. Baker. He was born in Maine in 1835 and died October 28, 1921. In 1862, he enlisted in Company D, 72nd Illinois Infantry. He was commissioned captain, Company H, 3rd Heavy Artillery, on April 20, 1864, and served in the Army until 1876. Captain Baker served as superintendent of the cemetery from November 4, 1885, to February 12, 1892, and from May 10, 1905, to November 1, 1909.

Section S Grave 5900 contains the remains of Baptiste Garnier, known as Little Bat. He was the son of a French trapper and a Sioux mother. Little Bat was one of the most noted frontier characters during the 1870s, and an excellent scout and tracker. He scouted for General Crook during his Indian campaigns. He was murdered at Crawford, Nebraska, on December 16, 1900, and was originally buried at Fort Robinson in a grave just a few feet away from his friend, "California Joe."

In Section S Grave 5921 are the remains of Moses Milner, known as California Joe. He left his Kentucky home at age 14 and started west. His first winter in Nebraska was spent on the North Platte River learning to hunt, trap, and shoot Indians. He became a good friend of Jim Bridger and other noted frontiersmen. Milner fought in the Mexican War; joined the gold rush to California; was with Kit Carson at Adobe Wells; scouted for General Custer in the Battle of Washita; and scouted for General Crook in the Wyoming campaigns. In 1848, he and other trappers built a cabin on Brady's Island. From there they traded with friendly Indians on the Loup, Daniel, Platte, and Republican rivers. In 1876, while riding from one camp to another, California Joe was shot in the back by an unknown assailant. He was originally interred at Fort Robinson.

On May 27, 1873, a detachment of Company F, 3rd U.S. Cavalry, left Fort McPherson to patrol the Republican River Valley. They camped for the night of May 31 on Blackwood Creek. About 9 P.M. a terrible flash flood swept down the valley, carrying everything before it, and drowned 6 men and 26 horses. These six Edward P. Doe, blacksmith; Daniel H. Taylor, private; Lewis Cohn, private; Theodor Froendle, private; William G. Mars, recruit; and Dennis I. Mahoney, private are interred in Section A Graves 385–89.

On June 11, 1865, Captain Fouts with 135 men of the 7th Iowa Cavalry left Fort Laramie escorting a band of Indians to Fort Kearney, Nebraska. Apparently the Indians had some misgivings about being taken into the land of their enemies, the Pawnees. At Horse Creek, on the morning of June 14, they turned on their escort, and after killing Captain Fouts and three soldiers, they fled across the North Platte River. The victims were buried at Fort Mitchell, about 18 miles east of Horse Creek, but were disinterred and moved to Fort McPherson National Cemetery.

About a mile southeast of the cemetery is a monument with a statue of a Civil War soldier marking the site of the flagstaff of Fort McPherson, the old military post. The monument is inscribed on each side with the following:

Side 1:

> This monument marks
> The site of old
> Fort McPherson
> Flag Staff
> Said Fort established
> February 20, 1866
> June 20, 1880

Side 2:

> This fort made
> Possible the first
> White settlement in
> Lincoln County
> Located here
> And known as
> Cottonwood Springs

Side 3:

> Lincoln County's
> Surviving soldiers of
> Old Fort McPherson
> May 30, 1928
> Cyrus Fox
> Chas. Hendy
> Theodor Lowe
> R. McMurray

Side 4:

> Erected by the people
> of Lincoln County
> In the year 1928 to
> Perpetuate the site of
> Old Fort McPherson
> And The Oregon Trail

Directly underneath is a plaque inscribed:

> Through the efforts of
> Cyrus Fox
> This monument was erected
> In memory of
> The Seventh Iowa Cavalry
> First Troops in Cottonwood Springs
> Later named Fort McPherson

A marker two miles northwest of the cemetery marks the route taken by the Pony Express over the Oregon Trail, which passed through the cemetery.

The Grattan Massacre (see Fort Leavenworth National Cemetery) on August 19, 1854, was the spark that started the great Sioux war which continued, with short intermissions, until December 29, 1890. Lt. Grattan and his men were initially interred at Fort Laramie, Wyoming. In 1891, the remains of Lt. Grattan were moved to Fort Leavenworth National

Cemetery, while the remains of the enlisted men were disinterred and brought to Fort McPherson where they were interred in a common grave. The monument marking their grave is inscribed on three sides with their names. On the fourth side, the inscription reads, "In memory of Enlisted men Co. C, 6th Inf. Killed in action near Ft. Laramie, Wyo. (Grattan Massacre) August 19, 1854."

Spotted Horse, a famous Pawnee Indian scout, is interred in Section C, Grave 258. In his youth he possessed a troublesome weakness for white scalps, but he later became a friend of the soldiers and entered their service.

A third former superintendent of the cemetery, John Neukirch, is interred in Section I, Grave 61. He was a veteran of World War I, and served as superintendent from April 19, 1946, until he retired January 31, 1957.

The last Civil War veteran in Lincoln County, Nebraska, Cyrus Fox, died on June 12, 1942, and was interred in Section C, Grave 1270. Fox was a private in Company C, 7th Iowa Cavalry, and had served under General McPherson.

As of September 30, 2008, a total of 9,127 interments had been made in the cemetery. Included among the decedents of World War II, whose remains were returned from overseas, are 81 group burials of 350 remains. The cemetery is projected to remain open for interments until 2030.

Four Medal of Honor recipients are interred in the cemetery. A dagger before the name indicates that the recipient was killed in action.

†**James W. Fous**, Sec G, Grave 685. Private First Class, U.S. Army, Company E, 4th Battalion, 47th Infantry, 9th Infantry Division. Place and date: Kien Hoa Province, Republic of Vietnam, 14 May 1968.
Citation: For conspicuous gallantry and intrepidity in action at the risk of his life above and beyond the call of duty. Private Fous distinguished himself at the risk of his life while serving as a rifleman with Company E. Private Fous was participating in a reconnaissance-in-force mission when his unit formed its perimeter defense for the night. Private Fous, together with three other American soldiers, occupied a position in a thickly vegetated area facing a woodline. Private Fous detected three Viet Cong maneuvering toward his position and, after alerting the other men, directed accurate fire upon the enemy soldiers, silencing two of them. The third Viet Cong soldier managed to escape in the thick vegetation after throwing a hand grenade into Pfc. Fous' position. Without hesitation, Pfc. Fous shouted a warning to his comrades and leaped upon the lethal explosive, absorbing the blast with his body to save the lives of the three men in the area at the sacrifice of his life.

George Jordan, Sec F, Grave 1131. Sergeant, Company K, 9th U.S. Cavalry. Place and date: At Fort Tularosa, New Mexico, 14 May 1880; at Carrizo Canyon, N. Mex., 12 August 1881.
Citation: While commanding a detachment of 25 men at Fort Tularosa, New Mexico, repulsed a force of more than 100 Indians. At Carrizo Canyon, New Mexico, while commanding the right of a detachment of 19 men, on 12 August 1881, he stubbornly held his ground in an extremely exposed position and gallantly forced back a much superior number of the enemy, preventing them from surrounding the command.

Daniel H. Miller, Sec A, Grave 380. Private, Company F, 3d U.S. Cavalry. Place and date: At Whetstone Mountains, Ariz., 5 May 1871.
Citation: Gallantry in action.

Emanuel Stance, Sec F, Grave 1040. Sergeant, Company F, 9th U.S. Cavalry. Place and date: At Kickapoo Springs, Tex., 20 May 1870.
Citation: Gallantry on scout after Indians.

Former superintendents/directors of the cemetery are:

George Griffen, March 1873–December 1873	Carl O. Gruel, May 1939–June 1943
John Ridgely, January 1874–February 1874	Dorman B. Hall, June 1943–October 1943

Thomas Mulcaney, February 1874–June 1877

Patrick J. O'Rourke, August 1877–January 1885

J. J. O'Rourke, January 1885–November 1885

Benjamin F. Baker, November 1885–February 1892

George W. Allen, February 1892–October 1895

Ludwig Beege, October 1895–August 1897

L. H. Dow, August 1897–May 1904

L. B. May, May 1904–May 1905

Benjamin F. Baker, May 1905–November 1909

E. T. Engle, November 1909–May 1914

John Harrigan, May 1914–November 1915

Mart Howe, November 1915–May 1918

William Houser, May 1918–July 1918

Leonard A. Heil, July 1918–June 1920

John McCarthy, June 1920–April 1921

Othello O. H. Weidner, April 1921–November 1926

Frank V. Fehl, December 1926–February 1927

George L. Snider, February 1927–August 1927

Elmer Chase, September 1927–February 1928

James W. Dell, February 1928–January 1929

John W. Moss, February 1929–September 1930

Elmer Chase, September 1930–January 1931

Charles E. Wingert, January 1931–May 1937

Clarence H. Otis, May 1937–May 1939

Thomas O. Moore, October 1943–September 1944

Hans P. Larsen, September 1944–January 1945

Edward J. Larkin, January 1945–October 1945

Dorman B. Hall, October 1945–April 1946

John Neukirch, April 1946–January 1957

William F. Spivey, February 1957–August 1960

James D. Simms, August 1960–August 1967

Gerald C. Nelson, September 1967–November 1970

Richard H. Crouse, November 1970–August 1974

Walter F. Blake, August 1974–June 1976

Ronald G. Andrews, June 1976–February 1978

Joseph Russell, February 1978–August 1978

Dale Shaner, August 1978–September 1978

Joseph Russell, October 1978–December 1982

Dale Shaner, April 1983–March 1990

Robert E. Poe, April 1990–June 1991

Everett J. Schwartz, July 1991–December 1991

Shirley Mileinski, January 1992–July 1995

Everett J. Schwartz, July 1995–July 2004

Jeffrey B. Barnes, July 2004–September 2004

Gene B. Linxwiler, October 2004–September 2006

George Bacon, September 2006–Present

Fort Meade National Cemetery
Fort Meade, South Dakota 57741

The cemetery is located on top of a hill approximately two miles south of the Department of Veterans Affairs Fort Meade Hospital. Access to the cemetery is a gravel road maintained by the Bureau of Land Management off Highway 34/79 East, or from Interstate 90, exit at the Black Hills National Cemetery, south of Sturgis, South Dakota.

The two-acre cemetery was established on September 24, 1878, on the Fort Meade Reservation by the Quartermaster Corps, 7th U.S. Cavalry. The first interment was made that day. The cemetery was closed 70 years later in October 1948, after only 188 interments had been made.

The fort was named in honor of Major General George G. Meade. It was the home of the horse Comanche, the lone cavalry survivor of the Battle of Little Big Horn. It might well be better known as the birthplace of the U.S. national anthem. When Colonel Caleb Carlton was commanding officer at Fort Meade in 1892, he was appalled by the lack of a national anthem. His musically talented wife suggested the "Star Spangled Banner" and the colonel ordered it played at the close of all concerts and parades, and later brought it to the attention of authorities in Washington. Sometime later, Secretary of War Daniel E. Lamont issued an order requiring the "Star Spangled Banner" to be played at every Army Post every evening at retreat. In 1931, Congress made the "Star Spangled Banner" the national anthem.

In addition to the 7th Cavalry, other units, including the 1st, 3rd, 4th, 6th, 8th, 9th, 10th, and 13th cavalry regiments and the 25th Infantry, whom the Cheyennes called "black white men," were stationed at Fort Meade at various times.

In early 1942, the 4th Cavalry was converting from horses to armored vehicles. Two squadrons went to Fort Robinson, Nebraska, to participate in the Army Day parade in Omaha. After passing in review on April 9, the horses were turned over to the post, and the troopers returned to Fort Meade the next day to begin training as mechanized cavalry. This signaled the end of the horse-mounted cavalry as a part of the U.S. armed forces, but history will long remember the pictures and stories of mounted troopers charging into battle with sabers flashing.

The cemetery contains both government-furnished headstones and monuments obviously furnished by family or friends. Some of the gravesites are enclosed by wire fencing, wooden board fencing, and ornate pipe fencing. Individual stories are not known, but one must wonder about the lives of the people buried here and how they came to rest in this

Fort Meade post cemetery (now part of the national cemetery).

hallowed ground. Two graves, side by side, are marked "Child of Civilian Refugee" and "Lucy, Child, Sioux Indian." A grave marked "William Fool Soldier, Co. L, 7th Cav." is located near the ornate marble monument of "Alexander Brown, Late Sgt., Troop A, 7th Cav, Born Aberdeen, Scotland, 1844, Died Fort Meade, Dakota Territory, 1884."

Enclosed by a wrought iron fence is the gravesite of "Otto Von Wargowski, 1889–1909." The poetic inscription on his monument is in Ger man. He evidently was a member of Prussian nobility, but was only 30 years old when he died. An obelisk monument was erected by members of D Troop, 8th Cavalry, in memory of two of their comrades who, according to legend, died as a result of drinking wood alcohol while on patrol near Belle Fouche. One of the most elaborately carved monuments reads "Pvt. Frank Weg, Co. M, 7th Cav., Sacred to the Memory of Our Late Comrade, June 3rd, 1883 Aged 27 Years." One wonders what he did to become so important to his friends that they would erect so elaborate a monument to him.

Among those interred here is one Medal of Honor recipient.

Albert Knaak, Sec 2, Grave 101. Private, Company B, 8th U.S. Cavalry. Place and date: Arizona, August to October 1868.
Citation: Bravery in scouts and actions against Indians.

The cemetery is assigned to the director of Black Hills National Cemetery, Sturgis, South Dakota, for operation and management.

Fort Mitchell National Cemetery
Highway 165
553 Highway 165
Fort Mitchell, Alabama 36856

Sixteen miles south of Phoenix City, on state Route 165, the cemetery is adjacent to the state owned and operated Fort Mitchell Park. The Georgia Militia originally constructed Fort Mitchell in order to show a military presence during the Creek War of 1813–1814. It was named in honor of David B. Mitchell, who was governor of Georgia from 1809 to 1813, and served as an Indian Agent from 1819 to 1825. Fort Mitchell gradually emerged as the center of trade with Native Americans. The Fort also became central to the protection of Native Americans as new settlers constantly violated the Creek territory as defined under the 1814 Treaty of Fort Jackson. In response to the Creek Indian protests, a new fort was constructed and was occupied by the 4th U.S. Infantry in the summer of 1825.

President Andrew Jackson was committed to a policy of moving Native Americans beyond the "white settlement line," the Mississippi River, and was reluctant to use force against settlers who were supported by the laws of Georgia and Alabama. For every trespasser removed by the troops of Fort Mitchell, ten others would cross the river into Creek Territory. In 1836, about 1,600 Creek Indians were held in Fort Mitchell in preparation for a forced march to the west. Between 2,000 and 3,000 people were forced to march from Fort Mitchell to Montgomery. This route, as well as the routes of the five major tribes forcibly removed from their land, became known as the "Trail of Tears."

There are five archaeological sites located within the Fort Mitchell Cemetery: prehistoric upland campsites, historic period Creek settlements, the Fort Mitchell Military Post area, a Creek Indian factory and agency, and antebellum-to-recent plantation and tenant farming. All sites are well marked.

Fort Mitchell National Cemetery

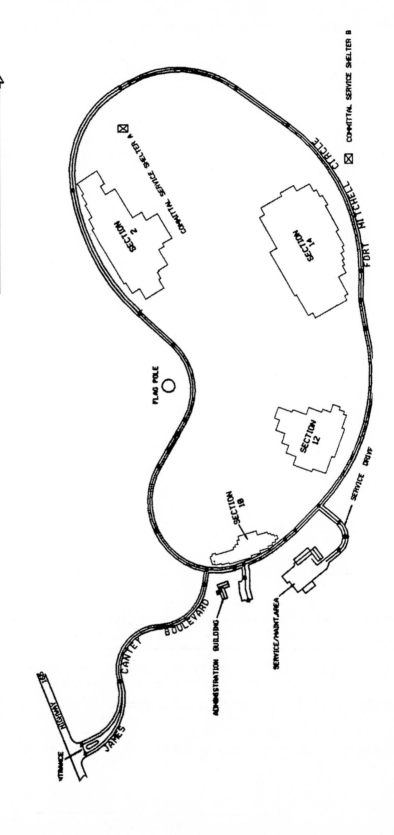

VA Administrator Max Cleland had selected Fort Gillem, in east Atlanta, to be the site of the Region IV national cemetery. When Robert Nimmo became Administrator, he changed the site to Fort Mitchell.

The 280 acre cemetery opened in May 1987, and as of September 30, 2008, there have been 6,736 interments. There is one Medal of Honor recipient interred here:

†**Matthew Leonard**, Platoon Sergeant, U.S. Army, Company B, 1st Battalion, 16th Infantry, 1st Infantry Division. Place and Date: Near Suoi Da, Republic of Vietnam, 28February 1967.
Citation: For conspicuous gallantry and intrepidity in action at the risk of his life above and beyond the call of duty. (The complete citation may be found on the Congressional Medal of Honor website.)

Former directors of the Cemetery are:

Robert Brake, 1986–1988
Jimmy T. Jackson, 1988–1994
William Trower, December 1994–October 1997
Sharon Goodrich, November 1997–May 2000
Timothy Spain, March 2000–April 2002

Gregory Whitney, May 2002–December 2004
Tommy Monk, December 2004–September 2005
John Corsi, September 2005–June 2007
Deborah L. Kendrick, June 2007–Present

Fort Richardson National Cemetery
P.O. Box 5-498
Fort Richardson, Alaska 99505

The cemetery is located on the Fort Richardson Military Reservation in Anchorage, Alaska.

During World War II, approximately 39 acres were set aside for cemetery purposes at Fort Richardson. The site, just north of Davis Highway, then a major route between Anchorage, Fort Richardson, and Palmer, was a temporary U.S. military cemetery where deceased soldiers, regardless of nationality, were interred until either their next of kin or their government took custody of their remains. This cemetery was one of two concentration points for World War II personnel who died in Alaska. Most of the remains were repatriated under the Return of World War II Dead Program. Some remains were not claimed because the next of kin could not be located, and in some cases, the families wished the bodies to stay in Alaska. The site was designated a post cemetery in December 1946, and the first interment made that day.

Two sections were initially developed, one for allies inside the fence and one for Japanese soldiers killed in the Aleutians, located outside the fenced area. Wartime burials included 235 Japanese soldiers, 14 Russians and 12 Canadians. The foreign burials, unidentified Allied and enemy soldiers, were made prior to 1946. Although the section outside the fence was referred to as the Allied Plot and Enemy Plot Adjacent to Fort Richardson Post Cemetery, it is part of the post cemetery. These plots were set aside solely to accommodate those Allied and enemy World War II dead who could not be repatriated because the government concerned did not desire to secure custody of the remains. There was no intent that the plots would be used to provide burial places for foreign nationals dying subsequent to World War II, and there is no authority for such utilization. There was one exception: in 1953, a British Army physician who died in a plane crash en route to Ladd Air Force Base, now Fort Wainwright, was buried in the post cemetery.

Major Kermit Roosevelt, son of President Theodore Roosevelt, was interred in the cemetery on June 8, 1943. His widow, Mrs. Belle Roosevelt, advised the quartermaster general, General T.B. Larkin, and the chief of staff, General Dwight D. Eisenhower, that she desired that her husband's remains be permanently interred at Fort Richardson. General Eisenhower personally approved her request. In 1949, Mrs. Roosevelt wrote to General George C. Marshall stating her desire to erect some sort of memorial to her husband. She proposed a memorial gateway, with the idea that the Army might then build a permanent fence around the cemetery. The gate was completed in 1951. One pillar post of the gate bears a plaque in honor of her husband.

In July 1953, the 235 Japanese dead were disinterred for proper cremation under the supervision of Mr. Shigeru Inada, third secretary of the Japanese Embassy in Washington. Shinto and Buddhist ceremonies were performed at the cremation ritual. There were 18 identified and 217 unidentified remains. The ashes were reinterred in coffin crates and a single headstone placed at the head of the plot. The plot is recorded in cemetery records as Section Y, graves 246–250. The stone bears the names of the 18 identified soldiers and "Two Hundred and Seventeen Unknown." Included in a group of 18 Japanese who made a pilgrimage to Alaska in July 1964 was Mr. Kuneo Sato, one of the 27 survivors of the battle for Attu Island. A group of Japanese citizens in Anchorage had a new marker made in Japan and placed in the plot in May 1981.

For over 15 years there were efforts made to have the post cemetery designated a national cemetery. On May 28, 1984, Brigadier General Gerald H. Bethke, senior Army commander in Alaska, presented a certificate of transfer to Paul T. Bannai, director of the National Cemetery System, and Fort Richardson National Cemetery became the 109th cemetery in the system. About a month prior to the official transfer of the land to the National Cemetery System, a top military official at Fort Richardson called the author to determine if burials could be made in the cemetery prior to its transfer. When asked why, he replied that there were a number of bodies getting "ripe." Asked to explain, he stated that during the long, extremely cold winter, no graves could be dug and bodies were stored until the spring thaw, and the thaw had started nearly a month early that year. Needless to say, permission was granted. Since the transfer, several hundred graves are dug each fall and prepared for the winter interments.

At the time of the transfer, all but 700 of the 2,000 gravesites had been used or reserved. With the addition of 20 acres secured from the state of Alaska, the municipality of Anchorage and Eklutna Inc., there will be sufficient land for burials beyond the year 2030. The State, City and Village Corporation agreed not to claim the property pursuant to the North Anchorage Land Agreement of 1982, which would have given them claim to properties being excessed by the government.

There is one Medal of Honor recipient interred here:

James L. Bondsteel, Sec H, Grave 19. Staff sergeant, U.S. Army; died April 6, 1987.

As of September 30, 2008, there were 4,920 interments. The cemetery is maintained by contract with the U.S. Army, Fort Richardson. Former directors, or persons in charge, of the Fort Richardson National Cemetery are:

Willie F. Crosby, March 1987–September 1989
David G. Dimick, September 1989–October 1991
James L. Fitzgerald, October 1991–September 1993

Yvonne V. Payne, September 1993–November 1999
Virginia M. Walker, November 1999–Present

Fort Rosecrans National Cemetery

Point Loma, P.O. Box 6237
San Diego, California 92106

Situated in San Diego County, in the Fort Rosecrans Military Reservation, Point Loma, California, the cemetery is on Cabrillo Memorial Drive approximately 10 miles west of San Diego, overlooking the bay and the city.

When the Spanish explorer Juan Rodrigues Cabrillo began his search for the fabled "city made of gold" in 1542 along the coast of California, he made one of his many stops at the site of present-day San Diego. Soon after Cabrillo's explorations, the Spanish padres moved up the coast from Mexico to civilize the region and bring Christianity to the Indians. Shortly after the United States declared war on Mexico, in May 1846, Brigadier Stephen Watts Kearny was assigned the task of conquering Mexico's northern provinces, New Mexico and California. Taking New Mexico by a show of strength and diplomacy, rather than by doing battle, Kearny divided his forces and led the smallest of the three units toward California. Along the way, Kearny met Kit Carson, who was bringing him the news that the large American community in California had already established the Bear Flag Republic and had control of the area. Relying on this new information to be correct, Kearny again divided his forces, and with Carson and 100 men, continued to California. As they traveled, the situation Carson had reported reversed itself and the Californians were again supporting Mexico. As Kearny and his troops approached San Diego, the Californians came out in full force to meet them. In the ensuing battle of San Pasqual, on December 6, 1846, the American troops were soundly defeated, with 18 killed and 15 wounded before the Californians withdrew. Captain Benjamin Moore, the first commander of Fort Scott, Kansas, was killed during this battle.

Fort Rosecrans National Cemetery.

The cemetery grounds are part of the 1,000 acres set aside in February 1852 for the development of a military reservation. The reservation was named Fort Rosecrans in 1899 in honor of Major General William Starke Rosecrans, United States Volunteers, brigadier general, United States Army. General Rosecrans military career began in 1861 when he was appointed colonel of the Ohio Volunteer Infantry. During the Civil War he rose to the rank of major general due to his astute judgment and strategic planning of military actions. After the war, he served as United States minister to Mexico for one year, and retired to his home in California. He died on March 1, 1898, at the age of 78, and is interred in Arlington National Cemetery.

Fort Rosecrans National Cemetery, the second cemetery area in California to achieve national cemetery status, was so designated by the War Department on October 5, 1934. The initial area of the cemetery comprised eight acres and included the long established post cemetery of the military reservation. Subsequent accretions of land from within the military reservation have extended the boundaries of the cemetery to 77.5 acres.

Many of the interments made in the post cemetery date back to the early years of the territory of California and include former members of the Navy and Marine Corps, retired officers and enlisted men, one sailor of the English Royal Navy, a number of Mexican soldiers who died while interned at Fort Rosecrans, and the remains of 2 officers and 16 enlisted men killed in the battle of San Juan. The graves of the Mexican soldiers have been re-marked with headstones similar to those of U.S. personnel.

The remains of the casualties of the battle of San Pasqual were initially buried where they fell in 1846. In 1874, their remains were removed to the San Diego Military Reservation, and finally reinterred in the post cemetery when it was established in 1882. As the remains could not be individually identified, the gravesite was marked only as the burial place of 18 unknowns. In 1922 the San Diego Parlors of Native Sons and Daughters of the Golden West had a large boulder brought from the San Pasqual battlefield and placed at the gravesite. A bronze plaque listing the names of 17 soldiers and 1 civilian was affixed to the boulder. In 1949 a new plate bearing the names of the decedents was placed over the original nameplate, which had become worn through exposure to the elements.

Another outstanding monument in the Fort Rosecrans National Cemetery commemorates the dead from an explosion and fire involving the *USS Bennington*, which suffered a boiler explosion in San Diego Harbor on July 21, 1905. The *Bennington* was at anchor in the harbor preparing for departure to search for the *USS Wyoming*, which was reported broken down at sea. About 10:30 A.M. an explosion in the ship's boiler killed one officer and 65 enlisted crew members, with severe injuries to the majority of the ship's complement. On July 23, the remains of 47 of the unfortunate men were brought to the post cemetery and interred in an area which has come to be known as the Bennington Plot. Each of the graves in this area is marked by an individual headstone. The Bennington Monument is a granite obelisk, 75 feet high. The front face is inscribed, "To the Bennington's Dead, July 21, 1905." An inscription on the rear of the monument indicates that it was "Erected by the Officers and Men of the Pacific Squadron to the Memory of Those Who Lost Their Lives in the Performance of Duty."

On July 29 the *Bennington* was pumped out, floated and made ready to be towed to the Navy yard at Mare Island, where she remained until September 1910, when she was stricken from the Navy list.

Many acts of heroism were performed by the officers and crew of the stricken *Bennington* in removal of the dead and rescue of the wounded. On January 5, 1906, Secretary of the Navy Charles J. Bonaparte directed that 11 members of the *Bennington*'s crew be awarded the Navy's Medal of Honor and a gratuity of $100 in cash. One of the awards went to Willie Cronan, boatswain's mate, USN, a native of Illinois whose service dated from 1902 through World Wars I and II until his retirement in 1946, with the rank of lieutenant commander. He died on October 22, 1959, and is interred in Section T, Grave 534.

During the period from 1905 until 1934 numerous high-ranking Army and Navy officials attempted to have the post cemetery designated as a national cemetery. By 1934 changes in legislation had greatly increased the number of persons eligible for interment in a national cemetery, and in many cemeteries available grave space was becoming limited. The historic San Francisco National Cemetery, the first national cemetery established on the Pacific coast, was one of these. These conditions along with the increasing growth of the Southern California area helped to bring about the establishment of the Fort Rosecrans National Cemetery on October 5, 1934. Mr. King C. Tolles, who had served with the U.S. Army during World War I as a Captain, was appointed the first superintendent. He served from August 1935 until his retirement in July 1943.

Memorial markers are erected in all national cemeteries in solemn remembrance of members of the Armed Forces dying in service whose remains were not recovered or identified, or were buried at sea. There are 158 such markers within the 3 memorial areas which attest to the dedication and sacrifice of these men. The entrance to the memorial area near the administration building is marked by a bronze tablet with a dedicatory inscription to their memory.

Fort Rosecrans National Cemetery is the honored burial place of many Army, Navy, Marine Corps and Air Force personnel from the San Diego area. General Holland M. Smith, USMC, famed for his leadership in some of the toughest battles in the Pacific area during World War II, is among many high-ranking Navy and Marine Corps officers interred here. General Smith was interred in Officers Section, Grave 279-A, on January 14, 1967.

On December 1, 1989, the remains of Air Force Captain Daniel Carrier were interred. He had been missing in action for 22 years. On July 31, 1989, the Vietnamese government returned his remains and those of four other U.S. servicemen. Captain Carrier was the radar officer in a Phantom jet shot down near Da Nang in June 1967.

As of September 30, 2008, there were 96,626 interments. The cemetery was closed to interments on September 15, 1966, except for those in reserved gravesites or second interments in existing graves under the single gravesite per family policy. Garden niches were established in June 1982 for the in-ground burial of cremated remains. The National Cemetery System is currently negotiating with the U.S. Navy for additional strips of land around the cemetery, which would permit the cemetery to expand the areas used for interment of cremated remains.

There are 22 Medal of Honor recipients interred in the cemetery. Daggers appear before the names of men killed in action.

Name	Service	War/Place/Date of Action	Section & Grave
Charles Francis Bishop	USN	Vera Cruz	O-4562
Willis W. Bradley	USN	WWI	O-2925
Mason Carter	USA	Indian	Post-4-102
†Peter S. Connor	USMC	Vietnam	AE-1005
William Cronan	USN	USS *Bennington*	T-534
James L. Day	USMC	WWII	P-1748
†Albert L. David	USN	WWII	OS-125-A
Jesse Farley Dyer	USMC	Vera Cruz	P-1606

Name	Service	War/Place/Date of Action	Section & Grave
Middleton Stuart Elliott	USN	Vera Cruz	P-2628
†Michael John Estocin*	USN	Vietnam	MA-112
Donald A. Gary	USN	WWII	A-13-B
Ora Graves	USN	WWI	W-1208
Herman H. Hanneken	USMC	Haiti	C-1166-D
Jimmie E. Howard	USMC	Vietnam	D-3759
Ross Lindsay Iams	USMC	Haiti-1915	P-2930
†Herbert Charplet Jones	USN	WWII	G-76
†John Edward Murphy	USN	Sp.-Amer.	OS-363
James Irsley Poynter	USMC	Korea	O-729
Anund Charles Roark	USA	Vietnam	O-1855
Henry Frank Schroeder	USA	Phil.	S-854
Robert Semple	USN	Vera Cruz	OS-A-192
William Zuiderveld	USN	Vera Cruz	A-19-B

Former superintendents/directors of the cemetery are:

King C. Tolles, August 1935–July 1943

Carl J. Sonstelie, July 1943–August 1945

Claybourne F. Kearney, August 1945–December 1949

Eugene B. Taylor, December 1949–May 1953

Ralph L. Fischetti, June 1953–November 1963

James M. Griffin, February 1964–November 1966

Ernest C. Schanze, December 1966–June 1971

Winston J. Stratton, July 1971–January 1975

Harold F. Hammer, March 1975–March 1976

George C. Miller, March 1976–October 1977

Charles R. Weeks, November 1977–July 1980

Milo D. Hayden, August 1980–January 1984

Robert E.L. St. Clair, February 1984–1990

Jack Shaw, 1990–2007

Kirk Leopard, December 2007–Present

Fort Sam Houston National Cemetery

1520 Harry Wurzbach Road

San Antonio, Texas 78209

The cemetery is situated in Bexar County, adjoining the northeast section of the Fort Sam Houston Military Reservation.

Since the beginning of the 18th century, soldiers of some nation have been stationed at the head of the Rio San Antonio. The Spanish invaded Texas from the south and the French came from the Mississippi River. The Tejas Indians, from whom the state derives its name, were subjected to the preaching and teaching of missionaries of both nations, and each mission was protected by well-trained fighting men. The first military force to establish itself in San Antonio was a unit of 30 soldiers sent by the Spanish Viceroy of Mexico to protect the padres at the small mission set up at the source of the Rio San Antonio in 1718. This new mission was called the Alamo.

Since before the Civil War, Fort Sam Houston has been an important Army post. When the 2nd Cavalry came to the fort, following the Mexican War, among its officers were Colonel Albert Sidney Johnson, Lieutenant Colonel Robert E. Lee, Major George H. Thomas and Major William J. Hardee. All became famous during the Civil War, Lee as commander of the Army of Northern Virginia, Johnson by commanding the Confederate forces opposing Grant at Shiloh and losing his life there, Thomas as the "Rock of Chickamauga," and Hardee as commander of the Confederate armies in the west. At the close of the Civil War the present site of the fort was chosen and named after General Sam Houston, commander-

Memorial headstone only. Captain Estocin is still listed as missing in action.

in-chief of the Army of the Republic of Texas, the first president of that republic, and the first governor of the state of Texas.

Although the Military Reservation was established in 1865, the ground upon which Fort Sam Houston National Cemetery is located did not become a burying ground until over half a century later. Interments from the post were made in a portion of the city cemetery until 1867 when the United States acquired the tract by donation from the city government and designated it San Antonio National Cemetery. Even at that early date, the city completely surrounded the new national cemetery and the possibilities for expansion were very limited. As the years passed, the number of military personnel grew with a corresponding increase in the number of deaths occurring on the post, which created a need for more burial facilities. In recognition of this need, 2nd Division headquarters on March 13, 1924, set aside a portion of the military reservation to be used as a post cemetery. The first interment was not made until 1926. On August 6, 1931, the War Department announced the transfer of 60.11 acres, including the post cemetery, from the military reservation and designated the tract as an addition to San Antonio National Cemetery. This status remained until March 4, 1937, when the War Department designated the tract as a national cemetery for the burial of veterans of past wars and deceased members of the service and their eligible dependents, and formally named it Fort Sam Houston National Cemetery.

Remains from the cemeteries of the one-time frontier posts Fort Ring gold, Fort Clark and Fort McIntosh, Texas, were interred in the national cemetery in 1947 when those posts were discontinued. The remains of 27 Buffalo Soldiers from the 9th and 10th Cavalry were brought to Fort Sam Houston National Cemetery and reinterred in Section PE.

Captain William Randolph, for whom Randolph Air Force Base is named, is interred here. Captain Randolph died in a plane crash in 1928, and his remains were reinterred in the cemetery in 1949. Here too lies a distinguished forerunner of the space age, Colonel Daniel Tyler Moore, founder and first commandant of the United States Army Artillery and Missile Center and School at Fort Sill, Oklahoma. Raymond Hatfield Gardner, alias Arizona Bill, a famous Indian scout, was interred in the cemetery in 1878.

There are many unsung heroes interred in these hallowed grounds. More than 1,500 graves hold the remains of those who paid the supreme sacrifice for their country: 1,365 World War II dead, 135 killed in action in Korea, and 369 Vietnam casualties. Five of the Southeast Asia burials are the remains of men missing in action who were returned home many years after the war ended. Lieutenant Colonel Richard Castillo, United States Air Force, missing in action since 1972, was brought to his final resting place on October 29, 1986. The most recent, U.S. Air Force Colonel Woodrow H. Wilburn, who was listed as missing in action over Vietnam 22 years ago, was interred on February 5, 1990.

Four Air Force Reservists who were killed when their C-5 cargo plane crashed at Ramstein Air Base in West Germany on August 29, 1990, were interred on September 6 and 7, 1990. They were flying round-the-clock missions deploying troops and supplies as part of Operation Desert Shield in Saudi Arabia. Technical Sergeant Daniel Perez, loadmaster, was interred on September 6th, as was Major Richard M. Chase, pilot; Master Sergeant Rosenda Herrera, flight engineer; and Staff Sergeant Daniel Garza, crew chief, were buried on September 7.

General Frank Thomas Mildren, U.S. Army (Retired), was buried on September 19, 1990. In 1944 General Mildren served as commander of the 1st Battalion, 38th Infantry during the landing at Omaha Beach and the Allied advance through France and Germany. During the Korean War, he commanded the 38th Infantry Regiment in the battles of Heartbreak Ridge, the taking of the Punchbowl, and the fight for Mun-Dung-Ni Valley. Promoted to brigadier general in 1960, he became assistant division commander of the 24th Infantry Divi-

Ft. Sam Houston National Cemetery

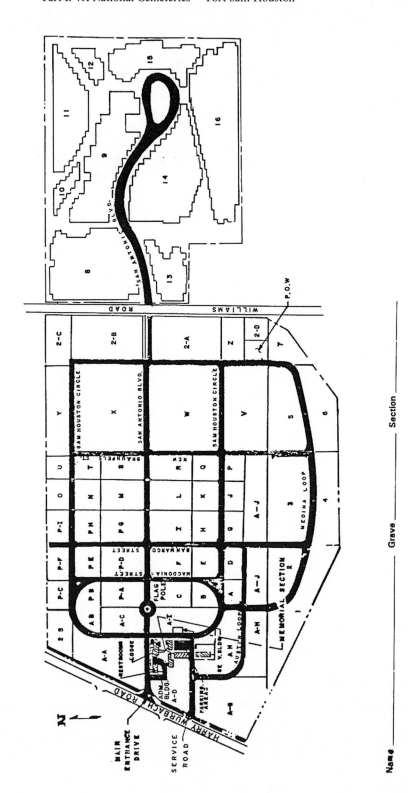

sion in Germany. He received his fourth star as commanding general, Allied Land Forces, Southeastern Europe.

U.S. Congressman Frank Tejeda, who served as a major in the U.S. Marine Corps in Vietnam in interred in Section AI, Grave 554. There are 370 General Officers buried here.

A prisoner of war section was established in October 1946, in the southeast corner of the cemetery. The initial burial was made on February 17, 1947. There are now 132 Germans, 5 Italians, 3 Japanese, and 1 Austrian buried in this section. Ninety-one of the 141 total were reinterments from the cemetery at Dodd Field, Texas. The remaining 50 bodies were brought here from Camp Swift, Camp Hood and Camp Maxey, Texas; from Camp J.T. Robinson and Camp Chaffee, Arkansas; from Camp Polk and Camp Livingston, Louisiana; and from Camp Gruber, Oklahoma.

Additional transfers of land from the military reservation have increased the size of the cemetery to 154.7 acres. As of September 30, 2008, there were 120,982 interments in the cemetery.

There are 12 Medal of Honor recipients interred in the cemetery. Daggers appear before the names of men who were killed in action.

Name	Service	War/Place/Date of Action	Section & Grave
Roy P. Benavidez	USA	Vietnam	AI-553
Cecil Hamilton Bolton	USA	WWII	PC-22-J
William J. Bordelon	USMC	WWII	AI-558
William George Harrell	USMC	WWII	W-3247
†Lloyd H. Hughes	USA (AM)	WWII	U-53
Raymond L. Knight	USAAC	WWII	HB-11
†Milton A. Lee	USA	Vietnam	X-2475
Cleto Luna Rodriguez	USA	WWII	A-I-700
†James E. Robinson, Jr.	USA	WWII	T-98
Lucien Adams	USA	WWII	AI-555
Luis R. Rocco	USA	Vietnam	AI-549
Seth Lathrop Weld	USA	Phil.	A-H-189

Former superintendents/directors of the cemetery are:

Charles Schraegler, January 1932–June 1932
Sgt. R.A. Brown, June 1932 only
James P. Madigan, August 1932–March 1939
Placide Rodriquez, March 1939–June 1939
Marion M. Coffee, June 1939–October 1955
Adolph P. Bernhardt, November 1955–August 1957
Raymond J. Costanzo, September 1957–January 1962

Curtis W. Spence, January 1962–December 1976
Allen H. Long, March 1977–April 1978
Claude E. Arnold, July 1978–August 1980
Thomas E. Costanzo, August 1980–April 1986
Stephen H. Jorgensen, 1986–1990
Donald Fritz, 1990–1994
Joe A. Ramos, January 1994–December 2002
William A. Trower, February 2003–Present

Fort Scott National Cemetery
Fort Scott, Kansas

Fort Scott National Cemetery, located about two miles from the post office in Fort Scott, Kansas, on the eastern outskirts of the city, is a visual reminder of the expansion and development of the middle west when it was the frontier. Like so many of the present-day cities and towns of the middle west, Fort Scott owes not only its name but its very existence to the military post established at that point for the protection of the newly developed trade routes from the east to the southwest.

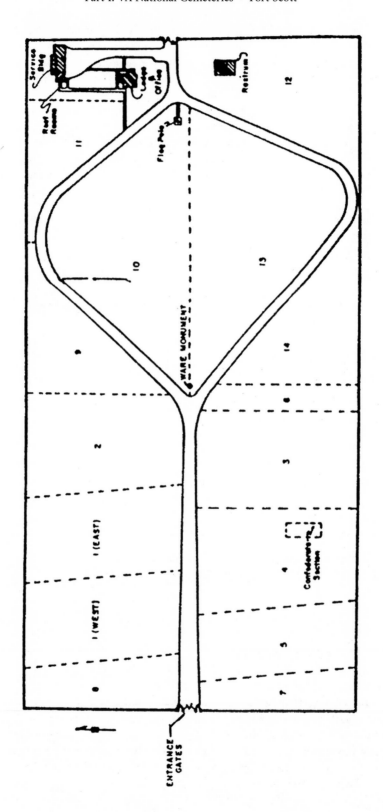

Fort Scott National Cemetery, Fort Scott, Kansas.

The fort was erected in 1842 approximately halfway between Fort Leavenworth, Kansas (built in 1827), and Fort Gibson, Oklahoma (built in 1824), on the route generally known as the Military Road. It was named for Lieutenant General Winfield Scott, then general-in-chief of the Army. The first post commander was Captain Benjamin Moore, who helped select the site. Captain Moore was killed in 1846 at the battle of San Pasqual while serving under General Stephen Kearney. The fort's primary purpose was to keep peace between the relocated Indians from the east, the nomadic tribes, and white settlers. The Indians were quiet and the soldiers' main duties were to guard caravans on the Santa Fe Trail and to patrol the vast Indian country. The post quartermaster, Captain Thomas Swords, directed most of the construction, which was done by the soldiers themselves assisted by a few skilled craftsmen. They used raw materials which were close by, and when construction stopped in 1850, the cost of the fort was only about $32,000.

By 1853 the frontier had moved farther west and there was little need for a military garrison here. The garrison was moved to Fort Leavenworth. In 1855 the government abandoned the post, selling the lumber in the stockade and auctioning off the buildings. Federal troops returned in 1857 and again in 1858 to quiet local civilian unrest caused by the struggle over whether Kansas would be a slave or a free state.

The outbreak of the Civil War caused Fort Scott to again assume military importance and the fort was reestablished. It became a concentration center for troops as well as the storage place for large quantities of supplies intended for the use of troops stationed as far south as the Red River. The 1st Kansas Colored Infantry, one of the first black regiments raised during the war, was established here in 1863. This unit took part in five engagements and suffered more casualties than any other Kansas regiment.

For a short time after the Civil War, the fort continued to be used for handling movements of displaced Indians to the western territories. As the frontier continued moving westward and new military posts were established, its usefulness ceased and Fort Scott was again abandoned, this time permanently. However, the Army did return to the town of Fort Scott in the 1870s to protect workers building a railroad across disputed land. The establishment and development of the Fort Scott National Cemetery was tied closely to its surroundings and the times. The first graveyard was established in the early days of the fort on the west side of town to accommodate the burial of soldiers stationed at the garrison, and a few citizens. In 1861 approximately four acres of land located about 1½ miles southeast of the old military post were purchased by subscription of the town officers and the citizens of Fort Scott for use as a new burying ground. Since it was controlled by the Presbyterian church, it was known as the Presbyterian Graveyard. After the Civil War broke out and the fort was reestablished, the new burying ground was used for the burial of soldiers who died while stationed at Fort Scott. On November 15, 1862, the Presbyterian Graveyard and an adjoining tract owned by the Town Company were designated as Fort Scott National Cemetery.

Following the cessation of hostilities in 1865, the remains of those who died in the skirmish fields of Vernon County, Missouri, and Bourbon and Linn Counties, Kansas, and of those interred in the old military cemetery at Fort Scott were concentrated in the national cemetery. The post cemetery at Fort Lincoln, Kansas, was closed and those remains as well as those from the surrounding countryside were removed and reinterred at Fort Scott National Cemetery. The earliest recorded death was that of Captain Alexander Morrow, who died on July 1, 1851.

One of the most famous poets from Kansas, Eugene Fitch Ware, is interred in Grave 1, in the Heart Section of the cemetery. As a young man, Ware served his country during the Civil War as a captain in the 7th Iowa Cavalry. Throughout the years he lived in Kansas and composed many poems, including the famous "Ironquill" and "John Brown." The site of Ware's and his wife's graves is marked by a large native sandstone boulder. Ware had noticed this particular boulder, and its natural beauty appealed to him. One of his final requests was that it be used as his grave marker.

Interred in the cemetery are 16 Indian soldiers, some of whose colorful, vividly descriptive names belie the importance of the service they rendered the United States. Stick-out-Belly, Deer-in-Water, Young Chicken, Setthem-Up, and Coming Deer were all privates in the Indian Regiments of the Union Army during the Civil War. These men were scouts for the Army, drawing upon their keen senses to aid in tracking the enemy. Their talents were of vital necessity to the Army, especially in unknown, hostile territory. Of the 16 Indian scouts, 10 were interred between November 24, 1862, and January 5, 1863. Unfortunately, history does not record the circumstances surrounding their deaths. They were originally buried at the Fort Scott Post Cemetery and later moved to the national cemetery. The 16 are:

Name	Burial Date	Section & Grave
Set-Them-Up	September 22, 1862	Sec 1 Grave 20
Stick-Out-Belly	November 24, 1862	Sec 1 Grave 8
Rich'd. Hand	December 5, 1862	Sec 1 Grave 91
Jno. Binche	December 11, 1862	Sec 1 Grave 77
Joseph Drinker (Indian Joe)	December 14, 1862	Sec 1 Grave 65
Coming Deer	December 14, 1862	Sec 1 Grave 80
Deer-In-Water	December 15, 1862	Sec 1 Grave 22
Dave	December 16, 1862	Sec 1 Grave 7
Woodward	January 5, 1863	Sec 1 Grave 89
Henry Vaun	December 3, 1863	Sec 5 Grave 433
Johnson Springston	December 14, 1863	Sec 1 Grave 214
Chas. Fleetwood	Unknown	Sec 3 Grave 344
Parhosa	March 18, 1864	Sec 1 Grave 220
Issac Ord	June 15, 1864	Sec 1 Grave 246
Young Chicken	February 6, 1865	Sec 1 Grave 175
Unknown	Unknown	Unknown

During the Civil War Fort Scott was one of the many Union internment camps for Confederate soldiers. Life in Civil War prison camps was harsh, and the conditions at Fort Scott were no different. Disease and illness were common and the mortality rate was high. Fourteen Confederate soldiers were originally interred in the post cemetery and later moved to the national cemetery. Thirteen are interred in the Confederate section and one in Section 1. They are:

Name	Unit	Burial Date
Fountain G. Bristow	Co. D, 10th Mo. Cav. Chornes' Co.	November 12, 1864
G. Springer	Unknown	February 15, 1863
Patrick Mullens	Douglass, Tex.	January 19, 1864
Joel Franklin	Unknown	March 11, 1864
J.C.M. Harris	Shank's Mo. Reg	November 4, 1864
Fay Price	Unknown	November 4, 1864
J. Teague	Unknown	November 4, 1864
Wm. Tucker	Co. A, Gordon's Mo. Reg.	November 4, 1864
Lewis Thomas	Co. C, 4th Ala. Cav.	November 5, 1864
Fountain G. Bristow	Marmaduke's Escort, Ark.	November 9, 1864
Thomas F. Wells	Co. E, 14th Mo. Cav.	November 12, 1864
Peter A.J. Embree	Co. A, Perkin's Mo. Reg.	November 17, 1864
Jos. A.W. Page	Co. A, McGehees' Ark.	November 20, 1864
Hiram Stafford	Baber's Ark. Reg.	November 22, 1864
Robert Martin	Co. D, 10th Mo. Cav. Chornes' Co.	January 23, 1865

The Fort Scott National Cemetery encompasses 21.8 acres and as of September 30, 2008, included 6217 interments.

Former cemetery superintendents/directors are:

John A. Commerford, April 1881–November 1883

Joseph F. Morrow, January 1930–February 1949 (Ret.)

Pearl O. Crawford, February 1949–March 1956

Lionel M. Rippy, March 1956–September 1956

Pearl O. Crawford, September 1956–September 1971 (Ret.)

Thomas F. Morehead, September 1971–April 1987 (Dec.)

Upon the death of Mr. Morehead in 1987, the cemetery was assigned for administration and management to the director of Leavenworth National Cemetery.

Fort Sill National Cemetery

2648 NE Jake Dunn Road
Elgin, Oklahoma 73538

Fort Sill National Cemetery lies in southwestern Oklahoma, approximately 75 miles from Oklahoma City and five miles north of Lawton. Land for the 391 acre national cemetery was transferred from the Department of the Army's Fort Sill Military Reservation in 1998. The Fort Sill National Cemetery was dedicated on November 2, 2001, and interments began on November 5. The cemetery is situated on land that was once Indian Territory. A military reservation was staked out in January 1869 by Maj. Gen. Philip H. Sheridan and was formally established as Camp Wichita the following month. Sheridan later renamed the garrison as Fort Sill in honor of fellow West Point classmate, Brigadier General Joshua W. Sill, who died in the Battle of Stones River during the Civil War. Fort Sill's mission was one of law enforcement for the expanding American frontier. The arrival of the Quohada Comanches to Fort Sill in June 1875 marked the end of Indian warfare in the south Plains.

In the 1890s, Apache Chief Geronimo and 341 other Apache prisoners of war were brought to Fort Sill by the government. Geronimo was granted permission to travel briefly with Pawnee Bill's Wild West Show and also visited President Theodore Roosevelt. Geronimo died of pneumonia at Fort Sill on February 17, 1909, at the age of 83, and is buried in the post cemetery at Fort Sill. Lt. Hugh L. Scott instructed the remaining Apache prisoners of war on how to build houses, raise crops, and herd cattle. Many of them spent the remainder of their lives at Fort Sill.

The last Native American lands in Oklahoma opened for settlement in 1901 and 29,000 homesteaders registered at Fort Sill for the land lottery during July. On August 6 of that year, the town of Lawton sprang up and quickly grew to become the third largest city in Oklahoma. As of 2005, Lawton was the fourth largest city, having fallen behind Norman in the last census. With the disappearance of the frontier, the mission of Fort Sill gradually changed from cavalry to field artillery. The first artillery battery arrived at Fort Sill in 1902 and the last cavalry regiment departed in 1907.

The School of Fire for the Field Artillery was founded at Fort Sill in 1911, and continues to operate today as the world-renowned U.S. Army Field Artillery School. At various times, Fort Sill has also served as home to the Infantry School of Musketry, the School for Aerial Observers, the Air Service Flying School, and the Army Aviation School. Today, the U.S. Army Field Artillery Center remains the only active Army installation to continuously serve the Southern Plains since the Indian Wars. (The above historical data on Fort

Sill was researched and furnished to the author by Carla Stipe Williams, cemetery director. It is included here with her permission.)

The cemetery has a Scattering Garden for scattering ashes with eligibility to place a memorial marker in the Memorial Section. A Memorial Section is designated on cemetery grounds to honor veterans and their families whose remains have never been recovered, who were buried at sea, whose bodies were donated to science, or whose ashes were scattered.

As of December 1, 2008, there have been 2,011 interments in the cemetery. Larry Williams was appointed the first cemetery director, and served from 2001 to 2004. Carla Stipe Williams succeeded him and has served from 2005 to the present time.

Fort Smith National Cemetery
522 South Garland Avenue
Fort Smith, Arkansas 72901

The Fort Smith National Cemetery is located in Sebastian County, Fort Smith, Arkansas. The cemetery is three blocks due south of the corner of Garrison Avenue and South 6th Street in the city of Fort Smith.

About 14 years after the Louisiana Purchase and 3 years after the War of 1812 ended, immigrants were arriving in the United States by the boatload, and white settlers were streaming westward to build new homes and new lives. Arkansas had been acquired by the United States as part of the Louisiana Purchase. As settlers moved into Indian lands in large numbers bitter quarrels developed between the Indians and the white men. These quarrels often led to the death of an Indian or one of the settlers. In order to maintain peace and to protect the settlers, the Army established a string of military outposts along the Mississippi River. Fort Smith was the first and most westerly of these posts.

General Andrew Jackson had returned to his plantation in Tennessee after the Battle of New Orleans in 1815, but he remained in command of the Army's Southern Division. On August 19, 1817, he issued orders through General Thomas A. Smith to Major William Bradford and Major Stephen H. Long, a topographical engineer, to descend the Mississippi River to the mouth of the Ohio River. There they met a detachment of 82 men of the rifle regiment at Philadelphia who had descended the Ohio River from Pittsburgh, and Major Bradford took command of the group. At that point, 30 of the men were sick. The command proceeded down the Mississippi and reached Arkansas Post on October 15, 1817. Arkansas Post was the first permanent white settlement in Arkansas, having grown from a camp established in 1686 by Henri de Tonti. It was located at the mouth of the Arkansas River. So many of the men were sick at this time that Major Bradford was required to remain at the post for some time. In the meantime, Major Long proceeded by skiff down the Arkansas River to the mouth of the Verdigris River, which is northeast of what is now Muskogee, Oklahoma. After observing the area, he returned to the mouth of the Poteau River. Here, on a point of land just below the confluence of the Poteau and Arkansas rivers which commanded a clear view of both rivers, he selected a site for the erection of a stockade fort. The place was known as Belle Point, a name given by French explorers because of its natural beauty.

As soon as the sick troops had sufficiently recovered to travel, Major Bradford and the detachment left Arkansas Post and proceeded up the Arkansas River to Belle Point. They arrived on Christmas Day, 1817. Here on Belle Point near a point dividing Arkansas from the Choctaw Nation, the command constructed a stockade fort sufficient for one company

Fort Smith National Cemetery.

in conformity with plans prepared by Major Long. The small fort was only about 132 feet on each side, and was never manned by more than 130 men. The garrison, always too small for its peace-keeping function, was named for Brigadier General Thomas A. Smith. Major Bradford became the first commander. In March 1821, the rifle company was discontinued and the soldiers at Fort Smith were absorbed into companies of the 7th U.S. Infantry.

In order to maintain peace and prevent hostilities between the Cherokee and the Osage, it was decided to increase the strength of the command at Fort Smith. In July 1821, Colonel Matthew Arbuckle at New Orleans was ordered to hold the 7th Infantry in readiness to occupy the southwest frontier. In November 1821, Colonel Arbuckle and companies B, C, G, and H left New Orleans, but because of low water at the mouth of the Arkansas River, they did not reach Arkansas Post until early in 1822. At Arkansas Post, Colonel Arbuckle was joined by Company K, which had been stationed at Fort Scott, Georgia. The five companies then proceeded up the Arkansas River and reached Fort Smith in February 1822. A large number of men died on this long journey. On arrival at Fort Smith, there remained only 139 officers and men of this command. On February 28 of that year, there were 235 officers and men on duty. The inspection returns indicate that 39 men were sick. The returns also show that rations were drawn for eight women, and though no names were given, it is possible that they were laundresses who in those days accompanied the troops.

On November 27, 1823, a band of 200 Osage Indians under Chief Mad Buffalo surprised and attacked a white hunting camp near the Blue River. Major Curtis Welborn of Hempstead County and four men were killed, their heads cut off, and their bodies badly mangled. This outrage produced great excitement and uneasiness among the white settlers and they banded together for defense. In Crawford County a company of cavalry was organized under Captain Frederick Fletcher, and the Miller County Militia, Ninth Regiment, under Colonel Jacob Pennington, was organized. (There is a J. Pennington interred in the national cemetery, but the records show him as a citizen, and the date of death is unknown.)

Colonel Arbuckle at Fort Smith was ordered to bring the offenders to justice. He sent Major Alexander Cummings to demand that the Osage Tribe surrender the murderers. This demand was met with considerable evasion and promises, but no action. Colonel Arbuckle recommended that should the government decide to chastise the Osage, the campaign be launched in the spring or early summer. Upon receipt of this recommendation, General Winfield Scott, in command of the Western Department at New Orleans, ordered Colonel Arbuckle, on March 8, 1824, to move his five companies from Fort Smith to a location at the mouth of the Verdigris River and take position there. This new location became Fort Gibson. The move was dictated in part, said General Scott, by the great amount of sickness among the troops at Fort Smith. Fifty men, or about 25 percent of the command, had died in 1823, with 44 of the deaths occurring during the summer months. Colonel Arbuckle received these orders on April 2, and departed from Fort Smith on April 9, 1824. Doors, windows, and all other movable equipment at Fort Smith were transported by water to Fort Gibson for use in construction of that post.

Little is known about Major William Bradford, the first commanding officer of Fort Smith, prior to 1799, except that he was born in Virginia. In 1799, his name appeared on the tax rolls of Muhlenberg County, Kentucky. He was commissioned from the state of Kentucky on March 12, 1812, as captain of the 17th Infantry. On May 5, 1813, while engaged in a battle at or near Fort Meigs, Michigan Territory, he received a gunshot wound in his left thigh. He never fully recovered from his wounds. He died at Fort Smith on October 20, 1826, of yellow fever and was buried in the little cemetery which later became part of the national cemetery.

In a newspaper article on the subject of burial grounds in Fort Smith, Mr. W.J. Weaver stated that shortly after he located in Fort Smith in 1841 he visited a burying ground on the highest point on the east bank of the Poteau River, quite a distance above the stockade built by Major Bradford in 1817. It was about 30 feet square and in a very dilapidated condition. It contained a few graves, three of which were marked by marble slabs. One of the slabs was in memory of a surgeon, and the other two marked the resting places of lieutenants. The unmarked graves were occupied by soldiers who had died in the hospital. He further stated that it is reasonable to conclude that the surgeon whose grave was marked by one of the marble slabs was Doctor Thomas Russell.

It is evident that this was the first post cemetery, and must have been established at the time of, or just prior to, the death of surgeon Thomas Russell in 1819. The northwest corner of the national cemetery contains the highest point on the east bank of the Poteau River.

After Colonel Arbuckle moved his troops to Fort Gibson in April 1824, the old stockade fort remained unoccupied until March 22, 1833.

During the early days a very sizable whiskey business had sprung up with the bulk of it being sold to the Indians and to troops stationed here. When the U.S. government took steps to stop the sale of whiskey to the Indians, Captain John Stuart and Company C of the 7th U.S. Infantry were ordered from Fort Gibson to take station at the abandoned fort. It was thought that they would be able to intercept intruders and shipments of liquor coming up the river. Captain Stuart ordered all boats traveling west of Fort Smith to dock and be inspected to assure that they were not transporting liquor to the Indians or to persons residing with them.

Within one year after the troops' return, eight soldiers and one surgeon died, in addition to six citizens on the point and a family of seven on the opposite side of the Arkansas River a total of 22 out of a population of about 100. On June 16, 1834, the troops were ordered to Swallow Rock, also known as Harold's Bluff, on the south bank of the Arkansas River about ten miles above Fort Smith. The place was named Fort Coffee in honor of General Coffee of Seminole Indian War fame. After the departure of Captain Stuart and his men the old stockade fort was abandoned and there were no troops at Fort Smith for about four years until July 27, 1838.

In 1838, Captain B.L.E. Bonneville, commanding Company F, 7th U.S. Infantry, arrived and camped about 1½ miles northeast of the old stockade fort. In July, Major Charles Thomas arrived to supervise construction of a new garrison, and took possession of the land at the head of the present Garrison Avenue. A temporary encampment was built known as Cantonment Belknap. The soldiers' quarters were log huts with mud chimneys, and an officers' log house was built across the road. General Zachary Taylor lived in this house from 1841 until 1845. In October 1838, Captain William G. Belknap, commanding Companies B and H of the 3rd U.S. Infantry arrived at the fort.

General Zachary Taylor had his headquarters at Camp Belknap when he was in command of the Department of the Southwest. From this camp he left to gain fame in the War with Mexico, which resulted later in his becoming the 12th president of the United States. It is said that here, also, Lieutenant Jefferson Davis, who subsequently became the only president of the Confederate States of America, first met his future wife, Sarah, the daughter of General Taylor. This same story, however, is told around at least four old military posts.

While he was in command of Camp Belknap, old "Rough and Ready" liked to rise early and walk down Garrison Road through the woods to wake the fishermen at the river and get a fish from his trotline, or meet a newly arrived steamboat. On this particular morning some young brevets just out of West Point saw him board the steamer upon their arrival. The young men had risen early and seeing the old gentleman, whom they took for a farmer, greeted him with, "Good morning, old fellow, how's crops?" General Taylor responded, "Purty good." They pressed him to take a drink and amused themselves at his expense for a time and as he left they sang out, "Give our love to the old woman and the gals," which he promised to do. Imagine their surprise and embarrassment when later in the day they called in full dress to pay their respects to the commanding general and found him to be their "old fellow" of the morning. General Taylor presented his wife and daughter Sarah, remarking to them, "Here are the old woman and my gal."

About a month before the arrival of Captain Bonneville, the government purchased 306 acres of land from War of 1812 veteran Captain John Rogers and his wife. This land was east of the Arkansas and Poteau rivers and south of what is now Garrison Avenue. On the northwest corner of this reservation, near the banks of the Arkansas River and slightly north and east of the location of the old stockade fort, was laid out a substantial garrison which took the name Fort Smith. The buildings in this second Fort Smith were completed about 1842, and were first occupied by Companies D and F of the 6th U.S. Infantry under the command of Captain William Hoffman. In that year the city was incorporated under the same name as the fort and became the city of Fort Thomas Smith.

The troops were withdrawn from the garrison on July 2, 1850, but the citizens of Fort Smith and the surrounding communities raised such a strong protest that the government sent soldiers to reoccupy the fort in March 1851.

When the Civil War broke out the fort was garrisoned by two troops, about 150 men, of the 1st U.S. Cavalry under the command of Captain S.D. Sturgis. On April 23, 1861, two steamers arrived at Van Buren from Little Rock carrying 300 Confederates under the command of Colonel Borland. From scouting parties Captain Sturgis learned that these troops were moving toward Fort Smith. Because of the small number of men in his command, he evacuated the fort. On that day Confederate forces occupied the garrison. In May the Arkansas legislature ceded the fort to the Confederate States of America.

After the Confederates occupied the fort, many Confederate troops began to gather there. In 1861, Colonel DeRosa Carroll was in command of the fort. Many Confederate units were organized there but it is said that they were devoid of even the slightest knowledge of military training. This deficiency was overcome, however, through the services of several men living in the town who had formerly served in the regular Army. Among the old regulars who helped train them were John Degan and John Porter.

There were no great battles fought at Fort Smith, although there was considerable bushwhacking. The principal battle in the western part of Arkansas was the first on Arkansas soil and occurred at Pea Ridge in the northern part of Benton County. During the three days of fighting, March 6–8, 1862, 500 men were killed, 900 wounded, and 600 reported missing. Another battle occurred at Prairie Grove, southwest of Fayetteville, in Washington County, in December 1862.

On September 1, 1863, Union troops under the command of Colonel W.F. Cloud, 1st Kansas Cavalry, took possession of Fort Smith.

During the period that Fort Smith was held by Confederate troops, many burials of Confederate soldiers were made in the post cemetery. There are 473 Confederates interred in the national cemetery. Included among these are two Confederate generals who were graduates of West Point and veterans of many campaigns with the United States Army prior to their change of allegiance.

General James B. McIntosh, born in Florida, participated in numerous Indian campaigns in Texas and Kansas. He was on duty as a captain at Fort Smith on May 7, 1861, when he resigned his commission and joined the Army of the Confederacy. He became a colonel of the Confederate forces and commanded the 2nd Mounted Rifles at the Battle of Oak Hill, Missouri, on August 10, 1861. In 1862 Colonel McIntosh was appointed a brigadier general and took part in the battle fought at Pea Ridge. On the second day of this engagement, General McIntosh, then only 34 years old, was killed. His remains were brought to Fort Smith for burial. He is interred in Section 3, Grave 1267. General McCulloch of the Confederate Army also lost his life in this battle.

General Alexander E. Steen, who was born in Missouri, was another Confederate general who perished during the Civil War and was interred in the post cemetery. He had served with distinction in the United States Army during the Mexican War, and was a first lieutenant in the 3rd U.S. Infantry when he resigned his commission on May 10, 1861. The *Dallas Morning News* feature section, Sunday, October 11, 1925, tells his story.

> Steen was a young Northerner living in Arkansas at the time the Civil War was declared. Immediately sympathizing with the South in its secession, Steen wrote his family that he was joining the Southern forces. His family immediately answered that if he did so he would be disowned. Steen followed his convictions however, became a Brigadier General in the Confederate Army and was on the way to a brilliant record when he was killed at the Battle of Prairie Grove in December [7] 1862.

His final resting place is Section 4, Grave 1822, at the national cemetery.

It is presumed that at some time between June 17, 1838, when Company F of the 7th U.S. Infantry arrived at Camp Belknap, and September 17, 1842, when the second Fort Smith was occupied, the original post cemetery was rehabilitated and enlarged. A short time after the Civil War, in 1867, the old post cemetery became a national cemetery. It contained 5½ acres of land and was enclosed by a sturdy whitewashed picket fence. Removal of the dead from the battlefields was carried out with reinterment in the national cemetery. At about this time many of the military dead were moved from private cemeteries in the city of Fort Smith, Van Buren and other locations. Among these was a Sergeant Heckle of the Army Ordnance Department, who died in 1848 and was entombed in an old-fashioned vault covered with a marble slab. In connection with this vault the following story comes from an old newspaper clipping:

> This vault at one time afforded the people of the town a subject for a period of exciting gossip. As the story ran, a citizen of the town had been informed by an old lady fortune teller that there was in one corner of the vault a keg of money that had been secreted there by somebody who had died after hiding it. The fortune teller and her friend went one night to investigate. They pushed a corner of the vault covering aside and reaching down discovered the object of their search. Suddenly the fortune teller's companion heard approaching footsteps. This alarmed them and they fled. Both returned a night or two afterward but the keg and its precious contents had disappeared. This incensed the fortune teller, she preached at the same time accusing her partner of having returned after her flight and made away with the treasure.

In 1871 the second Fort Smith was abandoned and the reservation turned over to the Department of the Interior. By executive order dated May 22, 1871, President U.S. Grant directed that so much of the reservation of Fort Smith as was encompassed by the national cemetery be retained for the purpose of military burials and restored to the custody of the War Department.

A simple government headstone in Section 9 of the cemetery marks the final resting place of a man whose firm beliefs in law and order earned him a notoriety which extended far beyond his immediate circle of friends and acquaintances. Isaac C. Parker was known throughout the West as the "hanging judge."

Isaac C. Parker was born in 1838 in Belmont County, Ohio, and began practicing law in 1859 in St. Joseph, Missouri. He served as a corporal in Company A of the 61st Missouri Infantry during the Civil War. After the war he became circuit judge for the Twelfth Circuit of Missouri and was elected to Congress twice, his last term expiring in 1875. In 1875 President Grant appointed Parker chief justice of the newly created Territory of Utah. Before the Senate could act on the appointment President Grant withdrew it and appointed Parker United States district judge for the Western District of Arkansas. This second appointment was promptly confirmed. At the age of 37 years, he became judge of probably the most unusual tribunal which has ever functioned in the United States. The area over which Judge Parker presided was mainly frontier territory and included the Indian Territory, now Oklahoma, an area totaling 74,000 square miles. He served for more than 21 years, during which time over 13,000 criminal cases were docketed in his court. Seventy percent, or more than 9,000, of the defendants in these cases were convicted by a jury or entered pleas of guilty. Of these, 344 were capital offenses. One hundred and fifty-one were convicted and sentenced to be hanged. Eighty-three of these were actually executed, while the sentences of the majority of the balance were commuted by the president, usually to life imprisonment. Parker's efforts brought law and order and made it possible for decent citizens to live in safety. His court broke up lawless gangs and meted out sure and swift justice to murderers, robbers and bootleggers.

On November 17, 1896, only two months after Judge Parker lost jurisdiction over the Indian Territory due to the settlers' insistence on having their own local courts, he died of Bright's disease. His doctor said his death was hastened by 21 years of overwork. Private and public business activities were suspended during the elaborate funeral and burial services. The national cemetery was too small to hold the thousands who accompanied his remains to its last resting place. The most fitting and appropriate tribute of all came when Chief Plesant Porter of the Choctaws placed upon his grave a simple garland of wildflowers.

Five of the U.S. deputy marshals who "rode" for Judge Parker, performing their jobs of bringing criminals to justice with courage and daring, are also interred in the national cemetery. These frontier law officers, who were also veterans of the Civil War were, Randolph B. Creekmore, Joseph Gramlich, James Anderson Johnson, Calvin Whitson, and Jacob Yoes.

James McCann was an officer's steward on the *USS Powhatan* and served under the alias of James Lopinto. When he died on August 16, 1928, at the age of 115 years, he was the oldest man in Arkansas. He had served 53 years with the U.S. Navy.

The city of Fort Smith is the birthplace of William O. Darby, known to many for his World War II exploits and as the organizer of the Rangers. Darby, a West Point graduate, patterned his Rangers after the British commandos. The courage and boldness of these Rangers earned Darby and themselves an enviable combat reputation for their very first campaign in Tunisia. Several battalions were added to the Ranger force and the entire organization took part in the Sicilian landings and campaign. Only five days before Germany's surrender in 1945, Colonel Darby died in Italy's Po Valley. His courageous actions and military prowess were recognized by the Army, which posthumously raised him to the rank of brigadier general. Darby's remains were returned to his birthplace, and a simple monument at Section 9, Grave 3991, bears testimony to his military accomplishments.

A number of private monuments in the national cemetery face west in the opposite direction of government furnished headstones. This is in accordance with a religious custom in some Arkansas communities to bury the dead with the feet to the east so that on Resurrection Day the body arising will face the east. The inscription is facing west as it is a belief that a person when reading the headstone would be in a proper position (facing east) to say a prayer for the deceased.

The small cemetery at Fort Smith has been expanded until today it encompasses 22.3 acres. As of September 30, 2008, there were 14,275 interments in the cemetery.

Former superintendents/directors of Fort Smith National Cemetery are:

Patrick Hart, 1867–1876
William Dillon, 1876–November 1884
Baker, November 1884–November 1885
Richard G. Bulgin, November 1885–December 1902
William Dillon, December 1902–September 1930
John W. Moss, September 1930–December 1937
Frank O. Stallings, December 1937–June 1940
Elmer E.E. Swanton, June 1940–November 1943
Thomas Swain, December 1943–July 1945
Joseph Kowalski, July 1945–September 1948
Martin T. Corley, October 1948–April 1955
Walter M. Mick, May 1955–March 1961
Duane I. Walsh, March 1961–September 1971
Mack Cochenour, Jr., September 1971–July 1974

Raymond B. Schuppert, August 1974–August 1975
James D. Simms, August 1975–March 1977
Lyle E. Norby, October 1977–November 1979
Stephen H. Jorgensen, December 1979–September 1981
Oakland A. DeMoss, 1981–1990
Candice L. Underwood, February 1990–August 1992
L. Karen Brown, August 1992–September 1996
John A. Bacon, September 1996–January 1999
John R. Smith, May 1999–March 2000
Darrell W. Lindsey, Mar 2000–February 2001
Paul H. Martin, February 2001–June 2005
Bernard A. Blizzard, June 2005–January 2008
Tommy Monk, January 2008–Present

Fort Snelling National Cemetery
7601 34th Avenue South
Minneapolis, Minnesota 55450

The cemetery is located adjacent to the St. Paul–Minneapolis Airport on 34th Avenue between Post Road and Interstate 494.

Although the national cemetery was not established until the first half of the 20th century, it is particularly appropriate that it should bear the name of the fort and military reservation that played a significant role in the development of Minnesota as a territory and a state.

A frontier post was established in 1805 near the junction of the Minnesota and Mississippi rivers, but it was not until 1820 that a permanent post, designated Fort St. Anthony, was constructed by soldiers of the 5th United States Infantry under the command of Colonel Josiah Snelling. The first official inspection of the fort was made in May or June 1824 by Brigadier General Winfield Scott, who was so impressed with conditions at Fort St. Anthony that he recommended in his report that the installation be named Fort Snelling as a "just compliment to the meritorious officer under whom it has been erected." The War Department directed that the recommended change be made on January 7, 1825.

One period in the life of Fort Snelling, that of an active post charged with keeping the peace in a frontier environment, ended in 1855 when the troops were withdrawn. However, with the onset of the Civil War, Fort Snelling was again the scene of activity as the site of an assembly ground and training camp for Minnesota volunteers preparing to defend the Union. Minnesota's governor, Alexander Ramsey, was the first state executive to offer troops to President Lincoln, and more than 22,000 men from Minnesota served in the Union Army. After the war ended, troops continued to be stationed at Fort Snelling. The military reservation post cemetery was established in 1870. During the brief Spanish-American War and later during World War I, the fort served as a troop training center. In 1947 the Fort Snelling Military Reservation was deactivated as an active military reservation. Today, nearly two centuries after it was established, Fort Snelling serves a vital pur-

Committal shelter at Fort Snelling National Cemetery.

pose as headquarters for the 88th Army Reserve Command (ARCOM) and several other components of the military reserves.

Following World War I, legislation was passed which expanded the eligibility requirements for burial in a national cemetery. This prompted the people of the St. Paul–Minneapolis area to organize a National Cemetery Committee and petition Congress for the establishment of a national cemetery in their area. Congress responded in 1936 and 1937 with legislation that authorized the Secretary of War to earmark certain land at the Fort Snelling Military Reservation for use as a national cemetery. The cemetery was established in 1939, and the first burial was made on July 5, 1939.

This first burial honored Captain George H. Mallon whose acts of heroism during the Meuse-Argonne drive of September 1918 were recognized by his being awarded the Medal of Honor. The citation notes his deeds of September 18, 1918, which resulted in the capture of 100 prisoners, 11 machine guns, four 155-millimeter howitzers and one antiaircraft gun. Captain Mallon died in 1934 and was interred in a private cemetery. His remains were reinterred in Section B DS 1-S of the new national cemetery. Captain Mallon was selected by General John J. Pershing as one of the outstanding soldiers of World War I.

Following the dedication of the new cemetery on July 14, 1939, arrangements were made for exhumation of the remains of those buried in the post cemetery and reinterment in the Fort Snelling National Cemetery. The remains of 680 soldiers who served from 1820 to 1939 were accorded burial honors in Section A, Block 23. Their graves are marked by white marble headstones, each inscribed "Unknown."

The Fort Snelling Air Force Station transferred 323.3 acres of land, 146 acres on May 6, 1960, and 177.3 on June 12, 1961, to the national cemetery, bringing it to its present size of 436.3 acres. As of September 30, 1990, there were 96,025 interments. Even though the cemetery is one of the most active in the National Cemetery System, it is projected to remain open beyond the year 2030. A single six by ten foot gravesite per family policy was implemented on May 15, 1970. Because of the frigid winters, about 1,000 graves are dug each fall to be used for interments during the winter.

Some of the drives in the cemetery are named in honor of distinguished service members. These are: Colvill, William, brigadier general, Civil War, 1st Minn. H. Artillery; Klanska, Freddric L., private, World War I, 4th Infantry, 3rd Division (killed in action October 12, 1918); LaBelle, James D., private, USMC, 5th Marine Division (killed in action March 1945, Iwo Jima); Mallon, George H., captain, World War I, American Expeditionary Force, 132nd Infantry, 33rd Division; Nelson, Oscar F., MM1C, USN, *USS Bennington*; Peck, William R., sergeant, World War I, American Expeditionary Force, Company C, 354th Infantry, 89th Division (heroism in action near Remonville, France, November 1, 1918); Peterson, Theodore, sergeant, World War I, MD, 151st FA (killed in action March 1918); Pruden, Robert J., staff sergeant, Vietnam, Company G, 75th Infantry, American Division (killed in action November 20, 1969); Rosenwald, John P., 1st lieutenant, World War I, MD, 151st FA (killed in action May 1918); and Wold, Neis, private, World War I, Company I, 138th Infantry, 35th Division (killed in action September 26, 1918).

The activities of the many volunteer groups and individuals who provide support to the national cemeteries have already been discussed, but special note must be made of the Fort Snelling Memorial Rifle Squad. This group started in June 1979 with barely enough men to form one day's squad. They now provide military honors for the funeral of every veteran whose next of kin requests it. It is a truly remarkable achievement that they have performed military honors, sometimes under the most adverse weather conditions, for over 10,000 veteran interments in Fort Snelling National Cemetery.

There are eight Medal of Honor recipients interred in the cemetery. Three of them were killed in action as indicated by daggers before their names.

Richard E. Fleming, Captain, Marine Scout–Bombing Squadron 241, U.S. Marine Corps Reserve. World War, Memorialized in Section F-1.

†Richard E. Kraus, Private First Class, USMC, World War II, Grave DS-61A.
Citation: Action with the 8th Amphibious Tractor Battalion at Peleliu, Palau Islands, on October 5, 1944. He volunteered to evacuate a wounded comrade from the front lines. As he and three companions were making their way through enemy lines they were attacked by an "intense, devastating barrage of hand grenades which caused the stretcher party to take cover." While trying to retreat to a safer position they were approached by two Japanese soldiers who threw a hand grenade into the group. Private Kraus heroically flung himself on the grenade, thereby saving the remaining members of the rescue party.

†James D. LaBelle, Private First Class, USMC, World War II, Grave B-1 422S.
Citation: Action on Iwo Jima on March 8, 1945. He was in a foxhole with two other Marines when a hand grenade landed in the midst of them. He shouted a warning and instantly dived onto the grenade, saving his fellow Marines.

George H. Mallon, Captain, USA, World War I, Grave DS 1-S. (Captain Mallon's citation is included above.)

Oscar Frederick Nelson, Machinist Mate 1C, USN, Grave DS 64-N.
Citation: Heroism during a boiler explosion on board the *USS Bennington* at San Diego, California, on July 21, 1905.

Arlo Olson, Captain, 15th Infantry, 3rd Infantry Division, U.S. Army. Place and Date: Crossing of the Volturno River, Italy, 31 August 1944. Section C-24, Grave 13787.

†Robert J. Pruden, Staff Sergeant, USA, Vietnam, Grave M-5710.
Citation: Action in Quang Ngai Province, Republic of Vietnam on November 29, 1969. As reconnaissance team leader during an enemy ambush from two units, SSgt. Pruden left his concealed position to attack the enemy, drawing hostile fire. Although wounded twice, he drove off the enemy, directed his men into defensive positions and called for evacuation helicopters which safely withdrew the reconnaissance team at the cost of Sgt. Pruden's life.

Robert Keith Sorenson, First Lieutenant, USMC. Place and Date: Namur Island, Kwajalein Atoll, Marshall Islands, 1–2 February 1944. Section B, Grave 149–1.

Former superintendents/directors of the cemetery are:

Harvey A. Olsen, June 1938–August 1948
John A. Boender, July 1948–January 1950
Oscar P. Findley, January 1950–December 1950
Ralph R. Dea, January 1951–June 1962
Martin T. Corley, July 1962–January 1964
Donald L. Garrison, January 1964–November 1966

James M. Griffin, November 1966–March 1970
Wilborn D. Burdeshaw, June 1970–June 1980
Howard J. Ferguson, July 1980–November 1983
William D. Napton, December 1984–1995
Steve Muro, 1995–1998
Robert McCollum, 1998–2005
William A. Owensby, Jr., 2005–2007

Georgia National Cemetery
2025 Mount Carmel Church Lane
Canton, Georgia 30114

This 775 acre cemetery is located in western Cherokee County, Georgia, about eight miles west of Canton on Georgia Highway 20. The entrance is just across the Knox Bridge over the Etowah River.

The property for the cemetery was donated in 2001 by Scott Hudgens, an Atlanta World War II veteran, land developer, and philanthropist. It lies along the Etowah River and from many areas in the cemetery, one can see beautiful views of the Blue Ridge Mountains and Lake Allatoona. It has been determined that about one-half of the land is too steep for interments. The cemetery is surrounded by large horse farms and country estates.

The Georgia National Cemetery is located near the site of the Etowah burial mounds created by American Indians of the Mississippian culture between A.D. 1000 and 1550. This site is one of the largest Indian burial mounds in North America, and archaeological studies have been conducted on these mounds for over 100 years.

The cemetery was opened for burials on April 24, 2006, and formally dedicated on June 4, 2006. As of September 30, 2008, there have been 2,154 interments.

In March 2003, Sandra Beckley was appointed the first Director of the cemetery. She had previously served as Director of the Barrancas National Cemetery. In October 2007, Mrs. Beckley was reassigned to oversee the development and opening of the Sarasota National Cemetery in Florida. Deborah L. Kendrick succeeded her as Director. Brian Moore was appointed Director in September 2007, and serves currently.

Gerald B. H. Solomon National Cemetery
200 Duett Road
Schuylerville, New York 12871-1721

The Gerald B. H. Solomon National Cemetery was established in July 1999. The 351 acre cemetery lies along the Champlain Canal Trail, and is famous for its military Route used by Native Americans during pre-colonial times, and the colonists during the French and Indian War and the American Revolution. At full capacity, the cemetery can provide burial space for 175,500 veterans and their eligible dependents. There have been 7,832 interments in the cemetery through September 30, 2008.

President George W. Bush signed legislation on January 24, 2002, changing the name of the Saratoga National Cemetery to its present name. Congressman Solomon was widely known as a strong advocate of veterans' programs. He spearheaded the effort to elevate the Veterans Administration to the Cabinet-level, Department of Veterans Affairs, and successfully led the drive to establish this cemetery. Congressman Gerald Brook Hunt Solomon was interred in Section 20, Site 7, on October 31, 2001. A pyramid black-mist granite memorial honoring Congressman Solomon was erected in 2002.

The ship's bell from the USS *Saratoga*, CV-3, was installed as a memorial in 1999.

There are three Medal of Honor recipients interred here.

†**Thomas A. Baker,** Sec. 8, Site 530. Sergeant, U.S. Army, Company A, 105th Infantry, 27th Infantry Division. Place and Date: At Saipan, Mariana Islands, June 19 to July 7, 1944.
Citation: "For conspicuous gallantry and intrepidity at the risk of his life above and beyond the call of duty...."

†**Peter J Dalessandro,** Sec. G12, Site 1. Technical Sergeant, U.S. Army, Company #, 39th Infantry, 9th Division. Place and Date: Near Kalterherberg, Germany, December 22, 1944.
Citation: "The gallantry and intrepidity shown by T/Sgt. Dalessandro against an overwhelming enemy attack saved his company from a complete rout."

Raymond R. Wright, Sec. 7, Site 1035. Specialist Fourth Class, Company A, 3rd Battalion, 60th Infantry, 9th Infantry Division. Place and Date: In the Ap Bac Zone, Vietnam, May 2, 1967.
Citation: For conspicuous gallantry and intrepidity ... while serving as a Rifleman with Co. A,

Sp4c Wright distinguished himself during a combat patrol in an area where an enemy attack had occurred earlier…. Sp4c Wright's extraordinary heroism, courage, and indomitable fighting spirit saved the lives of many of his comrades and inflicted serious damage on the enemy."

Former directors of the cemetery are:

Roseann Santore April 2005–March 2007
Dan Cassidy November 2007–Present

Glendale National Cemetery
8301 Willis Church Road
Richmond, Virginia 23231

The cemetery is situated in Henrico County, Virginia, 13 miles southeast of Richmond, on state Highway No. 156.

The existence of Glendale National Cemetery reflects another aspect of General McClellan's "on to Richmond" campaign of 1862. Strategic retreat back to the James River and the protection of Union gunboats now became the objective of the Army, whose balloon crews had sighted the spires of Richmond churches only a few short weeks before.

Bitter and hotly contested rear guard actions at Savage Station, White Oak Swamp, and Glendale (Frayer's Farm) marked McClellan's retreat from Richmond, culminating in the final battle of the Seven Days campaign at Malvern Hill on July 1, 1862. There McClellan's superior and well-placed artillery forces were able to withstand General Lee's bold attacks, and on July 2 the Union forces moved down the James River to Harrison's Landing. McClellan's Peninsula Campaign failed, and Richmond, capital of the Confederacy, was saved but only at a frightful cost to both sides. During the Seven Days campaign, Union forces numbering some 91,000 men suffered losses of 1,734 killed, 8,062 wounded, and 6,053 missing. The Confederate forces, numbering 85,000 men, lost 3,478 killed, 16,261 wounded, and 875 missing as the Seven Days campaign concluded.

The country in this vicinity is truly historical ground. The Battle of Nelson's Farm, on June 30, 1862, was fought on ground in the immediate area of the Glendale National Cemetery, and the battle of Malvern Hill, on July 1, was fought within two miles of the cemetery.

The cemetery was established on May 7, 1866, but the 2.1 acres of land were not purchased until June 16, 1869. The land was purchased from Lucy C. Nelson. The cemetery name is taken from the farm on this property, used as a Union headquarters during the Civil War. Original interments were the remains of Union soldiers recovered from Malvern Hill, Frayers Farm, Harrison's Landing, and other areas in the vicinity. The inspector of national cemeteries reported on July 26, 1871, that a total of 1,189 interments, including 236 known and 953 unknown, had been made in the cemetery. As of September 30, 2008, the total number of interments was 2,074. The cemetery is closed for interments except for second interments in existing graves under the single gravesite per family policy.

There is one Medal of Honor recipient interred in the cemetery. He was killed in action.

†**Michael Fleming Folland,** Sec H, Grave 846. Corporal, U.S. Army, Company D, 2d Battalion, 3d Infantry, 199th Infantry Brigade. Place and date: Long Khanh, Providence, Republic of Vietnam, 3 July 1969.
Citation: For conspicuous gallantry and intrepidity at the risk of his life above and beyond the call of duty. Corporal Folland distinguished himself while serving as an ammunition bearer with the weapons platoon of Company D, during a reconnaissance patrol mission. As the patrol was moving through a dense jungle area, it was caught in an intense crossfire from heavily fortified

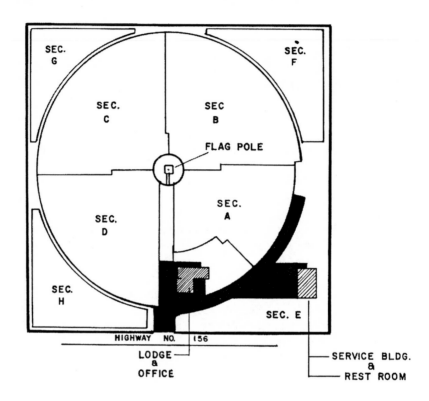

Map of the Glendale National Cemetery, Richmond, Va., October 1969.

and concealed enemy ambush positions. As the patrol reacted to neutralize the ambush, it became evident that the heavy weapons could not be used in the cramped fighting area. Corporal Folland dropped his recoilless rifle ammunition and ran forward to join his commander in an assault on the enemy bunkers. The assaulting force moved forward until it was pinned down directly in front of the heavily fortified bunkers by machine gun fire. Corporal Folland stood up to draw enemy fire on himself and to place suppressive fire on the enemy position while his commander attempted to destroy the machine gun positions with grenades. Before the officer could throw a grenade, an enemy grenade landed in the position. Corporal Folland alerted his comrades and the commander hurled the grenade from the position. When a second grenade landed in the position, Corporal Folland again shouted a warning to his fellow soldiers. Seeing that no one could reach the grenade and realizing that it was about to explode, Corporal Folland, with complete disregard for his safety, threw himself on the grenade. By his dauntless courage, Corporal Folland saved the lives of his comrades although he was mortally wounded by the explosion. Corporal Folland's extraordinary heroism, at the cost of his life, was in keeping with the highest traditions of the military service and reflects great credit upon himself, his unit, and the U.S. Army.

Former superintendents/directors of the cemetery are:

Amos J. Potter, Unknown–1871
Edwin G. Ragsdale, August 1944–September 1950

James E. Wolstenholme, September 1960– February 1964
William E. Norton, February 1964–April 1965

John J. Hackett, November 1950–October 1952   Leland W. Potter, Sr., April 1965–1978
Wallace W. Myers, November 1952–August 1960

Glendale National Cemetery is assigned to the director of Richmond National Cemetery for administration and management.

Golden Gate National Cemetery
1300 Sneath Lane
San Bruno, California 94066

The cemetery is located in San Mateo County, at the corner of Junipero Serra Boulevard (Interstate 280) and Sneath Lane. San Bruno is about 12 miles south of the San Francisco city limits.

In the days when the Spanish Empire spread up the western coast of North America, the Golden Gate National Cemetery site was known as the Rancho Buriburi. The Rancho land grants in Spanish California were made to disabled veterans to encourage colonization of the New World. Land grants, such as the Rancho Buriburi, were often made by the Mexican governors to their supporters in order to dissolve the extensive mission holdings of the time. This property later became part of the Sneath Ranch until purchased by the U.S. government.

The cemetery was authorized by Congress in 1937, shortly after San Franciscans voted to remove cemeteries from the city proper. Exempt from that order were the ancient cemetery of the Mission Delores, the final resting place of many of the early padres who brought European civilization to the area, and the San Francisco National Cemetery, located on federal property at the Presidio of San Francisco.

The 161.55-acre tract was purchased by the War Department in 1938, and its official

Golden Gate National Cemetery.

name was conferred upon it the following year. It was John C. Fremont, an early and dedicated proponent of California entry into the United States, who first named the San Francisco Bay area the Golden Gate.

The first interment in the new cemetery, in 1941, was Leroy Crosley, private, Company B, 4th Infantry. Formal dedication ceremonies were held on Memorial Day 1942, with Earl Warren, then attorney general of California and later chief justice of the United States Supreme Court, as the dedication speaker.

The Golden Gate National Cemetery was established prior to the United States' entry into World War II because the San Francisco National Cemetery, which had served the area since 1884, would soon be filled. As the deceased from the Pacific theater of World War II began to fill the cemetery, it became apparent that the original planning and projections for this cemetery to serve until the year 2000 would have to be revised. The impact of World War II, the Korean War, and Vietnam resulted in increased interments which could not have been predicted in the mid–1930s.

In the 1950s the Army found on two occasions that proposals to expand the cemetery lacked the support of influential local officials. Funds appropriated in 1951 to purchase about 120 contiguous acres north of the cemetery could not be obligated because of local opposition. The funds reverted to the treasury. In 1958, the Navy declared 55 acres of government-owned land adjoining the cemetery surplus to its needs. The Army began an investigation to see if 30 of these acres might be transferred to expand the cemetery. The city of San Bruno, the local chamber of commerce, and even the United Veterans Coordinating Committee of San Mateo County joined in opposing the project. They informed the Army that the land was the last open area within the county into which San Bruno could expand and that all official bodies preferred to have the land used for tax-producing purposes. All plans to expand Golden Gate were terminated in 1959.

These hallowed grounds serve as the final resting place for one of America's most valiant naval officers, Fleet Admiral Chester W. Nimitz. Admiral Nimitz was named commander-in-chief, U.S. Pacific Fleet, after the surprise attack on Pearl Harbor. It fell to him hold back the Japanese advance with limited resources at his command until the nation's war effort could pro vide the men and materiel needed to go on the offensive. Not only did Nimitz have to deter this immediate threat to the United States, but he also bore the burden of retaining strategic access to Australia and New Zealand.

It was from the aircraft carrier *USS Hornet* that Colonel Jimmy Doolittle took off one morning in April 1942 to lead the first air attack on the Japanese homeland. The Battle of the Coral Sea, in May 1942, forced the Japanese to end their effort to cut the Australian lifeline. The trap laid by Admiral Nimitz and his staff at Midway in June 1942 has been called one of the most decisive battles in naval history. It was the first major defeat for the Japanese in three and one-half centuries, and stopped their advance after only six months.

Admiral Nimitz was promoted to the five-star rank of fleet admiral in December 1944. At the war's end, he was aboard the *USS Missouri* in Tokyo Bay when the Japanese signed the surrender documents. He was awarded two Distinguished Service medals and two Gold Stars in lieu of two more medals. After the war, he served as chief of naval operations, and later as plebiscite administrator for the United Nations during the clash between India and Pakistan over Kashmir.

On February 24, 1966, on what would have been his 81st birthday, Admiral Nimitz was given his nation's final salute when he was interred in Section C. It is interesting to note that Chester Nimitz went to the U.S. Naval Academy because he could not get an appointment to West Point and that he became "frightfully seasick" on his first voyage.

Three distinguished Navy officers who served with Fleet Admiral Nimitz and shared the tremendous responsibilities of command and strategy in the Pacific are also interred in Section C. Admiral Richard K. Turner, commander of the amphibious forces, died on February 7, 1961, and is interred in Grave 7. Vice Admiral Charles A. Lockwood, commander of submarines, died on June 6, 1967, and is interred in Grave 5. Admiral Raymond A. Spruance, close friend of his commanding officer, died December 13, 1969, and is interred in Grave 3.

There are 44 German and Italian prisoners of war buried here. These Axis soldiers were captured in North Africa after the collapse of Rommel's Afrika Korps in 1943. Buried originally at Camp Beale, near Marysville; Camp Cook, near Santa Maria; and Camp Rupert, Idaho, they were reinterred here when those posts were closed.

One of the unusual features of the cemetery is the large mound near the front entrance. The flagpole stands in the midst of a grey granite structure which rests on top of the cemetery reservoir.

There are 15 Medal of Honor recipients interred in the cemetery. Daggers appear before the names of men who were killed in action.

Name	Rank	Service	War/Place/Date of Action	Section & Grave
Edward A. Bennet	CPL	USA	WWII	2-B-1071-A
Vito R. Bertoldo	SGT	USA	WWII	C-52-A
John Joseph Clausey	CGM	USN	*USS Bennington*	C-121-B
John O. Dahlgren	CPL	USMC	Boxer	Z-1950
John Francis DeSwan	PVT	USA	Sp.-Amer.	R-195-A
Mosheim Feaster	PVT	USA	Indian	O-319
†Paul H. Foster	SGT	USMC	Vietnam	V-4764
Edward H. Gibson	SGT	USA	Phil.	L-5-7791
†Harold Gonsalves	PFC	USMC	WWII	B-61
Nelson M. Holderman	CAPT	USA	WWI	R-17
William R. Huber	MecM	USN	1926	2-B-4085
†Reinhardt J. Keppler	BM1C	USN	WWII	C-379
Hugh Patrick Mullin	Seaman	USN	1899	A-2-294
†Stuart S. Stryker	PFC	USA	WWII	B-719
†Robert H. Young	PFC	USA	Korea	O-8

Golden Gate National Cemetery was closed for interments on June 7, 1967, except for those in reserved gravesites and second interments in existing graves. Garden niches were established in 1982 for the burial of cremated remains. As of September 30, 2008, there were 139,037 interments.

Former superintendents/directors of the cemetery are:

Warren L. Pierson, May 1941–November 1943
Elmer E.E. Swanton, November 1943–August 1944
Thomas O. Moore, September 1944–September 1945
Anthony J. Nettke, September 1945–April 1961
Robert H. Schmidt, May 1961–September 1963
Joseph V. Darby, January 1964–November 1964
John T. Spelman, December 1964–August 1976
Mack Cochenour, Jr., August 1976–November 1977
Henry A. Hartwig, December 1977–June 1979
John C. Metzler, Jr., July 1979–July 1980
Charles R. Weeks, July 1980–February 1982

William D. Napton, February 1982–January 1984
Milo Hayden, February 1985–June 1985
Dennis E. Kuehl, July 1985–January 1990
Cynthia Nunez, January 1990–1996
Gloria Gamez, 1996–1999
Steve Muro, 1999–2001
James Fitzgerald, 2001–2003
James Metcalfe II, 2003–2006
Ronald Wondolowski, 2006–Present (Dir., Field Opns.)
Kathleen McCall, 2006–Present (Dir. Admin. Opns.)

Grafton National Cemetery
421 Walnut Street
Grafton, West Virginia 26354

The cemetery is located in Taylor County in West Grafton.

Acting under orders from the War Department in 1867, Major R.C. Bates searched for a site to concentrate the Union soldiers who had died in various hospitals and battlefields in West Virginia. He apparently chose the Grafton site because it was relatively level, although the entire area appears to be mountainous country. It was located near the Maple Avenue Cemetery, where many war dead had already been buried, the Beech Street military hospital, and the Parkersburgh branch of the Baltimore and Ohio Railroad, which would provide transportation for the remains to be brought here.

The 3.21 acre site was appropriated in 1867, condemned in 1871, and finally purchased from the heirs of James A. Yates in 1874. The steep slope of the land was graded into three terraces with a walkway down the center which divides the cemetery into two equal parts. Initial interments were made on the lower two terraces. The report of the inspector of national cemeteries dated June 16, 1871, states that 1,252 Union soldiers, 639 known and 613 unknown, had been interred in the cemetery. The unknown remains are marked with six-inch square markers, but records in the cemetery office list the state from which each decedent came. The remains reinterred in 1867 and 1868 included 68 from the Maple Avenue Cemetery.

Approximately half of the original interments came from Clarksburg. Other remains were brought from Wheeling, Rich Mountain, and other places in the state mostly in the counties of Fayette, Kanawha, Marion and Grant and some from Kentucky. The dead represented 24 states, including 12 soldiers of the famous Volunteer Regiment of the Army who dressed like the Zouaves, a French infantry unit noted for its dash and bravery.

In 1903, relatives of Thornesberry Bailey Brown gave their permission for his remains to be disinterred from a private cemetery and reinterred in Grafton National Cemetery. He is said to be the first Union casualty of the Civil War. He was killed on May 22, 1861, near a B & O railroad bridge in the village of Fetterman, allegedly by a Confederate sentry named Daniel Knight, when Brown and his companion refused the sentry's order to halt. The story goes that Brown then shot the sentry in the ear, and Knight responded by shooting Brown through the heart with his musket. He is interred on the first terrace, and a special monument marks his gravesite.

Grafton is probably the site of the oldest continuing Memorial Day parade and program in the United States. The first parade and service was scheduled for May 30, 1868, but heavy rains postponed the event until June 14. It has been held each Memorial Day since then. The parade starts in downtown Grafton with schoolchildren, bands, veterans' organizations, military units, patriotic groups, and public officials marching through town and out to the national cemetery where the Memorial Day services are held.

The cemetery was closed in fiscal year 1961 except for interments in reserved gravesites or second interments in existing graves. As of September 30, 2008, there were a total of 2,155 interments. The cemetery is managed by the director of West Virginia National Cemetery.

Former superintendents/directors of the cemetery are:

James B. Martin, January 1923–March 1924
Marion B. Coffee, February 1927–November 1937
James M. Griffin, July 1946–January 1948

Thomas M. Cathcart, Jr., August 1963–July 1965
Wilborn D. Burdeshaw, August 1965–August 1969

Terraced banks of Grafton National Cemetery.

Aaron C. Gordon, January 1948–November 1949
John A. Boender, January 1950–April 1959
Roland E. Lex, April 1959–July 1963

Charles R. Weeks, September 1969–July 1973
Earl R. White, July 1973–February 1975
James L. Turner, Unknown

Some years ago an elderly lady who lived in a house with a clear view of the cemetery related the story that on warm summer evenings, just about dark, she often saw a couple strolling arm in arm through the cemetery. The man was fully dressed in his officer's uniform, and his lady was wearing an antebellum dress with a large hat. No one else has ever reported witnessing the evening stroll through the cemetery.

Great Lakes National Cemetery
4200 Belford Road
Holly, Michigan 48442

The 544 acre Great Lakes National Cemetery will serve veterans' needs for an estimated 50 years. Holly is located about 45 miles northwest of Detroit on Interstate 75 at exit 108. The ground-breaking and consecration ceremony was held on October 14, 2004, and interments began on October 17, 2005. Through September 30, 2008, there have been 5,406 interments. Richard C. (Rick) Anderson has served as director of the cemetery from April 2004.

The Department of Veterans Affairs purchased the land from the Egan Lake Development Corporation in 2002. The previous owners, the Horton family, had owned the property for over 160 years.

Hampton National Cemetery
Cemetery Road at Marshall Avenue
Hampton, Virginia 23669

Hampton National Cemetery occupies 27.1 acres in Elizabeth City County in Hampton, Virginia. Hampton is an independent city and includes the town of Phoebus and all of Elizabeth City County.

With the outbreak of the Civil War, signified by the fall of Fort Sumter on April 13, 1861, the area in the vicinity of Hampton, Norfolk, and Fort Monroe held special significance to both the Union and Confederate forces. The broad expanse of Hampton Roads was the scene of an historic naval battle on March 9, 1862, between two ironclad ships, the Confederate *Merrimac* and the Union *Monitor*. The Union forces had sunk the steam frigate *Merrimac* when they evacuated Norfolk. The Confederates promptly raised the ship, armored her with iron plate and a cast-iron ram, and renamed the vessel *Virginia*. On March 8, the *Virginia* rammed and sank the *USS Cumberland* and destroyed the *USS Congress*. The *Monitor* was the first of a new type of ironclad ship ordered early in the war by the Union Secretary of the Navy. It was designed and built by John Ericsson. Its hull was only a few inches above the water, but the ship had great mobility and a new type of central revolving gun turret. Neither ship did much damage to the other, and after several hours of fighting with only one casualty, both ships retired. While the battle itself has been exaggerated, it did mark a trend in the naval war, and the Union maintained supremacy on the water and was able to continue its blockade of Southern ports.

The inevitable toll of sick and wounded during the war necessitated the establishment of many military hospitals. One such hospital was at Fort Monroe, which had a capacity of 1,800 beds. Even though this hospital was better organized and staffed than some other Civil War hospitals, there was still a high mortality rate among those committed to its care. Land set aside as a burying ground for this hospital became the nucleus for the present-day Hampton National Cemetery.

An article in *Harper's New Monthly Magazine* for August 1864 describes in some detail the procedure followed for the burial of those who died in the Hampton Military Hospital. The dead were accorded reverent burial in wooden coffins, with the name, company, and date of death painted on both the inside and outside of the coffin lid. Each grave was marked by a wooden headboard similarly marked. All burials from the hospital were accorded suitable military honors with the firing of a volley of musketry over the grave at the conclusion of the burial service.

The original 11.61 acres of cemetery land were condemned and purchased in 1868. The land was already being used for burials, having been established as a national cemetery in 1866. In addition to interments of the deceased from the military hospital and from Fort Monroe, remains were brought to the cemetery from Big Bethel, Newport News, Jamestown, Craney Island, Deep Creek, Norfolk, Portsmouth, Blackwater, Smithfield, Suffolk, and Cherry Stone, Virginia.

The first superintendent, appointed August 6, 1867, was James Browning. He was a discharged principal musician of the Fifth Regiment of Artillery. Brevet Major General Lorenzo Thomas, inspector of national cemeteries, noted in his report of November 29, 1868, that Superintendent Browning was attentive to his duties and had the cemetery in good order. The report dated August 2, 1871, also noted that the cemetery was in "very good order." Interments at the time of the 1871 report were:

	Known	*Unknown*
Commissioned officers	25	0
White Union soldiers	3,519	402
White Union sailors	66	6
Colored Union soldiers	985	57
Women, children, etc.	83	0
Total	4,678	465

The care and attention to details incidental to burials from the Hampton Military Hospital no doubt accounted for the relatively small number of unknowns. Today, there is a total of 638 unknowns buried here, most of them Civil War soldiers who fell in combat and were given hasty burial on the battlefield.

There are 272 Confederate soldiers buried here in a separate section. The remains of those who died prior to the Civil War while stationed at Fort Monroe and were interred in the post cemetery were disinterred and brought here in 1891.

During the years following the Civil War additional legislation concerning national cemeteries was enacted, increasing the number eligible for interment. By 1891, the number of interments necessitated additional land for burial. In that year an eight-acre site at Phoebus, about three-fourths mile northeast of the original cemetery, was purchased. Further purchases of land at Phoebus were made in 1894 and in 1934.

In 1868, a memorial to Union soldiers known as the Soldiers Monument was erected in the cemetery. The monument is a roughhewn granite obelisk some 65 feet high, bearing the inscription, "In Memory of Union Soldiers Who Died to Maintain the Laws." Funds for the monument were raised by public subscription. The success of this campaign was attributed in large part to the efforts of Miss Dorothea Lynde Dix, superintendent of women nurses for the Union Army during the Civil War. Her work in the wartime hospitals was but one phase of a lifelong career devoted to humanitarian causes. Her continuing and strenuous campaigns, dating from 1841, for better treatment of paupers, prisoners, and the insane, brought about much needed and long overdue legislation for the relief and treatment of these persons.

Hampton National Cemetery is one of 13 national cemeteries in which World War II prisoners of war are interred. There are 55 German and 5 Italian POWs interred in the Phoebus Addition. On April 15, 1942, a full military honors funeral was held for the interment of 29 crew members of a German submarine sunk by an American destroyer on Atlantic patrol. The bodies and a few life jackets were all that surfaced after the submarine was sunk. Both Protestant and Catholic rites were performed at the service.

Among the honored dead who rest in these hallowed grounds are eight men who were awarded the Medal of Honor. A dagger before one name indicates that the recipient was killed in action.

Michael Cassidy, Sec B, Grave 9503. Landsman, U.S. Navy. G.O. No.: 45, 31 December 1864.
Citation: Served aboard the *USS Lackawanna* during successful attacks against Fort Morgan, rebel gunboats and the ram *Tennessee*, in Mobile Bay, 5 August 1864. Displaying great coolness and exemplary behavior as first sponger of a gun, Cassidy, by his coolness under fire, received the applause of his officers and the gun crew throughout the action which resulted in the capture of the prize ram *Tennessee* and in the destruction of batteries at Fort Morgan.

John Davis, Sec C, Grave 8534. Ordinary Seaman, U.S. Navy. G.O. No.: 326, 18 October 1884.
Citation: Onboard the *USS Trenton*, Toulon, France, February 1881. Jumping overboard, Davis rescued Augustus Ohlensen, coxswain, from drowning.

James R. Garrison, Sec B, Grave 9523. Coal Heaver, U.S. Navy. G.O. No.: 45, 31 December 1864.
Citation: Onboard the flagship, *USS Hartford*, during successful engagements against Fort Mor-

Hampton National Cemetery

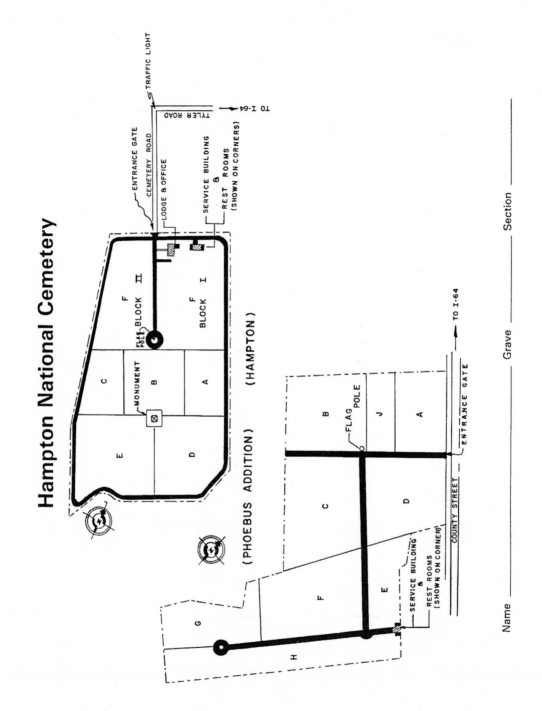

gan, rebel gunboats and the ram *Tennessee* in Mobile Bay, on 5 August 1864. When a shell struck his foot and severed one of his toes, Garrison remained at his station at the shell whip and, after crudely bandaging the wound, continued to perform his duties until severely wounded by another shellburst.

Alfred B. Hilton, Sec E, Grave 1231. Sergeant, Company H, 4th U.S. Colored Troops. Place and date: At Chapins Farm, Va., 29 September 1864.
Citation: When the regimental color bearer fell, this soldier seized the color and carried it forward, together with the national standard, until disabled at the enemy's inner line.

Harry J. Mandy, Sec B, Grave 8709. First Sergeant, Company B, 4th New York Cavalry. Place and date: At Front Royal, Va., 15 August 1864.
Citation: Capture of flag of 3d Virginia Infantry (C.S.A.).

†Ruppert Leon Sargent, Sec F, Grave 17596. First Lieutenant, U.S. Army, Company B, 4th Battalion, 9th Infantry, 25th Infantry Division. Place and date: Hau Nghia Province, Republic of Vietnam, 15 March 1967.
Citation: For conspicuous gallantry and intrepidity in action at the risk of his life above and beyond the call of duty. While leading a platoon of Company B, 1st Lt. Sargent was investigating a reported Viet Cong meetinghouse and weapons cache. A tunnel entrance which 1st Lt. Sargent observed was boobytrapped. He tried to destroy the boobytrap and blow the cover from the tunnel using hand grenades, but this attempt was not successful. He and his demolition man moved in to destroy the boobytrap and cover which flushed from the tunnel a Viet Cong soldier, who was immediately killed by the nearby platoon sergeant. First Lieutenant Sargent, the platoon sergeant, and a forward observer moved toward the tunnel entrance. As they approached, another Viet Cong emerged and threw two hand grenades that landed in the midst of the group. First Lieutenant Sargent fired three shots at the enemy then turned and unhesitatingly threw himself over the two grenades. He was mortally wounded, and his two companions were lightly wounded when the grenades exploded. By his courageous and selfless act of exceptional heroism, he saved the lives of the platoon sergeant and forward observer and prevented the injury or death of several other nearby comrades.

Charles Veal, Sec F, Grave 5097. Private, Company D, 4th U.S. Colored Troops. Place and date: At Chapins Farm, Va., 29 September 1864.
Citation: Seized the national colors, after two color bearers had been shot down close to the enemy's works, and bore them through the remainder of the battle.

David Warren, Sec C, Grave 7972. Coxswain, U.S. Navy. G.O. No.: 45, 31 December 1864.
Citation: Served as coxswain onboard the *USS Monticello* during the reconnaissance of the harbor and water defenses of Wilmington, N.C., 23–25 June 1864. Taking part in a reconnaissance of enemy defenses which lasted two days and nights, Warren courageously carried out his duties during this action which resulted in the capture of a mail carrier and mail, the cutting of a telegraph wire, and the capture of a large group of prisoners. Although in immediate danger from the enemy, Warren showed gallantry and coolness throughout this action, which resulted in the gaining of much vital information of the rebel defenses.

As of September 30, 2008, there were 28,003 interments in the cemetery. The cemetery is closed to new interments except for burial in the same gravesite as a previously interred family member.
Former superintendents/directors are:

James Browning, August 1867–Unknown
Robert R. Dye, 1905–1910
Herbert Rhodes, August 1939–August 1940
John S. Sargent, August 1940–May 1948
Oscar P. Findley, June 1948–November 1949
Aaron C. Gordon, December 1949–September 1960
Samuel H. Davis, Jr., September 1960–February 1964
William F. Spivey, February 1964–September 1965

Rudolph Staude, September 1965–December 1968
Harold A. Johnson, December 1968–September 1974
John T. Dowd, November 1974–September 1983
Bruce E. Dombkowski, December 1983–December 1985
Homer D. Hardamon, March 1986–December 2007
Ronald M. Hestdalen, December 2007–Present (Acting)

Hampton National Cemetery (VAC)
Veterans Administration Center
Hampton, Virginia 23667

This small parcel of land, a total of 0.3 acre, is located on the grounds of the Veterans Administration Center. It is the smallest of the national cemeteries, and the only one that has no connection whatsoever with the mission of the National Cemetery System.

The cemetery was established in 1898 on the hospital grounds as an emergency measure during a yellow fever epidemic which occurred on the station. A rigid quarantine was clamped on the station no one could enter and no one could leave. The cemetery was established for the sole purpose of burying those who died at the hospital during this epidemic, whether from the fever or from other causes. No interments were made before the epidemic and none have been made since the quarantine was lifted. There were 22 interments made in this plot while the quarantine was in effect.

The cemetery was transferred to the National Cemetery System in September 1973, when the system was transferred from the Department of the Army to the Veterans Administration (VA). This was one of the 21 VA cemeteries on medical center grounds that were combined with the 83 National cemeteries to form the VA National Cemetery System. It is under the jurisdiction of the director of Hampton National Cemetery.

Hot Springs National Cemetery
Department of Veterans Affairs Center
Hot Springs, South Dakota 57747

The cemetery is situated in Fall River County on the northeast edge of the city of Hot Springs. From the north on U.S. Highway 385, it appears as a green oasis, with the symmetrical white markers making a beautiful scene.

A National Home for Disabled Volunteer Soldiers was approved for Hot Springs in 1902. Construction was completed in 1907. It was originally named the Battle Mountain Sanitarium after a mountain peak that was once in the reservation area, but has since been given to the state as a recreation site. This area was the site of numerous engagements with Indians. The mountain looks down upon the cemetery at its base. The home was established to take advantage of the numerous warm springs of the area. The cemetery was established for the interment of veterans who died while residents of the home. The first interment, on May 4, 1907, was Civil War veteran Elijah F. Williams, Company A, 1st New Jersey Volunteer Infantry. The home became part of the Veterans Administration (VA) in 1930, and in 1973, the cemetery became one of the 21 VA cemeteries transferred to the National Cemetery System.

An obelisk approximately 32 feet high and 40 feet around the base, bearing the inscriptions "National Home, Disabled Volunteer Soldiers, Battle Mountain Sanitarium, 1914" and "In Memory of the Men Who Offered Their Lives in the Defense of Their Country," is situated on the southeast corner of the cemetery at its highest elevation.

There is one Medal of Honor recipient interred in Hot Springs National Cemetery.

Charles L. Russell, Sec 3–12, Grave R1. Corporal, Company H, 93rd New York Infantry. Place and date: Spotsylvania, Va., May 12, 1864.
Citation: Capture of flag of 42nd Virginia Infantry (C.S.A.).

There have been no interments in the cemetery since 1964, when the cemetery was closed. It is maintained by the Department of Veterans Affairs Medical Center. The cemetery is managed by the Director of the Black Hills National Cemetery. As of September 30, 2008, there were 1,484 interments.

Houston National Cemetery
10410 Veterans Memorial Drive
Houston, Texas 77038

The cemetery is situated in Harris County, 15 miles northwest of the downtown area of Houston, and 2 miles west of Interstate 45. The street on which the cemetery is located was originally named Stuebner-Airline Highway. The name was officially changed to Veterans Memorial Drive at the Veterans Day ceremony held November 11, 1985.

The establishment of the Houston Veterans Administration Cemetery resulted largely through the efforts of U.S. Representative Albert Thomas. The growth of the Houston area, the emergence of Houston as a major center for medical treatment, and the rapidly increasing veteran population brought clamors for the construction of a veterans cemetery. The Department of the Army had taken a position of nonexpansion of the National Cemetery System, leaving Congress to decide where and when any new cemeteries would be built.

On May 2, 1963, the Veterans Administration (VA) purchased a 419.2-acre tract of land for a VA cemetery. The first 50-acre development was opened and dedicated on Tuesday, December 7, 1965, the 24th anniversary of the Japanese attack on Pearl Harbor. Jeff F. Evans, private first class, U.S. Army, a veteran of World War II who was awarded several military citations for battles from New Guinea to the liberation of the Philippines, was interred in the cemetery on November 9, 1965.

The initial construction included over four miles of circular and winding roadways and a unique structure called a hemicycle. The hemicycle is the most prominent structure in the cemetery, and the only one of its kind in the National Cemetery System. Shaped like a horseshoe, it has a chapel with a 75-foot bell tower at the center of 2 sweeping arches which enclose a courtyard where 3,000 spectators can be comfortably seated for ceremonies. At the base of the bell tower is a raised platform where ceremonies sponsored by the local veterans organizations are held. The two arches were constructed with upper walkways which serve as a cover for the ground-level walkways. The chapel features mosaic cut glass windows that display the designs of the official seals of the Armed Services and the Veterans Administration. A bas-relief portraying two men carrying a fallen comrade is situated above the chapel entrance.

Less than three months after he had seen the new cemetery dedicated, Congressman Albert Thomas, 2nd lieutenant, U.S. Army, World War I, was buried in the mall area of the cemetery. He had served almost 30 years in the U.S. House of Representatives. He died in Washington, D.C., on February 16, 1966, and was interred on February 18.

One of the largest and finest carillon bell sets in the world was installed in the side rooms of the chapel, and the beautiful music is amplified through an organ console within the chapel and through bell-shaped speakers outside in the bell tower. The set has 330 hand-cast bells, with sufficient power and amplification to be heard for several miles. The volume has been adjusted and the sound confined to the cemetery area. The funds to purchase this carillon were raised through the combined efforts of the All Veterans Memorial Carillon Committee, chaired by Lieutenant General Stuart Haynsworth, USAF Reserve, and composed of the commanders and leaders of all local veterans, military, military-oriented organizations and their auxiliaries. The set was presented to the cemetery at the Memorial Day service on May 30, 1970.

Major John Gordon, USAF Reserve, was buried on September 6, 1990. Major Gordon was one of the pilots of a C-5 cargo plane that crashed on August 29 at Ramstein Air Base in West Germany, killing nine of its crew of 17. The reservists were flying round-the-clock missions in the deployment of troops and supplies to Saudi Arabia in support of Operation Desert Shield.

The Houston VA Cemetery was one of the 21 transferred to the National Cemetery System in 1973 by the VA, and was designated the Houston National Cemetery. The director of the VA cemetery, William F. Spivey, had resigned as superintendent of a national cemetery in August 1965 to become director here. With the cemetery's transfer he came back into the system, and remained at the Houston National Cemetery until his retirement in June 1986. Ronald R. Pemberton succeeded him as director.

The lawn area between the outer extremity of the hemicycle and the circular roadway was landscaped with shrubs and trees adapted to this area. A portion of this area was designated as a Medal of Honor section by John W. Mahan, director of the National Cemetery System.

The remains of the two Medal of Honor recipients interred in the cemetery were relocated to this area in 1976. The remains of a third Medal of Honor recipient were relocated to the cemetery on April 25, 1992.

James H. Fields, Sec. H-B-6. 1st Lieutenant, U.S. Army, 10th Armored Infantry, 4th Armored Division. Place and date: At Rechicourt, France, on 27 September 1944.
Citation: During sharp action with the enemy infantry and tank forces, 1st Lt. Fields personally led his platoon in a counterattack on the enemy position. Seeing that one of his men had been wounded, he left his slit trench and with complete disregard for his safety, administered first aid to the wounded man. While returning to his slit trench he was seriously wounded by a shell burst,

Hemicycle at Houston National Cemetery.

the fragments of which cut through his face and head, tearing his teeth, gums, and nasal passage. Although rendered speechless by his wounds, he refused to be evacuated and continued to lead his platoon by the use of hand signals. When two enemy machine guns had a portion of his unit under deadly crossfire, he left his hole, wounded as he was, ran to a light machine gun, picked it up and fired from his hip with such deadly accuracy that the enemy gun positions were silenced. Only when his objective had been taken and the enemy scattered did 1st Lt. Fields consent to be evacuated to the battalion command post. At this point he refused to move farther back until he had explained to his battalion commander by drawing on paper the position of his men and the position of the enemy forces. First Lieutenant Fields died on June 17, 1970.

Marcario Garcia, Sec. H-A-1. Staff Sergeant, U.S. Army, Company B, 22nd Infantry, 4th Infantry Division.
Citation: While acting as a squad leader on 27 November 1944 near Grosshau, Germany, he singlehandedly assaulted two enemy machine gun emplacements. Although painfully wounded, he fought on with his unit until the objective was taken, and only then did he permit himself to be removed for medical care. Staff Sergeant Garcia died on December 24, 1972.

Raymond L Wright, Sec. H-B-11. First Lieutenant, U.S. Army Air Corps. Place and Date: Northern Po Valley, Italy, April 25, 1945.

As of September 30, 2008, there were 67,793 interments in Houston National Cemetery.

Indiantown Gap National Cemetery
Box 187
Annville, Pennsylvania 17003

The cemetery is situated on the southern portion of Fort Indiantown Gap, about 16 miles northeast of Harrisburg, Pennsylvania, on Interstate 81.

Indiantown Gap draws its name from the many Indian communities that flourished here in bygone days. The first inhabitants of the area were the Susquehannocks, an Iroquois tribe first encountered by white men early in the 17th century. During the years of the French and Indian War, the Indian allies of the French colonists raided many of the frontier settlements. The section from Manada Gap to Swatara Gap, now the site of Indiantown Gap, was fiercely attacked. As a defense measure, the pioneers built many forts and blockhouses in the Indiantown Gap area.

The 1930s were active years for this site. The Pennsylvania National Guard first held cavalry exercises here and later decided to acquire the land for training purposes. The area was designated a National Guard campsite in 1940. During World War II the Gap, as it was commonly known, was one of the nation's most important military camps. It was a staging area for the New York Port of Embarkation for many units prior to going overseas, and at the end of the war, a separation center for troops returning from Europe. In September 1946, Indiantown Gap was deactivated as a federal base.

The post returned to active status in February 1951, when the 5th Infantry Division and the headquarters of the Pennsylvania Military District became tenants. The 5th Division stayed at the Gap only two years carrying out its mission to train replacements for assignment to Korea. The military district became the Army's representative with the added responsibility of maintenance of the post and support of the reserve training. In 1957, when most military districts were abolished, an Army Corps headquarters here supervised and administered the Army Reserve program in several surrounding states.

From 1962 to 1973 Indiantown Gap was the host installation for the largest Reserve

Administration Building, Indiantown Gap National Cemetery.

Officers Training Corps advanced summer camp nationwide. During this 11-year period 41,158 cadets completed training and 4,931 were commissioned as second lieutenants. To add prestige to the reserve components, the Army, and the community, the Secretary of the Army designated the post as Fort Indiantown Gap on May 1, 1975. At this time the fort became a camp for Southeast Asian refugees. During the next 8 months, 22,027 Vietnamese and Cambodian refugees were resettled through the fort. Today, Fort Indiantown Gap covers over 18,000 acres and is a major training site for reserve components. It is occupied by the United States Army Garrison and the Pennsylvania Department of Military Affairs.

In 1976, a section of Fort Indiantown Gap was selected as the regional national cemetery for Standard Federal Region III, which serves the states of Delaware, Maryland, New Jersey, Virginia and West Virginia. The 677-acre site was donated to the Veterans Administration by the commonwealth of Pennsylvania.

Dedication of the cemetery was scheduled for September 19, 1982, until Robert Stone, national commander of the Jewish War Veterans, complained to Administrator Robert Nimmo that the 19th was a holy day and no Jewish veterans would attend. Nimmo agreed to his objection and cancelled the 4,000 invitations and arrangements with the military and other organizations. The ceremony was held later.

The first interment, on September 20, 1982, was that of Brigadier General Allen J. Stevens, U.S. Army National Guard (Retired). The body of the former Pennsylvania state representative in Philadelphia and community leader from Carlisle was removed from a mausoleum in central Pennsylvania. His widow said that her husband had indicated a desire to be buried in the national cemetery when it opened.

Spanish-American War veteran Walter Pleate was interred on December 9, 1985. He served in the Army from 1899 to 1902, and when he died at age 109, he was the nation's oldest veteran.

The main feature of the cemetery is the administration building. This unique design is intended to represent an old barn that may have burned or fallen apart. The walls are constructed of native stone quarried from the mountains north of the cemetery. The stone silo adjacent to the administration building is actually an observation tower and is capped with a transparent dome. A spiral staircase rises to the observation deck.

As of September 30, 2008, there were 31,929 interments. Charles R. Weeks was appointed the first director of the cemetery and served from February 1982 until January 1985. He was succeeded by Dennis P. Gura. In 1990, Willie Crosby was appointed director when Gura was assigned to open a new national cemetery in California.

Jacksonville National Cemetery
4083 Lannie Road
Jacksonville, Florida 32218

The new Jacksonville National Cemetery will cover 569 acres when it is fully developed. It is located on Lannie Road north of the Jacksonville Airport, about five miles from Intestate 295.

When the Phase 1 development of 62 acres is completed, there will be 7,500 full casket gravesites, including 7,200 pre-placed crypts, 5,000 cremation sites, and 4,500 columbarium niches.

The cemetery was dedicated on September 21, 2007, and the first interments were seven simultaneous interments on January 7, 2009. The Consecration service was held on January 5, 2009, with 14 religious faith traditions participating The cemetery will provide interment space for an estimated 189,000, veterans and dependents in the northeastern area of Florida and southeastern Georgia.

Arleen Ocasio De La Rosa-Vincenty was appointed in January 2008 to be the first Cemetery Director. She is the first Hispanic-American woman to be named to oversee the opening of a new cemetery. She came to Jacksonville National Cemetery after serving as Director of the Puerto Rico National Cemetery.

Jefferson Barracks National Cemetery
101 Memorial Drive
St. Louis, Missouri

Jefferson Barracks National Cemetery, 11 miles south of St. Louis, Missouri, was established by Congress during the Civil War as a military burial ground for Union dead. Since then, this beautiful site overlooking the Mississippi River has memorialized the final resting places of heroic dead of all the nation's wars, from the Civil War forward.

Following the Louisiana Purchase in 1803, which expanded the territory of the United States from the Mississippi River to the Rocky Mountains and from the Gulf of Mexico to the Canadian border, the federal government moved to establish a permanent military base near the confluence of the Missouri and Mississippi rivers. This new military post was needed to replace Fort Bellefontaine on the Missouri which had become unhealthy because of disease and flooding, and was unsatisfactory as a military garrison. The site of the new post was selected in 1826, and land for the military reservation was purchased from various citizens of the village of Corondelet. On October 23, 1826, orders were issued to name the new post Jefferson Barracks in honor of President Thomas Jefferson, who died six days before the post was occupied. It was during his term in office that the Louisiana Purchase

Jefferson Barracks National Cemetery, 1933.

was made. As was the custom at that time, a plot of 29 acres was set aside for the burial of military and civilian personnel who died at the garrison.

During the years prior to the Civil War, Jefferson Barracks served as a distribution point for troops and munitions destined for isolated posts scattered throughout the frontier. At various times it was the duty station for many officers of the U.S. Army who were destined to become bitter enemies in the War between the States. Lieutenant Jefferson Davis first came to Jefferson Barracks in 1828 after graduation from West Point. In 1832 he returned with the captured Indian Chief Black Hawk as his prisoner. He later became president of the Confederate States of America. West Point graduate Second Lieutenant Ulysses S. Grant was stationed here in 1843. He later commanded the Union Army that defeated the Confederacy. Another West Pointer, Colonel Robert E. Lee, assumed command of Jefferson Barracks in 1855. Colonel Lee resigned his commission in the United States Army and was named a general in the Confederate forces. He surrendered to General Grant at Appomattox Court House on April 9, 1865, to end the Civil War.

Military activities in and about Missouri during the Civil War reflected its position as a border state with conflicting loyalties among its citizenry, with frequent skirmishes throughout the state between Union and Confederate forces. Many hospitals were established around St. Louis to care for the sick and wounded in the area as well as from other Southern battlefields. By 1863, the post cemetery at Jefferson Barracks, originally intended only for the garrison's dead, had to be enlarged to provide burial places for Union soldiers.

The first burial in the Jefferson Barracks post cemetery is believed to be Eliza Ann Lash, the infant child of an officer stationed at the garrison. She was interred on August 5,

1827. Union soldiers originally buried at Cape Girardeau, Pilot Knob, Warsaw, Rolla, and other places in Missouri were reinterred in the national cemetery. This original section of the cemetery contains the remains of 12,000 Union soldiers of the Civil War and 1,140 members of the Confederate Army.

The cemetery at Jefferson Barracks became a national cemetery in 1866 by authority of a joint resolution of Congress whereby the Secretary of War was authorized and required "to take immediate measures to preserve from desecration the graves of soldiers of the United States who fell in battle or died of disease ... so that the resting place of the honored dead may be kept sacred forever." During the years immediately following cessation of hostilities, the efforts of Quartermaster Corps search and recovery teams brought the remains of many Union soldiers initially buried in various locations throughout the state to the cemetery for reinterment. Additional reinterments were made from the Wesleyan and Christ Church cemeteries in St. Louis.

Identification of the thousands of remains recovered after the war was extremely difficult. Many were identified as soldiers only by bits of blue uniform and other small clues. They were buried in the cemetery as unknowns. Included among these Union unknowns are the remains of 470 soldiers that were brought to the national cemetery in 1876 from Arsenal Island in the Mississippi River. This island, known during the war days as Smallpox Island, was the site of the military contagious disease hospital. The 470 who died there were victims of smallpox. During the years following the war, river floods washed away the wooden headboards in the hospital cemetery with the result that when remains were disinterred for removal to the national cemetery, individual identification was impossible.

There are three Revolutionary War veterans interred in the cemetery.

Richard Gentry (Section OPS-2, Grave 2093A) was born in the Colony of Virginia on September 26, 1763. A private in the Continental Army at the age of 17, he was present at the capture of Lord Cornwallis at the Battle of Yorktown on October 19, 1781. After the Revolution he moved westward, fighting in the various Indian wars. He died on February 12, 1843, near Richmond, Kentucky, and was buried in a private cemetery. His remains were reinterred in the national cemetery on June 20, 1958.

Thomas Hunt (Section OPS-1, Grave 2289C) was born in the Colony of Massachusetts. He was a sergeant in Captain Croft's Company of Minutemen at the Battle of Lexington and Concord in April 1775. He enlisted in a Massachusetts Regiment from May to December 1775. On January 1, 1776, he became a member of the 25th Continental Infantry. He transferred to Jackson's Continental Regiment as a captain on February 1, 1777. At the Battle of Stoneypoint on July 16, 1779, he was wounded. On January 1, 1781, he transferred to the 9th Massachusetts Regiment and was wounded again at the Battle of Yorktown on October 14, 1781. After the Revolution he remained in the Army. He transferred to the 3rd Massachusetts Regiment on January 1, 1783, and returned to Jackson's Continental Regiment in November 1783. He became a captain in the 2nd U.S. Infantry on March 4, 1791, and was promoted to the rank of major on February 18, 1793. He was reassigned to the 1st U.S. Infantry on November 1, 1793, was promoted to lieutenant colonel on April 1, 1802, and to colonel on April 11, 1803. He died on August 18, 1808, and was buried at Fort Bellefontaine. His remains were removed to Jefferson Barracks National Cemetery in April 1904.

Russell Bissell (Section OPS-1, Grave 2289B) was born in the Colony of Connecticut. He was a lieutenant in the 2nd Infantry from March 4, 1791, to the end of the Revolutionary War. He was promoted to captain on February 19, 1793. He transferred to the 1st U.S. Infantry on April 1, 1802, and was promoted to major upon his transfer to the 2nd U.S.

Infantry on December 9, 1807. He was commanding officer at Fort Bellefontaine when he died on December 18, 1807. His remains were removed to Jefferson Barracks National Cemetery in April 1904.

Major Aeneas Mackey (Section OPS-1, Grave 2287B), was a veteran of the War of 1812, the Indian wars, and the Mexican War.

The infant son of Colonel Zebulon Pike is buried in Section OPS-1, Grave 2288E.

The early growth of the cemetery was most rapid in 1869 when the remains of 10,217 Union soldiers, recovered from isolated burial grounds scattered throughout the Missouri area, were placed at rest at Jefferson Barracks. Records indicate that 13,174 Civil War casualties are buried in this national shrine.

The 1,140 Confederate dead interred in sections 19, 20, 22, 66, and 67 include 824 soldiers, 161 civilians, one female civilian, 116 not classified as either soldier or civilian, one gunboat man and one conscript. The lone female is Mrs. Jane N. Foster from Randolph County, Arkansas. She died on November 4, 1864, and is interred in Section 20, Grave 4613. John Lyden (Section 22, Grave 5257) was a fireman on the gunboat *Star of the West*. John Murraim (Section 20, Grave 4655) was a conscript. Records from that time indicate that he probably was a soldier detained to gunboat service. Interred in Section 21, Grave 4841, is Samuel Marion Dennis. He was a founder of Sigma Alpha Epsilon fraternity at the University of Arkansas.

In graves 4605–10, Section 20, are six Confederate prisoners of war executed by the Union Army to avenge the death of Major James Wilson (Section 39, Grave 4319) and a six-man patrol massacred by Confederate guerrillas under the command of Major Tim Reeves during the Battle of Pilot Knob on October 3, 1864.

The second period of rapid growth came after World War II. Because of the central location of the cemetery in the United States, Jefferson Barracks is a major burial place for group interments resulting from national disasters or for large groups of remains that cannot be individually identified for separate burials. Included among these decedents are 564 group burials, consisting of the remains of two or more servicemen interred in a common grave. The largest single group burial consists of 123 victims of a massacre of prisoners of war by the Japanese in December, 1944, on Palawan Island in the Philippines. This burial is in Section 85, graves 14–20, 25–31, 40–46, and 60–66. On July 23, 1968, 41 remains in 8 caskets were interred. Remains in the burial were from a U.S. Marine CH-53A Sea Stallion helicopter which crashed on January 8, 1968, in the Dong Nagi mountains northeast of Hue Phu Bai, South Vietnam, killing all 46 persons aboard (44 American servicemen and 2 civilians). Five remains were positively identified and individual services were held for them.

The other group burials are in sections 78, 79, 81, 82, 84, 85, and B. Seven World War II prisoners of war are buried in Section 57½. Two are German and five are Italian.

Three men are interred here who were identified by DNA testing and relocated to Jefferson Barracks:

First Lieutenant Michael Joseph Blassie was interred in Arlington National Cemetery's Tomb of the Unknown Soldier from May 28, 1984 to May 14, 1998. He was interred in Sec. 85, Grave 1.

Sergeant Robert N. Lincoln, a turret gunner on a B-17G Flying Fortress, shot down near Furth, Germany, on September 13, 1944. His remains were identified and returned for interment in Sec 84, Grave 193, on June 20, 2000.

Second Lieutenant Sherman J. Andrews, Navigator/Bombardier on a B-24 J Bomber, lost over France December 11, 1944. His remains were identified and returned for interment in Sec 86, Grave 12A on September 10, 2001.

Eight men buried at Jefferson Barracks were awarded the Medal of Honor. Their names and citations are listed below. A dagger appears before the name of each man who was killed in action.

Lorenzo D. Immell, Sec 4, Grave 12342. Corporal, Company F, 2nd U.S. Artillery. Place and date: At Wilsons Creek, Mo., 10 August 1861.
Citation: Bravery in action.

Martin Schubert, Sec 4, Grave 12310. Private, Company E, 26th New York Infantry. Place and date: At Fredericksburg, Va., 13 December 1862.
Citation: Relinquished a furlough granted for wounds and entered the battle, where he picked up the colors after several bearers were killed or wounded, and carried them until himself again wounded.

Alonzo Stokes, Sec 63, Grave 11450. First Sergeant, Company H, 6th U.S. Cavalry. Place and date: At Wichita River, Tex., 12 July 1870.
Citation: Gallantry in action.

David Ryan. Sec 59, Grave 11715. Private, Company G, 5th U.S. Infantry. Place and date: At Cedar Creek, etc., Mont., 21 October 1876.
Citation: Gallantry in action.

†**Ralph Cheli** (1 of 21 in group burial, Sec 78, graves 930–34). Major, U.S. Army Air Corps. Place and date: Near Wewak, New Guinea, 18 August 1943.
Citation: For conspicuous gallantry and intrepidity above and beyond the call of duty in action with the enemy. While Maj. Cheli was leading his squadron in a dive to attack the heavily defended Dagua Airdrome, intercepting enemy aircraft centered their fire on his plane, causing it to burst into flames while still two miles from the objective. His speed would have enabled him to gain the necessary altitude to parachute to safety, but this action would have resulted in his formation becoming disorganized and exposed to the enemy. Although a crash was inevitable, he courageously elected to continue leading the attack in his blazing plane. From a minimum altitude, the squadron made a devastating bombing and strafing attack on the target. The mission completed, Maj. Cheli instructed his wingman to lead the formation and crashed into the sea.

George Hobday, Sec. 59, Grave 1890. Private, Company A, 7th U.S. Calvary (Indian Campaigns). Place and Date: Wounded Knee, S.D., 29 December 1890.

†**Donald D. Puckett** (1 of 6 in group burial, Sec 84, graves 270–72). First Lieutenant, U.S. Army Air Corps, 98th Bombardment Group. Place and date: Ploesti Raid, Rumania, 9 July 1944.
Citation: Took part in a highly effective attack against vital oil installation in Ploesti, Rumania, on 9 July 1944. Just after "bombs away," the plane received heavy and direct hits from antiaircraft fire. One crew member was instantly killed and six others severely wounded. The airplane was badly damaged, two were knocked out, the control cables cut, the oxygen system on fire, and the bomb bay flooded with gas and hydraulic fluid. Regaining control of his crippled plane, 1st Lt. Pucket turned its direction over to the copilot. He calmed the crew, administered first aid, and surveyed the damage. Finding the bomb bay doors jammed, he used the hand crank to open them to allow the gas to escape. He jettisoned all guns and equipment but the plane continued to lose altitude rapidly. Realizing that it would be impossible to reach friendly territory he ordered the crew to abandon ship. Three of the crew, uncontrollable from fright or shock, would not leave. First Lieutenant Pucket urged the others to jump. Ignoring their entreaties to follow, he refused to abandon the three hysterical men and was last seen fighting to regain control of the plane. A few moments later the flaming bomber crashed on a mountainside. First Lieutenant Pucket, unhesitatingly and with supreme sacrifice, gave his life in his courageous attempt to save the lives of three others.

†**Bruce Avery Van Voorhis**, (1 of 6 in group burial, Sec 79, graves 279–81). Lieutenant Commander, U.S. Navy.
Citation: For conspicuous gallantry and intrepidity at the risk of his life above and beyond the call of duty as squadron commander of Bombing Squadron 102 and as plane commander of a PB4Y-1 patrol bomber operating against the enemy on Japanese-held Greenwich Island during the battle of the Solomon Islands, 6 July 1943. Fully aware of the limited chance of surviving an urgent

mission, voluntarily undertaken to prevent a surprise Japanese attack against our forces, Lt. Cmdr. Van Voorhis took off in total darkness on a perilous 700-mile flight without escort or support. Successful in reaching his objective despite treacherous and varying winds, low visibility and difficult terrain, he fought a lone but relentless battle under fierce antiaircraft fire and overwhelming aerial opposition. Forced lower and lower by pursuing planes, he coolly persisted in his mission of destruction. Abandoning all chance of a safe return he executed six bold ground-level attacks to demolish the enemy's vital radio station, installations, antiaircraft guns, and crews with bombs and machinegun fire, and to destroy one fighter plane in the air and three on the water. Caught in his own bomb blast, sacrificing himself in a singlehanded fight against almost insuperable odds, he made a distinctive contribution to the continued offensive in driving the Japanese from the Solomons and, by his superb daring, courage and resoluteness of purpose, enhanced the finest traditions of the U.S. Naval Service. He gallantly gave his life for his country.

Within the Jefferson Barracks National Cemetery are located a number of commemorative monuments placed to honor specific groups of individuals. A bronze female figure was erected by the state of Minnesota in 1922, in memory of 164 soldiers from that state who lost their lives in the Civil War. This is located at Longstreet and Monument Drive.

A large red granite boulder was donated by the St. Louis chapter of the Daughters of the American Revolution in November 1904 to commemorate the burial place of the unknown officers and soldiers who died while in camp between 1806 and 1826 at Fort Bellefontaine. The boulder is located in Old Post Section 1.

A monument honors the memory of 175 non-commissioned officers and privates of AG 56 U.S. Colored Troops Infantry who died of cholera in August 1866. The monument and remains were removed from Quarantine Station, Missouri, by authority of the War Department cooperating with a citizens committee. It was dedicated in May 1939.

A memorial to the Unknown Dead 1861–1865, dedicated by the Annie Whittermeyer Tent No. 3, Daughters of Veterans, USA, can be found in Section 14. A water fountain donated by the 35th Division Association in 1952 is located on Monument Drive. Finally, a Confederate monument, donated by the Sons of the Confederate Veterans and dedicated on May 1, 1988, is located in Section 62.

In 1970 the Korean and Vietnam Gold Star Mothers and Fathers sought a perpetual living memorial to remember the sons and daughters who paid the supreme sacrifice in defense of the principles in which they believed. As a result of their efforts, a memorial chapel was dedicated on April 30, 1974, to all veterans. The Jefferson Barracks Chapel Association, a volunteer group, has contributed to the chapel a 60 by 8 foot stained glass skylight en titled "The History of Man," 20 venetian nave windows, and a 30 by 10 foot laminated glass panel.

As of September 30, 2008, a total of 172,254 interments had been made in Jefferson Barracks National Cemetery, including 3,255 unknown decedents.

Former superintendents/directors of the cemetery are:

Harrison C. Magoon, Unknown–1905
Clarence E. Otis, June 1940–April 1947
Andrew K. Hill, April 1947–June 1949
Louis B. Hellmeyer, June 1949–February 1951
Frank A. Lockwood, February 1951–June 1953
Eugene B. Taylor, June 1953–November 1954 (Ret.)
Joseph V. Darby, December 1954–February 1958
Martin T. Corley, March 1958–July 1962
James M. Griffin, July 1962–February 1964
Samuel H. Davis, February 1964–December 1964

Walter N. Mick, February 1965–April 1967 (Dec.)
William J. Boyer, June 1967–September 1979 (Ret.)
Ronald F. Houska, September 1979–July 1984
Delles Atchinson, 1984–1989
Ralph E. Church, 1989–1990
Larry Williams, 1990–2008
Jeff S. Barnes, 2008–Present

Jefferson City National Cemetery

1024 East McCarty Street
Jefferson City, Missouri 65101

Jefferson City National Cemetery is situated in Cole County within the city limits of Jefferson City, Missouri. The 2.01-acre site, enclosed by a stone wall, lies about 1 mile southeast of the state capitol.

This cemetery was apparently established during the summer of 1861, as there are records of burials as early as that time. The purpose was evidently for the burial of soldiers engaged in the Civil War, principally from militia organizations from Missouri, Iowa and Illinois. It appears that approximately 350 interments had been made before the cemetery was designated a national cemetery in 1867. The precise date that the cemetery was designated a national cemetery is not known; nor is it known whether it was operated by municipal or private interests. The entire plot now occupied by the cemetery was sold to the government by Israel B. and Mary A. Read on December 7, 1867.

Old records from the archives files state that the land was surveyed and fenced in for a U.S. cemetery during the Civil War under the direction of Adj. Pound of the Regular Army of the United States, who was the commanding officer in Jefferson City. After the cemetery was established, remains were brought here from Boonville, Brunswick, Georgetown, Glasgow, Ledalin, Otterville, Sedalia, Smithton, and Warrensburg. The report of the inspector of national cemeteries dated May 26, 1871, states, "No labor has been hired this year, or last, the prison authorities having sent convicts to help the superintendent whenever he asked for assistance." There are three Confederate prisoners of war buried in the cemetery.

On September 27, 1864, a guerrilla force under William Anderson burned a train and

Jefferson City National Cemetery, Facing Rostrum.

killed 17 Union soldiers and several civilians who were passengers. Many of the soldiers had been wounded and were returning home to recover. Later that day Major A.V.E. Johnston followed Anderson and his men to their camp where a bloody battle ensued. Johnston's forces were routed and he was killed. In 1873 their remains were removed to Jefferson City National Cemetery. Anderson was killed less than one month later by Federal forces commanded by Assistant Lieutenant Colonel Samuel P. Cox.

A special monument was erected about 1868 in memory of the 118 members of companies A, G and H, 39th Regiment, Missouri Infantry Volunteers, who were killed in action at Centralia, Missouri, September 27, 1864. The names of those killed are inscribed on the monument. When the remains were brought to the cemetery, the monument was placed at the foot of the trench in which they were interred.

As of September 30, 2008, there were 1,802 interments. The cemetery is closed except for interments in reserved gravesites and second interments in existing graves.

Former superintendents/directors of the cemetery are:

John M. Jones, 1918–December 1923
D.R. Wilcox, December 1923–November 1924
John A. Bebber, November 1924–March 1926
Wm. S. Snyder, March 1926–July 1927
Vivian Bell, July 1927–December 1928
James Wilson, December 1928–January 1930
John M. Jones, January 1930–October 1932
Ernest Hippe, November 1933–Unknown

John A. Myers, Unknown–November 1939
Leon P. Leonard, December 1939–May 1940
Walter M. Gardner, November 1945–January 1967
Ray C. Van Tassell, March 1967–August 1968
Rudolph A. Lujan, August 1968–June 1970
Raymond B. Schuppert, July 1970–August 1974

The cemetery is maintained by private contract, supervised by the director of Jefferson Barracks National Cemetery.

Keokuk National Cemetery
1701 "J" Street
Keokuk, Iowa 52632

This cemetery was originally part of the city-owned Oakland Cemetery, and was known as the Soldiers' Burial Ground. It occupied an area of 2.75 acres which was donated to the United States by the city of Keokuk. Subsequent donations and purchases have increased the area to 22.7 acres. As of September 30, 2008, a total of 4,924 interments had been made in the cemetery.

Although Keokuk National Cemetery is far removed from the battlefields of the Civil War, its history exemplifies in some measure the impact of that war upon the area in which it is located. The location of Keokuk at the confluence of the Des Moines and Mississippi rivers afforded facilities for transportation of the produce of Iowa farms so necessary for the war's execution. Many young men from Iowa farms and villages passed through Keokuk en route down the "Father of Waters" to the battlefields of the South.

The first Civil War camp in Iowa was Camp Ellsworth, established near Keokuk in May 1861. It was here on May 14, 1861, that members of the First Iowa Volunteer Infantry were mustered into service. Camps Rankin, Halleck, and Lincoln were also established in 1861 and 1862. The Third Regiment of the Iowa Volunteer Infantry was mustered into service in June 1861. Between August 30 and September 14, the Third Regiment Iowa Volunteer Cavalry was formed. In 1862 the 17th and 19th regiments Iowa Volunteer Infantries were organized at Keokuk.

As the war progressed casualty lists of the sick and wounded brought a more somber aspect to the war effort activities at Keokuk. Five Army general hospitals, capable of accommodating more than 1,500 sick and wounded soldiers, were established to care for casualties brought up the Mississippi River from the battlefields of the South. Original interments were the dead from these hospitals. The report of the inspector of national cemeteries dated April 25, 1871, lists only a total of 627 burials 600 known white Union soldiers and 27 unknown white Union soldiers. The report does not include the remains of eight Confederate soldiers who died in the military hospitals while they were prisoners of war and were buried in the national cemetery. A cemetery lodge was constructed in 1870, and though not in use, it still stands today. Clayton Hart was appointed the first superintendent in May 1870. The first interment in the national cemetery was Private Pat Sullivan, 9th Iowa, whose marker bears a date of October 16, 1861.

In 1908, subsequent to abandonment of the post cemetery at Fort Yates, North Dakota, 73 remains were brought to Keokuk for reinterment. An account in *The Daily Constitution Democrat* (Keokuk) of Friday, November 13, 1908, describes in some detail the reverent tribute paid by the citizens of Keokuk as the flag-draped boxes containing the remains were escorted to the national cemetery by members of the Grand Army of the Republic, Spanish American War veterans, members of the Daughters of the American Revolution and the Sons of the American Revolution, and city dignitaries. The following tribute by Miss Mary C. Collins, who had been an Indian missionary and preacher at Fort Yates, fittingly eulogized the services of those who had served in the frontier outpost at Fort Yates:

> We are prone to think of soldiers only as brave when they have been drawn up in battle line before an enemy and have been killed in the heat of battle. Have any of you soldiers here ever been stationed on a frontier post, with nothing but the wheezing little steamer coming once a month with new troops or hardtack or coffee to relieve the monotony? There is no excitement, there is nothing to make the blood run hot. These men died on a frontier post, poor homesick boys and men grown gray, serving in silence on the frontier. Some of them were veterans of the Civil War; others have died in service on the frontier. They have all died in the service of their country.

In 1948, 156 remains were disinterred from the post cemetery at Des Moines, Iowa, and reinterred in the national cemetery. Subsequent to World War II, 15 group burials of 74 remains were interred here.

In 1912, the Women's Corps of Keokuk erected a monument to 48 unknown soldiers of the Civil War. This monument is a large granite shaft surmounted by the figure of a Confederate soldier standing at parade rest. The date when the American War Dads and Auxiliaries of Iowa erected a bronze wreath "Dedicated to the Unknown Soldier" is not known.

Another interesting historical monument in the cemetery is a copper and glass case containing the cornerstone of the Estes House Hospital, the largest of the Keokuk military hospitals maintained during the Civil War. When the building was razed in 1929, the cornerstone was removed and brought to the cemetery in memory of those who died in the hospital.

The only known Medal of Honor recipient interred in the Keokuk National Cemetery is John F. Thorson. He was killed in action.

†**Thorson, John F.**, Sec D, Grave 71. Private First Class, U.S. Army, Company G, 17th Infantry, 7th Infantry Division. Place and date: Dagami, Leyte, Philippine Islands, 28 October 1944.

Citation: He was an automatic rifleman on 28 October 1944, in the attack on Dagami, Leyte, Philippine Islands. A heavily fortified enemy position consisting of pill boxes and supporting trenches held up the advance of his company. His platoon was ordered to out-flank and neutralize the strong point. Voluntarily moving well out in front of his group, Pvt. Thorson came upon an enemy fire trench defended by several hostile riflemen and, disregarding the intense fire directed at him, attacked single handed. He was seriously wounded and fell about six yards from the trench.

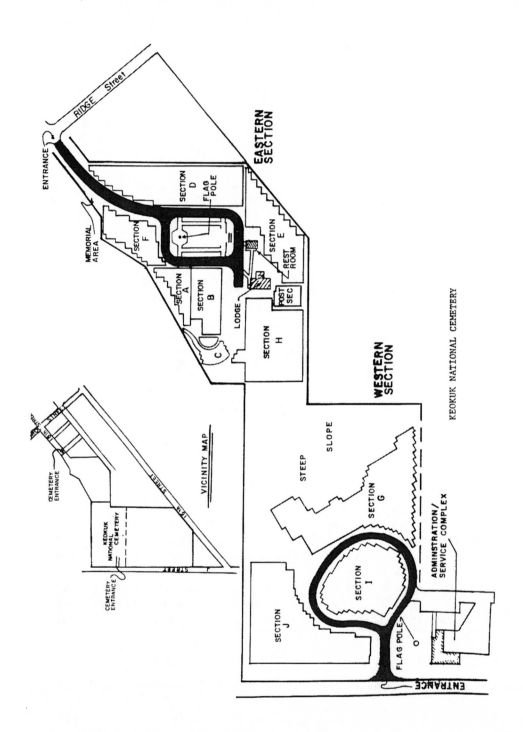

Just as the remaining 20 members of the platoon reached him, one of the enemy threw a grenade into their midst. Shouting a warning and making a final effort, Pvt. Thorson rolled onto the grenade and smothered the explosion with his body. He was instantly killed, but his magnificent courage and supreme self-sacrifice prevented the injury and possible death of his comrades, and remains with them as a lasting inspiration.

All administrative functions for the cemetery are performed by the Rock Island National Cemetery.

Former superintendents/directors of the Keokuk National Cemetery are:

Clayton Hart, May 1870–Unknown
Harold Montague, November 1940–April 1942
John Bierman, April 1942–March 1943
James Davis, April 1943–September 1949
Harold Montague, September 1949–October 1951
Paul B. Porter, November 1951–February 1953
Albin McLellan, March 1953–April 1955
Lester C. Smith, April 1955–August 1955
Donald L. Garrison, August 1955–February 1958
Donald L. Peterson, February 1958–July 1968
Claude E. Arnold, August 1968–July 1973

Robert L. Whitfield, August 1973–September 1974
Harlon R. Sheets, October 1974–January 1978
Thomas J. Beauchane, January 1978–January 1979
Arthur J. Conklin, May 1979–February 1982
Lucille Fisher, February 1982–September 1987
Douglas D. Miner, November 1987–January 1989
Candice L. Underwood, January 1989–1990
Dane B. Freeman, 1990–

Kerrville National Cemetery
Spur Route 100
Kerrville, Texas 78028

The cemetery is situated in Kerr County, about two miles southeast of Kerrville, adjacent to the grounds of the Department of Veterans Affairs (DVA) Medical Center. It is located on Spur Route 100, ½ mile north off Highway 27.

In June 1923, A.P. Brown and J.S. Brown, trustees of the Brown Cemetery (a private cemetery used by the Brown family, descendents and relatives of Joshua Brown), executed an instrument giving the Women's Auxiliary of the Garrett-Baker Post of the American Legion permission to bury any "white ex-service man dying in the vicinity of Kerrville, for whose burial they have assumed responsibility." The auxiliary had assumed the responsibility of providing a burial place for ex-servicemen and World War I veterans who died in the Kerrville community without having anyone to provide for burial.

In December 1932, the Brown trustees sold the portion of the family cemetery used for veteran burials to the Department of Texas, American Legion, and the auxiliary relinquished its rights and claims to the property. The American Legion Department of Texas donated the 1.7-acre cemetery to the Veterans Administration (VA) in February 1943, along with all burial records.

The first recorded burial, on April 12, 1923, was that of Clifford C. Hurlbert. He is interred in Section 1, Row C, Grave 14. His grave has no marker, and the burial record notes that a Department of the Army letter dated December 27, 1967, says that he had no active military duty. The last recorded interment in the cemetery took place on October 28, 1957, when James M. Brittain was interred in Section 2, Row A, Grave 18. The cemetery contains 463 occupied gravesites.

The VA cemetery was transferred to the National Cemetery System in September 1973, and is still maintained by personnel of the Department of Veterans Affairs Medical Center. The Fort Sam Houston performs all administrative functions for the cemetery.

Knoxville National Cemetery
939 Tyson Street, N.W.
Knoxville, Tennessee 37917

The cemetery is located in Knox County, Knoxville, Tennessee, in the northern section of the city. The 9.83 acres were appropriated in September 1863 from John Damon and purchased on June 10, 1867. The burying ground was established as a national cemetery in 1863.

The original cemetery was laid out with a small circular mound in the center, 30 feet in diameter and 4 feet high, on which a flagstaff was erected. A drive surrounded the mound, with branches leading to the center of each of the four sides of the square burial area laid out in the eastern part of the property. The graves were arranged in circles, concentric with the drive around the mound.

The cemetery was established by General Ambrose E. Burnside, the Union commander during the siege of Knoxville, who was once characterized as "a general with a genius for slowness." Captain E.B. Chamberlain, assistant quartermaster, laid out the cemetery in 1863. It was described in 1866 by Major E.B. Whitman, in charge of mortuary records as "the only burial ground of Union soldiers in this department originally laid out and conducted to the present time in a manner and on a system that render it suitable to be converted into a National Cemetery without material alteration or change, or removal of a single body."

The first interments were remains removed from Cumberland Gap, Tazewell, Concord, and many other places in Tennessee, Kentucky, Virginia, and North Carolina. As of December 2, 1870, the cemetery contained a total of 3,153 interments; 2,078 known, and 1,075 unknown. As of September 30, 2008, the number of interments was 9,023.

In the northeast corner of the cemetery is a large monument, of Tennessee marble with a base about 15 feet square, known as the Tennessee but referred to locally as the Wilder Monument. It was erected between 1896 and 1901. The Grand Army of the Republic raised funds through public subscription and dedicated the monument to the Tennessee Union soldiers.

There are Medal of Honor recipients interred in the cemetery. The dagger denotes that one was killed in action.

†**Troy A. McGill**, Sec B, Grave 6294. Sergeant, U.S. Army, Troop G, 5th Cavalry Regiment, 1st Cavalry Division. Place and date: Los Negros Islands, Admiralty Group, 4 March 1944.

Citation: For conspicuous gallantry and intrepidity above and beyond the call of duty in action with the enemy at Los Negros Islands, Admiralty Group, on 4 March 1944. In the early morning hours Sgt. McGill, with a squad of 8 men, occupied a revetment which bore the brunt of a furious attack by approximately 200 drink-crazed enemy troops. Although covered by crossfire from machine guns on the right and left flanks he could receive no support from the remainder of our troops stationed at his rear. All members of the squad were killed or wounded except Sgt. McGill and another man, whom he ordered to return to the next revetment. Courageously resolved to hold his position at all costs, he fired his weapon until it ceased to function. Then, with the enemy only five yards away, he charged from his foxhole in the face of certain death and clubbed the enemy with his rifle in hand-to-hand combat until he was killed. At dawn 105 enemy dead were found around his position. Sergeant McGill's intrepid stand was an inspiration to his comrades and a decisive factor in the defeat of a fanatical enemy.

Timothy Spillane, Sec. A, Grave 3319. Private, Company C, 16th Pennsylvania Calvary. Place and Date: T Hatchers Run, Virginia, 27 February 1865.

Citation: Gallantry and good conduct in action, bravery in a charge and reluctance to leave the field after being twice wounded.

Tennessee Monument, Knoxville National Cemetery, 1953.

As of May 1, 1973, the cemetery was closed for future interments except for interments in previously reserved gravesites and second interments in existing gravesites under the single gravesite per family policy. The cemetery may be able to inter cremated remains.

Former superintendents/directors of the Knoxville National Cemetery are:

Robert R. Dye, April 1908–August 1908
Owen H. Kell, June 1945–February 1959
John A. Boender, April 1959–October 1960
Edward E. Douglas, Jr., October 1960–May 1966
Brice E. Bowen, June 1966–July 1983
Richard L.R. Boyd, November 1983–January 1986

Lawrence T. Mitchell, March 1986–August 1987
Ramona L. Vaughn, 1987–1990
Rodney Dunn, 1990–1999
Candice Underwood, August 1999–February 2005
Sandra Beckley, March 2005–June 2005
Paul H. Martin, June 2005–Present

The cemetery is assigned to the director, Chattanooga National Cemetery for administration and management.

Leavenworth National Cemetery
P.O. Box 1694
Leavenworth, Kansas 66048

The cemetery is located approximately three miles southeast of downtown Leavenworth in Leavenworth County, Kansas. It is bounded on the east by a Missouri Pacific railroad line and overlooks the Missouri River. The grounds of the Department of Veterans Affairs Medical Center (DVAMC) form the northern and western boundaries.

In the spring of 1878, the Grand Army of the Republic held a reunion at Leavenworth. The idea of establishing a western branch of the National Home for Disabled Volunteer Soldiers was born during this reunion. After much effort on the part of the political leaders in Leavenworth and the state of Kansas, the Board of Managers announced on September 26, 1884, that the home would be built in Leavenworth. Construction was started in 1886. The first member to be admitted to the home on July 11, 1885, was Alexander Maines, formerly a private in Company A, First Rhode Island Light Artillery. He had served three years during the Civil War, and transferred from the Eastern Branch at Togus, Maine. His disabilities were listed as "Rheumatism, Fever, and Ague."

For many years, the "Old Soldiers Home" was a principal center of the community. The first trolley line ran from Fort Leavenworth through town to the front of the mess hall. In the summer, the home band gave concerts every weekend at the bandstand in Lake Jeanette, and in winter, ice skating on the frozen lake attracted large crowds. The home was transferred to the Veterans Administration when it was formed in 1930, and is now officially named the Dwight D. Eisenhower Department of Veterans Affairs Medical Center.

The cemetery at the western branch was established with the burial of Thomas Brennan on January 22, 1886. It was transferred to the National Cemetery System in September 1973. The memorial spire, which overlooks the Missouri River valley from the highest ridge of the cemetery, was brought here on the Santa Fe Railroad siding and moved to its present location in 1919 by prisoners and a team of oxen from the state prison in Lansing. Among the graves in the section near the spire are those of early governors (managers) of the home and their families. Also located in this section is an obelisk monument in memory of the soldiers who have died for their country.

During the construction of Building 122 on the Medical Center grounds, the remains of 12 Indians were uncovered. They were reinterred in a single grave, Section 34, Row 21,

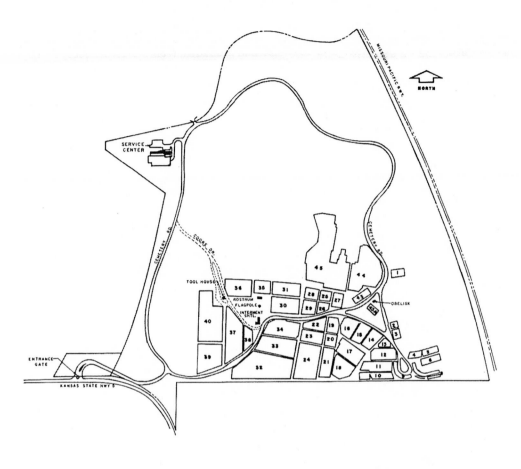

Name _____ Grave _____ Section _____

Grave 8, the only group burial in the cemetery. It is believed that they belonged to a small band of Christian Indians, the Munsees, who during the early 1800s were permitted to settle on land now occupied by the DVAMC.

The cemetery covers 128.8 acres, and as of September 30, 2008, there were 33,395 interments. There are six Medal of Honor recipients interred here:

William W. Burritt, Sec 16, Row 5, Grave 7. Private, Company G, 113th Illinois Infantry. Place and date: At Vicksburg, Miss., 27 April 1863.

Citation: Voluntarily acted as a fireman on a steam tug which ran the blockade and passed the batteries under a heavy fire.

Daniel Allen Dorsey, Sec 11, Row 19, Grave 8. Corporal, Company H, 33d Ohio Infantry. Place and date: Georgia, April 1862.

Citation: One of the 19 of 22 men* (including 2 civilians) who, by direction of General Mitchell (or Buell), penetrated nearly 200 miles south into enemy territory and captured a railroad train at Big Shanty, Ga., in an attempt to destroy the bridges and track between Chattanooga and Atlanta.

*Though the meaning of this phrase is uncertain, it is believed that the "22 men" included 19 soldiers and 2 civilians who participated in the raid, as well as another soldier who slept through the raid.

John S. Durham, Sec 33, Row 10, Grave 18. Sergeant, Company F, 1st Wisconsin Infantry. Place and date: At Perryville, Ky., 8 October 1862.

Citation: Seized the flag of his regiment when the color sergeant was shot and advanced with the flag midway between the lines, amid a shower of shot, shell, and bullets, until stopped by his commanding officer.

William Garrett, Sec 32, Row 3, Grave 26. Sergeant, Company G, 41st Ohio Infantry. Place and date: At Nashville, Tenn., 16 December 1864.

Citation: With several companions dashed forward, the first to enter the enemy's works, taking possession of four pieces of artillery and capturing the flag of the 13th Mississippi Infantry (C.S.A.).

John Gray, Sec 9, Row 1, Grave 23. Private, Company B, 5th Ohio Infantry. Place and date: At Port Republic, Va., 9 June 1862.

Citation: Mounted an artillery horse of the enemy and captured a brass six pound piece in the face of the enemy's fire and brought it to the rear.

John H. Shingle, Sec 22, Row 4, Grave 2. First Sergeant, Troop I, 3d U.S. Cavalry. Place and date: At Rosebud River, Mont., 17 June 1876.

Citation: Gallantry in action.

Lebanon National Cemetery
Route 1, Box 616
Lebanon, Kentucky 40033

Situated in Marion County, on the outskirts of Lebanon, Kentucky, the cemetery is located on Kentucky Highway 208, about one-half mile from the intersection of Kentucky highways 55 and 208. This intersection is about one mile southwest of Lebanon.

Official records indicate that the United States appropriated the land for the cemetery in 1862, but it was not designated a national cemetery until 1867. Dr. J.F. McElroy in his "History of Lebanon," written about 1870, states, "A cemetery for soldiers was established in January 1863, about one mile south of town...." A letter written to the superintendent in 1963 says, "I was born just 31 years after the end of the Civil War and in past years I have been told by many old timers that many of the dead from the Perryville battle [October 8, 1862] were brought here just a few months after the battle." On April 6, 1867, part of the 2⅜ acres purchased from James F. and Wm. E. McElroy, and the remainder was purchased from Charles Gale on August 18, 1875. A donation of 3.4 acres in 1984, and a donation of 9 acres brought the cemetery to its present size of 14.8 acres.

Construction of the cemetery was under the direction of the quartermaster general, but the cemetery was laid out and the work supervised by Lt. J.R. King, 2d Infantry, commanding a detachment then stationed at Lebanon.

Along the route of his Ohio Raid during the summer of 1863, General John Hunt Morgan swept through Lebanon, and on July 5, 1863, burned the county clerk's office and all county records.

Original interments were the scattered remains of Union soldiers from Lebanon and vicinity, Campbellsville, Crab Orchard, Green River Bridge, Neatsville, Calvary Church, Salama, and from within a radius of 50 miles or more from Lebanon. The total number of original interments was 865, including 281 unknowns. The report of the inspector of national cemeteries dated November 25, 1870, stated that the names of all are known, but the bodies of the "unknowns" could not be identified. As of September 30, 2008, there were 5,128 interments in the cemetery. The original 1,367-foot stone wall around the cemetery was constructed in 1867 by J.G. Campbell, at a cost of $4.60 per lineal foot.

Approach to Lebanon National Cemetery (lodge in background), June 1931.

Former superintendents/directors of the cemetery are:

Mrs. Peter McKenna (Actg), October 1895–1896
Hiram S. Towne, 1896–1900
Harry C. Varble, May 1944–September 1958
James D. Simms, September 1958–August 1960
Norman W. Baumgardner, August 1960–May 1961
Clarence A. Lambert, June 1961–July 1962
Steve L. Bukovitz, July 1962–March 1964
Ray C. Van Tassell, March 1964–March 1965
Raymond C. Cordell, April 1965–June 1967
William G. Kaiser, June 1967–August 1968
Ralph L. Hamilton, September 1968–April 1969
Richard H. Crouse, April 1969–November 1970

Walter F. Blake, November 1970–August 1974
Juanita Walker, November 1974–May 1976
Walter J. Degnan, May 1976–July 1976
Robert L. Scoggins, November 1977–November 1978
Kevin J. Taylor, November 1979–November 1980
Oakland A. DeMoss, January 1981–September 1982
Robert Bennett, November 1982–February 1984
Daniel L. Nelson, February 1984–March 1985
Matt Cornett, April 1985–April 1987
Eileen G. Harrison, June 1987–March 1988

Since March 1988, the cemetery has been assigned to the Director, Zachary Taylor National Cemetery for maintenance, administration and management.

Lexington National Cemetery
833 West Main Street
Lexington, Kentucky 40508

The cemetery is situated in Fayette County, in the city of Lexington, and is located on the southern border of the 168-acre City of Lexington Cemetery, approximately 1,500 feet from the main entrance and cemetery office.

The land used as a burying ground was established as a soldiers' lot in 1861, and as a national cemetery in 1863. The United States lot contains approximately 0.75 acre of sloping land purchased from the Cemetery Association on July 1, 1867. The original reservation consisted of 0.37 acre donated by the Lexington Cemetery Company, which was included in the purchase of 1867. When arrangements for the care of the scattered dead in Kentucky provided for their reinterment in this cemetery, an agreement was made with the cemetery corporation to purchase the unoccupied portion of the section or lot in which original interments had been made.

In his Ohio raid in the summer of 1863, Confederate General John Hunt Morgan swept through Lexington on the way to Cincinnati. His force of about 2,500 mounted infantrymen robbed, plundered, and looted as they went. As they swept through Lexington, they captured elements of the 3rd and 4th Ohio Cavalry. General Morgan was pursued and captured on the up per Ohio near Blennerhassett's Island in late July 1863. He was confined in a northern prison at Columbus, Ohio, from which he escaped in November. Ten months later, he was killed near Greenville, Tennessee, while trying to escape from Northern troops. While not inside the national cemetery, he is buried in the Lexington Cemetery.

The first burial, on November 28, 1861, was that of Amos Barr, 14th Infantry. The 671 original interments were from hospitals established in Lexington to receive patients sent back from the front, and transient troops who camped from time to time in the area. In addition to these original burials, the scattered bodies of Union soldiers were collected from an area 40 by 50 miles in extent, including those killed at Falmouth, Cynthiana, Mount Sterling, Paris, and from various bridges and trestle works along the line of the Kentucky Central Railroad.

On May 26, 1868, the Lexington Cemetery Corporation perpetually bound itself to care for the government lot. Therefore, no superintendent was ever appointed. In 1874, ten white marble posts were erected to mark the boundary of the national cemetery. The director of Camp Nelson National Cemetery is responsible for administration of this cemetery. As of September 30, 2008, there were 1,390 interments. The cemetery has been closed since 1939.

Little Rock National Cemetery
2523 Confederate Boulevard
Little Rock, Arkansas 72206

Little Rock National Cemetery is located in Pulaski County, Little Rock, Arkansas, about two miles southeast of the state capitol. Little Rock is the largest city in the state and an important manufacturing center. The French explorer Bernard de la Harpe explored the Arkansas River in 1722 and named the river bluff *La Petite Roch*, "the Little Rock."

After the government established Fort Smith to keep peace among the Indian tribes in the area, numerous settlements began to spring up between Arkansas Post, in southeast Arkansas, and Fort Smith in the west. In 1819 the northern part of the Louisiana Purchase, the Missouri Territory, was divided and the Arkansas Territory was created. It included all of Arkansas and part of what is now Oklahoma. In 1820 a land speculator laid out a town site at "the Little Rock" which was incorporated into a city in 1831.

When Arkansas became a state on June 15, 1836, it was a slave state, but Arkansans were almost equally divided about staying in the Union or joining the Confederacy. In 1861, after the state refused to send troops to fight in the Union Army, a convention met and voted to secede from the Union, reversing a convention vote taken two months earlier. Following the battle of Pea Ridge in 1862, the Union Army captured Little Rock on September 10, 1863.

During the early part of the Civil War, the land now occupied by the national cemetery was located approximately 1½ miles outside the city limits. It was used as a camping ground for Union troops. Later the space was used as a city cemetery for the purpose of burying the Civil War dead. While the United States troops were occupying the city, in 1866, a portion of the new city cemetery was purchased by the government and set aside as a military burial ground.

The military plot in the Little Rock City Cemetery was purchased by the government in two parcels: 9.1 acres in September 1866, and 3.2 acres on April 9, 1868. On April 9, 1868, this land was designated a national cemetery. The purpose was to concentrate the remains of the Union dead who had been buried throughout the state. At the time of its designation as a national cemetery, there were 5,425 interments in the cemetery, of which 3,092 were known and 2,333 unknown. During the 1868 fiscal year 1,482 remains were reinterred in the cemetery after being moved from Dardanelle, Lewisburg, Jenkins Ford, Princeton, Marks Mill, Pine Bluff, and DeValls Bluff. This would indicate that by September 1869, a total of 6,907 interments had been made in the cemetery. However, the report of the inspector of national cemeteries dated June 3, 1871, states that "The whole number of interments, according to records in the office, is 5,439." No records are available to resolve the discrepancy between the figures. Perhaps the reinterred remains were not included in the inspector's report, which would then leave only 14 remains unaccounted for.

In 1884, a Confederate cemetery of 11 acres was established adjoining the national cemetery. The remains of 640 Confederate soldiers were removed from Mt. Holly Cemetery and reburied in the new cemetery. An imposing monument to their memory was erected in the same year by the trustees of Mt. Holly Cemetery. In 1913, Congress authorized the Secretary of War to accept from the city of Little Rock a deed to the Confederate cemetery with the restriction that only Confederate veterans could be interred in the new

Confederate section at Little Rock National Cemetery.

acquisition. This restriction was removed in 1938, and the Confederate cemetery became the Confederate Section in the Little Rock National Cemetery. This removed the last traces of distinction between veterans of our bloodiest war. There are 1,797 Confederate soldiers interred in the cemetery. One of the outstanding features of the cemetery is the handsome monument erected in 1916 by the state of Minnesota in memory of its soldiers who lost their lives in the Civil War and are buried there.

Affixed to the rostrum in the Confederate Section is a plaque dated 1907 which reads, "Erected by Memorial Chapter United Daughters of the Confederacy." This organization is the successor organization to the Ladies Memorial Aid Society. In December 1890, the city of Little Rock passed an ordinance granting that group a strip of land west of the national cemetery for the purpose of establishing a Confederate Cemetery.

Today the cemetery encompassed 31.7 acres and includes 25,471 interments. The cemetery is closed for initial interments.

There is one Medal of Honor recipient interred in the cemetery:

Maurice L. Britt, Sec. 20, Grave 319, Lieutenant, U.S. Army, 3rd Infantry Division. Place and Date: Near Mignano, Italy, 10 November 1943.
Citation: For conspicuous gallantry and intrepidity at the risk of his life above and beyond the call of duty.

Former superintendents/directors of the national cemetery are:

Martin Burkes, June 1869–December 1869
Wesley Markwood, January 1870–March 1872
John Flynn, December 1872–March 1876
Ed M. Main, March 1876–January 1880
William F. Graham, March 1880–June 1880
Thomas Daniels, May 1881–April 1887
J.V. Davis, April 1887–September 1887
Charles F. Eichwurzel, October 1887–March 1888
Ed. Taubenspeck, May 1888–April 1898
D.F. Stevens, April 1898–February 1904
Thomas Krementz, February 1904–June 1915
J.M. Bryant, September 1915–September 1927
H.D. Stanley, November 1927–April 1932
Sidney Guard, April 1932–February 1941
Walter Hanns, February 1941–September 1942
Floyd Wilcox, September 1942–July 1944
Herbert Rhodes, July 1944–February 1955
Oberlin H. Carter, February 1955–September 1959
Donald L. Garrison, September 1959–December 1962
William J. Boyer, December 1962–April 1964

Rudolph F. Staube, April 1964–September 1965
Harold A. Johnson, October 1965–November 1968
Howard J. Ferguson, December 1968–August 1969
Wilborn D. Burdeshaw, August 1969–June 1970
Grover R. Neal, August 1970–February 1972
Jack A. Morris, March 1972–April 1975
Joe D. Willard, May 1975–November 1977
Velva L. Melton, January 1978–November 1979
Dennis E. Kuehl, February 1980–November 1983
Eugene L. Chambers, January 1984–January 1985
Rodney L. Dunn, July 1985–March 1986
Robert F. McCollum, June 1986–November 1988
Douglas Minor, 1989–February 1992
Alvin Sanders, April 1992–1994
Mary Ann Fisher, April 1994–April 1999
Ron Zink, May 1999–October 2000
Gary N. Overall, January 2001–April 2007
Darrin White, August 2007–Present

Long Island National Cemetery
Farmingdale
Long Island, New York 11735

The cemetery is situated in Suffolk County at Pinelawn, Long Island, New York; its entrance is on Wellwood Avenue.

The establishment of the Long Island National Cemetery in 1936 reflected one aspect of the rapid urbanization of American society. With nearly 5 million veterans of World War I eligible for future interment in a national cemetery, it was evident that existing national cemeteries in the vicinity of large cities would not be able to provide sufficient gravesites.

The situation was particularly critical in New York City and the surrounding metropolitan area. The only national cemetery in the area, Cypress Hills National Cemetery in Brooklyn, had been established in 1862 and was of limited acreage with only a small number of gravesites remaining. In recognition of this problem, Congress passed legislation on May 18, 1936, authorizing the Secretary of War "to acquire by purchase, condemnation or otherwise such suitable lands in the vicinity of New York City as in his judgment are required for enlargement of existing national cemetery facilities...." Pursuant to this act and supplementary legislation on June 22, 1936, action was started for acquiring land for the projected national cemetery. Many sites in New York City were investigated and considered by the War Department prior to making a final decision to purchase land offered by the Pinelawn Cemetery, a private corporation in Farmingdale. The initial purchase was 175 acres. A subsequent purchase of adjoining land in 1951 in creased the total area of the cemetery to its present size of 364.7 acres. The cemetery was named Long Island National Cemetery by War Department General Orders No. 2 in 1938.

The United States took possession of the area to be developed as a cemetery in January 1937, though it did not acquire actual title until May. Special legislation by the state of New York and approval of the governor were necessary to permit the Pinelawn Cemetery to sell part of its land to the United States for use as a cemetery.

The lack of available grave space in Cypress Hills National Cemetery made it necessary that the new land be developed very quickly. Accordingly, the land was sufficiently cleared to permit the first burials to be made in the new cemetery in March 1937. During the eight-month period from March 16, 1937, to November 15, 1937, a total of 426 inter-

Memorial Fountain, Long Island National Cemetery.

ments were made in a new and only partially developed cemetery. This was a good indication of the need for a national cemetery in the New York metropolitan area.

During the first eight years of its existence, Long Island National Cemetery received 10,167 interments. Repatriation of remains of decedents of World War II and the Korean conflict rapidly increased the number of interments. On November 1, 1963, Private First Class Ernest B. Palmer, a veteran of World War II, became the 100,000th interment. Less than 10 years later, on February 7, 1973, Chief Torpedo man's Mate William Rodgers, a veteran of both World Wars I and II, became the 200,000th interment. As of September 30, 2008, there were 333,592 interments. Urban development of the property around the cemetery following World War II prohibits any further expansion of this cemetery. This was a major consideration in the establishment of Calverton National Cemetery in 1978.

Among the interments in the cemetery are 39 group burials containing 112 decedents. The largest group burial contains the remains of three officers, one technical sergeant, two sergeants, and four corporals. They were all members of the U.S. Army Air Force who died together in a plane crash on May 4, 1945.

Another group burial marks the final resting place of four American servicemen and two members of the British armed forces. Their plane crashed in the Burmese jungle in April 1945. Immediate attempts to locate the wreckage were futile. It was not until 1957 that the Army, acting on information supplied by Burmese tribesmen who had found a wreck in the jungle, finally discovered the plane and its ill-fated passengers. After an agreement with the British government and arrangements with the families of the deceased were completed, the remains of the six men were interred on February 5, 1958.

The World War II Prisoner of War Section contains 91 remains, those of 37 Germans and 54 Italians. The remains of 36 Italian prisoners of war are interred in one grave as unknowns. They were among 1,800 prisoners on board a British ship en route from Bone, in northeast Algeria, to Oran in northwest Algeria, when the ship was struck by an aerial torpedo on August 16, 1943, at or below the water line. A great number of prisoners confined in the holds of the ship were injured, killed outright, or drowned. Initial search of the ship upon its return to Bone after the torpedoing failed to locate all of the casualties. When the ship subsequently returned to the United States, the remains of the 36 prisoners were recovered from holds 1 and 2 of the ship. Since it was not possible to identify them individually, they were interred in a single grave.

In 1948 the remains of 16 Civil War soldiers of the 14th Rhode Island Heavy Artillery were removed from an abandoned cemetery at Fort Greble, Rhode Island, and interred in a single grave in the cemetery. Additional reinterments were made in 1952 when 104 remains were moved from an abandoned post cemetery at Fort McKinley, Maine.

A simple memorial containing a bronze tablet studded with emblems of various veterans organizations was dedicated at Long Island National Cemetery on May 30, 1940. The memorial, located in the northwest corner of Section E, was erected by the veterans organizations of Nassau and Suffolk counties of New York. These veterans groups also raised the necessary funds to purchase and install an electronic carillon that was dedicated on May 27, 1962. The carillon is played three times daily and for services each Memorial Day.

There are 20 Medal of Honor recipients interred the cemetery. Daggers appear before the names of men who were killed in action.

Heinrick Behnke, Sec DDS, Grave 20-A. Fireman First Class, U.S. Navy. G.O. No.: 182, 20 March 1905.
Citation: Onboard the *USS Iowa*, 25 January 1905. Following the blowing out of the manhole plate of boiler D of that vessel, Behnke displayed extraordinary heroism in the resulting action.

Anthony Casamento, Sec DSS, Grave 79-A. U.S. Marine Corps; died July 18, 1987.

John Everetts, Sec DDS, Grave 36. Gunner's Mate, Third Class, U.S. Navy. G.O. No.: 489, 20 May 1898.
Citation: Serving aboard the *USS Cushing,* 11 February 1898, Everetts displayed gallant conduct in attempting to save the life of the late Ens. Joseph C. Breckinridge, U.S. Navy, who fell overboard at sea from that vessel.

Robert Gailbraith, Sec DSS, Grave 17. Gunner's Mate, Third Class, U.S. Navy. G.O. No.: 531, 21 November 1900.
Citation: For extraordinary heroism and gallantry while under fire of the enemy at El Pardo, Cebu, Philippine Islands, 12 and 13 September 1899.

William Henry Gowan, Sec DSS, Grave 7. Boatswain's Mate, U.S. Navy. G.O. No.: 18, 1909.
Citation: For bravery and extraordinary heroism displayed by him during the conflagration in Coquimbo, Chile, 20 January 1909.

Sydney G. Gumpertz, Sec DSS, Grave 65. First Sergeant, U.S. Army, Company E, 132d Infantry, 33d Division. Place and date: In the Bois-de-Forges, France, 29 September 1917.
Citation: When the advancing line was held up by machine gun fire, 1st Sgt. Gumpertz left the platoon of which he was in command and started with two other soldiers through a heavy barrage toward the machine gun nest. His two companions soon became casualties from bursting shells, but 1st Sgt. Gumpertz continued on alone in the face of direct fire from the machine gun, jumped into the nest and silenced the gun, capturing nine of the crew.

August Holtz, Sec F, Grave 916. Chief Watertender, U.S. Navy. G.O. No.: 83, 4 October 1910.
Citation: Onboard the *USS North Dakota,* for extraordinary heroism in the line of his profession during the fire on board that vessel, 8 September 1910.

†**Joseph Rodolph Julian,** Sec DSS, Grave 12. Platoon Sergeant, U.S. Marine Corps Reserve.
Citation: For conspicuous gallantry and intrepidity at the risk of his life above and beyond the call of duty as P/Sgt. while serving with the 1st Battalion, 27th Marines, 5th Marine Division, in action against enemy Japanese forces during the seizure of Iwo Jima in the Volcano Islands, 9 March 1945. Determined to force a breakthrough when Japanese forces occupying trenches and fortified positions on the left front laid down a terrific machine gun and mortar barrage in a desperate effort to halt his company's advance, P/Sgt. Julian quickly established his platoon's guns in strategic supporting positions, and then, acting on his own initiative, fearlessly moved forward to execute a one-man assault on the nearest pillbox. Advancing alone, he hurled deadly demolitions and white phosphorus grenades into the emplacement, killing two of the enemy and driving the remaining five out into the adjoining trench system. Seizing a discarded rifle, he jumped into the trench and dispatched the five before they could make an escape. Intent on wiping out all resistance, he obtained more explosives and, accompanied by another Marine, again charged the hostile fortifications and knocked out two more cave positions. Immediately thereafter, he launched a bazooka attack unassisted, firing four rounds into the one remaining pillbox and completely destroying it before he fell, mortally wounded by a vicious burst of enemy fire. Stouthearted and indomitable, P/Sgt. Julian consistently disregarded all personal danger and, by his bold decision, daring tactics, and relentless fighting spirit during the critical phase of the battle, contributed materially to the continued advance of his company and to the success of his division's operations in the sustained drive toward the conquest of this fiercely defended outpost of the Japanese Empire. He gallantly gave his life for his country.

†**Steven Edward Karopczyc,** Sec DSS, Grave 5-A. First Lieutenant, U.S. Army, Company A, 2d Battalion, 35th Infantry, 25th Infantry Division. Place and date: Kontum Province, Republic of Vietnam, 12 March 1967.
Citation: For conspicuous gallantry and intrepidity in action at the risk of his life above and beyond the call of duty. While leading the 3d Platoon, Company A, on a flanking maneuver against a superior enemy force, 1st Lt. Karopczyc observed that the lead element was engaged with a small enemy unit along his route. Aware of the importance of quickly pushing through to the main enemy force in order to provide relief for a hard-pressed friendly platoon, he dashed through the intense enemy fire into the open and hurled colored smoke grenades to designate the foe for attack

by helicopter gunships. He moved among his men to embolden their advance, and he guided their attack by marking enemy locations with bursts of fire from his own weapon. His forceful leadership quickened the advance, forced the enemy to retreat, and allowed his unit to close with the main hostile force. Continuing the deployment of his platoon, he constantly exposed himself as he ran from man to man to give encouragement and to direct their efforts. A shot from an enemy sniper struck him above the heart but he refused aid for this serious injury, plugging the bleeding wound with his finger until it could be properly dressed. As the enemy strength mounted, he ordered his men to organize a defensive position in and around some abandoned bunkers where he conducted a defense against the increasingly strong enemy attacks. After several hours, a North Vietnamese soldier hurled a hand grenade to within a few feet of 1st Lt. Karopczyc and two other wounded men. Although his position protected him, he leaped up to cover the deadly grenade with a steel helmet. It exploded to drive fragments into 1st Lt. Karopczyc's legs, but his action prevented further injury to the two wounded men. Severely weakened by his multiple wounds, he continued to direct the actions of his men until he succumbed two hours later. First Lieutenant Karopczyc's heroic leadership, unyielding perseverance, and selfless devotion to his men were directly responsible for the successful and spirited action of his platoon throughout the battle.

†**John J. Kedenburg,** Sec 2H, Grave 3684. Specialist Fifth Class, U.S. Army, 5th Special Forces Group (Airborne), 1st Special Forces. Place and date: Republic of Vietnam, 13 June 1968.

Citation: For conspicuous gallantry and intrepidity in action at the risk of his life above and beyond the call of duty. Specialist Kedenburg, U.S. Army, Command and Control Detachment North, Forward Operating Base 2, 5th Special Forces Group (Airborne), distinguished himself while serving as adviser to a long-range reconnaissance team of South Vietnamese irregular troops. The team's mission was to conduct counter-guerilla operations deep within enemy held territory. Prior to reaching the day's objective, the team was attacked and encircled by a battalion-size North Vietnamese Army force. Specialist Keden burg assumed immediate command of the team which succeeded after a fierce fight, in breaking out of the encirclement. As the team moved through thick jungle to a position from which it could be extracted by helicopter, Sp5c. Kedenburg conducted a gallant rear guard fight against the pursuing enemy and called for tactical air support and rescue helicopters. His withering fire against the enemy permitted the team to reach a pre-selected landing zone with the loss of only one man, who was unaccounted for. Once in the landing zone, Sp5c. Kedenburg deployed the team into a perimeter defense against the numerically superior enemy force. When tactical air support arrived, he skillfully directed air strikes against the enemy, suppressing their fire so that helicopters could hover over the area and drop slings to be used in the extraction of the team. After half of the team was extracted by helicopter, Sp5c. Kedenburg and the remaining three members of the team harnessed themselves to the sling on a second hovering helicopter. Just as the helicopter was to lift them out of the area, the South Vietnamese team member who had been unaccounted for after the initial encounter with the enemy appeared in the landing zone. Sp5c. Kedenburg unhesitatingly gave up his place in the sling to the man and directed the helicopter pilot to leave the area. He then continued to engage the enemy who were swarming into the landing zone, killing six enemy soldiers before he was overpowered. Specialist Kedenburg's inspiring leadership, consummate courage and willing self-sacrifice permitted his small team to inflict heavy casualties on the enemy and escape almost certain annihilation.

†**Carlos James Lozada,** Sec T, Grave 2295. Private First Class, U.S. Army, Company A, 2d Battalion, 503d Infantry, 173d Airborne Brigade. Place and date: Dak To, Republic of Vietnam, 20 November 1967.

Citation: For conspicuous gallantry and intrepidity in action at the risk of his life above and beyond the call of duty. Private Lozada distinguished himself at the risk of his life above and beyond the call of duty in the battle of Dak To. While serving as a machine gunner with the 1st Platoon, Company A, Pfc. Lozada was part of a four-man early warning outpost, located 35 meters from his company's lines. At 1400 hours a North Vietnamese Army company rapidly approached the outpost along a well-defined trail. Private Lozada alerted his comrades and commenced firing at the enemy who were within 10 meters of the outpost. His heavy and accurate machine gun fire killed at least 20 North Vietnamese soldiers and completely disrupted their initial attack. Private Lozada remained in an exposed position and continued to pour deadly fire upon the enemy despite the urgent pleas of his comrades to withdraw. The enemy continued their assault, attempting to envelop the outpost. At the same time enemy forces launched a heavy attack on the forward west flank of Company A with the intent to cut them off from their battalion. Company A was given the order to withdraw. Private Lozada apparently realized that if he abandoned his position there would be nothing to hold back the surging North Vietnamese soldiers and the entire company withdrawal would be jeopardized. He called for his comrades to move back and stated that he would stay and provide cover for them. He made his decision realizing that the enemy was converging on three sides of his position and only meters away, and a delay in withdrawal meant almost certain death. Private Lozada continued to deliver a heavy, accurate volume of suppressive fire against the enemy until he was mortally wounded and had to be carried during the withdrawal. His heroic deed served as an example and an inspiration to his comrades throughout the ensuing four-day battle.

Thomas Mitchell, Sec M, Grave 27661. Landsman, U.S. Navy. G.O. No.: 326, 18 October 1864.
Citation: Serving on board the *USS Richmond,* Mitchell rescued from drowning, M.F. Caulan, first class boy, serving with him on the same vessel, at Shanghai, China, 17 November 1879.

Lauritz Nelson, Sec DDS, Grave 2. Sailmaker's Mate, U.S. Navy. G.O. No.: 521, 7 July 1899.
Citation: Onboard the *USS Nashville* during the operation of cutting the cable leading from Cienfuegos, Cuba, 11 May 1898, facing the heavy fire of the enemy, Nelson displayed extraordinary bravery and coolness throughout this action.

†**Bernard James Ray,** Sec DSS, Grave 6. First Lieutenant, U.S. Army, Company F, 8th Infantry, 4th Infantry Division. Place and date: Hurtgen Forest near Schevenhutte, Germany, 17 November 1944.
Citation: He was a platoon leader with Company F, 8th Infantry, on 17 November 1944, during the drive through Hurtgen Forest near Schevenhutte, Germany. The American forces attacked in wet, bitterly cold weather over rough, wooded terrain, meeting brutal resistance from positions spaced throughout the forest behind minefields and wire obstacles. Small arms, machine gun, mortar, and artillery fire caused heavy casualties in the ranks when Company F was halted by a concertina-type wire barrier. Under heavy fire, 1st Lt. Ray reorganized his men and prepared to blow a path through the entanglement, a task which appeared impossible and from which others tried to dissuade him. With implacable determination to clear the way, he placed explosive caps in his pockets, obtained several bangalore torpedoes, and then wrapped a length of highly explosive primer cord about his body. He dashed forward under direct fire, reached the barbed wire and prepared his demolition charge as mortar shells, which were being aimed at him alone, came steadily nearer his exposed position. He had placed a torpedo under the wire and was connecting it to a charge when he was severely wounded by a bursting mortar shell. Apparently realizing that he would fail in his self-imposed mission unless he completed it in a few moments, he made a supremely gallant decision. With the primer cord still wound around his body and the explosive caps in his pockets, he completed a hasty wiring system, and unhesitatingly thrust down on the handle of the charger, destroying himself with the wire barricade in the resulting blast. By the deliberate sacrifice of his life, 1st Lt. Ray enabled his company to continue its attack, resumption of which was of positive significance in gaining the approaches to the Cologne Plain.

Joseph E. Schaeffer, Sec DSS, Grave 80. Staff Sergeant, U.S. Army; died March 16, 1987.

William Shea, Sec. DSS, Grave 71A, Second Lieutenant, U.S. Army, Company F, 350th Infantry, 88th Infantry Division. Place and Date: Near Mount Damiano, Italy, 12 May 1944.

†**William Thompson,** Sec DDS, Grave 19. Private First Class, U.S. Army, 24th Company M, 24th Infantry Regiment, 25th Infantry Division. Place and date: Near Haman, Korea, 6 August 1950.
Citation: Private Thompson distinguished himself by conspicuous gallantry and intrepidity above and beyond the call of duty in action against the enemy. While his platoon was reorganizing under cover of darkness, fanatical enemy forces in overwhelming strength launched a surprise attack on the unit. Private Thompson set up his machine gun in the path of the onslaught and swept the enemy with withering fire, pinning them down momentarily, thus permitting the remainder of his platoon to withdraw to a more tenable position. Although hit repeatedly by grenade fragments and small-arms fire, he resisted all efforts of his comrades to induce him to withdraw, steadfastly remained at his machine gun and continued to deliver deadly, accurate fire until mortally wounded by an enemy grenade.

Michael Valente, Sec DDS, Grave 60-A. Private, U.S. Army, Company D, 107th Infantry, 27th Division. Place and date: East of Ronssoy, France, 29 September 1918.

Citation: For conspicuous gallantry and intrepidity above and beyond the call of duty in action against the enemy during the operations against the Hindenburg Line, east of Ronssoy, France, 29 September 1918. Finding the advance of his organization held up by a withering machine gun fire, Pvt. Valente volunteered to go forward. With utter disregard of his own personal danger, accompanied by another soldier, Pvt. Valente rushed forward through an intense machine gun fire directly upon the enemy nest, killing two and capturing five of the enemy and silencing the gun. Discovering another machine gun nest close by which was pouring a deadly fire on American forces, preventing their advance, Pvt. Valente and his companion charged upon this strong point, killing the gunner and putting this machine gun out of action. Without hesitation they jumped into the enemy's trench, killed 2 and captured 16 German soldiers. Private Valente was later wounded and sent to the rear.

James Aloysius Walsh, Sec DDS, Grave 47-A. Seaman, U.S. Navy. G.O. No.: 101, 15 June 1914.

Citation: On the *USS Florida;* for extraordinary heroism in the line of his profession during the seizure of Vera Cruz, Mexico, 21 and 22 April 1914.

†**John E. Warren, Jr.,** Sec O, Grave 33144. First Lieutenant, U.S. Army, Company C, 2d Battalion, (Mechanized), 22d Infantry, 25th Infantry Division. Place and date: Tay Ninh Province, Republic of Vietnam, 14 January 1969.

Citation: For conspicuous gallantry and intrepidity in action at the risk of his life above and beyond the call of duty. First Lieutenant Warren distinguished himself at the cost of his life while serving as a platoon leader with Company C. While moving through a rubber plantation to reinforce another friendly unit, Company C came under intense fire from a well-fortified enemy force. Disregarding his safety, 1st Lt. Warren with several of his men began maneuvering through the hail of enemy fire toward the hostile positions. When he had come to within six feet of one of the enemy bunkers and was preparing to toss a hand grenade into it, an enemy grenade was suddenly thrown into the middle of his small group. Thinking only of his men, 1st Lt. Warren fell in the direction of the grenade, thus shielding those around him from the blast. His action, performed at the cost of his life, saved three men from serious or mortal injury.

Long Island National Cemetery is closed except for interments in reserved gravesites or second interments in existing graves under the single gravesite per family policy.

Former superintendents/directors of the cemetery are:

Robert A. Spence, May 1945–June 1946
John A. Boender, June 1946–July 1948
John C. Metzler, July 1948–November 1951
Joseph J. Walsh, Sr., November 1951–October 1963
Frank A. Lockwood, October 1963–October 1966
Robert H. Schmidt, October 1966–June 1972
Donald L. Garrison, July 1972–May 1980

Ernest C. Schanze, September 1980–March 1984
Howard J. Ferguson, April 1984–September 1985
Steve L. Muro, October 1985–July 1988
Dennis J. Johnson, 1989–1990
Dennis E. Kuehl, March 1990–May 1992
David M. Cariota, September 1992–March 1995
Jim Adamson, September 1995–March 1998
Arthur Smith, July 1998–May 2003
Nadine Bruh-Schiffer, October 2007–Present

In September 2003 Long Island and Cypress Hills National Cemeteries became a complex with Calverton National Cemetery. On October 1, 2007, the complex split and Nadine Bruh-Schiffer became the director of Long Island and Cypress Hills National Cemeteries.

Los Angeles National Cemetery
950 Sepulveda Boulevard
Los Angeles, California 90049

The cemetery is located in the western section of Los Angeles, approximately four miles from the Pacific Ocean and one mile from Santa Monica, California. The entrance gates are on the western side of the cemetery at the intersection of Sepulveda Boulevard and Constitution Avenue. Constitution Avenue is the main road running west to east through the cemetery. The cemetery is across Sepulveda Boulevard from the Department of Veterans Affairs complex which contains the Wadsworth and Brentwood hospitals.

The Pacific branch of the National Homes for Disabled Volunteer Soldiers was established in 1887 on 300 acres of land donated by Senator John P. Jones and Arcadia B. de Baker. The land was part of their Rancho San Vicente y Santa Monica. Along with the land, they agreed to donate $100,000 in installments of $20,000 per year. On November 27, 1888, 200 more acres were acquired in lieu of payment for $75,000 of the $100,000 due the home. At that time, another 20 acres were added for use as a cemetery. In 1890, the Board of Governors took the remaining 80 acres of the original tract when the signers of the notes could not make payment. The original 300-acre site has been expanded to over 700 acres today.

By 1889, over 1,000 members were living in the home. The Barry Hospital was built in 1900, and replaced in 1927 by the Wadsworth Hospital, named for Major James Wadsworth, an early president of the Board of Managers. The Brentwood Hospital was constructed in the 1920s. Of the original Victorian buildings, only the Domiciliary Chapel remains today. In the 1980s the White House Office of Management and Budget attempted to pressure the Veterans Administration to sell some of the acreage. The 14 homeowner groups surrounding the complex joined forces to push Congress to prevent such an action. A plan has been developed that will preserve the open space for both veterans and westsiders.

Los Angeles National Cemetery became part of the National Cemetery System in 1973 when the Veterans Administration took over the responsibility for the system. From its original 20 acres, it has been expanded to 114.5 acres today. The first interment in the cemetery took place on May 11, 1889, when Abner Prather was buried. The site was dedicated on May 22, 1889. As of September 30, 2008, there were 85,448 interments, including over 5,000 remains inurned in the columbarium.

The cemetery closed for interments in 1960, except for second interments in existing graves, previously reserved graves, and cremated remains. Garden niches for in-ground burial of cremated remains were established in June 1962.

The indoor columbarium is the only one in the National Cemetery System. This structure contains 5,616 niches for cremated remains. The design of the structure and its matching pergola are of Spanish architecture, reflecting the city's rich Spanish heritage. It was opened on June 7, 1941. Two plaques adorn the outside walls of the columbarium. One is inscribed, "Veterans of Foreign Wars of the United States Ladies Auxiliary Department of California Humbly Honor the Memory of the Brave Men and Women of the United States Armed Forces Who Offered Their Lives in the Service of Our Country 1946," and the second plaque is inscribed, "1898–1902 United Spanish War Veterans in Tribute to Our Boys Who Left Their Homes in Defense of Their Country."

In the southeast corner of the cemetery is an impressive monument bearing a plaque with the inscription, "To Those Who Volunteered and Extended the Hand of Liberty to Alien Peoples 1902." This commemorative monument was funded and erected by the Spanish-American War Veterans in 1902. On Buena Vista Hill an obelisk monument is dedicated "In Memory of the Men Who Offered Their Lives in Defense of Our Country." At the end of Antietam Road on the east side of the cemetery, in the center of Geranium Circle, there is a bronze monument "Dedicated to Women Who Served for God and Country." A statue of a Revolutionary War soldier stands in a park-like burial section near the rostrum. The statue, which is dedicated to "The Department of California and

Los Angeles National Cemetery.

Nevada Grand Army of the Republic," was erected by the Women's Relief Corps Auxiliary in 1942.

There are at least two dogs buried here: Old Bonus, a mutt adopted as a pet by soldiers of the home, and Blackout, a war dog wounded in the Pacific during World War II. Blackout was buried with full military honors.

Nicholas P. Earp, the father of western lawman Wyatt Earp, was buried in the cemetery on February 16, 1907.

The repatriated remains of U.S. Air Force Lt. Col. Gordon B. Blackwood, a senior pilot of the 333rd Tactical Fighter Squadron in the 355th Tactical Fighter Wing, and his wife, Patricia, were interred on June 8, 1990. The remains of Col. Blackwood were repatriated in April 1989 along with the remains of 20 other U.S. service members. He had been missing in action since 1967 when a surface-to-air missile hit his F-105 Thunderchief on a bombing mission over Hanoi, North Vietnam. His plane broke apart and went down in the North Vietnam city of Phu Lang Thuong, Ha Bac province. Other pilots in the area observed his parachute deploy but the colonel was never heard from again. During his Air Force career, he received numerous awards and decorations, including the Distinguished Flying Cross. The cremated remains of Patricia Blackwood, held by family members since her death in 1987, were buried in the same gravesite with her husband.

There are 14 Medal of Honor recipients interred in these hallowed grounds. A dagger appears before the name of one man who was killed in action.

Chris Carr (Name legally changed from Christos H. Karaberis, under which name the medal was awarded.) Sec 275, Row G, Grave 15. Sergeant, U.S. Army, Company L, 337th Infantry, 85th Infantry Division. Place and date: Near Guignola, Italy, 1–2 October 1944.
Citation: Leading a squad of Company L, he gallantly cleared the way for his company's approach along a ridge toward its objective, the Casoni di Remagna. When his platoon was pinned down by heavy fire from enemy mortars, machine guns, machine pistols, and rifles, he climbed in advance of his squad on a maneuver around the left flank to locate and eliminate the enemy gun positions. In a one-man attack, heroically and voluntarily undertaken in the face of tremendous risks, Sgt. Karaberis captured 5 enemy machine gun positions, killed 8 Germans, took 22 prisoners, cleared the ridge leading to his company's objective, and drove a deep wedge into the enemy line, making it possible for his battalion to occupy important, commanding ground.

George H. Eldridge, Sec 37, Row B, Grave 1. Sergeant, Company C, 6th U.S. Cavalry. Place and date: At Wichita River, Tex., 12 July 1870.
Citation: Gallantry in action.

Harry Harvey, Sec 60, Grave E-4. Sergeant, U.S. Marine Corps.
Citation: Served in battle against the enemy at Benictian, 16 February 1900. Throughout this action and in the presence of the enemy, Harvey distinguished himself by meritorious conduct.

Luther Kaltenbach, Sec 43, Row A, Grave 15. Corporal, Company F, 12th Iowa Infantry. Place and date: At Nashville, Tenn., 16 December 1864.
Citation: Capture of flag, of 44th Mississippi Infantry (C.S.A.).

William F. Lukes, Sec 7, Row F, Grave 19. Landsman, U.S. Navy. G.O. No.: 180, 10 October 1872.
Citation: Served with Company D during the capture of the Korean forts, 9 and 10 June 1871. Fighting the enemy inside the fort, Lukes received a severe cut over the head.

George McKee, Sec 1, Row G, Grave 2. Color Sergeant, Company D, 89th New York Infantry. Place and date: At Petersburg, Va., 2 April 1865.
Citation: Gallantry as color bearer in the assault on Fort Gregg.

Edward Murphy, Sec 44, Row I, Grave 22. Private, Company G, 1st U.S. Cavalry. Place and date: At Chiricahua Mountains, Ariz., 20 October 1869.
Citation: Gallantry in action.

Edwin Phoenix, Sec 67, Row H, Grave 22. Corporal, Company E, 4th U.S. Cavalry. Place and date: Near Red River, Tex., 26–28 September 1874.
Citation: Gallantry in action.

Samuel Porter, Sec 40, Row E, Grave 6. Farrier, Company L, 6th U.S. Cavalry. Place and date: At Wichita River, Tex., 12 July 1870.
Citation: Gallantry in action.

Charles W. Rundle, Sec 34, Row I, Grave 11. Private, Company A, 116th Illinois Infantry. Place and date: At Vicksburg, Miss., 22 May 1863.
Citation: Gallantry in the charge of the "volunteer storming party."

Griffin Seward, Sec 15, Row D, Grave 10. Wagoner, Company G, 8th U.S. Cavalry. Place and date: At Chiricahua Mountains, Ariz., 20 October 1863.
Citation: Gallantry in action.

Timothy Sullivan, Sec 18, Row H, Grave 2. Coxswain, U.S. Navy. G.O. No.: 11, 3 April 1863.
Citation: Served onboard the *USS Louisville* during various actions of that vessel. During the engagements of the *Louisville,* Sullivan acted as first captain of a nine-inch gun and throughout his period of service was "especially commended for his attention to duty, bravery, and coolness in action."

James Sweeney, Sec 78, Row P, Grave 3. Private, Company A, 1st Vermont Cavalry. Place and date: At Cedar Creek, Va., 19 October 1864.
Citation: With one companion captured the state flag of a North Carolina regiment, together with three officers and an ambulance with its mules and driver.

†**Robert H. Von Schlick,** Sec 81, Row G, Grave 20. Private, Company C, 9th U.S. Infantry. Place and date: At Tientsin, China, 13 July 1900.
Citation: Although previously wounded while carrying a wounded comrade to a place of safety, he rejoined his command, which partly occupied an exposed position upon a dike, remaining there after his command had been withdrawn, singly keeping up the fire, and presenting himself as a conspicuous target until he was literally shot off his position by the enemy.

From its establishment in 1889 until 1973, the cemetery was operated by the Soldiers' Home and its successors, the Veterans Bureau and the Veterans Administration Medical Center. The first superintendent was assigned at that time. Former superintendents/directors are:

Theodore J. Nick, Jr., December 1973–March 1976
Henry A. Hartwig, June 1976–December 1977
Ronald F. Houska, January 1978–September 1979
Juanita Walker, October 1979–December 1983
Therese J. Bush, January 1984–August 1987

Patricia Hagler, September 1987–1989
Helen Szumylo, 1989–1994
Lucy Devenney, 1994–1998
William Livingston, 1998–2004
Gloria Mote, 2004–2006
Paula Haley, 2006–2007
Cynthia Nunez, 2007–Present

Loudon Park National Cemetery
3445 Frederick Avenue
Baltimore, Maryland 21229

The cemetery, located in the southwest section of the city of Baltimore, was originally a military cemetery within Loudon Park Cemetery, a private cemetery established in 1853. The land, 5.6 acres, was acquired in 1874, 1875, 1882, 1883, and 1903 from Loudon Park Cemetery Co. and owners of individual lots therein.

The national cemetery was established in 1862, and original interments came from the general hospitals in Baltimore, the Relay House, and Elkridge Landing. Approximately 200 remains from the soldiers' lots in Laurel Cemetery were removed to Loudon Park National Cemetery in 1884. While the records of the cemetery do not show reinterments from Laurel Cemetery (colored), they do show that about 1,000 interments, mostly colored, were made about that time.

The report of the inspector of national cemeteries dated July 21, 1871, shows total interments of 1,790. Among these were only 166 unknowns. Also included in the total at that time were 139 "Rebel soldiers, prisoners of war" who died at Fort McHenry, Maryland. The

G.A.R. Monument, Loudon National Cemetery.

inspector also reported that the superintendent had recently been discharged, and the cemetery was in very poor condition.

Five special monuments have been erected in the cemetery.

The Maryland Daughters Monument, erected in 1884, is inscribed, "To the Sons of Maryland who perished in preserving to us and our posterity the 'Government of the people, by the people, for the people,' secured by our fathers through the Union, this memorial is erected by her loyal and grateful daughters."

The G.A.R. Monument was erected in 1898 by the A.W. Dodge Post 44 "In memory of our Comrades."

The Unknown Dead Monument, erected in 1895 by the Women's Relief Corps of the Grand Army of the Republic is dedicated, "to the memory of the unknown dead."

The Maryland Naval Monument was erected in 1896 by the Naval Veterans Association of Maryland and dedicated as "Maryland['s] tribute to her loyal sons who served in the United States Navy during the war of preservation of the Union."

Finally, the Confederate Monument, erected in 1912 by the United States, marks the burial place of 29 Confederate soldiers who died at Fort McHenry while prisoners of war.

There are four Medal of Honor recipients interred in the cemetery. Daggers appear before the names of two men who were killed in action.

†**Henry G. Costin,** Sec B, Grave 460. Private, U.S. Army, Company H, 115th Infantry, 29th Division. Place and date: Near Bois-de-Consenvoye, France, 8 October 1918.
Citation: When the advance of his platoon had been held up by machine gun fire and a request was made for an automatic rifle team to charge the nest, Pvt. Costin was the first to volunteer. Advancing with his team, under terrific fire of enemy artillery, machine guns, and trench mortars, he continued after all his comrades had become casualties and he himself had been seriously wounded. He operated his rifle until he collapsed. His act resulted in the capture of about 100 prisoners and several machine guns. He succumbed from the effects of his wounds shortly after the accomplishment of his heroic deed.

†**James T. Jennings,** Sec A, Grave 1410. Private, U.S. Army; died March 22, 1865.

Henry Newman, Post Section, Grave 739. First Sergeant, Company F, 5th U.S. Cavalry. Place and date: At Whetstone Mountains, Ariz., 13 July 1872.
Citation: He and two companions covered the withdrawal of wounded comrades from the fire of an Apache band well concealed among the rocks.

William Taylor, Officers Section, Grave 16. Sergeant, Co. H, and 2d Lt. Co. M, 1st Maryland Inf. Place and date: At Front Royal, Va., 23 May 1862. At Weldon Railroad, Va., 19 August 1864.
Citation: When a sergeant, at Front Royal, Va., he was painfully wounded while obeying an order to burn a bridge, but, persevering in the attempt, he burned the bridge and prevented its use by the enemy. Later, at Weldon Railroad, Va., then a lieutenant, he voluntarily took the place of a disabled officer and undertook a hazardous reconnaissance beyond the lines of the army; was taken prisoner in the attempt.

There were 7,141 interments as of September 30, 2008. The cemetery was closed for interments on September 30, 1970, except for those in reserved gravesites, or in existing graves under the single gravesite per family policy. The cemetery is under the supervision of the Director, Baltimore National Cemetery.

Former superintendents/directors of the cemetery are:

Shelby A. Robbins, June 1933–April 1950
Clarence E. Suders, April 1950–June 1961
John H. Richardson, September 1961–November 1962

Gartrell J. McRae, November 1962–April 1964
Eugene G. Goodman, April 1964–November 1970

Marietta National Cemetery

500 Washington Avenue
Marietta, Georgia 30060

The cemetery is located in Cobb County, one block off the main street of Marietta, Georgia. Marietta National Cemetery was established in 1866 to provide a suitable final resting place for soldiers of the Union Armies killed in battle or dying in hospitals during the advance from Chattanooga through Georgia in 1864 and early 1865. Rows of white marble headstones offer mute testimony to the great price paid during this advance.

Henry G. Cole, a citizen of Marietta who had remained loyal to the Union throughout the Civil War, offered land to be used as a burial ground for both Union and Confederate fatalities. His hope was that by honoring those who had fallen together, the living might learn to live in peace together. Unfortunately, the bitter differences which remained during the early days of Reconstruction made it impossible for either the North or the South to accept Mr. Cole's offer toward reconciliation. When this effort failed, 24 acres were offered to General George H. Thomas for use as a national cemetery. The land was conveyed to the United States on July 31, 1866. A second donation by Mr. Cole in 1867 and a purchase in 1870 of an outstanding dower interest brought the cemetery to its present size of 23.256 acres.

This site was at one time the projected site of the capitol of the Confederate States of America. Mr. Cole had refused an offer of $50,000 for the property for that purpose. He rejected the offer with the comment that he "expected to put it to a better purpose."

In recognition of Mr. Cole's gift, the government made express provision that a burial plot be set aside for members of the Cole family, irrespective of relationship. Mr. Cole died on April 18, 1875, and was interred in Grave 1 of the Cole Plot. Further recognition of the gift came in 1909 when Congress authorized a bronze plaque to be placed at the gate of the cemetery to commemorate the gift.

Daniel Webster Cole, son of the donor, lived for many years in the family home across the street from the cemetery. He maintained an active interest in the cemetery and supervised the interment of other members of the Cole family. He was a construction engineer by profession, and in 1892, made the first layout map of the cemetery. His drawing was the basis for later official layout maps. Daniel Cole died on June 2, 1958, at the age of 95 years and was interred in the Cole Plot.

The cemetery was laid out by Chaplain Thomas B. Van Horne and for a long period interments were made under his supervision. He was succeeded by Lieutenant A.W. Corliss, 33rd U.S. Infantry, and then by a Lieutenant Farnsworth.

The Office of the Superintendent of National Cemeteries, Head quarters, Department of the Cumberland, in a document dated June 21, 1869, refers to the cemetery as the "Marietta and Atlanta National Cemetery."

From the summit of that would be *Capitol Hill* now floats the Stars and Stripes and around it lie.... Union dead whose remains have been gathered by careful and tender hands from all the battlefields and hospital grounds of Sherman's advance upon Atlanta, from the banks of Oostanaula at Resaca to Jonesboro below Atlanta and east to Augusta.... Here lie those who fell with McPherson at Atlanta; with Harker at Kennesaw; on the fields of "Peachtree Creek" and in the forests of New Hope Church; and here too lie those martyrs who so freely sacrificed their lives on the heights of Allatoona to make Sherman's march to the sea possible.

The original sections were laid out in concentric circles around the flag staff with paths radiating through the circles. Original interments were remains found through an extremely detailed search of every farm, churchyard, and town from Chattanooga through the southern outskirts of Atlanta. The dead from central Alabama, at first collected and interred in the national cemetery at Montgomery, Alabama, were transferred here prior to 1871, and that cemetery abandoned. On the granite arch over the cemetery gate is the following inscription: "Here rest the remains of 10,312 Officers and Soldiers who died in defense of the Union 1861–1865."

One of the honored dead interred in these hallowed grounds is John Clark, who distinguished himself not only as a soldier but also as a civil servant during the early years of the United States. Clark was born in February 1766, the son of General Elijah Clark and Hannah Harrington Clark. He fought in many battles during the Revolutionary War, and during his career rose from the rank of lieutenant to major general. He served in the Georgia House of Representatives, 1801–1803, and in the Georgia Senate, 1803–1804. He was elected governor twice, in 1819 and in 1823, and, after completing his terms as governor of Georgia, was appointed Indian Agent for Florida by President Andrew Jackson. Clark and his wife contracted yellow fever and died in Florida within 14 days of each other. In 1923 the Daughters of the American Revolution had the remains of John and Nancy Clark moved to Marietta National Cemetery. The original marker was replaced in 1963 by the state of Georgia.

By May 1870, the Twentieth Army Corps had erected a monument in the cemetery dedicated to their comrades. On Memorial Day 1926, a monument donated by the state of Wisconsin was dedicated to the 405 sons of that state who had perished in Georgia during the Civil War and who are interred in the cemetery. The 12-foot-high monument of Wisconsin granite, surmounted by the image of a beaver, is inscribed, "Dedicated to the Memory of Wisconsin Soldiers Who Gave Their Lives in Defense of the Union 1861–1865."

In 1960, the Atlanta chapter of the Gold Star Mothers donated a marble monument inscribed, "In memory of Members of the Armed Forces of the United States Missing in Action." The monument is placed near the Memorial Section.

Arbor in Marietta National Cemetery.

Major General Crump Garvin, U.S. Army, was buried on September 10, 1990. General Garvin served in the Army for 38 years, retiring in 1958 as deputy commander, Third U.S. Army, and commanding general of reserve forces in the Third Army area. As a colonel in World War II, he served as chief of staff of the American Division in the battle of Guadalcanal Island, commanded the division's 164th Infantry Regiment at Bougainville Island, and then joined General Douglas MacArthur's forces in the invasion of Leyte in the Philippine Islands. He was promoted to brigadier general while in combat on Okinawa. As major general, he commanded the Pusan Logistical Command and the 2nd Logistical Command in the early months of the Korean War. His decorations include the Distinguished Service Medal with oak leaf cluster, the Legion of Merit with oak leaf cluster, the Army Commendation Ribbon with oak leaf cluster, the Combat Infantryman's Badge, and numerous service ribbons with ten battle stars.

The cemetery was closed for interments on October 28, 1970, except for those in reserved gravesites, or second interments in existing graves under the single gravesite per family policy. As of September 30, 2008, there were 18,709 interments in the cemetery. The cemetery is administered by the Director, Georgia National Cemetery.

Among the memorial markers erected in Marietta National Cemetery is one to honor the memory of Corporal Lee H. Phillips. He is the sole Medal of Honor recipient memorialized here. Corporal Phillips survived the mission described below but was killed in action 23 days later.

†**Lee Hugh Phillips,** Sec B, Grave 8. Corporal, U.S. Marine Corps, Company E, 2d Battalion, 7 Marines, 1st Marine Division (Rein). Place and date: Korea, 4 November 1950. Corporal Phillips was killed in action 27 November 1950.

Citation: For conspicuous gallantry and intrepidity at the risk of his life above and beyond the call of duty while serving as a squad leader of Company E, in action against enemy aggressor forces. Corporal Phillips assumed the point position in the attack against a strongly defended and well-entrenched, numerically superior enemy force occupying a vital hill position which had been unsuccessfully assaulted on five separate occasions by units of the Marine Corps and other friendly forces. Corporal Phillips fearlessly led his men in a bayonet charge up the precipitous slope under a deadly hail of mortar, small-arms, and machine gun fire. Quickly rallying his squad when it was pinned down by a heavy and accurate mortar barrage, he continued to lead his men through the bombarded area and, although only five members were left in the casualty-ridden unit, gained the military crest of the hill where he was immediately subjected to an enemy counterattack. Although greatly outnumbered by an enemy squad, Cpl. Phillips boldly engaged the hostile force with hand grenades and rifle fire and, exhorting his gallant group of Marines to follow him, stormed forward to completely overwhelm the enemy. With only three men now left in his squad, he proceeded to spearhead an assault on the last remaining strongpoint, which was defended by four of the enemy on a rocky and almost inaccessible portion of the hill position. Using one hand to climb up the extremely hazardous precipice, he hurled grenades with the other and, with two remaining comrades, succeeded in annihilating the pocket of resistance and in consolidating the position. Immediately subjected to a sharp counterattack by an estimated enemy squad, he skillfully directed the fire of his men and employed his own weapon with deadly effectiveness to repulse the numerically superior force. By his valiant leadership, indomitable fighting spirit and resolute determination in the face of heavy odds, Cpl. Phillips served to inspire all who observed him and was directly responsible for the destruction of the enemy stronghold.

Former superintendents/directors of the cemetery are:

Chaplain Thomas Van Horne, July 1866–
  Unknown
Lieutenant A.W. Corliss, Unknown
Lieutenant Farnsworth, Unknown

Gerald C. Nelson, November 1970–July 1973
Donald R. Peterson, July 1973–June 1976
Thomas E. Costanzo, June 1976–January 1978
Therese J. Bush, April 1978–August 1979

Mr. Hughes, 1869–Unknown
Andrew B. Drum, July 1888–November 1892
John A. Commerford, November 1892–
　November 1914
Robert A. Spence, January 1937–May 1937
Russell V. Ridenour, October 1943–August 1957
Charles J. Horton, August 1957–June 1967
John W. Clemons, July 1967–November 1969
Theodore J. Nick, December 1969–November
　1970

Donald R. Peterson, August 1979–September
　1980
Lonnie M. Nelms, September 1980–August 1981
Patricia Hagler, August 1981–November 1985
Jack D. Shaw, January 1986–October 1987
David D. Dimick, 1987–1989
Douglas W. Smith, Jr., 1990–

Marion National Cemetery
1700 East 38th Street
Marion, Indiana 46952

The cemetery is located on the east side of the Department of Veterans Affairs Medical Center (DVAMC). The DVAMC is in the southeast section of the city, and is bounded by 38th Street and Lincoln Boulevard.

In 1888, Colonel George W. Steele, attorney and legislator, convinced Congress of the need to establish a Soldiers' Home in Grant County, Indiana. The facility, one of six National Homes for Disabled Volunteer Soldiers established in the United States, was opened in 1889. In 1920, the home became known as the Marion Sanatorium, and on July 3, 1930, it was transferred to the newly created Veterans Administration (VA).

Colonel Steele served as the first governor of the home, and later became the first territorial governor of Oklahoma.

The cemetery was established for burial of those who died at the home. The first interment occurred in May 1890. Some of the early administrators of the home are interred in the cemetery. Standing guard near the Silent Circle is a monument dedicated to the Marion branch of the National Home by an act of Congress on July 23, 1888. Atop the monument are three militiamen with rifles and flag. The inscription reads, "In Memory of the Men Who Offered Their Lives in Defense of Their Country." In July 1990, the Watchfire Committee dedicated a memorial "To Those Who Died in Vietnam."

With the passage of the Cemetery Act of 1973 (Public Law 93–43), the cemetery was one of the 21 VA cemeteries transferred to the National Cemetery System.

As of September 30, 2008, the cemetery encompassed 45.1 acres and contained 8,988 interments.

There are three Medal of Honor recipients interred here:

Henry J. Hyde, Sec 1, Grave 97. Sergeant, Company M, 1st U.S. Cavalry. Place and date: Winter of 1872–1873.
　Citation: Gallant conduct during campaigns and engagements with Apaches.

Nicholas Irwin, Sec 1, Grave 382. Seaman, U.S. Navy. G.O. No. 45, December 31, 1864.
　Citation: Onboard the *USS Brooklyn* during action against rebel forts and gun boats and with the ram *Tennessee* in Mobile Bay, August 5, 1864. Despite severe damage to his ship and the loss of several men on board as enemy fire raked her decks from stem to stern, Irwin fought his gun with skill and courage throughout the furious battle which resulted in the surrender of the prize rebel ram *Tennessee* and in the damaging and destruction of batteries at Fort Morgan.

Jeremiah Kuder, Sec 4, Grave 2464. Lieutenant, Company A, 74th Indiana Infantry. Place and date: At Jonesboro, Georgia, September 1, 1864.
　Citation: Capture of flag of 8th and 9th Arkansas (C.S.A.).

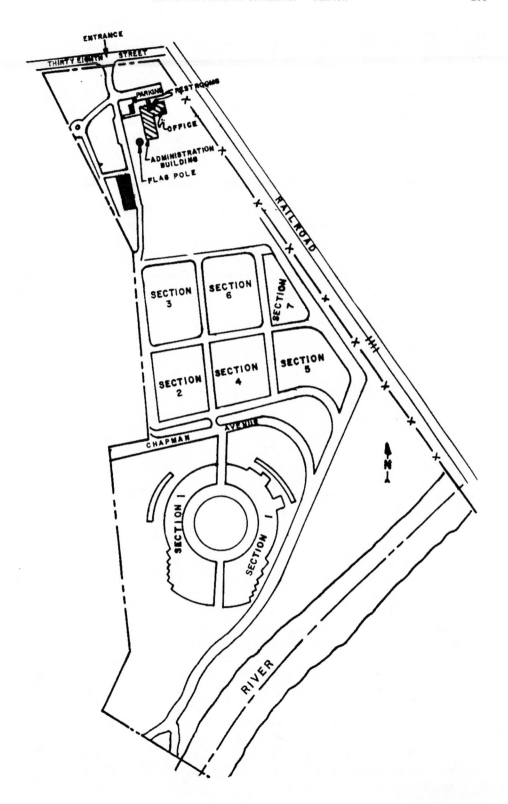

Former directors of the cemetery are:

Charles R. Weeks, September 1974–February
  1976
Robert W. John, June 1976–December 1981
Arthur J. Conklin, March 1982–July 1984
Helen B. Szumylo, October 1984–May 1987

Gerald T. Vitela, June 1987–?
Brian G. Moore, January 2004–January 2006
Edward Marshall, Jan 2006–October 2007
Elfrieda Robinson, December 2007–Present

Massachusetts National Cemetery
Connery Avenue
Bourne, Massachusetts 01532

The cemetery is situated in Barnstable County on Cape Cod, about 65 miles southeast of Boston. It is adjacent to the Otis Air Force Base, and east of the village of Pocasset.

After the National Cemetery System was transferred to the Veterans Administration in 1973, and the regional cemetery concept adopted in 1974, a search began for a site in New England on which to locate a large national cemetery to serve Standard Federal Region I. The New England region had no active national cemeteries at that time. The veteran population center was Boston, so the search was somewhat localized. This search for available land which could be acquired at no cost to the government resulted in the identification of a 749-acre tract on the 22,000-acre Otis Air Force Base. The base was state-owned land leased to the Department of Defense, which terminated its lease with the state on that portion of land transferred to the NCS.

Massachusetts National Cemetery, dedicated on October 11, 1980, was the third new national cemetery to be established in over 25 years (Calverton and Riverside were the first and second). The designated name was the Veterans Administration National Cemetery of Bourne, Massachusetts, but was soon changed through usage, not officially, to its present name.

The history of what is today referred to as Otis Air Force Base incorporates the history of two distinct entities, Otis Field and Camp Edwards. The land for the Camp Edwards Military Reservation, named for Major General Clarence D. Edwards, commander of the famed 26th Yankee Division of World War I, was acquired by the Massachusetts state legislature from what was then the Shawnee Forest.

In 1933, in one corner of the reservation, the initial aircraft runway was constructed for what would eventually become Otis Air Force Base. After expansion in 1936, the facility was officially designated Otis Field in honor of 1st Lieutenant Frank Jesse Otis, Jr., MD, pilot and flight surgeon. He was assigned to the 101st Observation Squadron in the Massachusetts National Guard, the forerunner of the 102nd Fighter Interceptor Wing (Air National Guard), presently based at Otis.

With the growing threat of war, the United States in 1940 leased the land encompassing Camp Edwards and Otis Field and began an expansion to accommodate a full division with all of its support units. In 1941, the 26th Yankee Division and the cadre of the American Division trained at Camp Ed wards prior to embarking for Europe and the South Pacific. Aircraft from Otis Field flew daily patrols against the German U-boats which threatened the eastern coast.

After World War II, Otis Field was deactivated and stood idle until 1949, when it was transferred to the U.S. Air Force and redesignated Otis Air Force Base. Today, the Massachusetts Army National Guard and the Air National Guard have operational control of both facilities. It serves in air defense missions, the Coast Guard mission, and as training sites for National Guard and Army Reserve units.

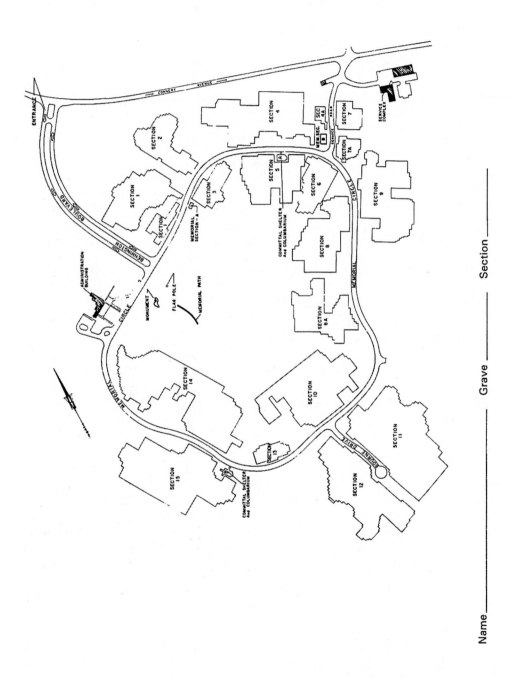

Massachusetts National Cemetery.

The cemetery is located in the northwest corner of Otis Air Force Base. Natural hollows in the hilly terrain are referred to as kettles. A large kettle hole, locally called the Natural Amphitheater, is situated just south of the administration building. It is about ½ mile wide and 150 feet deep. The interesting feature of the kettle is its climate, which varies greatly from its rim to the floor.

The first interment, on October 14, 1980, was that of Olive Shaw, telephone operator, U.S. Army, a female veteran of World War I. The two columbaria at the committal shelters were opened on October 28, 1982. As of September 30, 2008, there were 46,380 interments.

On October 14, 1987, the remains of Richard David Dewert, recipient of the Medal of Honor, were disinterred from Woodlawn National Cemetery and reinterred here.

> †**Richard David Dewert,** Hospital Corpsman, U.S. Navy. Hospital Corps man attached to Marine infantry company, 1st Marine Division. Place and date: Korea, 5 April 1951.
>
> Citation: For conspicuous gallantry and intrepidity at the risk of his life above and beyond the call of duty while serving as a HC, in action against enemy aggressor forces. When a fire team from the point platoon of his company was pinned down by a deadly barrage of hostile automatic weapons fire and suffered many casualties, HC Dewert rushed to the assistance of one of the more seriously wounded and, despite a painful leg wound sustained while dragging the stricken Marine to safety, steadfastly refused medical treatment for himself and immediately dashed back through the fire-swept area to carry a second wounded man out of the line of fire. Undaunted by the mounting hail of devastating enemy fire, he bravely moved forward a third time and received another serious wound in the shoulder after discovering that a wounded Marine had already died. Still persistent in his refusal to submit to first aid, he resolutely answered the call of a fourth stricken comrade and, while rendering medical assistance, was himself mortally wounded by a burst of enemy fire. His courageous initiative, great personal valor, and heroic spirit of self-sacrifice in the face of overwhelming odds reflect the highest credit upon HC Dewert and enhance the finest traditions of the U.S. Naval Service. He gallantly gave his life for his country.

Brigadier General Paul E. Kincaid, a retired officer of the Massachusetts National Guard, was interred on February 26, 1990. The highly decorated general served as a first lieutenant in the 23rd Infantry Regiment, 2nd Division, during World War II, and took part in the Normandy landings and the Battle of the Bulge. He wrote a 1987 book, *Lines of Departure,* about his experiences in the war.

On August 4, 1990, an unknown Civil War soldier was buried, more than 125 years after his death. A county road crew unearthed his remains near Sumter, S.C. From bones, buttons and bits of cloth, the FBI and other investigators identified the remains as those of a young man, 19 to 21 years old, who was a member of a Massachusetts regiment operating in South Carolina during the closing months of the Civil War. Local historians determined that the soldier died after General Robert E. Lee surrendered at Appomattox on April 9, 1865. He apparently died in one of a series of skirmishes that occurred during the week following Lee's surrender. Civil War re-enactors of the 12th Massachusetts Cavalry served as the honor guard at his burial.

Former Directors of the cemetery are:

Ralph E. Church, November 1979–April 1987
Gary W. Smith, 1987–1992
David Wells, 1993–1995

Kurt Rotar, 1995–2005
Paul McFarland, 2005–Present

Memphis National Cemetery

3568 Townes Avenue
Memphis, Tennessee 38122

Memphis National Cemetery is located in Shelby County, Memphis, Tennessee, in the northeastern part of the city. The cemetery was established in 1867 as a concentration point for the remains of those who were buried in the military hospital cemeteries in and around Memphis, and from many isolated combat sites on both sides of the Mississippi River.

On June 8, 1861, Tennessee became the last state to secede from the Union. It was the first state to be readmitted on July 24, 1866, due largely to the efforts of Andrew Johnson, the 17th president of the United States. The location of Memphis, one of the great commercial centers on the Mississippi River, was of considerable strategic importance to the Confederacy. But the Confederacy lost New Orleans in April 1862, and on June 6, 1862, strong land and naval forces combined to seize the city of Memphis. Thus, the Confederacy was severely pinched by loss of control of both ends of the Mississippi, although complete Union domination of the "Father of Waters" did not come until the fall of Vicksburg on July 4, 1863. At Vicksburg, General Pemberton surrendered his entire command of 30,000 troops. General Grant provided rations to Pemberton's troops and, instead of taking them captive, released them as prisoners of war on parole.

The inevitable toll of sick and wounded necessitated the establishment of many military hospitals. Memphis, once it had come under control of the Union forces, furnished a convenient location to care for the wounded and sick from the Mississippi River area of combat. General hospitals capable of caring for 5,000 men were set up in and around the city. The more serious cases were sent to these hospitals in three river steamers assigned

Memphis National Cemetery, 1944.

to the medical department as hospital transports. These hospitals, though better staffed and organized than some Civil War facilities, nonetheless had a high death rate among the ill and wounded committed to their care.

The site for the cemetery was chosen by a board of officers consisting of Chaplain William R. Earnshaw; Brevet Lieutenant Colonel A.W. Wills, assistant quartermaster; and Brevet Major G.W. Marshall, assistant quartermaster. The 32.62 acres purchased for the cemetery were then about 7 miles northeast of the city. The first superintendent was John F. Carl, a discharged corporal of Company A, Fourth Artillery Regiment. He was appointed on August 6, 1867.

Old records indicate that the national cemetery was at one time known as the Mississippi River National Cemetery. This was a most appropriate designation since a very large number of the initial burials were of members of the Union forces who participated in the battles and engagements during the early years of the war, which contributed to eventual control of the Mississippi River. Following the close of the war, reinterments were made in the cemetery from camps and hospitals in and around Memphis, Island No. 10, New Madrid, Fort Pillow, numerous places on the Memphis and Charleston and the Memphis and Louisville railroads, and from Hickman, Kentucky, to Helena, Arkansas.

During the early Civil War period, riverboats of the U.S. Navy performed an effective and important role in gaining and maintaining control of the Mississippi River. Interred at Memphis National Cemetery are the identified remains of nearly 200 crew members from many of the ships of this river flotilla.

In sections A, B, C, D, E, H, J, and K are 8,866 Civil War graves marked "unknown." This is the second largest group of unknowns interred in any national cemetery. The large number of interments of unknowns may be attributed to the facts that the cemetery was not established until 1867, two years after the close of the Civil War, and remains were brought from so many places. During the interval from initial burial of these decedents to the time of disinterment for removal to Memphis, many of the crude wooden burial markers had been removed or destroyed through exposure to the elements. Since there was no mandatory form of personal identification carried by these soldiers, identification of disinterred remains was extremely difficult.

There are six isolated graves marked with the Confederate Cross. In addition, several sections are devoted to Southern states.

Memphis National Cemetery is the burial place of many of the victims, both known and unknown, of one of the nation's most tragic maritime disasters the explosion and burning of the Mississippi River steamboat USS Sultana during the night of April 26, 1865. This well-known river craft had limited cabin space for 75 to 100 passengers and by law could carry a total of 376 persons, including the crew. The ship left New Orleans on April 21, 1865, with stops scheduled upriver at Vicksburg, Memphis, Cairo, Evansville, Louisville, and Cincinnati. The Vicksburg landing was made on April 24 to take on passengers and cargo.

At Vicksburg a huge throng of Union soldiers, lately released from Confederate prison camps, anxiously awaited the arrival of the Sultana, which was to take them to Cairo, Illinois. From there they would make their way home. An estimated 1,800 to 2,000 crowded onboard the ship. The men were so eager to go on board that the authorities decided to delay making out muster rolls until after the ship had left Vicksburg. A leaking boiler had been hastily repaired at Vicksburg, and the overloaded steamer pressed on upriver to Memphis, bucking strong river currents reinforced by heavy spring rains. Memphis was reached during the evening of April 26, and some of the returning soldiers disembarked and went out to see the sights of the town while the ship was readied for the journey upriver, and further repairs made to the boilers. A few of the men missed the boat when it sailed from Memphis. As the *Sultana* pushed on through the night to a point above Memphis near a group of islands known as the Hen and Chickens, the overburdened and weakened boilers exploded. Fire broke out on the ship, and hundreds of hapless passengers were forced to jump into the swift current of the Mississippi. Some were drowned. Others were rescued and taken to various Memphis hospitals, where many died as a result of burns, exposure to the elements, or weakened physical condition brought about by long incarceration in Confederate prison camps. The death toll of this Mississippi River tragedy has been estimated at more than 1,700 persons.

Three years after its establishment, Memphis National Cemetery was ranked fifth in number of interments among the 73 national cemeteries under the control of the War Department. The cemetery contained the remains of 13,965 Civil War decedents. Members of Civil War volunteer organizations from 28 states, as well as members of the U.S. Army, the U.S. Navy, the U.S. Colored Troops, and the Mississippi River Marine Brigade are interred here. Some 537 Civil War regiments are represented among the honored dead in these hallowed grounds.

Located within the cemetery are two large and imposing monuments, one erected by the state of Minnesota in 1916 and the second by the state of Illinois in 1928.

The Minnesota monument, in Section C of the cemetery, depicts in bronze the figure of a Union soldier, his rifle reversed, standing with head bowed in tribute to fallen comrades. The marble base upon which the statue rests has carved upon it the following inscription:

> Erected A.D. 1916 by the
> State of Minnesota
> in Memory of Her Soldiers
> Here Buried Who Lost Their
> Lives in the Service of the
> United States in the War for
> the Preservation of the Union
> A.D. 1861–1865

The tribute of the state of Illinois, located in Section B, is a sarcophagus monument of granite and bronze showing the shrouded figure of a soldier lying in state. The monument bears replicas of the seals of the United States and the state of Illinois, and the following two inscriptions:

> When President Lincoln Called for Volunteers to Defend the Life of Our Imperiled Nation, These Valiant Sons of Illinois, Together with Other Heroes Offered Their Lives with Patriotism Unsurpassed. With Unflinching Bravery They Fought the Bloody Battle of the Great Civil War for Union and Liberty. Upon Them Therefore, a Grateful State Bestows the Crown of Undying Affection and the Laurel of Victory.

*   *   *

> This Monument Erected by the State of Illinois in 1928 to the Glorious Memory of the Soldiers of Illinois Who Fought in the Civil War.

Over the years Memphis National Cemetery has been expanded, and to day it covers 44.2 acres. As of September 30, 2008, there were 42,324 interments. The cemetery has space for cremated remains, but is closed for initial interments.

The post section of the cemetery was established to fulfill the requirements of Camp McCain, Mississippi (World War II camp activated October 14, 1942, and declared surplus on January 1, 1946). In 1946, Headquarters recommended abolishing the post section, but the recommendation was not favorably considered by the Office of the Quartermaster General.

There is one known Medal of Honor recipient interred in the cemetery:

James H. Robinson, Sec H, Grave 4131. Private, Company B, 3d Michigan Cavalry. Place and date: At Brownsville, Ark., 27 January 1865.

Citation: Successfully defended himself, single-handed against seven guerrillas, killing the leader (Capt. W.C. Stephenson) and driving off the remainder of the party.

Known former superintendents/directors of Memphis National Cemetery are:

John F. Carl, August 1867–Unknown
Bernard J. Slade, January 1939–February 1949
Robert A. Spence, March 1949–April 1954
Harold L. Keogh, May 1954–July 1955
Raymond J. Costanzo, August 1955–August 1957
John T. Spelman, September 1957–August 1959
Oberlin H. Carter, September 1959–February 1964
Louis B. Hellmeyer, February 1964–May 1968
Grover R. Neal, June 1968–June 1970
Lewis J. King, June 1970–November 1977

Juanita Walker, November 1977–September 1979
Velva Melton, November 1979–February 1981
Raymond L. Cordell, March 1981–December 1982
Dennis P. Gura, February 1983–April 1985
David M. Cariota, 1985–August 1992
Mark E. Maynard, September 1992–June 1999
Mary J. Dill, June 1999–June 2005
Gary N. Overall, June 2005–April 2007
Darrin W. White, July 2007–Present

Little Rock National Cemetery supervises the Memphis National Cemetery.

Mill Springs National Cemetery
Rural Route 2, P.O. Box 172
Nancy, Kentucky 42544

Mill Springs National Cemetery is located near Logan's Cross Roads in Pulaski County, approximately eight miles west of Somerset, Kentucky, off state Route 80 at Nancy, Kentucky.

The cemetery was originally designated Logan's Cross Roads National Cemetery. It is situated on the site of the Battle of Mill Springs, sometimes known as the Battle of Fishing Creek. On January 19, 1862, this battlefield was the scene of a brief but bloody skirmish occasioned by the invasion of Kentucky by a Confederate army led by General Felix K. Zollicoffer of Nashville, Tennessee. The Union forces were led by Major General George H. Thomas, who was to become known after the September 19–20, 1863, battle in Tennessee as the "Rock of Chickamauga." General Zollicoffer was killed in the engagement, some say by his own men, and the Confederate army was forced to retreat. The victorious Union soldiers, under the direction of General Thomas, gathered their dead and buried them in single graves in what is now the national cemetery. These graves were located just opposite the position of batteries B and C, 1st Ohio Volunteer Artillery, and about 500 yards north of the first battle position of the Union army.

After he had personally explored all of central and southern Kentucky, the site was selected for a national cemetery by Brevet Major E.B. Whitman, assistant quartermaster and superintendent of cemeteries in the Department of the Cumberland. Major Whitman felt that the spot marked a most decisive and important battle. The land, 3.5 acres, was donated to the United States on July 5, 1867, by William H. Logan, on whose farm the battle had been fought. Both Mr. Logan, who died in 1884, and his wife Nancy, who died in 1896, are buried in the national cemetery. Their gravesites are marked by private monuments.

Mills Springs National Cemetery.

In addition to the original battlefield casualties, the remains of Union soldiers found within a radius of 40 miles were concentrated in the cemetery. They were recovered from Somerset and its vicinity, Burnside Point, Waitsboro, Stegall's Ferry, Mill Springs, Horseshoe Bend, Greasy Creek, Monticello, Gap in the Ridge, Columbia and vicinity, from all points on the Cumberland River between Burnside Point and Jamestown, and from "almost inaccessible mountain country" where soldiers died of illness or were killed in skirmishes with guerrillas.

Mill Springs National Cemetery was established in 1862. The report of the inspector of national cemeteries dated November 22, 1870, indicated 341 known and 367 unknown interments in the cemetery. The names of over 200 of the Unknowns were known, but the bodies could not be individually identified. The dead included representatives of 11 states.

Approximately one mile from the national cemetery, a stone marker commemorates the grave of the Confederate casualties who were buried where they fell. Although General Zollicoffer's body was returned to his home in Tennessee, a monument near the mass grave commemorates the spot where he was killed.

As of September 30, 2008, there were 3,243 interments in the 6.3 acre cemetery. The cemetery is maintained by private contract, supervised by the director of Camp Nelson National Cemetery.

There is one Medal of Honor recipient interred in the cemetery. His remains were removed from a private cemetery and interred here in 1984.

Brent Woods, Sec A, Grave 930. Sergeant, Company B, 9th U.S. Cavalry. Place and date: New Mexico, 19 August 1881.
Citation: Saved the lives of his comrades and citizens of the detachment.

Former superintendents/directors of the cemetery are:

Peter McKenna, 1890–April 1895

Mrs. Peter McKenna (Acting), April 1895–
October 1895

Hiram S. Towne, 1896–1900

William C. MacMurray, July 1942–November
1943

Ever E. Rice, May 1946–September 1959

John E. Johnson, November 1959–December
1961

Lewis J. King, January 1962–February 1964

Earl R. White, February 1964–July 1964

William R. Rossbach, August 1964–October
1965

Andrew F. Szilvasi, October 1965–January 1968

Henry A. Hartwig, January 1968–August 1968

Donald D. Ratliff, October 1968–August 1977

Lewis J. King, November 1977–October 1982

Douglas M. Gibbs, November 1982–November
1983

Floyd E.A. Keck, February 1984–April 1985

Mobile National Cemetery
1202 Virginia Street
Mobile, Alabama 36604

Mobile National Cemetery was established in 1865. Since August 1864, when Mobile fell into Union hands after the assault by Flag Officer David G. Farragut, the U.S. Army had been making burials in a portion of the city-owned Magnolia Cemetery. Following a request from the Army for additional burial space for Federal dead, the city of Mobile readily complied. The original deed reads, "Resolved that the Mayor, Aldermen and Common Council hereby donate to the United States Government three acres of land in the extension of the new burying ground as a place of burial for United States soldiers to include the ground as occupied by the Federal Dead...." This resolution was unanimously adopted.

Original interments were remains moved to Mobile from Fort Morgan, Fort Gaines, Mobile, Spanish Fort, Fort Blakely, Fort Powell, Pollard, Conemuh, and other places in Alabama.

An additional donation of land was received in 1894, and a purchase was made in 1935. In 1936, a 1.67-acre tract which was unfit for burials (under water) was sold to the city. This plot was known as Freedman's Lot, or Parcel No. 2. The cemetery contains a total of 5.24 acres, in two parcels straddling Virginia Street. As of September 30, 2008, a total of 5,345 interments had been made in the cemetery.

The report of the inspector of national cemeteries dated February 15, 1871, states that a total of 902 interments had been made. Of these, 31 white soldiers, 2 sailors, and 91 black soldiers were reported known, and the rest were unknown. This report indicated that the information was taken from grave markers since there were no records in the office. Records available today indicate the Civil War dead as follows:

Union soldiers	628
Civilian employees of the U.S. Army	23
Unknowns	112
Colored soldiers representing 10 infantry regiments from various states	78
Total	841

These burials represent soldiers from 20 different states and 128 different regiments.

Also buried in the cemetery are the remains of 35 seamen and sailors from various vessels operating in and about Mobile Bay during the Civil War. The names of these vessels are: schooner *Cecilia*, ship *Harry of the West*, steamer *Huntsman*, British ship *J.R. Jarvis*, steamer *Kate Dale*, schooner *L.S. Davis*, steamboat *Mary Conley*, flat *Mary Louise*, British ship *Maxwell*, ship *Mountaineer*, British ship *Norwood*, *Ocean Wave*, schooner *Scout Q.M.E.*,

Confederate Fortification, Mobile National Cemetery, 1946.

brig *Star Orleans,* U.S. monitor *Winnebago, USS Brooklyn, USS Chicasaw, USS Cincinnati, USS Elk, USS Kittaning, USS Lebago, USS Port Royal, USS Winnebago.*

There are four Confederate soldiers interred in the cemetery: Jonathon Bibbs, Sec 2, Grave 560, died February 22, 1862; John Cander, Sec 2, Grave 532, died January 18, 1862; John LeCron, Sec 2, Grave 563, died January 18, 1862; and Jim Reed, Sec 3, Grave 713, date of death unknown. Reed was a private, Co. H, 48th Alabama Infantry.

In Section 7, there is a mound which is the remains of an old Confederate breastwork, known as Confederate Fortifications. A retaining wall was built around it in 1936. In 1940, the Electra Semmes Colston Chapter of the United Daughters of the Confederacy erected a granite monument between sections 7 and 8 to mark the Confederate Fortifications.

While the Apache Indians were at Vernon Barracks, Alabama, 13 of them died and were interred in Mobile National Cemetery (see Barrancas National Cemetery). Among them was Chappo, son of Geronimo, interred in Section 1, Grave 621-B, and Larry (or Lanny) Fun, cousin of Geronimo, interred in Section 3, Grave 656-C.

There is a large monument in the cemetery erected in 1892 by the survivors of the 76th Illinois Volunteer Infantry Regiment, in memory of their comrades who died in the Battle of Port Blakely, Alabama, April 9, 1865.

There is one known Medal of Honor recipient interred in Mobile National Cemetery. The dagger indicates that he was killed in action.

†**John Dury New,** Sec 7, Grave 2147. Private First Class, U.S. Marine Corps.
Citation: For conspicuous gallantry and intrepidity at the risk of his life above and beyond the call of duty while serving with the 2d Battalion, 7th Marines, 1st Marine Division, in action against enemy Japanese forces on Peleliu Island, Palau Group, 25 September 1944. When a Japanese soldier emerged from a cave in a cliff directly below an observation post and suddenly hurled a grenade into the position from which two men were directing mortar fire against enemy emplacements, Pfc. New instantly perceived the dire peril to the other Marines and, with utter disregard for his own safety, unhesitatingly flung himself upon the grenade and absorbed the full impact of the explosion, thus saving the lives of the two observers. He gallantly gave his life for his country.

During fiscal year 1963 the cemetery was closed except for interments in reserved gravesites and second interments in existing graves under the single gravesite per family policy. Cemetery maintenance is performed by a private contractor. The cemetery has been assigned to the director of Barrancas National Cemetery for administration and management since September 1983.

Former superintendents/directors of the cemetery are:

John A. Commerford, April 1869–April 1870
Mark L. Jacobs, March 1929–December 1947
Chester R. Lightfritz, January 1948–August 1948
Harold L. Keogh, September 1948–May 1954
Joseph V. Darby, May 1954–December 1954
James M. Griffin, December 1954–August 1955

Clifford E. Larkins, August 1955–December 1961
John E. Johnson, December 1961–June 1973
Willie B. Smith, January 1973–November 1977
Lonnie M. Nelms, December 1977–May 1980
Gilberto Lopez, May 1980–October 1981
Rodney L. Dunn, May 1982–September 1983

Mound City National Cemetery
P.O. Box 128
Mound City, Illinois 62963

Situated in Pulaski County, approximately one mile from Mound City, Illinois, the cemetery is on Illinois Highway No. 37 at its junction with U.S. Highway 51, seven miles north of Cairo, Illinois.

During the Civil War there were a navy yard and several general hospitals in Mound City. These factors determined the site selected for a cemetery. Burials began in 1864, and the national cemetery was established that year. The 1,644 original interments were the remains of those who died in the general hospitals.

The 10.5 acres of land were purchased in two separate parcels from S.S. Taylor and Edwin Parsons, trustees. The initial 10 acres were purchased in 1867, and ½ acre was acquired in 1873. The total price paid for the land was $825. The cemetery was completely surrounded by a strong dike to keep the back-water from the Ohio River from flooding it. Until U.S. Highway 51 was completed, the entrances to the cemetery were roadways over the dike. Part of this levee, or dike, still remains on the southwest side of the cemetery. The remainder was removed in 1968, making 1,228 gravesites available.

In addition to burials from the general hospitals of Mound City, remains were brought from Cairo, Illinois, Belmont, Missouri, and Paducah and Columbus, Kentucky. The report of the inspector of national cemeteries dated June 12, 1871, listed interments at that time as:

White soldiers and sailors, known	2,060
White soldiers and sailors, unknown	2,460
Colored soldiers and sailors, known	307
Rebel prisoners of war, unknown	41
Total	4,868

Current cemetery records indicate that there are 2,759 unknown decedents and 27 Confederate soldiers interred in the cemetery. As of September 30, 2,008, there was a total of 8,262 interments. The projected closing date for initial interments is beyond the year 2020.

In 1874 the state of Illinois erected the Illinois Soldiers Monument near the center of the cemetery. The base of the monument, 25 feet square and 4 feet high, is of granite and marble. Upon this base a pedestal 15 feet high supports a marble shaft on which is mounted a marble statue of the goddess of liberty. At the foot of the shaft stand two marble statues,

Illinois Soldiers Monument, Mound City National Cemetery.

one of a soldier and one of a sailor. The monument was placed to honor the Illinois soldiers and sailors interred in the national cemetery, some known and 2,637 unknown. In the early 1970s the statue of the goddess of liberty was toppled from the pedestal and broken. A replacement statue was shipped from the quarry in Italy but never reached the United States. The second replacement was received in 1974 and placed on the original pedestal.

Former superintendents/directors of the cemetery are:

Andrew K. Hill, January 1939–November 1945
Louis B. Hellmeyer, March 1946–April 1947
Clarence Otis, April 1947–September 1949
James Davis, September 1949–Unknown
John W. Cox, November 1951–April 1957
Walter Hanns, April 1957–May 1961
Norman W. Baumgardner, June 1961–October 1969
Thomas F. Morehead, December 1969–September 1971

Robert L. Whitfield, September 1971–July 1973
Richard L. Dodson, August 1973–October 1974
Willard A. Johnson, June 1976–May 1977
Lucille A. Fisher, November 1977–November 1979
Jimmy T. Jackson, November 1979–December 1980
Wilfred Messier, April 1985–July 1985

During the period from 1981 to April, 1985, Charles D. Pirtle, cemetery caretaker, supervised the operations of the cemetery. Since July 1985, the cemetery has been assigned to the director of Jefferson Barracks National Cemetery for administration and management.

Mountain Home National Cemetery
P.O. Box 8
Mountain Home, Tennessee 37684

Situated in the northeastern section of Tennessee in the foothills of the Appalachian Mountains within the city limits of Johnson City, the cemetery is on the grounds of the Mountain Home Veterans Administration (VA) Center. The area around Johnson City is rich in history; here are found the mustering place of the Overmountain Men for the march on Kings Mountain and Daniel Boone's birthplace and his "b'ar" killing site. Nearby Jonesborough is the oldest town in Tennessee.

The facility was originally known as the Mountain Home of the National Home for Disabled Volunteer Soldiers. It was through the efforts of First District Congressman Walter Preston Brownlow (1851–1910) that the facility was established. In 1901 Congress approved a bill, appropriated funds for construction, and established criteria for admission, "to provide that all honorably discharged soldiers and sailors who served in the war of rebellion and the Spanish-American War, and the provisional army and volunteer soldiers and sailors of the War of 1812 and the Mexican War, who are disabled by age, disease, or otherwise, and by reason of such disability are incapable of earning a living, shall be admitted into the Home for Disabled Volunteer Soldiers."

This was the ninth, and last, home provided by Congress for Union veterans of the Civil War.

The Board of Managers chose a 450-acre site and commissioned New York architect J.H. Freedlander to design 36 French Renaissance–style buildings to be constructed of native timber, brick and limestone. The buildings included domiciliaries, hospital, administration, theater, chapel, store houses, canteen, morgue, laundry, post office, and others. These buildings are still in use today, and in most instances are used for the same purpose as they were when the facility opened on October 15, 1903. The cemetery began interments later that same year. Interments were limited to the residents of the home or those who died in the hospital.

Special dispensation granted by the Board of Managers in October 1908 permitted the interment of Congressman Brownlow. He and his wife occupy the only graves inside Monument Circle, which is marked by a large monument.

George C. Maledon, a resident of the Mountain Home domiciliary, died on June 5, 1911, and was interred in the cemetery. Maledon was linked with Judge Isaac C. Parker, the "hanging judge" (see Fort Smith National Cemetery), in ensuring that justice for crimes committed in the Indian Territory was both swift and certain. George Maledon was known as the "prince of hangmen." Of the 79 men sentenced by Judge Parker to be hanged, Maledon is credited with hanging 60 of them, plus 5 that he shot while they were trying to escape. Maledon is something of a mystery: some writers picture him as a cold-blooded, sadistic legal killer who pulled the lever with joy in his heart; others picture him as a gentle family man with great compassion for those around him. They contend his oft-quoted boast that he "always broke the neck of his victim" was not a boast of his prowess with a rope, but a vow that no man suffered unnecessarily during the hanging process. Maledon was a deputy U.S. Marshall under Judge Parker, but there is no evidence to prove that he received anything more for the hangings than his pay as a guard. The cause of his death in 1911 at the age of 81 was listed as "dementia."

Colonel John Powell Smith, who served as the first "governor" of the national home, is also interred here. He served from 1903 until 1917.

The cemetery became a national cemetery in 1973, when the National Cemetery System was transferred to the Veterans Administration. The VA accepted 83 national cemeteries from the Department of the Army and designated the 21 cemeteries operated by VA Medical Centers as part of the system. This action opened up the 99.7 acre cemetery for the interment of all eligible persons listed in Public Law 93–43.

As of September 30, 2008, there were 13,212 interments in the cemetery. There are three Medal of Honor recipients among those buried here.

Frederick Clarence Buck, Sec. F, Row 1, Grave 9, Lieutenant, U.S. Army, Company A, 21st Connecticut Infantry. Place and Date: Near Chapins Farm, Virginia, 29 September 1864.
Citation: Although wounded, refused to leave the field until the fight closed.

Henry G. Buhrman, Sec. C, Row 2, Grave 12. Sergeant, Company H, 54th Ohio Infantry. Place and Date: At Vicksburg, Miss., 22 May 1863.
Citation: Gallantry in the charge of the "volunteer storming party."

Junior J. Spurrier, Sec HH, Grave 15–8. Staff Sergeant, U.S. Army, Company G, 134th Infantry, 35th Infantry Division. Place and date: Achain, France, 13 November 1944.
Citation: For conspicuous gallantry and intrepidity at risk of his life above and beyond the call of duty in action against the enemy at Achain, France, on 13 November 1944. At 2 P.M., Company G attacked the village of Achain from the east. Sergeant Spurrier, armed with a BAR, passed around the

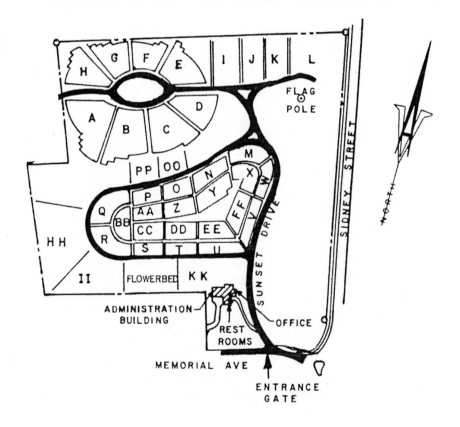

Name_____ Grave_____ Section _____

Mountain Home National Cemetery.

village and advanced alone. Attacking from the west, he immediately killed three Germans. From this time until dark, S/Sgt. Spurrier, using at different times his BAR and M1 rifle, American and German rocket launchers, a German automatic pistol, and hand grenades, continued his solitary attack against the enemy regardless of all types of small-arms and automatic-weapons fire. As a result of his heroic actions he killed an officer and 24 enlisted men and captured 2 officers and 2 enlisted men.

From the time of its establishment in 1903 (though records indicate that interments actually began in 1904) until it was transferred to the National Cemetery System, the cemetery was operated by personnel at the national home, and later by the VA Medical Center. During this time, most of the grounds maintenance work was performed by member-residents of the domiciliary. Those members also served as honor guards at funeral services for other members.

Superintendents/directors assigned since the cemetery has been a part of the National Cemetery System are:

Richard H. Crouse, August 1974–June 1975
Juanita D. Walker, August 1975–November 1977
Fred I. Haselbarth, December 1977–July 1980
Raymond L. Cordell, September 1980–March 1981

Kenneth D. LaFevor, September 1981–February 1986
Rodney L. Dunn, April 1986–February 2001
Kenneth D. LaFevor, July 2001–January 2008
Artis L. Parker, October 2007–Present

Nashville National Cemetery

1420 Gallatin Road, South
Madison, Tennessee 37115

Nashville National Cemetery is situated on the south boundary of Madison, Tennessee, in Davidson County. It is approximately six miles northeast of the metropolitan center of Nashville, and about two miles from the world-famous Grand Ole Opry. The tracks of the Louisville and Nashville Railroad run through the middle of the cemetery. The easement for the right of way was granted in perpetuity to the railroad on November 9, 1912.

The 64.5 acres of undulating land the cemetery occupies were acquired at 3 different times. On July 3, 1866, the Craighead Tract of about 45¼ acres was transferred to the United States in fee simple by Morton B. Howell, master of the Chancery Court of Nashville, in accordance with the decree of the court. On January 28, 1867, 17¾ additional acres were conveyed in the same manner. The final portion, about 1½ acres, was sold to the United States on October 17, 1879, by J. Watts Judson. The total cost of 64.5 acres was $10,058.65.

The original interments were the remains of those removed from temporary burial grounds around the general hospitals in Nashville; from nearby battlefields at Franklin and Gallatin, Tennessee; from Bowling Green and Cave City, Kentucky; and from numerous other localities in Kentucky and Tennessee. In the battle at Franklin, eight miles south of Nashville, on November 30, 1864, the Union army under General Schofield suffered 2,000 casualties, and the Confederate forces under General Hood lost 6,000 men.

The report of the inspector of national cemeteries dated November 29, 1870, listed interments in the cemetery as follows:

	Known	Unknown
Commissioned officers	38	0
White Union soldiers	10,300	3,098
Colored Union soldiers	1,447	463
Employees	703	29
Total	12,488	4,001

Entrance to Nashville National Cemetery.

There are 4,141 unknown remains interred in the cemetery. The most recent took place on July 26, 1974. During excavation for a new administration building, the remains of an infant in an iron casket with a glass face plate were unearthed. It was determined that that type of casket was used prior to the turn of the century, but no information about the remains could be located. Cemetery records did not indicate that interments had ever been made in that area. The remains were reinterred in another section, and an "unknown" marker was placed at the gravesite.

As of September 30, 2008, a total of 35,148 interments had been made in the cemetery, including 16,485 Civil War interments. There are 7 group burials accounting for 28 remains. The stone wall around the cemetery and the beautiful limestone archway at the entrance were both constructed in 1870. At one time, rumors held that the remains of three Union soldiers were entombed at the top of the archway, but no evidence to support this claim could ever be found. The service building also has an interesting history. It was built about 1870 to accommodate the mules, carts, and wagons which were part of the cemetery equipment. The front portion was originally the stables. In 1932 one room and a toilet were added to the left wing of the building from salvaged materials. Most recently, a service garage has been added which includes a hydraulic lubricating hoist. The present lodge, the third constructed here, was built near the site of the original lodge, near the stables, and was completed in 1931. The second lodge was built near the front entrance. The outside comfort station, completed in 1933, was recently converted to a storage building.

One of the former superintendents told the story that as he walked the grounds of the cemetery one evening after dark, he was joined by a man with a dog who came from somewhere in one of the burial sections. He tried to make conversation with the man, to no avail. Their walk continued in silence around the cemetery until they returned to the point where the man had joined him. Without a word, the man and dog turned back into the burial section, and walked away into the darkness. The superintendent who told the story was not known for telling tall tales, but he had no explanation for his visitor.

In 1920, the state of Minnesota erected a monument in Section MM inscribed, "In memory of her soldiers here buried who lost their lives in the service of the United States in the war for Preservation of the Union A.D. 1861–1865."

Chaplain Erastus M. Cravath, 101st Regiment, Ohio Volunteer Infantry, was interred in Section MM, Grave 16,694, in 1900. Chaplain Cravath was one of the founders of Fisk University in Nashville, Tennessee, and served for 25 years as its president.

Colonel Edward S. Jones, commander of the 3rd Pennsylvania Cavalry, was interred in Section MM, Grave 16,520, in November 1866. He was the founder, and for many years the commander, of the Department of Tennessee and Georgia Grand Army of the Republic. He was also the founder of the George H. Thomas Post No. 1, G.A.R., in Nashville, Tennessee.

Colonel James W. Lawless, 5th Kentucky Cavalry, was buried in Section MM, Grave 10,662, on June 25, 1899. Colonel Lawless was born in Ireland and came to the United States at the age of 16. His marker is fittingly inscribed, "His loyalty to the Stars and Stripes could not be surpassed having fought for four years under the same and at all times stood ready to defend them with his life."

Major General George Hilton Butler was interred in Section OO, Grave 700, in November 1974. General Butler served as adjutant general of Tennessee, and in other posts, during the administration of Governor Ellington.

Two former cemetery superintendents are buried here: Corporal Harrison E. Pond, who served until his death in 1921, and his successor, Sergeant John B. Wilson, QMC, who served from 1921 until his death in 1929. Pond is buried in Section M, Grave 16,813, and Wilson in Section A, Grave 5,237A.

There are so many men interred here who were decorated for their bravery in action that it is impossible to list all of them. Among these heroes is Lieutenant Colonel Oscar Little Farris, Section MM, Grave 337, who was awarded the Distinguished Service Cross. Captain Eugene L. Goodrich, 11th Infantry, Section MM, Grave 140, was decorated with the Silver Star. Distinguished Flying Crosses were awarded to Captain Charles Smith Melton, USAF, Section MM, Grave 339; Ensign Lucien George Geldreich, USNR, Section MM, Grave 15; and, First Lieutenant Thomas Hamilton Opsomer, USAF, Section MM, Grave 125.

There are three Medal of Honor recipients interred in the cemetery. A dagger appears before the name of one man who was killed in action.

Charles P. Cantrell, Sec 1, Grave 132. Private, Company F, 10th U.S. Infantry. Place and date: At Santiago, Cuba, 1 July 1898.
Citation: Gallantry assisted in the rescue of the wounded from in front of the lines and under heavy fire from the enemy.

John Carr, Sec KK, Grave 16,550. Private, Company G, 8th U.S. Cavalry. Place and date: At Chiricahua Mountains, Ariz., 29 October 1869.
Citation: Gallantry in action.

†**William Franklin Lyell,** Sec 1, Grave 151. Corporal, U.S. Army, Company F, 17th Infantry Regiment, 7th Infantry Division. Place and date: Near Chup'ari, Korea, 31 August 1951.
Citation: Corporal Lyell, a member of Company F, distinguished himself by conspicuous gallantry and outstanding courage above and beyond the call of duty in action against the enemy. When his platoon leader was killed, Cpl. Lyell assumed command and led his unit in an assault on strongly fortified enemy positions located on commanding terrain. When his platoon came under vicious, raking fire which halted the forward movement, Cpl. Lyell seized a 57-mm. recoilless rifle and unhesitatingly moved ahead to a suitable firing position from which he delivered deadly accurate fire, completely destroying an enemy bunker and killing its occupants. He then returned to his platoon and was resuming the assault when the unit was again subjected to intense hostile fire from two other bunkers. Disregarding his personal safety, armed with grenades he charged forward hurling grenades into one of the enemy emplacements, and although painfully wounded in this action he pressed on, destroying the bunker and killing six of the foe. He then continued his

attack against a third enemy position, throwing grenades as he ran forward, annihilating four enemy soldiers. He then led his platoon to the north slope of the hill where positions were occupied from which effective fire was delivered against the enemy in support of friendly troops moving up. Fearlessly exposing himself to enemy fire, he continuously moved about directing and encouraging his men until he was mortally wounded by enemy mortar fire.

Former superintendents/directors of Nashville National Cemetery are:

Edward M. Main, February 1880–March 1884
Harrison E. Pond, Unknown–1921
John B. Wilson, 1921–1929
John P. Sasser, September 1934–March 1946
Henry R. Cole, February 1946–January 1955
Herbert L. Rhodes, February 1955–April 1964
William J. Boyer, April 1964–April 1965
Clifton Cockrell, April 1965–June 1974
Donald L. Polston, August 1974–January 1975

William G. Kaiser, February 1975–September 1983
Kenneth D. LaFevor, February 1986–August 1988
Kevin J. Taylor, 1988–1992
Sandra Noguez, September, 1992–February 1996
Joseph Nunnally, February 1996–December 2000
William Owensby, May 2001–June 2005
Paul H. Martin, June 2005–Present

Natchez National Cemetery

61 Cemetery Road
Natchez, Mississippi 39120

The cemetery is situated in Adams County in Natchez, on a bluff overlooking the Mississippi River, about two miles north of the old landing at Natchez.

The city of Natchez lies on the southwestern border of Mississippi and is the oldest city on the Mississippi River. In 1717, Jean Baptiste le Moyne, then the French governor of Louisiana, built Fort Rosalie here, which the Natchez Indians destroyed in 1729. The city derives its name from the Natchez Indians who inhabited the area until they were nearly wiped out by the French in 1729. One of the interesting beliefs of the Natchez was that their chiefs descended from the sun, which they worshiped. Their chief was carried about so that his feet never touched the ground, and when he died, his wives were strangled.

The city was reestablished by settlers in 1771. Prior to the Civil War, when cotton was king, Natchez was an important center of wealth and culture and was the capital of the Territory of Mississippi, which consisted of what is now Mississippi and Alabama. Kings Tavern, probably the oldest building in Natchez, was the southern terminus of the Natchez Trace, an important route between Nashville, Tennessee, and Natchez. Northern merchants and traders often floated their goods on rafts down the Mississippi River to New Orleans and returned by way of the Trace. Settlers heading into the southwest often used this route. In 1800, after its designation as a post road, the Army improved it. Since 1938 it has been designated the Natchez Trace National Parkway.

During World War II and since that time, industry has moved south and created many new developments, including many new industrial plants and the petroleum industry located in Natchez. There are over 300 producing oil wells in Adams County. Natchez National Cemetery is in the middle of an oil field. Two producing wells east of the cemetery are within a few hundred yards of the wall, and there are four wells to the west between the cemetery and the Mississippi River.

Though there was comparatively little fighting in the immediate vicinity of Natchez, there were engagements in the area in November and early December 1863 and again in April 1864.

The cemetery was established in 1866 on 11.7 acres of land appropriated, and later purchased, from Margaret Case, Thomas D. Purnell, Louisa C. Purnell, Walter R. Irvine and Martha M. Irvine. In 1886, the city of Natchez deeded to the United States the land for the

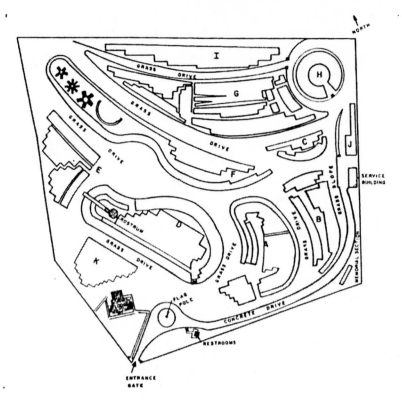

Natchez National Cemetery, Natchez, Mississippi.

approach road to the cemetery. In 1948, the United States returned the property to the city. Original interments were brought from various places in Louisiana and Mississippi within a radius of 50 miles around Natchez. One of the old Natchez homes, "The Gardens," served as a military hospital for Federal troops, and some of the original interments are those who died in this hospital. In his report for the year ending June 30, 1866, Quartermaster General Montgomery C. Meigs informed Secretary of War Edwin M. Stanton that many bodies were buried in the levees near the west shore of the Mississippi at and above Vidalia. Removal and reinterment of these remains began in the fall of 1866. Other locations from which remains of Union soldiers and sailors were disinterred included gravesites at Port Gibson and Prio's Race Track in Mississippi, and Concordia Parish, Cross Bayou Ferry, Red River Landing, and Turnbull's Island in Louisiana.

The report of the inspector of national cemeteries dated March 4, 1871, indicated that a total of 3,086 interments had been made. Of these, only 253 were known.

Information available from old burial records indicates that the remains of a considerable number of Union Navy personnel were among those reinterred at Natchez after the cemetery was established. Now interred in Section D are William Preston, Grave 459, quartermaster of the *USS Hartford,* who died on May 9, 1862, and was originally buried at Quitman's Landing, Mississippi; Seaman John Keese, Grave 423, *USS Osage,* who died on May 7, 1864; and T.W. Roberts, Grave 421, acting ensign, *USS Ozark,* who died on August 17, 1864. Keese and Roberts were originally interred at Acklin's Plantation, Louisiana.

There is one Medal of Honor recipient interred in the cemetery. Wilson Brown died on January 24, 1900.

Wilson Brown, Sec G, Grave 3152. Landsman, U.S. Navy. G.O. No.: 45, 31 December 1864. Citation: Onboard the flagship *USS Hartford* during the successful attacks against Fort Morgan, rebel gunboats and the ram *Tennessee* in Mobile Bay on 5 August 1864. Knocked unconscious into the hold of the ship when an enemy shellburst fatally wounded a man on the ladder above him, Brown, upon regaining consciousness, promptly returned to the shell whip on the berth deck and zealously continued to perform his duties although four of the six men at this station had been either killed or wounded by the enemy's terrific fire.

As of September 30, 2008, there were 7,486 interments in the 25.7 acre cemetery. Former superintendents/directors of the cemetery are:

Charles Fitcheit, November 1883–Unknown
Roger J. Puckett, Unknown–February 1945
Benjamin H. Puritt, March 1945–November 1946
Wilfred W. Horne, November 1946–June 1966
David C. Corson, July 1966–April 1972
Clifford C. Filteau, June 1972–May 1973
David C. Corson, June 1973–October 1977
Richard J. Pless, January 1978–March 1980
Jimmy T. Jackson, January 1981–September 1983
Donald H. Fritz, February 1984–March 1985
Homer D. Hardamon, April 1985–March 1986

Gloria C. Gamez, April 1986–January 1987
Jorge L. Lopez, March 1987–November 1988
Curtis E. Hardamon, December 1988–1991
William Trower, 1992–1994
John Bacon, 1996–1996
Sharon Goodrich, 1996–1998
Tim Spain, 1998–2000
Arleen Vincenty, 2001–2002
Peter Young, 2002–2004
Gene Linxwiler, 2004–2004
Gregory Whitney, 2005–2007
Phyllis M. Speed, 2007–Present

One afternoon, some years ago, one of the former superintendents brought a pistol to the service area and started firing at tin cans and a garbage can, and threatening another individual who, fortunately, was not present. He is the only superintendent ever arrested for incidents occurring on federal property during duty hours.

National Cemetery of the Alleghenies

1158 Morgan Road
Bridgeville, Pennsylvania 15017

The 292 acre National Cemetery of the Alleghenies is located in Bridgeville, Pa., south of Pittsburgh. It is anticipated that it will serve 323,000 veterans in western Pennsylvania for the next 50 years.

The formal dedication was held on October 9, 2005, and burials began on August 15, 2005, in a 10 acre initial development site. This is separate from the Phase 1 development, which covers 80 acres and will include full casket gravesites, in-ground crypts, and columbarium niches for cremated remains. As of September 30, 2008, there were 2,113 interments in the cemetery.

Before being converted to a cemetery site, the land has been constantly farmed since the 2800s. This region is considered the flash-point of the Whiskey Rebellion of 1794.

Interred in Section 1, Grave 1118, is Charles William Tater, Captain, U.S. Army, and First Lieutenant U.S. Army Air Force, Fighter Pilot, Squadron B2143 RD, "Tuskegee Airman," Tuskegee Army Air Field, Alabama, European Theatre, February 29, 1944. Air Medal with four Oak Leaf Clusters, Distinguished Flying Cross.

National Memorial Cemetery of Arizona

23029 N. Cave Creek Road
Phoenix, Arizona 85024

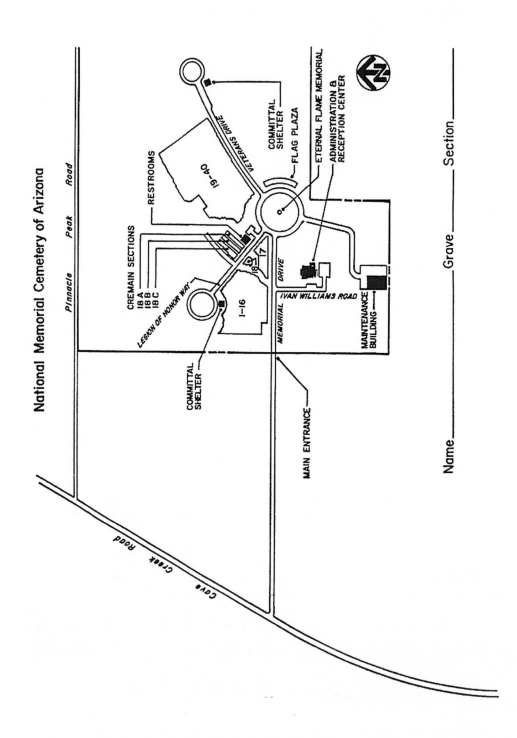

National Memorial Cemetery of Arizona

On April 15, 1989, the Arizona Veterans Memorial Cemetery was transferred to the Veterans Administration and became the 113th cemetery in the National Cemetery System. Senators Dennis DeConcini and John McCain, Governor Rose Mofford and federal, state, and local officials, including the author, were participants in the transfer ceremony.

Local support for development of a veterans cemetery in Arizona began in the 1930s. The late Senator Carl Hayden was among the early supporters of the concept. Renewed efforts in the late 1960s resulted in the formation in 1971 of an organization called the Veterans Memorial Cemetery of Arizona, Inc., whose purpose was to acquire land for a veterans cemetery to be operated by municipal, state or federal authority. The corporation board of directors was composed of three members each from the American Legion, the Disabled American Veterans and the Veterans of Foreign Wars. The corporation leased a section of state land in the southeast corner of the intersection of Cave Creek Road and Pinnacle Peak Road in Phoenix. State legislation passed in 1976 authorized the development of up to 640 acres for a veterans cemetery, and $50,000 was appropriated for initial development costs.

In Arizona at that time, veterans affairs were the responsibility of the Department of Economic Security (DES), which was given oversight of the cemetery. Seventeen acres of the leased land were conveyed to DES, and 12.5 acres were developed. Veterans organizations donated more than $60,000 to begin developing the site. The cemetery was dedicated on December 9, 1978, and the first interment was made on March 14, 1979.

The State Cemetery Grants Program was authorized by Congress in 1979 to assist states in establishing, expanding or improving state-owned veterans cemeteries. Arizona later received $291,700 through this federal-state matching funds grant program.

In the mid–1980s, an in-house study by the National Cemetery System included Phoenix among the ten areas in the United States with the largest veteran populations not served by a national cemetery. The study was never officially released. A subsequent study mandated by Congress did not include Phoenix since the Office of Management and Budget insisted that veteran burial needs were being adequately met through the Arizona Veterans Memorial Cemetery, and since the regional cemetery concept was still official policy, the Riverside National Cemetery, over 300 miles west, served veterans of the Phoenix area.

The Arizona Veterans Service Commission was created in 1982, and the cemetery was transferred to the commission. An additional 212-acre parcel was conveyed to the commission in 1985, bringing the total acreage to 225, of which 23 are developed. Operating expenses were provided by the Arizona legislature along with periodic appropriations for development. Veterans organizations continued to donate large sums for construction and special projects, such as the Eternal Flame, dedicated in 1981. Donated funds have permitted the building of ramadas and security fencing, the renovation and furnishing of the interior of the administration/visitors building, the placement of lights at the flagpole, and the landscaping of the flag plaza.

Prompted by the veterans organizations, the entire Arizona Congressional delegation supported legislation to make this cemetery a national cemetery. On May 20, 1988, President Ronald Reagan signed a House of Representatives bill as Public Law 100–322, which transferred the 225-acre Arizona Veterans Memorial Cemetery to the Veterans Administration and designated it as the National Memorial Cemetery of Arizona.

As of September 30, 2008, there were over 52,513 veterans and family members interred here, and it is estimated that grave space will be available for nearly a century to come.

Former Directors of the cemetery are:

William Rogers, 1989–1991
Karen Brown, 1991–1993
Eileen Harrison, 1993–1994
Arthur Smith, 1994–1996

Mary Dill, 1996–1999
Mark Maynard, 1999–2004
Larry Williams, 2004–2006
Wayne E. Ellis, 2006–Present

National Memorial Cemetery of the Pacific

2177 Puowaina Drive
Honolulu, Hawaii 96813

The cemetery is situated in Honolulu County in central Honolulu, about midway between the Honolulu International Airport and the Waikiki hotel area.

The National Memorial Cemetery of the Pacific, usually called the Punchbowl, is located in Punchbowl Crater, the remnant of a long-extinct volcano. The crater was named by early seamen who noted its similarity to a punchbowl. From the heights of the cemetery, the 360-degree panorama permits one to view the green Hawaiian mountains, the blue Pacific Ocean, and the majestic Diamond Head.

No more symbolic site could be imagined for a national cemetery. For centuries the Punchbowl has had a deep religious meaning for the people of Hawaii. Long before the islands were discovered by explorers from western civilizations, Punchbowl was known as *Puowaina,* which translates roughly as "Consecrated Hill" or "Hill of Sacrifice." The crater was the site of many secret *Alii* (royalty) burials as well as the place where offenders of certain *kapus* (taboos) were taken to be sacrificed. The Punchbowl was an important stronghold for the army of Oahu, under King Kalanikupule, who tried in vain to resist the invading army of Kamehameha, the young king from the island of Hawaii. Kamehameha was successful in unifying the Hawaiian Islands in 1810. He established a kingdom that lasted until Queen Lilioukalani was deposed in 1893 by the supporters of a Hawaiian republic. The decisive battle took place at the Punchbowl when Captain Samuel Nowlein, commanding the queen's guards, surrendered his forces rather than be annihilated by the cannons placed at the top of the crater. The revolution was allegedly led by nine Americans and four Europeans. The United States had been given exclusive rights to use Pearl Harbor as a naval station in 1887. The Republic of Hawaii was established in 1894, was annexed to the United States in 1898, became the Territory of Hawaii in 1900, and finally, in 1959, became the 50th state of the Union.

This area was later used as a training ground for the Hawaiian National Guard. From 1940 until the end of World War II it served as an observation and fire control point in the harbor defense system.

During the late 1890s a committee was formed to find a site for a new cemetery for the growing city of Honolulu, and it recommended the Punch bowl. The recommendation was rejected based on the fear of polluting the water supply and emotional aversion to putting a city of the dead above a city of the living. These same objections were raised 50 years later when the Punchbowl was selected as the site for a national cemetery.

In 1941, the 77th Congress authorized a small appropriation for the establishment of a national cemetery in Honolulu with the provision that a site acceptable to the War Department would be made available without cost to the United States. In 1943, the governor of Hawaii offered the Punchbowl area as a site. The $50,000 appropriation proved insufficient to establish the cemetery, and the matter was deferred until the conclusion of World War II. During the war, the Navy's dead were buried in a newly established cemetery in Halawa, and the Army designated Schofield Barracks Cemetery as the interment site for Army dead.

ABMC Memorial, National Memorial Cemetery of the Pacific.

In 1947, the Army began planning for a Punch bowl cemetery. Strong pressure from the congressional delegation, veterans groups, and the military was exerted to find a permanent burial place for the thousands of bodies of servicemen stored in Hawaii and thousands more on the island of Guam being held for burial instructions. Finally, on February 24, 1948, Congress approved funds for the cemetery, and construction began in August. On October 13, 1948, the War Department designated the area as the National Memorial Cemetery of the Pacific.

Prior to the opening of the cemetery for public burials, remains from Oahu, Guam, Wake Island, Guadalcanal, Saipan, Iwo Jima, Formosa, prisoner of war camps in Japan, and other locations in the Pacific were brought to the Punchbowl for interment. These initial interments totaled nearly 13,000 World War II dead. The first interment, on January 4, 1949, was the remains of an unknown serviceman killed in the attack on Pearl Harbor on December 7, 1941.

The cemetery was opened to the public on the morning of July 19, 1949, with services for five war dead: an unknown serviceman, two Marines, an Army lieutenant and one civilian, Ernie Pyle. The remains of Ernest Taylor Pyle were interred in Section D, Grave 109. Pyle, a Pulitzer Prize–winning war correspondent, was beloved and admired by American servicemen the world over for his accurate portrayal of the GI's life under combat conditions. He was killed by Japanese machine gun fire on April 18, 1945, on Ie Shima, a small island off the northern tip of Okinawa. He served in the U.S. Navy during World War I.

Initially, the graves were marked with white wooden crosses and Stars of David in preparation for the dedication ceremony on September 2, 1949, the fourth anniversary of V-J Day which ended World War II. Despite the Army's extensive efforts to inform the public that the crosses and Stars were only temporary, a public outcry arose when, in 1951, flat granite markers were put into place and the temporary markers were removed.

Poignant memories of World War II were revived on October 23, 1953, when committal services were held marking the group burial of the remains of 44 Marines, 3 Navy men, and 131 civilians who perished in defense of Wake Island. A specially designed group marker listing the names of the 178 decedents, whose remains could not be individually identified, has been placed at the site in Section G, Grave 68.

On May 15, 1958, the remains of 4 of the 848 unknown dead from Korea were presented as candidates for interment in Arlington National Cemetery, in the Tomb of the Unknowns. Army Master Sergeant Ned Lyle, a decorated Korea veteran, was given the honor of making the selection.

The American Battle Monuments Commission dedicated a memorial in the cemetery on May 1, 1966. This memorial is an eloquent and moving tribute commemorating the lives and deeds of members of the Armed Forces of the United States during World War II and the Korean Conflict who were recorded as missing, lost, or buried at sea in the Pacific Region. It consists of a beautiful chapel, a gallery of specially designed mosaic mural maps of the Pacific theaters of action, and a monumental stairway bordered by eight Courts of the Missing. On the marble walls of these courts are engraved the names of 18,094 American servicemen of World War II and 8,195 American servicemen of the Korean Conflict. In 1980, the memorial was enlarged by adding two half courts with the names of 2,489 missing during the Vietnam War. The dedicatory stone, centered at the base of the stairway, is inscribed, "In These Gardens Are Recorded the Names of Americans Who Gave Their Lives in the Service of Their Country and Whose Earthly Resting Place Is Known Only to God."

Lieutenant Colonel Ellison Onizuka, USAF, is interred in Section D, Grave 107. He was a crew member of the space shuttle *Challenger* and perished in the tragic explosion of the shuttle in January 1986.

Senator Spark M. Matsunaga was interred on April 19, 1990. Nine members of a joint-service honor guard accompanied the body of the senator from Washington, D.C. Senator Matsunaga was an original member of the famous Nisei 100th Infantry Battalion, later designated the 100th Battalion, 442nd Infantry Regiment, one of the most decorated military units in history. He served 14 years in the U.S. House of Representatives and 13 years in the Senate.

On January 11, 1976, the cemetery was entered on the National Register of Historic Places under its Hawaiian name, *Puowaina*.

A columbarium for the inurnment of cremated remains was opened on August 16, 1982. The tunnels under the rim of the crater were considered during the 1970s as sites for columbaria, but the cost of development was deemed prohibitive.

No story of the Punchbowl would be complete without a comment about the Overlook. This area is one of the reasons that more than 5 million visitors come to the cemetery each year. It is the highest point on the rim of the crater, and it offers a breathtaking panoramic view of the island of Oahu.

The National Memorial Cemetery of the Pacific was the first national cemetery to place Bicentennial Medal of Honor headstones. On May 11, 1976, 23 of these special monuments were placed on the gravesites of the recipients, all but one of whom were killed in action. In addition to the 32 interred and 1 memorialized recipients in the cemetery, the names of

26 recipients are in scribed in the Courts of the Missing. The Medal of Honor recipients interred or memorialized in the cemetery are:

Name	Rank	Service	War/Place/Date of Action	Section
Thomas Alexander Baker, Jr.	SGT	USA	WWI	F-162
Willibald C. Bianchi*	1LT	USA	WWII	MA-39
William James Bordelon	SSGT	USMC	WWII	A-481
Erwin Jay Boydston†	PVT	USMC	Boxer	G-703
William Robert Caddy	PFC	USMC	WWII	C-81
George Ham Cannon	1LT	USMC	WWII	1644
Anthony Peter Damato	CPL	USMC	WWII	A-334
William Grant Fournier	SGT	USA	WWII	C-462
William D. Halyburton, Jr.	PhM2	USN	WWII	O-274
William Deane Hawkins	1LT	USMC	WWII	B-646
Mikio Hasemoto	PVT	USA	WWII	D338
Edwin Joseph Hill	CBM	USN	WWII	A-895
Robert Howard McCard	GSGT	USMC	WWII	B-1024
Larry Leonard Maxam	CPL	USMC	Vietnam	J-388
Martin O. May	PFC	USA	WWII	N-1242
Leroy Anthony Mendonca	SGT	USA	Korea	Q-1408
Joseph E. Muller	SGT	USA	WWII	N-1259
Joseph William Ozbourn	PVT	USMC	WWII	F-77
Herbert K. Pililaau	PFC	USA	Korea	P-127
Thomas James Reeves	RaElec	USN	WWII	A-884
Joseph R. Sarnoski	2LT	USA	WWII	A-582
Elmelindo Rodriques Smith	P1SGT	USA	Vietnam	W-131
Grant F. Timmerman	SGT	USMC	WWII	A-844
Benjamin F. Wilson	1LT	USA	Korea	A-1060A
Rodney J.T. Yano	SFC	USA	Vietnam	W-614
Kaoru Moto	PVT	USA	WWII	Court 2, Wall F, Row 400, Niche 422
Allan M. Ohata	SGT	USA	WWII	III-w47
Francis B. Wai	Captain	USA	WWII	Q-1194
Yeiki Kobashigawa	TSGT	USA	WWII	Court 8, Wall E, Row 500, Niche 536
Robert T. Kuroda	SSGT	USA	WWII	D-92
Masato Nakae	PVT	USA	WWII	U-1446
Shinyei Nakamine	PVT	USA	WWII	D-402

Memorial marker only. Buried at sea.
†*Not killed in action.*

Medal of Honor recipients memorialized in the Courts of the Missing of the American Battle Monuments Commission Memorial located in the National Memorial Cemetery of the Pacific are:

Name	Rank	Service	Date of Death	Court No.
Charles H. Barker	PFC	USA	5 June 1954	4
Alexander Bonnyman, Jr.	1LT	USMC	22 November 1943	2
John P. Cromwell	CAPT	USN	19 November 1943	5
George A. Davis	LTC	USAF	10 February 1952	8
Don C. Faith, Jr.	LTC	USA	2 December 1950	4
Francis C. Flaherty	ENS	USN	7 December 1941	3
Richard E. Fleming	CAPT	USMC	6 June 1942	2
Fernando Luis Garcia	PFC	USMC	5 September 1952	8
Charles L. Gilliland	CPL	USA	7 April 1951	6
Louis James Hauge, Jr.	CPL	USMC	14 May 45	4
Frederick F. Henry	CAPT	USA	31 December 1953	6
James E. Johnson	SGT	USMC	2 November 1953	8

Name	Rank	Service	Date of Death	Court No.
Isaac C. Kidd	RADM	USN	7 December 1941	3
Charles J. Loring	MAJ	USA	22 November 1952	8
Leonard F. Mason	PFC	USMC	23 July 1944	4
Frank N. Mitchell	1LT	USMC	26 November 1950	8
Edward H. O'Hare	LCDR	USN	27 November 1944	1
Lee H. Phillips*	CPL	USMC	27 November 1950	8
Dan Swain Schoonover	CPL	USA	10 July 1953	6
Luther H. Story	CPL	USA	1 September 1950	8
Clyde Thomason	SGT	USMC	17 August 1942	4
Peter Tomich	CWT	USN	7 December 1941	2
Franklin Van Valkenburgh	CAPT	USA	7 December 1941	2
John S. Walmsley	CAPT	USA	14 September 1951	8
James Richard Ward	S1C	USN	7 December 1941	2
Lewis George Watkins	SSGT	USMC	7 October 1952	8

Also memorialized in the Marietta National Cemetery.

As of September 30, 2008, there were 49,203 interments. The cemetery has space for cremated remains and may accommodate casketed remains in the same gravesite of previously interred family members. Former superintendents/directors of the cemetery are:

Alvin G. Baker, October 1948–October 1950
Taro Suzuki, November 1950–October 1957
Joseph V. Darby, February 1958–January 1964
Martin T. Corley, January1964–July 1971
Ernest C. Schanze, July 1971–September 1980
Claude E. Arnold, September 1980–April 1983

Mack Cochenour, Jr., April 1983–February 1985
Kevin J. Taylor, September 1985–September 1988
William E. Rodgers, Jr., March 1985–1989
Gene Castagnetti, February 1990–Present

New Albany National Cemetery
1943 Ekin Avenue
New Albany, Indiana 47150

The cemetery is situated in Floyd County, New Albany, Indiana, across the Ohio River from Louisville, Kentucky.

New Albany is one of seven cemeteries established in 1862 near large troop recruitment and training sites. It was designed to accommodate the reinterment of Union soldiers who died in general hospitals and were buried nearby in city and soldiers' graveyards. Reinterments came from West Virginia, Virginia, Kentucky and Indiana, and most of the deaths were in the hospitals established near those places.

The 5.46 acres of land were purchased from Dr. Charles Bowman early in 1862. The report of the inspector of national cemeteries dated November 15, 1870, shows interments as follows:

	Known	*Unknown*
White Union soldiers	1,341	490
Colored Union soldiers	757	208
Employees	11	0
Total	2,109	698

The inspector also reported that the colored Union soldiers were buried in a section by themselves.

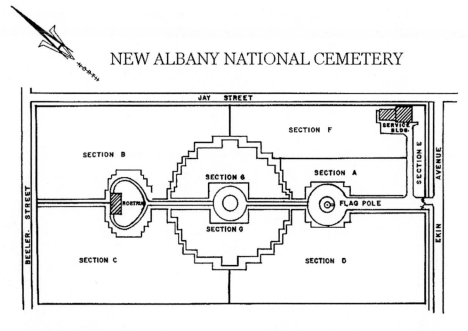

NEW ALBANY NATIONAL CEMETERY

The cemetery was closed for interments on April 7, 1960, but the removal of the unoccupied lodge, which was constructed in 1942, enabled the cemetery to reopen in 1985 .The cemetery has space for cremated remains, and may accommodate casketed remains in the same gravesite with a previously interred family member. As of September 30, 2008, there were 7,066 interments.

In 1982, the Veterans Administration (VA) proposed to remove the rostrum in the cemetery, which had been constructed prior to 1880. The public protest, even though the rostrum was used only on Memorial Day, reached such a peak that the VA decided to restore it to its original condition.

Former superintendents/directors of the cemetery are:

Simpson Clark, May 1946–Unknown
Ervin Ross, June 1946–September 1958
Harry C. Varble, October 1958–March 1962
Doyle N. Yates, April 1962–November 1968

Dorrance A. Long, Sr., February 1969–January 1975
Robert W. John, March 1975–June 1976
Lyle E. Norby, June 1976–October 1977

Since October 1977 cemetery operations and management have been the responsibility of the director of Zachary Taylor National Cemetery.

New Bern National Cemetery
1711 National Avenue
New Bern, North Carolina 28560

The cemetery is situated in Craven County in the city of New Bern, North Carolina. The ground upon which this cemetery is located was appropriated and the cemetery established on February 1, 1867. The plot contains 7.68 acres of land, the right and title to which was acquired at different times. The original purchase, on March 13, 1869, was from William P. Moore, who conveyed about 7.5 acres to the United States. The property had previously been attached by D. Golden Murray and others for non-payment of debts by Moore. On the date of purchase from Moore, the United States paid Murray et al. the sum of $10 to release their interest in the land. On July 1, 1874, Isaac W. Hughes conveyed to the government a narrow strip of land adjoining the cemetery, bringing the cemetery to its present size.

Coastal North Carolina came under Union control early in the Civil War. The inlets

Massachusetts Monument, New Bern National Cemetery, 1915.

to Pamlico Sound were secured after forts Clark and Hatteras were captured in August 1861. In February and March 1862, General A.E. Burnside and Commodore L.M. Golds-bourough seized Confederate positions on Roanoke Island and at New Bern. This control of the inner coastal positions tightened the blockade of the North Carolina coast.

The report of the inspector of national cemeteries dated April 28, 1870, indicated interments at that time as follows:

	Known	Unknown
Commissioned officers	22	1
White Union soldiers	1,726	806
White Union sailors	130	49
Colored Union soldiers	209	195
Employees and citizens	1,120	0
Total	2,199	1,051

Some of these burials were made here originally. Other interments were remains removed from New Bern, Beaufort, Morehead City, Kinston, Hatteras, Roanoke Island, and many other places along the coast of North Carolina. The original interments were made by state, and the 1,051 unknowns were buried in a separate section.

As of September 30, 2008, a total of 7,616 interments had been made. The cemetery is closed for initial interments.

Four special monuments have been erected in the cemetery: 15th Connecticut Volunteers, erected by the state of Connecticut in 1898, Section 13; state of New Jersey, erected in 1905, Section 12; state of Massachusetts, erected in 1908, Section 8; and state of Rhode Island, erected in 1909, Section 9.

Former superintendents/directors of the cemetery are:

John A. Commerford, January 1880–November 1881
Thomas Shea, 1892–1894
A. Hyde, 1894–1894
J.M. Bryant, 1894–1904
G.P. Thorton, 1904–1905
John A. Reeves, 1905–1913
W.H.H. Garrott, 1913–1916
Frederick Wagner, 1916–1920
J.B. Lovelace, 1922–1940
William Sparrow, July 1940–April 1946

Leo E. Weems, August 1946–May 1974
Joe D. Willard, May 1974–March 1975
Milo D. Hayden, May 1975–January 1978
Eugene L. Chambers, January 1978–March 1980
Patricia A. Hagler, March 1980–July 1981
Oliver Creswick, October 1981–October 1984
Robert F. McCollum, October 1984–July 1986
Joe A. Ramos, July 1986–August 1987
Kurt W. Rotar, 1987–1990
Karen J. Duhart, 1990–Present

Ohio Western Reserve National Cemetery
10175 Rawiga Road
Rittman, Ohio 44270

The 273 acre cemetery lies approximately 45 miles south of Cleveland in Medina County near the town of Rittman. The cemetery name refers to part of the Northwest Territory, once known as the Connecticut Western Reserve. This tract of land in northeast Ohio was reserved by the State of Connecticut when it ceded its claims to western land to the U.S. government in 1786.

The cemetery was opened in 2000. The first phase of construction covered 65 acres and included 15,000 gravesites, 2,000 columbarium niches, and 1,000 in-ground burial sites for cremated remains. As of September 30, 2008, there have been 11,984 interments. At full capacity the Ohio Western Reserve National Cemetery can provide burial space for 106,000 eligible veterans and dependents.

The cemetery contains a pathway that is lined with over 100 memorials that honor America's veterans. Former directors of the cemetery are:

Sean Baumgartner, November 2003–October 2005
Maria E. Garza, February 2007–Present

Perryville National Cemetery
Perryville, Kentucky 40468

The Perryville National Cemetery was established in 1928, remained in the National Cemetery System for 50 years, and was donated to the commonwealth of Kentucky in 1978. It is located in Boyle County, approximately 2.6 miles northwest of the town of Perryville, off U.S. Route 68 at the Perryville Battlefield State Park.

There are no deceased buried in this cemetery. The land on which the original cemetery was situated did not belong to the United States, and owing to the peculiarities of a will under which it was left to heirs, no title to it could be obtained. The 974 Union soldiers interred here were removed to Camp Nelson National Cemetery. The exact date is unknown, but it was probably in 1868.

Public Law 87–70, March 3, 1928, authorized the United States to accept a tract containing 4.03 acres, with a roadway running to the tract, and directed that a national cemetery be established thereon. The property was donated by the Perryville Battlefield Commission. The Kentucky officials who prompted the legislation advised later that it was their original intention to have this area set aside as a national military park rather than a national cemetery.

The cemetery contains only one monument, which was erected in 1928 to the memory of the 974 Union soldiers killed in the Battle of Perryville. The cemetery is bounded on the north, south and east by the Perryville Battlefield State Park, which contains 137 acres. On the southeast is a Confederate burial lot, 70 feet by 100 feet surrounded by a stone wall. There are 290 Confederates interred in the lot, probably in a single grave. The lot is marked by a monument which is inscribed "Confederate Memorial" and is surmounted by a statue of a Confederate soldier.

In March 1948, at the request of the National Cemetery System, Mr. J.B. Gentry, teacher of agriculture at Perryville High School, made an investigation to determine the existence of rocks beneath the soil within the cemetery area. Six test pits were excavated. Excavations indicated rock outcroppings at depths of 33 inches to 57 inches below grade. The superintendent of Camp Nelson National Cemetery reported that it took 288 hours to excavate and backfill the test pits with hand tools, and that opening and closing graves in rock strata, using hand tools, would necessitate approximately 4½ times more work than opening and closing graves under average soil conditions. As a result of this investigation, it was determined that approximately 95 percent of the cemetery area was unsuitable for interment purposes.

In 1978, after lengthy negotiations, the cemetery was abandoned and removed from the roster of national cemeteries. The land was donated to the commonwealth of Kentucky and became a part of the Perryville Battlefield State Park. During the 50 years that it was a national cemetery, Perryville was maintained by contract with the Department of Parks, commonwealth of Kentucky. It was under the supervision of the superintendent of Camp Nelson National Cemetery.

Philadelphia National Cemetery

Haines Street and Limekiln Pike
Philadelphia, Pennsylvania 19138

The cemetery is situated in Philadelphia County, two miles north of Germantown in Philadelphia.

The national cemetery was one of the original 14 established in 1862. It was also one of seven established near large troop recruitment and training areas. Actually, in 1862 the "cemetery" consisted of burial lots in seven different cemeteries, which were either donated to or were purchased by the United States. These lots were established for burial of soldiers who died in the general hospitals near Philadelphia. The seven cemeteries Lafayette, Lebanon, United American Mechanics Association, Odd Fellows, Woodland, Glenwood, and Mt. Moriah together with those at Bristol, Chester, and Whitehall, made up the Philadelphia Group in the reports of the inspector of national cemeteries in 1871 and 1874.

In 1885, the United States purchased 13.32 acres at the present site from Henry J. and Susan B. Freeman, to concentrate these scattered remains. Remains from the first five of the above cemeteries were disinterred and moved to Philadelphia in 1885. The remains from Glenwood were reinterred in 1891, and remains from Bristol, Chester, and Whitehall in 1892. Only a few remains were disinterred from Mt. Moriah, and it is still maintained as a soldiers' lot. Other reinterments were from Potter's Field, Philadelphia (1890), Machpelah Cemetery (1895), and Fort Mifflin Post Cemetery (1897). The cemetery has a Confederate section in which 416 interments were made.

There are four special monuments in the cemetery: the Mexican War Monument, marking the graves of 65 Mexican War soldiers; the Confederate Marker, erected by the General Dabney H. Maury Chapter, U.D.C.; the Confederate Monument, erected in 1911 by the United States; and the Revolutionary War Memorial Marker, erected in 1928 by the residents of Germantown and vicinity.

Two Medal of Honor recipients are interred in the cemetery:

Alphonse Girandy, Sec N, Grave 66. Seaman, U.S. Navy. G.O. No.: 85, 22 March 1902.
Citation: Serving onboard the *USS Bennington,* for extraordinary heroism displayed at the time of the explosion of a boiler at San Diego, California, 21 July 1905.

Galusha Pennypacker, Officers Section, Grave 175. Colonel, 97th Pennsylvania Infantry. Place and date: At Fort Fisher, N.C., 15 January 1865.
Citation: Gallantly led the charge over a traverse and planted the colors of one of his regiments thereon; was severely wounded.

Philadelphia National Cemetery is maintained by private contract under the supervision of the director of Beverly National Cemetery. The cemetery was closed for interments in September 1962, except for those in reserved gravesites or second interments in existing gravesites. As of September 30, 2008, there were 13,202 interments.

Former superintendents/directors of the cemetery are:

T.D. Goodman, Unknown–1882
Frederick Kaufman, February 1884–October 1892
King C. Tolles, Unknown–August 1943
Carl J. Sonstelie, August 1935–July 1943

James H. Malloy, August 1962–October 1967
Milton T. Kelly, Jr., October 1967–August 1968
Henry A. Hartwig, August 1968–July 1973
Claude E. Arnold, July 1973–September 1974
James D. Simms, March 1975–August 1975

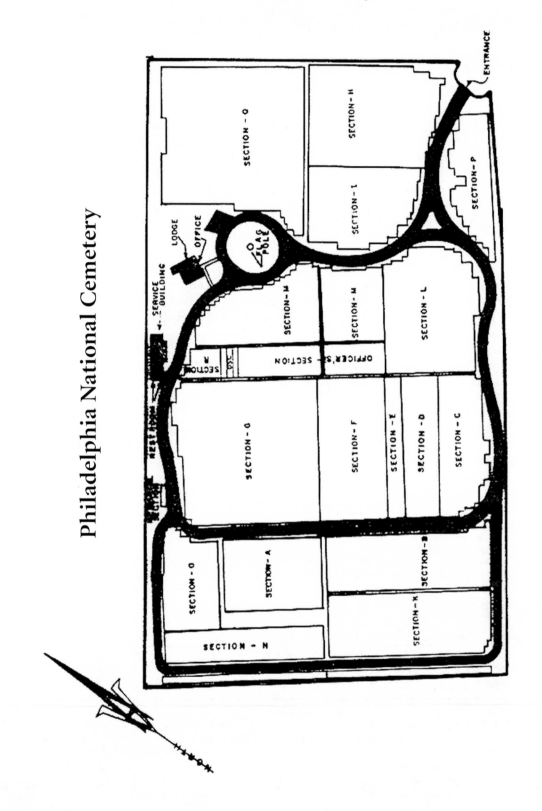

Philadelphia National Cemetery

Harry Painting, May 1945–December 1954
Kenneth E. Ridley, January 1955–August 1961
Metro Kowalchick, August 1961–August 1962

Robert L. Scoggins, December 1978–February 1980

Port Hudson National Cemetery
Route No. 1, P.O. Box 185
Zachary, Louisiana 70791

The cemetery is located approximately 7 miles west of Zachary, Louisiana, about 2 miles east of a bend in the Mississippi River, and some 20 miles north of Baton Rouge. Situated in East Baton Rouge Parish, it is 1 mile from Port Hickey and 1¾ miles from the town of Port Hudson.

The national cemetery is located near the site where the Union and Confederate forces engaged in the siege of Port Hudson in 1862. It is estimated that nearly 4,000 Union soldiers were killed in the siege, and nearly all of them were interred in the cemetery. Only 600 of them have been positively identified. Historians generally agree that the 500 Confederate soldiers who were killed during the battle were buried in the trenches where they fell. The land for the cemetery was used, beginning in 1863, as a burial ground. In 1866 the federal government appropriated 8.4 acres of land and purchased it in 1869.

Port Hudson was for many years an important trading post on the Mississippi River. It was well-known for its white cliffs that were reportedly 2½ to 3 miles long. The name of the community has changed five times since 1699: Thompson's Creek, Old Port Hudson, Alto, Port Hickey, and New Port Hudson. The Mississippi River channel shifted to the west and the community moved with it. The original appropriation by the United States included

Port Hudson National Cemetery, 1948.

a strip of land 60 feet wide extending from the main entrance of the national cemetery to the bluffs overlooking the Mississippi River. This land is now a public road and part of the Georgia Pacific employee recreation area.

The attack on Baton Rouge in July 1862 afforded the Confederacy the opportunity to fortify Port Hudson. With its 100-foot-high bluffs, it provided cannon range up and down the river. Original plans called for a fortification line nine miles long, but when Brigadier General W.W.R. Bell took command, it was limited to 4½ miles. The original fortification would have required about 35,000 men; the contracted fortification, taking advantage of the irregular terrain, required 20,000 men. It was never manned by more than one quarter of that number. The Confederate batteries that lined the bluffs were Union artillery pieces, captured and brought overland to Port Hudson.

On December 28, 1862, Major General Frank Gardner took command of the post. One week earlier, General Nathaniel P. Banks, U.S. Army, had landed 10,000 troops at Baton Rouge and occupied the city. On March 12, 1863, General Banks marched from Baton Rouge, expecting to find Port Hudson evacuated, but on finding it heavily fortified, he returned to Baton Rouge. After learning that the Confederates intended to defend Vicksburg and Port Hudson, Admiral David G. Farragut decided that it was necessary to patrol the river above Port Hudson. General Banks brought three divisions to a position east of Port Hudson to distract the Confederate garrison while the ships moved past the batteries with as little damage as possible. Their aim was to patrol the river only and not to start a naval battle. Banks' maps were in error and he had to build bridges for his troops. They were still building when the shore batteries started firing on the naval fleet late in the evening of March 13, 1863. The engagement was a disaster for the Union fleet. The *Richmond* and the *Tennessee* turned back, the *Monongahela* and the *Kineo* were grounded, and the sloop of war *Mississippi* was grounded and set afire. After more than thirty minutes under heavy fire, Captain Smith of the *Mississippi* decided to abandon ship. Captain Smith ordered the engines destroyed, the sick and wounded moved to shore, and fuses laid to the ship's magazine. The ship blew to pieces at the foot of Profit Island. There were 64 crewmen missing after the battle, and the remains of the vessel have never been located. This was the last attempt to take Port Hudson by water.

The *Mississippi* is of historical importance for two reasons. First, the *Mississippi* was the flagship of Commodore Matthew C. Perry when he made his voyage to Japan in 1853 to open trade between the United States and Japan. Second, during the battle of Port Hudson, the executive officer of the *Mississippi* was Lt. George Dewey, who later became an admiral and was the hero of Manila Bay.

Early in May 1863, General Banks again headed to Port Hudson, and the siege of Port Hudson began on May 24. By the time the Confederates surrendered on July 9, 1863, they were reduced to eating parched corn, dogs and rats. The battle was the first time that the Union army used USCTs (United States Colored Troops) in combat. Many hundreds of them fought valiantly, and were reportedly "wiped out to a man." The siege of Port Hudson was the longest lasting battle of the Civil War, but the Confederacy had been split into two parts, and the Union had gained control of the Mississippi River. When President Lincoln heard the news, he reportedly said, "The Father of Waters again goes unvexed to the sea."

The battlefield at Port Hudson is probably the only naturally preserved Civil War battleground still remaining. The breastworks, gun pits, and trenches remain today almost as they were during the battle.

The burying ground was established as a national cemetery in 1866. The report of the inspector of national cemeteries dated February 27, 1871, listed interments at that time as:

Commissioned officers	7
White Union soldiers and sailors	274
Colored Union soldiers	256
Citizens	4
Unknown and unclassified	<u>3,262</u>
Total	3,803

Besides those killed in the siege of Port Hudson and those who died in military hospitals, remains were brought to the cemetery from Bayou Sara, Morganzia, and other places around the area. The inspector reported in 1871 that the owner of the adjacent land was hostile and would not permit a drainage ditch to be run across his property to drain the cemetery.

During 1978, the Port Hudson National Cemetery was closed to initial interments. That same year the Georgia Pacific Corporation donated approximately four acres which allowed it to be reopened for interments. As of September 30, 2008, the cemetery consisted of approximately 19.9 acres and included 13,095 interments.

Former superintendents/directors of the cemetery are:

Captain William Fletcher, December 1867–1869
P.P. Carroll, 1869–March 1871
George B. Craft, March 1871–July 1875
William Dillan, 1875–1877
W.H. Louis, 1878–1878
Henry Mason, March 1878–June 1882
Major Patrick Hart, 1882–1882
George A. Sanno, 1882–February 1891
Edward Harrison, February 1891–December 1893
L.B. May, December 1893–October 1900
Hiram S. Towne, October 1900–August 1901
George P. Dean, August 1901–March 1903
B.S. Harvey, 1903–January 1904
George W. Ford, February 1904–November 1906
George W. Mathews, November 1906–July 1918
D.D. Rhoads, 1918–1922
Robert Petrum, 1923–1927
Placide Rodriguez, 1928–1933
Frank W. Baker, April 1934–September 1938
Thomas E. Swain, July 1939–October 1940
J.K. Spencer, 1940–December 1941

Philip Cowell, December 1941–July 1945
James H. Blanchard, July 1945–July 1946
Charles S. Stroup, July 1946–December 1946
John W. Cox, January 1947–November 1951
Winston J. Stratton, November 1951–June 1954
Paul B. Porter, June 1954–February 1960
Vernon J. Cram, February 1960–February 1961
Albion H. McLellan, Jr., April 1961–May 1962
Clarence A. Lambert, July 1962–September 1963
Harry W. Blake, October 1963–May 1967
Raymond L. Cordell, June 1967–June 1970
Paul B. Porter, June 1970–March 1977
Richard J. Pless, March 1977–December 1977
Donald H. Fritz, March 1985–August 1987
Clyde E. Rowney, 1987–1990
Virgil M. Wertenberger, 1990–1999
Jorge Baritar, 1999–2001
Gloria Mote, March 2001–March 2004
John Rosentrater, May 2004–September 2005
Gary Ackerman, September 2005–October 2006
Sharon K. Boozer, July 2006–Present

During the period December 1977 to March 1985, the cemetery was under the jurisdiction of the director of Baton Rouge National Cemetery.

Prescott National Cemetery
Department of Veterans Affairs Medical Center
Prescott, Arizona 86313

The cemetery is located in Yavapai County, on Highway 69 east of Prescott, adjacent to the Department of Veterans Affairs Medical Center (DVAMC). The cemetery is oblong in shape and is paralleled on both sides by deep dry washes. It was never officially established as a cemetery. Burials were simply made a conveniently safe distance from Fort Whipple due to the Indian warfare prevalent at the time.

One of the expeditions launched by the government during the 1850s to explore and survey the American West was commanded by First Lieutenant Amiel W. Whipple, a top-

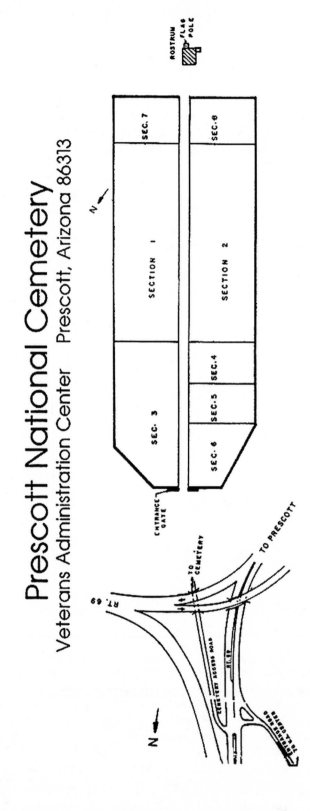

Prescott National Cemetery
Veterans Administration Center   Prescott, Arizona 86313

ographical engineer. He and 110 men left Fort Smith on July 13, 1853, to conduct a survey along the 35th parallel to locate a route for a railroad from Fort Smith, Arkansas, to Los Angeles, California. His party traveled over 1,800 miles of plains, deserts and mountains, encountering 21 different Indian tribes and leaving an important trail across Arizona. The Atcheson, Topeka and Santa Fe Railroad follows this route, as does Interstate 40.

In 1863, members of an exploration party into the Prescott area, led by Captain Joseph Walker, discovered gold in Lynx Creek. Hostile Indians made settlement impossible without military protection. On October 23, 1863, Brigadier General James R. Carleton, headquartered in Santa Fe, issued orders to establish a military post to be known as Fort Whipple in honor of Brigadier General Amiel W. Whipple, who was killed at the Battle of Chancellorsville. A Major Willis and his party established a camp in Chino Valley at Del Rio Springs in December 1863, but moved it 21 miles south to Granite Creek in May 1864. In 1869, the president declared it a military post.

Fort Whipple served as the headquarters for General George Crook during the Indian Wars when the general was best known for his pursuit of Geronimo. The fort was the center of social life in the Prescott area. Among those who lived here during the 1870s and 1880s was the future mayor of New York City, Fiorello LaGuardia. His father was bandmaster at the fort.

The fort was declared obsolete in 1912 when Arizona achieved statehood. After World War I, Fort Whipple became a U.S. Army Hospital for the treatment of tuberculosis. The hospital was transferred from the Army to the U.S. Public Health Service in 1920 and to the Veterans Bureau in 1922; in 1930, with the consolidation of all veterans services, it became part of the Veterans Administration.

The cemetery is thought to be in its third location. The original cemetery was established when Fort Whipple was a camp near Del Rio Springs in 1864. The present location is not the same as shown on the Wheeler survey map in 1869. The cemetery was reportedly relocated to the present site in the mid–1880s because flash floods along Granite Creek had washed out numerous burials in the earlier cemetery. This probably accounts for the majority of the 25 unknown graves in the present cemetery.

Prescott National Cemetery covers 15.35 acres, and as of September 30, 2008, contained 3,714 interments. It was transferred to the National Cemetery System in September 1973. The date of the first interment is not known since 145 burials were made before the first one was recorded. The first recorded burial is Joseph Sands, private, Company F, 5th Infantry. He died of wounds received in action on February 22, 1865. One Medal of Honor recipient is buried here:

Nicholas Foran, Sec 1, Grave 2–54. Private, Company L, 8th U.S. Cavalry. Place and date: Arizona, August to October 1868.
Citation: Bravery in Scouts and actions against Indians.

The cemetery is operated and maintained by the DVAMC.

Puerto Rico National Cemetery
Avenida Cemeterio Nacional # 50
Barrio Hato Tejas
Bayamon, Puerto Rico 00960

The Puerto Rico National Cemetery is the only national or military cemetery on the island. As such, it is primarily intended to serve as a final resting place for Puerto Rican veterans who served in the World Wars, Korea and Vietnam. The national cemetery occupies a unique position: it is simultaneously a symbol of American presence on the island and of Puerto Rican participation in world-shaping events.

The cemetery is located on a dramatic site 1½ miles northwest of Bayamon, a fast-growing subcenter of the San Juan metropolitan area, which is about 13 miles away. From the hills on the site, an observer can see the ocean and in the distance old San Juan and El Moro, the ancient Spanish fort. The site is limited to its present size of 108.2 acres by the surrounding topographic features and land uses.

The site was used during World War II as a U.S. Navy Machine Gun Range. On July 12, 1948, the land was transferred to the Department of the Army for construction of the Puerto Rico National Cemetery. The land was originally acquired by the Navy Department in 1942 through condemnation proceedings. The cemetery was officially dedicated on Veterans Day 1949. Governor Luis Munoz-Marin and Major General Herman Feldman, quartermaster general of the Army, were principal speakers. General Feldman said during his remarks that "practically every family in Puerto Rico had a representative in uniform during World War II."

Over the years since its dedication, Puerto Rico National Cemetery has become a shrine to Puerto Ricans who served in the armed forces. Special patriotic observances are held on Veterans Day and Memorial Day, with attendance usually numbering about 10,000 people, and all military commanders on the island as well as large numbers of government officials are present. There are many visitors on Easter, All Souls Day, All Saints Day, Mother's Day,

Flag Plaza, Puerto Rico National Cemetery.

and Father's Day. On any given day, practically every gravesite in the cemetery is decorated with fresh flowers.

There are several individuals interred here who are very dear to the people of Puerto Rico. These include Major General Juan Cesar Cordero, Major General Carlos Fernando Chardon, Dr. Bailey Kelly Ashford, and Carlos Garcia-Curbelo.

Major General Cordero was a prominent Puerto Rican who distinguished himself in the military with the U.S. Army during World War II. Later, during the Korean War, Cordero fought with the 65th Infantry Regiment. He rose to the rank of major general as adjutant general of Puerto Rico. General Cordero met an untimely death at the age of 61 and was interred with full military honors in Grave 1, Section C.

Major General Chardon was a former secretary of state and later adjutant general of the Commonwealth of Puerto Rico. He was chairman and the inspiring force in the project to obtain congressional approval to fly the flag of Puerto Rico at the same height as the American flag in the cemetery. He also served as chairman of the project to raise funds for the expansion of the Court of Honor. General Chardon died at the age of 74 on December 9, 1981, and was interred in Grave 6, Honor Section, on December 10, 1981.

Dr. Bailey Kelly Ashford, a native of Washington, D.C., earned the gratitude of the thousands of people living in the tropics due to his role in combating hookworm. When Dr. Ashford came to Puerto Rico with the occupying forces of the U.S. Army during the Spanish-American War, he soon realized the prevalence of hookworm and became determined to find a cure. Ashford, a retired colonel, died in 1934 and was interred in Fort Brooke Military Cemetery. In 1954 his remains, along with all others in the Fort Brooke cemetery, were transferred to Puerto Rico National Cemetery. He is interred in Grave 1204, Section A.

Carlos Garcia-Curbelo served as director of Puerto Rico National Cemetery from June 12, 1950, until his death, at age 70, on December 30, 1986. In addition, he served as U.S. Army mortuary and survivor assistance officer for Puerto Rico and the Caribbean. While he was actually the second superintendent of the cemetery Ralph Dea had served from July 1949 to June 1950 Garcia was known throughout the island and was referred to as Don Carlos by everyone. He and his wife, Lydia, personally planted the royal palms that lined the main drive in the cemetery until they were destroyed by Hurricane Hugo in 1989. He is interred in Grave 7, Honor Section, next to his longtime friend Carlos Chardon.

There are two Medal of Honor recipients interred in the cemetery. The daggers indicate that they were killed in action.

†**Fernando Luis Garcia-Ledesma,** Sec MB, Grave 4. Private First Class, U.S. Marine Corps, Company I, 3rd Battalion, 1st Marine Division (Rein). Place and date: Korea, 5 September 1952.
Citation: For conspicuous gallantry and intrepidity at the risk of his life above and beyond the call of duty while serving as a member of Company I, in action against enemy aggressor forces. While participating in the defense of a combat outpost located more than one mile forward of the main line of resistance during a savage night attack by a fanatical enemy force employing grenades, mortars, and artillery, PFC Garcia, although suffering painful wounds, moved through the intense hail of hostile fire to a supply point to secure more hand grenades. Quick to act when a hostile grenade landed nearby, endangering the life of another Marine, as well as his own, he unhesitatingly chose to sacrifice himself and immediately threw his body upon the deadly missile, receiving the full impact of the explosion. He gallantly gave his life for his country.

†**Euripides Rubio, Jr.,** Sec HS, Grave 5. Captain, U.S. Army, Head quarters and Headquarters Company, 1st Battalion, 28th Infantry Division, RVN. Place and date: Tay Ninh Province, Republic of Vietnam, 8 November 1966.
Citation: For conspicuous gallantry and intrepidity in action at the risk of his life above and beyond the call of duty. Captain Rubio was serving as communications officer, 1st Battalion, when

a numerically superior enemy force launched a massive attack against the battalion defense position. Intense enemy machine gun fire raked the area while mortar rounds and rifle grenades exploded within the perimeter. Leaving the relative safety of his post, Capt. Rubio received two serious wounds as he braved the withering fire to go to the area of most intense action where he distributed ammunition, reestablished positions, and rendered aid to the wounded. Disregarding the painful wounds, he unhesitatingly assumed command when a rifle company commander was medically evacuated. Captain Rubio was wounded a third time as he selflessly exposed himself to devastating enemy fire to move among his men to encourage them to fight with renewed effort. While aiding the evacuation of wounded personnel, he noted that a smoke grenade which was intended to mark the Viet Cong position for air strikes had fallen dangerously close to the friendly lines. Captain Rubio ran to reposition the grenade but was immediately struck to his knees by enemy fire. Despite his several wounds, Capt. Rubio scooped up the grenade, ran through the deadly hail of fire to within 20 meters of the enemy position and hurled the already smoking grenade into the midst of the enemy before he fell for the final time. Using the repositioned grenade as a marker, friendly air strikes were directed to destroy the hostile positions. Captain Rubio's singularly heroic act turned the tide of battle, and his extraordinary leadership and valor were a magnificent inspiration to his men.

Many changes have taken place in this cemetery since it opened in 1949. On May 25, 1975, the flag of Puerto Rico was hoisted to the same height as the American flag in the Court of Honor. This unique event was made possible by the contributions of the Puerto Rican people and businesses. The funds were used to enlarge the Court of Honor, to erect a second flagpole, and to install an illumination system. A bronze plaque was placed in the Court of Honor to commemorate this event. An electronic 54-bell carillon was donated and installed by the American Legion, Department of Puerto Rico, on January 12, 1969. Two unique committal shelters were designed by the VA Cemetery Service and constructed by cemetery personnel in 1982. A new maintenance service building was completed in 1980, and a new administration building was completed in November 1984. At the request of the veterans of Puerto Rico, the building was dedicated to Garcia-Curbelo. Finally, a public restroom building was completed in 1987.

Fort Buchanan has provided extensive support since the cemetery was established. At various times, it has provided honor guards, firing squads, and a bugler for veterans' funerals.

The cemetery has expanded from the original 19 acres to over 108 acres. As of September 30, 2008, there were 49,309 total interments. All gravesites are marked with flat granite markers.

There are several stories of the supernatural associated with this cemetery. One of them occurred one day when the wife of the superintendent answered a knock on the door of their quarters. A man dressed from head to toe in white introduced himself as Senor Lopez and asked for directions to his grave. She told him that her husband was out in the cemetery and when he returned he would help him locate the grave. At that time she saw her husband coming toward the office and pointed him out to the gentleman. She watched as the man walked up to her husband, talked for a moment, and then walked with him back to a gravesite where an interment had been made that morning. When they reached the grave, the superintendent shook hands with the man, then turned and started walking back to the office. She continued to watch as the man lay down on the new grave and disappeared.

Former superintendents/directors of the cemetery are:

Ralph Dea, July 1949–June 1950
Carlos Garcia-Curbelo, June 1950–December 1986
Rafael Acosta, 1987–March 1995
Jorge Lopez, August 1995–February 1999

William Trower, September 1999–August 2001
Jorge R. Baltar, January 2002–October 2006
Arleen Ocasio DeLa Rosa Vincenty, November 2006–December 2007
Stephen E. Fezler, December 2007–Present

Quantico National Cemetery
18424 Joplin Road (Route 619)
Triangle, Virginia 22172

Quantico National Cemetery is located approximately 25 miles south of Washington, D.C., at exit 50B off Interstate 95. The cemetery consists of 726.6 rolling, wooded acres crossed by two streams running north to south draining into Chopawamsic Creek.

The area was first used as a base for military operations by the navy of the commonwealth of Virginia in 1775. During the Civil War, it was a blockade point for the Confederacy. Still later, it was used by the 12th commandant of the Marine Corps, Major General George Barnett, as a training camp for Marines. Thousands of Marines trained at Quantico during World War I, including the famed Fourth Marine Brigade whose members were awarded six Medals of Honor for action in Europe.

The Quantico site was purchased in December 1918 when the secretary of the Navy authorized the Marine Corps to develop Quantico as a permanent training base. In 1921, the Marine Corps Schools, forerunner of the Marine Corps Development and Education Command, was established here. Since 1941 the primary mission of the base has been individual education and training as distinguished from unit training.

When the National Cemetery System (NCS) adopted the regional cemetery concept in 1974, the plan was to establish a large regional cemetery in each of the 10 standard federal regions, plus one in the Washington, D.C., metropolitan area. The site at Quantico was chosen as the best location for the Washington, D.C., cemetery, and the Marine Corps transferred the land to the NCS in January 1977.

The cemetery was dedicated on May 15, 1983, and the first interment was made the following day. As of September 30, 2008, there were 24,209 interments. There will be available gravesites beyond the year 2030.

A number of distinguished veterans are interred here, including General Lewis M. Walt, assistant commandant, U.S. Marine Corps, and Louis R. Lowery, a World War II Marine combat photographer who took the picture of the U.S. flag being raised atop Mount Suribachi on the island of Iwo Jima. The flag was said to be the first stars and stripes to fly over Japanese territory in World War II.

Brigadier General Warren Sweetser was the first general officer buried at Quantico. During World War II, General Sweetser was in the first B-25 training group at Edenton and Cherry Point, and saw service in the Pacific. He commanded two Marine air groups during the Korean War.

Captain Michael S. Haskell, Corporal Douglas E. Held, HTFN (Hull Technician Fireman) David Hyder, and Captain Vincent Smith were all casualties of the bombing of the American Embassy in Lebanon. They were buried in October 1983. Major John Giguere, also interred in October 1983, was killed during the Grenada invasion.

The cemetery history handout includes the stories of other notable individuals interred her. A copy may be obtained at the Quantico National Cemetery Administration Office.

John D. Comer III, a decorated veteran, was the first Manassas, Virginia, police officer to be slain in the line of duty. His funeral was attended by over 1,400 police officers from the Carolinas to New England, plus 300 police officials from the FBI National Academy representing over 150 communities around the world.

There are three private cemeteries located within the Quantico grounds; Abel, Minnie Doyle Place and the Other Minnie Doyle Place. The Abel family cemetery consists of ½ acre containing 12 graves with the possibility of 10 additional burials. The Minnie Doyle

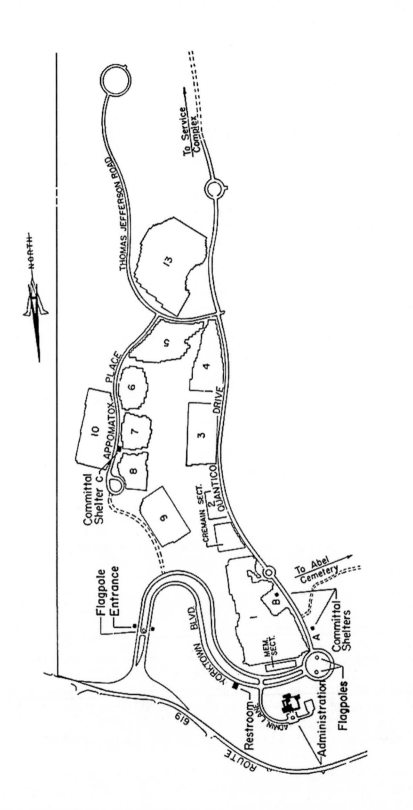

Name ——————— Grave ——————— Section ———————

Place consists of seven to ten unmarked graves, and the Other Minnie Doyle Place contains only two or three graves. All are maintained by the Quantico staff.

Former directors of the cemetery are:

Joe D. Willard, April 1982–October 1985   George Allen, 2005–2006
Fred I. Haselbarth, Jr., 1985–1989   James Metcalf, 2006–2007
Patricia K. Novak, 1989–2001   Karl McDonald, 2007–Present
Michael Picerno, 2001–2005

Quincy National Cemetery
36th & Main Streets
Quincy, Illinois 62301

The cemetery is situated in Adams County in the Forest Lawn Memorial Gardens, formerly called the Graceland Cemetery.

As early as 1861, Union soldiers were being buried in the soldier's lot of the Woodland Cemetery. In 1870 the city of Quincy donated to the United States the half-acre in which were buried 221 soldiers.

In the years following the close of the Civil War, both Congress and the War Department were very sensitive to the demands of the Grand Army of the Republic (G.A.R.). It is little wonder that when William W. Berry wrote to Secretary of War R.T. Lincoln on July 3, 1882, urging the establishment of a national cemetery in Quincy, Secretary Lincoln responded in late July by designating the soldiers' lot a national cemetery.

A superintendent who was strongly recommended by the local G.A.R. post was appointed on October 20, 1882. Soon after his appointment, allegations were made that the superintendent had agreed to share his salary with the G.A.R. post. The quartermaster general ordered an investigation and it was found "that the superintendent had received the endorsement of the Post for his appointment upon the condition that he was to pay to the Post fund the whole of his annual salary ($720) except $200." On January 30, 1883, the secretary of war cancelled the superintendent's appointment and again contracted with the Woodland Cemetery association to care for the grounds at a cost of $25 per annum.

In 1899, the government purchased a site in the Graceland Cemetery and transferred approximately 300 remains to the new location, but still used the name Quincy National Cemetery.

Corporal Martin J. Hawkins, one of the Andrews' Raiders (see Chattanooga National Cemetery) was interred in the cemetery on February 7, 1886. He was awarded the Medal of Honor for his participation in the raid.

> **Martin J. Hawkins,** Corporal, Company A, 33d Ohio Infantry. Place and date: Georgia, April 1862.
> Citation: One of the 19 of 22 men (including 2 civilians)* who, by direction of Gen. Mitchell (or Buell), penetrated nearly 200 miles south into enemy territory and captured a railroad train at Big Shanty, Ga., in an attempt to destroy the bridges and track between Chattanooga and Atlanta.

The cemetery is supervised by the Director of Rock Island National Cemetery. As of September 30, 2008, there were 584 interments. The cemetery is closed for initial interments.

This phrase is taken to refer to the fact that one man (a soldier) slept through the raid.

Raleigh National Cemetery
501 Rock Quarry Road
Raleigh, North Carolina 27610

The cemetery is situated in Wake County, Raleigh, North Carolina, about ten blocks from the state capitol building. It occupies 6.95 acres which were appropriated in 1865. In 1871 Governor Tod R. Caldwell, pursuant to direction of the North Carolina legislature, deeded the entire property to the United States.

The city of Raleigh, known as the City of Oaks, has the unique distinction among the 50 state capitals of having been planned and established on land bought by the state as the location of its seat of government. It was established in 1792. The city was named in honor of Sir Walter Raleigh, whose ill-fated colony settled on the coast of North Carolina in 1587. Wake County, bearing the maiden name of Royal Governor Tryon's wife, was created in 1771.

In 1864, Governor Zebulon Vance directed that an entrenchment be erected around Raleigh to defend the capital city from what he felt to be an inevitable battleground as the Civil War continued. The entrenchment was later removed to establish what is now known as Rock Quarry Road. The street derived its name from the rock quarry located directly across from the cemetery. Rocks were extracted from this quarry to build the state capitol building.

On April 13, 1865, General Sherman's army entered Raleigh as the Confederates

Raleigh National Cemetery

(Approximate location of grave is indicated on the map)

Name _____ Grave _____ Section _____

retreated westward from the city. Surrounding fortifications had been thrown up, but due to the wisdom of B.F. Moore, Major John Devereux, and others, the city was surrendered unconditionally. As a result, the city was spared the devastation and destruction wreaked upon other Southern cities. Federal guards were furnished at all homes and there was no widespread destruction of property. A few days later, following the surrender of General Joseph E. Johnson at Durham Station, 27 miles west of Raleigh, General U.S. Grant went to Raleigh and reviewed General Sherman's troops in a "great parade."

When the Union Army occupied the city, Camp Green was established on a site near the cemetery as its headquarters. A post cemetery, on the site of the present national cemetery, was established wherein were buried 32 troops and members of their families. When the national cemetery was established in 1865, remains were brought here from Averysboro, Smithville, Bentonville County, Goldsboro, Greensboro, Franklin, Henderson, and other places within the state. The first burial sections were established by states, with 14 states represented.

Records indicate that the first superintendent of the cemetery was appointed on June 1, 1868. He was G.A. Dichtl, a discharged sergeant of Company A, 42d Regiment of Infantry. The report of the inspector of national cemeteries prepared August 16, 1871, showed that 621 known and 539 unknown had been interred in the cemetery. As of September 30, 2008, there had been 6,066 interments.

There is one known Medal of Honor recipient interred in Raleigh National Cemetery. The dagger denotes that he was killed in action.

†**William Maud Bryant,** Sec 15, Grave 1227. Sergeant First Class, U.S. Army, Company A, 5th Special Forces Group, 1st Special Forces. Place and date: Long Khanh Province, Republic of Vietnam, 24 March 1969.

Citation: For conspicuous gallantry and intrepidity in action at the risk of his life above and beyond the call of duty. Sergeant Bryant, assigned to Company A, distinguished himself while serving as commanding officer of Civilian Irregular Defense Group Company 321, 2d Battalion, 3d Mobile Strike Force Command, during combat operations. The battalion came under heavy fire and became surrounded by the elements of three enemy regiments. Sergeant Bryant displayed extraordinary heroism throughout the succeeding 34 hours of incessant attack as he moved throughout the company position heedless of the intense hostile fire while establishing and improving the defensive perimeter, directing fire during critical phases of the battle, distributing ammunition, assisting the wounded, and providing leadership and an inspirational example of courage to his men. When a helicopter drop of ammunition was made to resupply the beleaguered force, Sfc. Bryant with complete disregard for his safety ran through the heavy enemy fire to retrieve the scattered ammunition boxes and distributed needed ammunition to his men. During a lull in the intense fighting, Sfc. Bryant led a patrol outside the perimeter to obtain information of the enemy. The patrol came under intense automatic weapons fire and was pinned down. Sergeant Bryant singlehandedly repulsed one enemy attack on his small force and by his heroic action inspired his men to fight off other assaults. Seeing a wounded enemy soldier some distance from the patrol location, Sfc. Bryant crawled forward alone under heavy fire to retrieve the soldier for intelligence purposes. Finding that the enemy soldier had expired, Sfc. Bryant crawled back to his patrol and led his men back to the company position where he again took command of the defense. As the siege continued, Sfc. Bryant organized and led a patrol in a daring attempt to break through the enemy encirclement. The patrol had advanced some 200 meters by heavy fighting when it was pinned down by the intense automatic weapons fire from heavily fortified bunkers and Sfc. Bryant was severely wounded. Despite his wounds he rallied his men, called for helicopter gunship support, and directed heavy suppressive fire upon the enemy positions. Following the last gunship attack, Sfc. Bryant fearlessly charged an enemy automatic weapons position, overrunning it and singlehandedly destroying its three defenders. Inspired by his heroic example, his men renewed their attack on the entrenched enemy. While regrouping his small force for the final assault against the enemy, Sfc. Bryant fell mortally wounded by an enemy rocket. Sergeant Bryant's selfless concern for his comrades at the cost of his life above and beyond the call of duty are in keeping with the highest traditions of the military service and reflect great credit upon himself, his unit, and the U.S. Army.

This cemetery is administered by the director, New Bern National Cemetery. Former superintendents/directors of the national cemetery are:

G.A. Dichtl, June 1868–Unknown

Jonah C. Pumphrey, October 1943–January 1947

Oberlin H. Carter, January 1947–June 1953

Andrew K. Hill, June 1953–February 1956

Edward B. McFarland, February 1956–March 1962

Winston J. Stratton, March 1962–September 1964

William M. Miller, September 1964–August 1970

George C. Miller, August 1970–January 1975

Winston J. Stratton, January 1975–June 1978

David Rivera-Guzman, July 1978–April 1980

Gary W. Smith, May 1980–August 1981

Gilberto Lopez, October 1981–March 1984

Delores T. Blake, March 1984–October 1985

Virgil M. Wertenberger, February 1986– September 1987

Leon B. Murphy, 1987–1990

Richard Anderson, April 1990–October 1991

Richmond National Cemetery
1701 Williamsburg Road
Richmond, Virginia 23231

The land on which this cemetery is located was appropriated by the United States and the cemetery established on September 1, 1866. It is situated in Henrico County, Virginia, about 1½ miles from the James River and 3 miles east of the state capitol. It is just within the lines of fortification thrown up by the Confederates during the defense of Richmond. The site contains ten acres and originally afforded a commanding view of the city and the valley of the James River. The United States purchased 3 acres from Mr. and Mrs. William Slater on July 29, 1867; 5 acres from William L. Williams, trustee, et al., on July 10, 1868; and 1.74 acres from George Geffert on June 23, 1906. The approach road was acquired by quit claim deed on November 28, 1939.

Only about 100 miles separate Richmond, Virginia, and Washington, D.C., respective capitals of the Confederacy and the United States. Yet it took four long years of hard fought campaigns and more loss of life than any other conflict on the North American continent for the Union forces to capture Richmond on April 3, 1865. With the fall of Richmond, and a few days later on April 9, 1865, the surrender of General Robert E. Lee's valiant Army of Northern Virginia, the Civil War was at last over.

Reinterments in the national cemetery were made from Oakwood and Hollywood cemeteries in Richmond, the cemetery of the Belle Island Confederate Prison (for Union prisoners of war), from the battlefields of Cold Harbor and Seven Pines, and from locations in Chesterfield and Hanover counties. Some 70 different locations within a distance of 25 miles surrounding the cemetery were searched for Union remains to be removed to the cemetery.

The report of the inspector of national cemeteries dated July 24, 1871, listed interments in the cemetery as follows:

	Known	Unknown
White Union soldiers	803	5,665
Marines		
Citizens	8	0
Employees	3	0
Servants (colored)	2	0
Total	818	5,665

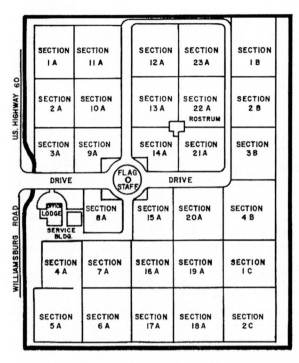

Map of the Richmond National Cemetery, Richmond, VA, October 1969.

The inspector also reported that a few Union soldiers were still buried outside the cemetery but would soon be brought in and buried with their comrades.

As of September 30, 2008, there had been 9,337 interments in Richmond National Cemetery. The cemetery is closed for interments, except for those in reserved gravesites or second interments in existing graves under the single gravesite per family policy.

Richmond National Cemetery is headquarters for what the National Cemetery System calls the Richmond Complex. The cemeteries at City Point, Cold Harbor, Fort Harrison, Glendale, and Seven Pines are under the jurisdiction of the director of Richmond National Cemetery for operation, administration, and management. All 6 of the cemeteries were established in 1866, and they contain a total of 23.8 acres of land. The single management concept was implemented in 1978.

Former superintendents/directors of the cemetery are:

Patrick Hart, Unknown–1871
Nathan E. Numbers, September 1936–August 1947
John J. Carr, September 1947–April 1950
William Robert Rossbach, April 1950–March 1956
James E. Wolstenholme, March 1956–September 1960
Howard J. Ferguson, September 1960–November 1968

Theodore J. Nick, December 1968–August 1969
Allan H. Long, December 1969–August 1970
Leland W. Potter, Sr., September 1970–March 1981
Arthur E. Bath, April 1981–October 1988
Lillian V. Couch, October 1988–1990
Leon B. Murphy, 1990–

Riverside National Cemetery
22495 Van Buren Boulevard
Riverside, California 92508

The cemetery is located on a gentle eastern-facing slope in the Moreno Valley in Riverside, California, adjacent to March Air Force Base. It is 55 miles east of Los Angeles, 42 miles west of Palm Springs, and 85 miles north of San Diego.

One reason veterans service organizations raised such a hue and cry to convince Congress to transfer the National Cemetery System (NCS) from the Department of the Army to the Veterans Administration was that cemeteries in many areas of the country were rapidly filling and the Army was following a non-expansion policy. About a year after the transfer had been made, the system adopted the so-called regional concept, which would establish one large national cemetery in each standard federal region. Fort Rosecrans, established in San Diego in 1934, and Golden Gate, established in 1941 in San Bruno, could not handle the staggering casualties of World War II, Korea and Vietnam. All of these things started the NCS looking for a site for Standard Federal Region IX, preferably in California. Eventually the site, part of March Air Force Base, was selected, and 740 acres were transferred to the NCS at a site dedication ceremony on June 27, 1976. An additional 181 acres was transferred by the Air Force in 2003.

The property, formerly Camp William G. Haan, was an Army camp during World War II. During this period, many thousands of troops trained in antiaircraft defense with searchlights, 50 caliber machine guns, 37, 40, and 90 millimeter antiaircraft guns. The antiaircraft units sometimes were known as "moonlight cavalry." The training center was a flourishing active camp with all the facilities of a first-class military installation, and the Service Club and USO hosted many of Hollywood's outstanding talents. Other units stationed and trained at Camp Haan during the war years included troops of Quartermaster, Signal Corps and DEML units.

When the war ended and Camp Haan was no longer required by the Army, it was turned over to the Air Force.

Riverside National Cemetery is the most active in the NCS. It was dedicated on November 11, 1978. Since the first interment on Dedication Day until September 30, 2008, there were 185,957 total interments, including over 3,000 inurnments in the columbarium. The cemetery is projected to have gravesites available beyond the year 2030.

Recognizing that cremation was fast becoming acceptable to more people, and that space was available, new thinking in the NCS dictated that a columbarium be constructed at Riverside. Of the total burials in fiscal year 1989, 23 percent were of cremated remains. The columbarium is a stone-faced structure consisting of eight courts located across a lake from the Memorial Amphitheater.

The Memorial Amphitheater was constructed on a hillside sloping to one of the lakes, with the stage set on the shoreline. It provides seating for about 2,000 and is fully accessible to the handicapped. Partial funding was raised by the Cemetery Support Committee, with the VA providing the balance.

The lakes hold treated effluent water which is purchased from March Air Force Base and used in irrigating the cemetery grounds. Committal shelters are constructed in the style of a ramada, a structure associated with southwestern climates.

The first interment was that of Staff Sergeant Ysmael R. Villegas. He is one of three Medal of Honor recipients interred in the cemetery.

Riverside National Cemetery

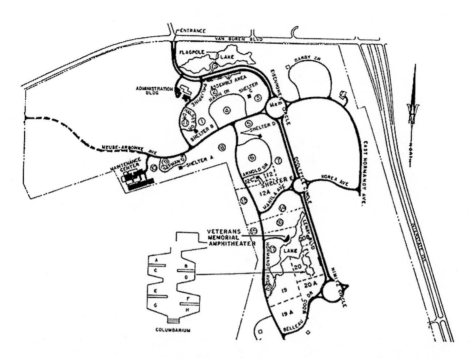

†**Ysmael R. Villegas,** Sec.5, Grave 1178. Staff Sergeant, U.S. Army, Company F, 127th Infantry, 32nd Infantry Division. Place and date: At Ville Verde Trail, Luzon, Philippine Islands on March 20, 1945.

Citation: For charging enemy foxholes, under heavy and intense fire, and destroying five of them. He was hit and killed as he charged the sixth position.

John H. Balch, Sec. 2, Grave 1926. Commander (then Pharmacist's Mate First Class), U.S. Navy, 6th Regiment U.S. Marines. Place and Date: Vierzy & Somme-Py, France, July 19, 1918 and October 9, 1918.

Mitchell Paige, Sec. 20A, Grave 533. Colonel (then Platoon Sergeant), U.S. Marine Corps, 1st Marine Division. Place and Date: Solomon Islands, October 26, 1942.

U.S. Air Force Major General Chesley G. Peterson, a highly decorated flying ace and member of the prestigious American Eagle Squadron 71 that flew in the Battle of Britain, was interred on January 28, 1990. Squadron 71 was an elite group of American volunteers who fought for the British before the United States entered World War II. The Eagle Squadrons were transferred to the U.S. Army Air Corps in September 1942. In August 1943, General Peterson assumed command of the 4th Fighter Group, which became the highest-scoring Air Corps fighter unit in the war.

Captain Lillian Kinkela Keil, U.S. Air Force Flight Nurse Pioneer, is interred in Section 20A Site 1235. She flew on 425 combat missions and took part in 11 major campaigns that included the D-Day invasion, and the Battle of the Bulge in World War II and the Battle of Chosin Reservoir during the Korean War. She is one of the most decorated women in American military history. She was awarded 19 medals including a European Theater medal with four battle stars, a Korean service medal with seven battle stars, four air medals, and a Presidential Citation from the Republic of Korea.

Former directors of the cemetery are:

Roland E. Lex, January 1978–April 1986
Thomas E. Costanzo, April 1986–May 1987
Therese J. Bush, June 1987–

Rock Island National Cemetery
Building 118, Rock Island Arsenal
Rock Island, Illinois 61299

Rock Island National Cemetery was established in 1863 within the area of the United States Arsenal, located on Rock Island in the Mississippi River near the cities of Davenport, Iowa, and Rock Island and Moline, Illinois. The area set aside within the arsenal grounds provided burial space for those who died in the general hospital at Davenport, Iowa, and Union soldiers who died while serving as guards at the large Confederate prisoner of war camp established on Rock Island.

On August 28, 1868, Brevet Major General Lorenzo Thomas, inspector of national cemeteries, visited the national cemetery. He noted in his report that the cemetery was in the shape of a rectangle, 216 feet by 96 feet; that it was enclosed with a paling fence; that the graves and walks were covered with a blue grass; and that the graves were marked with

Original Entrance to Rock Island National Cemetery.

wooden headboards. There were 136 interments, which included 74 white soldiers of various state volunteer regiments, 49 members of the 108th Regiment U.S. Colored Troops, 6 women and children, and 7 unknowns.

At the time of the 1868 inspection, the commanding officer of the arsenal, Brevet Brigadier General Thomas J. Rodman, indicated that the location of the burial area would ultimately conflict with his plans for expansion of the arsenal. He recommended that the remains be removed to higher ground on the upper end of the island. General Thomas concurred with this plan and further suggested that the remains of 159 Civil War decedents interred in the back part of the Oakdale Cemetery in Davenport, Iowa, be removed to the burial site on Rock Island.

The original site of approximately one acre has been increased by property transfers in 1926, 1936, 1950, and 1988. Today the site encompasses 66 acres and includes, as of September 30, 2008, 25,815 interments.

During the years 1863–65, another cemetery about 2,500 yards northwest of Rock Island National Cemetery was established on the reservation. This cemetery is known as the Rock Island Confederate Cemetery, wherein are interred 1,951 members of the Confederate forces who died while confined as prisoners of war in the prison camp established in 1863. The first contingent of prisoners, taken during the battles of Lookout Mountain and Missionary Ridge on November 25 and 26, 1863, arrived at Rock Island in December 1863. During the ensuing months until the end of the war in 1865, additional prisoners were brought to Rock Island from the battlefields of the south. More than 12,000 prisoners of war were at some time confined here. Many of the prisoners died from a variety of causes: the cold northern winters, inadequate food and housing, and disease especially smallpox, which also killed many of the Union soldiers appointed as prison guards.

Brigadier General Thomas J. Rodman, distinguished Civil War officer and commanding officer of the arsenal from 1865 until his death in 1871, is interred in the cemetery. General Rodman has been called the father of Rock Island Arsenal as the arsenal was planned and constructed under his supervision. His gravesite, designated by the secretary of war, is marked by a large obelisk monument. The Civil War–era cannon surrounding General Rodman's grave are especially significant as they were cast by a process invented by General Rodman. Iron cannon fabricated by this method were cast around a water or air-cooled core so that the barrel cooled first and was compressed by contraction of the outside metal. Crystallization of the metal was regulated thereby so that guns made in this manner would withstand considerable internal pressure without breaking. General Rodman also improved the propellant quality of black powder by molding it into large grains that burned more steadily than corned powder and gave the projectile a steady shove from a gun or cannon rather than a sudden impulse. General Rodman graduated from West Point in 1841 and was commanding officer of the Watertown Arsenal, New York, prior to assuming command of the Rock Island Arsenal in 1865.

The grave of Colonel David Matson King, commanding officer of the Rock Island Arsenal from 1921 to 1932, is located near the grave of General Rodman. He graduated from West Point in 1893 and died at Rock Island Arsenal on January 27, 1932.

Thirty-three group burials for 154 decedents have been made in the cemetery. The group burial sites are located in sections D and E. The largest group burial, in Section E, marks the honored resting place of 19 servicemen who died on January 10, 1945, following an explosion onboard the *USS Warhawk,* a troop-landing carrier at anchor in the Lingayen Gulf of Luzon, largest of the Philippine Islands. The group burial was made on June 23, 1950.

A local artist, Dorothy Pate, has donated many historical paintings which hang in the administration building. One of the paintings is of Captain Frederick E. Woodward, a Navy Kingfisher pilot. Captain Woodward helped spot and rescue Eddie Rickenbacker and his crew, who had been down in the Pacific Ocean for 24 days and were near death.

Two Medal of Honor recipients are interred in the cemetery. The daggers before their names indicate that they were killed in action.

†**Edward J. Moskala,** Sec E, Grave 293. Private First Class, U.S. Army, Company C, 383d Infantry, 96th Infantry Division. Place and date: Kakazu Ridge, Okinawa, Ryukyu Islands, 9 April 1945.

Citation: He was the leading element when grenade explosions and concentrated machine gun and mortar fire halted the unit's attack on Kakazu Ridge, Okinawa, Ryukyu Islands. With utter disregard for his personal safety, he charged 40 yards through withering, grazing fire and wiped out 2 machine gun nests with well-aimed grenades and deadly accurate fire from his automatic rifle. When strong counterattacks and fierce enemy resistance from other positions forced his company to withdraw, he voluntarily remained behind with eight others to cover the maneuver. Fighting from a critically dangerous position for 3 hours, he killed more than 25 Japanese before following his surviving companions through screening smoke down the face of the ridge to a gorge where he discovered that one of the group had been left behind, wounded. Unhesitatingly, Pvt. Moskala climbed the bullet-swept slope to assist in the rescue, and, returning to lower ground, volunteered to protect other wounded while the bulk of the troops quickly took up more favorable positions. He had saved another casualty and killed four enemy infiltrators when he was struck and mortally wounded himself while aiding still another disabled soldier. With gallant initiative, unfaltering courage, and heroic determination to destroy the enemy, Pvt. Moskala gave his life in his complete devotion to his company's mission and his comrades' well-being. His intrepid conduct providing a lasting inspiration for those with whom he served.

†**Frank Peter Witek,** Sec E, Grave 72. Private First Class, U.S. Marine Corps Reserve.

Citation: For conspicuous gallantry and intrepidity at the risk of his life above and beyond the call of duty while serving with the 1st Battalion, 9th Marines, 3d Marine Division, during the Battle of Finegayen at Guam, Marinas, on 3 August 1944. When his rifle platoon was halted by heavy surprise fire from well camouflaged enemy positions, Pfc. Witek daringly remained standing to fire a full magazine from his automatic at point-blank range into a depression housing Japanese troops, killing eight of the enemy and enabling the greater part of his platoon to take cover. During his platoon's withdrawal for consolidation of lines, he remained to safeguard a severely wounded comrade, courageously returning the enemy's fire until the arrival of stretcher bearers, and then covering the evacuation by sustained fire as he moved backward toward his own lines. With his platoon again pinned down by a hostile machine gun, Pfc. Witek, on his own initiative, moved forward boldly to the reinforcing tanks and infantry, alternately throwing hand grenades and firing as he advanced to within five to ten yards of the enemy position, and destroying the hostile machine gun emplacement and an additional eight Japanese before he himself was struck down by an enemy rifleman. His valiant and inspiring action effectively reduced the enemy's firepower, thereby enabling his platoon to attain its objective, and reflects the highest credit upon Pfc. Witek and the U.S. Naval Service. He gallantly gave his life for his country.

The first superintendent was appointed in June 1970. Prior to that time the cemetery was operated and maintained initially by the quartermaster, and later, the post engineer, Rock Island Arsenal. Former superintendents/directors are:

Raymond L. Cordell, June 1970–June 1973	Mary Dill, 1991–1994
Donald L. Polston, June 1973–June 1974	Robert Poe, 1994–1996
Claude Arnold, September 1974–February 1977	Larry Williams, 1996–2001
Eddie Walker, August 1977–February 1978	Rick Anderson, 2001–2004
Ronald B. Andrews, February 1978–May 1981	Robert Poe, 2004–2005
William E. Cox, July 1981–June 1984	Sean Baumgardner, 2005–2008
Arthur L. Conklin, 1984–1991	Marty Fury, 2008–Present

Roseburg National Cemetery
Department of Veterans Affairs Medical Center
Roseburg, Oregon 97470

The cemetery is located between the South Umpqua River and Harvard Avenue, approximately one-half mile from the Department of Veterans Affairs Medical Center (DVAMC).

The Oregon State Soldiers' Home was established in 1893 "to provide a home for honorably discharged soldiers, sailors and marines who had served in any wars in which the United States was engaged, or who served in the Indian Wars of Oregon, Washington or Idaho, provided they were or might become citizens of Oregon." The cemetery was established as an "Old Soldiers Cemetery" in 1897, as part of the home.

In 1933, the home was turned over to the National Soldiers' Home Bureau, and the 69 members were transferred to the new Veterans Administration (VA) facility. The cemetery became a VA cemetery. In September 1973, this was one of the 21 VA cemeteries transferred to the National Cemetery System, becoming the Roseburg National Cemetery.

The cemetery is 4.1 acres in size and contains, as of September 30, 2008, 3,944 interments. It closed for burials in 1981 except for second interments in existing gravesites. Section A contains upright headstones with the earliest dated 1901. Graves in sections B and C are marked with flat granite markers. The cemetery is managed by the Eagle Point National Cemetery.

Roseburg National Cemetery

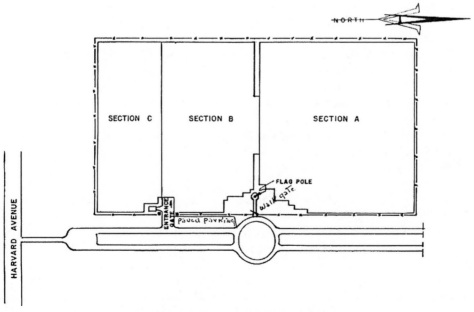

Approximate location of grave is indicated on the map

Name _____ Row _____ Grave _____ Section _____

The grave of Mother Mary Pennie, a Roman Catholic nun, is marked with a vault shaped memorial. She apparently worked for many years at the Oregon Soldiers' Home, and died on September 14, 1924, at the age of 83.

Sacramento Valley National Cemetery
5810 Midway Road
Dixon, California 95620

The Sacramento Valley National Cemetery contains 561 acres, located in Solano County, about 27 miles southwest of Sacramento along Interstate 80 between Dixon and Vacaville.

The cemetery was dedicated on April 27, 2007. Interments began in October 2006 in an area of about 14 acres with 8,466 gravesites, including 3,070 pre-placed crypts, 1,642 standard gravesites, and 3,754 in-ground cremation sites. The first phase development will cover 110 acres and will include 17,200 casket gravesites, 12,000 pre-placed crypts, 3,000 columbarium niches, and 765 in-ground cremation sites.

As of September 30, 2008, a total of 3,588 interments have been made.

St. Augustine National Cemetery
104 Marine Street
St. Augustine, Florida

The cemetery is located in St. Johns County, in the city of St. Augustine, adjacent to the headquarters of the Florida National Guard.

Although the St. Augustine burial ground was not designated a national cemetery until 1881, this hallowed ground played a role in the entire colorful history of the oldest city in the United States. In the days of the first Spanish colony of St. Augustine, a Franciscan monastery and convent stood near the south end of the city. The land which is now the national cemetery was part of the property held by the religious community. The southern boundary of the cemetery marks the periphery of the old Spanish walled city.

Under the English rule of Florida, 1763–83, the convent was occupied by the military and barracks were constructed on the site. During the second Spanish occupation of Florida, 1783–1821, the property remained in the hands of the military.

When the United States gained possession of Florida in 1821, the St. Francis Barracks housed the military of the third nation to stand guard over the city, already three centuries old. Shortly after, land at the Barracks was set aside for a post cemetery. According to old burial records, the first interment took place in 1828. Most of the early interments were of soldiers who died during the Florida Indian Wars, either in battle or due to sickness and disease, not uncommon in this subtropical climate.

The Seminole Indians resisted the mass emigration to the west imposed upon the tribes by the U.S. government. Seven years of fighting followed the signing of the deportation treaties.

On December 23, 1835, Major Francis L. Dade, commanding Company B, 4th Regiment of Infantry, with 108 officers and men, began the journey from Fort Brook at Tampa to offer reinforcement to General Wiley Thompson, stationed at Fort King, at Ocala. His sense of geography confused, Dade announced to his men on the 28th that they had passed the danger zone. He failed to take precautions to post an advance or flank guard. The heavy winter garments of the soldiers covered their weapons, so that when the Seminoles staged

St. Augustine National Cemetery, 1946.

an attack, Dade's troops were virtually wiped out; only one soldier survived. A few months later, when travel in the area was again possible, a command under General Gaines came up from Tampa and buried the fallen men on the site of the massacre.

In 1842, when hostilities ceased, it was proposed to transfer the remains of the men who fell with Major Dade, and of all who died within the territory, to one burial ground. Reinterment, with proper ceremonies, took place at the St. Augustine post cemetery. In addition to Dade's command, more than 1,400 soldiers were interred in 3 collective graves, over which 3 pyramids of native coquina stone were erected in their memory. Nearby, several plain white markers designate the graves of Indian scouts.

By 1845, when Florida became the 27th state in the Union, the city was quickly developing as a modern resort, offering a warm climate and a contrasting Latin culture especially attractive to Northern visitors. In 1861, when Florida seceded from the Union and Confederate troops raised the fourth flag to fly over the city, sentiment in St. Augustine was about equally divided between the North and the South. Fort Marion and St. Francis Barracks were appropriated by the Confederate army.

The city suffered greatly from the interruption of trade. In March 1862, a Federal gunboat, the *Wabash,* entered St. Augustine harbor, and the mayor surrendered the city rather than attempt a surely devastating battle. St. Augustine again became part of the Union and never reverted to Confederate hands during the course of the war.

In 1881, St. Augustine was once again a flourishing city, and the commanding officer of the St. Francis Barracks recognized the need to assure the proper care and respectful treatment of the old post cemetery. That same year, Brevet Brigadier General Montgomery Meigs proposed that, "As Florida is now a resort of many thousands of citizens with their families in search of benefit from its mild winter climate, it will be only becoming to put this cemetery, too long neglected and falling lately into decay, into as good condition as the other national cemeteries." The adjutant general concurred, and the old post burial grounds were declared a national cemetery.

It was also proposed at this time that a monument be erected to the soldiers who died in the Florida wars. It would be a tall obelisk to stand before the three pyramids, the cost of which would be met by a donation of one day's pay from each soldier stationed at the barracks. A wall of coquina stone was constructed to enclose the cemetery properly. In 1912 and 1913, additional land from the military reservation was added to the cemetery, nearly doubling its size to its present 1.36 acres.

In 1908, 27 remains were removed from Egmont Key and reinterred in the cemetery.

In 1938, a new superintendent's lodge was constructed according to designs approved by the city council, which has always sought to preserve the unique heritage of St. Augustine. Built of coquina with an overhanging balcony and weathered shingle roof, the building boasts architecture strictly in keeping with the style of the old Spanish homes in the historic district. The lodge is presently leased to the Military Department of Florida. A coquina rostrum, the stage for all official ceremonies, at the northern end of the cemetery echoes the curving roofline silhouettes of the Spanish Baroque style, seen in other prominent structures in the city.

St. Augustine National Cemetery was one of the first National Cemeteries to install lighting so that the U.S. flag could be flown 24 hours a day. Mrs. Russell B. Palmes, past president of Volusia County Gold Star Mothers and the mother of two sons lost in action in World War II, threw the switch to turn on the lights on August 26, 1975. One of her sons is interred in the cemetery. The remains of the other son were never recovered, but he is memorialized in the cemetery.

Commander Randolph Wright Ford was interred in the cemetery on November 21, 1985. He was reported missing in action over North Vietnam in 1968, and his remains were returned by the Hanoi government. His date of death is listed as June 20, 1968.

As of September 30, 2008, there were 2,797 interments. The cemetery was closed in 1949 for interments except for those in reserved gravesites or second interments in existing graves. The cemetery is maintained by private contract under the supervision of the director of Florida National Cemetery.

Today this cemetery remains a link between the past and the present, reminding one of the first colony and of its growth with a new nation, through the courage and dedication of the men and women buried here.

Former superintendents/directors of the cemetery are:

Edward J. Larkin, August 1946–November 1947
John C. Metzler, Sr., November 1947–July 1948
Leon P. Leonard, July 1948–June 1949

Andrew K. Hill, June 1949–January 1951
Delmar Stewart, January 1951–October 1987

Salisbury National Cemetery
202 Government Road
Salisbury, North Carolina 28144

Salisbury National Cemetery is located in the city of Salisbury, Rowan County, North Carolina, about one block off U.S. Highway 29, in the center of the city. In 1863, about 5½ acres of land were appropriated from Joseph Horah by Confederate authorities. The land was used as a burial ground for Union prisoners of war who died in the stockade located at Salisbury. The cemetery was designated a national cemetery in 1865, and the United States purchased the land in 1870.

Salisbury, the largest town in western North Carolina at that time, was chosen for the prison site because of its proximity to the railroad. The cemetery itself is only about 250

Salisbury National Cemetery, 1970.

yards south of the railroad. An 1841 cotton mill and several brick workers' cottages were the first buildings of the 16-acre prison. The Confederacy erected mess halls, hospital quarters, and a "dead house." The facilities were considered adequate as long as the agreement arranged by General John A. Dix, U.S. Army, and General D.H. Hill, Confederate Army, in July 1862, remained in effect. This agreement was to release all prisoners of war. If one side had more than the other, the excess number could not take up arms again. For those involved in an even trade, they could go back to fighting. There were, of course, charges and countercharges of parole violations, and the agreement lasted only about six months before it completely broke down. From early 1863 the number of prisoner exchanges grew fewer and the number of prisoners of war multiplied on each side. Some exchanges were negotiated by the military commanders on the battlefield, until General Grant ordered this practice stopped in 1864. In 1865, realizing that the war was coming to a close, Grant relented and consented to a policy of even exchange.

It should be pointed out that historians are in agreement that prison conditions were no better or worse on either side. Northern politicians used Southern prisoner of war camp atrocities to inflame the electorate, and Southern politicians did the same. Food, clothing, sanitation, health care, and other facilities were generally about the same for both the captives and their captors.

When the exchange of prisoners was stopped, the Salisbury Confederate prison facility was no longer adequate for the large number of prisoners and conditions rapidly deteriorated. In early October 1864 there were 5,000 prisoners at Salisbury. By mid–November, this number had swelled to about 10,000. Hardships were caused by the shortage of food, clothing, medicine and other supplies. With the onset of an unusually cold, wet winter and the lack of adequate shelter, the death rate soared. With the exception of Andersonville, it was the highest of any prison stockade. Out of the 10,000 prisoners confined here, over 5,000 fell victim to starvation and disease.

When it became apparent that the Confederacy was losing the war, the remaining Union prisoners were sent to Richmond, Virginia, and Wilmington, North Carolina. General George Stoneman was sent to Salisbury to destroy the prison. He arrived on April 12, 1865, and after a terrifying night of burning and looting, all that remained of the prison was a small guard's cottage and the flag which had flown over the gates. The cottage still stands today on Bank Street in Salisbury. The flag was taken by Union soldiers, but was returned and is on display in the Rowan Museum. An old escape tunnel still runs under the streets of Salisbury as a grim reminder of the desperate need to escape the terrible conditions of the prison.

Records indicate that 11,700 men are buried in 18 trenches, each about 240 feet long, located in the southeast end of the cemetery. These men perished at the prison during 1864 and 1865. The wooden fence erected around these mass graves by General Stoneman has been replaced by granite curbing around each trench. Brevet Colonel Oscar A. Mack, inspector of cemeteries, says in his report of 1870–1871 that "The bodies were placed one above the other, and mostly without coffins. From the number of bodies exhumed from a given space it was estimated that the number buried in these trenches was 11,700. The number of burials from the prison pen cannot be accurately known, as no records have been found; but the above estimate is considered as being under the real number of deaths." In his report, Colonel Mack is most scathing in discussing the Southern prison stockades, and overly benevolent toward the treatment of Southern prisoners in Northern prisons.

Among the unknowns interred somewhere in the 18 trenches are the remains of Robert Livingstone, the oldest son of Dr. David Livingstone, the noted African missionary and explorer. He enlisted in the Union Army under the name of Rupert Vincent. He was wounded near Laurel Hill, Virginia, was captured, and died in the prison camp on December 5, 1864.

Following the end of the Civil War, in 1866, 412 remains were moved to the national cemetery from Lexington, Charlotte, Morgantown, and other places.

In his report of the inspector of national cemeteries dated April 20, 1872, Colonel Mack recommended that the government erect a suitable memorial to the Union dead buried in the 18 trenches. On March 3, 1873, Congress approved the proposal. The contract, awarded in December 1874, provided for its erection by December 31, 1876. The monument consists of a granite obelisk and base, 39 feet high. The shaft is crowned with a laurel wreath and the four sides are ornamented with laurel leaves. At the foot of the shaft are a helmet, sword, and shield, bearing respectively the national crest, coat of arms, and stars. Grouped with these is a chain with broken bracelets, suggesting the condition of dead prisoners and the happy release from captivity. Just above the shield is a tablet, veiled, indicating that the dead were unknown, while below is the number of those buried in the trenches. Above the tablet or shield is a small laurel crown enclosing the words "Pro Patria."

The state of Maine erected a monument in 1908 honoring its soldiers who died while prisoners at Salisbury. The people of Pennsylvania erected a monument to that state's soldiers in 1910.

James Joyce Fitzgerald, famed race car driver who died in the St. Petersburg Grand

Prix on November 8, 1987, is interred in Section H-1, Grave 16. He was the winningest driver in the history of the Sports Car Club of America. Fitzgerald won more than 350 national races during his 32 years of racing. He had been a racing partner of actor Paul Newman and chief driving instructor at Road Atlanta Drivers Training Center in Braselton, Georgia. He served in the U.S. Navy during World War II.

As of September 30, 2008, the national cemetery encompassed 63.5 acres of land and included 22,548 interments. The Salisbury National Cemetery Annex, including the new administrative office and maintenance shop, is located at 501 Statesville Boulevard, behind the VA Medical Center.

Former superintendents/directors of Salisbury National Cemetery are:

Herbert D. Stanley, February 1947–August 1947
William M. Darby, September 1947–August 1954
Norman W. Kelly, May 1954–November 1956
Andrew K. Hill, November 1956–November 1959
Charles E. Kilgore, November 1959–September 1979

Lucille A. Fisher, September 1979–March 1982
Sharon K. Smith, June 1982–March 1985
Matt D. Cornett, April 1985–December 1987
Diane F. Jorgensen, 1988–1990
Marcus Lee Richards, 1990–

San Antonio National Cemetery
517 Paso Hondo Street
San Antonio, Texas 78202

The cemetery is situated in Bexar County in San Antonio, Texas, between East Commerce Street and East Houston Street and three blocks west of New Braunfels Avenue on Paso Hondo Street.

The original cemetery site, part of the city cemetery, was donated to the United States by the city of San Antonio in 1867 for the establishment of a national cemetery. The original deed was lost and the transfer never recorded. A new deed was executed by the city on April 14, 1871, conveying approximately 1.89 acres of land to the United States. In 1884, the United States purchased an additional 1.75 acres from the city. The national cemetery is completely surrounded by improved private cemeterial property, and further expansion of the cemetery is not possible.

Interment of deceased Union soldiers commenced in December 1867 and was considered to be completed in April 1868. The total number interred at that time was 122 known and 61 unknown. Original burials were remains removed from the city cemetery, from Austin, Indianola, the Solado and Medina rivers, and other places within the state. Included in the transfer from the outlying frontier were 314 unknowns, whose remains are buried in a common grave in Section H. A monument inscribed "To the Unknown Dead" was erected by the United States in 1912 to mark the grave.

The report of the inspector of national cemeteries dated February 6, 1871, contains a comment that "The remains of some of the old officers of the Army, who died in San Antonio years ago, have recently been exhumed and re-interred here; among them, Brevet Brigadier General George M. Brooke." General Brooke, a colonel at the time, was the founder of Tampa, Florida, as a military fort. The inspector also reported that graves were being marked with limestone blocks, ten inches square and two feet long, placed flush with the top of the mounded graves, with the number, name, regiment, etc. cut into the top. The stone was soft, easily worked, and more durable than wooden stakes or headboards.

Notable individuals interred in the cemetery include Second Lieutenant George E.M.

San Antonio National Cemetery, Memorial Day 1953.

Kelly, for whom Kelly Air Force Base was named. Lieutenant Kelly was killed in 1911 at Fort Sam Houston, the second U.S. Army aviator to lose his life in a military airplane accident.

Harry M. Wurzbach, a five-term U.S. congressman from San Antonio, is also buried here. One of the major thoroughfares of the city is named for him.

Guston Schleicher, a German-born immigrant who became a Texas state representative and senator and was elected to the U.S. House of Representatives, is buried here, as well.

Brigadier General John L. Bullis, for whom Camp Bullis, Texas, was named, retired in 1905, the day after he was promoted to brigadier general, and is also interred here.

Friday Bowlegs and several other Indian scouts are buried in Section F.

Of special note also is the fact that a grandson of English royalty rests in the cemetery. A son, presumably illegitimate, of the Prince of Wales, later King George IV of England, was adopted by Mr. and Mrs. James Ord, while they were in England. The adopted son was the father of Major Placidus Ord, interred in Section A, and General Edward Otho Cresap Ord, whose wife Mary Mercer Ord is also interred in Section A.

On Decoration Day, May 30, 1885, the principal speaker at San Antonio National Cemetery and at San Pedro Springs was Captain Orsemus Bronson Boyd, captain, 8th U.S. Cavalry. In speaking at both places, he recognized both the boys in blue and in gray who fought the Civil War. Seven weeks later, Captain Boyd was killed in New Mexico while campaigning against Geronimo. Captain Boyd is interred in Section A.

There are 12 Chinese civilian employees of the Quartermaster Corps buried in Section H. Five of them are listed both as Chinese refugees and as Quartermaster employees. They accompanied the American Expeditionary Forces commanded by General John J. Pershing out of Mexico.

There are 267 private headstones erected in San Antonio National Cemetery, ranging from simple markers to elaborate monuments, dating back to 1853. These monuments were erected at private expense and are of many designs constructed of durable stone, granite and marble. The private monument to Colonel G.M. Brooke was removed in 1947 or 1948. It was of concrete and stucco construction with a marble inscription plate and had deteriorated badly. A regulation government headstone now marks his grave.

One of the most fascinating stories connected with the National Cemetery System is that of Simon Suhler, one of the ten Medal of Honor recipients interred here (he was awarded the Medal of Honor under the name Charles Gardner). Suhler was born in Bavaria and immigrated to the United States sometime before 1861, when he enlisted in the 32nd Indiana Volunteers. He was wounded at Shiloh, captured at the Battle of Chickamauga, and paroled to a Union hospital at St. Louis. He disappeared and was classified as a deserter. In June 1863, he enlisted in the 4th New York Heavy Artillery using his mother's maiden name, Newstattel. He served until the end of the war and was mustered out in September 1865. He then traveled west to San Francisco, where on October 15, 1866, he joined the 8th Cavalry under the name Charles Gardner. Private Gardner was awarded the Medal of Honor in 1868 and was recommended for promotion to second lieutenant, although this did not happen. After being discharged in 1878, Suhler moved to San Antonio. He died on May 16, 1895. His true story finally came to light in 1987 through the efforts of a Suhler family historian and a frontier history buff in Texas. A Medal of Honor headstone inscribed with his correct name now marks his grave in the cemetery.

The ten Medal of Honor recipients interred in the cemetery are as follows. A dagger before one name indicates that the recipient was killed in action.

William H. Barnes, Private, Company C, 38th U.S. Colored Troops. Place and date: At Chapins Farm, Va., 29 September 1864.
Citation: Among the first to enter the enemy's works, although wounded.

†David B. Barkeley, Sec G, Grave 1302. Private, U.S. Army, Company A, 356th Infantry, 89th Division. Place and date: Near Pouilly, France, 9 November 1918.
Citation: When information was desired as to the enemy's position on the opposite side of the Meuse River, Pvt. Barkeley, with another soldier, volunteered without hesitation and swam the river to reconnoiter the exact location. He succeeded in reaching the opposite bank, despite the evident determination of the enemy to prevent a crossing. Having obtained his information, he again entered the water for his return, but before his goal was reached, he was seized with cramps and drowned.

Frederick Deetline, Sec G, Grave 921. Private, Company D, 7th U.S. Cavalry. Place and date: At Little Big Horn, Mont., 25 June 1876.
Citation: Voluntarily brought water to the wounded under fire.

John Harrington, Sec F, Grave 1012. Private, Company H, 6th U.S. Cavalry. Place and date: At Wichita River, Tex., 12 September 1874.
Citation: While carrying dispatches was attacked by 125 hostile Indians, whom he and his comrades fought throughout the day. He was severely wounded in the hip and unable to move. He continued to fight, defending an exposed dying man.

Henry Falcott, Sec F, Grave 918. Sergeant, Company L, 8th U.S. Cavalry. Place and date: Arizona, August to October 1868.
Citation: Bravery in scouts and actions against Indians.

Henry A. McMasters, Sec D, Grave 729. Corporal, Company A, 4th U.S. Cavalry. Place and date: At Red River, Tex., 29 September 1872.
Citation: Gallantry in action.

James J. Nash, Sec T, Grave 1461-A. Private, Company F, 10th U.S. Infantry. Place and date: Santiago, Cuba, 1 July 1898.
Citation: Gallantly assisted in the rescue of wounded from in front of the lines and under heavy fire from the enemy.

Solon D. Neal, Sec G, Grave 1323. Private, Company L, 6th U.S. Cavalry. Place and date: At Wichita River, Tex., 12 July 1870.
Citation: Gallantry in action.

Simon Suhler (Cited while serving under the alias of Charles Gardner), Private, Company B, 8th U.S. Cavalry. Place and date: Arizona, August to October 1868.
Citation: Bravery in scouts and action against Indians.

Lewis Warrington, Sec A, Grave 60. First Lieutenant, 4th U.S. Cavalry. Place and date: At Muchague Valley, Tex., 8 December 1874.
Citation: Gallantry in combat with five Indians.

Four Medal of Honor recipients are interred in the cemetery as unknowns and are memorialized in the Memorial Section. They are:

William H. Barnes, Sec. MA, Grave 86, Private, U.S. Army, Company C 38th U.S. Colored Troops. Place and Date: Chapins Farm, Virginia, September 29, 1864.

George W. Smith, Sec. MA, Grave 87, Private, U.S. Army, Company M, 6th U.S. Cavalry. Place and Date: Wichita River, Texas, September 12. 1874.

John J. Givens, Sec. MA, Grave 88, Corporal, U.S. Army, Company K, 6th U.S. Cavalry. Place and Date: Wichita River, Texas, July 12, 1870

William DeArmond, Sec. MA, Grave 89, Sergeant, U.S. Army, Company I, 5th U.S. Infantry. Place and Date: Upper Washita, Texas, September 9–11, 1874.

As of September 30, 2008, there had been 3,163 interments made here. The cemetery is closed for interments except for those in existing graves under the single gravesite per family policy.

At first there was no regularly appointed superintendent for this cemetery. The post quartermaster of Fort Sam Houston had jurisdiction over the cemetery and employed a caretaker to perform the grounds maintenance. Former superintendents/directors of the cemetery are:

Peter McKenna, 1874–1877	Clarence Henry Otis, October 1949–June 1952
Charles Schroegler, 1929–1931	Kenneth E. Ridley, July 1952–January 1955
Placide Rodriguez, 1931–1939	William E. Spivey, January 1955–January 1957
R.I. McMillan, 1939–1942	Louis B. Baughman, January 1957–January 1969
Frank L. Williamson, 1942–1945	Forrest W. Gore, February 1969–September 1974
Harold Montague, February 1945–October 1949	Arthur W. Kerr, October 1974–1975

Since 1975, the cemetery has been assigned to the director of Fort Sam Houston National Cemetery for administration and management. Grounds maintenance is performed by a private contractor.

San Francisco National Cemetery
1 Lincoln Blvd., Presidio of San Francisco
San Francisco, California 94129

The cemetery is located in San Francisco County, within the military reservation of the Presidio of San Francisco, one-half mile south of the Golden Gate Bridge, off Highway 101.

The Presidio is the oldest military post in the United States. It was established in 1776 by explorers of the Spanish rulers of Mexico as their northernmost outpost. The original parade ground is still in use as is one of the abode buildings constructed near the parade. It is now the Officers' Club, and is the oldest building in the city of San Francisco. The Presidio continued to be used by the Spaniards until 1822 when Mexico gained independence. The Mexicans garrisoned the post until the United States forcibly ejected them during the Mexican War. The post was occupied by Captain F.J. Lippitt's Company of the 1st New York Volunteers on March 7, 1849. Until the gold rush started the post was never garrisoned by more than 50 men since the Indians were friendly and no foreign power threatened the area. With the large number of people seeking gold, the city suddenly grew from a small village to a city of several thousand, and the post was reinforced with additional personnel. It continued to grow until it became one of the large important army posts. Nearly all of the special branches of the U.S. Army are represented by detachments at the Presidio.

The cemetery includes the site of the old post cemetery and was established as a national cemetery on December 12, 1884. The War Department General Orders designated 9.5 acres of land and gave the cemetery its name. Further accretions of land from the Presidio area have increased its size to the present 28.34 acres. The establishment of the national cemetery marked the first such cemetery on the Pacific coast, and further evidenced the growth and development of a system of national cemeteries extending beyond the area of conflict of the Civil War.

Initial interments included the remains of decedents interred in the predecessor post cemetery as well as those removed from cemeteries at abandoned forts and camps along

San Francisco National Cemetery.

the Pacific coast and other parts of the far West. Reinterments from these sources included remains from forts Halleck and McDermit, Nevada; Fort Yuma, California; forts Colville and Townsend, Washington Territory; Fort Klamath, Oregon; and Camp Crittenden and Fort McDowell, Arizona Territory. Records of those reinterred indicate dates of death ranging from the late 1850s through the period of the early 1890s. In 1934, all unknowns interred in the cemetery were disinterred and reinterred in one plot. During the period 1899–1902, 1,922 remains were received from overseas for reinterment here. During the years following, many of the armed forces personnel who died while serving in the Philippines, Hawaii, China and other areas of the Pacific were interred in San Francisco National Cemetery.

Major General Irwin McDowell, commander of the Union forces at the first Battle of Bull Run in 1861, is interred in the Officer's Section, Grave 1. After the war, General McDowell was the commanding general of the Pacific Division, Western Defense Command, and subsequent to his retirement in 1882 was a park commissioner of San Francisco. He died on May 4, 1885.

The remains of Major Thomas Cowan Bell, one of the founders of Sigma Chi fraternity, are interred in Grave 3, Plot 43-A, OS Section. A private monument was erected on his grave by the fraternity.

Colonel Edward Dickinson Baker, killed on October 21, 1861, while leading his troops in the Battle of Balls Bluff, is interred in Officer's Section D, Grave 488. Baker, a close personal friend of President Abraham Lincoln, had served in the Illinois legislature and later as a United States congressman. He emigrated to the West from Illinois in 1852, became a well-known lawyer in California, subsequently went to Oregon, and was serving in the United States Senate when he entered the Union Army at the start of the Civil War (see Balls Bluff National Cemetery). Baker's remains were interred in the Laurel Hill Cemetery until May 1940 when that cemetery became part of a real estate development. The remains of Colonel Baker and his wife were reinterred in San Francisco National Cemetery. His son, Major Edward Baker, Jr., U.S. Army, who died in 1883, was reinterred in grave 489, beside his parents.

A small white marble headstone at Grave 1, Plot 18, Officer's Section, near the flagpole bears the inscription "Pauline C. Fryer, Union Spy." Here lie the remains of Pauline Cushman, an actress of the 1860s and a sometime espionage agent for the Union Army during the Civil War.

Biographical accounts indicate that she was born in New Orleans on June 10, 1833. Her merchant father moved the family to Grand Rapids, then a frontier settlement, where she was reared with the Indian children. At 18, she visited New York City where she met Thomas Placides, manager of the New Orleans "Varieties," and she later joined his troupe. While a member of the cast of *Seven Sisters* at Wood's Theater, Louisville, Kentucky, in March 1863, Pauline Cushman was approached by two paroled Confederate officers who offered her $500 to propose a toast to Jefferson Davis during her performance in the play. With strong Union sentiments, she was outraged by the proposal and reported it to the provost marshall of Louisville. He urged her to accept the offer as a possible opening for secret service work. In the midst of her performance that evening, she walked to the front of the stage and said in a loud clear voice "Here's to Jeff Davis and the Southern Confederacy. May the South always maintain her honor and her rights." Immediately discharged and ordered to leave the city, she entered the United States secret service, and became the confidante and favorite of many who supported the Confederate cause. With her charm and ability as an actress, she was able to provide the Union authorities with considerable information such as troop movements and fortifications strength. She was wounded twice and twice sentenced to die after being identified as a Northern spy. She escaped from prison on the eve of her scheduled execution with the aid of an enamored Southern officer, or so rumor says. She was arrested by the Confederates near Nashville for proceeding beyond the lines without a pass. When arrested, she was carrying valuable information hidden between the double soles of her shoes. She was taken to General Bragg's headquarters and sentenced to be hanged. While confined at Shelbyville, Tennessee, she became ill (or skillfully feigned illness), thus delaying her execution. Union forces captured Shelbyville on June 27, 1863, and released her, but her career as an espionage agent was ended. In recognition of her services General Garfield gave her the rank of brevet major and acclaimed her as the "spy of the Cumberland." She resumed her career as an actress and lectured on her experiences while wearing the Federal army uniform. She was married three times to Charles Dickinson, who died in 1862; to August Fichtner in 1872; and to Jerry Fryer, an Arizona sheriff, in 1879. All her children died in childhood, and she died in San Francisco on December 2, 1893, of an overdose of narcotics, allegedly taken to relieve rheumatism. The Grand Army of the Republic arranged for her burial with full military honors in a private cemetery. Her remains were reinterred in San Francisco National Cemetery in 1907.

Like many others interred in national cemeteries, General Edward McGarry, buried in Officer's Circle, left many unanswered questions about his death. An outstanding soldier in the Mexican War, he rose in rank during the Civil War to brigadier general. A fort in northwestern Nevada, now long abandoned, was named for him. After the war he commanded the 32nd Infantry at the Presidio. In 1867, he was assigned to command the new Subdistrict of Santa Cruz in southern Arizona, a post which was especially created for him by his friend Major General Henry Halleck. In July he became drunk on duty, was relieved of his command, and was sent to San Francisco to await further orders. On the night of December 31, 1867, he committed suicide by stabbing himself in the throat with a pocket knife and twisting it until the windpipe and arteries were severed. There was no indication that he was contemplating such an action, and no reason for it has ever been discovered. He is buried in Officer's Section, Grave 7, Plot 8.

Among the remains brought to the Presidio from Fort Yuma is another notable woman of early Americana, Sarah A. Bowman, buried in Post Plot East, Grave 55. Bowman followed her husband to war in 1846 as a cook and laundress. Over six feet two inches tall, with red hair, and wearing two pistols, she was known to the troops as "Great Western." After her husband died she switched "husbands" frequently. When the war ended, she ran a brothel in El Paso for several months, then followed the troops to California. Along the way she set up business in Arizona City (Yuma), in a "dirt-roofed adobe house." In 1861 she was the only resident of Yuma. Historians have described her as generous, loyal, devoted and brave. One historian has described her as "the greatest whore in the West," but the old-timers in Yuma call her their first citizen.

The adventures and misadventures of many of America's fighting men are often buried with them. Such is the little-known story of Charles C. De Rudio. Born of minor Italian nobility as Carlo Camilius di Rudio, he gravitated to London and later to Paris where, in 1858, he joined in an assassination attempt against Emperor Napoleon III and Empress Eugenie. Three bombs were set off as Napoleon's carriage arrived at the Paris Opera House. Several persons died and over 150 were wounded in the blasts, but Napoleon and his empress were barely harmed. De Rudio and two accomplices were found guilty after a jury trial and sentenced to death by guillotine. His fellow conspirators were executed but Napoleon spared De Rudio's life and had him banished to the infamous French penal colony, Devil's Island. De Rudio escaped (arguably the only prisoner ever to flee Devil's Island successfully). In

1864 he made his way to the United States, enlisted in the Union Army, then garnered a commission with the 2d U.S. Colored Troops. He soon gained a Regular Army commission in the 7th Cavalry. When Custer and 260 men of the 7th Cavalry perished at Little Bighorn, De Rudio was two miles distant with Captain Reno's troops and thus once again cheated death. He eventually retired from the Army as a major, died November 1, 1910, was cremated and buried in the San Francisco National Cemetery in Officers Section, Grave 6, Plot 109.*

Many other noteworthy persons in American history are interred in the cemetery.

Major General William R. Shafter was awarded the Medal of Honor at Fair Oaks on May 31, 1862. During the Spanish-American War, General Shafter commanded the U.S. Army forces in Cuba. He is buried in Grave 2, Officer's Section Plot 20.

Major General Frederick Funston received the Medal of Honor for heroic action at Rio Grande de la Pampanga, Luzon, on April 27, 1899. Another exploit in General Funston's career was his capture of the Philippine insurgent leader Emilio Aguinaldo on March 23, 1901. He directed the administration of the city of Vera Cruz during the occupation by U.S. Marines and sailors in 1914. He is buried in Grave 3, Officer's Section, Plot 68.

Lieutenant General Hunter Liggett commanded an army during World War I in France and is also buried here.

Brigadier General John Henry Parker was known as Machine Gun Parker for his efforts in advancing Army use of the machine gun.

Captain Norman Nelson, U.S. Coast Guard, on duty at Golden Gate and Eureka stations, was renowned for saving more than 200 lives.

Brigadier General Robert O. Van Horn commanded the 9th Infantry in France during World War I.

Brigadier General Harry O. Rethors was in charge of all U.S. Army Quartermaster activities in the British Isles and, as commanding officer of the American Graves Registration Service, had charge of removing the American dead after the Armistice on November 11, 1918. In October 1921 he selected one unknown soldier from each of four overseas cemeteries as candidates for the symbolic "Unknown." Sergeant Edward F. Younger chose one of the four for interment in Arlington National Cemetery.

Sergeant Reginald Arthur Bradley, Troop C, 4th U.S. Cavalry, who died on February 5, 1971, was the last of 104,000 Indian War veterans.

Private William Hood, who died in 1928, was regarded as one of the greatest railroad engineers of the West.

Major General William F. Dean was commanding general, 24th Infantry Division, when he was awarded the Medal of Honor for action at Taejon, Korea, on July 20–21, 1950. He refused to abandon his men and was captured by the enemy and held as a prisoner of war.

On January 10, 1991, the repatriated remains of USAF Major Stephen Cuthbert, listed as missing during the Vietnam War, were interred in the cemetery. Major Cuthbert was deployed to the 432nd Tactical Reconnaissance Wing, Udorn Royal Thai Air Base in Thailand. On July 3, 1972, hostile fire hit Major Cuthbert's F4E Phantom jet fighter 37 miles south of Vinh, Vietnam. Both Major Cuthbert and his weapons system analyst ejected from the aircraft. North Vietnamese captured the weapons system analyst and later released him. In September 1990, the Socialist Republic of Vietnam repatriated the remains of 20 Americans, but only 6, including Major Cuthbert, have been identified.

*This information was furnished for inclusion here by Colonel Wilfred L. Ebel, U.S. Army, retired. Colonel Ebel has done considerable research on Charles C. De Rudio.

Sixteen other flag officers of the Army or Navy are buried in San Francisco National Cemetery, as is Indian Scout Two Bits.

Special monuments in the cemetery include the Pacific Garrison Memorial, dedicated to the Regular Army and Navy Union of the United States of America to the Pacific Coast Garrison, Memorial Day 1897; the G.A.R. Memorial, erected by George H. Thomas Post #2 and dedicated May 30, 1893; the Unknown Soldier Dead, erected to commemorate the 517 remains regrouped from locations throughout the cemetery in 1934; the American War Mothers Monument, erected by the San Francisco Chapter, located in Section B; and a simple monument erected by the crew of the *USS Oregon* in memory of the Marines who gave their lives at the Tartar Wall in Pakia, China, in 1900.

There are 35 recipients of the Medal of Honor interred in the cemetery. One of them, Sergeant William Wilson, received two awards, and one, Captain Reginald B. Desiderio, was killed in action.

Name	Service	War/Place/Date of Action	Section & Grave No.
William Allen	USA	Indian	OS, 48-2
William Badders	USN	1939	A, 788-A
James Coey	USA	Civil	OS, 89-1
James Congdon*	USA	Civil	OS, A-7
Matthias W. Day	USA	Indian	OS, 2-11
William F. Dean	USA	Korea	OS, 353-B
Reginald B. Desiderio	USA	Korea	OS, 20-128
Abraham DeSomer†	USN	Vera Cruz	MA, 15
Kern W. Dunagan	USA	Vietnam	WS, 117-I
William Foster	USA	Indian	WS, 197
Frederick Funston, Sr.	USA	Phil.	OS, 68-3
Rade Grbitch	USN	*USS Bennington*	A, 44
Oliver D. Greene	USA	Civil	OS, 49-8
John Chowning Gresham	USA	Indian	OS, 4-A-5
Franz Anton Itrich	USN	Sp.-Amer.	OS, A-83-5
Robert S. Kennemore	USMC	Korea	HCA, 404
John Sterling Lawton	USA	Indian	NAWS, 1392
Cornelius J. Leahy	USA	Phil.	NA, 970
John Mitchell	USA	Indian	NAWS, 411
Albert Moore	USMC	Sp.-Amer.	WS, 1032-A
Louis Clinton Mosher	USA	Phil.	NA, 1408
Adam Neder	USA	Indian	NAWS, 1805
William Parnell	USA	Indian	OS, 68-8
Reuben Jasper Phillips	USMC	Boxer	OS, D-3
Norman W. Ressler	USA	Sp.-Amer.	WS, 134-A
Lloyd Martin Seibert	USA	WWI	OS, 10-128
William Rufus Shafter	USA	Civil	OS, 30-2
George Matthew Shelton, Sr.	USA	Phil.	OS, D-799
Andrew V. Stoltenberg	USN	Phil.	A, 242
Bernard Taylor	USA	Indian	WS, 1090
William H. Thompkins	USA	Sp.-Amer.	WS, 1036-A
Charles A. Varnum	USA	Indian	OS, 3-3-A
George Weed Wallace	USA	Phil.	OS, 3917
Axel Westermark	USN	Boxer	A, 32
William Wilson	USA	Indian	WS, 527

*Served under the name of James Madison.
†Buried at sea. Memorial headstone only.

In 1956 the Army transferred 26.84 acres to the national cemetery for expansion. Local outcry, whipped up by real estate developers, over the use of the land for cemeterial purposes forced cancellation of the expansion. The developers' only stated reason for objecting was that the eucalyptus trees would be removed and the esthetics of the area destroyed. The Army had planted the trees some years earlier. Despite pressure from the White House, the Army surprised the developers by not declaring the land excess and returned it to the Presidio.

As of September 30, 1990, there were 31,633 interments. The cemetery was closed for interments in 1962, except for cremated remains, those in reserved gravesites, and second interments in existing graves.

Former superintendents/directors of the cemetery are:

Henry W. Richit, January 1886–March 1918
Max Weinberger, October 1918–November 1918
Richard B. Hill, November 1918–June 1919
William Davis, June 1919–June 1927
Charles C. Church, August 1927–January 1930
William Davis, February 1930–1930
W.O. Allen Reinhart, March 1930
Thomas J. Stangier, March 1930–August 1939
Warren L. Pierson, August 1939–May 1941
C. Kearney, May 1941–May 1943
Warren L. Pierson, May 1943–August 1955
James M. Griffin, September 1955–July 1962
Ernest C. Schanze, July 1962–February 1964
John Cox, February 1964–June 1969
Donald R. Peterson, July 1969–October 1970
Roland E. Lex, November 1970–March 1976

Robert Whitfield, June 1976–December 1976
James D. Simms, March 1977–August 1977
Robert E. Bevering, November 1977–March 1980
David Rivera-Guzman, April 1980–September 1982
Stephen H. Jorgensen, October 1982–April 1985
Cynthia Nunez, April 1985–November 1987
Matt D. Cornett, 1988–1988
Gloria Gamez, 1998–1998
Gil Gallo, 1998–August 2001
Don Rincon, December 2001–January 2004
Rosanne Santore, April 2004–March 2006
Wesley Jones, August 2005–January 2008
Gary Ackerman, February 2008–Present

San Joaquin Valley National Cemetery
32053 West McCabe Road
Santa Nella, California 95322

The 322 acres of land for the cemetery was donated by the Romero Ranch Company in February 1989. The first phase of construction, covering 105 acres began in July 1990, was completed in May 1992. This phase yielded about 15,000 gravesites and 8,000 in-ground cremation sites.

The California Korean War Veterans Memorial was dedicated August 1, 1998. It contains the names of 2,495 Californians who gave their lives fighting in the Korean War.

The 11th Airborne Memorial was dedicated on May 11, 2002, in honor of all airborne soldiers.

As of September 30, 2008, there have been 30,054 interments in the cemetery.

One Medal of Honor recipient is interred here:

William Troy, Sec. M-1, Grave 53. Seaman, U.S. Navy. Place and Date: On board the USS Colorado during the capture of the Korean forts. June 11, 1871.
Citation: Fighting at the side of Lt. McKee, by whom he was especially commended, Troy was badly wounded by the enemy.

Former directors of the cemetery are:

Dennis Gura, 1990–1991
Dennis Kuehl, 1992–1996

Carla Williams, 1996–2005
Ralph Bennett, 2005–Present

Santa Fe National Cemetery

501 North Guadalupe Street
Santa Fe, New Mexico 87501

Situated within the Santa Fe city limits, approximately one mile northwest of the plaza, the cemetery faces St. Francis Drive on the west.

With the start of "Mr. Polk's war" with Mexico in May 1846, Brigadier General Stephen Kearny, commander of the Army of the West, was ordered to capture the northern provinces of Mexico and California. He marched out of Fort Leavenworth on June 26 with 10 regiments and on August 19, 1846, accepted the formal surrender of New Mexico in the plaza at Santa Fe, apparently without firing a shot. In order to carry out the second part of his orders, the conquest of California, General Kearny split his forces into three groups. He would lead the troops heading west; Colonel Alexander W. Doniphan would lead troops to subdue nearby Indians and then move south to conquer the province of Chihuahua; and Colonel Sterling Price would continue the occupation of Santa Fe.

Private Dennis O'Leary's marker in Santa Fe National Cemetery.

Colonel Doniphan commanded what was formally called the First Missouri Regiment, but that was where formality ended. The colonel disliked both formality and discipline. His men, recruited from the Missouri backwoods, were the despair of regular army officers. The exploits of the Doniphan Expedition form one of the sagas of the Far West. The regiment, composed of 856 men, traveled 6,000 miles in 1 year, defeated 2 armies, and lost only 1 man. They served without supplies, orders, or pay.

During the period of the Civil War, there was little armed conflict in the territory of New Mexico. Engagements were principally in the area of Santa Fe, the territorial capital, and represented attempts on the part of the Confederacy to control the capital as well as other frontier posts with a view toward establishing a route westward to the Pacific coast. Such an undertaking, if successful, would vastly increase the prestige of the Confederacy. There was also the possibility that some of the gold from California might come under their control. But events in the vicinity of Santa Fe during the early months of 1862 quite definitely proved the futility of this bit of Confederate strategy.

The commanding officers of both Union and Confederate forces during the brief New Mexico campaign had served in the U.S. Army during the Mexican War and at several frontier posts. Henry H. Sibley resigned his commission as major in the U.S. Army on May 13, 1861, and three days later was commissioned a colonel in the Confederate States Army. Less than one month later, he was promoted to brigadier general. The commander of Union forces in New Mexico, Edward R.S. Canby, was promoted to the rank of colonel, 19th United States Infantry, on May 14, 1861. He subsequently was promoted to brevet brigadier general in recognition of his services during the New Mexico campaign.

A Confederate force of some 2,400 men led by Brigadier General Sibley, who was known as a "walking whiskey keg," entered New Mexico from Texas. At Valverde, New Mexico, on February 21, 1862, they were met by Union forces, numbering about 3,800 men, under the command of Colonel Canby. After a hard fought day-long battle, the victorious Confederate forces moved on to occupy Santa Fe without opposition on March 16. As the Confederate forces approached the city, territorial officials fled. The Union forces attacked the Confederates at Apache Canyon, near Glorieta, 15 miles south of Santa Fe. During a fierce engagement many Confederate prisoners were captured. In another skirmish, on March 28 at Pigeon's Ranch, the Confederate supply train was destroyed and their forces fell back to Santa Fe, and the Union forces retired to Fort Union. General Sibley's troops abandoned Santa Fe on April 8, 1862, and Union forces reoccupied the city three days later. An engagement at Peralta on April 15 found the forces under General Sibley continuing their retreat down the Rio Grande back to Texas. Additional Union reinforcements arrived in July and August 1862, and Civil War activities in New Mexico were over.

With the close of the Civil War, action was taken to establish a burial ground in the vicinity of Santa Fe for the reinterment of the remains of Union soldiers who died during the brief military activity in this area. The site initially chosen for a burying ground was 0.39 acre located about one-fourth mile west of the town of Santa Fe. This property, now included within Santa Fe National Cemetery, is within the city limits of Santa Fe. Title to the property was held by the Roman Catholic Diocese of Santa Fe. On July 2, 1870, Bishop John B. Lamy donated the land to the United States for use as a military cemetery. In October 1875, an additional parcel of 1.95 acres adjoining the first tract was purchased from the Diocese of New Mexico. In 1894, an additional 7.10 acres were obtained by decree of condemnation and title was vested in fee simple in the United States.

By 1870, the remains of nearly 300,000 Union Civil War dead had been reinterred in national cemeteries established in the vicinity of battlefields and wartime military hospitals. As a result of legislation in 1873, additional national cemeteries were established in areas beyond the principal Civil War battlefields. Establishment of the Santa Fe National Cemetery in 1875 expanded the scope of the National Cemetery System to include the upper Rio Grande Valley.

The initial designation of Santa Fe as a national cemetery was of short duration. In July 1876 the War Department decided that, for economic reasons, the cemetery should be maintained as the Fort Marcy post cemetery. The superintendent appointed in 1875 was transferred to Mound City National Cemetery, and the Fort Marcy post quartermaster took over the operation of the cemetery. On September 10, 1892, the cemetery was again designated a national cemetery by the adjutant general.

Santa Fe National Cemetery now comprises 78.6 acres and, as of September 30, 2008, included 44,478 interments. On November 11, 1989, the city of Santa Fe donated 40.0 acres to the U.S. Department of Veterans Affairs to expand the cemetery. The initial interments in the cemetery were the remains of 265 Union soldiers from the battlefields of Glorieta, Koslouskys, and old Fort Marcy, which was the site of General Kearny's camp in 1847. After its second designation as a national cemetery in 1892, remains from abandoned frontier post cemeteries were moved to Santa Fe. These include Fort Stanton, in 1896; Fort Sumner and Fort Marcy, in 1906; Fort Grant, Arizona, in 1907; Fort Wingate, New Mexico, and Fort Craig, in 1912; Fort Duchesne, Utah, in 1913; Fort Apache, Arizona, in 1932; and Fort Hatch, New Mexico, in 1933.

The remains of Governor Charles Bent, first American territorial governor of New Mexico, were among the 47 remains removed from the old Masonic Cemetery in Santa Fe and reinterred in the cemetery. Governor Bent was killed on January 19, 1847, during an Indian uprising at Taos.

The remains of five Confederate soldiers who died in April 1862 were among those removed from the Masonic Cemetery. Captain Isaac Adair, 7th Texas Cavalry; Thomas Cater and William Ohram, Texas Rangers; Private Hugh Harris, 7th Texas Cavalry; and Private Jesse W. Jones, 4th Texas Cavalry, are now interred in Section K. Another Confederate soldier, John H. Bencke, 35th Battalion Virginia Cavalry, who died of natural causes on August 7, 1879, is also interred in Section K.

Within the cemetery are 17 group burials of 52 World War II casualties whose remains were returned from overseas but could not be individually identified.

Major General Patrick J. Hurley, secretary of war in the cabinet of President Herbert Hoover, was interred in Section 5, Grave 149, on August 2, 1963. General Hurley served with distinction in World Wars I and II and as United States ambassador to China during the period 1944–45. His wife, Ruth Wilson Hurley, was interred with him on August 9, 1984.

Oliver LaFarge was interred in Section O, Grave 300 on August 5, 1963. His book *Laughing Boy,* a story of an Indian youth caught between the forces of modern society and his tribe's traditional life, won the Pulitzer Prize for literature in 1930. He was the author of many books and articles concerning the American Indian, and a special friend and champion of the Navajo Indians in New Mexico and Arizona. He served as a lieutenant colonel with the Army Air Corps during World War II.

A unique monument in Section A-2, Grave 956, marks the grave of Private Dennis O'Leary, Company I, 23rd Infantry. The monument depicts an almost life-size reclining soldier, carved in sandstone, leaning against a tree trunk and wearing boots and a cartridge belt. Private O'Leary was stationed at Fort Wingate when he disappeared for a few weeks. When he returned, he was court-martialed and served his sentence without complaint. On April 1, 1901, Private O'Leary shot himself to death. A suicide note explained that he had left a memento of his death in the mountains, and he asked the Army to send a wagon to retrieve it. Perhaps out of curiosity, the Army did. Following his direction, they located the monument, and found that he had even carved his date of death on it. When the remains from Fort Wingate were reinterred in Santa Fe National Cemetery in 1912, the unique monument was also brought to the cemetery.

In 1987, during the excavation of the foundation for a new house near Glorieta, the skeletal remains of 33 men were found. Some of them have been identified from buttons as members of the 4th Regiment Texas Mounted Volunteers. As of March 1990, three of their number have been individually identified: Major John Shropshire; Pvt. Ebineezer "Abe" Hanna, Jr., age 17; and J.S.L. Cotton, age 20. It is anticipated that many of these remains will be reinterred in the cemetery unless pending legislation is approved to designate the recovery area a historic site.

The surnames of the eight Medal of Honor recipients interred in Santa Fe National Cemetery provide a cross section of New Mexico's heritage. Daggers before three names indicate that the recipients were killed in action.

†Alexander Bonnyman, Jr., Sec MA, Grave 84. First Lieutenant, U.S. Marine Corps Reserves.
Citation: For conspicuous gallantry and intrepidity at the risk of his life above and beyond the call of duty as executive officer of the 2d Battalion Shore Party, 8th Marines, 2d Marine Division, during the assault against enemy Japanese-held Tarawa in the Gilbert Islands, 20–22 November 1943. Acting on his own initiative when assault troops were pinned down at the far end of Betio Pier by the overwhelming fire of Japanese shore batteries, 1st Lt. Bonnyman repeatedly defied the blasting fury of the enemy bombardment to organize and lead the besieged men over the long, open pier to the beach and then, voluntarily obtaining flame throwers and demolitions, organized his pioneer shore party into assault demolitionists and directed the blowing of several hostile installations before the close of D-day. Determined to effect an opening in the enemy's strongly organized defense line the following day, he voluntarily crawled approximately 40 yards forward on our lines and placed demolitions in the entrance of a large Japanese emplacement as the initial move in his planned attack against the heavily garrisoned, bombproof installation which was stubbornly resisting despite the destruction early in the action of a large number of Japanese who had been inflicting heavy casualties on our forces and holding up our advance. Withdrawing only to replenish his ammunition, he led his men in a renewed assault, fearlessly exposing himself to the merciless slash of hostile fire as he stormed the formidable bastion, directed the placement of demolition charges in both entrances, and seized the top of the bombproof position, flushing more than 100 of the enemy who were instantly cut down, and effecting the annihilation of approximately 150 troops inside the emplacement. Assailed by additional Japanese after he had gained his objective, he made a heroic stand on the edge of the structure, defending his strategic position with indomitable determination in the face of the desperate charge and killing three of the enemy before he fell mortally wounded. By his dauntless fighting spirit, unrelenting aggressiveness, and forceful leadership throughout three days of unremitting, violent battle, 1st Lt. Bonnyman had inspired his men to heroic effort, enabling them to beat off the counterattack and break the back of hostile resistance in that sector for an immediate gain of 400 yards with no further casualties to our forces in this zone. He gallantly gave his life for his country.

Edward Alvin Clary, Sec O, Grave 335. Watertender, U.S. Navy. G.O. No.: 59, 23 March 1910.
Citation: Onboard the USS Hopkins for extraordinary heroism in the line of his profession on the occasion of the accident to one of the boilers of that vessel, 14 February 1910.

Edwin L. Elwood, Sec H, Grave 705. Private, Company G, 8th U.S. Cavalry. Place and date: At Chiricahua Mountains, Ariz., 20 October 1869.
Citation: Gallantry in action.

†Daniel D. Fernandez, Sec S, Grave 246. Specialist Fourth Class, U.S. Army, Company C, 1st Battalion, 5th Infantry (Mechanized) 25th Infantry Division. Place and date: Cu Chi, Hau Nghia Province, Republic of Vietnam, 18 February 1966.
Citation: For conspicuous gallantry and intrepidity at the risk of his life above and beyond the

call of duty, Sp4c. Fernandez demonstrated indomitable courage when the patrol was ambushed by a Viet Cong rifle company and driven back by the intense enemy automatic weapons fire before it could evacuate an American soldier who had been wounded in the Viet Cong attack. Specialist Fernandez, a sergeant, and two other volunteers immediately fought their way through devastating fire and exploding grenades to reach the fallen soldier. Upon reaching his fallen comrade, the sergeant was struck in the knee by machine gun fire and immobilized. Specialist Fernandez took charge, rallied the left flank of his patrol, and began to assist in the recovery of the wounded sergeant. While first aid was being administered to the wounded man, a sudden increase in the accuracy and intensity of enemy fire forced the volunteer group to take cover. As they did, an enemy grenade landed in the midst of the group, although some men did not see it. Realizing there was no time for the wounded sergeant or the other men to protect themselves from the grenade blast, Sp4c. Fernandez vaulted over the wounded sergeant and threw himself on the grenade as it exploded, saving the lives of his four comrades at the sacrifice of his life.

Y.B. Rowdy, Sec A, Grave 894. Sergeant, Company A, Indian Scouts. Place and date: Arizona, 7 March 1890.
Citation: Bravery in action with Apache Indians.

†**Jose F. Valdez,** Sec Q, Grave 29. Private First Class, U.S. Army. Company B, 7th Infantry, 3d Infantry Division. Place and date: Near Rosenkrantz, France, 25 January 1945.
Citation: He was on outpost duty with five others when the enemy counterattacked with overwhelming strength. From his position near some woods 500 yards beyond the American lines he observed a hostile tank about 75 yards away, and raked it with automatic rifle fire until it withdrew. Soon afterwards he saw three Germans stealthily approaching through the woods. Scorning cover as the enemy soldiers opened up with heavy automatic weapons fire from a range of 30 yards, he engaged in a fire fight with the attackers until he had killed all 3. The enemy quickly launched an attack with two full companies of infantrymen, blasting the patrol with murderous concentrations of automatic and rifle fire and beginning an encircling movement which forced the patrol leader to order a withdrawal. Despite the terrible odds, Pfc. Valdez immediately volunteered to cover the maneuver, and as the patrol one by one plunged through a hail of bullets toward the American lines, he fired burst after burst into the swarming enemy. Three of his companions were wounded in their dash for safety and he was struck by a bullet that entered his stomach and, passing through his body, emerged from his back. Overcoming agonizing pain, he regained control of himself and resumed his firing position, delivering a protective screen of bullets until all others of the patrol were safe. By field telephone he called for artillery and mortar fire on the Germans and corrected the range until he had shells falling within 50 yards of his position. For 15 minutes he refused to be dislodged by more than 200 of the enemy; then, seeing that the barrage had broken the counterattack, he dragged himself back to his own lines. He died later as a result of his wounds. Through his valiant, intrepid stand and at the cost of his life, Pfc. Valdez made it possible for his comrades to escape, and was directly responsible for repulsing an attack by vastly superior enemy forces.

Jacob Gunther, Sec. A-3, Grave 1055, Corporal, Company E, 8th U.S. Cavalry. Place and Date: Arizona, 1868 and 1869.
Citation: Bravery in scouts and actions against Indians.

Robert S. Scott, Sec. 9, Grave 460. Captain, U.S. Army, 172nd Infantry, 43rd Infantry Division. Place and Date: Near Munda Air Strip, New Georgia, Soloman Islands, July 29, 1943.

Former superintendents/directors of the cemetery are:

Theodore Joseph, March 1895–March 1899
C.D. Crittentan, March 1899–May 1905
L.B. May, May 1905–November 1905
A.J. Chapman, November 1905–September 1909
K.W. Kendall, September 1909–June 1912
A.C.R. von Nyvenheim, June 1912–July 1924
Mrs. A.C.R. von Nyvenheim, July 1924–October 1924 (Actg.)
D.R. Wilcox, October 1924–November 1925

John A. Boender, March 1934–June 1945
Carl O. Gruel, June 1945–June 1959
Clement A. Byrne, June 1959–June 1959 (Actg.)
Charles H. Culver, June 1959–August 1964
Winston J. Stratton, August 1964–June 1968
John W. Lawrence, June 1968–July 1968 (Actg.)
Oscar P. Findley, July 1968–August 1969
Louis B. Baughman, August 1969–February 1970

Herbert D. Stanley, November 1925–November 1927

C.W. Dial, November 1927–January 1929

G.W. Rose, January 1929–January 1932

Fred Muller, January 1932–May 1932 (Actg.)

Fern C. Maugar, May 1932–May 1932

Fred Muller, May 1932–July 1932 (Actg.)

Joseph A. Zeller, July 1932–December 1933

Fred Muller, December 1933–March 1934 (Actg.)

John W. Lawrence, February 1970–August 1970 (Actg.)

Allen H. Long, August 1970–July 1973

Henry A. Hartwig, August 1973–July 1974

Rudolpho A. Lujan, July 1974–October 1986

Gloria C. Gamez, 1986–1998

Roseann Santore April 2004–April 2005

Gregg Whitney, 2007–Present

A former superintendent related the story that one time while his son was visiting and spent the night in the lodge, the son was awakened during the night by the sensation that someone was holding his ankles. He opened his eyes and saw a man standing at the foot of the bed, one hand around each of his ankles. The man did not respond when the son asked who he was or what he was doing. The son turned on the light, and the man disappeared. When he described the man the next day, he almost perfectly described a superintendent who had died in that room over 50 years earlier. Was it a dream? The son said it was not. The superintendent's lodge is occupied by the present director of the cemetery, but no ghostly visits have been reported.

Sarasota National Cemetery

9810 State Route 72
Sarasota, Florida 34241

The new Sarasota National Cemetery will include 296 acres when completed. It is located on State Route 72 about five miles east of Interstate 75.

Phase 1 development consists of about 60 acres which will include nearly 18,200 casket gravesites with 16,200 pre-placed crypts, 500 in-ground cremation sites, and about 7,000 columbarium niches. The cemetery was dedicated on June 1, 2008.

Sandra Beckley was appointed the first director of the cemetery. Mrs. Beckley came to Sarasota in October 2007, after completing a similar assignment of overseeing the development and opening of the Georgia National Cemetery.

Seven Pines National Cemetery

400 East Williamsburg Road
Sandston, Virginia 23150

The cemetery is situated in Henrico County, Sandston, Virginia, approximately eight miles southeast of Richmond. The 1.9 acres of land are a portion of a battlefield of great significance in the Civil War. Here was fought the Battle of Fair Oaks, better known as the Battle of Seven Pines. Great heroism was exemplified by both sides, one to capture and the other to defend the capital of the Confederacy at Richmond. This capital city was regarded as a symbol of the South and throughout the conflict between the states, Federal armies made repeated attempts to capture it.

One of the first attempts was made by General George B. McClellan, when in the spring of 1862, with the Army of the Potomac, he began his march on the Confederate capital. By the end of May the Union forces had advanced from Fort Monroe up the York-James Rivers peninsula to a point almost within sight of the Confederate capital. In fact, Union observers sent up in balloons were able to see the church spires of the city. Acting on his belief that

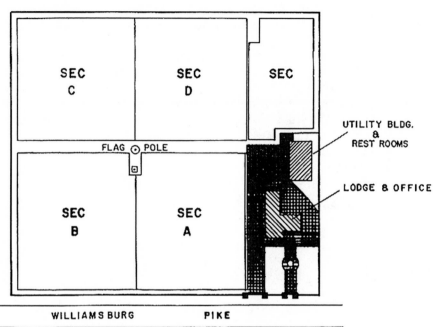

Map of the Seven Pines National Cemetery, Sandston, Va., October 1969.

McClellan planned to stay north of the James River, General Joseph E. Johnston, the Confederate commander, decided to attack. McClellan's forces were divided by the Chickahominy River, a low, marshy stream bordered by swamps. Heavy rains had further complicated the situation, and the area in the vicinity of the Chickahominy was almost impassable. McClellan therefore established his main line of defense at the junction of Nine Mile Road and Williamsburg Road. On the morning of May 31, General Joseph E. Johnston attacked McClellan's forces on this front and thus the Battle of Seven Pines began. For two days the battle was bitterly contested and both sides lost heavily. The Confederates were repulsed and Johnston was wounded. McClellan's heavy losses made him even more cautious than usual, and no further progress in the 1862 Richmond campaign was made until the Seven Days battles of late June and early July. An important result of the battle was Confederate President Jefferson Davis' appointment of General Robert E. Lee to succeed the wounded Johnston as commander of the forces which became the famed and valiant Army of Northern Virginia.

After the close of the Civil War, Lieutenant Colonel James H. Moore, assistant quartermaster, was authorized to select a site for a permanent national cemetery for concentration of the dead from the battlefields of Seven Pines (Fair Oaks), Gaines Hill, and Malvern Hill. The original site of 1.3 acres was appropriated in 1866 and purchased in 1867 from Richard Hilliard. Two small strips of land containing 10,580 square feet were added in 1874 and 1875. The cemetery name is derived from the seven pine trees planted along the inside of the cemetery wall in 1869. One of the trees died about 1975, and cemetery personnel have been unsuccessful in growing any of the several trees planted to replace it.

The program of concentrating the battlefield remains was started in May 1866. More than four years had elapsed since the first war casualties had occurred, and great difficulty was experienced in the identification of the dead and of the location of isolated graves. Remains were removed from the battlefields noted above, from Savage's Station, and from farms within a four mile area surrounding the cemetery. By June 27, all reinterments had been made and each grave marked. Original interments numbered 1,358, with 141 known and 1,216 unknown. As of September 30, 2008, the total number of interments was 1,813.

In October 1868, James Kelly, a discharged Civil War veteran, was appointed the first superintendent of Seven Pines National Cemetery. The present lodge was erected in 1874, and the brick wall around the cemetery was constructed in 1876.

The cemetery was closed July 24, 1964, except for interments in reserved gravesites or second interments in existing graves under the single gravesite per family policy. Since 1975, the cemetery has been assigned to the director of Richmond National Cemetery for maintenance and administration.

Former superintendents/directors of the cemetery are:

James Kelly, October 1868–Unknown
Francis Henry Osbourne, 1897–1904
Robert R. Dye, December 1908–April 1909
Francis Henry Osbourne, 1912–1915
Harry Osbourne, October 1921–November 1921
Willis R. DuPree, December 1921–May 1928
Charles B. Trotter, 1928–1931
Thomas C. Lacey, December 1931–1939
Thomas M. Holton, May 1939–July 1945
Harold A. Johnson, July 1945–July 1946
John S. Sargent, July 1946–August 1948
William R. Rossbach, November 1948–April 1950

Edward J. Smith, April 1950–April 1950
Charles J. Horten, May 1950–October 1955
Ernest L. Fusse, October 1955–March 1956
James H. Malloy, February 1957–August 1962
Harry W. Blake, August 1962–October 1963
David C. Corson, October 1963–July 1966
Claude E. Arnold, August 1966–August 1968
Eddie Walker, December 1968–May 1969
Donald L. Polston, September 1969–July 1973
Charles R. Weeks, July 1973–September 1974
Robert L. Whitfield, September 1974–March 1975

Sitka National Cemetery
803 Sawmill Creek Road
Sitka, Alaska 99835

The cemetery is situated in an area of high elevation, dominated by the natural grandeur of the mountains and the waters of Sitka Bay, at the intersection of Saw Mill Creek Road and Observatory Way, approximately 0.4 mile east of the center of town. The only access to Sitka is by air or by weekly ferry boat from Seattle, Washington.

When Baron Baranov arrived in 1790 and built the village on the hill, he named it New Archangel, but the Indian word *sitka,* thought to mean "by the sea," was never lost.

From March 30, 1867, when Secretary of State William H. Seward bought Alaska from Russia for $7,200,000 (about two cents per acre), until 1906, Sitka was the district capital. Alaska was called a district until 1912 when it became an organized territory. The U.S. flag was first raised over Alaska in Sitka on October 18, 1867, by troops under the command of General Jefferson Columbus Davis. But it was not until 1884 that Congress provided for any form of government through the passage of the first Organic Act, establishing Alaska as "a civil and judicial district." For those intervening 17 years the territory was administered by the War Department, then the Treasury Department, and finally by the Navy Department. None of these departments had any interest in local problems except the Army, which had the responsibility of keeping the Tlingit Indians under control.

Sitka National Cemetery, 1962.

The cemetery was originally laid out by General Davis during the military occupation of the District of Alaska from 1868 to 1880. Original interments were members of the occupation forces and the deceased from a Marine base and a Naval hospital during the period 1884 to 1912. Subsequently the land was loaned to the Department of the Interior as a home for indigent prospectors. From 1912 until 1921 the cemetery was practically abandoned, and a dense growth of trees and underbrush sprang up, almost obscuring the site. In 1920, Sitka Post No. 13, American Legion, wrote to the secretary of war calling attention to the neglected condition of the cemetery and asking for some remedial action. They were told that no funds were available. In 1921, they appealed to the secretary of the Navy, who expended $1,200 in reconditioning the site.

In 1922, the secretary of the Navy took up the question of maintenance of this cemetery with the War Department, since the Navy felt that it had no jurisdiction over it. The Navy requested that the War Department take over the care and maintenance under the laws pertaining to national cemeteries. The designation of Sitka Cemetery as a national cemetery was recommended by Governor Bone of Alaska and by the American Legion. On June 12, 1924, President Calvin Coolidge, by executive order, designated the cemetery a national cemetery. The executive order was amended in 1925 to reduce the size from 3.98 acres to 1.19 acres. In 1957, Sheldon Jackson Junior College donated approximately one acre of land; a donation of 0.20 acre by the Board of National Missions of the Presbyterian Church of the United States followed on September 17, 1959; and a transfer of approximately two acres from the Department of the Interior in the mid–1980s brought the cemetery to its present size of 4.3 acres.

During 1929, 49 remains from abandoned post cemeteries at Fort St. Michael, Fort

Davis, Fort Egbert, and Fort Gibson were reinterred in the national cemetery. In 1947, 52 remains from Chilkoot Barracks; 21 from Bayview Cemetery, Ketchikan; and 1 from Evergreen Cemetery, Juneau, were brought here. During World War II, there were 51 temporary military cemeteries in Alaska. Among those who died while serving in Alaska during World War II, the remains of 1,570 decedents were repatriated to the United States on August 27, 1948. On September 5, 1948, the remains of 99 of those originally interred in the temporary cemeteries were brought to Sitka and reinterred in the national cemetery.

John Green Brady was governor of the territory of Alaska, a presidential appointment, from 1897 to 1906. At his death in 1918 he was buried in the military cemetery in Section R, Grave 4. Governor Brady had come to Sitka as a Presbyterian missionary and later became commissioner and ex officio registrar of the Land Office, where he served until he was appointed governor. In the fall of 1924, Mrs. Brady returned to the territory and placed a large boulder over his grave and affixed to it the plate which formerly marked his grave. The Governor Brady plot occupied the most desirable and prominent site in the cemetery. It contained the graves of the governor, his son, and his parents-in-law, Mr. and Mrs. Hugh Patton. Other than Mrs. Brady, no further interments were allowed in the plot after the cemetery became a national cemetery.

Captain Charles W. Paddock, USMC, who died on July 21, 1943, is buried in Section Q, Grave 7. A native of California, Captain Paddock was an outstanding amateur athlete during the early 1920s.

There is a romantic legend attached to one headstone in the cemetery. During the days of military occupation, a Russian maiden named Nadia was courted by both a captain and a lieutenant who had been the closest of friends. When Nadia indicated that she preferred the lieutenant, the captain appeared to accept his loss. Some time later, they left on a hunting trip together. Several hours later, the captain staggered back to the village carrying the body of his companion on his shoulders. He said that the lieutenant had accidentally shot himself. After unsuccessfully trying to win the beautiful Nadia, he gave a party at the officers' club. The next morning the captain was found dead, still in his dress uniform, with a note under his body. In the note he explained that he had challenged the lieutenant to a duel and they used the hunting trip as an excuse. He had lost his sweetheart and his best friend, and did not have the courage to live. In the cemetery stands the headstone where Nadia wept for her lover. The inscription reads "B.W. Livermore, Lieut., 2nd U.S. Art." His was one of the first burials made in the military cemetery.

As of September 30, 2008, there were 1,115 interments. The cemetery is maintained by private contract under the supervision of the director of Fort Richardson National Cemetery. It is projected to remain open for interments beyond the year 2030. There is one Medal of Honor recipient memorialized here. Staff Sergeant Archie Van Winkle, U.S. Marine Corps Reserve, Company B, 1st Battalion, 7th Marines, 1st Marine Division. Place and Date: Sudong, Korea, November 2, 1960. SSgt Van Winkle's ashes were scattered and a memorial headstone was placed at the top of the hill in the historical part of the cemetery.

South Florida National Cemetery
6501 S. State Road 7
Lake Worth, Florida 33449

The 313 acre South Florida National Cemetery is located in Palm Beach County on State Road/U.S. 441, just south of Lantana Road and north of Boynton Beach Boulevard.

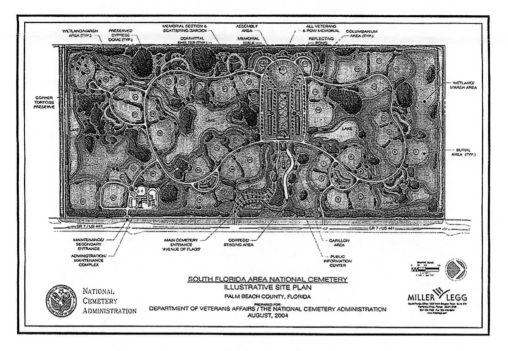

South Florida National Cemetery, Palm Beach County, Florida.

The Department of Veterans Affairs purchased the site from private citizens in August 2002.

The first burials began on April 16, 2007, in a small section that provided 1,708 casket gravesites, and approximately 4,000 plots for cremated remains. This construction is separate from the major Phase 1 development, and allowed burials to begin during the construction of the cemetery. It is anticipated that this cemetery will serve veterans' needs for the next 50 years.

There were 23 interments the first day, and 108 the first week the cemetery was open. As of September 20, 2008, there have been 3,138 interments. The cemetery property contains numerous species of wildlife, including a protected area around an eagle's nest in a tall tree.

David Wells was appointed the first director. He was succeeded by Kurt Rotar, who is the current director.

Springfield National Cemetery
1702 East Seminole Street
Springfield, Missouri 65804

Springfield National Cemetery, located on what was once the Kickapoo prairie, is situated in Greene County, Missouri.

Missouri was the center of national interest in 1861 as the nation wondered whether Missouri would secede and join the Confederacy or remain in the Union. At a convention called by Governor Claiborne F. Jackson, who was strongly pro–South, the members voted to remain in the Union. Governor Jackson refused President Lincoln's call for troops from Missouri. Most Missourians wanted to stay neutral.

Monument to General Nathaniel Lyon, Springfield National Cemetery.

The Battle of Wilson's Creek, some 10 miles southwest of Springfield, pitted the 11,600 Union troops commanded by Brigadier General Nathaniel Lyon against 5,400 Confederate soldiers commanded by General Sterling Price, a former governor of Missouri. During the battle, on August 10, 1861, both sides sustained heavy losses. The Union Army lost 233 killed, 721 wounded and 291 missing. General Lyon was among those killed. The Confederate losses were 297 killed, 900 wounded and 27 missing. Though technically a Confederate victory, the battle did nothing to resolve the issue of divided loyalties in Missouri, and the state remained in the Union.

The initial five acres for the cemetery were purchased from the city of Springfield in 1867, and the national cemetery established. An additional 1.92 acres were purchased from the city in 1885. In 1911, the Confederate Cemetery Association conveyed 6.3 acres, of which 2 were within a stone wall and 4.3 were undeveloped. There was a provision in the donation restricting burials to men who had served in the military or naval service of the Confederate States of America. This provision was removed in 1948 by the Confederate Cemetery Association of Missouri for that portion of the property lying outside the wall. Congress amended the 1911 legislation in 1957 to remove the restriction to permit interments in this ground. In February 1984, Congress approved legislation permitting burial of any eligible veteran in the vacant gravesites in the enclosed section. This was subject to the provisions that the stone wall separating the two sections would never be removed, and that all grave markers would be placed flat on the ground, rather than upright. In this way, the original appearance of the cemetery would not be altered. The present area of Springfield National Cemetery totals 18.1 acres.

The remains of many who perished at Wilson's Creek were reinterred in the cemetery after its establishment. Other remains were brought to the cemetery from Urbana, Springfield, and various other places in southwestern Missouri where fighting took place.

The report of the inspector of national cemeteries dated May 21, 1871, indicated that 832 known and 689 unknown interments had been made in the cemetery. The inspector also stated that, "A very worthless superintendent was in charge last year, and the cemetery was sadly neglected. This year it has been put in good order."

The exact number of Confederate dead in Springfield National Cemetery is not known. The cemetery director reported 463 gravesites in 1988. A 1915 report compiled by the Superintendent from the burial register of the Confederate Cemetery shows 77 known and 483 unknown, for a total of 560. A slab of concrete measuring 6 feet by 16 feet in the Confederate section marks the mass grave of an unknown number of decedents. In 1956, the Army made a recommendation that an appropriate inscription be placed on the slab and contacted a large number of individuals hoping to obtain authentic information about how many, if any, were interred under the slab. Their efforts were fruitless, and no further action was taken. The last burial of a Confederate soldier took place on June 12, 1939. The widow of a Confederate veteran was interred on October 15, 1940.

Several special monuments have been erected in the cemetery:

The Lyon Cenotaph, whose date of erection is unknown, is about ten feet tall with a knight's helmet, battle axe and a wreath on top of a four-foot pillar. General Lyon is not interred in the cemetery. The inscription reads, "Erected by the citizens of Springfield in memory of General Nath'l Lyon who fell in the battle of Wilson Creek while commanding the Union Army August 10, 1861."

The Springfield Monument, whose date of erection is also unknown, is approximately 20 feet tall and topped by a likeness of a Union soldier about 6 feet tall. The inscription reads: "In honor to and in memory of the citizens and volunteer soldiers who were killed or who died of wounds received in defense of Springfield, Missouri, against the Rebels, January 8, 1863. This monument was erected under the provisions of the last will of Dr. Thomas J. Bailey to show his love for the Union and its gallant Defenders."

The Price Monument, erected in 1901, is approximately 35 feet tall and is topped by a bronze likeness of a Confederate soldier about 10 feet tall. Below the soldier is a bronze bas-relief portrait, allegedly of General Price, and on each side of the monument are replicas of the Confederate battle flag. The inscription reads: "In memory of the Missouri Soldier in the Army of the Confederate States of America, Major General Sterling Price. Erected AD 1901 by the United Confederate Veterans of Missouri and the Daughters of the Confederacy of Missouri."

The UDC Monument is inscribed, "In memory of the gallant Confederate dead who fell at Wilson Creek on August 10, 1861, and whose place of burial is not known, this marker was erected by the United Daughters of the Confederacy on September 27, 1958."

Another item of interest in the cemetery is the time capsule buried north of the rostrum during the nationally televised Bicentennial celebration July 4, 1976, by the Lakes Counties 4H Clubs of America. The author was the principal speaker at this ceremony.

As of September 30, 2008, a total of 15,063 interments had been made. This includes William Freeman, a Revolutionary War veteran; Henry Walters, who served as a scout for "the Gray Ghost," John Singleton Mosby, during the Civil War; and five recipients of the Medal of Honor. A dagger before his name indicates that one recipient was killed in action.

Harrison Collins, Sec 26, Grave 1357-B. Corporal, U.S. Army; died December 25, 1890.

Orion P. Howe, Sec 4, Grave 207-A. Musician, Company C, 55th Illinois Infantry. Place and date: At Vicksburg, Miss., 19 May 1863.
Citation: A drummer boy, 14 years of age, and severely wounded and exposed to heavy fire from the enemy, he persistently remained upon the field of battle until he had reported to Gen. W.T. Sherman the necessity of supplying cartridges for the use of troops under command of Colonel Malmborg.

Fred Henry McGuire, Sec 29, Grave 332. Hospital Apprentice, U.S. Navy. G.O. No.: 138, 13 December 1911.
Citation: While attached to the *USS Pampang,* McGuire was one of a shore party moving in to capture Mundang, on the island of Basilan, Philippine Islands, on the morning of 24 September 1911. Ordered to take station within 100 yards of a group of nipa huts close to the trail, McGuire advanced and stood guard as the leader and his scout party first searched the surrounding deep grasses, then moved in the open area before the huts. Instantly enemy Moros opened point-blank fire on the exposed men and approximately 20 Moros charged the small group from inside the huts and from other concealed positions. McGuire, responding to the calls for help, was one of the first on the scene. After emptying his rifle into the attackers, he closed in with rifle, using it as a club to wage fierce battle until his comrades arrived on the field, when he rallied to the aid of his dying leader and other wounded. Although himself wounded, McGuire ministered tirelessly and efficiently to those who had been struck down, thereby saving the lives of two who otherwise might have succumbed to enemy-inflicted wounds.

Patrick H. Pentzer, Sec 24, Grave 1696. Captain, Company C, 97th Illinois Infantry. Place and date: At Blakely, Ala., 9 April 1865.
Citation: Among the first to enter the enemy's entrenchments, he received the surrender of a Confederate general officer and his headquarters flag.

†Jack Williams, Sec 30, Grave 2375. Pharmacist's Mate Third Class, U.S. Naval Reserve.
Citation: For conspicuous gallantry and intrepidity at the risk of his life above and beyond the call of duty while serving with the 3d Battalion, 28th Marines, 5th Marine Division, during the occupation of Iwo Jima, Volcano Islands, 3 March 1945. Gallantly going forward on the front lines

under intense enemy small-arms fire to assist a Marine wounded in a fierce grenade battle, Williams dragged the man to a shallow depression and was kneeling, using his own body as a screen from the sustained fire as he administered first aid, when struck in the abdomen and groin three times by hostile fire. Momentarily stunned, he quickly recovered and completed his ministration before applying battle dressings to his own multiple wounds. Unmindful of his own urgent need for medical attention, he remained in the perilous fire-swept area to care for another Marine casualty. Heroically completing his task despite pain and profuse bleeding, he then endeavored to make his way to the rear in search of adequate aid for himself when struck down by a Japanese sniper bullet which caused his collapse. Succumbing later as a result of his self-sacrificing service to others, Williams, by his courageous determination, unwavering fortitude and valiant performance of duty, served as an inspiring example of heroism, in keeping with the highest traditions of the U.S. Naval Service. He gallantly gave his life for his country.

Former superintendents/directors of the cemetery are:

R.C. Taylor, 1874–1875
Peter McKenna, 1877–1890
Clayton Hart, 1908–1911
Thomas B. Robinson, 1911–1914
James Burns, 1914–1916
K.W. Kindall, 1916–1920
John McCarthy, 1921–1929
Drue C. Wilkes, 1929–1932
J.C. Pumphrey, 1932–Unknown
Samuel E. Sharp, 1946–November 1946

Fred Rover, November 1946–1949
Leon P. Leonard, June 1949–October 1951
Harold Montague, October 1951–February 1957
John W. Cox, March 1957–February 1964
Lewis J. King, February 1964–June 1970
Rudolpho A. Lujan, June 1970–July 1974
Forrest W. Gore, September 1974–September 1987
James Wallace III, 1987–2001

The cemetery has been assigned to Jefferson Barracks for administration.

Staunton National Cemetery
901 Richmond Avenue
Staunton, Virginia 24401

The cemetery is located approximately one mile east of downtown Staunton on U.S. Highway 250. The 1.15 acres of land for the cemetery were appropriated in 1866, and the site was established as a national cemetery. The land was purchased in September 1868.

Staunton, located at the southern end of the Shenandoah Valley, just south of the Massanutten Mountains, was of critical importance to the Confederacy. While headquartered near here in early 1862, General Thomas J. "Stonewall" Jackson was ordered to operate in the Shenandoah Valley, to harass Union forces and appear to threaten Washington, D.C. His strategy was not to win or hold any place, but to strike at the Union commanders before they could unite, thereby creating a panic over the safety of Washington. His success took considerable pressure off General Robert E. Lee's defense of Richmond when President Lincoln detached 40,000 troops from General McClellan's army to try to trap Jackson in the valley. Reported numbers of troops engaged in actions during the Civil War are almost always subject to disagreement, but it is generally agreed that Jackson's forces were only about half the Union forces deployed in the Shenandoah Valley during this time. Jackson later joined Lee in time to add his strength to the main Confederate defense. In 1864, General Philip Sheridan lay waste to the city during his campaign to scourge the Shenandoah Valley.

Staunton is also the birthplace of Woodrow Wilson, 28th president of the United States. He was born December 28, 1856, and his minister father moved the family to Augusta,

Staunton National Cemetery

(Approximate location of grave is indicated on the map)

Name _____ Grave _____ Section _____

Georgia, less than two years later. During the Civil War, Wilson's father was a strong Southern supporter who turned his church into a Confederate hospital.

Original interments in the national cemetery were remains removed from the city cemetery at Staunton and from Cross Keys, Port Republic, Waynesboro, and from other places in that section. Of the original 749 interments, 231 were known and 518 were unknown. There are 104 group burials of 219 remains.

As of September 30, 2008, there was a total of 997 interments. The cemetery is closed for interments except for those in reserved gravesites or second interments in existing graves under the single gravesite per family policy. It is maintained by private contract under the supervision of the director of Culpeper National Cemetery.

Former superintendents/directors of the cemetery are:

Doss V. Porter, May 1943–October 1951
Leon P. Leonard, November 1951–June 1954
Winston J. Stratton, June 1954–March 1957
Doyle N. Yates, March 1957–September 1959
Duane T. Walsh, September 1959–March 1961
Herschell E. Davidson, Jr., March 1961–April 1962
Wilborn D. Burdeshaw, April 1962–August 1965

Allen G. Farabee, August 1965–September 1968
Thomas F. Morehead, October 1968–December 1969
Mack Cochenour, Jr., December 1969–September 1971
Arthur W. Kerr, September 1971–October 1974
Thomas J. Beauchane, May 1975–January 1978
John D. Simons, February 1978–October 1979

Tahoma National Cemetery
18600 Southeast 240th Street
Kent, Washington 98042-4868

From the flag assembly area looking in a southerly direction, Mount Rainier is ever present. This is a magnificent setting for the final resting place of America's heroes.

The 158 acre cemetery was established May 11, 1993, dedicated on September 26, 1997, and opened for interments on October 1, 1997. Phase II of construction was completed in March 2006, and includes 5,000 pre-placed crypts and 12,000 new columbarium niches. The Memorial Walkway contains 23 memorials commemorating veterans of various twentieth century wars.

There are two Medal of Honor recipients interred here:

Jesse T. Barrick, Sec. 8, Grave 108. Second Lieutenant, 57th Regiment of the U.S. Colored Infantry Division. Place and Date: Near Duck River, Tenn., May 26–June 2, 1963.
Citation: While on a scout, captured single-handed two desperate Confederate guerilla officers who were together and well armed at the time. (Note: The Congressional Medal of Honor records show the following: Corporal, Company H, 3rd Minnesota Infantry. The Medal was issued in 1917.)

Dexter J. Kerstettar, Section 9, Grave 12. Private First Class, Company C, 130th Infantry, 33rd Infantry Division. Place and Date: Near Galiano, Luzon, Philippine Island, April 13, 1945.
Citation: He was with his unit in a dawn attack against hill positions approachable only along a narrow ridge paralleled on each side by steep cliffs which were heavily defended by enemy mortars, machine guns, and rifles.... PFC Kerstetter's dauntless and gallant heroism was largely responsible for the capture of this key enemy position, and his fearless attack in the face of great odds was an inspiration to his comrades in their dangerous task.

Sergeant First Class Nathan Ross Chapman, Section 6, Grave 33, was the first American serviceman to die from hostile fire in the war in Afghanistan in 2002.

Francis Agnes, Section 24, Grave 717, was a former POW from 1941 to 1945, survivor of the Bataan Death March and founder of the Tahoma National Cemetery Support Group.

As of September 30, 2008, there were 23,479 interments in the cemetery. Former directors of the cemetery are:

Sandra Noguez, April 1996–April 2000
Mary Ann Fisher, July 2000–April 2003

Joseph Turnbach, June 2003–October 2006
James R. Trimbo, Apr, 2007–Present

Togus National Cemetery
Medical and Regional Office Center
Togus, Maine 14330

The cemetery is situated in Kennebec County, in the town of Chelsea, Maine, on the grounds of the Department of Veterans Affairs Medical and Regional Office Center. The center is equidistant between Gardiner and Augusta, Maine, six miles from each.

The center is the oldest Department of Veterans Affairs (DVA) facility in the country. It was established in October 1866, under authority of the Soldiers Act of March 3, 1865, as the Eastern Branch of the National Asylum (later changed to Home) for Disabled Volunteer Soldiers. The name Togus comes from the Indian name *Worromontogus*, which means mineral water. The Togus property was originally a summer resort known as Togus Springs. The facility became part of the Veterans Administration (VA) in July 1930 when all agencies administering benefits to veterans were consolidated.

The Togus National Cemetery is actually divided into a West Cemetery and an East Cemetery, with a total acreage of 31.2 acres. The West Cemetery, established in 1865 and moved to its present location west of the Asylum about 1867, contains 3,803 interments. It was closed for interments in 1936. The East Cemetery was established in 1936 and closed in 1961. It contains 1,569 interments. No interments have been made here for at least 25 years. The cemetery was one of the Veterans Administration cemeteries transferred to the National Cemetery System in 1973 when the system was transferred from the Department of the Army to the VA. The cemetery is maintained by personnel of the DVA Center.

In 1899, the government erected a monument to the veterans who had served in the United States military forces.

One Medal of Honor recipient is interred in the West Cemetery.

David John Scannell, Sec W-2-42, Grave 3955. Private, U.S. Marine Corps. G.O. No.: 55, 19 July 1901.

Citation: In the presence of the enemy during the action at Peking, China, 21 July to 17 August 1900. Throughout this period, Scannell distinguished himself by meritorious conduct.

Washington Crossing National Cemetery
Bucks County, Pennsylvania

The 205 acre Washington Crossing National Cemetery is located in Bucks County, north of Philadelphia, about three miles from the Washington Crossing Historic Park.

Phase 1A of the construction program is a 12 acre early interment area with temporary facilities. The complete 64 acre Phase 1 development will provide 15,500 full casket gravesites, including 13,500 pre-placed crypts, 6,500 in-ground cremation sites, and 4,100 columbarium niches.

West Virginia National Cemetery
Route 2 Box 127
Grafton, West Virginia 26354

The cemetery is situated in Taylor County, about 17 miles east of Clarksburg and about 5 miles west of Grafton, West Virginia.

This cemetery is clear evidence of the political clout of Senator Robert Byrd. In the mid–1980s, he had the Senate appropriate $1,750,000 for a cemetery to be constructed in West Virginia, and language was put into the appropriation bill requiring the Veterans Administration (VA) to build it. No site in West Virginia had even been considered in the search for sites under the regional cemetery concept because, while West Virginians are very patriotic with a high percentage of veterans, the population is sparse and widely spread throughout the state.

From the moment it became apparent that the nearby Grafton National Cemetery would reach its capacity in 1961, veterans organizations began a strong effort to get another national cemetery in the state. In 1975, after extensive studies to determine whether or not Grafton could be expanded by purchasing property across Walnut Street, it was determined that the property was too steep and would be extremely costly to develop. The West Virginia United Veterans National Cemetery Committee was formed and began to

West Virginia National Cemetery

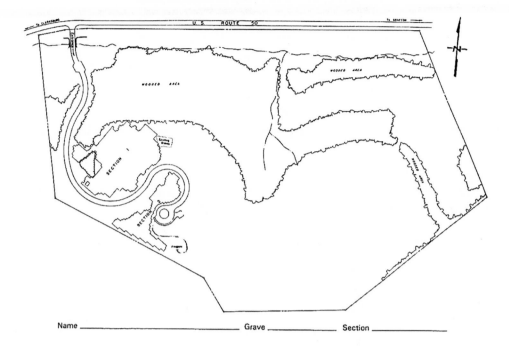

Name _____ Grave _____ Section _____

pressure the governor and members of the congressional delegation for a new national cemetery.

After extensive negotiations between the VA and the state over acreage and boundary lines, a tract of 58 acres part of the land occupied by the West Virginia Industrial School for Boys was agreed upon. The frequent calls and inquiries from Senator Byrd's office to the VA were strong motivational factors. The land was transferred, but construction was held up by the winter weather and by negotiations over and with a small contractor.

Finally, the cemetery was dedicated on September 27, 1987, and opened for interments the following day. None of the structures was finished, and the cemetery was run from the office of Grafton National Cemetery, five miles away. The principal speakers at the dedication were Senator Byrd, Governor Arch Moore, and National Cemetery System Director Wilfred Ebel.

Through September 30, 2008, there were 3,713 interments. Because of steep hills, only 6,500 gravesites will be usable in the original 58 acres. The cemetery has been expanded and now covers 89.7 acres.

The site is characterized by steep hillsides and plateaus, where gravesites will be developed. The flagpole is 1,335 feet above sea level, creating a dramatic 200-foot vertical rise from the entrance to the cemetery's focal point. The location of the upper committal shelter offers panoramic views of West Virginia's rolling hills from this valley overlook.

Former directors of the cemetery are:

James L. Turner, April 1986–September 1988
William Livingston, September 1988–1990
Terry Ellison, November 1990–December 1995
Patrick H. Lovett, October 1997–October 1998

Deborah L. "Cindy" Poe, November 1999– February 2008
Gerald Vitela, February 2008–Present (Acting)

Willamette National Cemetery

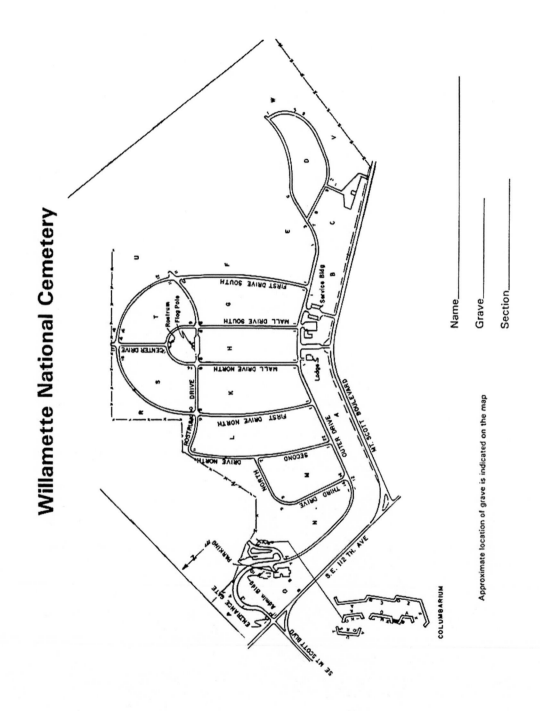

Name_____

Grave_____

Section_____

Approximate location of grave is indicated on the map

Willamette National Cemetery
11800 Southeast Mount Scott Boulevard
Portland, Oregon 97266

The cemetery is located about 10 miles southeast of Portland in Multnomah and Clackamas counties.

After long, continuous efforts on the part of veterans organizations, the 77th Congress passed Public Law 388 on December 29, 1941, authorizing the secretary of war to establish a national cemetery in the vicinity of Portland, Oregon. When he signed the bill into law, President Franklin Roosevelt sent a note to the secretary of war "to indicate to you my view that under present conditions funds for land purchases should be limited to urgent defense needs, and ... I would not expect that there would be a need for sending forward at any early date any estimate of appropriation under the authorization provided by this enactment."

With the conclusion of World War II, action was again taken toward the establishment of a national cemetery in the Portland area. In 1949, the state of Oregon donated to the United States 51.59 acres of land in Multnomah County and an adjoining tract of 51.04 acres in Clackamas County for use as a national cemetery. A subsequent donation of 98.82 acres in 1952, and acquisitions since 1989 have brought the cemetery to its present size of 269.4 acres. Construction work at the site began in 1950, and the area was officially designated Willamette National Cemetery on December 14, 1950.

A dedication ceremony was held on Sunday, July 22, 1951. At that time there were 117 interments in the new site. The first interment, on February 14, 1951, was that of Private Blaine Clayton Van Ausdeln, a veteran of World War I. As of September 30, 2008, there were 137,013 interments, including over 3,000 inurnments in the columbarium, which was opened on April 18, 1983.

The cemetery has been the beneficiary of many significant contributions by individuals and organizations working toward its beautification and development. In conjunction with the nation's bicentennial in 1976, local Veterans Administration units held a ceremony at Willamette National Cemetery in support of the national VA program. They donated a dawn redwood tree and bronze plaque to honor all Medal of Honor recipients. Members of the Eastmoreland Garden Club and the Oregon Federation of Garden Clubs have contributed and planted many fine trees and shrubs which add greatly to the beauty of the cemetery grounds. They also donated an electronic carillon system to the cemetery on Memorial Day 1975. Permanent seating for the area in front of the rostrum was sponsored and funded by the American Legion in 1970. The project to illuminate the flagpole so that the flag may be flown 24 hours a day was contributed by the Veterans of Foreign Wars in 1975. A marble plaque honoring unknown soldiers was donated by the Federated Veteran's Council of Multnomah County in May 1977.

There are four Medal of Honor recipients interred in these hallowed grounds. Daggers appear before the names of two who were killed in action.

Stanley T. Adams, (then Master Sergeant), Sec H, Grave 3623-O, Lieutenant Colonel, U.S. Army, 1st Platoon, Company A, 1st Battalion, 19th Infantry Regiment, 24th Infantry Division. Place and Date: Near Sesim-ni, Korea, February 4, 1951.
Citation: Master Sergeant Adams, Company A, distinguished himself by conspicuous gallantry and intrepidity above and beyond the call of duty in action against the enemy.

Arnold L. Bjorklund, Sec O, Grave 3446. First Lieutenant, U.S. Army, 36th Infantry Division. Place and date: Near Altavilla, Italy, 13 September 1943.
Citation: When his company attacked a German position on Hill 424, his platoon was pinned

down by a heavy concentration of machine gun and rifle fire. With only three hand grenades, he crawled forward under intense enemy fire and hurled one grenade into the first nest, killing the three Germans manning the gun. He then crawled 20 yards to the right on a higher terrace and using his second grenade, destroyed the second position. As the platoon advanced up the hill, it was again pinned down, this time by mortar fire. First Lieutenant Bjorklund located the mortar and worked his way to within 10 yards and threw his third grenade, destroying the mortar.

†**Larry G. Dahl,** Sec S, Grave 3512. Specialist Fourth Class, U.S. Army, 359th Transportation Company, 27th Transportation Battalion, U.S. Army Support Command. Place and date: An Khe, Binh Dinh Province, Republic of Vietnam.

Citation: While serving as a machine gunner on a gun truck assisting in the defense of a convoy that had been ambushed by an enemy force, Sp4c Dahl was riding in a truck into which an enemy hand grenade was thrown. He called a warning to his companions and threw himself directly onto the grenade. He sacrificed his life while saving the lives of the other members of the truck crew.

†**Loren R. Kaufman,** Sec G, Grave 2812. Sergeant First Class, U.S. Army, Company G, 9th Infantry Regiment. Place and date: Near Yongsan, Korea, 4 and 5 September 1950.

Citation: His platoon was ordered to reinforce the company when it was attacked by an enemy battalion. As his unit moved along a ridge it encountered a hostile encircling force. Sergeant Kaufman, running forward, bayoneted the lead scout and engaged the column in a rifle and grenade assault. His quick, vicious attack so surprised the enemy that they retreated in confusion. When his platoon joined the company he discovered that the enemy had taken commanding ground and pinned the company down in a draw. Without hesitation Sfc. Kaufman charged the enemy lines, firing his rifle and throwing grenades. He bayoneted two enemy and, seizing an unmanned machine gun, delivered deadly fire on the defenders. Leading the assault, he reached the ridge and routed the remaining enemy. He was killed in subsequent action on February 10, 1951.

Across the boulevard from the national cemetery are two veterans burial tracts; one contains five acres owned by the Soldiers, Sailors, and Marines Cemetery Association, and the other contains 12.57 acres owned by the state of Oregon, of which 4.47 acres are developed. These tracts adjoin each other. Prior to 1973, there was some congressional interest in transferring the two tracts as an addition to the national cemetery, but the Department of the Army indicated that they were not interested in such a transfer. The purchase of 65 acres contiguous to the cemetery was completed in the fall of 1990, adding nearly 30 years' life to the cemetery.

Former superintendents/directors of the cemetery are:

Fred Rover, January 1951–June 1952
William J. Costine, June 1952–August 1969
Howard J. Ferguson, August 1969–October 1970
Samuel H. Davis, Jr., October 1970–June 1974
Martin T. Corley, June 1974–October 1975
Samuel H. Davis, Jr., December 1975–August 1979

John R. Richardson, August 1979–December 1982
Claude E. Arnold, April 1983–August 1984
Billy D. Murphy, September 1984–1998
Lucy Devenney, July 1998–January 2005
Gil Gallo, April 2005–May 2006
George Allen, May 2006–Present

Wilmington National Cemetery
2011 Market Street
Wilmington, North Carolina 28401

The cemetery is located in New Hanover County, on U.S. Highways 17 and 74, near downtown Wilmington.

Purchases of land in 1867 and 1877 from J.D. Ryttenberg, and a donation of 0.07 acre from the city of Wilmington in 1953, brought the area to its present size of 5.065 acres.

Wilmington's harbor was considered the great importation depot of the South during the Civil War. The harbor was protected by mines and underwater explosives devised under the direction of Confederate Secretary of the Navy Stephen R. Mallory. In addition, a heavily armed Fort Fisher with elaborate coastal defenses guarded the entrance to the harbor. Union forces captured much of the eastern coast early in the Civil War, but the Wilmington port remained open to supply the Confederacy until January 1865.

In December 1864, a combined effort by the Navy, under Admiral David Porter, and the Army, under General Benjamin F. Butler, could not take Fort Fisher. A second attempt in January 1865, with a huge naval force under Admiral Porter, and an army of 8,000, under General A.H. Terry, succeeded in capturing the fort. The extended bombardment finally silenced its guns and ended the blockade running that had supplied subsistence for General Lee's army. Wilmington was evacuated on February 22.

Original interments in the cemetery were remains removed from the city of Wilmington, the Lutheran cemetery in Wilmington, Fort Fisher, Fort Johnson, Fayetteville, Smithville, and from 12 miles along the Wilmington and Weldon and the Wilmington and Manchester railroads. The first superintendent, Matthew Dellingham, is interred in the cemetery. The report of the inspector of national cemeteries dated May 13, 1870, lists 2,039 interments, 698 known and 1,341 unknown. The report also notes that there were 2,057 graves marked by headboards. There are 6 group burials containing 224 remains 3 from Fort Fisher, 2 from Burgam, North Carolina, and a group from an airplane crash in Alabama in 1945.

Wilmington National Cemetery

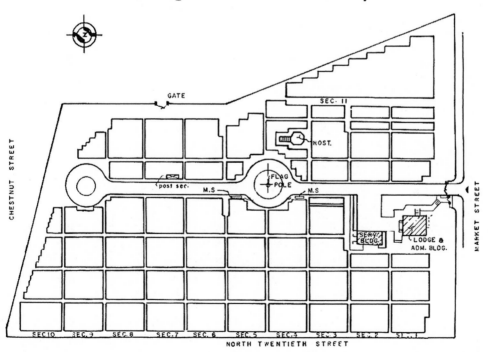

Name_____ Grave_____ Section_____

Many tragic events occurred in Old Wilmington during the great influenza epidemic of 1918, but none so tragic as the deaths of a group of Puerto Ricans. The first report of this event appeared in the *Morning Star,* November 14, 1918. Pneumonia-influenza was reported aboard the government ship *City of Savannah,* which had arrived in the Cape Fear River two days earlier carrying 1,900 Puerto Ricans to Fayetteville to aid in the construction of Camp Bragg. On November 18, nine bodies were brought to Wilmington for interment in the national cemetery. "The islanders were all pneumonia victims." Today there are 28 Spanish names carved on grave markers in the Wilmington National Cemetery, in neat rows in Sections 8 and 9.

On Saturday, March 3, 1990, Commander Frank C. Elkins, a Navy pilot, was interred. The 27-year-old officer from Bladenboro, N.C., was declared missing in action on October 12, 1966, after he failed to return from a combat mission over North Vietnam. His remains were returned by the Vietnamese with those of 27 other American servicemen in June 1989. To date only nine of the servicemen have been identified.

As of September 30, 2008, there were 6,228 interments. The cemetery closed in February 1987, except for those in reserved gravesites, or in existing graves under the one gravesite per family policy.

Former superintendents/directors of the cemetery are:

Matthew Dellingham, 1867–1869
R.C. Taylor, 1883–1884
L.B. May, 1885–1888
E.L. Grant, 1888–1889
Henry C. Lacy, 1894–1905
William Vandre, 1906–1906
George H. Taylor, 1909–1916
Charles Luck, 1917–1917
Jerome Romine, 1918–1920
Rodriquez Placide, 1922–1926
James M. Freeman, 1928–1929
Joseph LaRue, 1930–1932
Maurice Kelly, August 1933–August 1948

Chester R. Lightfritz, August 1948–January 1958
John W. Clemons, February 1958–August 1961
Norman W. Kelley, August 1961–May 1973
Clifford E. Filteau, May 1973–December 1977
Robert E.L. St. Clair, December 1977–April 1980
Kenneth D. LaFevor, July 1980–September 1981
Elizabeth L. Whitaker, November 1981–April 1984
Gary Peak, June 1984–June 1985
Jim Adamson, June 1985–January 1986
Vickie Smith, March 1986–August 1986
James H. Wallace III, September 1986–October 1987

The cemetery is maintained by private contract under the supervision of the director of New Bern National Cemetery.

Winchester National Cemetery
401 National Avenue
Winchester, Virginia 22601

Winchester National Cemetery is situated in Frederick County in Winchester, Virginia, about 80 miles west of Washington, D.C. The cemetery was dedicated on April 8, 1866, on 4.89 acres of appropriated land. The land was purchased in 1871 from Jacob Baker of Winchester.

The strategic importance of the city of Winchester has been recognized since George Washington, at the age of 16, was hired by Lord Fairfax as one of a party to survey his property 5.2 million acres known as the "Northern Neck of Virginia." The town was "plotted" by Colonel James Wood in 1744. In 1752 the name was changed from Frederick to Winchester, after the old English capital that was Colonel Wood's birthplace. The town was a center of commerce where pioneers obtained their wagons and provisions for traveling south and west. Frederick County was the staging area for actions against the French dur-

Massachusetts Monument, Winchester National Cemetery, 1956.

ing the French and Indian War. General Edward Braddock outfitted his troops here before marching to attack Fort Duquesne in Pennsylvania.

Both Union and Confederate generals were well acquainted with Washington's exploits in and around Winchester prior to the Revolutionary War. They were also aware that the city was the gateway to the Shenandoah Valley, which, from a military viewpoint, was very valuable to the army that controlled it. It was an ideal outfitting area, for in this fertile valley there were numerous mills and factories, and cattle and crops were plentiful. The Confederates recruited many troops from this area. For these reasons, it is easy to understand why the city of Winchester changed hands 71 times during the Civil War. There were three major engagements in the area which were of great significance in the general pursuit of the war.

General Thomas Jonathan "Stonewall" Jackson maintained his headquarters in Winchester during 1861 and 1862. General Jackson earned his nickname "Stonewall" at the First Battle of Manassas in 1861. General Barnard E. Bee was trying to rally his troops when he saw Jackson's strong line holding its ground. He shouted to his troops, "There is Jackson standing like a stone wall. Let us determine to die here, and we will conquer." From that moment, Jackson became known as Stonewall, and his troops were called the Stonewall Brigade. Jackson died on May 10, 1863, after being mistakenly shot by one of his own men on the night of May 2 near Chancellorsville, Virginia.

From the many bitterly fought engagements to secure the "Granary of the Confederacy" in the Shenandoah Valley, both Union and Confederate dead were eventually brought to their final rest in the cemeteries in Winchester. Most of the casualties of the five battles fought in and around the city are interred in the Stonewall Confederate Cemetery located within the Mt. Hebron Cemetery, across the road from the national cemetery.

A *Philadelphia Inquirer* article dated April 21, 1862, states that a graveyard on the east side of town contains about 100 bodies of Union soldiers, consisting of those killed in battle and those who died of wounds and sickness. These could very well be the first interments at this cemetery. The first planned burials in the cemetery were soldiers reinterred from battlefields near Winchester, New Market, Front Royal and Snicker's Gap, Virginia, and from Harpers Ferry, Martinsburg and Romney, West Virginia. The bronze plaque implanted at the base of the large Dahlgren cannon near the flagpole states that 4,448 Union soldiers, including 2,338 of them unknown, are buried in this final resting place. Cemetery records indicate that most of the Union dead were killed in the Third Battle of Winchester during September and October 1864. A state of Virginia plaque in the cemetery states that two future presidents of the United States, James A. Garfield and Rutherford B. Hayes, served in the Union forces during this battle. It further states that Confederate General Jubal A. Early was finally driven from Winchester on September 19, 1864.

Winchester National Cemetery was closed on July 11, 1969, except for interments in reserved gravesites, or second interments in existing graves under the single gravesite per family policy. As of September 30, 2008, there were 5,577 interments in the cemetery. The lodge is leased to the Winchester Frederick County Historical Society.

There are 13 special monuments erected in this cemetery, 6 of them by the states of Ohio, Pennsylvania, Vermont, New Hampshire, New York, and Massachusetts. Each one commemorates fallen soldiers with the names of various battles in the valley, and, in some cases, the names of those being honored. These special monuments are as follows: 123rd Regiment Ohio Volunteer Infantry, 8th Corps–24th Corps, 1899; Pennsylvania; 6th Army Corps, 1890; 8th Regiment Vermont Infantry; 8th Vermont Volunteers, 1885; 12th Regiment Connecticut Volunteers, 1896; 18th Connecticut Volunteers Regiment; Sheridan's Valley Campaign of 1864, 3rd Massachusetts Calvary, 19th Corps, 1888; monuments to nine soldiers killed in the Shenandoah Valley Campaign of 1864, erected by their comrades (no other information is available); Colonel George D. Wells, erected by comrades in memory of members of the 34th Massachusetts Infantry Regiment who were killed in the Shenandoah Valley; Massachusetts, 1907; 114th New York Volunteer Infantry; 14th New Hampshire Regiment, erected prior to 1869.

Former superintendents/directors of the cemetery are:

P. Sedwick, 1866–August 1874

J.M. Witty, August 1874–January 1881

Andrew B. Drum, June 1881–August 1888

W.A. Donaldson, August 1888–February 1895

T.H. Savage, February 1895–June 1903

Charles R. Sanford, July 1903–October 1903

E.J. Lewis, October 1903–March 1913

Charles Gaddas, March 1913–May 1913

Robert R. Dye, May 1913–January 1914

F.W. Davis, January 1914–June 1917

J.W. Bodley, June 1917–August 1918

O.H. Weidman, August 1918–March 1921

E.C. Phillips, April 1921–February 1925

S.S. Hershman, February 1925–April 1928

Charles Spitler, April 1928–October 1929

James R. Martin, October 1929–September 1934

Dallas M. Sprinkle, November 1934–June 1950

Raymond J. Costanzo, June 1950–February 1955

Lester C. Harvey, February 1955–September 1956

Samuel H. Davis, Jr., September 1956–February 1958

Metro Kowalchick, February 1958–August 1961

Kenneth Ridley, August 1961–May 1969

Roland E. Lex, May 1969–October 1970

John T. Dowd, November 1970–November 1974

Thomas E. Costanzo, March 1975–June 1976

William E. Rogers, Jr., July 1976–December 1977

Robert L. Brake, January 1978–November 1979

Dennis P. Gura, December 1979–August 1980

David M. Cariota, October 1980–April 1983

Elmer D. Nygaard, May 1983–January 1985

Daniel L. Nelson, March 1985–November 1985

Since November 1985, the cemetery has been assigned to the director of Culpeper National Cemetery for administration and management.

Wood National Cemetery

5000 West National Avenue, Bldg. 1301
Milwaukee, Wisconsin 53295-4000

The cemetery is located on the grounds of the Clement J. Jablocki VA Medical Center, adjacent to the Milwaukee County Stadium, between National and Bluemound avenues. Interstate Highway 94 passes through the cemetery.

During the Civil War, Lydia Hewitt resolved to have a soldiers home in Milwaukee. Under her leadership, volunteer women's groups rented quarters to returning veterans who needed care. The first makeshift quarters held up to 155 residents and was called the Milwaukee Soldiers Home. Ms. Hewitt organized a fair to raise funds to construct a suitable building to house the increasing number of veterans. The fair raised $110,000.

A state charter was granted to the facility in 1865, and it became known as the Wisconsin Soldiers Home. After Congress had passed legislation authorizing the creation of five national soldiers homes, the federal government was seeking a suitable site for the Northwestern Branch for Disabled Volunteer Soldiers. Wisconsin sent a representative to Washington to plead its cause, and the money raised by the fair was turned over to the federal government. This is considered to have been a factor in locating one of the national homes in Milwaukee. The Wisconsin Soldiers Home closed its doors in May 1867, having served 31,650 veterans during its two years of operation.

The Northwestern Branch Home for Disabled Volunteer Soldiers was located on 410 acres of land, of which 250 acres were set apart for farming purposes. The remaining part, on which buildings were located, was laid as a park.

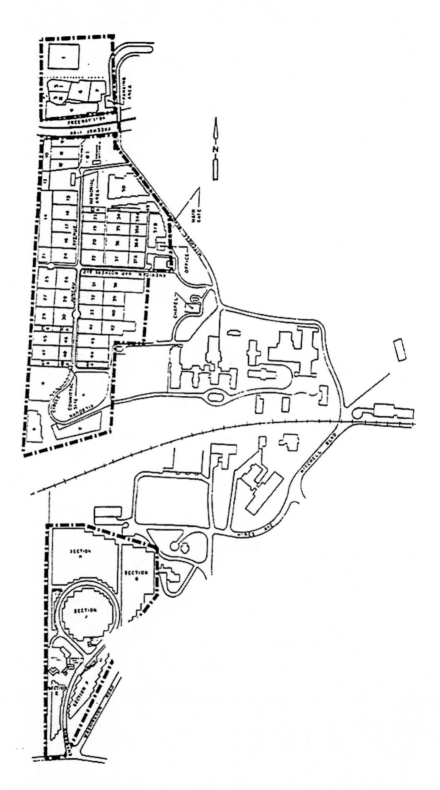

Wood National Cemetery

From the time it opened in 1867 until 1871, the home buried its dead in private cemeteries in the Milwaukee area. In 1871, a cemetery was opened on the grounds, and John K.
Afton was the first interment on May 22, 1871. It was then known as Soldiers Home Cemetery. In 1937, the name was changed to Wood Veterans Cemetery in honor of General George
Wood, a longtime member of the Board of Managers of the soldiers home. It became a
national cemetery in 1973 when the National Cemetery System was transferred from the
Department of the Army to the Veterans Administration. The first interment made under
the National Cemetery System was of Andrew F. Brestrup, a World War I veteran, on September 4, 1973.

Wood National Cemetery, as of September 30, 2008, contained 52.2 acres of land and
37,661 interments. The cemetery is closed to new interments. All the land except for a small
section was transferred from the VA Medical Center to the National Cemetery System. Section 1 of the cemetery is located in Calvary Cemetery, which is adjacent to the national cemetery. This section consists of 690 graves and was donated to the United States in 1876 by
the Archdiocese of Milwaukee for the burial of Catholic veterans.

A 70-foot-tall monument with a Civil War soldier at "Parade Rest" was donated in
1903 by the Soldiers' and Sailors' Monument Association. The cemetery flagpole was donated
by the Gold Star Mothers in 1956. The Soldiers Home Chapel is adjacent to, but not part
of, the cemetery. Approximately 40 percent of all burial services at Wood are held in this
chapel, constructed in 1889 with funds saved by former soldiers who passed away while at
the soldiers home and left no heirs. The chapel is Queen Anne in style, and its irregular
shape is essentially that of a cross, with a few appendages. Other interesting characteristics
of its finely detailed exterior and interior are stained-glass windows, a turreted tower, dec-
orative iron work, honey-toned oak pews, and interior columns and woodwork. A pipe
organ was installed in 1896 and a new altar erected in 1909.

There are nine veterans of the War of 1812 and five Medal of Honor recipients, all from
the Civil War, buried here. There are also some civilians, including doctors who worked for
the old soldiers home, and their families. The largest private monument in the cemetery
marks the grave of General Kilbourn Knox. He was the sixth governor of the Northwestern
Branch of the Home for Disabled Volunteer Soldiers. Shortly after the end of the Civil War,
General Knox was transferred to the 22nd Infantry, but soon was detached and assigned to
the White House as military secretary to President Andrew Johnson. General Knox served
as governor of the Wood complex from May 1, 1889, until his death on April 8, 1891.

The five Medal of Honor recipients interred here are:

James K.L. Duncan, Sec 19, Grave 41. Ordinary Seaman, U.S. Navy. G.O. No.: 32, 16 April 1864.
Citation: Served onboard the *USS Fort Hindman* during the engagement near Harrisonburg, La.,
2 March 1864. Following a shell-burst at one of the guns which started a fire at the cartridge tie,
Duncan immediately seized the burning cartridge, took it from the gun and threw it overboard
despite the immediate danger to himself. Carrying out his duties through the entire engagement,
Duncan served courageously during this action in which the *Fort Hindman* was raked severely with
shot and shell from enemy guns.

Milton Matthews, Sec 11, Grave 61. Private, Company C, 61st Pennsylvania Infantry. Place and
date: At Petersburg, Va., 2 April 1865.
Citation: Capture of flag of 7th Tennessee Infantry (C.S.A.).

Winthrop D. Putnam, Sec 16, Grave 109. Corporal, Company A, 77th Illinois Infantry. Place
and date: At Vicksburg, Miss., 22 May 1863.
Citation: Carried, with others, by hand, a cannon up to and fired it through an embrasure of
the enemy's works.

Lewis Rounds, Sec 20, Grave 256. Private, Company D, 8th Ohio Infantry. Place and date: At Spotsylvania, Va., 12 May 1864.
Citation: Capture of flag.

Michael McCormick, Sec. MA, Grave 10A. Boatswain's Mate, U.S. Navy, USS Signal. Place and Date: Red River, May 19, 1865.
Citation: Proceeding up the Red River, the USS Signal engaged a large force of enemy field batteries and sharpshooters, returning the fire until the ship was totally disabled, at which time the white flag was raised. Serving as gun captain and wounded early in the battle, McCormick bravely stood by his gun in the face of the enemy fire until ordered to withdraw.

From the time of the first interment in 1871 until the cemetery was transferred to the National Cemetery System in September 1973, the cemetery was operated and managed by the personnel of the soldiers home and the VA Medical Center. Superintendents/directors assigned since the transfer are:

Allen H. Long, July 1974–July 1975
Mack Cochenour, Jr., July 1975–August 1976
Claude E. Arnold, February 1977–July 1979
Therese J. Bush, August 1979–January 1984
Robert L. Brake, January 1984–November 1984
Gary W. Smith, January 1985–June 1987
Elmer D. Nygaard, 1987–1991

Richard Anderson, 1991–2001
Joe Turnbach, 2001–2003
Quincy Whitehead, 2004–2005
Maria Garza, 2005–2007
Michael Lewis, 2007–April 2008
Sean Baumgartner, 2008–Present

Woodlawn National Cemetery
1825 Davis Street
Elmira, New York 14901

The cemetery is located in the northern section of Elmira, in Chemung County, New York.

In 1861 Elmira was a training and marshalling center for Union soldiers. There were three camps with two hospitals and a large warehouse. As the barracks emptied and the trainees were assigned to units, it was decided to use the buildings as a prisoner of war camp. Between July 1864 and August 1865, about 12,000 Confederate prisoners were confined at different times. Of these, about 2,950 died. Many were in poor physical condition when they arrived, and the first winter in camp was unusually severe.

At first, the United States government made no provision for the burial of prisoners, so the officials of the city of Elmira gave the commanding officer of the camp permission to use one-half acre in the city-owned Woodlawn Cemetery. The half-acre plot was soon filled, and before the camp closed, two and one-half acres had been used for the graves of Confederate prisoners. Original burials in the cemetery were 3,343 Confederate prisoners of war and approximately 140 Union soldiers, most of whom were prison guards who died in the general hospital. The federal government established the plot as Woodlawn National Cemetery in 1874.

At the time of the Confederate burials, John Jones, an escaped slave who had found freedom in Elmira, was sexton of Woodlawn Cemetery. He kept a meticulous record of each Confederate burial so that when, in 1907, the federal government erected a small marble marker at each grave, it was possible to mark each stone with the soldier's name, company regiment, date of death, and grave number. Among the men whom John Jones buried was one from the household in which he had lived as a slave in Virginia. Jones received $2.50 from the government for each burial, and the fees helped him amass a comfortable fortune after the war.

Confederate Soldiers Monument, Woodlawn National Cemetery, 1963.

All gravesites in the cemetery were used or reserved by May 26, 1969, and the cemetery was closed. In 1987 the Chemung County Veterans Council donated almost three acres, enabling the Veterans Administration to reopen the cemetery. The cemetery has space available in the columbarium. As of September 30, 2008, a total of 9,087 interments had been made in the cemetery.

There are four German prisoners of war interred here. They were reinterred in the national cemetery from Fort Niagara, New York, in May 1949.

The Shohola Monument was erected by the United States in 1911 to mark the burial place of 49 Confederate prisoners of war who were killed in a railroad accident near Shohola, Pennsylvania, and whose remains were buried there but subsequently removed to this cemetery, where the individual graves cannot now be identified. The 49 prisoners were from Virginia, North Carolina, and Georgia units. The monument also commemorates the privates of the Eleventh Veteran Reserve Corps of Union Guard who were killed with their Confederate prisoners of war on July 15, 1864, at Shohola. Their individual remains are also unidentified.

In 1938, the Daughters of the Confederacy erected a monument in memory of those who died in Elmira. The monument overlooks the entire length of the Confederate area.

Former superintendents/directors of the national cemetery are:

Clarence E. Suders, May 1941–December 1942 (superintendent of the adjoining private cemetery, January 1943–December 1947)

John J. Richardson, December 1962–June 1968
Ray C. Van Tassell, Sr., August 1968–November 1978

Aaron C. Gordon, December 1947–January 1948
James M. Griffin, January 1948–December 1954
Edwin C. Cooper, December 1954–January 1959
Roland E. Lex, January 1959–March 1959
William J. Boyer, March 1959–December 1962

Dennis J. Johnson, November 1978–November 1979
Robert L. Brake, November 1979–December 1983

Since January 1984, Woodlawn National Cemetery has been assigned to the director of Bath National Cemetery for administration and management.

Zachary Taylor National Cemetery

4701 Brownsboro Road
Louisville, Kentucky 40207

The cemetery is situated in Jefferson County, Kentucky, on U.S. Highway 42 (Brownsboro Road) just west of the intersection with Interstate 264, in northeast Louisville.

Zachary Taylor National Cemetery, established in 1928, was actually authorized by an act of Congress on February 24, 1925. This act was apparently the result of the efforts of a niece of Robert Taylor to have the government take title to the Taylor family burying ground since it was the burial place of Zachary Taylor, twelfth president of the United States. The state of Kentucky donated 4.76 acres of land in 1927. An additional donation by the state of 11.17 acres, in 1928, plus the half-acre Taylor plot, increased the size of the national cemetery to its present 16.43 acres. The cemetery is surrounded by houses, and no further expansion is possible.

Even though the Taylor family plot is enclosed within the stone wall of the cemetery, it does not belong to the United States. Robert Taylor's niece was unsuccessful in her efforts to have the United States take title to the property. The Army judge advocate general ruled that it was impossible to determine the names of all living heirs, and condemnation proceedings due to public necessity, the only alternate course of action, was not believed warranted. The Taylor family burying ground is cared for and maintained by the government, however, out of respect for the former president.

Colonel Richard Taylor, a Revolutionary War soldier and father of a President Taylor, founded this family burying ground. He died on January 13, 1829, and is interred in the plot. The remains of some 50 members of the Taylor family are also interred here. It is owned by the heirs at law of the late Robert Hornsby Taylor, son of President Taylor's brother, Hancock Taylor.

Zachary Taylor was born in Orange County, Virginia, on November 24, 1784, shortly before his father and mother moved to Kentucky. He was a soldier in the war of 1812, the Black Hawk Indian War, and the Florida wars with the Seminole Indians, and was one of the outstanding generals in the war with Mexico (1846–48). Taylor spent most of his adult life in military service or as a Louisiana planter, and he had little experience in political matters. However, his military exploits and colorful career as a soldier were sufficient to gain for him the presidential nomination of the Whig Party in the campaign of 1848. He was elected president in 1848, defeating Lewis Case of Michigan, the Democratic candidate, and former President Martin Van Buren of the Free-Soil Party. Taylor's election as the candidate of the Whigs with virtually no party platform other than his military abilities marked the final triumph at the polls for that party in a national election.

Zachary Taylor's presidency was of short duration. He died of typhus on July 9, 1850, after only 16 months in office. It was a turbulent time whose central issues included national

Gravesite and statue of Zachary Taylor in Zachary Taylor National Cemetery, 1929.

expansion and slavery. The outcome of the Mexican War meant the opening of land available for settlement, and interest in California was heightened by the discovery of gold. Opening of these areas made the question of slavery a critical issue. Taylor, being a slaveholding Southerner, shocked the South by taking a strong stand against the extension of slavery. His 40 years in the army had imbued him with a strong nationalist spirit, and he was trying to preserve the Union when he died. He was the second president of the United States to die while in office. Vice President Millard Fillmore succeeded him as president.

President Taylor's remains and those of his wife, Margaret Mackall Smith, who died in 1852, were initially interred in the Taylor family burying ground. The state of Kentucky erected a 50-foot granite shaft surmounted by a life size figure of Zachary Taylor in 1883. It is located about 30 feet from the new Taylor tomb, which was erected by the United States in 1926. The original vault is still in the family burying ground. The new mausoleum, of classic Roman design, is constructed of limestone, and the interior is lined with marble. Over double glass-paneled bronze doors is the inscription "1784 Zachary Taylor 1850."

Only four former presidents are interred in national cemeteries: Taylor; John F. Kennedy and William Howard Taft, both of whom are interred in Arlington National Cemetery; and Andrew Johnson, who is interred in the cemetery that bears his name in Tennessee. Each year on November 24, President Taylor's birthdate, a wreath laying ceremony is conducted at the Taylor mausoleum by military personnel from Fort Knox, Kentucky, under authority of the President's Committee on Commemoration of Former Presidents.

It is interesting to note that Zachary Taylor served as an aide to General Andrew Jackson and President James Monroe. Abraham Lincoln and Jefferson Davis, who married Taylor's daughter, served under him. Both Ulysses S. Grant and Robert E. Lee were with Taylor in the Mexican War.

Ten years after the cemetery was established, only 286 interments had been made. With the close of World War II and the return of the remains of many decedents from overseas for final burial, however, the cemetery was used more. Zachary Taylor National Cemetery has accommodated 340 group burials of 1,587 remains. The only unknown decedent interred in the cemetery is included in one of these group burials. The largest group burial is of 23 decedents whose remains are individually unidentifiable.

In late 1974, a tornado ripped through Louisville and uprooted or destroyed many trees in the cemetery. Two large trees guarding the Taylor mausoleum were uprooted and broken off. The mausoleum sustained only minor damage to a small section of the back right corner. When Robert Taylor, the administrator of the Taylor estate, was called to be informed of the damage to the Taylor plot and how the cemetery system proposed to repair it and replace the trees, he commented, "You fellows have been doing a good job of caring for the old gentleman and his lady for nearly 50 years, and I see no reason to meddle now."

As of September 30, 2008, a total of 13,530 interments had been made in the cemetery. Along with President Zachary Taylor, a Marine killed in the Beirut massacre on October 23, 1983, three soldiers who died in the Gander, Newfoundland air crash on December 12, 1985, and two Medal of Honor recipients are interred here. The cemetery is closed for interments except for those in reserved gravesites and second interments in existing graves under the single gravesite per family policy.

The Medal of Honor recipient, John C. Squires, was killed in action subsequent to the engagement in which he was awarded the medal.

†**John C. Squires,** Sec A, Grave 1359. Sergeant (then Private First Class), U.S. Army, Company A, 30th Infantry, 3d Infantry Division. Place and date: Near Padiglione, Italy, 23–24 April 1944.
Citation: For conspicuous gallantry and intrepidity at risk of life above and beyond the call of duty. At the start of his company's attack on strongly held enemy positions in and around Spaccasassi Creek, near Padiglione, Italy, on the night of 23–24 April 1944, Pfc. Squires, platoon messenger, participating in his first offensive action, braved intense artillery, mortar, and antitank gun fire in order to investigate the effects of an antitank mine explosion on the leading platoon. Despite shells which burst close to him, Pfc. Squires made his way 50 yards forward to the advance element, noted the situation, reconnoitered a new route of advance and informed his platoon leader of the casualties sustained and the alternate route. Acting without orders, he rounded up stragglers, organized a group of lost men into a squad and led them forward. When the platoon reached Spaccasassi Creek and established an outpost, Pfc. Squires, knowing that almost all of the noncommissioned officers were casualties, placed eight men in position of his own volition, disregarding enemy machine gun, machine-pistol, and grenade fire which covered the creek draw. When his platoon had been reduced to 14 men, he brought up reinforcements twice. On each trip he went through barbed wire and across an enemy minefield, under intense artillery and mortar fire. Three times in the early morning the outpost was counterattacked. Each time Pfc. Squires ignored withering enemy automatic fire and grenades which struck all around him, and fired hundreds of rounds of rifle, Browning automatic rifle, and captured German Spandau machine gun ammunition at the enemy, inflicting numerous casualties and materially aiding in repulsing the attacks. Following these fights, he moved 50 yards to the south end of the outpost and engaged 21 German soldiers in individual machine gun duels at point-blank range, forcing all 21 enemy to surrender and cap-

turing 13 more Spandau guns. Learning the function of this weapon by questioning a German officer prisoner, he placed the captured guns in position and instructed other members of his platoon in their operation. The next night when the Germans attacked the outpost again he killed three and wounded more Germans with captured potato-masher grenades and fire from his Spandau gun. Private Squires was killed in a subsequent action.

Willie Sandlin, Sec. E, Grave 10A. Sergeant, U.S. Army, Company A, 132nd Infantry, 33rd Division. Place and Date: At Bois-de Forges, France, 26 September 1918.

Citation: He showed conspicuous gallantry in action by advancing alone directly on a machine-gun nest which was holding up the line with its fire.

Former superintendents/directors of the cemetery are:

James W. Dell, July 1932–June 1935
Thomas P. Boston, June 1935–December 1942
Clarence E. Suders, January 1943–April 1950
John J. Carr, April 1950–March 1955
Martin T. Corley, May 1955–March 1958
Albion H. McLellan, Jr., March 1958–March 1961
Walter M. Mick, April 1961–January 1962
Louis B. Hellmeyer, January 1962–February 1964
Clifton Cockrell, February 1964–April 1965
Metro Kowalchick, May 1965–August 1967
James D. Simms, August 1967–January 1969
Louis B. Baughman, January 1969–August 1969

Oscar P. Findley, August 1969–August 1970
Jack A. Morris, August 1970–April 1972
Andrew F. Szilvasi, April 1972–July 1973
William G. Kaiser, July 1973–January 1975
Joe D. Willard, March 1975–May 1975
Robert E. Bevering, December 1975–November 1977
Milo D. Hayden, January 1978–August 1980
Dennis P. Gura, August 1980–February 1983
David M. Cariota, April 1983–May 1985
Gary Peak, 1985–2005
Patrick Lovett, 2005–Present

The cemetery is now part of the Kentucky National Cemetery Complex.

Confederate Cemeteries

Camp Chase Confederate Cemetery

2900 Sullivant Avenue
Columbus, Ohio 43204

The cemetery is situated in Franklin County, approximately six miles west of downtown Columbus. The 1.84 acres of ground were originally established as Camp Chase Confederate Cemetery in 1862. It was officially designated a Confederate cemetery in 1879. The government condemned the land in 1952 and acquired title to the property.

The remains of Confederate prisoners of war at Camp Chase were originally buried in the City Cemetery at Columbus, and were later removed to the Camp Chase Confederate Cemetery, which was established on a portion of the prison grounds. Remains of 31 Confederates buried at Camp Dennison were also removed to this cemetery shortly after the end of the Civil War.

The Boulder Monument in the Memorial Arch at the entrance to the cemetery was erected in July 1902 and bears the inscription "2260 Confederate Soldiers of the War 1861–1865 buried in this enclosure." The March 23, 1955, report of inspection indicates that there are 2,122 gravesites marked by headstones for known dead and one marked unknown, and that there are 2,168 deceased interred in this cemetery.

Each year memorial services for the Confederate dead are held by the United Daughters of the Confederacy on the Sunday nearest the birthday of Jefferson Davis (June 3).

Camp Chase Confederate Cemetery, 1962.

Confederate Mound, Oak Woods Cemetery
1035 E. 67th Street
Chicago, Illinois 60637

The cemetery is situated in Cook County, in Oak Woods Cemetery, Section K, Divisions 1 and 2, in Hyde Park, Chicago, Illinois.

The Mound (1.58) acres is the present burial place of the remains of Confederate dead originally buried in the City Cemetery and near the smallpox hospital at Camp Douglas.

Confederate Mound, Oak Woods Cemetery.

It was first occupied in 1866 when the remains from the latter burial grounds were removed. The following year, those buried in the City Cemetery were also removed. The individual graves are not marked, but Confederate associations under the leadership of the United Confederate Veterans solicited funds and erected on the Mound a granite monument which was dedicated in 1896. An act approved in 1910 extended the time for the marking of Confederate graves and provided for the raising of the monument and mound, while stipulating that to mark the graves, the United States should provide a sub-base. On the monument erected by the Confederate associations and on the sub-base, 16 bronze plaques were placed listing the names of 4,243 known and 32 unknown Confederate soldiers, together with a general inscription referring to the raising of the monument. The cemetery register shows the names of 39 citizens and 143 soldiers removed in addition to the names listed on the monument (per report of commissioner for marking Confederate graves, 1912).

Twelve Union guards who died at Camp Douglas are also interred in the plot. Their graves are marked by individual headstones. The total number of interments in the cemetery is 6,229.

Confederate Stockade Cemetery
Johnson's Island
Sandusky, Ohio 44870

Situated in Ottawa County on Johnson's Island, Sandusky Bay, Ohio, approximately four miles from Sandusky, the cemetery occupies land donated to the United States in 1931

Confederate Stockade, Johnson's Island, Ohio.

by the United Daughters of the Confederacy. In 1862, the 1.22-acre tract was used as a prison burial ground for Confederate commissioned officers, and was established that year as a Confederate plot.

The original deed to the property gives the acreage as 1.07. A 1905 survey shows 1.22 acres because of the changing bay line which is the boundary on the east.

The prison was primarily for the confinement of Confederate officers although a few enlisted men were also interred in the cemetery. There are 153 known and 52 unknown graves, but the cemetery register shows 246 names, of which 20 were citizens and 22 were later removed. Other records state that there are 206 Confederates buried in the cemetery. A Confederate statue was erected by the United Daughters of the Confederacy in 1910.

Crown Hill Confederate Burial Plot
700 W. 38th Street
Indianapolis, Indiana 46208

The 0.016 acre plot, situated in Marion County in Crown Hill Cemetery, Section 32, Lot 285, was purchased from the Crown Hill Cemetery in 1931.

Crown Hill Confederate Lot.

As stated in an annual inspection report dated August 7, 1950, "the Mission of the Crown Hill Confederate Cemetery is a memorial and burial plot for 1,616 Unknown Confederate Soldiers removed from Greenlawn Cemetery, Indianapolis, Indiana, October 27, 1931." The Confederate soldiers interred in the plot died at Camp Morton during the Civil War. A monument erected on the plot in 1933 bears the inscription "Remains of 1616 Unknown Confederate Soldiers who died at Indianapolis while Prisoners of War." One unknown Confederate soldier was removed from Greenlawn Cemetery on June 30, 1945, and interred in gravesite 26. There are 26 gravesites for the 1,617 remains.

The genealogy division and the archives division of the Indiana State Library, 140 N. State Avenue, Indianapolis, IN 46204, have records through which the names of the Confederate soldiers who died in the prison camp at Camp Morton have been identified. These are from inscriptions on stones which were in the old Greenlawn Cemetery; clippings from Indianapolis newspapers; books written about Camp Morton; a newspaper list of the soldiers who died there; an article by William Herschel in the *Indianapolis News* on October 3, 1931, about their removal from Greenlawn Cemetery to Crown Hill Cemetery; and information from the records of Charles Williams, government undertaker at Camp Morton.

North Alton Confederate Cemetery
635 Rozier Street
Alton, Illinois 62003

The cemetery is situated in Madison County in the northern part of the city of Alton, in the area originally established in 1855 as a cemetery to serve the Illinois State Prison. It was established as a Confederate cemetery in 1867.

Confederate Monument, North Alton Confederate Cemetery, 1955.

The cemetery occupies 2.45 acres inside the fence and 1.5 acres outside. Records indicate that the government acquired some of the land by donation and purchase in 1867, and more by purchase in 1941. Ownership of 0.29 of the 1.5 acres purchased is questionable. On December 22, 1954, the Office of the Chief of Engineers advised, "It is believed that all boundaries ... are correct, with the exception of the westerly boundary, which will require a survey to clarify," but recommended that no survey be accomplished "since the records indicate that there is no intent to acquire Cemetery property westerly of the road...." This recommendation was approved by the Office of the Quartermaster General on January 5, 1955.

There are 1,635 interments and, technically, 900 gravesites available in the cemetery. The Confederate Monument, erected in 1910, marks the graves collectively. It is 58 feet high, and on 6 bronze plaques attached to the monument are the names of 1,354 Confederate soldiers which include those buried on Smallpox Island. There is one headstone to mark one individual grave.

Point Lookout Confederate Cemetery
Point Lookout, Maryland

The cemetery is located on Maryland Highway 5, approximately 80 miles from Washington, D.C.

Confederate remains are interred in a common mound. Originally, these Confederate prisoners of war were buried in two cemeteries near the prison camp. In 1870, the state of Maryland had the remains removed to a better location about one mile inland. They were buried in a common mound as the individual graves could not be identified, the wooden headboards which marked the graves having been destroyed by fire several years earlier. In 1910, the state requested the federal government to assume the care of these dead in the same manner as that practiced elsewhere and, toward that end, passed an act relinquishing all right, title, and interest in the cemetery. The United States marked the common grave with a granite monument of reinforced concrete approximately 85 feet high. Twelve bronze tablets giving the names and command of 3,383 known Confederate soldiers, and 1 unknown, were affixed to the monument.

Rock Island Confederate Cemetery
Rock Island Arsenal
Rock Island, Illinois 61202

The cemetery is situated in Rock Island County, on the island of Rock Island Arsenal, about 2,500 yards northwest of Rock Island National Cemetery. The land was transferred from the military reservation in 1863.

During the Civil War a military prison was established on Rock Island for the confinement of Confederate prisoners. The first prisoners, taken at the Battle of Lookout Mountain, Tennessee, arrived from Chattanooga in December 1863. In a period of about 2½ years more than 12,000 prisoners were confined here, and 1,900 of them died. The total number of interments is 1,950, and burials were discontinued on July 11, 1865.

Rock Island Confederate Cemetery.

Soldiers' Lots

Albany Rural Cemetery Soldiers' Lot
Albany Cemetery Assn.
Rural Cemetery
Albany, New York 12204

The lot is situated in Albany County in Rural Cemetery, Lot 7, Section 75, an elevated plateau overlooking the Hudson River near Albany, New York.

The property (0.16 acre) was set aside by the Albany Cemetery Association on June 17, 1862, for deceased members of the Union Army. Although no deed was ever issued, the property was donated to the United States "for the burial of soldiers who have fallen or may fall in the Civil War." It has never been officially named.

Interments were made mostly from the military hospitals near Albany, although a few bodies were brought from the South and a few burials were made after the war. There are 149 interments in the Lot and none have been made since 1897. The Grand Army of the Republic erected a special monument in 1870.

The grave of Chester A. Arthur, 21st president of the United States, is located in this cemetery, although not on government property.

Allegheny Cemetery Soldiers' Lot
4734 Butler Street
Pittsburgh, Pennsylvania 15201

Soldiers' monument, Allegheny Soldiers' Lot, ca. 1961.

The lot is situated in Allegheny County in Lot 66, Section 33, of the Allegheny Cemetery, which is located at 47th and Butler streets in Pittsburgh.

The property (0.232 acre) was donated to the United States by the cemetery corporation in 1875. Burials were mostly Civil War veterans, including 15 Confederates and some veterans of the Spanish-American War and World War I. There have been no interments since 1927. The lot contains 303 graves; 290 are known persons, 11 individual graves are of unknowns, and 2 graves numbers 175 and 176 contain the remains of 7 unknown U.S. Volunteers brought from Mexico. A 16-foot special monument was erected by the Allegheny County Ladies Memorial Association.

Ashland Cemetery Soldiers' Lot
Ashland Cemetery
Carlisle, Pennsylvania 17013

The lot is situated in Cumberland County, in lots 212–265, Section D, in Ashland Cemetery, about one-fourth mile southeast of Carlisle, Pennsylvania, on East High Street.

The 0.198 acre soldiers' lot was sold to the United States in 1865, as a burial place for deceased soldiers from Carlisle Barracks.

The soldiers' lot includes a common grave for 500 decedents. Around 1934 a government Civil War–type headstone was erected at the site bearing the inscription "500 Unknown U.S. Soldiers" as it was believed that the decedents were unknown casualties of the Battle of Gettysburg. Subsequent investigation and research indicated that the remains of 35 known decedents are interred in this common grave with the unknown remains, and that none of the known decedents was a casualty of the Gettysburg campaign. In July 1960, the government erected a specially designed new monument at the site. A bronze plaque on the new granite monument bears the inscription "500 U.S. Soldiers of the Civil War Are Here Interred (names of the 35 decedents). The Others Are Known But to God." In addition, 23 graves are marked with individual headstones, 19 known and 4 unknown. These are soldiers who died at Carlisle Barracks.

Baxter Springs Soldiers' Lot
Baxter Springs, Kansas 66713

The Soldiers' Lot, occupying a total of 0.714 acre, was donated to the United States in 1869, 1875, 1877, and 1887, by the city of Baxter Springs. It is situated in the Baxter Springs City Cemetery (north central portion). Baxter Springs is approximately 60 miles south of Fort Scott, Kansas.

One hundred sixty-three of the soldiers killed in Quantrell's Massacre in 1863 were interred in the plot. It was the intent of the government to remove the bodies to the Springfield National Cemetery, but citizens of Baxter Springs petitioned to have them remain, giving the government the privilege of selecting the necessary grounds in a tract of land they had purchased for a cemetery, donating the land, and agreeing to keep the graves in good order. The deceased were buried as Knowns and the graves marked with wooden headboards, which for unknown reasons were later removed. The government erected a special monument in 1886 to the 163 Unknowns buried in the unmarked graves. The names of 108 soldiers appear on the monument which is 8 feet by 8 feet and 20 feet high, with a statue of a soldier on top.

There are 254 interments in 121 gravesites.

Evergreen Cemetery Soldiers' Lot
25 South Alexandria Pike
Newport, Kentucky 41072

The lot is situated in Campbell County in Section 25 of Evergreen Cemetery in Southgate, Kentucky, which is about two miles from Newport. The lots were set aside in 1892 for burial of deceased soldiers at Fort Thomas. The fort was deactivated in 1947, and in 1950 the post cemetery was declared a soldiers' lot. Although it has never been officially named, it contains 138 interments.

Baxter Springs Soldiers' Lot, 1954.

In 1952, the government released to the Evergreen Cemetery Company 188 unused gravesites. These are presently being sold for the burial of honorably discharged veterans, and monuments on these sites are restricted to government headstones.

Forest Hill Cemetery Soldiers' Lot
1 Speedway Road
Madison, Wisconsin 53705

The 0.36-acre lot was donated by the city of Madison in 1886, and an additional 20-foot strip was donated in 1908. It is situated in Dane County, in Section 34 of Forest Hill Cemetery. It was established as a soldiers' lot in 1862.

The original burial of 222 was from the general hospital in the city. Interments now include Civil War, Spanish-American War, and World War I veterans. The last interment was made in 1931. Approximately 100 yards distant is a plot known as Confederate Rest wherein are interred 140 Confederates who died while prisoners of war at Camp Randall. Most of them were from Alabama, but a few were from Louisiana and Arkansas. For many years, up to the time of her death in 1897, Mrs. Alice W. Waterman, formerly of Baton Rouge, Louisiana, cared for these graves at her own expense. Her remains, at her request, are within the enclosure. The marker over her grave was furnished by the U.D.C., which also erected a monument to the Confederate dead. The plot is not owned by the govern-

Forest Hill Soldiers' Lot, 1964.

ment, but in the early 1900s, the graves were marked by the Commission for Marking Graves of the Confederate Dead.

There are two other special monuments in the lot: the Soldiers' Orphans Monument, erected in 1873, and a monument "To the Unknown Dead" erected in 1891 by the Woman's Relief Corps No. 37.

Forest Home Cemetery Soldiers' Lot
2405 West Forest Home Avenue
Milwaukee, Wisconsin 53215

Situated in Milwaukee County within Forest Home Cemetery, the 0.038-acre soldiers' lot, established in 1863, consists of lots 5, 6, 7, and 8 in Block 5, Section 24, of the cemetery. The lots were purchased in 1872 from Forest Home Episcopal Cemetery.

Original burials were of deceased from the general hospitals in the city. According to the cemetery records, 21 Civil War veterans are interred here. The 1896 report of the inspector of national cemeteries indicated that there were 24. The late Brigadier General William "Billy" Mitchell, U.S. Army, is buried in a family lot in this cemetery. He organized the I Corps Air Service in France in 1918, ushering in the era of the modern air force.

Forest Lawn Cemetery Soldiers' Lot
40th Street, Forest Lawn Avenue
Omaha, Nebraska 68112

The lot is situated in Douglas County in Forest Lawn Cemetery, lots 15, 21, and 22, in Section 9, on 0.039 acre that was set aside without a written agreement in 1881, and established as a soldiers' lot in 1887. The lot is not owned by the government, and it has never been officially named.

The land was established as a post cemetery for Fort Omaha, which was renamed Fort Crook in 1891. When Fort Crook was established as a military reservation in 1889, a post cemetery was also established and use of Forest Lawn Cemetery was discontinued. No interments have been made in the soldiers' lot since 1920. The Forest Lawn Cemetery register contains the names of 41 deceased who are interred in the soldiers' lot.

Fort Crawford Cemetery Soldiers' Lot
413 South Beaumont Road
Prairie du Chien, Wisconsin 53821

The lot is situated in Crawford County, in Block 13 of Fort Crawford Military Tract, on part of lots 3, 7, and 8, in the heart of the city.

The cemetery is on the former site of the Fort Crawford Military Reservation, where the first interment took place in 1829. The federal government purchased the 0.59-acre site in 1904 and 1905. Original interments were of members of the 1st and 5th Infantry regiments stationed at Fort Crawford. The cemetery contains eight aboveground tombs of beautiful design which appear to have been erected by the regiments. Authentic records on interments do not exist, and there is no burial register listing the 64 burials. In August 1947,

Fort Crawford Cemetery Soldiers' Lot, 1964.

four remains were removed from the Protestant Cemetery at Prairie du Chien and reinterred here.

Near the entrance to the cemetery is a monument to Jefferson Davis which was erected by the United Daughters of the Confederacy. Fort Crawford is one of at least four places that claim that Davis met and eloped with the daughter of Zachary Taylor while stationed here. A good story, but not true (see Fort Gibson and Fort Smith national cemeteries. Fort Scott is the fourth location). There is also a bronze plaque mounted on an iron post, inscribed "U.S. Military Cemetery Fort Crawford Est. 1816."

Fort Mackinac Post Cemetery
Mackinac Island, Michigan

The cemetery is situated in the Mackinac Island State Park, located on Mackinac Island in Lake Huron. In 1990, Congressman Bob Traxler secured the passage of Public Law 101-237, which required the Department of Veterans Affairs to contract with the state of Michigan for the operation and maintenance of the small cemetery.

Fort Mackinac was established as a U.S. military post in 1796. Burials here were of soldiers and family members only. The first battle of the War of 1812 fought on U.S. soil took place at Fort Mackinac, and 17 U.S. and 6 British soldiers from that encounter were buried in the cemetery in 1814. Seventy of the 142 graves are unidentified. Two sailors who drowned in a 19th century shipwreck off the island are buried here. There have been no interments since 1895, when the U.S. military left the island.

Fort Winnebago Cemetery Soldiers' Lot
Portage, Wisconsin 53901

The lot is situated in Columbia County, near the site of Old Fort Winnebago, approximately 2½ miles north of Portage, Wisconsin.

Originally established as the Fort Winnebago Post Cemetery in 1835, the two-acre site was designated a soldiers' lot in 1862. The entire reservation was sold in 1853 at public sale. Although the cemetery property was not specifically exempted from the sale, its area was not included in the area given in the deed and, hence, the United States appears to possess a valid title to the property.

There are 75 interments in the lot, including Silas Wentworth, who died July 6, 1819, and Elisha Parmerton, who died October 11, 1819. Alexander Porter, a Revolutionary War veteran who died in 1833 and was originally interred in a cemetery in Freedom, New York, was reinterred in Grave No. 3 in 1924. Other interments include veterans of various Indian wars, the Revolutionary War, War of 1812, Civil War, Spanish-American War, and World War I.

A granite boulder monument to the unknown dead was erected by the "Wau-Bun" chapter of the D.A.R. in 1924. The monument also marks the site of the 1827 surrender of Winnebago Indian Chief Red Wing after a foray against the settlers.

Fort Winnebago Cemetery Soldiers' Lot.

Green Mount Cemetery Soldiers' Lot

250 State Street
Montpelier, Vermont 05602

Situated in Washington County, Lot 324 in Green Mount Cemetery, the lot was donated to the United States in 1866 after having been established in 1865. The lot contains 450 square feet and 8 interments. The original interments were four Union soldiers.

Green Mount Soldiers' Lot, 1960.

Lake Side Cemetery Soldiers' Lot

3781 Gratiot Street
Port Huron, Michigan 48060

The lot is situated in St. Clair County in Lake Side Cemetery, lots 144 through 159. The 0.174 acre was donated to the United States in 1881 when the 135 remains from Old Fort Gratiot were removed to this cemetery. A Concord granite monument 23 feet high was erected by the government in 1884.

Mound Cemetery Soldiers' Lot

1147 West Boulevard
Racine, Wisconsin 53405

Situated in Racine County, in Mound Cemetery, lots 1, 5, and 6 in Block 18, the lot occupies 0.03 acre purchased from the city of Racine in 1868 with a guarantee of perpetual care by the city.

Of the 14 remains interred, 13 are known and 1 unknown. The 13 known were members of Wisconsin units. According to the 1869 and 1870–71 reports of the inspector of national cemeteries, original interments were of deceased from the hospitals in the city and from nearby Camp Utley. The cemetery maintains records of the known interments.

Mound City Soldiers' Lot
Mound City, Kansas 66056

The lot is situated in Linn County in Woodlawn Cemetery, lots 262 and 263. Mound City is about 30 miles from Fort Scott, Kansas.

The deed for the original purchase in 1874 covered a lot 48 feet by 158 feet. An enclosing wall and chain link fence erected by the WPA in 1940 encompassed an additional tri-

Mound City Soldiers' Lot.

angular section measuring 10 feet by 46 feet by 40 feet, which has not been deeded to the United States.

When 39 soldiers were killed in the area in 1864, Woodlawn Cemetery set aside the lot now known as the Mound City Soldiers' Lot for their interment. In 1888, the bodies of other Union soldiers buried in Linn County, including some unknowns, were removed to this cemetery. There are 80 interments. In 1889, the United States erected a granite monument in honor of the Civil War dead. The record of interments in the soldiers' lot is maintained at Fort Scott National Cemetery.

Mount Moriah Cemetery Soldiers' Lot
62nd St. and Kingsessing Avenue
Philadelphia, Pennsylvania

Situated in Mount Moriah Cemetery, Lot 1, Section 200. The original deed to the lot cannot be located. In 1927, the recorder of deeds of Philadelphia County refused to accept a duplicate deed and insisted on having an original or confirmation deed. As a result of prolonged negotiations, the Cemetery Association executed a deed on January 19, 1957, which vested title to the soldiers' lot in the United States government.

Original burials were the deceased from a Civil War hospital, including six Confederates. A few bodies were removed to Philadelphia National Cemetery, but in 1906 the Office of the

Mount Moriah Cemetery Soldiers' Lot, 1963.

Quartermaster General advised the depot quartermaster that since the private cemetery was not abandoned and neither the Cemetery Association nor outside parties had requested it, there appeared to be no valid reason to remove the bodies to Philadelphia National Cemetery. There is 1 Unknown interred in Grave 2, among the 404 interments in the soldiers' lot.

Mount Pleasant Cemetery Soldiers' Lot
North Street
Augusta, Maine 04330

The lot is situated in Kennebec County in Mount Pleasant Cemetery. In 1862, the cemetery donated lots 262, 263, 294, and 295 in the western division, an area measuring 30 feet by 50 feet. In 1870, it made an additional donation of lots 17, 18, 19, 40, 49, and 51 in the eastern division, an area of 30 feet by 75 feet. The deed for the lots donated in 1862 was lost, and a new deed was issued in 1933.

There are 60 interments in the eastern division, 15 known and 45 unknown, and 29 interments in the western division, 13 known and 16 unknown.

In 1906, the United States erected a monument "In Memory of Union Soldiers (40 Known and 15 Unknown) who died in the hospitals of Augusta in 1861–1865." This monument is located in the eastern division. A granite monument inscribed "Set Williams Post #13, G.A.R." is located in the center of the western division. Unknown gravesites in this division are marked only with G.A.R. metal markers.

Bronze identifying signs were placed in the western division (1966) and eastern division (1967). The inscription on each reads "United States of America Soldiers' Lots."

Oakdale Cemetery Soldiers' Lot
2501 Eastern Avenue
Davenport, Iowa 52807

The lot is situated in Scott County in Lot 14 of Oakdale Cemetery.

Interments include 71 Civil War dead, 1 Spanish-American War dead, and 1 child. Originally, burials were made in Lot 140, Section 2, in the center of Section 2, and in a portion of Section 13. Those buried in the center of Section 2 (seven remains) were soldiers killed during the Battle of Fort Donelson, Tennessee, on February 15, 1862. They were the first Iowa victims of the Civil War.

Around 1888, roughly 160 bodies were removed to the Rock Island and Keokuk national cemeteries. In 1900, the rest of the bodies were removed to the G.A.R. Plot, where all subsequent government burials were made. In 1940, the G.A.R. conveyed all interest in its plot (Lot 14) to the Oakdale Cemetery Association. In 1941, the United States exchanged the lots it had acquired in 1866 for Lot 14.

Prospect Hill Cemetery Soldiers' Lot
94 South Main Street, Box 653
Brattleboro, Vermont 05301

The lot is situated in Windham County, in the southern portion of Prospect Hill Cemetery.

The 19 interments were decedents from the hospital at Brattleboro. All but one are known.

Prospect Hill Soldiers' Lot
700 North George Street
York, Pennsylvania 17404

The lot is situated in York County in Prospect Hill Cemetery, Lot 689, Section A.

Burials were made from the general hospital in York. There is no record of exact date of establishment, but historical records indicate burials were made as early as 1862. The soldiers' lot was first located on the west slope of a hill but was moved to a more favorable location on the eastern slope. A monument in the center was erected by the citizens of York in 1874. There are 161 known and 2 unknown veterans of the Civil War buried in the lot.

There are no headstones; instead, the names are inscribed on 2 continuous circular curbs with breaks only for gateways.

Prospect Hill Soldiers' Lot, 1960.

Woodland Cemetery Soldiers' Lot
6901 Woodland Avenue
Cleveland, Ohio 44104

The lot is situated in Cuyahoga County in Woodland Cemetery. Lot 48 in Section 14, containing 16 gravesites in an area of 28 feet by 23 feet, was purchased in 1863. Lots 59 and 60, in Section 10, containing 32 gravesites in an area of 40 feet by 16 feet, were purchased in 1868. The two lots are not contiguous.

Original interments consisted of the remains of 41 Union soldiers, 38 known and 3 unknown, which were removed to the Woodland Cemetery from a cemetery on the west side of the Cuyahoga River.

Woodlawn Cemetery Soldiers' Lot
Harvard Street
Ayer, Massachusetts 01432

The lot is situated in Middlesex County in Woodlawn Cemetery, Section 1, lots 195, 203, 206, and 211. Ayer, Massachusetts, is near Fort Devens. The lots were purchased from Woodlawn Cemetery in 1918, and cover 1,056 square feet.

The majority of the 52 men interred in the soldiers' lot died at Fort Devens in 1918. The last interment was made in 1931. In 1937, it was strongly recommended that the remains be removed to the Fort Devens post cemetery, but no action was taken. All deceased are known and their graves are marked by government headstones.

Monuments

Fort Phil Kearny Monument Site

The monument site is located about one-tenth mile from U.S. Highway 87 in Sheridan County, near Sheridan, Wyoming.

The site was ceded to the United States by an act of the Wyoming legislature on February 19, 1903. The monument, known locally as the Fetterman Monument, was erected in 1904 to the memory of the soldiers who were killed in the Fetterman Massacre by Sioux Indians on December 21, 1866, approximately five miles north of Fort Phil Kearny. The area, 0.757 acre, will accommodate 400 gravesites, but the deed states that it is "to be used as a site for the erection of a monument to the memory of the soldiers in the Fort Phil Kearny Massacre."

In December 1953, the Office of the Quartermaster General took action to effect a transfer of the site to the Department of the Interior, but the offer was rejected by the acting secretary of the interior. The monument site is maintained by the director of Black Hills National Cemetery, Sturgis, South Dakota.

Union Confederate Monument Site
227 East 28th Street Terrace
Kansas City, Missouri 64108

The monument is located in Jackson County in the Union Cemetery. The 7.84-square-foot site was donated to the United States by Union Cemetery in 1912.

It consists of a monument to 15 Confederate prisoners of war who died in Kansas City and are buried in unknown graves in Union Cemetery. The names of the soldiers are on two tablets fastened to the monument. The monument site is administered by the city park department, Kansas City, Missouri, at no cost to the government.

Woodlawn Cemetery Confederate Monument Site
North 3rd Street & 4th Avenue
Terre Haute, Indiana 47802

The Confederate monument, situated in Vigo County in Woodlawn Cemetery, was first erected in 1912 on a six by eight foot site donated by Woodlawn Cemetery. The monument marked the burial place of 11 Confederate soldiers who died at Terre Haute while prisoners of war, and whose individual graves could not be identified. The names of the 11, plus 2 civilians, are inscribed on bronze tablets affixed to the monument. On February 27, 1951, an alternate site in the cemetery was obtained from the Board of Cemetery Regents, city of Terre Haute, in exchange for the original lot, and the monument was moved to the new site in October 1953. The new lot, at the intersection of Wabash and Central avenues in the southwest section, is 50 feet in diameter. The monument is maintained at no federal expense by Woodlawn Cemetery.

Special Installations

Congressional Cemetery
1801 E. Street, S.E.
Washington, D.C. 20003

The government lots are within the area of the Washington Parish Burial Grounds in Washington, D.C., formerly known as the Cemetery of Christ Church.

The original 100 burial sites were intended for members of Congress who died while in office. Interred in these lots, however, are not only congressmen but other high government officials: Henry Stephen Fox, British envoy to the United States; a number of famous Indians, including Push-Ma-Ta-Ha, a Choctaw Indian Chief; soldiers and sailors of the Revolution; and Confederate prisoners of war. There have been no interments in government owned lots since 1902.

There are 113 cenotaphs erected as memorials to individuals who are buried elsewhere. These cenotaphs, which are alike, occupy usually three gravesites, and in some cases four. The same design was used for 52 monuments erected as grave markers. Placement of cenotaphs as memorials in this cemetery was forbidden after 1876, primarily for aesthetic reasons.

In addition to Chief Push-Ma-Ta-Ha, who was known as "the White Man's Friend," eight other Indians are buried in the cemetery. They were members of various delegations to Congress who died while in Washington. Thirteen Confederates are buried in government-owned lots in Square 1104.

There is a large monument in the cemetery marking the burial place of 21 girls killed in an explosion at the Washington, D.C., arsenal on June 17, 1864. Someone had temporarily stored a large quantity of fireworks in the open next to the building where the girls were making cartridges. The heat of the summer sun apparently set off the fireworks, and a burning fuse blew through an open window igniting the exposed gunpowder where the girls were working.

The original donation of lots in 1816 was added with another donation in 1823 and the purchase of several lots in 1856. In 1856 and 1954, the government exchanged lots within the cemetery. The government now owns 806 lots, including 467 interments, 113 cenotaphs and 8 lots encroached on by monuments and cenotaphs. The cemetery is under the jurisdiction of the director of Quantico National Cemetery.

Two noted Americans buried in Congressional Cemetery but not in government-owned plots are John Philip Sousa, leader of the U.S. Marine Corps band who was noted worldwide as "the March King," and J. Edgar Hoover, director of the Federal Bureau of Investigation from 1924 until his death in 1972.

Mount Moriah Naval Plot
62nd Street & Kingsessing Avenue
Philadelphia, Pennsylvania 19142

This plot was originally part of the U.S. Naval Asylum. The name was changed to the U.S. Naval Home in 1889. In 1809, Paul Hamilton, secretary of the Navy, became concerned over the poor hospital conditions that existed to provide relief for indigent seamen who had served with honor and distinction during the Revolutionary War. In 1811 Congress approved an act establishing the asylum, but it was not until 1826 that a 24-acre tract once

Congressional Cemetery; Monument to victims of explosion at Washington arsenal.

belonging to the Penns was purchased. A Quaker family, the Pembertons, occupied the property (which they called the Manor) at that time. When the property was acquired, Navy patients were transferred from the hospital at the Philadelphia Naval Shipyard to the Pemberton Manor. From the time of the establishment of the Naval Asylum, half of the main building (Biddle Hall) was the Naval hospital and the other half housed the beneficiaries. The graveyard was used by both activities, as well as ships at the Naval yard.

In the following years, the asylum was also used for training Navy officers in navigation, language, mathematics, and similar subjects. In 1839, Secretary of the Navy James K. Paulding ordered 11 officers to enroll at the Naval Asylum for training in the above fields. Thus, the first Naval Academy was established in the north wing of the first floor. In 1845, the Naval Academy was moved to Annapolis, Maryland.

In 1846, the cemetery was moved to the northwest corner of the grounds and 51 bodies and a quantity of loose bones were transferred to the new site. The Civil War wounded overtaxed the capacity of the Naval hospital, and burial space in the cemetery was rapidly being depleted. The board of managers of the Naval Asylum in 1864 purchased a 10-acre tract in Mount Moriah Cemetery to handle future burials. At the asylum, a cemetery record was opened in which was to be entered information on all deceased buried in the new ground. The first burial in the new grounds was made on March 26, 1865. In February 1866, 351 bodies were removed from the old cemetery on the asylum grounds and reinterred in the new cemetery at Mount Moriah.

From about 1869 until 1880, the grounds fell into disrepair and records, except for beneficiaries of the home, were not maintained. In 1880, the grounds maintenance situation was corrected, and careful research and hard labor brought the records up to date.

The last burial from a ship at the Navy yard is believed to have been in the early 1920s. Since that time, burials have been restricted to residents of the Naval Home. On July 21, 1976, the Navy declared the Naval Home Cemetery as excess to the General Services Administration. The Naval Home was officially moved to Gulfport, Mississippi, on September 30, 1976, and the cemetery was transferred to the Veterans Administration (VA). A physical count of graves and headstones was made by VA personnel at the time of the transfer, and 2,400-plus interments were entered in VA records.

The plot is maintained by contract with the Mount Moriah Cemetery Association, under the supervision of the director of Beverly National Cemetery.

There are 10 Medal of Honor recipients interred in the Naval Plot:

Name	Service	War/Place/Date of Action	Section & Grave No.
Charles Baker	USN	Civil	2, 22-22
Albert E. Beyer	USN	Sp.-Amer.	1, 9-19
Joseph Killackey	USN	Boxer	4, 3-23
John Laverty	USN	Civil	3, 3-17
Nicholas Lear	USN	Civil	3, 3-3
Thomas G. Lyons (Alias Edward McBride)	USN	Civil	3, 4-3
James Martin	USMC	Civil	2, 24-19
Henry Shutes	USN	Civil	2, 22-1
August P. Teytand	USN	1909	5, 4-5
William Thompson	USN	Civil	2, 14-12

Lost Cemeteries

The 1870–71 report of the inspector of national cemeteries (dated April 20, 1872) stated that were a number of cemeteries inspected and or reported on that were no longer included in the records of the National Cemetery System. There were also a number of individual cemeteries or soldiers' lots reported on that were subsequently abandoned and the remains removed to other national cemeteries. In cases where the remains were moved, this information is included in this book with the cemeteries in which the bodies were reinterred.

The cemeteries and lots listed below are those on which records are no longer maintained by the federal government. Except for a few instances where the price was negligible, the land was donated to the United States for burial of Union soldiers. The grounds were acquired for burial of specific decedents and have been maintained over the years at no cost to the government.

This information is included only to make complete the record of national cemeteries and memorials.

Connecticut

Evergreen Cemetery, New Haven (inspected September 1, 1870). The 48 by 63 foot soldiers' lot is owned by the state and contains the remains of 117 Union soldiers who died in the general hospital in New Haven. Seventy other soldiers are buried with their families.

Roman Catholic Cemetery (Saint Bernard's), New Haven (inspected September 1, 1870). The 10 by 12 foot lot, owned by the federal government, contains the unmarked remains of 8 soldiers. Twenty-five other Union soldiers are buried here with their friends.

Delaware

In the incorporated cemeteries in the vicinity of Wilmington, there are reported to be 72 known and 13 unknown Union soldiers interred.

Illinois

Rose Hill Cemetery, Chicago (inspected June 25, 1870). The 317 Union dead are buried in several lots donated to the United States by the Cemetery Association. The burials were principally from the general hospital near the city, but some bodies were brought from the South. There were, in 1870, five monuments erected in or near these lots.

Graceland Cemetery (not inspected). About 100 Union soldiers buried in private lots by their friends.

Indiana

Oak Hill Cemetery, Evansville (not inspected). The United States purchased a lot in the incorporated cemetery for $300 and interred 588 known and 8 unknown soldiers who died in the general hospital at Evansville.

There are 340 Union soldiers, all known, reported to be buried in 92 local cemeteries throughout the state. They were buried by their families or friends.

Maine

Eastport (inspected July 20, 1870). This is a small lot in which U.S. soldiers who died at Fort Sullivan were buried. It contains 10 graves. A monument was erected in memory of 18 members of Company K, Sixth Maine Volunteer Infantry.

Calais Cemetery (inspected August 23, 1870). The cemetery is about 2 miles northwest of the old steamboat wharf, and contains the graves or memorials of 24 Union soldiers. They are not together but with the families of the deceased.

Winthrop Street Cemetery, Augusta (inspected August 24, 1870). The cemetery contains the graves of 59 Union soldiers. The cemetery has never been subject to the control of the United States, nor were the burials made by the government. Five other soldiers are buried in this cemetery with their friends.

Forest City Cemetery, on Cape Elizabeth, Portland (inspected August 19, 1870). The cemetery contains 24 burials in a plot 90 feet by 54 feet.

Union soldiers are buried at other places in the state as well — 20 known and 10 unknown enlisted men.

Massachusetts

Garden Cemetery, Chelsea (inspected August 11, 1870). The citizens of Chelsea purchased a tract 48 feet by 28 feet, in which are interred 19 of the town's Union soldiers. There are 17 other Union soldiers buried in this cemetery with their friends.

Cambridge Cemetery (inspected August 11, 1870). There are 23 Union soldiers buried in a circular soldiers' lot 50 feet in diameter. Twenty other Union soldiers are buried with their families. The city of Cambridge erected a large granite monument in a public park near Harvard University, inscribed with the names of 357 local soldiers who "died in the war for the maintenance of the Union."

Village Cemetery, Dedham (inspected August 12, 1870). The soldiers' lot in the southwest corner of this cemetery contains 65 graves in one row. The state of Massachusetts erected a large granite monument with marble slabs on the four faces of the shaft inscribed with the names of the deceased soldiers. The monument is dedicated to the soldiers who died at Reidsville during the Civil War. The state owns the land.

Rural Cemetery, Worcester (not inspected). The cemetery contains the graves of 45 Union soldiers buried with their families or friends.

Hope Cemetery, Worcester (not inspected). The cemetery contains the remains of 38 soldiers buried with their friends.

There are 44 Union soldiers who were officially reported as interred at other places in the state.

Michigan

Elmwood Cemetery, Detroit (inspected September 21, 1870). The soldiers' lot, situated near the center of the cemetery, contains 74 interments. Sixty-two soldiers died in the general hospital in Detroit and the remaining 12 were interred between the end of the Civil War and the date of the cemetery inspection.

Other officially reported burials of Union soldiers in the state include 66 in the cemeteries near Grand Rapids, 30 in the City Cemetery at Jackson, and 23 in the post cemetery at Fort Wayne.

New Hampshire

"**Old Cemetery,**" Concord (inspected August 29, 1870). No soldiers' graves were found, but 10 were reported to be in the cemetery.

Valley Cemetery, Manchester (inspected August 30, 1870). There are 59 Union soldiers buried here with their friends.

Pine Grove Cemetery, Manchester (inspected August 30, 1870). There are nine Union soldiers buried in the potter's field. Also, nine Union soldiers are buried with their friends.

Proprietors' Cemetery, Portsmouth (inspected August 19, 1870). There are 55 Union soldiers buried here with their friends.

"**Old Cemetery,**" near Eastern Railway Station, Portsmouth (inspected August 19, 1870). There are seven soldiers buried among their friends.

Twelve known soldiers were officially reported as buried at other places in the state.

New Jersey

Fairmount Cemetery, Newark (inspected October 22, 1870). The 150 by 60 foot soldiers' lot contains the graves of 164 Union soldiers. The lot is maintained by the Cemetery Association.

New York

Mount Hope Cemetery, Rochester (inspected September 17, 1870). There are said to be 150 Union soldiers buried in the cemetery, nearly all with their families. There are also 10 soldiers buried in the potter's field. All graves are unmarked.

Forest Lawn Cemetery, Buffalo (inspected September 18, 1870). There are reportedly 26 Union soldiers buried here, probably with their families or friends.

Limestone Cemetery, Buffalo (not inspected). There are reported to be 10 Union soldiers buried here with their friends.

Official reports indicate 105 soldiers buried at other places in the state, excluding military posts.

Ohio

Green Lawn Cemetery, Columbus (inspected June 16, 1870). The soldiers' lot was purchased by the state of Ohio, and it contains the remains of 486 known and 6 unknown Union soldiers.

Spring Grove Cemetery, near Cincinnati (inspected June 17, 1870). The lot was donated to the federal government by the state. It contains 3 sections, each originally marked with a 32-pound iron gun. Under each of these guns is buried a general or field grade officer: Section A, General Robert McCook; Section B, Colonel F. Jones; and Section C, General T.J. Williams. The lot contains 994 remains in 932 graves. Of these, 339 were removed from Camp Dennison, where they were originally interred. The balance of the deceased came from hospitals in or near Cincinnati.

Cemetery at Gallipolis (not inspected). The soldiers' lot within the town cemetery contains the remains of 157 Union soldiers and 1 citizen.

Oakwood Cemetery, Sandusky (not inspected). Eleven Union soldiers are buried here.

Roman Catholic Cemetery, Cleveland (not inspected). Three officers and nine enlisted Union soldiers, all known, are interred here.

Pennsylvania

Harrisburgh Cemetery (inspected October 26, 1870). There are said to be 155 soldier burials in this cemetery, but very few graves are marked. Among them are the remains of 15 Confederate prisoners of war. All of the deceased are from Camp Curtin.

Cedar Grove Cemetery, Chambersburgh (inspected October 26, 1870). The small lot, 12 feet by 18 feet, contains the remains of 19 soldiers who died here soon after the Battle of Gettysburg. Only five of the graves were marked in 1870.

There were 330 known and 40 unknown soldier burials officially reported at other places in the state, excluding military posts.

Vermont

Prospect Hill Cemetery, Brattleborough (inspected August 31, 1871). The 50 by 30 foot lot purchased by the U.S. in the southwestern portion of the grounds contains 18 graves.

Six soldiers were officially reported as buried at other places within the state.

PART II

Other Cemeteries and Monuments

Department of the Army National Cemeteries

When the National Cemetery System came into existence in July 1862, management of cemeteries quite naturally came within the purview of the quartermaster general and quartermasters of local military commands. The Army had for many years been operating small burial grounds, called post cemeteries, at nearly every garrison where troops were stationed. The new national cemeteries were simply added to the quartermaster workload. The early history of the Department of the Army national cemeteries has been recounted in the history of the National Cemetery System, for in fact the Army had jurisdiction of all national cemeteries until the Government Reorganization Act of 1933 transferred 11 national cemeteries located on or adjacent to Civil War battlefields to the National Park Service of the Department of the Interior. In 1973, 83 of the remaining 85 national cemeteries were transferred to the Veterans Administration.

In September 1973, with the passage of Public Law 93-43, the National Cemeteries Act of 1973, all national cemeteries except Arlington, Soldiers' Home, and military post cemeteries were transferred to the Veterans Administration. The military continues to operate these cemeteries. Histories of Arlington and Soldier's Home national cemeteries are included here. Other Army post cemeteries and Navy installation cemeteries are listed below only if a Medal of Honor (MOH) recipient is interred there. The Naval base cemeteries are under the jurisdiction of the Department of the Navy. It should be noted that many servicemen and women and their dependents are interred in these and all other post and naval cemeteries.

Culebra Naval Station Cemetery, San Juan, PR. MOH: Alexander J. Foley, USMC, Boxer Rebellion (1910).

Guantanamo Bay Naval Station Cemetery, Guantanamo Bay, Cuba. MOH: Frederick T. Fisher, USN, Philippines (1906).

Post cemetery, Fort Benning, GA. MOH: Donald R. Johnson, USA, Vietnam. Grave C-636.

Post cemetery, Fort Bragg, N.C. MOH: Glenn Harry English, Jr., USA, Vietnam. Grave I-288-A.

Post cemetery, Fort Riley, KS. MOH: James F. Ayers, USA, Indian Wars, Grave F-27; John E. Clancy, USA, Indian Wars, Grave I-5.

Post cemetery, Fort Sill, OK. MOH: Jack L. Treadwell, USA, World War II, Grave XII-8.

Post cemetery, Plattsburg Barracks AFB, N.Y. MOH: Thomas Kelly, USA, Sp.-Amer. War, Grave Q-6.

Post cemetery, Vancouver Barracks, WA. MOH: James Madison Hill, USA, Indian War, Grave 4-W-650; William Wallace McCammon, USA, Civil War, Grave 4-W-412; Herman Pfisterer, USA, Sp.-Amer. War, Grave 4-E-448; Moses Williams, USA, Indian Wars, Grave 8-W-393.

Post cemetery section, Columbus Barracks, Greenlawn Cemetery, Columbus, OH. MOH: Stanislas Roy, U.S. Army, Indian Wars, Grave 51-A-183.

U.S. Military Academy, West Point, N.Y. MOH: William S. Beebe, USA, Civil War, Grave N-15; William H.H. Benyaurd, USA, Civil War, Grave T-1; Daniel Adams Butterfield, USA, Civil War, Grave R-15; Eugene Asa Carr, USA, Civil War, Grave K-14; Samuel Streit Coursen, USA, Korea, Grave 7-230; George Lewis Gillespie, Jr., USA, Civil War, Grave S-37; Moses Harris, USA, Civil War, Grave 4-C-60; John William Heard, USA, Sp.-Amer. War, Grave 8-39; Robert Lee Howze, USA, Indian Wars; Bernard John D. Irwin, USA, Indian Wars, Grave D-17; Andre C. Lucas, USA, Vietnam, Grave 7-C-160; Albert Leopold Mills, USA, Sp.-Amer. War, Grave 4-7; Joseph A. Sladen, USA, Civil War, Grave 4-22; Alexander Stewart Webb, USA, Civil War, Grave M-18; William H. Wilbur, USA, World War II, Grave 7-C-148; John Moulder Wilson, USA, Civil War, Grave K-9.

U.S. Naval Academy, Annapolis, MD. MOH: Thomas C. Cooney, USN, Sp.-Amer. War, Lot 254; Bruce McCandless, USN, World War II, Lot 1021; Frederick V. McNair, Jr., USN, Vera Cruz, Lot 406; Daniel Montague, USN, Sp. Amer. War, Lot 275; Robert Sommers, USN, Civil War, Lot 235; William Peterkin Upshur, USMC, Haiti-1915, Lot 250-A.

U.S. Naval Cemetery, Mare Island, CA. MOH: James Cooney, USMC, Boxer Rebellion, Grave 10-93; William Halford, USN, 1870, Grave A-34.

U.S. Navy Hospital Cemetery, Norfolk, VA. MOH: James Avery, USN, Civil War; Daniel Atkins, USN, 1898.

Arlington National Cemetery
Arlington, Virginia 22211

On the Virginia side of the Potomac River across from Washington, D.C., lies Arlington National Cemetery, the burial place of many great Americans and a revered shrine to America's war dead. The cemetery was established in 1864. On June 30, 1865, approximately a year after its establishment, Quartermaster General Montgomery C. Meigs, in his report to Secretary of War Edwin C. Stanton, referred to the cemetery as "the National Soldiers Cemetery at Arlington." While not the first national cemetery, it is the best known. Nearly 5 million each year visit this national shrine.

The cemetery was originally part of a 6,000-acre tract granted in 1669 by the governor of Virginia to a ship's captain, Robert Howsing, in payment for transporting settlers to the New World. Howsing soon sold his acres, reportedly for six hogsheads of tobacco, to John Alexander, whose family held the land until 1778. At that time, John Parke Custis, son of Martha Washington by her first marriage, bought 1,100 acres—the land now occupied by Arlington Cemetery and Fort Myer Military Reservation. From then on, the land would be associated with famous names in American history.

John Parke Custis died of illness during the siege of Yorktown in 1781, while serving as an aide to George Washington. The future first president then adopted two of Custis' four children, Eleanor and George Washington Parke Custis, and took them to live at Mount Vernon. The boy became devoted to his stepfather, and when the Custis estate passed into his hands, he made it part of his effort to perpetuate Washington's memory. After first naming the property Mount Washington, he built a mansion suited to house his mementos of the first president. The mansion was renamed Arlington House after the Custis family's original property on Virginia's eastern shore, acquired by grant from the Earl of Arlington.

George Washington Parke Custis and his wife had four children. Only one lived to maturity—Mary Ann Randolph Custis, born in 1808. In 1831, she married Lieutenant Robert Edward Lee, a childhood friend and recent West Point graduate. The Lees, being a military family, traveled much, but the house at Arlington always remained their home. Title was to pass to Mrs. Lee's eldest son, George Washington Custis Lee, upon her death. The Civil War intervened and the future of Arlington, like so much else, was changed.

Robert E. Lee returned to Arlington for the last time on April 18, 1861, four days after the firing on Fort Sumter. He had refused to take command of the federal armies being marshalled to crush the revolt. On April 20 he resigned his commission from the United States Army, saying, "Save in the defense of my native State, I never again desire to draw my sword." Soon after, the Lees left Arlington forever, having dispatched as much as possible of the family pictures, silver, and furniture to a safe place.

The former home of the commander of the Army of Northern Virginia soon became a Union Army headquarters, and fortifications were erected on its high ground. Forts Whipple and McPherson were the first military installations set up on the Arlington land. They were succeeded by the present day Fort Myer.

The U.S. government took possession of Arlington under an 1862 "Act for the Collection of Direct Taxes in the Insurrectionary Districts within the United States." Mrs. Lee, who was living within the Confederate lines, attempted to pay the taxes of $92.07 plus penalties through an agent. The payment was refused on the grounds that Mrs. Lee had to pay it in person. On January 11, 1864, the tax commissioners bid on the estate at a tax auction to the federal government at an evaluation of $26,800 "for Government use, for war, military, charitable, and educational purposes." There was no other bidder.

After the National Cemetery System was established on July 17, 1862, burial grounds were established in Alexandria, Virginia, and on the grounds of the Soldiers' Home in Washington, D.C. Burial space at these locations quickly became scarce. On June 15, 1864, Secretary of War Edwin M. Stanton formally designated Arlington House and 200 surrounding acres as a military cemetery. The Army quartermaster general, Montgomery C. Meigs, was charged with creating and administering the new facility. Arlington would remain under the quartermaster general's jurisdiction until the abolition of that office in the 1960s.

The first military burial in Arlington took place on May 13, 1864 — a month before Secretary Stanton's order — when Private William Christman, Company G, 67th Pennsylvania Infantry, was interred. Those buried immediately thereafter were principally soldiers who died in Washington and Alexandria hospitals during the war. Subsequently the remains of Union soldiers were gathered from the battlefields of Bull Run, Bristol Station, Chantilly, and Aldie, Virginia; from abandoned cemeteries in the District of Columbia; from other points within a 40-mile radius of Washington; and from the military post cemetery at Point Lookout, Maryland. There were some wartime interments of Confederate dead, but most of the more than 500 Confederates now buried in Arlington were veterans who died in Washington after the conflict was over. Many former Southern soldiers are grouped around a Confederate monument erected by the United Daughters of the Confederacy in 1914. It is the work of Sir Moses Ezekial, a well known sculptor who served with the Southern forces in his youth. He is buried at the foot of the monument.

Arlington was well established as a national cemetery by the end of the Civil War, yet the Custis-Lee family still had substantive claims to the land. General Lee died in 1870 and his wife three years later. Their son, George Washington Custis Lee, who served as a major general in the Confederate Army, sued in 1877 to regain the Arlington estate, claiming right to inheritance under the will of his grandfather, George Washington Parke Custis. After

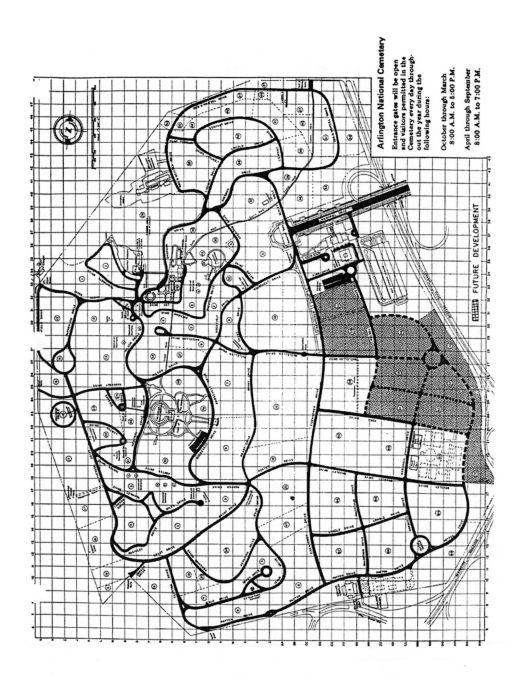

Arlington National Cemetery

Entrance gates will be open and visitors permitted in the Cemetery every day throughout the year during the following hours:

October through March
8:00 A.M. to 5:00 P.M.

April through September
8:00 A.M. to 7:00 P.M.

FUTURE DEVELOPMENT

five years of litigation the U.S. Supreme Court declared him the legal owner of the estate, thus making the U.S. government in effect a trespasser, and a very substantial one at that. Thousands of interments had been made at Arlington, and a sizable part of the land had been developed as Fort Myer. Mr. Lee finally solved the dilemma by accepting $150,000 as full compensation for the Arlington estate. Congress appropriated funds for payment on March 3, 1883, and Mr. Lee signed the deed on March 31. The United States government thereby acquired legal title to the Arlington estate.

After the Civil War, Arlington House served as the office and living quarters of the cemetery superintendent until 1925. That year Congress directed the War Department to restore the mansion to its pre–1861 condition. By Executive Order No. 6228, July 18, 1933, Arlington House was transferred from the War Department to the Department of the Interior. The Custis-Lee Mansion is now administered by the National Park Service and remains a major attraction on any tour of the cemetery.

The grave of Pierre Charles L'Enfant, engineer, artist, and soldier, lies in front of the mansion and overlooks the federal city he designed. It is marked by a table-like monument provided for by Congress. South of the Arlington House a massive granite sarcophagus stands over a vault containing the remains of 2,111 dead recovered from the battlefields of Bull Run and the route to the Rappahannock. The Confederate Monument, mentioned earlier, is on the west side of the cemetery, in Jackson Circle.

The Maine Memorial is on Sigsbee Drive. By act of Congress, May 9, 1910, the mast of the *USS Maine* was raised from the Havana harbor and brought to Arlington to honor those who lost their lives in the disastrous explosion and sinking which touched off the Spanish-American War. There are 229 crewmen buried in the surrounding section, 167 unknown and 62 known. The names of all those killed are inscribed on the memorial. In the vault at the base of the memorial rest, temporarily, the remains of Ignace Jan Paderewski, Polish patriot and musician. Paderewski died in New York City in 1941 while his country was under Nazi occupation. President Roosevelt stipulated that he could lie at Arlington "until Poland is free." The extended Communist rule in his native land caused Paderewski's temporary rest at Arlington to be a long one.

Three other monuments honor Spanish-American War dead: a Spanish War Monument dedicated to all soldiers and sailors who died in that war, a Spanish War Nurses Monument, and a monument to Teddy Roosevelt's famed Rough Riders. Other memorials of interest include the Canadian Cross of Sacrifice, erected by the Canadian government in honor of U.S. citizens who lost their lives serving in the Canadian armed forces during the World and Korean wars; the Argonne Cross, erected by the Argonne Unit of the American Women's Legion in memory of World War I dead; and a Chaplains Memorial erected by World War I chaplains in memory of 23 comrades who died in that conflict. Recent monument dedications include a memorial to the eight American servicemen who died attempting to free the American hostages held in Iran in April 1980 and a memorial to the seven crew members of the space shuttle *Challenger* who lost their lives in the tragic explosion of the shuttle in January 1986. A flagpole near the Memorial Amphitheater is dedicated to the memory of Commander Maxwell Woodhull, USN, and his son, Brevet Brigadier General Maxwell Van Zandt Woodhull, in accordance with General Woodhull's will. It supplements the cemetery's principal flagpole near the Arlington House.

Preeminent among Arlington's many memorials are the Memorial Amphitheater, and on its plaza, the Tomb of the Unknowns. Likely through the influence of the Grand Army of the Republic, Congress appropriated funds for its construction in 1913, five years after first authorizing it. President Woodrow Wilson laid the cornerstone in 1915, construction was completed on June 30, 1919, and the final dedication took place on May 15, 1920. The amphitheater, an imposing white marble structure of classical design, occupies 1½ acres and is enclosed by a marble colonnade with entrances at the east and west ends of its principal axes. The west entrance gives the public access to seating within the amphitheater for ceremonies and other events. At the east entrance there is an outdoor stage. Behind the stage, within the amphitheater itself, are display rooms at the main and second floor levels and a chapel in the basement. The latest major addition to the main level display room, which also serves as a reception area for visiting dignitaries, is a plaque dedicated by President Jimmy Carter to all who served in the Vietnam War.

The Tomb of the Unknowns is one of the principal attractions for the millions of visitors who come to Arlington each year. The placing of wreaths at the tomb by foreign dignitaries and representatives of schools and civic and fraternal organizations has become a familiar occurrence. The first Unknown, a soldier from World War I, was laid to rest on the plaza during ceremonies presided over by President Warren Harding on Armistice Day, November 11, 1921. A sarcophagus of pure white Colorado marble was erected over the grave in 1932. It bears this inscription: "Here Rests in Honored Glory an American Soldier Known but to God."

To the left of the tomb, a white marble slab marked "1950–1953" indicates the resting place of an unknown American serviceman of the Korean Conflict. To the right, a similar marble slab marked "1941–1945" lies over the grave of an Unknown from World War II. The Unknowns of World War II and Korea were interred on Memorial Day 1958, during ceremonies presided over by President Eisenhower and Vice President Nixon. A marble slab inscribed with the dates 1958–75, centered between the crypts of the World War II and Korean Unknowns, marks the grave of the Unknown Serviceman from the Vietnam War. President Ronald Reagan presided over the dedication of this slab on Memorial Day, May 28, 1984.

More than 250,000 former service members and their spouses and children are buried in Arlington. The dead from all of America's wars are represented. Many who achieved personal distinction, whether in the military or in civilian life, have found a final resting place here. Major military figures of the nineteenth century include Montgomery C. Meigs, the quartermaster general who first had jurisdiction over the cemetery; General Phillip "Fighting Phil" Sheridan; General George Crook; Major General Leonard Wood; and Admirals David D. Porter and William T. Sampson. Others whose reputations in American history are most attributable to their civilian careers include Captain Oliver Wendell Holmes, Colonel William Jennings Bryan, and Captain Robert Todd Lincoln, son of the slain president.

Major figures of the twentieth century include Admiral Robert E. Peary; Major Walter Reed; General of the Armies John J. Pershing; Rear Admiral Richard E. Byrd; General of the Air Force Henry H. "Hap" Arnold; General of the Army George C. Marshall; General of the Army Omar N. Bradley; General Jacob L. Devers; Lieutenant General Claire Chennault, USAF; General Jonathon M. Wainwright; Fleet Admiral William F. Halsey, Jr.; Fleet Admiral William D. Leahy; Major Audie Murphy, the most decorated soldier of World War II; Major John Foster Dulles, secretary of state 1953–59; Lieutenant James V. Forrestal (USNR), the first secretary of defense, 1947–49; astronauts Lieutenant Commander Virgil I. Grissom, USAF, and Lieutenant Commander Roger B. Chaffee, USN, victims of the Apollo training fire in 1967; Lieutenant Colonel Francis R. "Dick" Scobee, USAF, and Captain Michael J. Smith, USN, crew members of the space shuttle *Challenger* General Daniel "Chappie" James, Jr., the first black four star general in the Air Force; General Nathan Twining,

USAF, General George S. Brown, USAF, and General Maxwell D. Taylor, USA, former chairmen of the Joint Chiefs of Staff; Admiral Hyman Rickover, father of the nuclear Navy; and Supreme Court justices William O. Douglas, a private during World War I, and Potter Stewart, a Navy lieutenant during World War II, who join four other Supreme Court justices interred in Arlington.

Former heavyweight boxing champion Joe Louis, an Army veteran of World War II, was buried at Arlington in April 1981.

In recent years, Arlington has become the final resting place for American victims of terrorism throughout the world. Twenty-one members of the U.S. Marine Corps killed in the bombing of the Marine compound in Beirut, Lebanon, on October 23, 1983, are buried in Arlington. Seven victims of the terrorist bombing of the American embassy in Beirut on April 18, 1983, are also buried here, as are Navy Seabee Robert D. Stetham, murdered by hijackers of a TWA jetliner in June 1985, and 24 soldiers of the 101st Airborne Division, killed in an aircraft accident in Gander, Newfoundland.

Arlington National Cemetery is the burial place of two presidents of the United States. As commander-in-chief of the armed forces, any president is eligible for burial in Arlington, whether or not he had any previous military service.

William Howard Taft, 27th president and later chief justice of the Supreme Court, was buried on March 11, 1930. Mrs. Taft was interred beside him on May 25, 1943. Before her death, Mrs. Taft arranged for her husband's grave to be marked by a monument designed by sculptor James E. Fraser.

John Fitzgerald Kennedy, 35th president and a Navy lieutenant during World War II, was buried in a special lot in Section 45 on November 25, 1963, three days after his assassination in Dallas, Texas. While president, Kennedy visited Arlington on several occasions. His last visit was on Veterans Day 1963, just 11 days before his assassination, when he placed a wreath at the Tomb of the Unknowns. On an earlier visit, he stood before the Custis-Lee Mansion and commenting on the beauty and serenity of the scene before him, remarked, "I could stay here forever." His grave is some 300 feet from the terrace of the mansion, in a direct line with the Memorial Bridge spanning the Potomac and the Lincoln Memorial on the Washington side of the bridge.

Mr. John C. Warnecke, a distinguished architect and a member of the Commission of Fine Arts, designed the president's permanent memorial and gravesite. The remains of the president and the two infant Kennedy children were interred in the permanent site on the evening of March 14, 1967. Boston's Cardinal Cushing blessed the gravesite the following day. Construction and other expenses in the immediate area of the gravesite were paid for by the Kennedy family.

Senator Robert F. Kennedy, brother of the slain president, was buried in Section 45 after graveside services on the evening of June 8, 1968, two days after he was assassinated following a victory in the California Democratic primary. As a United States senator with prior military service in the Navy during World War II, Kennedy was eligible for burial in Arlington as a veteran, as an electee to national office, and as a presidential appointee to a position requiring Senate confirmation.

Recent years have seen the development and integration of an expanded 612-acre Arlington. Both the Memorial Amphitheater and the Tomb of the Unknowns have been refurbished, and a new administration building constructed. Two phases of a columbarium for the inurnment of cremated remains have been completed. It is open to all honorably discharged veterans, their spouses, and dependent children. Eventually there will be 50,000 niches for cremated remains. A new visitors center and parking facility was opened in the spring of 1988. These and the additional expansion still ongoing of new facilities provide better service to the visiting public and reduce interference with funeral services.

Since 1967, following the great increase in the demand of gravesites after the interment of President John F. Kennedy, eligibility for ground burial in Arlington has been restricted to a relatively small portion of those who have served in the armed forces, their spouses, and minor or dependent children. The purpose of these restrictions is to keep Arlington an active cemetery for as long as possible.

There are 387 Medal of Honor recipients interred in Arlington National Cemetery, including the 4 interred in the Tomb of the Unknowns. Four of these individuals received two Medals of Honor each. In addition, there are two memorial Medal of Honor headstones one from the Navy and one from the Marine Corps. Space does not permit listing here each individual and the citation for their brave act.

Former superintendents of Arlington National Cemetery are:

Captain James M. Moore, May 1864–June 1864
William Murphy, June 1864–June 1864
F.B. Medlar, July 1864–October 1866
E.J. McLean, November 1866–May 1867
Thompson R. East, August 1867–October 1869
Charles Fitcheit, November 1869–December 1870
Edwin H. Harner, December 1870–January 1872
Frederick Kaufman, January 1872–February 1884
Edwin M. Main, February 1884–October 1886
John A. Commerford, October 1886–November 1892

Andrew B. Drum, November 1892–August 1906
Harrison C. Magoon, November 1906–May 1918
Robert R. Dye, July 1918–March 1942
Lamont A. Williams, April 1942–June 1946
Robert Ashley Spence, June 1946–January 1948
Joseph J. Walsh, February 1948–November 1951
John C. Metzler, November 1951–Unknown
Frank A. Lockwood, Unknown–May 1975
Raymond J. Costanzo, May 1975–December 1990
John C. Metzler, Jr., January 1991–Present

Soldiers' Home National Cemetery
21 Harewood Road, N.W.
Washington, D.C. 20011

The rout of Union forces following the First Battle of Bull Run, or First Manassas, on July 21, 1861, brought the Civil War very close to home for the residents of Washington, D.C. There were 28,432 soldiers engaged in that battle, of whom 481 were killed, 1,011 wounded, and 1,216 missing. Many churches and public buildings were requisitioned to serve as military hospitals along with hastily erected hospital buildings located throughout the city.

Burial of the dead from these hospitals soon became a very real problem for the military. The small cemetery established in Alexandria, Virginia, could not meet the crucial needs for burial space. Days after the Battle of Bull Run, the commissioners of the United States Asylum (Soldiers' Home) offered six acres of land within the grounds to the secretary of war for use as a burial place for officers and soldiers, both regular and volunteer. The offer was acknowledged and accepted by War Department Special Orders No. 198, July 25, 1861, signed by Brigadier General Lorenzo Thomas, the adjutant general. The first burials in this area were made on August 3, 1861. It was designated as one of the original 14 national cemeteries in 1862.

Old burial registers for the Soldiers' Home National Cemetery show numerous soldier burials during the late summer and early fall of 1861. Grave 1330, Section F, is the last

SOLDIERS' HOME NATIONAL CEMETERY
Washington, D.C.

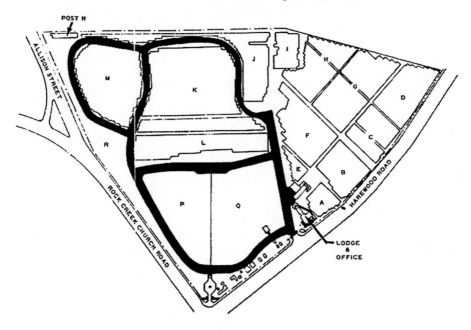

resting place of Private John Williams, Company G, 71st New York Infantry, who died on August 3, 1861. Nearby, in Section G, Grave 3387, are the remains of Private Lowell W. Gibson, Company K, 3rd Vermont Infantry, who also died on August 3, 1861. Private Robert McKenney, Company K, 2nd Maine Infantry, died on August 8, 1861, and is buried in Grave 656, Section F. They all died far from home and their loved ones.

During the period 1861–64, more than 5,000 interments were made in Soldiers' Home National Cemetery. Burial records show that nearly all of the Civil War casualties were privates, corporals, sergeants, storekeepers, cooks, musicians, and ambulance drivers. Volume I of the *Roll of Honor* prepared by the quartermaster general after the Civil War includes an impressive roster of regulars and volunteers interred in the cemetery. They came from the District of Columbia and 17 of the 25 states loyal to the Union.

By 1864 there appeared to be no more space available in the six-acre plot. This circumstance influenced the establishment and development of another, larger cemetery across the Potomac River in Virginia. The area chosen for the new national cemetery was the estate of General Robert E. Lee in Arlington.

The report of the inspector of national cemeteries, based on an inspection on October 18, 1871, listed interments as follows:

	Known	*Unknown*
Commissioned officers	20	0
Enlisted men	5,070	278
United States sailors	2	0
Citizens, employees, etc.	117	0
Rebel prisoners of war	125	0
Total	5,334	278

The inspector also noted that several marble slabs had been erected by friends of the deceased. To date, nearly 13,000 interments have been made in the cemetery.

On April 17, 1883, the board of commissioners of the Soldiers' Home approved a resolution whereby approximately nine acres adjoining the original acreage of the cemetery were assigned to the War Department for enlargement of the cemetery. This additional land brought Soldiers' Home National Cemetery to its present size of 15.8 acres.

Visitors entering the cemetery by way of the main gate at Rock Creek Church Road and Harewood Road will note the impressive Logan mausoleum, one of the landmarks of the cemetery. It is of Norman architecture and is constructed of grey granite from Belfast, Maine. A.B. Mullett, one-time supervising architect of the Treasury Department, designed the mausoleum, which cost about $18,000 at the time of its construction in 1888. The structure was erected at no cost to the government by direction of Mrs. Mary S. Logan as a memorial to her husband, Major General John A. Logan. The remains of General Logan; his wife, Mary S. Logan; a daughter, Mary Logan Tucker; and two grandsons, Captain Logan Tucker, USMC, and George E. Tucker, are entombed within the mausoleum. General Logan died on December 26, 1886, at the age of 60. His remains were temporarily entombed at Rock Creek Cemetery pending completion of the mausoleum.

Major General John A. Logan fought in the Mexican War and was a member of the U.S. House of Representatives from Illinois just prior to the Civil War. When the war broke out, he organized a volunteer regiment in Illinois and became its colonel. He participated in the Fort Donelson campaign, gaining the rank of brigadier general. Service during the siege of Vicksburg brought him promotion to major general. After the war he returned to Congress, serving in both the House and the Senate. In 1884, General Logan was the Republican candidate for vice president on the ticket with James G. Blaine. As commander-in-chief of the Grand Army of the Republic, he decreed in his famous General Order No. 11 on May 5, 1868, that the G.A.R. should inaugurate the practice of spreading flowers on the graves of Union soldiers on a designated date. May 30 was the date suggested in the order. The first grave decoration on that date was observed in 1869. The influence and example of this powerful veterans organization gave impetus to the custom of memorializing the nation's war dead by appropriate ceremonies on a designated day. This was an important factor leading to the choice of May 30 as Memorial Day and to the practice of placing small American flags at the graves of all service persons interred in national cemeteries.

By reason of its location and close association with the historic United States Soldiers' and Airmen's Home, the cemetery holds many interments of retired enlisted personnel who were residents of the home. The cemetery is the burial place of Colonel Henry J. Hunt, Brigadier General John C. Kelton, and Brigadier General David S. Stanley, former governors of the home. Brigadier General Samuel B. Holabird, quartermaster general of the Army from 1883 to 1890, is also interred here.

There are 22 recipients of the Medal of Honor buried here. They are:

Name	Rank	War	Section & Grave
Richard Barrett	Pvt.	Ind.	K-6765
Thomas Boyne	Pvt.	Ind.	J-5859
James Brophy	Pvt.	Ind.	L-9086
Benjamin Brown	Pvt.	Ind.	K-7519
John Connor	Sgt.	Ind.	K-7258
John Denny	Sgt.	Ind.	K-7020
James Dowling	Pvt.	Ind.	J-6352
William Edwards	Sgt.	Ind.	K-7023
Louis Gedeon	Sgt.	Phil.	O-25

Name	Rank	War	Section & Grave
John James	Cpl.	Ind.	K-6991
John A. Kirkwood	Pvt.	Ind.	L-9102
Thomas Little	Bugler	Ind.	I-5627
Jeptha L. Lytton	Cpl.	Ind.	M-9370
Henry W.B. Mechlin	Blacksmith	Ind.	L-8861
Thomas Murray	Sgt.	Ind.	K-6502
Richard J. Nolan	Sgt.	Ind.	K-7179
Francis Oliver	1st Sgt.	Ind.	M-9905
William Osborne	Sgt.	Ind.	K-6512
Thomas J. Smith	Pvt.	Ind.	K-7492
David Sloane Stanley	Maj. Gen.	Civil	Off-20
Rudolph Stauffer	1st Sgt.	Ind.	K-8132
Charles Taylor	Sgt.	Ind.	K-6851

Former superintendents of the cemetery are:

Patrick Callaghan, August 1867–Unknown
James Ruby, Unknown–August 1938
Harry H. Williamson, November 1938–March 1939
Clarence H. Otis, May 1939–June 1940
Frank O. Stallings, May 1940–February 1948
Eugene B. Taylor, March 1948–December 1949
William J. Costine, December 1949–June 1952

Fred Rover, June 1952–January 1958
Donald L. Garrison, February 1958–September 1959
Doyle N. Yates, September 1959–April 1962
Hershell E. Davison, Jr., April 1962–June 1964
Earl E. White, July 1964–July 1974
Romaldo F. Lucero, December 1974–July 1988
Robert L. Brown, Jr., July 1988–

National Park Service National Cemeteries

The National Park Service (NPS) had its beginnings in 1790–91 when President George Washington appointed a commission to plan and lay out a 10-square-mile federal district on the Potomac River. Over a century later, while serving as director of the NPS, Horace N. Albright succeeded in bringing all national parks and monuments and all national military parks and cemeteries under the administration of the NPS. The Government Reorganization Act of 1933 is considered one of the most significant events in the growth and evolution of the present-day National Park Service. Outgoing President Herbert Hoover approved the legislation on March 3, 1933, and President Franklin Roosevelt signed executive orders on June 10 and July 28, directing the consolidation as of August 10, 1933.

In 1926, Congress went on one of its periodic conscience spells regarding the preservation of historic places. The War Department was directed to survey all historic battlefield sites within the United States and to prepare a plan for their preservation. As a result, a number of pre–Civil War sites were acquired by the government.

Prior to the Reorganization Act of 1933, most of the battlefield sites were operated and or maintained by the War Department. Under the act, the battlefields and national cemeteries at Antietam, Chattanooga, Fort Donelson, Fredericksburg, Gettysburg, Poplar Grove, Shiloh, Vicksburg, and Yorktown were transferred to the NPS. The national cemetery at Chattanooga was returned to the War Department in 1944.

The Andrew Johnson National Cemetery, a component of the Andrew Johnson National Monument, was acquired in 1935. Chalmette National Cemetery was transferred to the NPS by the War Department in 1939. The National Cemetery of Custer's Battlefield Reservation, established by the War Department in 1886, was transferred to NPS in 1940 and renamed

Custer Battlefield National Monument in 1946. In 1970, the NPS acquired the Andersonville National Cemetery, which is part of the Andersonville National Historic Site in Georgia.

Each of the national cemeteries maintained by the National Park Service is a Civil War creation. From the dates of their acquisition until 1975, the 14 cemeteries within the NPS were operated as separate units of the National Park Service. Since then, they have been listed as part of their associated parks even though they retain separate identities within the parks. All of the NPS battlefield cemeteries are listed on the National Register of Historic Places. Only two of the 14 cemeteries are open for interment. There are approximately 106,000 interments in the 14 cemeteries. Further information on any battlefield or cemetery may be obtained by writing to the address listed with each.

Andersonville National Cemetery
Andersonville National Historic Site
Rt. 1, Box 85
Andersonville, Georgia 31711

The national cemetery is located in the north-central portion of the Andersonville National Historic Site, about 10 miles northeast of Americus, Georgia, on State Highway 49. It is about ½ mile from the prison stockade.

During the Civil War, both Union and Confederate authorities had to deal with, and find ways to care for, thousands of prisoners. Neither side had expected a long conflict or the eventual problem of a large number of prisoners. As the number of prisoners increased, the South built special prison camps, and the North converted training centers into prison camps. During the war, 30,208 Union soldiers died in Southern camps, and 25,976 Confederates died in Northern camps, most during the latter part of the war. Between August 1862 and November 1863 captured men were either ex changed or paroled on their word of honor not to reenter their armed forces. This allowed the captured men to return to training camps as noncombatants, but more important, the conquering army did not have to provide for their needs. By October 1863, much disagreement over the exchange system had arisen, and it ceased to function. General Grant did not like the parole system because it eventually allowed the Southern soldiers to return to the army. He felt that the Northern soldiers could be replaced in the ranks if they were captured while the South had no such resources. Grant had little empathy for prisoners of war from either side.

The official name of the largest Confederate military prison was Camp Sumter, but everyone called it Andersonville. Built in early 1864 after Confederate officials decided to move the large number of Federal prisoners in and around Richmond to a place of greater security and more abundant food, it was a prison for enlisted men. After the first few months, officers were confined at Macon, Georgia. During the 14 months the prison existed, more than 45,000 Union soldiers were confined here, and almost 13,000 died from disease, poor sanitation, malnutrition, overcrowding, and exposure to the elements. The largest number confined at one time was 32,000 in August 1864. Handicapped by deteriorating economic conditions, an inadequate transportation system, and the need to concentrate all its resources on its army, the Confederacy was unable to provide adequate housing, food, clothing, and medical care to it captives.

When General William T. Sherman's forces occupied Atlanta on September 2, 1864, bringing Federal cavalry within easy striking distance, Confederate authorities moved most of the prisoners to other camps in South Carolina and Georgia. From then until April 1865, Andersonville was operated on a smaller scale. When the war ended, Captain Henry Wirz,

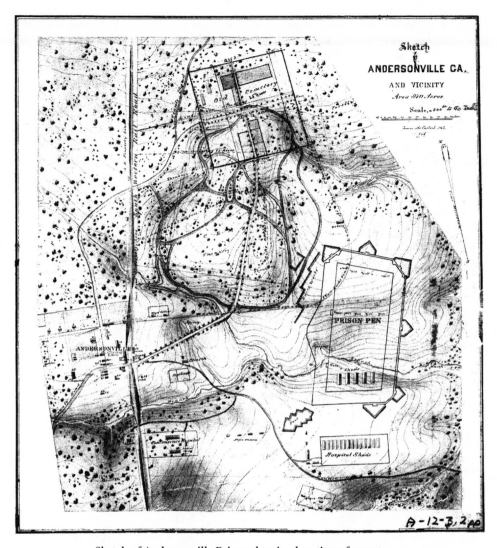

Sketch of Andersonville Prison showing location of cemetery.

the camp commandant, was arrested and rushed off to Washington, D.C., where he was tried before a military tribunal for conspiring with high Confederate officials to "impair and injure the health and destroy the lives ... of Federal prisoners" and "murder, in violation of the laws of war." He was found guilty and hanged on November 10, 1865. No such conspiracy existed, of course, but Northern anger demanded appeasement. One wonders why Sherman was never tried for his "violations of the rules of war" after his troops raped the people of Georgia on his march to the sea; or Grant and Philip Sheridan for laying waste to the Shenandoah Valley simply because they were not smart enough to capture Jubel Early. If the fortunes of war had been reversed, would the commandant of the Northern prison camp at Elmira, New York, where 25 percent of the prisoners died, have been tried and hanged? A monument honoring Captain Wirz, erected by the Georgia Division of the United Daughters of the Confederacy, stands in the town of Andersonville, and memorial services for him are held in a number of Southern towns.

The prison site reverted to private ownership in 1875. In December 1890, it was purchased by the Georgia Department of the Grand Army of the Republic. Unable to finance improvements needed to protect the property, this group sold it for $1 to the Women's Relief Corps, the national auxiliary of the G.A.R. In 1910, the Woman's Relief Corps donated the prison site to the United States. It was administered by the War Department and its successor, the Department of the Army, through 1970, when it was made a national historic site and placed under the jurisdiction of the National Park Service.

When an Andersonville prisoner died, he was moved outside the stockade to the Dead House, then hauled by wagon to the nearby cemetery. Paroled prisoners dug shallow trenches in which the bodies were placed side by side.

Quartermaster General Montgomery Meigs, by General Order Number 70, established Andersonville National Cemetery on July 26, 1865. The initial interments were those who died in the prison camp and were buried in sections E, F, H, J, and K. By 1868, more than 700 additional interments had been made in sections B and C of soldiers who had died in hospitals, other prisoner of war camps, and on the battlefields of central and southwest Georgia. Of these, more than 500 were unknown. Today, the cemetery is composed of 17 sections, A through R (there is no Section O), and contains over 16,000 interments. Many veterans of later wars and their eligible dependents are interred in the cemetery and grave space is still available.

In a small rectangular plot in Section J, near the flagpole at the main gate, are the graves of the six Andersonville Raiders. They were the ringleaders of a large, organized band of thieves, cut-throats and murderers who preyed on fellow prisoners. For four months the Raiders held sway inside the prison; robbery and murder were daily occurrences. Finally, with the help of General John Winder and Captain Wirz, the six ringleaders were captured. On July 11, 1864, after a quick trial by fellow inmates, they were hanged.

The report of the inspector of national cemeteries dated May 23, 1870, listed a total of 13,712 interments— 12,778 known and 934 unknown. It noted that "there are also interred in this cemetery the remains of one hundred eighteen rebel prisoners of war." Modern burials bring the total number of burials in the cemetery to 19,500. The cemetery is open for burials.

In 1900, 115 members of the prison guard detail who died at Andersonville were disinterred by the United Daughters of the Confederacy and reinterred in Oakgrove Cemetery in Americus, Georgia. These quite possibly are the remains of "rebel prisoners of war" mentioned in the inspector's report of 1870.

There is one Medal of Honor recipient interred here:

James Wiley, Sec H, Grave 12607. Sergeant, Company B, 59th Infantry. Place and date: At Gettysburg, Pa., 3 July 1863.
Citation: Capture of flag of a Georgia regiment.

Andersonville National Historic Site is unique in that it is the only park to serve as a memorial to all Americans ever held as prisoners of war. The purpose stated by Congress in the authorizing legislation is: "to provide an understanding of the overall prisoner of war story of the Civil War, to interpret the role of the prisoner of war camps in history, to commemorate the sacrifices of Americans who lost their lives in such camps and to preserve the monuments located within the site."

Fred Boyles is the superintendent of the Andersonville National Historic Site and National Cemetery.

Andrew Johnson National Cemetery
Andrew Johnson National Historic Site
Depot Street
Greenville, Tennessee 37743

The cemetery encompasses about 14.25 acres situated in the middle of the historic site at the end of Monument Avenue. The Johnson family burying ground was donated to the federal government in 1908 and designated a national cemetery. The cemetery was placed under the jurisdiction of the War Department with the first superintendent being appointed in 1908. In 1942, the Andrew Johnson Historic Site was established by Congress and the cemetery transferred to the National Park Service. The cemetery was created as a memorial to President Andrew Johnson, and superintendents assigned here have considered it unsuitable for burials. It is on steep terrain whose slopes measure up to 35 degrees, with a hill in the center. The soil is rocky with shale and limestone 6 to 18 inches below the surface.

On the hilltop about one mile from the homestead, the Johnson family raised a tall monument in memory of President Johnson. The Andrew Johnson Grave Marker is 27 feet high and measures 9 feet by 7 feet at the base. The grey granite base supports an arch which spans the graves of President and Mrs. Johnson. The pedestal is a shaft of white Italian marble. The upper half is draped with stars and stripes and surmounted by a globe on which an outspread eagle is perched. The pedestal is decorated with a scroll Constitution immediately above an open Bible, on the left hand page of which rests an open hand pointing toward the Constitution. The hand represents the act of taking the oath of office.

Despite the difficulty of opening graves and maintenance problems associated with the hilly terrain, the cemetery contains about 1,553 gravesites. It is open for interments. Mark Corey is Superintendent of the Andrew Johnson National Historic Site and National Cemetery.

Antietam National Cemetery
Antietam National Battlefield
Box 158
Sharpsburg, Maryland 21782

The Antietam National Battlefield lies north and east of Sharpsburg, Maryland, on state highways 34 and 65. The cemetery is situated in the center of the battlefield at the intersection of Boonsboro Pike and Rodman Avenue.

The Battle of Antietam, or Sharpsburg, on September 17, 1862, was the bloodiest single day of battle ever fought up to that time. The battle has been called a defeat for both sides, but the failure of General Robert E. Lee to carry the war into the North had two important consequences—both detrimental to the Southern cause—which greatly altered the course of the Civil War. First, Great Britain postponed recognition of the Confederate government, and second, the battle gave President Lincoln the opportunity to issue the Emancipation Proclamation on January 1, 1863. This gave the war two purposes: to preserve the Union and to end slavery in those states still in rebellion against the United States.

Following his great victory at Manassas in August 1862, General Lee marched his Army of Northern Virginia into Maryland, hoping to find vitally needed men and supplies. General George B. McClellan followed him, and at Frederick, a copy of the Confederate battle plan, Lee's Special Order No. 191, fell into Northern hands, probably preventing McClellan from losing the battle. General Thomas J. "Stonewall" Jackson captured Harpers Ferry on the 15th and joined Lee on the 16th. The battle lines were established west and east of Antietam Creek. About 40,000 Southerners were facing the 87,000-man Army of the Potomac under General McClellan.

The battle began at 6 A.M. on September 17 when Union General Joseph Hooker's artillery began a murderous fire on Jackson's men. The battle covered a 12-square-mile area and consisted of three phases. During the morning phase, three piecemeal Union attacks drove back Jackson's line but did not break it. Union General Joseph Mansfield was fatally wounded while leading his Corps into battle. General John Sedgwick's division lost more than 2,200 men in less than half an hour in a charge against General Jackson's troops in the West Woods. During the midday phase two Union divisions broke D.H. Hill's line in the sunken road (called Bloody Lane), but McClellan's failure to follow up lost him the advantage that had been gained. The afternoon phase was the key factor in McClellan's failure at Antietam. After being held off for most of the day by a few hundred Georgia riflemen, General Burnside began a slow pincer movement designed to cut off General Lee's line of retreat. General A.P. Hill's Confederate division arrived from Harpers Ferry about 4 P.M. and drove them back. When the battle ended about 5:30 P.M., there were 12,410 Federal and 10,700 Confederate casualties. The next day Lee began withdrawing his army across the Potomac.

The inspector of national cemeteries inspected the cemetery on September 26, 1870. He reported that the land for the cemetery was purchased and the cemetery incorporated by the state of Maryland. The cemetery is in charge of the Antietam Cemetery Association, composed of delegates from the several states having soldiers interred at Antietam. The 4,776 interments, 1,836 unknown, were in grave-plats laid out by states, with 19 states represented. One thousand four hundred seventy-five of these interments perished in the battle of Antietam and were originally buried nearby. The balance of the bodies were brought from the battlefields of Monocacy and South Mountain, and from Harpers Ferry and other places.

Most of the Confederate dead are buried in Hagerstown and Frederick, Maryland; Shepherdstown, West Virginia; and in local church and family cemeteries.

In 1870, the secretary of war was directed by Congress to take charge of the Antietam National Cemetery. Seven years later, Congress appropriated funds to pay the balance of indebtedness of the board of trustees of the cemetery. In 1933, under the Government Reorganization Act, the cemetery was transferred from the War Department to the National Park Service. The cemetery is closed for interments. John Howard serves as Superintendent of the Antietam National Cemetery.

Battleground National Cemetery
6625 Georgia Avenue
Washington, D.C.

Quartermaster General Montgomery C. Meigs ordered Captain James M. Moore to remove the dead from the battlefield in front of Fort Stevens and bury them in a site he had selected for the purpose. The 1-acre cemetery contains 4 unit memorials and 41 graves, all identified. Only one of the buried soldiers was not killed in the action on July 11–12, 1864. The last eligible Union veteran was interred in 1936, officially closing the cemetery to further interments.

On July 11, 1864, Jubel Early's Corps of the Army of Northern Virginia stood facing the northern defenses of Washington at Fort Stevens. Rumors of an impending attack by General Lee, coupled with Grant's decision to cross the James River for a strike at Richmond, caused a great deal of hysteria in the city. Grant detached H.G. Wright's VI Corps from City Point and sent them to defend Washington. Until the troops arrived, anyone physically able to carry a gun was enrolled in the defense. Civilian clerks from the quartermaster general's office formed a battalion, and brigades were formed by civilian quartermaster employees, by reserve corps units, and by convalescents from hospitals. Fortunately, Wheaton's Division, VI Corps, arrived in the afternoon of July 11, and the hurriedly formed defense force was never tested.

President Lincoln had been at Fort Stevens, standing on the ramparts watching the action of Early's troops. Union officers urged him, without success, to move back because he was such a conspicuous target. He received a message that the VI Corps would arrive at 4 P.M. and went to meet them. Lincoln's presence and the marching troops calmed the anxieties of the people of Washington.

The brief action on July 12 occurred when Wheaton attacked in an attempt to drive Confederate snipers from within rifle range of Fort Stevens. Had Early really intended to attack in force, the sortie by Wheaton would have touched off a violent battle for which neither side was prepared.

Captain Moore's unit was able to identify all the casualties of Wheaton's skirmish, remove them from the battlefield, and inter them properly. The site was designated a national cemetery in 1864. Adrienne Applewhaite-Coleman serves as Superintendent of the Battleground National Cemetery.

Chalmette National Cemetery

Chalmette National Historic Park
St. Bernard Highway
Chalmette, Louisiana 70043

The cemetery is located about six miles from the heart of New Orleans on Louisiana Highway 39. From Canal Street, a visitor should follow Ram part Street downriver until it merges with St. Claude Avenue, which leads directly to Chalmette National Historic Park.

Chalmette National Cemetery is the oldest below-ground cemetery in the New Orleans area. The federal government established the cemetery in 1864 for the burial of Union soldiers who died in Louisiana hospitals during the Civil War. Many of these soldiers had been buried in local city graveyards and were reinterred in the new national cemetery.

The cemetery is located on the Chalmette battlefield where British soldiers formed for their final, futile assault on Andrew Jackson's American defense line in the War of 1812. The battle, fought on January 8, 1815, need never have occurred as a peace treaty ending the war had been signed 15 days earlier in Ghent, Belgium. Only four burials in the cemetery are associated with the War of 1812, and only one veteran of the Battle of New Orleans was reinterred here. This unknown soldier was a Tennesseean who perished near Love Creek, Mississippi, on his march home after the campaign. None of the hundreds of British battlefield dead are buried in the cemetery and indeed, their remains have never been found.

The long, narrow property, consisting of 17.5 acres, is typical of early land divisions along the Mississippi River. The cemetery is bisected by a road which terminates at the levee in a cul-de-sac, in the center of which is an impressive Grand Army of the Republic (G.A.R.) monument. The G.A.R. was a Union veterans organization which erected numerous memorials to its comrades. Its inscription, "Dum tacent clamant," means "While they are silent, they cry aloud."

The variety of headstones testifies to the different periods of history represented in the cemetery. The vast majority of markers were supplied by the federal government, but their designs underwent many changes over the years. There are many large stones, some miniatures of the Chalmette victory monument, and others of unique style and appearance which were purchased privately by the soldiers' families or friends. The rows of six-inch square markers identify the graves of unknown soldiers.

The land for the cemetery was donated to the United States by New Orleans authorities on May 6, 1868. The cemetery was originally known as New Orleans National Cemetery. The report of the inspector of national cemeteries, General Lorenzo Thomas, dated December 12, 1868, gives a breakdown of interments listing 6,929 known and 5,615 unknown, for a total of 12,544. The report also states that 132 Confederate soldiers, prisoners of war, are interred in the cemetery but not included in the foregoing total. Remains in the cemetery were reinterred from cemeteries in New Orleans, bar racks hospitals, and various plantation burial grounds, some of which were more than 200 miles from the national cemetery area.

Brevet Colonel Oscar Mack, inspector of national cemeteries, in his report dated February 14, 1871, listed interments as 12,262 — 6,778 known and 5,484 unknown. The reduction of 282 interments over a 26-month period is probably explained by families disinterring loved ones and moving the remains to a family burying ground. Many civilian morticians widely advertised their availability to recover a soldier's remains from isolated burial sites, provide embalming services, and ship the casketed remains to the family. Colonel Mack also included a statement in his report that "This cemetery is visited by a great many people, and, being in an unfriendly country, great pains should be taken to keep it in excellent order."

The cemetery was closed for future interments except in reserved gravesites on June 30, 1945. Today, interments total over 15,000. Of this number 6,773 are unknown. Jurisdiction over the cemetery was transferred from the War Department to the National Park Service on October 9, 1939. David Luchsinger serves as Superintendent of the Jean Lefitte National Historic Park and the Chalmette Battlefield and National Cemetery.

Custer Battlefield National Cemetery
Custer Battlefield National Monument
P.O. Box 39
Crow Agency, Montana 59022

The cemetery is in Big Horn County, Montana, on the east bank of the Little Big Horn River. It marks the site of the most widely known and disastrous battle with the Indians in the whole northwest country, in which nearly half of the U.S. Seventh Cavalry was wiped out.

In 1875 serious troubles arose between the Sioux Indians and the white settlers and prospectors drawn by the newly discovered gold to the Black Hills of South Dakota. In December, the Department of the Interior ordered all Indians to come in to the reservations by January 31, 1876. The order was completely disregarded, and the Interior Department called upon the War Department for troops to enforce it. General Alfred H. Terry commanded three expeditions aimed at surrounding the Indians at the confluence of the

Big Horn and Little Big Horn rivers. Terry led a force from Fort Abraham Lincoln in Dakota Territory, General George Crook commanded troops from Fort Fetterman in Wyoming Territory, and Colonel John Gibbon led his troops from Fort Ellis in Montana Territory.

The Battle of Little Big Horn will not be recounted in detail here. That day, June 26, 1876, the 7th Cavalry lost five companies— C, E, F, I, and L — and its commander, Lt. Col. George Armstrong Custer. Two of Colonel Custer's brothers, Boston Custer and Captain Thomas Custer, who had previously been awarded two Medals of Honor, and a nephew, Autie Reed, were also killed that day. These five companies lost about 226 men, and Major Reno and Captain Benteen lost 47 killed and 52 wounded. The Indians lost no more than 100 killed. The only survivor of the force under Custer's direct command was Captain Keogh's horse Comanche, found astray and badly wounded. He was nursed back to health and by regimental order placed on the retired list. No one was allowed to ride him and he was paraded, saddled, and bridled at every regimental ceremony until his death in 1891 at the age of 28 years. When he died, he was "stuffed" and is now on display at the Museum of Natural History, University of Kansas, Lawrence, Kansas.

In an executive order dated December 7, 1886, President Grover Cleveland set aside an area of approximately one square mile for national cemetery purposes. At the northwestern end of the ridge where Custer formed his last line of battle and where most of his men were killed, the United States has erected a monument to commemorate the spot where Custer fell.

About a quarter mile from the monument, a 6.21-acre site has been enclosed. The first graves were dug with great haste over the entire battlefield where the soldiers fell. In 1881, as many graves as could be found were reopened and the bodies reinterred in a common grave around the base of the monument. The monument is of granite, 8 feet around the base and 12 feet high. The shaft is inscribed with the names of those who lost their lives. Custer's remains were reburied at the U.S. Military Academy Cemetery at West Point, New York, on October 10, 1877. Of those killed in the battle, only a few unidentified remains and the body of Lieutenant John C. Crittenden are in the cemetery enclosure.

After the cemetery was established and the small section enclosed, the remains of those buried in post cemeteries at various frontier posts and stations were reinterred here. Among these are the remains of those killed at the Phil Kearney Massacre on December 21, 1866. Also buried here are servicemen of the Spanish-American War, World Wars I and II, Korea, and Vietnam. The cemetery is now closed for interment except for eligible survivors of family members already interred. Darrell Cook currently serves as Superintendent of the Custer National Cemetery and the Little Bighorn Battlefield National Monument.

The brownstone lodge, built in 1894, served for many years as quarters for the superintendents, whom the Indians called "Ghost Herders."

There are seven Medal of Honor recipients interred here:

Aquilla Coonrod, Sec A, Grave 372. Sergeant, Company C, 5th U.S. Infantry. Place and date: At Cedar Creek, etc., Mont., during October 1876 to January 1877.
Citation: Gallantry in action.

James Fegan, Sec A, Grave 749. Sergeant, Company H, 3rd U.S. Infantry.
Citation: While in charge of a powder train en route from Fort Harker to Fort Dodge, Kans., Sgt. Fegan was attacked by a party of desperadoes who attempted to rescue a deserter in his charge and to fire the train. Sergeant Fegan, singlehanded, repelled the attacking party, wounding two of them, and brought his train through in safety.

Thomas Kelly, Sec A, Grave 559. Private, Company I, 5th U.S. Infantry. Place and date: At Upper Wichita, Tex., 9 September 1874.
Citation: Gallantry in action.

Wendlin Kreher, Sec A, Grave 466. First Sergeant, Company C, 5th U.S. Infantry. Place and date: At Cedar Creek, etc., Mont., 21 October 1876 to 8 January 1877.
   Citation: Gallantry in action.

Bernard McCann, Sec A, Grave 859. Private, Company F, 22nd U.S. Infantry. Place and date: At Cedar Creek, etc., Mont., 21 October 1876 to 8 January 1877.
   Citation: Gallantry in action.

The other two are Pvt. Joseph A. Cable (U.S. Army; died October 15, 1877) and Cpl. John Haddoo (U.S. Army; died September 30, 1877). Both may be in a group burial.

Fort Donelson National Cemetery
Fort Donelson National Battlefield
P.O. Box 434
Dover, Tennessee 37058

The cemetery is located on the northeastern side of the Fort Donelson National Battlefield, about one mile west of Dover on Church Street. It occupies about three acres of the total battlefield site.

The first victory for the North during the Civil War was the fall of Fort Donelson in February 1862. A stalemate had existed since the Southern victories at First Manassas and at Wilson's Creek during the summer of 1861, and attempts to break the Confederate defensive line had proven futile. The Union command was convinced that the most vulnerable points in the Confederacy's western line were forts Henry and Donelson, earthen works guarding the Tennessee and Cumberland rivers. A joint Navy/Army attack upon Fort Henry had been agreed to by Navy Flag Officer Andrew H. Foote and an obscure brigadier general named Ulysses S. Grant. Foote took his ironclad gunboats up the Tennessee River while Grant marched his troops overland. The plan called for the gunboats to engage the fort until the troops could arrive, but the fort was no match and was pounded into submission within an hour. The garrison surrendered, but nearly 2,500 soldiers escaped to Fort Donelson, Grant's next objective.

Confederate soldiers and slaves had built this 15-acre fort over a period of 7 months, using axes and shovels to make a wall of logs and earth 10 feet high. The fort's purpose was to protect the Cumberland River batteries from land attack. The Federal flotilla attacked Fort Donelson on the morning of February 14. This time, the battle lasted for about 1½ hours before the gunboats were forced to retreat. The Confederate generals—John Floyd, Gideon Pillow, Simon Buckner, and Bushrod Johnson—were informed that Grant was receiving reinforcements daily and had extended his right flank to an almost complete encirclement of the Confederates. If the Confederate forces did not move quickly, they would be starved into submission. They massed their troops against the Union right, hoping to clear a path to Nashville and safety. The North began to give way, but before the way was clear, the confusion and indecision among the Confederate generals resulted in an order to the troops to return to their entrenchments. Grant immediately launched a counterattack, regaining all the lost ground and taking new positions as well. The escape route was closed. Generals Floyd and Pillow immediately turned over command of Fort Donelson to General Buckner, and with over 2,000 troops slipped away to Nashville. Other troops followed Colonel Nathan Bedford Forrest across Lick Creek and escaped.

On February 16, General Buckner requested General Grant to state the conditions of capitulation. Grant replied that only an immediate and unconditional surrender would be accepted. General Buckner regarded the terms as "ungenerous and unchivalrous" but accepted them and surrendered the fort with a force of about 13,000 men and 40 pieces of artillery. The troops were loaded onto transports for shipment to Northern prisoner of war camps.

After the fall of Fort Donelson, the town of Dover was occupied by a Union garrison for the duration of the war. On two occasions, once in mid–1862 and again early in 1863, Confederate cavalry tried to drive Federal troops from the area. Both attempts failed, but the second attempt resulted in the destruction of all but four buildings in the town.

After the Battle of Dover in 1863, the Union garrison built a fortification which became the center of activity for black freedmen in the area. Four years later this site was selected by Chaplain William Earnshaw (see Dayton National Cemetery) for a national cemetery. In his inspection report dated June 14, 1871, the inspector of national cemeteries reported 670 interments, including 512 Unknowns. The soldiers had been buried on the battlefield, in local cemeteries, in hospital cemeteries, and in nearby towns. The high percentage of Unknowns can be attributed to the haste in cleaning up the battlefield.

Today, the national cemetery contains the remains of Civil War veterans and veterans who have served the United States since that time. Many spouses and dependent children are also buried here. The cemetery is closed except for interment of eligible survivors of family members already interred. Steven McCoy serves as Superintendent of the Fort Donaldson National Cemetery.

The Government Reorganization Act of 1933 transferred jurisdiction of the national cemetery from the War Department to the National Park Service.

Fredericksburg National Cemetery

Fredericksburg/Spotsylvania National Military Park
1013 Lafayette Boulevard
P.O. Box 679
Fredericksburg, Virginia 22404

The cemetery is located about one mile from the old railroad station in Fredericksburg on Marye's Heights, the celebrated entrenched position of the Confederate army under General Robert E. Lee in December 1862.

The Battle of Fredericksburg was a great victory for the South, and created severe doubt and depression in the North. President Lincoln was criticized by both moderates and radicals. His Emancipation Proclamation and suspension of the right of habeas corpus, coupled with the failure of the Union generals to win a decisive victory, made many people doubt his competence. In November 1862, he removed General George McClellan as commander of the Army of the Potomac and named General Ambrose E. Burnside to the post. Having endured McClellan's inertia for so long, no one knows why the president decided at that point to relieve him of his command. One reason may have been the news that Southern cavalry units under Colonel J.E.B. "Jeb" Stuart had on two occasions ridden completely around McClellan's army, gathering valuable information on troop strengths and locations. The second time, in October, his cavalry covered 80 miles in 27 hours, losing only 1 wounded and 2 missing.

Less than two months after Burnside took command of the Army of the Potomac, he committed one of the most monumental blunders of the Civil War by ordering his army of over 100,000 troops to attack the Southern forces at Fredericksburg. Confederate troops manned the almost impregnable Marye's Heights west of the city as well as a stone wall in the sunken road at the base of the hill. While General Lee had about 60,000 troops at his command, historians disagree as to the number actually engaged in the battle.

On December 11, Burnside's troops crossed the Rappahannock River just south of Fredericksburg. On the 13th, he ordered two attacks. The assault on the left, led by General George Meade, against Jackson's corps at Prospect Hill, was temporarily successful until Confederate reserves drove Meade back to his original position. The second attack was focused against the heart of Lee's defenses on Marye's Heights. Withering musket and artillery fire cut down repeated attempts to storm the hill. It was reported that Confederate batteries tore gaps in the troops charging the hill and sunken road. When the day ended, Lee had won his most one-sided victory of the war. Burnside's losses were 12,600 men, including 1,284 killed, 9,600 wounded and almost 2,000 missing. Lee lost about 600 killed and 4,700 wounded and missing.

In his report of July 7, 1871, the inspector of national cemeteries stated that the cemetery contained a little over 12 acres and 6,603 graves. Interments were listed as follows:

	Known	*Unknown*
Commissioned officers	98	35
White Union soldiers	2,293	12,807
White Union sailors	4	0
Colored Union soldiers	2	2
Total	2,397	12,844

The report stated that "The bodies were removed from battlefields of Fredericksburgh, Chancellorsville, the 'Wilderness,' and other places."

Old Salem Church, about three miles west of Fredericksburg, was built in 1844 to provide a more geographically convenient place of worship for the Baptists of upper Spotsylvania County. During the Battle of Fredericksburg, it served as a refugee center for scores of forlorn women and children who fled the city with a few meager belongings. Following the Battle of Salem Church, fought on May 3–4, 1863, during the Chancellorsville campaign, the church was used by Confederate surgeons to attend to the wounded of both sides.

There are two Medal of Honor recipients interred in the cemetery:

Edward Hill, Grave 6640. Captain, Company K, 16th Michigan Infantry. Place and date: At Cold Harbor, Va., 1 June 1864.
Citation: Led the brigade skirmish line in a desperate charge on the enemy's masked batteries to the muzzles of the guns, where he was severely wounded.

William Jones, Grave 2448. First Sergeant, Company A, 73rd New York Infantry. Place and date: At Spotsylvania, Va., 12 May 1864.
Citation: Capture of flag of 65th Virginia Infantry (C.S.A.).

The cemetery is closed for interments. The Government Reorganization Act of 1933 transferred jurisdiction over the cemetery from the War Department to the National Park Service.

Russ Smith serves as superintendent of the National Cemetery.

Gettysburg National Cemetery

Gettysburg National Military Park
P.O. Box 70
Gettysburg, Pennsylvania 17325

The cemetery is situated near the center of the battlefield, at the intersection of Baltimore Pike, Taneytown Road and Steinwehr Avenue. It is located on the northwest side of Cemetery Hill, where Union troops repelled a Confederate assault on July 2, 1863.

After his dramatic victory at Chancellorsville, General Robert E. Lee began marching his Army of Northern Virginia westward from Fredericksburg. Once through the Blue Ridge Mountains, he turned north into Maryland and Pennsylvania. The Union Army of the Potomac, led by General Joseph Hooker, followed. Lee's cavalry under Jeb Stuart was absent on a brash raid around the Federal forces, and Lee had no way of knowing of Hooker's whereabouts.

The two armies met by chance on June 30, but the main battle did not begin until the morning of July 1st when Confederate troops attacked Union troops on McPherson Ridge west of town. Though outnumbered, the Union troops commanded by General George Gordon Meade held their positions until the afternoon. In the afternoon, Jubel Early's Confederates smashed the Union defense at Barlow Knoll, and the Federal line north of Gettysburg collapsed. Union troops were overpowered and driven back to Cemetery Hill, south of town. During the night the Northerners built their defenses and the bulk of Meade's army arrived and took up positions.

On July 2, Lee ordered an attack against both Union flanks. James Longstreet's thrust on the left turned the area into a shambles strewn with dead and wounded. The evening attack on the Federal right, though successful, could not be exploited to Confederate advantage. Lee's artillery opened a two-hour bombardment to start the morning of July 3 but did little to soften the Union defensive position. Then, in a desperate attempt to repeat the success of the previous day, about 12,000 Confederates under George E. Pickett advanced across the open fields toward Cemetery Hill. Only about one-third of them survived. With the repulse of Pickett's charge, the Battle of Gettysburg ended. The Confederate army was physically exhausted. Never again would Lee attempt an offensive operation of such magnitude.

The Army of Northern Virginia and the Army of the Potomac marched from Gettysburg in the rain on July 5, 1863. They left behind more than 51,000 casualties. The wounded and dying were crowded into every building available. Most of the dead lay in hastily dug and inadequate graves; others were not buried at all. Among those who came to Gettysburg to view the carnage and the fields on which the war's most significant battle had been fought was Pennsylvania's governor, Andrew Curtin. Before leaving town, Governor Curtin appointed local attorney David Wills as his agent in creating a special cemetery. Wills solicited the support of other Union states, purchased 17 acres of battlefield land, hired landscape gardener William Saunders to design the grounds, and made arrangements for a dedication. The Honorable Edward Everett, the outstanding orator of the day, was invited to make the major speech. As a matter of protocol, Wills invited President Lincoln to dedicate the cemetery and make "a few appropriate remarks."

Less than half of the Union dead finally interred in the Soldiers' National Cemetery had been removed from their field graves by the day of dedication, November 19, 1863. That day, Edward Everett delivered a two-hour oration, rich in historical detail. President Lincoln in his two-minute address mourned for all battle dead, and asked his audience to remember not the soldiers' deeds in combat, but to recall the reasons for which they fought. His short but carefully prepared speech became one of the world's most significant political statements. In 1912, by act of Congress, a memorial to Lincoln's Gettysburg Address was erected. This is the only known memorial in existence dedicated to a speech.

Within a few years of the dedication, 3,700 Union soldiers killed in the Battle of Gettysburg were reinterred in the cemetery. In 1869, the Soldiers' National Monument, which marks the spot where Lincoln spoke, was the first monument to be erected on the battlefield. In 1872, the Commonwealth of Pennsylvania transferred the cemetery land to the U.S. War Department.

The report of the inspector of national cemeteries dated August 23, 1871, notes that "the bodies were removed soon after the battle from the places of original interment in the vicinity of the battlefield, and very great pains were taken to identify them." Soldiers in units from 17 states were among the original interments.

During the 25th anniversary of the battle, in 1888, veteran regimental organizations financed and dedicated over 100 monuments on the battlefield. Soldiers who fought in the Battle of Gettysburg gathered for the last time in 1938 on the 75th anniversary of the battle. Some 1,800 veterans whose average age was 91 years gathered on the fields overlooking the scene of the first day's action. Before a crowd of 200,000, President Franklin D. Roosevelt dedicated the monumental Eternal Peace Memorial.

There are two Medal of Honor recipients interred here:

Charles H.T. Collis, Grave H-1 (PA). Colonel, 114th Pennsylvania Infantry. Place and date: At Fredericksburg, Va., 13 December 1862.
Citation: Gallantly led his regiment in battle at a critical moment.

William Edward Miller, Grave OFF-8. Captain, Company H, 3rd Pennsylvania Cavalry. Date and place: At Gettysburg, Pa., 3 July 1863.
Citation: Without orders, led a charge of his squadron upon the flank of the enemy, checked his attack, and cut off and dispersed the rear of his column.

Today, the cemetery is closed for interments, but the remains of over 7,000 veterans of all later wars rest here. Some of them are buried in the five acre annex donated in 1953.

The Gettysburg National Military Park was created by Congress in 1895 and placed under the jurisdiction of the War Department. The Gettysburg Battlefield Memorial Association turned its holdings and projects over to the Federal Government. In 1933, the Government Reorganization Act transferred responsibility for Gettysburg National Military Park and Cemetery to the National Park Service. John Latschar currently serves as Superintendent of The Gettysburg National Cemetery.

Poplar Grove National Cemetery
Petersburg National Battlefield
Box 549
Petersburg, Virginia 23803

The cemetery is situated about five miles southeast of Petersburg on Highway 675. It is part of the battlefield on which were fought the last battles of the Civil War. When Robert E. Lee evacuated Petersburg on April 2, 1865, Appomattox was only one week away.

The campaign that brought the opposing armies to Petersburg began with the battles of the Wilderness, May 5–7, 1864, west of Fredericksburg, Virginia. During the late spring and early summer, the Union army under the immediate command of General George G. Meade, but in reality commanded by General Grant, engaged the Confederates in a series of hard fought battles. After each encounter, Grant moved farther south and closer to Richmond. Finally, on June 3, at Cold Harbor, only eight miles from the capital of the Confederacy, Grant tried a frontal attack to crush the Confederate army and take the city. His defeat, marked by extremely heavy casualties, caused Grant to abandon his plan to capture Richmond by direct assault. Instead he moved his army to the south side of the James River and on June 15 threw his forces against Petersburg.

Except for a series of Union blunders, the city might have fallen in the initial attack. Federal commanders failed to press their advantage, allowing the few Confederates to hold on until Lee transferred his army south from Richmond. On June 18, an all-out Union attempt to break the Southern line failed. In one assault, the 1st Maine Heavy Artillery, serving as infantrymen, went into battle with 850 men. It withdrew less than half an hour later with 632 casualties. Grant's abortive attempts to capture Petersburg cost him 10,000 men, but his efforts were not entirely wasted. Two railroads leading into Petersburg had been cut, and several main roadways were in Federal hands. Behind the Union forces was City Point, which they quickly converted into a huge supply base. Grant now settled down to the longest siege in American warfare, which lasted 10 months and claimed 70,000 American lives. In this grim struggle, Grant's army gradually but relentlessly encircled Petersburg and cut Lee's railroad supply lines from the south.

Hardly had the siege begun when coal miners of the 48th Pennsylvania Infantry began digging a tunnel under the Confederates at Pegram's Salient (also known as Elliott's Salient). Their plan was to blast a gap in the Confederate line by exploding four tons of gunpowder in the tunnel and then rushing in before the Southerners could recover from the shock. On the morning of July 30, they exploded the gunpowder under the salient, leaving a crater 170 feet long, 60 feet wide, and 30 feet deep. Union soldiers easily occupied the crater but failed to penetrate further. Had the infantry attack been executed as planned, Petersburg might have been captured in the summer of 1864. A Confederate counterattack led by General William Mahone successfully retook the crater, and by 1 P.M. it was over. More than 4,000 Union soldiers were casualties, and the South bought another 9 months of siege warfare.

By February 1865, Lee had only 60,000 cold and hungry troops to oppose the 110,000 well equipped Union troops. Lee hoped that by attacking Fort Stedman, he could gain access to Grant's military railroad and shorten the extended battle lines. On March 25, the Confederates overpowered Fort Stedman only to be crushed by a Union counterattack. Grant unleashed General Philip H. Sheridan on April 1 to take the Southside Railroad. Sheridan smashed the Confederate forces under George Pickett and took the tracks. On April 2, Grant ordered an all-out assault and Lee's right flank crumbled. Only an incredible defense that night at Confederate Fort Gregg (near the site of present-day Fort Lee) saved Lee from possible street fighting in Petersburg.

The 18-acre cemetery, now closed for interments, was established for the burial of the dead of the Petersburg campaign. Bodies were brought here from all around Petersburg, from Ream's Station, and from other places in the vicinity. The report of the inspector of national cemeteries dated July 27, 1871, listed total interments of 6,187. This total includes 2,035 Union and 15 Confederates known, and 4,114 Union and 23 Confederates unknown.

James Kirby currently serves as Superintendent of the Poplar Grove National Cemetery.

There is one Medal of Honor recipient buried here. The Medal of Honor Roll indicates that he was killed in action.

Henry M. Hardenbergh, Grave D-1283. Private, Company G, 39th Illinois Infantry. Place and date: At Deep Run, Va., 16 August 1864.‾
Citation: Capture of flag. He was wounded in the shoulder during this action. He was killed in action at Petersburg on 28 August 1864.

Shiloh National Cemetery

Shiloh National Military Park
P.O. Box 61
Shiloh, Tennessee 38376

The cemetery is located in the northeast corner of the Shiloh National Military Park on the west bank of the Tennessee River, overlooking Pittsburgh Landing, about 23 miles northeast of Corinth, Mississippi.

During the winter of 1861–62, the Confederacy had been forced to give up southern Kentucky and much of western and middle Tennessee, including Nashville. General Albert S. Johnson began concentrating his 40,000-man army at Corinth, Mississippi. He hoped to take the offensive and destroy General Ulysses S. Grant's Army of the Tennessee before it could be joined by General Don Carlos Buell's Army of the Ohio. The collapse of Southern defenses was so unexpected that Grant had moved south toward Pittsburgh Landing, where he was ordered to wait until Buell could join him. Concerned about the number of raw recruits in his army, Grant drilled his men rather than fortify the position he had taken at Shiloh Church.

When Johnson's Army of Mississippi attacked on Sunday morning April 6, 1862, the Confederates achieved complete surprise. The Union commanders had done little patrolling, and the senior commander, General William T. Sherman, treated all reports of Confederate troops in the area with contempt. The Southern army rolled over one Union position after another until noon. Along "Sunken Road" the Federal forces finally formed a line that stopped the Southern advance. The Confederate soldiers named it the "Hornets' Nest," and rather than seek a way around it, they repeatedly charged the position. None of the attacks succeeded until General Daniel Ruggles brought up 62 cannon, at that time the largest concentration of artillery ever seen on a North American battlefield. Under cover of the guns, Confederate infantry swept forward, surrounded the position, and captured General Benjamin Prentiss and more than 2,100 troops of his Sixth Division.

To the right and left of the Hornets' Nest, Federal forces fell back before the Confederate onslaught. On both sides, regiments became disorganized and companies disintegrated. General Johnson was killed while trying to push attacks on the river side of the battlefield to keep Union reinforcements from landing. General Pierre Gustave Toutant Beauregard took over the Confederate command. By late afternoon Grant's forces had established a line of 53 guns on the heights around Pittsburgh Landing, and beat off several attempts to breach it. Part of Buell's army crossed the river and filed into position on Grant's left covering the landing. During the night Federal gunboats provided protection as the rest of Buell's army crossed the river.

At dawn on April 7, unaware that all of Buell's army had arrived, Beauregard went on the offensive. Successful at first, the attack was slowly beaten back by the stronger Union armies. Realizing that he had lost the offensive, Beauregard tried a counterattack but failed to break the Union line. Low on ammunition and food, and with 15,000 of his men either killed, wounded, or missing, he knew he could go no further. He withdrew beyond Shiloh Church and began the weary march back to Corinth.

Pittsburgh Landing was a Federal base during the battle and for many years a landing for river steamers.

During the battle, Federal surgeons established one of the first tent hospitals of the Civil War. By gathering tents from all over the battlefield and concentrating medical services, they greatly improved patient care and lowered the death rate.

On the western side of the battlefield is the largest of five trenches in which Confederate dead were buried. More than 700 soldiers lie here.

The report of the inspector of national cemeteries dated June 9, 1871, lists 3,586 interments. Of these 1,227 were known and 2,359 were unknown. The cemetery is closed for interments. Jurisdiction over the cemetery was transferred from the War Department to the National Park Service in 1933. Haywood (Woody) Harrell serves as Superintendent of the cemetery.

Stones River National Cemetery
Stones River National Battlefield
Rt. 10, Box 495, Old Nashville Highway
Murfreesboro, Tennessee 37130

The National Battlefield is in the northwest corner of the city of Murfreesboro, about 27 miles southeast of Nashville. The cemetery occupies about 20 acres of land at the north end of the park, between the Nashville and Chattanooga Railway and the Old Nashville Highway (Nashville Pike).

In mid–1862 Confederate General Braxton Bragg was ordered to move his army into Kentucky in the hope that its presence would bring that state into the Confederacy. The plan failed, and Bragg retreated from Perryville, Kentucky, in October and set up a winter encampment at Murfreesboro. Major General William Rosecrans took command of the new Army of the Cumberland and was given the assignment of gaining control of middle Tennessee with its railroads and rich farms. General Rosecrans followed Bragg out of Kentucky as far as Nashville. At Nashville, he gathered supplies in case his communication should be cut. On December 2, 1862, Rosecrans, with 45,000 men, moved out of Nashville, intending to sweep Bragg and his 38,000 troops aside and drive on to Chattanooga.

On December 30, Rosecrans found Bragg's army, and the two forces spent the night within sound of each other. The next morning, the Confederates charged and pushed the Union troops back. By mid-morning Rosecrans was forced to bring up reserves, and by late afternoon had established a new line along the pike. The two armies remained in position the next day, but there was no fighting. Bragg was confident that Rosecrans would withdraw and was perplexed to find him still in position on January 2. Late in the afternoon, Bragg launched General John Breckinridge's infantry brigades in an attack that drove back the Federal lines, but the Confederate infantry was no match for the excellence of the Union artillery. The battle ended with both sides claiming victory. Losses were heavy on both sides, with an estimated 13,000 Union and 10,000 Confederates killed or wounded. Despite his numerical advantage, Rosecrans was hard pressed to contain the Confederate army. Only by sheer determination was he able to prevent defeat during the fighting on December 31. General Bragg was energetic but not persistent, and sometimes vague in carrying out his well made plans.

On the morning of January 3, 1863, General Bragg retreated 40 miles southeast to Tullahoma. Rosecrans occupied and fortified the city. The loss of the food producing section of middle Tennessee was a severe blow to the Confederacy. The huge supply base built within Fortress Rosecrans, as it was named, was the largest earthen fortification built during the Civil War. The attacks on Chattanooga and Atlanta and Sherman's March to the Sea were supplied from this base.

The national cemetery was established in June 1865. The inspector of national cemeteries noted in his report dated November 30, 1870, that there were 3,835 known and 2,304 unknown interments. "The bodies were brought from the battle-field adjoining, from the burying-grounds around Murfreesborough, wherein were buried the dead from the general hospitals near that place, and from Readyville, McMinnville, Shelbyville, and from many other places within a radius of sixty miles, including Franklin and Spring Hill. Dead from 17 States are buried here." The cemetery is landscaped according to an 1892 plan. It is closed for interments.

About 300 yards south of the cemetery is the Hazen Monument. It sits in the center of a small square lot in which are buried 56 men of Hazen's Brigade who fell in the battle of Stone River. After the war, members of the brigade provided the stone monument as well as a marble slab to mark each grave.

Confederate soldiers were not buried in the cemetery, but were taken to their hometowns, the nearest Southern community, or unmarked mass graves on the battlefield.

The Government Reorganization Act of 1933 transferred jurisdiction over the national cemetery from the War Department to the National Park Service. Stuart Johnson serves as Superintendent of the National Cemetery.

Vicksburg National Cemetery

Vicksburg National Military Park
3201 Clay Street
Vicksburg, Mississippi 39180

The cemetery is located in the northwestern portion of the Vicksburg National Military Park. The cemetery area was the location of the Confederate batteries which offered the most effective resistance to Union gunboats on the Mississippi River.

During the Civil War, control of the Mississippi River was of vital importance to both the North and the South. For the North, command of the river would allow uninterrupted passage of Union troops and supplies into the South. For the South, it kept open the avenue to Texas, Arkansas and most of Louisiana — nearly half the land area of the Confederacy. The South depended heavily on this region for supplies and recruits. President Lincoln called Vicksburg "the key" and believed that "the war can never be brought to a close until the key is in our pocket."

When the war began in 1861, the Confederates erected fortifications at strategic points along the river to protect this vital pipeline. Federal forces fought their way southward from Illinois and northward from the Gulf of Mexico, capturing post after post, until by late summer of 1862, only Vicksburg and Port Hudson (see Port Hudson National Cemetery) prevented total Union control of the Mississippi. Of the two, Vicksburg was considered stronger and more important. It sat on a high bluff overlooking a bend in the river, protected by artillery batteries along the river and by a maze of swamps and bayous to the north and south.

In October 1862, Ulysses S. Grant was appointed commander of the Department of the Tennessee. That same month, Lt. General John C. Pemberton assumed command of the roughly 50,000 widely scattered Confederate troops defending the Mississippi. Grant's orders were to clear the river of Confederate resistance, and Pemberton's orders were to keep the river open.

Grant failed to reduce Vicksburg through a series of amphibian operations, often called the Bayou Expeditions, during the winter of 1862–63. In the spring he decided to march his army of 45,000 men down the west (Louisiana) bank of the Mississippi, cross the river below Vicksburg, and then swing into position to attack the city from the south. The gunboats of Admiral David D. Porter failed to provide a safe crossing at Grand Gulf on April 29. Grant moved his troops further south to Bruinsburg, his crossing on April 30 unopposed. Moving eastward, Union troops defeated Confederate forces at Port Gibson and Raymond, and captured Jackson, Mississippi, the state capital, on May 14. He then turned westward toward Vicksburg, and when his advance units were in place against the Confederate defenses, he ordered an assault. This attack failed, as did another three days later.

Grant realized that it was futile to waste further lives in an attempt to storm the city. He reluctantly began formal siege operations. Batteries of artillery hammered the Confederate fortifications from the land side while Admiral Porter's gunboats cut off communications and blasted the city from the river. By the end of June, General Pemberton knew that he had no hope of relief and no chance to break out of the siege. On the afternoon of July 3, he met with Grant to discuss terms for the surrender of Vicksburg. Grant, of course, demanded unconditional surrender, and Pemberton refused. Later that afternoon, Grant modified his demands and agreed to let the Confederates sign paroles not to fight again until exchanged. In addition, officers could retain sidearms and a mount. Pemberton accepted these terms, and at 10 A.M. on July 4, 1863, Vicksburg was officially surrendered. Port Hudson surrendered five days later, and the Northern objectives of opening the Mississippi River and severing the Confederacy were realized.

Vicksburg National Cemetery was established in 1866. It encompasses 117.85 acres and includes over 18,000 interments. It was closed for further burials in 1961 when all gravesites were used. The inspector of national cemeteries inspected the cemetery on March 6, 1871. Interments at that time totaled 16,586, including 3,629 known and 12,957 unknown. The bodies were removed from the Union lines back of Vicksburg, from Jackson, Meridian, Grand Gulf, Chickasaw, Bayou, and from other places in Mississippi, Louisiana, and Arkansas. No Confederate soldiers are buried in the national cemetery; they were interred in the Vicksburg City Cemetery.

The national cemetery was maintained by the War Department until the Government Reorganization Act of 1933 transferred jurisdiction to the National Park Service. Monika Mayr currently serves as superintendent of the National Cemetery.

Yorktown National Cemetery

Yorktown Battlefield/Colonial National Historical Park
Box 210
Yorktown, Virginia 23690

The national cemetery is located in the Colonial Historical Park, about one mile south of the old Yorktown landing. It is about 330 feet square and contains about 2.7 acres. Initial interments were soldiers of the Army of the Potomac killed while besieging Yorktown, and victims from the battlefield of Williamsburg.

In early 1862, President Lincoln finally tired of the inactivity of General George McClellan and, bowing to public and political pressure, issued a special order for a general forward movement of the army by February 22. He had lost patience with General McClellan because of his seeming reluctance to attack the Confederates. Lincoln expected a direct move on Richmond, but McClellan decided to ignore the order and move his troops down to Fort Monroe and advance on Richmond up the peninsula between the York and James rivers.

Once the Union army was on the peninsula and ready to advance on Richmond, they found that the Confederates had established a heavily en trenched position at Yorktown. Rather than fight, McClellan settled down to a month long siege. Yorktown could probably have been taken immediately if Union troops had attacked. The Confederates withdrew on May 4, and McClellan occupied the abandoned fortifications. Union troops followed the retiring Confederates toward Richmond until Longstreet, commanding a rearguard action, disrupted McClellan's plan by routing the Union troops at the Battle of Williamsburg.

The cemetery inspection report dated August 15, 1871, showed 2,180 interments, including 745 known and 1,435 unknown. Dan Smith serves as superintendent of the Colonial National Historic Park and the Yorktown National Cemetery.

American Battle Monuments Commission (ABMC) Cemeteries and Monuments

Recognizing the need for a federal agency to be responsible for honoring American armed forces where they had served and for controlling the construction of military monuments and markers on foreign soil, Congress enacted legislation in 1923 creating the American Battle Monuments Commission (ABMC), a small, independent agency of the executive branch of the federal government. The ABMC administers, operates, and maintains on foreign soil 24 permanent American burial grounds, 14 separate monuments, 2 tablets (in Chaumont and Soilly, France, marking the general headquarters of the American Expeditionary Forces in World War I and the headquarters of the U.S. First Army in that war) and 4 memorials in the United States.

Presently 124,910 U.S. war dead are interred in these cemeteries: 30,920 from World War I, 93,240 from World War II, and 750 from the Mexican War. In addition, 5,608 American veterans and others are interred in the Mexico City and Corozal (Panama) American cemeteries. Commemorated by name on stone tablets at the World War I and II cemeteries and 3 memorials on U.S. soil are the 94,090 servicemen and women who were missing in action or lost or buried at sea in their general regions during the World, Korean, and Vietnam wars.

The commission's World War I commemorative program consisted of erecting a nonsectarian chapel in each of the 8 permanent American military burial grounds on foreign soil, erecting 11 separate monuments, 2 tablets elsewhere in Europe, and an AEF Memorial in the United States. In 1947, 14 sites in foreign countries which corresponded closely with the course of military operations were selected to become permanent burial sites. Like the World War I cemeteries, use of these sites as permanent burial ground was granted in perpetuity by the host country concerned, free of charge or taxation. All of ABMC's World War I and II cemeteries are closed for burials except for the remains of American war dead still found from time to time in the battle areas. This policy is dictated by the agreements with the host countries concerned.

Because of his stature, military background, and interest, President Warren Harding appointed General John J. Pershing to the commission in 1923, and Pershing was elected chairman by the other members. General Pershing served from 1923 until his death in 1948 and was succeeded by General George C. Marshall. Following General Marshall's death in 1959, General Jacob L. Devers became chairman, serving until 1969. General Mark W. Clark became chairman in 1969 and was succeeded by General Andrew J. Goodpaster in 1988. In 1990, General Goodpaster was succeeded by General P.X. Kelly, former commandant of the U.S. Marine Corps. The present Chairman is General Tommy Franks.

Further information on any of these cemeteries and memorials may be obtained from the American Battle Monuments Commission, Casimir Pulaski Building, 20 Massachusetts Ave. NW, Washington, D.C. 20314-0300.

Belgium

Ardennes Cemetery is located near the southeast edge of the village of Neupre (Neuville-en-Condroz), 12 miles southwest of Liege, Belgium. Many of the 5,327 graves in the 90-acre cemetery are of those who died in the Battle of the Bulge. Along the outside of the memorial, inscribed on granite slabs, are the names of 462 of the missing. Two World War II Medal of Honor recipients are interred here: Charles F. Carey, Jr., TSgt, 397th Inf., 100th Div. and John L. Jerstad, Maj, Hdqtrs, 2nd Bomber Wing. The name of a third, Darrell R. Lindsey, Capt, 585 Bomber Sqd, 394th Bomb Gp., is inscribed on the granite slabs.

Audenarde Monument is located in the town of Audenarde (Oudennaarde), Belgium. The monument is of golden-yellow limestone bearing the shield of the United States, flanked by two stone eagles. It commemorates the services and sacrifices of 40,000 American troops who, in October and November 1918, fought in the vicinity as units attached to the group of armies commanded by the king of Belgium.

Flanders Field Cemetery lies on the southeast edge of the town of Waregem, Belgium. The cemetery occupies a 6-acre site and contains the remains of 368 military dead. On the side walls of the chapel are inscribed the names of 43 whose remains were never recovered or identified.

Kemmel Monument is four miles south of Ypres (Ieper), Belgium. This small monument on a low platform consists of a rectangular white stone block, in front of which is carved a soldier's helmet upon a wreath. It commemorates the American troops who, in the late summer of 1918, fought nearby in units attached to the British Army.

France

Aisne-Marne Cemetery lies south of the village of Belleau (Aisne), France. The 42½-acre cemetery is at the foot of the hill of Belleau Wood, and contains the remains of 2,288 Americans, most of whom fought in the vicinity and in the Marne valley in the summer of 1918. On the interior walls of the chapel are inscribed the names of 1,060 who were missing in the region. Medal of Honor recipient Weedon E. Osbourne, Lt. Jg, U.S. Navy, is interred here.

Bellicourt Monument is nine miles north of St. Quentin (Aisne), France. Erected above a canal tunnel built by Napoleon I, it commemorates the achievements and sacrifices of 90,000 American troops who served in battle with the British armies in France during 1917 and 1918.

Brittany Cemetery lies 1½ miles southeast of the village of St. James (Manche), France. At this 28-acre cemetery rest 4,410 American dead, most of whom died in the Normandy and Brittany campaigns of 1944. Along the retaining wall of the memorial terrace are inscribed the names of 497 missing. Two World War II Medal of Honor recipients are buried here: Sherwood H. Hallman, SSgt, 175th Inf., 29th Div.; and Ernest W. Prussman, Pfc, 13th Inf., 8th Div.

Cantigny Monument is in the village of Cantigny (Somme), France. This battlefield monument, commemorating the first offensive operation in May 1918 by a large American unit, stands in the center of the village which was captured in that attack and which was completely destroyed by artillery fire. It consists of a white stone shaft on a platform.

Epinal Cemetery is located four miles south of Epinal (Vosges), France, on the west bank of the Moselle River. Within the 48-acre cemetery are 5,255 graves, and on the walls of the Court of Honor are listed the names of 424 others who are missing. Four men interred here were awarded the Medal of Honor in World War II: Victor L. Kandle, 1st Lt, 15th Inf., 3rd Div.; Gus J. Kefurt, SSgt, 15th Inf., 3rd Div.; John D. Kelly, TSgt, 314th Inf., 79th Div.; and Ellis R. Weicht, Sgt, 142nd Inf., 36th Div.

Henri-Chapelle Cemetery lies two miles northwest of the village of Henri-Chapelle. This 57-acre cemetery contains the graves of 7,989 soldiers, most of whom gave their lives during the advance of the American forces into Germany. On the rectangular piers of the colonnade are inscribed 450 names of the missing. Three World War II Medal of Honor recipients are interred here: Frederick W. Castle, Brig Gen, 4th Combt Bomb Wing; Truman Kimbro, Tech 4, 2nd Engr Combt Bn, 2nd Div.; and Francis S. McGraw, Pfc, 26th Inf., 1st Div.

Lorraine Cemetery is situated three-fourth mile north of the town of St. Avold (Moselle), France. The cemetery, which covers 113½ acres, contains 10,489 graves, the largest number of interments of U.S. World War II military dead. The walls of the memorial list the names of 444 missing Americans. Three recipients of the Medal of Honor in World War II are buried here: Andrew S. Miller, SSgt, 377th Inf., 95th Div.; Frederick C. Murphy, Pfc, 259th Inf., 65th Div.; and David C. Waybur, 1st Lt, 3rd Rcn Trp, 3rd Div.

Meuse-Argonne Cemetery is located east of the village of Romagne-Gesnes (Meuse), France. At this 130½-acre site rests the largest number of American military dead in Europe — 14,246. Most of those buried here gave their lives during the Meuse-Argonne offensive. There are 954 names of the missing inscribed on panels of the memorial loggias in the chapel, including those missing in the expedition to northern Russia in 1918–19. There are eight World War I Medal of Honor recipients interred here: Erwin R. Bleckley, 2nd Lt, 130 FA, 35th Div.; Marcellus H. Chiles, Capt, 356th Inf., 89th Div.; Matej Kocak, Sgt, 5th Reg., 2nd Marine Div. (received both Army and Navy medals); Frank Luke, Jr., 2nd Lt, 27th Aero. Sq.; Oscar F. Miller, Maj, 361st Inf., 91st Div.; Harold W. Roberts, Cpl, 344 Bn, Tk C; William Sawelson, Sup. Sgt, 312th Inf., 78th Div.; and Fred E. Smith, Lt Col, 308th Inf., 77th Div.

Montfaucon Monument at Montfaucon, France, is a granite Doric column surmounted by a statue symbolic of Liberty, towering more than 200 feet above the ruins of the former village. It commemorates the Meuse Argonne offensive in which, during 47 days of fighting between September 26 and November 11, 1918, the U.S. First Army forced a general retreat on this front.

Montsec Monument is situated on the isolated hill of Montsec, France. The monument is a classic circular colonnade which commemorates the American soldiers who fought in this area in 1917 and 1918.

Oise-Aisne American Cemetery and Memorial lies 1½ miles east of Fereen-Tardenois, Aisne, Picardy, France, and about 14 miles northeast of Chateau-Thierry. Plots A through D contain the graves of 6,012 American soldiers who died while fighting in this vicinity during World War I. The monument honors 241 Americans whose remains were never recovered. Plot E contains the 96 remains of the "Dishonored Dead." They were executed by the U.S. Army during World War II for crimes including rape and/or murder. Public access is extremely difficult.

Naval **Monument at Brest**, France stands on the ramparts of the city overlooking the harbor which was a major base of operations for American Naval vessels during World War I. The original monument was destroyed by the enemy on July 4, 1941, and was rebuilt in 1958. The rectangular rosegranite shaft is 145 feet above the lower terrace.

Normandy Cemetery is situated on a cliff overlooking Omaha Beach and the English Channel, just east of St. Laurent-sur-Mer and northwest of Bayeux in Colleville-sur-Mer. The 172½-acre cemetery contains 9,386 graves, and the names of 1,557 missing are inscribed on the walls of the semicircular garden on the east side of the memorial. Three World War II Medal of Honor recipients are buried in the cemetery: Jimmie W. Monteith, Jr., 1st Lt, 16th Inf., 1 Div.; Frank D. Peregory, TSgt, 116th Inf., 29th Div.; and Theodore Roosevelt, Jr., Brig Gen, U.S. Army.

Pointe du Hoc Ranger Monument is located on a cliff eight miles west of the Normandy Cemetery. It was erected by the French to honor elements of the 2nd Ranger Battalion under Lt. Col. James E. Rudder which scaled the 100-foot cliff, seized the objective and defended it against determined German counterattacks. It is a simple granite pylon atop a concrete bunker with inscriptions in both French and English on tablets at its base.

Rhone Cemetery is in the city of Draguignan (Var), France. In this 12-acre site rest 861 military dead, and the retaining wall of the terrace contains the names of 293 missing.

St. Mihiel Cemetery is situated at the west edge of Thiaucourt, France. The 40½-acre cemetery contains the remains of 4,153 military dead. The memorial consists of a small chapel, a peristyle with a large rose-granite urn in the center, and a museum. On the end walls of the museum are recorded 284 names of the missing. World War I Medal of Honor recipient J. Hunter Wickersham, 2nd Lt, 353rd Inf., 89th Div., is interred in this cemetery.

Somme Cemetery is situated one-half mile southwest of the village of Bony (Aisne), France. This 14-acre cemetery contains the graves of 1,844 American dead. Most of them lost their lives while serving in American units attached to British armies, or in operations near Cantigny. Inscribed on the walls of the chapel are the names of 333 missing in the area. Three World War I Medal of Honor recipients are interred here: Robert L. Blackwell, Private, 119th Infantry, 30th Division; Thomas E. O'Shea, Corporal, 107th Infantry, 27th Division; and William B. Turner, 1st Lt, 105th Infantry, 27th Division.

Sommepy Monument stands on Blanc Mont ridge, three miles northwest of Sommepy (Marne), France. The monument is essentially a tower of golden-yellow limestone. It commemorates the 70,000 Americans who served in this region during the summer and fall of 1918.

Suresnes Cemetery is in the suburbs of Suresnes, five miles west of the center of Paris. At this 7½-acre cemetery, there are 1,541 dead from World War I, together with 24 unknown American dead from World War II. Bronze tablets on the walls of the chapel record the names of 974 missing, buried, or lost at sea in 1917 and 1918.

Utah Beach Monument is located at the termination of highway N-13D, approximately three kilometers northeast of Sainte-Marie-du-Mont, France. It consists of a red granite obelisk commemorating the American forces of the VII Corps who fought in the liberation of the Cotentin Peninsula from June 6 to July 1, 1944.

Italy

Florence Cemetery is located on the west side of Via Cassia, about 7½ miles south of Florence, Italy. The 70-acre site contains 4,402 graves. The memorial has two open atria, or courts, joined by a wall upon which are inscribed the names of 1,409 of the missing.

Three World War II Medal of Honor recipients are memorialized here (two are interred and one is listed on the Wall of the Missing): Addison E. Baker, Lt Col, Hdqtrs 93rd Bomber Gp.; Roy W. Harmon, Sgt, 362nd Inf., 91st Div.; and George D. Keathley, SSgt, 338th Inf., 85th Div.

Sicily-Rome Cemetery lies at the north edge of the town of Nettuno, Italy. The cemetery covers 77 acres and contains 7,862 graves. On the white marble walls of the chapel are engraved the names of 3,094 of the missing. Two World War II Medal of Honor recipients are buried in this cemetery: Sylvester Antolak, Sgt, 15th Inf., 3rd Div.; and 1st Lt Robert T. Waugh, 339th Inf., 85th Div.

Luxembourg

Luxembourg Cemetery lies just within the limits of Luxembourg City. The cemetery encompasses 50½ acres and contains 5,076 interments. The names of 370 missing are inscribed on the two large stone pylons flanking the chapel. Two World War II Medal of Honor recipients—Pvt. William D. McGee, 304th Inf., 76th Div., and Staff Sgt. Day G. Turner, 319th Inf., 80th Div.—are interred in the cemetery.

Mexico

Mexico City National Cemetery is at 31 Calzada Melchor Ocampo, about two miles west of the cathedral and about one mile north of the American embassy. The cemetery was established in 1851 and contains the remains of 750 unidentified dead of the Mexican War.

Netherlands

Netherlands Cemetery, the only American military cemetery in the Netherlands, lies in the village of Margraten. The 65½-acre cemetery contains 8,301 graves, and two walls along the sides of the Court of Honor are inscribed with the names of 1,722 missing. The light fixture in the chapel and the altar candelabra and flower bowl were presented by the government of the Netherlands and by the local provincial administration. Five World War II Medal of Honor recipients are interred here: Robert G. Cole, Lt Col, 502nd Prcht Inf., 101st Abn. Div.; George J. Peters, Pvt, 507th Prcht Inf. Reg.; George Peterson, SSgt, 18th Inf., 1st Div.; Walter C. Wetzel, Pfc, 13th Inf., 8th Div.; and Walter J. Will, 1st Lt, 18th Inf., 1st Div.

Northern Mariana Islands

Saipan Monument is situated near the beach overlooking Tanapag Harbor on the Island of Saipan, Commonwealth of the Northern Mariana Islands. This monument specifically honors the 24,000 American Marines and soldiers who died recapturing the volcanic islands of Saipan, Tinian and Guam during the period June 15–August 11, 1944.

Panama

Corozal American Cemetery is located approximately three miles north of Panama City, Republic of Panama. There are 4,795 American veterans and others interred in this 16-acre cemetery.

Philippines

Manila Cemetery is situated about six miles southeast of Manila, Republic of the Philippines, within the limits of Fort Bonifacio. Most of the 17,206 who are interred in this 152-acre site gave their lives in the operations in New Guinea and the Philippines. On the rectangular piers of the hemicycles are inscribed the names of 36,280 of the missing. There are 28 World War II Medal of Honor recipients memorialized in this cemetery. The first 7 listed below are interred, and the 21 listed as missing follow: George Benjamin, Jr., Pfc, 306th Inf., 77th Div.; George W.G. Boyce, Jr., 2nd Lt, 112th Cav. Regt.; Dale E. Christensen, 2nd Lt, 112th Cav. Regt.; Leroy Johnson, Sgt, 126th Inf., 32nd Div.; Charles E. Mower, Sgt, 34th Inf., 24th Div.; Robert Allen Owens, Sgt, USMC; William H. Thomas, Pfc, 149th Inf., 38th Div.; Willibald C. Bianchi, Capt, 45th Inf. Regt. (PS); Elmer E. Fryar, Pvt, 511th Prcht Inf., 11th Abn. Div.; Alexander R. Nininger, Jr., 1st Lt, 57th Inf., (PS); Harl Pease, Jr., Capt, 93rd Bomber Sq., 19th Bomber Gp. (H); Kenneth N. Walker, Brig Gen, Hdqtrs, V Bomb Cmd.; Raymond H. Wilkins, Maj, 8 Bomber Sq., 3rd Bomber Gp. (L); Daniel J. Callaghan, Rear Adm, USN; George F. Davis, Cmdr, USN; Samuel D. Dealey, Cmdr, USN; Ernest E. Evans, Cmdr, USN; Howard W. Gilmore, Cmdr, USN; Oscar V. Peterson, CWT, USN; John J. Powers, Lt, USN; Milton E. Ricketts, Lt, USN; Albert H. Rooks, Capt, USN; Norman Scott, Rear Adm, USN; Cassin Young, Capt, USN; Harold William Bauer, Lt Col, USMC; Lewis K. Bausell, Cpl, USMC; Robert Murray Hanson, Capt, USMC; and Charles Howard Roan, Pfc, USMC.

Spain

Naval Monument at Gibraltar, the gateway to the Mediterranean, consists of a masonry archway bearing bronze seals of the United States and the Navy. It commemorates the achievements of the U.S. Navy in nearby waters and its comradeship with the Royal Navy during World War I.

Tunisia

North Africa Cemetery is located near the ancient city of Carthage, Tunisia. At this cemetery, 27 acres in extent, rest 2,841 American dead. The long Wall of the Missing contains the names of 3,724 other Americans. Private Nicholas Minue, 6th Inf., 1st Armored Div., a Medal of Honor recipient in World War II, is interred here.

United Kingdom

Brookwood Cemetery is located southwest of the town of Brookwood, Surrey, England. This small cemetery of 4½ acres lies within the large civilian cemetery of the London Necropolis Co., and contains the remains of 468 military dead. On the walls within the chapel are inscribed the names of 563 of the missing whose graves are in the sea. The name of one World War I Medal of Honor recipient is inscribed on the wall of the missing. He is Osmond K. Ingram, Gunner's Mate First Class, *USS Cassin.*

Cambridge Cemetery is situated three miles west of the university city of Cambridge, England. The 30½-acre site was donated by the University of Cambridge. It contains the remains of 3,811 dead, and 5,126 names are inscribed on the Great Wall of the Missing. The name of Lt. Col. Leon R. Vance, Jr., Army Air Corps, a Medal of Honor recipient in World War II, is inscribed on the wall of the missing.

United States

American Expeditionary Forces Memorial, located on Pennsylvania Ave. between 14th and 15th streets NW in Washington, D.C., commemorates the two million American military personnel and their commander-in-chief, General John J. Pershing, who made up the AEF in World War I. It consists of a stone plaza 52 feet by 75 feet, an 8-foot statue of General Pershing on a stone pedestal, a stone bench facing the statue, and two 10-foot walls along the east and south sides of the memorial.

East Coast Memorial is in Battery Park in New York City. This memorial commemorates those soldiers, sailors, Marines, Coast Guardsmen, and airmen who met their deaths in the western waters of the Atlantic during World War II. The names of 4,596 missing are carved on the 4 tall gray granite pylons.

Honolulu Memorial is located within the National Memorial Cemetery of the Pacific. Information on this memorial may be found under that national cemetery.

West Coast Memorial is located on a high point near the junction of Lincoln and Harrison boulevards in the Presidio of San Francisco. This memorial was erected in memory of the soldiers, sailors, Marines, Coast Guardsmen, and airmen who met their deaths in the American coastal waters of the Pacific during World War II. On the walls of the gray granite memorial, the names of 413 missing are engraved.

State Veterans Cemeteries

During the 1960s and early 1970s, the major national veterans service organizations exerted great pressure on Congress to establish a national cemetery in every state. This unrelenting pressure led to the inclusion of a provision in Public Law 93-43, the National Cemeteries Act of 1973, requiring the National Cemetery System to study methods of meeting veteran burial needs in this country.

The study submitted to Congress on January 24, 1974, and published as House Committee Print No. 110, reported that 42 of the 50 states provided some burial provisions for veterans as of 1973. These included financial benefits, burial plots and legal enactments that specified how veterans' burials would be conducted. Burial allowances ranged from unlimited county provisions for indigent veterans, to a $300 allowance in Michigan for all veterans and their spouses whose estates are $15,000 or less. Some states make no provisions, and at least one state repealed its payment after the federal cash benefit for all veterans was enacted. With respect to burial plots, a few states operated cemeteries for veterans, and some states authorized the purchase of lots for burial of indigent veterans.

The study pointed out that "experience has shown that the families of deceased veterans, in the vast majority of cases, have preferred and sought burial of the veterans within 50 miles of the family home." Subsequent studies by the National Cemetery System have shown that about 80 percent of those interred in national cemeteries lived within 50 miles of the cemetery.

One of the recommendations in the 1974 study was the establishment of a 50 percent grant-in-aid program with the states. The program came into existence with the enactment of the

Veterans Housing Benefits Act of 1978 (Public Law 95-476). The purpose of the program is to assist any state in establishing, expanding, or improving state-owned cemeteries for veterans. It encourages states to provide additional gravesites for veterans since the National Cemetery System cannot fully satisfy the burial needs of veterans. The program of state veteran cemeteries complements the national cemeteries and provides a vehicle whereby veterans who so desire can be buried with their comrades-in-arms in a cemetery in their home state.

While most states would probably prefer the establishment of a national cemetery in their state, the cost would be prohibitive. The initial cost of establishing a national cemetery ranges from $10 to $15 million, with long range costs of $80 to $100 million. From their inception up to 1990, state grants have ranged from $45,000 to $1.6 million, with the average grant being slightly more than $870,000. The only exception to the 50 percent provision was for the territory of Guam, where the VA waived the matching requirement and provided the entire $2.5 million to establish a veterans cemetery.

Since the program became operational in October 1980, 41 states and 2 territories have participated in the program. In addition to federal participation in the cost of establishing the cemetery, the state also receives the $150 plot allowance for burial of an eligible veteran, and a headstone or marker is furnished by the National Cemetery Administration. All states except Nevada, Wyoming, and Utah restrict burial in state cemeteries to residents. The National Cemetery Administration now pays for design, construction, administration, and for new equipment costs.

State veterans cemeteries, as of May 1990, are as follows, in order by state.

Southern Arizona Veterans' Memorial Cemetery
Sierra Vista, AZ 85635

Arkansas Veterans Cemetery
North Little Rock, AR 72120

Veterans Memorial Grove Cemetery
Yountville, CA 94599 (Closed)

Northern California Veterans Cemetery
Igo, CA 96047

Veterans Memorial Cemetery of Western Colorada
Grand Junction, CO

Colorado State Veterans Cemetery
Box 97 Homelake, CO 81135

Col. Raymond F. Gates Memorial Cemetery
287 West Street Rocky Hill, CT 06067

Middletown Veterans Cemetery
Rocky Hill, CT 06067

Spring Grove Veterans Cemetery
Darien, CT

Delaware Veterans Memorial Cemetery–New Castle
2465 Chesapeake City Road
Bear, DE 19710

Delaware Veterans Memorial Cemetery–Sussex
County
Hillsboro, DE 19966

Georgia Veterans Memorial Cemetery–Milledgeville
Milledgeville, GA 31061

Georgia Veterans' Memorial Cemetery–Glenville
Glenville, GA 30427

Hawaii Veterans Cemetery — Area I
Hawaii Veterans Cemetery — Area II
25 Aupuni Street
Hilo, HI 96720

Hawaii State Veterans Cemetery
Kaneohe, HI 96744

Kauai Veterans Cemetery
4396 Rice Street
Lihue, HI 96766

Makawao Veterans Cemetery
200 S. High Street
Wailuku, HI 96793

Kauai Veterans Cemetery
Makawao, HI 96768

Molokai Veterans Cemetery
Hoolehua, HI 96748

West Hawaii State Veterans Cemetery
Kailua-Kona, HI 96740

Lanai Veterans Cemetery
Lanai City, HI 96763

Idaho Veterans Cemetery
Boise, ID 83714

Sunset Cemetery
1707 N. 12th Street
Quincy, IL 62301

Indiana State Soldiers' Home Cemetery
W. Lafayette, IN 47906

Indiana Veterans Memorial Cemetery
Madison, IN 47250

Iowa Veterans Cemetery
Adel, IO 50003

Iowa Veteran's Home and Cemetery
13th & Summit Streets
Marshalltown, IO 50158

Kansas Veteran's Cemetery at Fort Dodge
Fort Dodge, KS 67843

Kansas Veterans Cemetery at Wakeeney
Wakeeney, KS 67672

Kansas Veterans Cemetery at Winfield
Winfield, KS 67156

Kentucky Veterans Cemetery–Central
Radcliff, KY 40160

Kentucky Veterans Cemetery–North
Williamstown, KY 41097

Northwest Louisiana Veterans Cemetery
Keithville, LA 71047

Maine Veterans Memorial Cemetery
Augusta, ME 04330

Maine Veterans Memorial Cemetery–Mt. Vernon
Rd.
Augusta, ME 04330

Maine Veterans Memorial Cemetery–Caribou
Caribou, ME 04736

Cheltenham Veterans Cemetery
Cheltenham, MD 20623

Crownsville Veterans Cemetery
Crownsville, MD 21032

Eastern Shores Veterans Cemetery
Hurlock, MD 21643

Garrison Forest Veterans Cemetery
Owings Mill, MD 21117

Rocky Gap Veterans Cemetery
Flintstone, MD 21530

Massachusetts State Veterans Cemetery–Agawam
Agawam, MA 01001

Winchendon Veterans Cemetery
Winchendon, MA 01475

Grand Rapids Home for Veterans Cemetery
Grand Rapids, MI 49505

Minnesota State Veterans Cemetery
Little Falls, MN 56345

Missouri State Veterans Cemetery in Higginsville
Higginsville, MO 64037

Missouri Veterans Cemetery–Springfield
Springfield, MO 65804

Missouri State Veterans Cemetery–Bloomfield
Bloomfield, MO 63825

Missouri State Veterans Cemetery–Jacksonville
Jacksonville, MO 65260

St. James Missouri Veterans Home Cemetery
St. James, MO 65559

Montana Veterans Home Cemetery
Columbia Falls, MT 59912

Montana State Veterans Cemetery
Helena, MT

Eastern Montana State Veterans Cemetery
Miles City, MT 59912

Nebraska Veterans Home Cemetery
Grand Island, NE 68803

Northern Nevada Veteran's Memorial Cemetery
Fernley, NV 89408

Southern Nevada Veteran's Memorial Cemetery
Boulder City, NV 89005

New Hampshire State Veterans Cemetery
Boscawen, NH 03303

Brigadier General William C. Doyle Veterans
Memorial Cemetery
Wrightstown, NJ 08562

New Jersey Memorial Home Cemetery
Vineland, NJ 08360

Coastal Carolina State Veterans Cemetery
Jacksonville, NC 28541

Sandhills State Veterans Cemetery
Spring Lake, NC 28390

Western Carolina State Veterans Cemetery
Black Mountain, NC 2871

North Dakota Veterans Cemetery
Mandan, ND 58554

Oklahoma Veterans Cemetery
Oklahoma City, OK 73111

Ohio Veterans Home Cemetery
Sandusky, OH 44870

Pennsylvania Soldiers and Sailors Home Cemetery
Erie, PA 16512

Rhode Island Veterans Cemetery
Exeter, RI 02822

M. J. Dolly Cooper Veterans Cemetery
Anderson, SC 29621

South Dakota Veterans Home Cemetery
Hot Springs, SD 57747

East Tennessee State Veterans Cemetery
Knoxville, TN 37919

Middle Tennessee Veterans Cemetery
Nashville, TN 37221

West Tennessee Veterans Cemetery
Memphis, TN 38125

Central Texas State Veterans Cemetery
Killeen, TX 76542

Rio Grande Valley State Veterans Cemetery
Mission, TX 78572

Utah State Veterans Cemetery
Bluffdale, UT 84065

Vermont Veterans Home War Memorial Cemetery
Bennington, VT 05201

Vermont Veterans Memorial Cemetery
Montpelier, VT 05620

Albert G. Horton, Jr. Memorial Veterans Cemetery
Suffolk, VA 23434

Virginia Veterans Cemetery at Amelia
Amelia, VA 23002

Washington Soldiers Home Colony and Cemetery
Orting, WA 98360

Washington Veterans Home Cemetery
Retsil, WA 98378

Central Wisconsin Veterans Memorial Cemetery
King, WI 54946

Northern Wisconsin Veterans Memorial Cemetery
Spooner, WI 54801

Southern Wisconsin Veterans Memorial Cemetery
Union Grove, WI 53182

Oregon Trail Veterans Cemetery
Evansville, WY 82636

Veterans Cemetery of Guam
Agatna Heights, Guam 96910

CNMI Veterans Cemetery
Saipan, MP 96950

Appendix A: Installations by State

Alabama
Alabama N/C
Fort Mitchell N/C
Mobile N/C

Alaska
Fort Richardson N/C
Sitka N/C

Arizona
National Memorial Cemetery
of Arizona
Prescott N/C

Akansas
Fayetteville N/C
Fort Smith N/C
Little Rock N/C

California
Bakersfield N/C
Fort Rosecrans N/C
Golden Gate N/C
Los Angeles N/C
Riverside N/C
Sacramento Valley N/C
San Francisco N/C
San Joaquin /Valley N/C

Colorado
Fort Logan
Fort Lyon

District of Columbia
Battleground N/C
Congressional Cemetery
Government Lot

Florida
Barrancas N/C
Bay Pines N/C
Florida N/C
Jacksonville N/C
St. Augustine N/C
Sarasota N/C
South Florida N/C

Georgia
Andersonville N/C
Georgia N/C
Marietta N/C

Hawaii
National Memorial Cemetery
of the Pacific (NMCP)

Illinois
Abraham Lincoln N/C
Alton N/C
Camp Butler N/C
Danville N/C
Mound City N/C
Quincy N/C
Rock Island N/C
Confederate Mound
Confederate Plot
North Alton Confederate
Cemetery
Rock Island Confederate
Cemetery

Indiana
Crown Hill N/C
Marion N/C
New Albany N/C
Crown Hill Confederate Plot
Woodlawn Confederate
Monument

Iowa
Keokuk N/C
Oakdale S/L

Kansas
Fort Leavenworth N/C
Fort Scott N/C
Leavenworth N/C
Baxter Springs S/L
Mound City S/L

Kentucky
Camp Nelson N/C
Cave Hill N/C
Danville N/C
Lebanon N/C
Lexington N/C
Mill Springs N/C
Zachary Taylor N/C
Evergreen S/L

Louisiana
Alexandria N/C
Baton Rouge N/C
Chalmette N/C
Port Hudson N/C

Maine
Togus N/C
Mt. Pleasant S/L

Maryland
Annapolis N/C
Antietam N/C
Baltimore N/C
Loudon Park N/C
Point Lookout Confederate
Cemetery

Massachusetts
Massachusetts N/C
Woodlawn S/L

Michigan
Fort Custer N/C
Fort Mackinac Post Cemetery
Lake Side S/L

Minnesota
Fort Snelling N/C

Mississippi
Biloxi N/C
Corinth N/C
Natchez N/C
Vicksburg N/C

Missouri
Jefferson Barracks N/C
Jefferson City N/C
Springfield N/C
Union Confederate
Monument

Montana
Custer N/C

Nebraska
Fort McPherson N/C
Forest Lawn S/L

New Jersey
Beverly N/C
Finn's Point N/C

New Mexico
Fort Bayard N/C
Santa Fe N/C

New York
Bath N/C
Calverton N/C
Cypress Hills N/C
Gerald B. H. Solomon
Saratoga N/C
Long Island N/C
Woodlawn N/C
Albany Rural S/L

North Carolina
New Bern N/C
Raleigh N/C
Salisbury N/C
Wilmington N/C

Ohio
Dayton N/C
Ohio Western Reserve N/C
Woodland S/L
Camp Chase Confederate
    Cemetery
Johnson's Island Confederate
    Stockade Cemetery

Oklahoma
Fort Gibson N/C
Fort Sill N/C

Oregon
Eagle Point N/C
Roseburg N/C
Willamette N/C

Pennsylvania
Indiantown Gap N/C
Philadelphia N/C
Allegheny S/L
Ashland S/L
Mount Moriah S/L
Prospect Hill S/L
Mount Moriah Goverment Lot

Puerto Rico
Puerto Rico N/C

South Carolina
Beaufort N/C
Florence N/C
Fort Jackson N/C

South Dakota
Black Hills N/C
Fort Meade N/C
Hot Springs N/C

Tennessee
Andrew Johnson N/C
Chattanooga N/C
Fort Donelson N/C
Knoxville N/C
Memphis N/C
Mountain Home N/C
Nashville N/C
Shiloh N/C
Stones River N/C

Texas
Fort Bliss N/C
Fort Sam Houston N/C
Houston N/C
Kerrville N/C
San Antonio N/C

Vermont
Green Mount S/L
Prospect Hill S/L

Virginia
Alexandria N/C
Arlington N/C

Balls Bluff N/C
City Point N/C
Cold Harbor N/C
Culpeper N/C
Danville N/C
Fort Harrison N/C
Fredericksburg N/C
Gettysburg N/C
Glendale N/C
Hampton N/C
Hampton (VAC) N/C
Poplar Grove N/C
Quantico N/C
Richmond N/C
Seven Pines N/C
Staunton N/C
Winchester N/C
Yorktown N/C

West Virginia
Grafton N/C
West Virginia N/C

Wisconsin
Wood N/C
Forest Hill S/L
Forest Home S/L
Fort Crawford S/L
Fort Winnebago S/L
Mound S/L

Appendix B: National Cemeteries
by Year of Establishment

1862
Alexandria, VA
Annapolis
Antietam
Camp Butler
Cypress Hills
Danville, KY
Fort Leavenworth
Fort Scott
Keokuk
Loudon Park
New Albany
Mill Springs
Philadelphia
Soldiers Home

1863
Beaufort
Camp Nelson
Cave Hill
Gettysburg
Knoxville

Lexington
Rock Island

1864
Beverly
Mound City

1865
Andersonville
Arlington
Balls Bluff
Florence
Fredericksburg
Mobile
Raleigh
Stones River
Salisbury

1866
Camp Nelson
City Point
Cold Harbor
Corinth

Crown Hill
Danville, VA
Fort Harrison
Glendale
Hampton
Jefferson Barracks
Marietta
Nashville
Natchez
Poplar Grove
Port Hudson
Richmond
Seven Pines
Staunton
Vicksburg
Yorktown
Winchester

1867
Alexandria, LA
Baton Rouge
Battleground

Chattanooga
Culpeper
Dayton
Fayetteville
Fort Donelson
Fort Lyon*
Fort Smith
Grafton
Jefferson City
Lebanon
Memphis
New Bern
San Antonio
Shiloh
Springfield
Wilmington

1868
Barrancas
Chalmette
Fort Gibson
Little Rock

1871
Wood*

1873
Fort McPherson

1874
Woodlawn

1875
Santa Fe
Finn's Point

1878
Fort Meade*

1879
Bath
Little Bighorn (Custer)

1881
St. Augustine

1882
Quincy

1884
San Francisco

1889
Los Angeles*

1898
Danville, IL*
Hampton(VAMC)

1899
Quincy

1903
Mountain Home*

1906
Andrew Johnson

1922
Fort Bayard*

1924
Sitka

1928
Zachary Taylor

1930
Dayton*
Hot Springs*
Leavenworth*
Los Angeles
Marion*

1931
Prescott*

1932
Roseburg*

1933
Bay Pines*

1934
Biloxi*
Fort Rosecrans

1936
Baltimore
Fort Bliss
Long Island
Togus*

1937
Fort Sam Houston

1938
Golden Gate

1939
Fort Snelling

1943
Kerrville*

1948
Alton
Black Hills
Pacific (NMCP)
Puerto Rico

1950
Fort Logan
Willamette

1952
Eagle Point*

1963
Houston*

1973
Bath*
Hampton (VAC)*

1978
Calverton
Riverside

1980
Massachusetts

1982
Indiantown Gap
Fort Custer

1983
Quantico

1986
Fort Richardson

1987
Fort Mitchell
West Virginia

1988
Florida

1989
Arizona (NMCA)†

1992
San Joaquin Valley

1997
Tahoma

1999
Gerald B.H. Solomon Saratog
Abraham Lincoln

2000
Dallas–Fort Worth
Ohio-Western Reserve

2001
Fort Sill

2005
Nat'l. Cem. of the Alleghenies
Great Lakes

2006
Georgia
Sacramento Valley

2007
South Florida

2008
Fort Jackson
Sarasota

2009
Alabama
Baskersfield
Fort Jackson
Jacksonville
Sarasota
Washington Crossing

*Cemetery transferred from VA Medical Center to the NCS by Public Law 93–43, September 1943.
†Cemetery transferred from state of Arizona to NCS on April 15, 1989.

Appendix C: Soldiers' Lots, Plots and Monuments by Year of Establishment

1856
Congressional Cemetery (DC)

1862
Albany Rural Cemetery S/L (NY)
Forest Hills Cemetery S/L (WI)
Fort Winnebago Cemetery S/L (WI)
Mt. Pleasant Cemetery S/L (MA)
Confederate Stockade Cemetery (OH)

1863
Forest Home Cemetery S/L (WI)
Woodland Cemetery S/L (OH)
Rock Island Confederate Cemetery (IL)

1864
Prospect Hill Cemetery S/L (VT)

1865
Ashland Cemetery S/L (PA)
Green Mount Cemetery S/L (VT)

1866
Oakdale Cemetery S/L (IO)
Confederate Mound, Oak Woods Cemetery (IL)

1867
North Alton Confederate Cemetery (IL)

1868
Mound Cemetery S/L (WI)
Prospect Hill Cemetery S/L (PA)

1869
Baxter Springs S/L (KS)

1874
Mound City S/L (KS)
Point Lookout Confederate Cemetery (MD)

1875
Allegheny Cemetery S/L (PA)

1878
Mt. Moriah Cemetery S/L (PA)

1879
Camp Chase Confederate Cemetery (OH)

1881
Lake Side Cemetery S/L (MI)

1887
Forest Lawn Cemetery S/L (NE)

1903
Fort Phil Kearney Monument Site (WY)

1904
Fort Crawford Cemetery S/L (WI)

1912
Union Confederate Monument Site (MO)

1918
Woodlawn Cemetery S/L (MA)

1931
Crown Hill Confederate Burial Plot (IN)

1950
Evergreen Cemetery S/L (KY)

1952
Woodlawn Cemetery Confederate Monument Site (IN)

1977
Naval Plot, Moriah Cemetery (PA)

1990
Fort Mackinac Post Cemetery (MI)

Appendix D: Headstones and Markers

The history of government headstones and markers has an identity of its own and was influenced in large measure by circumstances other than those that marked the development of the National Cemetery System. The original design of grave markers antedates the establishment of the National Cemetery System in 1862, and actually had its origin in the early frontier days of this country. United States military forces then served primarily as a constabulary, policing ever-expanding frontiers across Indian border lands in the West and Southwest. Garrison commanders were compelled to bury soldiers who died mainly in plots within cemeteries established on the military reservation. Those not so fortunate were buried where they died. In due time, a fairly common method of marking graves came into being: the rounded top wooden board bearing a registration number or inscription. There was, however, no uniformity in recording burials.

Within two months after Lee's capitulation at Appomattox, a reburial program was instituted by the U.S. Army to concentrate the Union dead in national cemeteries and to "cause each grave to be marked with a small headstone or block." In 1866, Colonel C.W. Folsom reported that from the casualty reports, burial records, and other records gathered by the Office of the Quartermaster General, Union soldiers were buried in 431 places classified as other than national cemeteries. By 1870, Quartermaster General Montgomery Meigs reported the project of concentrating the remains was virtually complete. The number of remains interred in national cemeteries, soldiers' lots, and private cemeteries, plus those marked for reinterment, totalled 315,555. Of these, 173,109, or 58 percent, were identified, and 143,446 were unknown.

Originally, the reinterments were marked with wooden headboards with the decedents' information either painted or carved thereon. The cost of maintaining the wooden headboards prompted considerations of a more durable type of marker. General Meigs proposed a small cast-iron monument, coated with zinc to prevent rusting, with raised letters cast in the solid. He adamantly resisted every proposal for marble or granite slabs in place of his unsightly design. The controversy between those favoring marble and those favoring iron lasted for six years until Congress resolved the issue on March 3, 1873, by appropriating $1 million "for the erection of a headstone at each grave in the national military cemeteries, to be made of durable stone and of such design and weight as shall keep them in place when set."

In 1873, two basic designs were adopted by Secretary of War William W. Belknap for stones to be erected in national cemeteries. For the known dead, a slab design of marble or durable stone 4 inches thick, 10 inches wide, and 12 inches above the ground was chosen. The part above the ground was polished and the top slightly curved. The number of the grave, rank and name of the soldier, and the name of his home state were cut into the face of the stone. For the unknown dead, the stone was a block of marble or durable stone 6 inches square, 2½ feet long. The top and four inches of the sides of the upper part were to be finished, and the number of the grave cut into the top. Contracts were awarded in December 1873 for approximately 255,000 stones, and by 1879 all graves in national cemeteries were marked.

While graves in national cemeteries were being marked, the public began protesting that the graves of veterans in private or village cemeteries were being ignored. In 1879 Congress authorized the furnishing of stones for the unmarked graves of Union veterans in private cemeteries.

One type of marker used for unknown interments.

As far as is known, these were the same type used for known dead buried in national cemeteries.

As the development of national cemeteries and the marking of graves continued, the originally designed stone was referred to as the Civil War type and was furnished for members of the Union Army only. The Civil War type of headstone was furnished for all the unmarked graves of eligible deceased soldiers of the Revolutionary War, War of 1812, Mexican War and the Indian campaigns. At the conclusion of the Spanish-American War, it was decided that the same type of headstone should be used to mark the graves of the eligible deceased from that war. This stone then became known as the Civil/Spanish–American War type.

In 1902 a study was made of the durability of the stone being used. After consideration, on March 24, 1903, the size of the stone was changed to 39 inches long, 12 inches wide and 4 inches thick, with a sunken shield in which the inscription, with raised lettering, was placed. No further change in design was made until after World War I when the subject once again came under heated discussion. The use of the six-inch square blocks for marking unknown graves was discontinued on October 21, 1903. These graves would thereafter be marked with the same type stone as for the known dead, with the grave number and the words "Unknown U.S. Soldier" on the face of the marker. This action established uniformity in marking graves in national cemeteries.

In order that all graves in military controlled cemeteries be appropriately marked, Congress, on April 28, 1904, authorized the furnishing of headstones for the unmarked graves of civilians interred in post cemeteries.

The question of permanently marking the graves of Confederate soldiers interred in national cemeteries and Confederate burial plots was resolved on March 9, 1906, when headstones for these graves were authorized by Congress. The design adopted was to be the same size and material as that used in the Civil/Spanish–American War type, except the top was to be pointed instead of rounded and the sunken shield was omitted. On May 26, 1930, a design stone was approved by Secretary of War P. Trubee Davis, which provided for the stone to be inscribed with the name of the soldier, rank, company, and regiment, with the Cross of Honor of the Confederate States' Army cut in a small circle on the front face of the stone above the inscription.

Following World War I, American military cemeteries were established overseas. Initially, graves were marked with a temporary marker in the form of a wooden cross or a Star of David. At that time, the question of adopting a new style of headstone or slab design for graves of all veterans was being studied by the War Department. There was strong protest from veterans of the Civil and Spanish-American wars since they had become sentimentally attached to the headstone with the sunken shield. After much discussion and consideration of public sentiment, the War Department directed that two types of headstones be furnished: the so-called old style, already in use, for veterans of the Civil and Spanish-American wars, and the new style for all other wars. The new style was a slab 2 inches thick, 40 inches long and 10 inches wide, with a rounded top.

After 2,200 new style headstones had been furnished and erected at graves in national cemeteries, it was decided that the headstones were not satisfactory. On April 26, 1922, a board of officers composed of Assistant Secretary of War J.M. Wainwright, General of the Armies and Chief of

Medal of Honor headstone.

Bahai Pointed Star.

Staff John J. Pershing, and Quartermaster General of the Army Harry L. Rogers, adopted a new design for headstones to be used for all graves except those of veterans of the Civil War, Spanish-American War, and the Confederate States Army. This stone was referred to as the General type. It was slightly rounded at the top, was made of white American marble, and was 42 inches long, 13 inches wide, and 4 inches thick. The inscription on the front face consisted of the name of the soldier, his rank, regiment, division, date of death, and his home state. This newly adopted headstone would be used also for the graves of war dead buried in overseas American military cemeteries.

As the overseas American military cemeteries neared completion, those who had visited the graves of veterans in Europe clamored to retain in permanent form the symbolic cross and Star of David. The American Battle Monuments Commission, an independent government agency which had been established in 1923, unanimously favored permanent headstones of white marble in the same form as the temporary wooden markers then in use. The secretary of war concurred and approved their use on December 12, 1924. This brought to four the number of different types of headstones furnished by the U.S. government.

In the years following World War I, burial practices in private cemeteries changed. Land prices dictated more efficient use of property and better maintenance and management techniques. The private sector turned to the development of park-like settings, using flat markers, and moved away from the large burial plots with huge family monuments, except in heavily endowed cemeteries. Congress and the War Department responded by authorizing three kinds of flat markers. The flat marble marker was authorized on October 11, 1936; flat granite on December 13, 1939; and the flat bronze on July 12, 1940. The flat markers are 24 inches long, 12 inches wide, and 4 inches thick, except for bronze, which is $\frac{3}{16}$ inches thick.

On December 1, 1948, the secretary of war authorized a 24 by 12 by 3 inch flat granite marker for use in the National Memorial Cemetery of the Pacific (the Punchbowl) and Puerto Rico National Cemetery, and subsequently for Willamette National Cemetery. In 1974, the three-inch thick-

ness was discontinued and all flat markers are now four inches thick. Upright granite headstones were approved for use in private cemeteries in 1941, and discontinued in 1947. An amendment to Title 38, U.S. Code 906, authorized the Veterans Administration to approve markers of any material "aesthetically compatible with the area of the cemetery in which it is to be placed." Slate markers are furnished upon request for use in private or local cemeteries, but their use in national cemeteries has not been authorized.

In 1922, for the first time, a religious emblem was adopted for use on government-furnished headstones. The emblem inscribed on the face of the stone consisted of the Latin cross for the Christian faith and the Star of David for the Jewish faith. The Buddhist Wheel of Righteousness was authorized in 1951. Since that time, 24 additional religious emblems and the atheist symbol have been authorized. In each case when a new emblem was requested, the head office of the corresponding church in the United States was required to approve the use of the emblem. There are three other emblems also approved, but their church authorities have requested that they not be publicized. They are the United Church of Christ, the Christian Science cross and crown, and the Islamic five-pointed star. The atheist emblem was added after the husband of Mrs. Madeline Murray O'Hare was interred in Arlington National Cemetery and she sued, based on freedom of religious expression, to have the government furnish an atheist symbol in lieu of a religious emblem. Mr. O'Hare's headstone in Arlington and two others in the Punchbowl are the only known atheist symbols in the national cemeteries.

Over the years the authorized inscription has been changed to permit the date of birth and death, period of war service, and abbreviations for the medals for valor. Next of kin may add short inscriptions or terms of endearment, space permitting, at their expense. Today, several of the more active cemeteries have a stone mason on their staff. By stocking blank stones and having them inscribed in the cemetery, the headstone to be placed on the grave within a short time after the interment, rather than several weeks later.

Appendix E: The Medal of Honor

The Medal of Honor is the highest military award for bravery that can be given to any individual in the United States. It is presented by the president in the name of Congress. For this reason, it has often been called the Congressional Medal of Honor.

On July 12, 1862, President Abraham Lincoln signed Senate and House of Representatives Resolution No. 52, authorizing 2,000 "medals of honor" to be prepared and presented to "such noncommissioned officers and privates as shall most distinguish themselves by their gallantry in action, and other soldier-like qualities, during the present insurrection." Previous to this resolution, an act passed on December 21, 1861, authorized the Secretary of the Navy to award "medals of honor" on "such petty officers, seamen, landsmen, and marines as shall distinguish themselves by gallantry in action and other seamanlike qualities during the present war." The Act of 1861 was the first time that the term "medal of honor" was used, and the 1862 resolution was the first to provide for the presentation "in the name of Congress." On March 3, 1863, the resolution was amended to include officers and made the provision retroactive to the beginning of the Civil War.

The establishment of the Medal of Honor was the work of many people who recognized the need to reward the deeds and efforts of American soldiers, sailors and Marines. The Army had long used a method for rewarding officers who were commended for gallantry or bravery. The brevet system of promotions, whereby the officer could be given a brevet rank higher than his actual rank, afforded the officer the privileges of the higher rank. By 1861, this system had fallen victim to political abuse and a more meaningful method of rewarding courage and bravery was needed. With the outbreak of the Civil War, considerable thought was again given to honoring the men who were fighting to preserve the nation, and who performed deeds far beyond the call of ordinary duty. Senator James W. Grimes of Iowa, chairman of the Senate Naval Committee, introduced the bill to create a Navy medal. Senator Henry Wilson, of Massachusetts, introduced the resolution providing for the Army medal.

The first Medal of Honor was presented by Secretary of War Edwin M. Stanton to Private Jacob Parrott, the youngest member of Andrew's Raiders. On that day, March 25, 1863, Secretary Stanton also presented medals to five other members of Andrew's Raiders (see Chattanooga National Cemetery). The first Navy medals were awarded on April 3, 1863, to sailors and marines.

The wording "...and other soldier-like qualities" in the resolution of 1862 created problems for Army officials in carrying out the intent of the law and determining who should receive the Medal of Honor. This vague statement resulted in medals being awarded to individuals whose actions did not justify the award. One medal, to Lieutenant Colonel Asa B. Gardiner, was given him by Secretary of War Belknap when he wrote to the secretary in 1872 requesting one as a souvenir of "memorable times past." By 1916, there had been 2,625 medals awarded, some of them for deeds which involved neither risk of life nor acts above and beyond the call of duty. A few had been awarded without any specific citation at all. It was not until an act of April 23, 1904, that a Medal of Honor recommendation was required to include evidence derived from official War Department records to justify the award.

One provision of the National Defense Act of 1916 required the secretary of war to appoint a board of five retired general officers to investigate and report on past awards of "the so-called congressional medal of honor" by or through the War Department. Their purpose was to determine what medals had been awarded for any cause other than distinguished conduct in action involving actual conflict with an enemy. Lieutenant General Nelson A. Miles was appointed president of the board. At the time, General Miles was 76 years of age. He had retired in 1903 after spending 42 years in the Army, having first attained general officer rank in 1864 at the age of 24.

The board reviewed all previous awards of the Medal of Honor, with the identity of the individual concerned removed, and in its final report listed 911 recipients whose actions did not meet the criterion specified in the new law. Among those whose names were removed from the list of recipients were William F. "Buffalo Bill" Cody and four other civilian scouts who were cited for service as guides and scouts during the Indian wars. General Miles made a special plea on behalf of Cody and the four others to Secretary of War Newton D. Baker and to the chairmen of the Military Affairs Committees of both the House and Senate, but no action was taken. The name of Lieutenant Colonel Asa Gardiner, who got his medal "as a souvenir," was also removed from the roll.

Another name stricken from the Medal of Honor roll was that of Dr. Mary E. Walker, the only woman ever to be awarded the medal. Dr. Walker was awarded the medal by President Andrew Johnson on November 11, 1865. The citation states that

> Dr. Walker ... has rendered valuable service to the Government, and her efforts have been earnest and untiring in a variety of ways, and that she served as assistant surgeon in charge of female prisoners at Louisville, Ky., upon the recommendation of Major Generals Sherman and Thomas ... and has devoted herself with patriotic zeal to the

Medals of Honor. Left to right, Army, Air Force, Navy–Marine Corps–Coast Guard.

sick and wounded soldiers, both in the field and hospitals, to the detriment of her own health, and has also endured hardships as a prisoner of war four months in a Southern prison while acting as a contract surgeon....

Secretary of War Edwin Stanton had refused to appoint her a contract surgeon in September 1865. On June 10, 1977, Secretary of the Army Clifford L. Alexander, Jr., approved a recommendation of the Army Board for Correction of Military Records to restore the Medal of Honor to Dr. Walker. One wonders if the congressional clamor caused the Army to overrule the careful deliberation of the board in 1916, since it provided no justification for the action.

Also stricken from the list were 864 members of the 27th Maine Volunteer Infantry. The unit was part of the defense of Washington, D.C., in 1863. The enlistment of the regiment was to expire in June 1863, and as an inducement to reenlist, President Lincoln authorized Medals of Honor to all who would extend their duty. Three hundred nine members did reenlist and received the medal. Through a clerical error, the 555 who had gone home despite Lincoln's plea also received the medal. Another 29 recipients stricken from the list were 4 officers and 25 first sergeants of the First Brigade, Veterans Reserve Corps, who escorted the remains of the President Lincoln to Springfield, Illinois.

There have been no cancellations of Navy Medal of Honor awards.

On July 9, 1918, Congress passed legislation authorizing the Medal of Honor to be awarded to a person who "shall hereafter, in action involving actual conflict with the enemy, distinguish himself conspicuously by gallantry and intrepidity at the risk of his life above and beyond the call of duty." This is still the criterion today.

It is not surprising that relatively few people have ever seen a Medal of Honor since only 3,409 were awarded from its establishment in 1862 up to 1978. Over one-fifth, 728, were awarded to individuals who were not born in this country. Over ten percent of the deceased recipients are interred in Arlington National Cemetery, and a total of 823 recipients are buried or memorialized in national or military post cemeteries. Their names and citations are included with the history of the cemetery where they are interred.

The youngest recipient of the Medal of Honor is Orion P. Howe, Musician, Company C, 55th Illinois Infantry. He was awarded the medal at

Vicksburg, Mississippi, on May 19, 1863. His citation reads: "A drummer boy, 14 years of age, and severely wounded and exposed to a heavy fire from the enemy, he persistently remained upon the field of battle until he had reported to General W.T. Sherman the necessity of supplying cartridges for the use of troops under command of Colonel Malmberg." Another 14-year-old recipient was John Angling, Cabin Boy, U.S. Navy. Angling was cited for gallantry, skill, and cool courage while serving aboard the *USS Pontoosuc* during the capture of Fort Fisher and Wilmington from 24 December 1864 to 22 January 1865.

Medals of Honor have been awarded by special legislation to the following: Floyd Bennett, Machinist, U.S. Navy; Richard Evelyn Byrd, Commander, U.S. Navy; George Robert Cholister, Boatswain's Mate 1c, U.S. Navy; Henry Clay Drexler, Ensign, U.S. Navy; Richard Pearson Hobson, Lieutenant, U.S. Navy; Charles A. Lindbergh, Captain, U.S. Army Air Corps Reserve; Adolphus W. Greeley, Major General, U.S. Army, Retired; William Mitchell, Colonel, U.S. Army (posthumous); Unknown Soldier of Belgium; Unknown Soldier of Great Britain; Unknown Soldier of France; Unknown Soldier of Italy; Unknown Soldier of Rumania; Unknown Soldier of the United States (1921)–World War I; Unknown American, World War II; Unknown American, Korean conflict; and Unknown American, Vietnam.

The number of Medals of Honor awarded in each war and campaign is as follows:

Civil War (1861–65)	1,522
Indian Campaigns (1861–98)	426
Korean Campaign (1871)	15
Spanish-American War (1898)	110
Samoa	4
Philippine Insurrection (1899–1913)	80
Boxer Rebellion (1900)	59
Action Against Philippine Outlaws (1911)	6
Mexican Campaign (Vera Cruz) (1911)	56
Haitian Campaign (1915)	6
Dominican Campaign (1916)	3
World War I (1917–18)	124
Haitian Campaign (1919–20)	2
Second Nicaraguan Campaign (1925)	2
World War II (1941–45)	464
Korean Conflict (1950–53)	133
Vietnam War	246
Samalia	2
Afghanistan	1
Iraq	4
Non-Combat	193
Unknowns	9
Total	3,467

Nineteen men received two awards. Fourteen men received two separate medals for two separate actions.

A complete history and list titled *Medal of Honor Recipients, 1863–1978* was published by the Committee on Veteran Affairs, United States Senate, 96th Congress, 1st Session, Senate Committee Print No. 3, dated February 14, 1979.

An excellent article, "Safeguarding the Medal of Honor," by Colonel Wil Ebel, USAR, published in *The Retired Officer* July 1977, was used as a reference on Dr. Walker.

Appendix F: Memorial Day Orders

I.

The 30th day of May, 1868, is designated for the purpose of strewing with flowers or otherwise decorating the graves of comrades who died in defense of their country during the late rebellion, and whose bodies now lie in almost every city, village, and hamlet churchyard in the land.—In this observance no form of ceremony is prescribed, but posts and comrades will in their own way arrange such fitting services and testimonials of respect as circumstances may permit.

We are organized, comrades, as our regulations tell us, for the purpose, among other things, "of preserving and strengthening these kind and fraternal feelings which have bound together the soldiers, sailors and Marines who united to suppress the late rebellion."

What can aid and more to assure this result than by cherishing tenderly the memory of our heroic dead who made their breasts a barricade between our country and the foes? Their soldier lives were the reveille of freedom to a race in chains and their deaths a tattoo of rebellious tyranny in arms. We should guard their graves with sacred vigilance.—All that the consecrated wealth and taste of the nation can add to their adornment and security is but a fitting tribute to the memory of her slain defenders. Let no wanton foot tread rudely on such hallowed grounds.— Let pleasant paths invite the coming and going of reverent visitors and fond mourners.

Let no vandalism of avarice or neglect, no ravages of time, testify to the present or to the coming generations that we have forgotten, as a people the cost of a free and undivided republic.

If other eyes grow dull and other hands slack, and other hearts cold in the solemn trust ours shall keep it well as long as the light and warmth of life remains in us.

Let us, then, at the time appointed, gather around their sacred remains and garland the passionless mounds above them with choicest flowers of springtime; let us raise above them the dear old flag they saved from dishonor; let us in this solemn presence renew our pledges to aid and assist those whom they have left among us as sacred charges upon the nation's gratitude — the soldier's and sailor's widow and orphan.

II.

It is the purpose of the Commander in Chief to inaugurate this observance with hope that it will be kept up from the memory of his departed comrades. We earnestly desire the public press to call attention to this order, and lend its friendly aid in bringing it to the notice of comrades in all parts of the country in time for simultaneous compliance therewith.

III.

Department Commanders will use every effort to make this Order effective.

By Command of
John A. Logan
Commander in Chief,
Grand Army of the Republic
May 5, 1868*

*General John A. Logan is interred in the Soldiers' Home National Cemetery.

Index